History of Modern Philosophy

by Richard Falckenberg

Copyright © 8/14/2015
Jefferson Publication

ISBN-13: 978-1516907243

Printed in the United States of America

All rights reserved. No part of this book may be reprinted or reproduced or utilized in any form or by any electronic, mechanical, or other means, now known or hereafter invented, including photocopying and recording, or in any form of storage or retrieval system, without prior permission in writing from the publisher.'

Contents

- PREFACE ... 3
- INTRODUCTION ... 4
  - CHAPTER I ... 9
- PART I ... 29
  - CHAPTER II ... 29
  - CHAPTER III ... 35
  - CHAPTER IV ... 48
  - CHAPTER V ... 55
  - CHAPTER VI ... 73
  - CHAPTER VII ... 80
  - CHAPTER VIII ... 87
- PART II. FROM KANT TO THE PRESENT TIME.% ... 94
  - CHAPTER IX ... 94
  - CHAPTER X ... 123
  - CHAPTER XI ... 130
  - CHAPTER XII ... 137
  - CHAPTER XIII ... 142
  - CHAPTER XIV ... 147
  - CHAPTER XV ... 159
  - CHAPTER XVI ... 170

PREFACE.

The aim of this translation is the same as that of the original work. Each is the outcome of experience in university instruction in philosophy, and is intended to furnish a manual which shall be at once scientific and popular, one to stand midway between the exhaustive expositions of the larger histories and the meager sketches of the compendiums. A pupil of Kuno Fischer, Fortlage, J.E. Erdmann, Lotze, and Eucken among others, Professor Falckenberg began his career as *Docent* in the university of Jena. In the year following the first edition of this work he became *Extraordinarius* in the same university, and in 1888 *Ordinarius* at Erlangen, choosing the latter call in preference to an invitation to Dorpat as successor to Teichmüller. The chair at Erlangen he still holds. His work as teacher and author has been chiefly in the history of modern philosophy. Besides the present work and numerous minor articles, he has published the following: *Ueber den intelligiblen Charakter, zur Kritik der Kantischen Freiheitslehre* 1879; *Grundzüge der Philosophie des Nicolaus Cusanus*, 1880-81; and *Ueber die gegenwärtige Lage der deutschen Philosophie*, 1890 (inaugural address at Erlangen). Since 1884-5 Professor Falckenberg has also been an editor of the *Zeitschrift für Philosophie und philosophische Kritik*, until 1888 in association with Krohn, and after the latter's death, alone. At present he has in hand a treatise on Lotze for a German series analogous to Blackwood's Philosophical Classics, which is to be issued under his direction. Professor Falckenberg's general philosophical position may be described as that of moderate idealism. His historical method is strictly objective, the aim being a free reproduction of the systems discussed, as far as possible in their original terminology and historical connection, and without the intrusion of personal criticism.

The translation has been made from the second German edition (1892), with still later additions and corrections communicated by the author in manuscript. The translator has followed the original faithfully but not slavishly. He has not felt free to modify Professor Falckenberg's expositions, even in the rare cases where his own opinions would have led him to dissent, but minor changes have been made wherever needed to fit the book for the use of English-speaking students. Thus a few alterations have been made in dates and titles, chiefly under the English systems and from the latest authorities; and a few notes added in elucidation of portions of the text. Thus again the balance of the bibliography has been somewhat changed, including transfers from text to notes and *vice versa* and a few omissions, besides the introduction of a number of titles from our English philosophical literature chosen on the plan referred to in the preface to the first German edition. The glossary of terms foreign to the German reader has been replaced by a revision and expansion of the index, with the analyses of the glossary as a basis. Wherever possible, and this has been true in all important cases, the changes have been indicated by the usual signs.

The translator has further rewritten Chapter XV., Section 3, on recent British and American Philosophy. In this so much of the author's (historical) standpoint and treatment as proved compatible with the aim of a manual in English has been retained, but the section as a whole has been rearranged and much enlarged.

The labor of translation has been lightened by the example of previous writers, especially of the translators of the standard treatises of Ueberweg and Erdmann. The thanks of the translator are also due to several friends who have kindly aided him by advice or assistance: in particular to his friend and former pupil, Mr. C.M. Child, M.S., who participated in the preparation of a portion of the translation; and above all to Professor Falckenberg himself, who, by his willing sanction of the work and his co-operation throughout its progress, has given a striking example of scholarly courtesy.

A.C.A., Jr.

Wesleyan University, June, 1893.

INTRODUCTION.

In no other department is a thorough knowledge of history so important as in philosophy. Like historical science in general, philosophy is, on the one hand, in touch with exact inquiry, while, on the other, it has a certain relationship with art. With the former it has in common its methodical procedure and its cognitive aim; with the latter, its intuitive character and the endeavor to compass the whole of reality with a glance. Metaphysical principles are less easily verified from experience than physical hypotheses, but also less easily refuted. Systems of philosophy, therefore, are not so dependent on our progressive knowledge of facts as the theories of natural science, and change less quickly; notwithstanding their mutual conflicts, and in spite of the talk about discarded standpoints, they possess in a measure the permanence of classical works of art, they retain for all time a certain relative validity. The thought of Plato, of Aristotle, and of the heroes of modern philosophy is ever proving anew its fructifying power. Nowhere do we find such instructive errors as in the sphere of philosophy; nowhere is the new so essentially a completion and development of the old, even though it deem itself the whole and assume a hostile attitude toward its predecessors; nowhere is the inquiry so much more important than the final result; nowhere the categories "true and false" so inadequate. The spirit of the time and the spirit of the people, the individuality of the thinker, disposition, will, fancy—all these exert a far stronger influence on the development of philosophy, both by way of promotion and by way of hindrance, than in any other department of thought. If a system gives classical expression to the thought of an epoch, a nation, or a great personality; if it seeks to attack the world-riddle from a new direction, or brings us nearer its solution by important original conceptions, by a subtler or a simpler comprehension of the problem, by a wider outlook or a deeper insight; it has accomplished more than it could have done by bringing forward a number of indisputably correct principles. The variations in philosophy, which, on the assumption of the unity of truth, are a rock of offense to many minds, may be explained, on the one hand, by the combination of complex variety and limitation in the motives which govern philosophical thought,—for it is the whole man that philosophizes, not his understanding merely,—and, on the other, by the inexhaustible extent of the field of philosophy. Back of the logical labor of proof and inference stand, as inciting, guiding, and hindering agents, psychical and historical forces, which are themselves in large measure alogical, though stronger than all logic; while just before stretches away the immeasurable domain of reality, at once inviting and resisting conquest. The grave contradictions, so numerous in both the subjective and the objective fields, make unanimity impossible concerning ultimate problems; in fact, they render it difficult for the individual thinker to combine his convictions into a self-consistent system. Each philosopher sees limited sections of the world only, and these through his own eyes; every system is one-sided. Yet it is this multiplicity and variety of systems alone which makes the aim of philosophy practicable as it endeavors to give a complete picture of the soul and of the universe. The history of philosophy is the philosophy of humanity, that great individual, which, with more extended vision than the instruments through which it works, is able to entertain opposing principles, and which, reconciling old contradictions as it discovers new ones, approaches by a necessary and certain growth the knowledge of the one all-embracing truth, which is rich and varied beyond our conception. In order to energetic labor in the further progress of philosophy, it is necessary to imagine that the goddess of truth is about to lift the veil which has for centuries concealed her. The historian of philosophy, on the contrary, looks on each new system as a stone, which, when shaped and fitted into its place, will help to raise higher the pyramid of knowledge. Hegel's doctrine of the necessity and motive force of contradictories, of the relative justification of standpoints, and the systematic development of speculation, has great and permanent value as a general point of view. It needs only to be guarded from narrow scholastic application to become a safe canon for the historical treatment of philosophy.

In speaking above of the worth of the philosophical doctrines of the past as defying time, and as comparable to the standard character of finished works of art, the special reference was to those elements in speculation which proceed less from abstract thinking than from the fancy, the heart, and the character of the individual, and even more directly from the disposition of the people; and which to a certain degree may be divorced from logical reasoning and the scientific treatment of particular questions. These may be summed up under the phrase, views of the world. The necessity for constant reconsideration of them is from this standpoint at once evident. The Greek view of the world is as classic as the plastic art of Phidias and the epic of Homer; the Christian, as eternally valid as the architecture of the Middle Ages; the modern, as irrefutable as Goethe's poetry and the music of Beethoven. The views of the world which proceed from the spirits of different ages, as products of the general development of culture, are not so much thoughts as rhythms in thinking, not theories but modes of intuition saturated with feelings of worth. We may dispute about them, it is true; we may argue against them or in their defense; but they can neither be established nor overthrown by cogent proofs. It is not only optimism and pessimism, determinism and indeterminism, that have their ultimate roots in the affective side of our nature, but pantheism and individualism, also idealism and materialism, even rationalism and sensationalism. Even though they operate with the instruments of thought, they remain in the last analysis matters of faith, of feeling, and of resolution. The aesthetic view of the world held by the Greeks, the transcendental-religious view of Christianity, the intellectual view of Leibnitz and Hegel, the pantheistic views of Fichte I and Schopenhauer are vital forces, not doctrines, postulates, not results of thought. One view of the world is forced to yield its pre-eminence to another, which it has itself helped to produce by its own one-sidedness; only to reconquer its opponent later, when it has learned from her, when it has been purified, corrected, and deepened by the struggle. But the elder contestant is no more confuted by the younger than the drama of Sophocles by the drama of Shakespeare, than youth by age or spring by autumn.

If it is thus indubitable that the views of the world held in earlier times deserve to live on in the memory of man, and to live as something better than mere reminders of the past—the history of philosophy is not a cabinet of antiquities, but a museum of typical products of the mind—the value and interest of the historical study of the past in relation to the exact scientific side of philosophical inquiry is not less evident. In every science it is useful to trace the origin and growth of problems and theories, and doubly so in philosophy. With her it is by no means the universal rule that progress shows itself by the result; the statement of the question is often more important than the answer. The problem is more sharply defined in a given direction; or it becomes more comprehensive, is analyzed and refined; or if now it threatens to break up into subtle details, some genius appears to simplify it and force our thoughts back to the fundamental question. This advance in problems, which happily is everywhere manifested by unmistakable signs, is, in the case of many of the questions which irresistibly force themselves upon the human heart, the only certain gain from centuries of endeavor. The labor here is of more value than the result.

In treating the history of philosophy, two extremes must be avoided, lawless individualism and abstract logical formalism. The history of philosophy is neither a disconnected succession of arbitrary individual opinions and clever guesses, nor a mechanically developed series of typical standpoints and problems, which imply one another in just the form and order historically assumed. The former supposition does violence to the regularity of philosophical development, the latter to its vitality. In the one case, the connection is conceived too loosely, in the other, too rigidly and simply. One view underestimates the power of the logical Idea, the other overestimates it. It is not easy to support the principle that chance rules the destiny of philosophy, but it is more difficult to avoid the opposite conviction of the one-sidedness of formalistic construction, and to define the nature and limits of philosophical necessity. The development of philosophy is, perhaps, one chief aim of the world-process, but it is certainly not the only one; it is a part of the universal aim, and it is not surprising that the instruments of its realization do not work exclusively in its behalf, that their activity brings about results, which seem unessential for philosophical ends or obstacles in their way. Philosophical ideas do not think themselves, but are thought by living spirits, which are something other and better than mere thought machines—by spirits who live these thoughts, who fill them with personal warmth and passionately defend them. There is often reason, no doubt, for the complaint that the personality which has undertaken to develop some great idea is inadequate to the task, that it carries its subjective defects into the matter in hand, that it does too much or too little, or the right thing in the wrong way, so that the spirit of philosophy seems to have erred in the choice and the preparation of its instrument. But the reverse side of the picture must also be taken into account. The thinking spirit is more limited, it is true, than were desirable for the perfect execution of a definite logical task; but, on the other hand, it is far too rich as well. A soulless play of concepts would certainly not help the cause, and there is no disadvantage in the failure of the history of philosophy to proceed so directly and so scholastically, as, for instance, in the system of Hegel. A graded series of interconnected general forces mediate between the logical Idea and the individual thinker—the spirit of the people, of the age, of the thinker's vocation, of his time of life, which are felt by the individual as part of himself and whose impulses he unconsciously obeys. In this way the modifying, furthering, hindering correlation of higher and lower, of the ruler with his commands and the servant with his more or less willing obedience, is twice repeated, the situation being complicated further by the fact that the subject affected by these historical forces himself helps to make history. The most important factor in philosophical progress is, of course, the state of inquiry at the time, the achievements of the thinkers of the immediately preceding age; and in this relation of a philosopher to his predecessors, again, a distinction must be made between a logical and a psychological element. The successor often commences his support, his development, or his refutation at a point quite unwelcome to the constructive historian. At all events, if we may judge from the experience of the past, too much caution cannot be exercised in setting up formal laws for the development of thought. According to the law of contradiction and reconciliation, a Schopenhauer must have followed directly after Leibnitz, to oppose his pessimistic ethelism to the optimistic intellectualism of the latter; when, in turn, a Schleiermacher, to give an harmonic resolution of the antithesis into a concrete doctrine of feeling, would have made a fine third. But it turned out otherwise, and we must be content.

* * * * *

The estimate of the value of the history of philosophy in general, given at the start, is the more true of the history of modern philosophy, since the movement introduced by the latter still goes on unfinished. We are still at work on the problems which were brought forward by Descartes, Locke, and Leibnitz, and which Kant gathered up into the critical or transcendental question. The present continues to be governed by the ideal of culture which Bacon proposed and Fichte exalted to a higher level; we all live under the unweakened spell of that view of the world which was developed in hostile opposition to Scholasticism, and through the enduring influence of those mighty geographical and scientific discoveries and religious reforms which marked the entrance of the modern period. It is true, indeed, that the transition brought about by Kant's noëtical and ethical revolution was of great significance,—more significant even than the Socratic period, with which we are fond of comparing it; much that was new was woven on, much of the old, weakened, broken, destroyed. And yet, if we take into account the historical after-influence of Cartesianism, we shall find that the thread was only knotted and twisted by Kantianism, not cut through. The continued power of the pre-Kantian modes of thought is shown by the fact that Spinoza has been revived in Fichte and Schelling, Leibnitz in Herbart and Hegel, the sensationalism of the French Illuminati in Feuerbach; and that even materialism, which had been struck down by the criticism of the reason (one would have thought forever), has again raised its head. Even that most narrow tendency of the early philosophy of the modern period, the apotheosis of cognition is,—in spite of the moralistic counter-movement of Kant and Fichte,—the controlling motive in the last of the great idealistic systems, while it also continues to exercise a marvelously powerful influence on the convictions of our Hegel-weary age, alike within the sphere of philosophy and (still more) without it. In view of the intimate relations between contemporary inquiry and the progress of thought since the beginning of the modern period, acquaintance with the latter, which it is the aim of this *History* to facilitate, becomes a pressing duty. To study the history of philosophy since Descartes is to study the pre-conditions of contemporary philosophy.

We begin with an outline sketch of the general characteristics of modern philosophy. These may be most conveniently described by comparing them with the characteristics of ancient and of mediaeval philosophy. The character of ancient philosophy or Greek philosophy,—for they are practically the same,—is predominantly aesthetic. The Greek holds beauty and truth closely akin and inseparable; "cosmos" is his common expression for the world and for ornament. The universe is for him a harmony, an organism, a work of art, before which he stands in admiration and reverential awe. In quiet contemplation, as with the eye of a connoisseur, he looks upon the world or the individual object as a well-ordered whole, more disposed to enjoy the congruity of its parts than to study out its ultimate elements. He prefers contemplation to analysis, his thought is plastic, not anatomical. He finds the nature of the object in its form; and ends give him the key to the comprehension of events. Discovering human elements everywhere, he is always ready with judgments of worth—the stars move in circles because circular motion is the most perfect; the right is better than left, upper finer than lower, that which precedes more beautiful than that which follows. Thinkers in whom this aesthetic reverence is weaker than the analytic impulse—especially Democritus—seem half modern rather than Greek. By the side of the Greek philosophy, in its sacred festal garb, stands the modern in secular workday dress, in the laborer's blouse, with the merciless chisel of analysis in its hand. This does not seek beauty, but only the naked truth, no matter what it be. It holds it impossible to satisfy at once the understanding and taste; nay, nakedness, ugliness, and offensiveness seem to it to testify for, rather than against, the genuineness of truth. In its anxiety not to read human elements into nature, it goes so far as completely to read spirit out of nature. The world is not a living whole, but a machine; not a work of art which is to be viewed in its totality and enjoyed with reverence, but a clock-movement to be taken apart in order to be understood. Nowhere are there ends in the world, but everywhere mechanical causes. The character of modern thought would appear to a Greek returned to earth very sober, unsplendid, undevout, and intrusive. And, in fact, modern philosophy has a considerable amount of prose about it, is not easily impressed, accepts no limitations from feeling, and holds nothing too sacred to be attacked with the weapon of analytic thought. And yet it combines penetration with intrusiveness; acuteness, coolness, and logical courage with its soberness. Never before has the demand for unprejudiced thought and certain knowledge been made with equal earnestness. This interest in knowledge for its own sake developed so suddenly and with such strength that, in presumptuous gladness, men believed that no previous age had rightly understood what truth and love for truth are. The natural consequence was a general overestimation of cognition at the expense of all other mental activities. Even among the Greek thinkers, thought was held by the majority to be the noblest and most divine function. But their intellectualism was checked by the aesthetic and eudaemonistic element, and preserved from the one-sidedness which it manifests in the modern period, because of the lack of an effective counterpoise. However eloquently Bacon commends the advantages to be derived from the conquest of nature, he still understands inquiry for inquiry's sake, and honors it as supreme; even the ethelistic philosophers, Fichte and Schopenhauer, pay their tribute to the prejudice in favor of intellectualism. The fact that the modern period can show no one philosophic writer of the literary rank of Plato, even though it includes such masters of style as Fichte, Schelling, Schopenhauer, and Lotze, not to speak of lesser names, is an external proof of how noticeably the aesthetic impulse has given way to one purely intellectual.

When we turn to the character of mediaeval thinking; we find, instead of the aesthetic views of antiquity and the purely scientific tendency of the modern era, a distinctively religious spirit. Faith prescribes the objects and the limitations of knowledge; everything is referred to the hereafter, thought becomes prayer. Men speculate concerning the attributes of God, on the number and rank of the angels, on the immortality of man—all purely transcendental subjects. Side by side with these, it is true, the world receives loving attention, but always as the lower story merely,[1] above which, with its own laws, rises the true fatherland, the kingdom of grace. The most subtle acuteness is employed in the service of dogma, with the task of fathoming the how and why of things whose existence is certified elsewhere. The result is a formalism in thought side by side with profound and fervent mysticism. Doubt and trust are strangely intermingled, and a feeling of expectation stirs all hearts. On the one side stands sinful, erring man, who, try as hard as he may, only half unravels the mysteries of revealed truth; on the other, the God of grace, who, after our death, will reveal himself to us as clearly as Adam knew him before the fall. God alone, however, can comprehend himself—for the finite spirit, even truth unveiled is mystery, and ecstasy, unresisting devotion to the incomprehensible, the culmination of knowledge. In mediaeval philosophy the subject looks longingly upward to the infinite object of his thought, expecting that the latter will bend down toward him or lift him upward toward itself; in Greek philosophy the spirit confronts its object, the world, on a footing of equality; in modern philosophy the speculative subject feels himself higher than the object, superior to nature. In the conception of the Middle Ages, truth and mystery are identical; to antiquity they appear reconcilable; modern thought holds them as mutually exclusively as light and darkness. The unknown is the enemy of knowledge, which must be chased out of its last hiding-place. It is, therefore, easy to understand that the modern period stands in far sharper antithesis to the mediaeval era than to the ancient, for the latter has furnished it many principles which can be used as weapons against the former. Grandparents and grandchildren make good friends.

[Footnote 1: On the separation and union of the three worlds, *natura, gratia, gloria*, in Thomas Aquinas, cf. Rudolph Eucken, *Die Philosophie des Thomas von Aquino und die Kultur der Neuzeit*, Halle. 1886.]

When a new movement is in preparation, but there is a lack of creative force to give it form, a period of tumultuous disaffection with existing principles ensues. What is wanted is not clearly perceived, but there is a lively sense of that which is not wanted. Dissatisfaction prepares a place for that which is to come by undermining the existent and making it ripe for its fall. The old, the outgrown, the doctrine which had become inadequate, was in this case Scholasticism; modern philosophy shows throughout—and most clearly at the start—an anti-Scholastic character. If up to this time Church dogma had ruled unchallenged in spiritual affairs, and the Aristotelian philosophy in things temporal, war is now declared against authority of every sort and freedom of thought is inscribed on the banner.[1] "Modern philosophy is Protestantism in the sphere of the thinking spirit" (Erdmann). Not that which has been considered true for centuries, not that which another says, though he be Aristotle or Thomas Aquinas, not that which flatters the desires of the heart, is true, but that only which is demonstrated to my own understanding with convincing force. Philosophy is no longer willing to be the handmaid of theology, but must set up a house of her own. The watchword now becomes freedom and independent thought, deliverance from every form of constraint, alike from the bondage of ecclesiastical decrees and the inner servitude of prejudice and cherished inclinations. But the adoption of a purpose leads to the consideration of the means for attaining it. Thus the thirst for knowledge raises questions concerning the method, the instruments, and the limits of knowledge; the interest in noëtics and methodology vigorously develops, remains a constant factor in modern inquiry, and culminates in Kant, not again to die away.

[Footnote 1: The doctrine of twofold truth, under whose protecting cloak the new liberal movements had hitherto taken refuge, was now disdainfully repudiated. Cf. Freudenthal, *Zur Beurtheilung der Scholastik*, in vol. iii. of the *Archiv für Geschichte der Philosophie*, 1890. Also, H. Reuter, *Geschichte der religiösen Aufklärung im Mittelalter* 1875-77; and Dilthey, *Einleitung in die Geisteswissenschaften*, 1883.]

This negative aspect of modern tendencies needs, however, a positive supplement. The mediaeval mode of thought is discarded and the new one is not yet found. What can more fittingly furnish a support, a preliminary substitute, than antiquity? Thus philosophy, also, joins in that great stream of culture, the Renaissance and humanism, which, starting from Italy, poured forth over the whole civilized world. Plato and Neoplatonism, Epicurus and the Stoa are opposed to Scholasticism, the real Aristotle to the transformed Aristotle of the Church and the distorted Aristotle of the schools. Back to the sources, is the cry. With the revival of the ancient languages and ancient books, the spirit of antiquity is also revived. The dust of the schools and the tyranny of the Church are thrown off, and the classical ideal of a free and noble humanity gains enthusiastic adherents. The man is not to be forgotten in the Christian, nor art and science, the rights and the riches of individuality in the interest of piety; work for the future must not blind us to the demands of the present nor lead us to neglect the comprehensive cultivation of the natural capacities of the spirit. The world and man are no longer viewed through Christian eyes, the one as a realm of darkness and the other as a vessel of weakness and wrath, but nature and life gleam before the new generation in joyous, hopeful light. Humanism and optimism have always been allied.

This change in the spirit of thought is accompanied by a corresponding change in the object of thought: theology must yield its supremacy to the knowledge of nature. Weary of Christological and soteriological questions, weary of disputes concerning the angels, the thinking spirit longs to make himself at home in the world it has learned to love, demands real knowledge,—knowledge which is of practical utility,—and no longer seeks God outside the world, but in it and above it. Nature becomes the home, the body of God. Transcendence gives place to immanence, not only in theology, but elsewhere. Modern philosophy is naturalistic in spirit, not only because it takes nature for its favorite object, but also because it carries into other branches of knowledge the mathematical method so successful in natural science, because it considers everything *sub ratione naturae* and insists on the "natural" explanation of all phenomena, even those of ethics and politics.

In a word, the tendency of modern philosophy is anti-Scholastic, humanistic, and naturalistic. This summary must suffice for preliminary orientation, while the detailed division, particularization, modification, and limitation of these general points must be left for later treatment.

Two further facts, however, may receive preliminary notice. The indifference and hostility to the Church which have been cited among the prominent characteristics of modern philosophy, do not necessarily mean enmity to the Christian religion, much less to religion in general. In part, it is merely a change in the object of religious feeling, which blazes up especially strong and enthusiastic in the philosophy of the sixteenth century, as it transfers its worship from a transcendent deity to a universe indued with a soul; in part, the opposition is directed against the mediaeval, ecclesiastical form of Christianity, with its monastic abandonment of the world. It was often nothing but a very deep and strong religious feeling that led thinkers into the conflict with the hierarchy. Since the elements of permanent worth in the tendencies, doctrines, and institutions of the Middle Ages are thus culled out from that which is corrupt and effete, and preserved by incorporation into the new view of the world and the new science, and as fruitful elements from antiquity enter with them, the progress of philosophy shows a continuous enrichment in its ideas, intuitions, and spirit. The old is not simply discarded and destroyed, but purified, transformed, and assimilated. The same fact forces itself into notice if we consider the relations of nationality and philosophy in the three great eras. The Greek philosophy was entirely national in its origin and its public, it was rooted in the character of the people and addressed itself to fellow-countrymen; not until toward its decline, and not until influenced by Christianity, were its cosmopolitan inclinations aroused. The Middle Ages were indifferent to national distinctions, as to everything earthly, and naught was of value in comparison with man's transcendent destiny. Mediaeval philosophy is in its aims un-national, cosmopolitan, catholic; it uses the Latin of the schools, it seeks adherents in every land, it finds everywhere productive spirits whose labors in its service remain unaffected by their national peculiarities. The modern period returns to the nationalism of antiquity, but does not relinquish the advantage gained by the extension of mediaeval thought to the whole civilized world. The roots of modern philosophy are sunk deep in the fruitful soil of nationality, while the top of the tree spreads itself far beyond national limitations. It is national and cosmopolitan together; it is international as the common property of the various peoples, which exchange their philosophical gifts through an active commerce of ideas. Latin is often retained for use abroad, as the universal language of savants, but many a work is first published in the mother-tongue—and thought in it. Thus it becomes possible for the ideas of the wise to gain an entrance into the consciousness of the people, from whose spirit they have really sprung, and to become a power beyond the circle of the learned public. Philosophy as illumination, as a factor in general culture, is an exclusively modern phenomenon. In this speculative intercourse of nations, however, the French, the English, and the Germans are most involved, both as producers and consumers. France gives the initiative (in Descartes), then England assumes the leadership (in Locke), with Leibnitz and Kant the hegemony passes over to Germany. Besides these powers, Italy takes an eager part in the production of philosophical ideas in the period of ferment before Descartes. Each of these nations contributes elements to the total result which it alone is in a position to furnish, and each is rewarded by gifts in return which it would be incapable of producing out of its own store. This international exchange of ideas, in which each gives and each receives, and the fact that the chief modern thinkers, especially in the earlier half of the era, prior to Kant, are in great part not philosophers by profession but soldiers, statesmen, physicians, as well as natural scientists, historians, and priests, give modern philosophy an unprofessional, worldly appearance, in striking contrast to the clerical character of mediaeval, and the prophetic character of ancient thinking.

Germany, England, and France claim the honor of having produced the first *modern* philosopher, presenting Nicolas of Cusa, Bacon of Verulam, and René Descartes as their candidates, while Hobbes, Bruno, and Montaigne have received only scattered votes. The claim of England is the weakest of all, for, without intending to diminish Bacon's importance, it may be said that the programme which he develops—and in essence his philosophy is nothing more—was, in its leading principles, not first announced by him, and not carried out with sufficient consistency. The dispute between the two remaining contestants may be easily and equitably settled by making the simple distinction between forerunner and beginner, between path-breaker and founder. The entrance of a new historical era is not accompanied by an audible click, like the beginning of a new piece on a music-box, but is gradually effected. A considerable period may intervene between the point when the new movement flashes up, not understood and half unconscious of itself, and the time when it appears on the stage in full strength and maturity, recognizing itself as new and so acknowledged by others: the period of ferment between the Middle Ages and modern times lasted almost two centuries. It is in the end little more than logomachy to discuss whether this time of anticipation and desire, of endeavor and partial success, in which the new struggles with the old without conquering it, and the opposite tendencies in the conflicting views of the world interplay in a way at once obscure and wayward, is to be classed as the epilogue of the old era or the prologue of the new. The simple solution to take it as a *transition period*, no longer mediaeval but not yet modern, has met with fairly general acceptance. Nicolas of Cusa (1401-64) was the first to announce *fundamental principles* of modern philosophy—he is the leader in this intermediate preparatory period. Descartes (1596-1650) brought forward the first *system*—he is the father of modern philosophy.

A brief survey of the literature may be added in conclusion:

Heinrich Ritter's *Geschichte der neueren Philosophie* (vols. ix.-xii. of his *Geschichte der Philosophie*), 1850-53, to Wolff and Rousseau, has been superseded by more recent works, J.E. Erdmann's able *Versuch einer wissenschaftlichen Darstellung der neueren Philosophie* (6 vols., 1834-53) gives in appendices literal excerpts from non-German writers; the same author's *Grundriss der Geschichte der Philosophie* (2 vols., 1869; 3d ed., 1878) contains at the end the first exposition of German Philosophy since the Death of Hegel [English translation in 3 vols., edited by W. S. Hough, 1890.—TR.]. Ueberweg's *Grundriss* (7th ed. by M. Heinze, 1888) is indispensable for reference on account of the completeness of its bibliographical notes, which, however, are confusing to the beginner [English translation by G.S. Morris, with additions by the translator, Noah Porter, and Vincenzo Botta, New York, 1872-74.—TR.]. The most detailed and brilliant exposition has been given by Kuno Fischer (1854 seq.; 3d ed., 1878 seq.; the same author's *Baco und seine Nachfolger*, 2d ed., 1875,—English translation, 1857, by Oxenford,—supplements the first two volumes of the *Geschichte der neueren Philosophie*). This work, which is important also as a literary achievement, is better fitted than any other to make the reader at home in the ideal world of the great philosophers, which it reconstructs from its central point, and to prepare him for the study (which, of course, even the best exposition cannot replace) of the works of the thinkers themselves. Its excessive simplification of problems is not of great moment in the first introduction to a system [English translation of vol. iii. book 2 (1st ed.), *A Commentary on Kant's Critick of the Pure Reason*, by J.P. Mahaffy, London, 1866; vol. i. part 1 and part 2, book 1, *Descartes and his School*, by J, P. Gordy, New York, 1887; of vol. v. chaps, i.-v., *A Critique of Kant*, by W.S. Hough, London, 1888.—TR.]. Wilhelm Windelband *(Geschichte der neueren Philosophie*, 2 vols., 1878 and 1880, to Hegel and Herbart inclusive) accentuates the connection of philosophy with general culture and the particular sciences, and emphasizes philosophical method. This work is pleasant reading, yet, in the interest of clearness, we could wish that the author had given more of positive information concerning the content of the doctrines treated, instead of merely advancing reflections on them. A projected third volume is to trace the development of philosophy down to the present time. Windelband's compendium, *Geschichte der Philosophie*, 1890-91, is distinguished from other expositions by the fact that, for the most part, it confines itself to a history of *problems*. Baumann's *Geschichte der Philosophie*, 1890, aims to give a detailed account of those thinkers only who have advanced views individual either in their content or in their proof. Eduard Zeller has given his *Geschichte der deutschen Philosophie seit Leibniz* (1873; 2d ed., 1875) the benefit of the same thorough and comprehensive knowledge and mature judgment which have made his *Philosophie der Griechen* a classic. [Bowen's *Modern Philosophy*, New York, 1857 (6th ed., 1891); Royce's *Spirit of Modern Philosophy*, 1892.—TR.]

Eugen Dühring's hypercritical *Kritische Geschichte der Philosophie* (1869; 3d ed., 1878) can hardly be recommended to students. Lewes (German translation, 1876) assumes a positivistic standpoint; Thilo (1874), a position exclusively Herbartian; A. Stoeckl (3d ed., 1889) writes from the standpoint of confessional Catholicism; Vincenz Knauer (2d ed., 1882) is a Güntherian. With the philosophico-historical work of Chr. W. Sigwart (1854), and one of the same date by Oischinger, we are not intimately acquainted.

Expositions of philosophy since Kant have been given by the Hegelian, C.L. Michelet (a larger one in 2 vols., 1837-38, and a smaller one, 1843); by Chalybaeus (1837; 5th ed., 1860, formerly very popular and worthy of it, English, 1854); by Fr. K. Biedermann (1842-43); by Carl Fortlage (1852, Kantio-Fichtean standpoint); and by Friedrich Harms (1876). The last of these writers unfortunately did not succeed in giving a sufficiently clear and precise, not to say tasteful, form to the valuable ideas and original conceptions in which his work is rich. The very popular exposition by an anonymous author of Hegelian tendencies, *Deutschlands Denker seit Kant* (Dessau, 1851), hardly deserves mention.

Further, we may mention some of the works which treat the historical development of particular subjects: On the history of the *philosophy of religion*, the first volume of Otto Pfleiderer's *Religionsphilosophie auf geschichtlicher Grundlage* (2d ed., 1883;—English translation by Alexander Stewart and Allan Menzies, 1886-88.—TR.), and the very trustworthy exposition by Bernhard Pünjer (2 vols., 1880, 1883; English translation by W. Hastie, vol. i., 1887.—TR.). On the history of *practical philosophy*, besides the first volume of I.H. Fichte's *Ethik* (1850), Franz Vorländer's *Geschichte der philosophischen Moral, Rechts- und Staatslehre der Engländer und Franzosen* (1855); Fr. Jodl, *Geschichte der Ethik in der neueren Philosophie* (2 vols., 1882, 1889), and Bluntschli, *Geschichte der neueren Staatswissenschaft* (3d ed., 1881); [Sidgwick's *Outlines of the History of Ethics*, 3d ed., 1892, and Martineau's *Types of Ethical Theory*, 3d ed., 1891.—TR.]. On the history of the *philosophy of history*: Rocholl, *Die Philosophie der Geschichte*, 1878; Richard Fester, *Rousseau und die deutsche Geschichtsphilosophie*, 1890 [Flint, *The Philosophy of History in Europe*, vol. i., 1874, complete in 3 vols., 1893 seq.]. On the history of *aesthetics*, R. Zimmermann, 1858; H. Lotze, 1868; Max Schasler, 1871; Ed. von Hartmann (since Kant), 1886; Heinrich von Stein, *Die Entstehung der neueren Aesthetik* (1886); [Bosanquet, *A History of Aesthetic*, 1892.—TR.]. Further, Fr. Alb. Lange, *Geschichte des Materialismus*, 1866; 4th ed., 1882; [English translation by E.C. Thomas, 3 vols., 1878-81.—TR.]; Jul. Baumann, *Die Lehren von Raum, Zeit und Mathematik in der neueren Philosophie*, 1868-69; Edm. König, *Die Entwickelung des Causalproblems von Cartesius bis Kant*, 1888, *seit Kant*, 1890; Kurd Lasswitz, *Geschichte der Atomistik vom Mittelalter bis Newton*, 2 vols., 1890; Ed. Grimm, *Zur Geschichte des Erkenntnissproblems, von Bacon zu Hume*, 1890. The following works are to be recommended on the period of transition: Moritz Carrière, *Die philosophische Weltanschauung der Reformationszeit*, 1847; 2d ed., 1887; and Jacob Burckhardt, *Kultur der Renaissance in Italien*, 4th ed., 1886. Reference may also be made to A. Trendelenburg, *Historische Beiträge zur Philosophie*, 3 vols., 1846-67; Rudolph Eucken, *Geschichte und Kritik der Grundbegriffe der Gegenwart*, 1878; [English translation by M. Stuart Phelps,

1880.—TR.]; the same, *Geschichte der philosophischen Terminologie*, 1879; the same, *Beiträge zur Geschichte der neueren Philosophie*, 1886 (including a valuable paper on parties and party names in philosophy); the same, *Die Lebensanschauungen der grossen Denker*, 1890; Ludwig Noack, *Philosophiegeschichtliches Lexicon*, 1879; Ed. Zeller, *Vorträge und Abhandlungen*, three series, 1865-84; Chr. von Sigwart, *Kleine Schriften*, 2 vols., 1881; 2d ed., 1889. R. Seydel's *Religion und Philosophie*, 1887, contains papers on Luther, Schleiermacher, Schelling, Weisse, Fechner, Lotze, Hartmann, Darwinism, etc., which are well worth reading.

Among the smaller compends Schwegler's (1848; recent editions revised and supplemented by R. Koeber) remains still the least bad [English translations by Seelye and Smith, revised edition with additions, New York, 1880; and J.H. Stirling, with annotations, 7th ed., 1879.—TR.]. The meager sketches by Deter, Koeber, Kirchner, Kuhn, Rabus, Vogel, and others are useful for review at least. Fritz Schultze's *Stammbaum der Philosophie*, 1890, gives skillfully constructed tabular outlines, but, unfortunately, in a badly chosen form.

CHAPTER I.

THE PERIOD OF TRANSITION: FROM NICOLAS OF CUSA TO DESCARTES.

The essays at philosophy which made their appearance between the middle of the fifteenth century and the middle of the seventeenth, exhibit mediaeval and modern characteristics in such remarkable intermixture that they can be assigned exclusively to neither of these two periods. There are eager longings, lofty demands, magnificent plans, and promising outlooks in abundance, but a lack of power to endure, a lack of calmness and maturity; while the shackles against which the leading minds revolt still bind too firmly both the leaders and those to whom they speak. Only here and there are the fetters loosened and thrown off; if the hands are successfully freed, the clanking chains still hamper the feet. It is a time just suited for original thinkers, a remarkable number of whom in fact make their appearance, side by side or in close succession. Further, however little these are able to satisfy the demand for permanent results, they ever arouse our interest anew by the boldness and depth of their brilliant ideas, which alternate with quaint fancies or are pervaded by them; by the youthful courage with which they attacked great questions; and not least by the hard fate which rewarded their efforts with misinterpretation, persecution, and death at the stake. We must quickly pass over the broad threshold between modern philosophy and Scholastic philosophy, which is bounded by the year 1450, in which Nicolas of Cusa wrote his chief work, the *Idiota*, and 1644, when Descartes began the new era with his *Principia Philosophiae*; and can touch, in passing, only the most important factors. We shall begin our account of this transition period with Nicolas, and end it with the Englishmen, Bacon, Hobbes, and Lord Herbert of Cherbury. Between these we shall arrange the various figures of the Philosophical Renaissance (in the broad sense) in six groups: the Restorers of the Ancient Systems and their Opponents; the Italian Philosophers of Nature; the Political and Legal Philosophers; the Skeptics; the Mystics; the Founders of the Exact Investigation of Nature. In Italy the new spiritual birth shows an aesthetic, scientific, and humanistic tendency; in Germany it is pre-eminently religious emancipation—in the Reformation.

%1. Nicolas of Cusa.%

Nicolas[1] was born in 1401, at Cues (Cusa) on the Moselle near Treves. He early ran away from his stern father, a boatman and vine-dresser named Chrypps (or Krebs), and was brought up by the Brothers of the Common Life at Deventer. In Padua he studied law, mathematics, and philosophy, but the loss of his first case at Mayence so disgusted him with his profession that he turned to theology, and became a distinguished preacher. He took part in the Council of Basle, was sent by Pope Eugen IV. as an ambassador to Constantinople and to the Reichstag at Frankfort; was made Cardinal in 1448, and Bishop of Brixen in 1450. His feudal lord, the Count of Tyrol, Archduke Sigismund, refused him recognition on account of certain quarrels in which they had become engaged, and for a time held him prisoner. Previous to this he had undertaken journeys to Germany and the Netherlands on missionary business. During a second sojourn in Italy death overtook him, in the year 1464, at Todi in Umbria. The first volume of the Paris edition of his collected works (1514) contains the most important of his philosophical writings; the second, among others, mathematical essays and ten books of selections from his sermons; the third, the extended work, *De Concordantia Catholica*, which he had completed at Basle. In 1440 (having already written on the Reform of the Calendar) he began his imposing series of philosophical writings with the *De Docta Ignorantia*, to which the *De Conjecturis* was added in the following year. These were succeeded by smaller treatises entitled *De Quaerendo Deum, De Dato Patris Luminum, De Filiatione Dei, De Genesi*, and a defense of the *De Docta Ignorantia*. His most important work is the third of the four dialogues of the *Idiota* ("On the Mind"), 1450. He clothes in continually changing forms the one supreme truth on which all depends, and which cannot be expressed in intelligible language but only comprehended by living intuition. In many different ways he endeavors to lead the reader on to a vision of the inexpressible, or to draw him up to it, and to develop fruitfully the principle of the coincidence of opposites, which had dawned upon him on his return journey from Constantinople (*De Visione Dei, Dialogus de Possest, De Beryllo, De Ludo Globi, De Venatione Sapientiae, De Apice Theoriae, Compendium*). Sometimes he uses dialectical reasoning; sometimes he soars in mystical exaltation; sometimes he writes with a simplicity level to the common mind, and in connection with that which lies at hand; sometimes, with the most comprehensive brevity. Besides these his philosophico-religious works are of great value, *De Pace Fidei, De Cribratione Alchorani*. Liberal Catholics reverence him as one of the deepest thinkers of the Church; but the fame of Giordano Bruno, a more brilliant but much less original figure, has hitherto stood in the way of the general recognition of his great importance for modern philosophy.

[Footnote 1: R. Zimmermann, *Nikolaus Cusanus als Vorläufer Leibnizens*, in vol. viii. of the *Sitzungsberichte der philosophisch-historischen Klasse der Akademie der Wissenschaften*, Vienna, 1852, p. 306 seq. R. Falckenberg, *Grundzüge der Philosophie des Nikolaus Cusanus mit besonderer Berücksichtigung der Lehre vom Erkennen*, Breslau, 1880. R. Eucken, *Beiträge zur Geschichte der neueren Philosophie*, Heidelberg, 1886, p. 6 seq.; Joh. Uebinger, *Die Gotteslehre des Nikolaus Cusanus*, Münster, 1888. Scharpff, *Des Nikolaus von Cusa wichtigste Schriften in deutscher Uebersetzung*, Freiburg i. Br., 1862.]

Human knowledge and the relation of God to the world are the two poles of the Cusan's system. He distinguishes four stages of knowledge. Lowest of all stands sense (together with imagination), which yields only confused images; next above, the understanding (*ratio*), whose functions comprise analysis, the positing of time and space, numerical operations, and denomination, and which keeps the opposites distinct under the law of contradiction; third, the speculative reason (*intellectus*), which finds the opposites reconcilable; and highest of all the mystical, supra-rational intuition (*visio sine comprehensione, intuitio, unio, filiatio*), for which the opposites coincide in the infinite unity. The intuitive culmination of knowledge, in which the soul is united with God,—since here even the antithesis of subject and object disappears,—is but seldom attained; and it is difficult to keep out the disturbing symbols and images of sense, which mingle themselves in the intuition. But it is just this insight into the incomprehensibility of the infinite which gives us a true knowledge of God; this is the meaning of the "learned ignorance," the *docta ignorantia*. The distinctions between these several stages of cognition are not, however, to be understood in any rigid sense, for each higher function comprehends the lower, and is active therein. The understanding can discriminate only when it is furnished by sensation with images of that which is to be discriminated, the reason can combine only when the understanding has supplied the results of analysis as material for combination; while, on the other hand, it is the understanding which is present in sense as consciousness, and the reason whose unity guides the understanding in its work of separation. Thus the several modes of cognition do not stand for independent fundamental faculties, but for connected modifications of one fundamental power which work together and mutually imply one another. The position that an intellectual function of attention and discrimination is active in sensuous perception, is a view entirely foreign to mediaeval modes of thought; for the Scholastics were accustomed to make sharp divisions between the cognitive faculties, on the principle that particulars are felt through sense and universals thought through the understanding. The idea on which Nicolas bases his argument for immortality has also an entirely modern sound: viz., that space and time are products of the understanding, and, therefore, can have no power over the spirit which produces them; for the author is higher and mightier than the product.

The confession that all our knowledge is conjecture does not simply mean that absolute and exact truth remains concealed from us; but is intended at the same time to encourage us to draw as near as possible to the eternal verity by ever truer conjectures. There are degrees of truth, and our surmises are neither absolutely true nor entirely false. Conjecture becomes error only when, forgetting the inadequacy of human knowledge, we rest content with it as a final solution; the Socratic maxim, "I know that I am ignorant," should not lead to despairing resignation but to courageous further inquiry. The duty of speculation is to penetrate deeper and deeper into the secrets of the divine, even though the ultimate revelation will not be given us until the hereafter. The fittest instrument of speculation is furnished by mathematics, in its conception of the infinite and the wonders of numerical relations: as on the infinite sphere center and circumference coincide, so God's essence is exalted above all opposites; and as the other numbers are unfolded from the unit, so the finite proceeds by explication from the infinite. A controlling significance in the serial construction of the world is ascribed to the ten, as the sum of the first four numbers—as reason, understanding, imagination, and sensibility are related in human cognition, so God, spirit, soul, and body, or infinity, thought, life, and being are related in the objective sphere; so, further, the absolute necessity of God, the concrete necessity of the universe, the actuality of individuals, and the possibility of matter. Beside the quaternary the tern also exercises its power—the world divides into the stages of eternity, imperishability, and the temporal world of sense, or truth, probability, and confusion. The divine trinity is reflected everywhere: in the world as creator, created, and love; in the mind as creative force, concept, and will. The triunity of God is very variously explained—as the subject, object, and act of cognition; as creative spirit, wisdom, and goodness; as being, power, and deed; and, preferably, as unity, equality, and the combination of the two.

God is related to the world as unity, identity, *complicatio*, to otherness, diversity, *explicatio*, as necessity to contingency, as completed actuality to mere possibility; yet, in such a way that the otherness participates in the unity, and receives its reality from this, and the unity does not have the otherness confronting it, outside it. God is triune only as the Creator of the world, and in relation to it; in himself he is absolute unity and infinity, to which nothing disparate stands opposed, which is just as much all things as not all things, and which, as the Areopagite had taught of old, is better comprehended by negations than by affirmations. To deny that he is light, truth, spirit, is more true than to affirm it, for he is infinitely greater than anything which can be expressed in words; he is the Unutterable, the Unknowable, the supremely one and the supremely absolute. In the world, each thing has things greater and smaller by its side, but God is the absolutely greatest and smallest; in accordance with the principle of the *coincidentia oppositorum*, the absolute *maximum* and the absolute *minimum* coincide. That which in the world exists as concretely determinate and particular, is in God in a simple and universal way; and that which here is present as incompleted striving, and as possibility realizing itself by gradual development, is in God completed activity. He is the realization of all possibility, the Can-be or Can-is (*possest*); and since this absolute actuality is the presupposition and cause of all finite ability and action, it may be unconditionally designated ability (*posse ipsum*), in antithesis to all determinate manifestations of force; namely, to all ability to be, live, feel, think, and will.

However much these definitions, conceived in harmony with the dualistic view of Christianity, accentuate the antithesis between God and the world, this is elsewhere much softened, nay directly denied, in favor of a pantheistic view which points forward to the modern period. Side by side with the assertion that there is no proportion whatever between the infinite and the finite, the following naïvely presents itself, in open contradiction to the former: God excels the reason just as much as the latter is superior to the understanding, and the understanding to sensibility, or he is related to thought as thought to life, and life to being. Nay, Nicolas makes even bolder statements than these, when he calls the universe a sensuous and mutable God, man a human God or a humanly contracted infinity, the creation a created God or a limited infinity; thus hinting that God and the world are at bottom essentially alike, differing only in the form of their existence, that it is one and the same being and action which manifests itself absolutely in God, relatively and in a limited way in the system of creation. It was chiefly three modern ideas which led the Cusan on from dualism to pantheism—the boundlessness of the universe, the connection of all being, and the all-comprehensive richness of individuality. Endlessness belongs to the universe as well as to God, only its endlessness is not an absolute one, beyond space and time, but weakened and concrete, namely unlimited extension in space and unending duration in time. Similarly, the universe is unity, yet not a unity absolutely above multiplicity and diversity, but one which is divided into many members and obscured thereby. Even the individual is infinite in a certain sense; for, in its own way, it bears in itself all that is, it mirrors the whole world from its limited point of view, is an abridged, compressed representation of the universe. As the members of the body, the eye, the arm, the foot, interact in the closest possible way, and no one of them can dispense with the rest, so each thing is connected with each, different from it and yet in harmony with it, so each contains all the others and is contained by them. All is in all, for all is in the universe and in God, as the universe and God in all. In a still higher degree man is a microcosm (*parvus mundus*), a mirror of the All, since he not merely, like other beings, actually has in himself all that exists, but also has a knowledge of this richness, is capable of developing it into conscious images of things. And it is just this which constitutes the perfection of the whole and of the parts, that the higher is in the lower, the cause in the effect, the genus in the individual, the soul in the body, reason in the senses, and conversely. To perfect, is simply to make active a potential possession, to unfold capacities and to elevate the unconscious into consciousness. Here we have the germ of the philosophy of Bruno and of Leibnitz.

As we have noticed a struggle between two opposite tendencies, one dualistic and Christian, one pantheistic and modern, in the theology of Nicolas, so at many other points a conflict between the mediaeval and the modern view of the world, of which our philosopher is himself unconscious, becomes evident to the student. It is impossible to follow out the details of this interesting opposition, so we shall only attempt to distinguish in a rough way the beginnings of the new from the remnants of the old. Modern is his interest in the ancient philosophers, of whom Pythagoras, Plato, and the Neoplatonists especially attract him; modern, again, his interest in natural science[1] (he teaches not only the boundlessness of the world, but also the motion of the earth); his high estimation of mathematics, although he often utilizes this merely in a fanciful symbolism of numbers; his optimism (the world an image of the divine, everything perfect of its kind, the bad simply a halt on the way to the good); his intellectualism (knowing the primal function and chief mission of the spirit; faith an undeveloped knowledge; volition and emotion, as is self-evident, incidental results of thought; knowledge a leading back of the creature to God as its source, hence the counterpart of creation); modern, finally, the form and application given to the Stoic-Neoplatonic concept of individuality, and the idealistic view which resolves the objects of thought into products thereof.[2] This last position, indeed, is limited by the lingering influence of nominalism, which holds the concepts of the mind to be merely abstract copies, and not archetypes of things. Moreover, *explicatio, evolutio*, unfolding, as yet does not always have the meaning of development to-day, of progressive advance. It denotes, quite neutrally, the production of a multiplicity from a unity, in which the former has lain confined, no matter whether this multiplicity and its procession signify enhancement or attenuation. For the most part, in fact, involution, *complicatio* (which, moreover, always means merely a primal, germinal condition, never, as in Leibnitz, the return thereto) represents the more perfect condition. The chief examples of the relation of involution and evolution are the principles in which science is involved and out of which it is unfolded; the unit, which is related to numbers in a similar way; the spirit and the cognitive operations; God and his creatures. However obscure and unskillful this application of the idea of development may appear, yet it is indisputable that a discovery of great promise has been made, accompanied by a joyful consciousness of its fruitfulness. Of the numberless features which point backward to the Middle Ages, only one need be mentioned, the large space taken up by speculations concerning the God-man (the whole third book of the *De Docta Ignorantia*), and by those concerning the angels. Yet even here a change is noticeable, for the earthly and the divine are brought into most intimate relation, while in Thomas Aquinas, for instance, they form two entirely separate worlds. In short, the new view of the world appears in Nicolas still bound on every hand by mediaeval conceptions. A century and a half passed before the fetters, grown rusty in the meanwhile, broke under the bolder touch of Giordano Bruno.

[Footnote 1: The attention of our philosopher was called to the natural sciences, and thus also to geography, which at this time was springing into new life, by his friend Paul Toscanelli, the Florentine. Nicolas was the first to have the map of Germany engraved (cf. S. Ruge in *Globus*, vol. lx., No. I, 1891), which, however, was not completed until long after his death, and issued in 1491.]

[Footnote 2: On the modern elements in his theory of the state and of right, cf. Gierke, *Das deutsche Genossenschaftsrecht*, vol. iii. § II, 1881.]

%2. The Revival of Ancient Philosophy and the Opposition to it%.

Italy is the home of the Renaissance and the birthplace of important new ideas which give the intellectual life of the sixteenth century its character of brave endeavor after high and distant ends. The enthusiasm for ancient literature already aroused by the native poets, Dante (1300), Petrarch (1341), and Boccaccio (1350), was nourished by the influx of Greek scholars, part of whom came in pursuance of an invitation to the Council of Ferrara and Florence (1438) called in behalf of the union of the Churches (among these were Pletho and his pupil Bessarion; Nicolas Cusanus was one of the legates invited), while part were fugitives from Constantinople after its capture by the Turks in 1453. The Platonic Academy, whose most celebrated member, Marsilius Ficinus, translated Plato and the Neoplatonists into Latin, was founded in 1440 on the suggestion of Georgius Gemistus Pletho[1] under the patronage of Cosimo dei Medici. The writings of Pletho ("On the Distinction between Plato and Aristotle"), of Bessarion (*Adversus Calumniatorem Platonis*, 1469, in answer to the *Comparatio Aristotelis et Platonis*, 1464, an attack by the Aristotelian, George of Trebizond, on Pletho's work), and of Ficinus (*Theologia Platonica*, 1482), show that the Platonism which they favored was colored by religious, mystical, and Neoplatonic elements. If for Bessarion and Ficinus, just as for the Eclectics of the later Academy, there was scarcely any essential distinction between the teachings of Plato, of Aristotle, and of Christianity; this confusion of heterogeneous elements was soon carried much farther, when the two Picos (John Pico of Mirandola, died 1494, and his nephew Francis, died 1533) and Johann Reuchlin (*De Verbo Mirifico*, 1494; *De Arte Cabbalistica*, 1517), who had been influenced by the former, introduced the secret doctrines of the Jewish Cabala into the Platonic philosophy, and Cornelius Agrippa von Nettesheim of Cologne (*De Occulta Philosophia*, 1510; cf. Sigwart, *Kleine Schriften*, vol. i. p. 1 seq.) made the mixture still worse by the addition of the magic art. The impulse of the modern spirit to subdue nature is here already apparent, only that it shows inexperience in the selection of its instruments; before long, however, nature will willingly unveil to observation and calm reflection the secrets which she does not yield to the compulsion of magic.

[Footnote 1: Pletho died at an advanced age in 1450. His chief work, the
[Greek: Nomoi], was given to the flames by his Aristotelian opponent,
Georgius Scholarius, surnamed Gennadius, Patriarch of Constantinople.
Portions of it only, which had previously become known, have been
preserved. On Pletho's life and teachings, cf. Fritz Schultze, *G.G.
Plethon*, Jena, 1874.]

A similar romantic figure was Phillipus Aureolus Theophrastus Bombast Paracelsus[1] von Hohenheim (1493-1541), a traveled Swiss, who endeavored to reform medicine from the standpoint of chemistry. Philosophy for Paracelsus is knowledge of nature, in which observation and thought must co-operate; speculation apart from experience and worship of the paper-wisdom of the ancients lead to no result. The world is a living whole, which, like man, the microcosm, in whom the whole content of the macrocosm is concentrated as in an extract, runs its life course. Originally all things were promiscuously intermingled in a unity, the God-created *prima materia*, as though inclosed in a germ, whence the manifold, with its various forms and colors, proceeded by separation. The development then proceeds in such a way that in each genus that is perfected which is posited therein, and does not cease until, at the last day, all that is possible in nature and history shall have fulfilled itself. But the one indwelling life of nature lives in all the manifold forms; the same laws rule in the human body as in the universe; that which works secretly in the former lies open to the view in the latter, and the world gives the clew to the knowledge of man. Natural becoming is brought about by the chemical separation and coming together of substances; the ultimate constituents revealed by analysis are the three fundamental substances or primitive essences, quicksilver, sulphur, and salt, by which, however, something more principiant is understood than the empirical substances bearing these names: *mercurius* means that which makes bodies liquid, *sulfur*, that which makes them combustible, *sal*, that which makes them fixed and rigid. From these are compounded the four elements, each of which is ruled by elemental spirits—earth by gnomes or pygmies, water by undines or nymphs, air by sylphs, fire by salamanders (cf. with this, and with Paracelsus's theory of the world as a whole, Faust's two monologues in Goethe's drama); which are to be understood as forces or sublimated substances, not as personal, demoniacal beings. To each individual being there is ascribed a vital principle, the *Archeus*, an individualization of the general force of nature, *Vulcanus*; so also to men. Disease is a checking of this vital principle by contrary powers, which are partly of a terrestrial and partly of a sidereal nature; and the choice of medicines is to be determined by their ability to support the Archeus against its enemies. Man is, however, superior to nature—he is not merely the universal animal, inasmuch as he is completely that which other beings are only in a fragmentary way; but, as the image of God, he has also an eternal element in him, and is capable of attaining perfection through the exercise of his rational judgment. Paracelsus distinguishes three worlds: the elemental or terrestrial, the astral or celestial, and the spiritual or divine. To the three worlds, which stand in relations of sympathetic interaction, there correspond in man the body, which nourishes itself on the elements, the spirit, whose imagination receives its food, sense and thoughts, from the spirits of the stars, and, finally, the immortal soul, which finds its nourishment in faith in Christ. Hence natural philosophy, astronomy, and theology are the pillars of anthropology, and ultimately of medicine. This fantastic physic of Paracelsus found many adherents both in theory and in practice.[2] Among those who accepted and developed it may be named R. Fludd (died 1637), and the two Van Helmonts, father and son (died 1644 and 1699).

[Footnote 1: On Paracelsus cf. Sigwart, *Kleine Schriften*, vol. i. p. 25 seq.; Eucken, *Beiträge zur Geschichteder neueren Philosophie*, p. 32 seq.; Lasswitz, *Geschichte der Atomistik*, vol. i. p. 294 seq.]

[Footnote 2: The influence of Paracelsus, as of Vives and Campanella, is evident in the great educator, Amos Comenius (Komensky, 1592-1670), whose pansophical treatises appeared in 1637-68. On Comenius cf. Pappenheim, Berlin, 1871; Kvacsala, Doctor's Dissertation, Leipsic, 1886; Walter Mueller, Dresden, 1887.]

Beside the Platonic philosophy, others of the ancient systems were also revived. Stoicism was commended by Justus Lipsius (died 1606) and Caspar Schoppe (Scioppius, born 1562); Epicureanism was revived by Gassendi (1647), and rhetorizing logicians went back to Cicero and Quintilian. Among the latter were Laurentius Valla (died 1457); R. Agricola (died 1485); the Spaniard, Ludovicus Vives (1531), who referred inquiry from the authority of Aristotle to the methodical utilization of experience; and Marius Nizolius (1553), whose *Antibarbarus* was reissued by Leibnitz in 1670.

The adherents of Aristotle were divided into two parties, one of which relied on the naturalistic interpretation of the Greek exegete, Alexander of Aphrodisias (about 200 A.D.), the other on the pantheistic interpretation of the Arabian commentator, Averroës (died 1198). The conflict over the question of immortality, carried on especially in Padua, was the culmination of the battle. The Alexandrist asserted that, according to Aristotle, the soul was mortal, the Averroists, that the rational part which is common to all men was immortal; while to this were added the further questions, if and how the Aristotelian view could be reconciled with the Church doctrine, which demanded a continued personal existence. The most eminent Aristotelian of the Renaissance, Petrus Pomponatius (*De Immortalite Animae*, 1516; *De Fato, Libero Arbitrio, Providentia et Praedestinatione*), was on the side of the Alexandrists. Achillini and Niphus fought on the other side. Caesalpin (died 1603), Zabarella, and Cremonini assumed an intermediate, or, at least, a less decided position. Still others, as Faber Stapulensis in Paris (1500), and Desiderius Erasmus (1520), were more interested in securing a correct text of Aristotle's works than in his philosophical principles.

* * * * *

Among the Anti-Aristotelians only two famous names need be mentioned, that of the influential Frenchman, Petrus Ramus, and the German, Taurellus. Pierre de la Ramée (assassinated in the massacre of St. Bartholomew, 1572), attacked the (unnatural and useless) Aristotelian logic in his *Aristotelicae Animadversiones*, 1543, objecting, with the Ciceronians mentioned above, to the separation of logic and rhetoric; and attempted a new logic of his own, in his *Institutiones Dialecticae*, which, in spite of its formalism, gained acceptance, especially in Germany.[1] Nicolaus Oechslein, Latinized Taurellus (born in 1547 at Mömpelgard; at his death, in 1606, professor of medicine in the University of Altdorf), stood quite alone because of his independent position in reference to all philosophical and religious parties. His most important works were his *Philosophiae Triumphus*, 1573; *Synopsis Aristotelis Metaphysicae*, 1596; *Alpes Caesae* (against Caesalpin, and the title punning on his name), 1597; and *De Rerum Aeternitate*, 1604.[2] The thought of Taurellus inclines toward the ideal of a Christian philosophy; which, however, Scholasticism, in his view, did not attain, inasmuch as its thought was heathen in its blind reverence for Aristotle, even though its faith was Christian. In order to heal this breach between the head and the heart, it is necessary in religion to return from confessional distinctions to Christianity itself, and in philosophy, to abandon authority for the reason. We should not seek to be Lutherans or Calvinists, but simply Christians, and we should judge on rational grounds, instead of following Aristotle, Averroës, or Thomas Aquinas. Anyone who does not aim at the harmony of theology and philosophy, is neither a Christian nor a philosopher. One and the same God is the primal source of both rational and revealed truth. Philosophy is the basis of theology, theology the criterion and complement of philosophy. The one starts with effects evident to the senses and leads to the suprasensible, to the First Cause; the other follows the reverse course. To philosophy belongs all that Adam knew or could know before the fall; had there been no sin, there would have been no other than philosophical knowledge. But after the fall, the reason, which informs us, it is true, of the moral law, but not of the divine purpose of salvation, would have led us to despair, since neither punishment nor virtue could justify us, if revelation did not teach us the wonders of grace and redemption. Although Taurellus thus softens the opposition between theology and philosophy, which had been most sharply expressed in the doctrine of "twofold truth" (that which is true in philosophy may be false in theology, and conversely), and endeavors to bring the two into harmony, the antithesis between God and the world still remains for him immovably fixed. God is not things, though he is all. He is pure affirmation; all without him is composed, as it were, of being and nothing, and can neither be nor be known independently: *negatio non nihil est, alias nec esset nec intelligeretur, sed limitatio est affirmationis.* Simple being or simple affirmation is equivalent to infinity, eternity, unity, uniqueness,—properties which do not belong to the world. He who posits things as eternal, sublates God. God and the world are opposed to each other as infinite cause and finite effect. Moreover, as it is our spirit which philosophizes and not God's spirit in us, so the faith through which man appropriates Christ's merit is a free action of the human spirit, the capacity for which is inborn, not infused from above; in it, God acts merely as an auxiliary or remote cause, by removing the obstacles which hinder the operation of the power of faith. With this anti-pantheistic tendency he combines an anti-intellectualistic one—being and production precedes and stands higher than contemplation; God's activity does not consist in thought but in production, and human blessedness, not in the knowledge but the love of God, even though the latter presupposes the former. While man, as an end in himself, is immortal—and the whole man, not his soul merely—the world of sense, which has been created only for the conservation of man (his procreation and probation), must disappear; above this world, however, a higher rears its walls to subserve man's eternal happiness.

[Footnote 1: On Ramus cf. Waddington's treatises, one in Latin, Paris, 1849, the other in French, Paris, 1855.]

[Footnote 2: Schmid Schwarzenburg has written on Taurellus, 1860, 2d ed., 1864.]

The high regard which Leibnitz expressed for Taurellus may be in part explained by the many anticipations of his own thoughts to be found in the earlier writer. The intimate relation into which sensibility and understanding are brought is an instance of this from the theory of knowledge. Receptivity is not passivity, but activity arrested (through the body). All knowledge is inborn; all men are potential philosophers (and, so far as they are loyal to conscience, Christians); the spirit is a thinking and a thinkable universe. Taurellus's philosophy of nature, recognizing the relative truth of atomism, makes the world consist of manifold simple substances combined into formal unity: he calls it a well constructed system of wholes. A discussion of the origin of evil is also given, with a solution based on the existence and misuse of freedom. Finally, it is to be mentioned to the great credit of Taurellus, that, like his younger contemporaries, Galileo and Kepler, he vigorously opposed the Aristotelian and Scholastic animation of the material world and the anthropomorphic conception of its forces, thus preparing the way for the modern view of nature to be perfected by Newton.

%3. The Italian Philosophy of Nature%.

We turn now from the restorers of ancient doctrines and their opponents to the men who, continuing the opposition to the authority of Aristotle, point out new paths for the study of nature. The physician, Hieronymus Cardanus of Milan (1501-76), whose inclinations toward the fanciful were restrained, though not suppressed, by his mathematical training, may be considered the forerunner of the school. While the people should accept the dogmas of the Church with submissive faith, the thinker may and should subordinate all things to the truth. The wise man belongs to that rare class who neither deceive nor are deceived; others are either deceivers or deceived, or both. In his theory of nature, Cardanus advances two principles: one passive, matter (the three cold and moist elements), and an active, formative one, the world-soul, which, pervading the All and bringing it into unity, appears as warmth and light. The causes of motion are attraction and repulsion, which in higher beings become love and hate. Even superhuman spirits, the demons, are subject to the mechanical laws of nature.

The standard bearer of the Italian philosophy of nature was Bernardinus Telesius[1] of Cosenza (1508-88; *De Rerum Natura juxta Propria Principia*, 1565, enlarged 1586), the founder of a scientific society in Naples called the Telesian, or after the name of his birthplace, the Cosentian Academy. Telesius maintained that the Aristotelian doctrine must be replaced by an unprejudiced empiricism; that nature must be explained from itself, and by as few principles as possible. Beside inert matter, this requires only two active forces, on whose interaction all becoming and all life depend. These are warmth, which expands, and cold, which contracts; the former resides in the sun and thence proceeds, the latter is situated in the earth. Although Telesius acknowledges an immaterial, immortal soul, he puts the emphasis on sensuous experience, without which the understanding is incapable of attaining certain knowledge. He is a sensationalist both in the theory of knowledge and in ethics, holding the functions of judgment and thought deducible from the fundamental power of perception, and considering the virtues different manifestations of the instinct of self-preservation (which he ascribes to matter as well).

[Footnote 1: Cf. on Telesius, Florentine, 2 vols., Naples, 1872-74; K. Heiland, *Erkenntnisslehre und Ethik des Telesius*, Doctor's Dissertation at Leipsic, 1891. Further, Rixner and Siber, *Leben und Lehrmeinungen berühmter Physiker am Ende des XVI. und am Anfang des XVII. Jahrhunderts*, Sulzbach (1819-26), 7 Hefte, 2d ed., 1829. Hefte 2-6 discuss Cardanus, Telesius, Patritius, Bruno, and Campanella; the first is devoted to Paracelsus, and the seventh to the older Van Helmont (Joh. Bapt.).]

With the name of Telesius we usually associate that of Franciscus Patritius (1529-97), professor of the Platonic philosophy in Ferrara and Rome *(Discussiones Peripateticae,* 1581; *Nova de Universis Philosophia,* 1591), who, combining Neoplatonic and Telesian principles, holds that the incorporeal or spiritual light emanates from the divine original light, in which all reality is seminally contained; the heavenly or ethereal light from the incorporeal; and the earthly or corporeal, from the heavenly—while the original light divides into three persons, the One and All *(Unomnia),* unity or life, and spirit.

The Italian philosophy of nature culminates in Bruno and Campanella, of whom the former, although he is the earlier, appears the more advanced because of his freer attitude toward the Church. Giordano Bruno was born in 1548 at Nola, and educated at Naples; abandoning his membership in the Dominican Order, he lived, with various changes of residence, in France, England, and Germany. Returning to his native land, he was arrested in Venice and imprisoned for seven years at Rome, where, on February 17, 1600, he suffered death at the stake, refusing to recant. (The same fate overtook his fellow-countryman, Vanini, in 1619, at Toulouse.) Besides three didactic poems in Latin (Frankfort, 1591), the Italian dialogues, *Della Causa, Principio ed Uno*, Venice, 1584 (German translation by Lasson, 1872), are of chief importance. The Italian treatises have been edited by Wagner, Leipsic, 1829, and by De Lagarde, 2 vols., Göttingen, 1888; the Latin appeared at Naples, in 3 vols., 1880, 1886, and 1891. Of a passionate and imaginative nature, Bruno was not an essentially creative thinker, but borrowed the ideas which he proclaimed with burning enthusiasm and lofty eloquence, and through which he has exercised great influence on later philosophy, from Telesius and Nicolas, complaining the while that the priestly garb of the latter sometimes hindered the free movement of his thought. Beside these thinkers he has a high regard for Pythagoras, Plato, Lucretius, Raymundus Lullus, and Copernicus (died 1543).[1] He forms the transition link between Nicolas of Cusa and Leibnitz, as also the link between Cardanus and Spinoza. To Spinoza Bruno offered the naturalistic conception of God (God is the "first cause" immanent in the universe, to which self-manifestation or self-revelation is essential; He is *natura naturans*, the numberless worlds are *natura naturata*); Leibnitz he anticipated by his doctrine of the "monads," the individual, imperishable elements of the existent, in which matter and form, incorrectly divorced by Aristotle as though two antithetical principles, constitute one unity. The characteristic traits of the philosophy of Bruno are the lack of differentiation between pantheistic and individualistic elements, the mediaeval animation and endlessness of the world, and, finally, the religious relation to the universe or the extravagant deification of nature (nature and the world are entirely synonymous, the All, the world-soul, and God nearly so, while even matter is called a divine being).[2]

[Footnote 1: Nicolaus Copernicus (Koppernik; 1473-1543) was born at Thorn; studied astronomy, law, and medicine at Cracow, Bologna, and Padua; and died a Canon of Frauenberg. His treatise, *De Revolutionibus Orbium Caelestium*, which was dedicated to Pope Paul III., appeared at Nuremberg in 1543, with a preface added to it by the preacher, Andreas Osiander, which calls the heliocentric system merely an hypothesis advanced as a basis for astronomical calculations. Copernicus reached his theory rather by speculation than by observation; its first suggestion came from the Pythagorean doctrine of the motion of the earth. On Copernicus cf. Leop. Prowe, vol. i. *Copernicus Leben*, vol. ii. (*Urkunden*), Berlin, 1883-84; and K. Lohmeyer in Sybel's *Historische Zeitschrift*, vol. lvii., 1887.]

[Footnote 2: Cf. on Bruno, H. Brunnhofer (somewhat too enthusiastic), Leipsic, 1882; also Sigwart, *Kleine Schriften*, vol. i. p. 49 *seq*.]

Bruno completes the Copernican picture of the world by doing away with the motionless circle of fixed stars with which Copernicus, and even Kepler, had thought our solar system surrounded, and by opening up the view into the immeasurability of the world. With this the Aristotelian antithesis of the terrestrial and the celestial is destroyed. The infinite space (filled with the aether) is traversed by numberless bodies, no one of which constitutes the center of the world. The fixed stars are suns, and, like our own, surrounded by planets. The stars are formed of the same materials as the earth, and are moved by their own souls or forms, each a living being, each also the residence of infinitely numerous living beings of various degrees of perfection, in whose ranks man by no means takes the first place. All organisms are composed of minute elements, called *minima* or monads; each monad is a mirror of the All; each at once corporeal and soul-like, matter and form, each eternal; their combinations alone being in constant change. The universe is boundless in time, as in space; development never ceases, for the fullness of forms which slumber in the womb of matter is inexhaustible. The Absolute is the primal unity, exalted above all antitheses, from which all created being is unfolded and in which it remains included. All is one, all is out of God and in God. In the living unity of the universe, also, the two sides, the spiritual (world-soul), and the corporeal (universal matter), are distinguishable, but not separate. The world-reason pervades in its omnipresence the greatest and the smallest, but in varying degrees. It weaves all into one great system, so that if we consider the whole, the conflicts and contradictions which rule in particulars disappear, resolved into the most perfect harmony. Whoever thus regards the world, becomes filled with reverence for the Infinite and bends his will to the divine law—from true science proceed true religion and true morality, those of the spiritual hero, of the heroic sage.

Thomas Campanella[1] (1568-1639) was no less dependent on Nicolas and Telesius than Bruno. A Calabrian by birth like Telesius, whose writings filled him with aversion to Aristotle, a Dominican like Bruno, he was deprived of his freedom on an unfounded suspicion of conspiracy against the Spanish rule, spent twenty-seven years in prison, and died in Paris after a short period of quiet. Renewing an old idea, Campanella directed attention from the written volume of Scripture to the living book of nature as being also a divine revelation. Theology rests on faith (in theology, Campanella, in accordance with the traditions of his order, follows Thomas Aquinas); philosophy is based on perception, which in its instrumental part comprises mathematics and logic, and in its real part, the doctrine of nature and of morals, while metaphysics treats of the highest presuppositions and the ultimate grounds,—the "pro-principles," Campanella starts, as Augustine before him and Descartes in later times, from the indisputable certitude of the spirit's own existence, from which he rises to the certitude of God's existence. On this first certain truth of my own existence there follow three others: my nature consists in the three functions of power, knowledge, and volition; I am finite and limited, might, wisdom, and love are in man constantly intermingled with their opposites, weakness, foolishness, and hate; my power, knowledge, and volition do not extend beyond the present. The being of God follows from the idea of God in us, which can have been derived from no other than an infinite source. It would be impossible for so small a part of the universe as man to produce from himself the idea of a being incomparably greater than the whole universe. I attain a knowledge of God's nature from my own by thinking away from the latter, in which, as in everything finite, being and non-being are intermingled, every limitation and negation, by raising to infinity my positive fundamental powers, *posse, cognoscere*, and *velle*, or *potentia, sapientia*, and *amor*, and by transferring them to him, who is pure affirmation, *ens* entirely without *non-ens*. Thus I reach as the three pro-principles or primalities of the existent or the Godhead, omnipotence, omniscience, and infinite love. But the infrahuman world may also be judged after the analogy of our fundamental faculties. The universe and all its parts possess souls; there is naught without sensation; consciousness, it is true, is lacking in the lower creatures, but they do not lack life, feeling, and desire, for it is impossible for the animate to come from the inanimate. Everything loves and hates, desires and avoids. Plants are motionless animals, and their roots, mouths. Corporeal motion springs from an obscure, unconscious impulse of self-preservation; the heavenly bodies circle about the sun as the center of sympathy; space itself seeks a content *(horror vacui)*.

[Footnote 1: Campanella's works have been edited by Al. d'Ancona, Turin, 1854, Cf. Sigwart, *Kleine Schriften*, vol. i. p. 125 *seq*.]

The more imperfect a thing is, the more weakened is the divine being in it by non-being and contingency. The entrance of the naught into the divine reality takes place by degrees. First God projects from himself the ideal or archetypal world *(mundus archetypus)*, *i.e.*, the totality of the possible. From this ideal world proceeds the metaphysical world of eternal intelligences *(mundus mentalis)*, including the angels, the world-soul, and human spirits. The third product is the mathematical world of space *(mundus sempiternus)*, the object of geometry; the fourth, the temporal or corporeal world; the fifth, and last, the empirical world *(mundus situalis)*, in which everything appears at a definite point in space and time. All things not only love themselves and seek the conservation of their own being, but strive back toward the original source of their being, to God; *i.e.*, they possess religion. In man, natural and animal religion are completed by rational religion, the limitations of which render a revelation necessary. A religion can be considered divine only when it is adapted to all, when it gains acceptance through miracles and virtue, and when it contradicts neither natural ethics nor the reason. Religion is union with God through knowledge, purity of will, and love. It is inborn, a law of nature, not, as Machiavelli teaches, a political invention.

Campanella desired to see the unity in the divine government of the world embodied in a pyramid of states with the papacy at the apex: above the individual states was to come the province, then the kingdom, the empire, the (Spanish) world-monarchy, and, finally, the universal dominion of the Pope. The Church should be superior to the State, the vicegerent of God to temporal rulers and to councils.

%4. Philosophy of the State and of Law%.

The originality of the modern doctrines of natural law was formerly overestimated, as it was not known to how considerable an extent the way had been prepared for them by the mediaeval philosophy of the state and of law. It is evident from the equally rich and careful investigations of Otto Gierke[1] that in the political and legal theories of a Bodin, a Grotius, a Hobbes, a Rousseau, we have systematic developments of principles long extant, rather than new principles produced with entire spontaneity. Their merit consists in the principiant expression and accentuation and the systematic development of ideas which the Middle Ages had produced, and which in part belong to the common stock of Scholastic science, in part constitute the weapons of attack for bold innovators. Marsilius of Padua (*Defensor Pacis*, 1325), Occam (died 1347), Gerson (about 1400), and the Cusan[2] (*Concordantia Catholica*, 1433) especially, are now seen in a different light. "Under the husk of the mediaeval system there is revealed a continuously growing antique-modern kernel, which draws all the living constituents out of the husk, and finally bursts it" (Gierke, *Deutsches Genossenschaftsrecht*, vol. iii. p. 312). Without going beyond the boundaries of the theocratico-organic view of the state prevalent in the Middle Ages, most of the conceptions whose full development was accomplished by the natural law of modern times were already employed in the Scholastic period. Here we already find the idea of a transition on the part of man from a pre-political natural state of freedom and equality into the state of citizenship; the idea of the origin of the state by a contract (social and of submission); of the sovereignty of the ruler (*rex major populo; plenitudo potestatis*), and of popular sovereignty[3] (*populus major principe*); of the original and inalienable prerogatives of the generality, and the innate and indestructible right of the individual to freedom; the thought that the sovereign power is superior to positive law (*princeps legibus solutus*), but subordinate to natural law; even tendencies toward the division of powers (legislative and executive), and the representative system. These are germs which, at the fall of Scholasticism and the ecclesiastical reformation, gain light and air for free development.

[Footnote 1: Gierke, *Johannes Althusius und die Entwickelung der naturrechtlichen Staatstheorien*, Breslau, 1880; the same, *Deutsches Genossenschaftsrecht*, vol. iii. § II, Berlin, 1881. Cf. further, Sigm. Riezler, *Die literarischen Widersacher der Päpste*, Leipsic, 1874; A. Franck, *Réformateurs et Publicistes de L'Europe*, Paris, 1864.]

[Footnote 2: Nicolas' political ideas are discussed by T. Stumpf, Cologne, 1865.]

[Footnote 3: Cf. F. von Bezold, *Die Lehre von der Volkssouveränität im Mittelalter*, (Sybel's *Historische Zeitschrift*, vol. xxxvi., 1876).]

The modern theory of natural law, of which Grotius was the most influential representative, began with Bodin and Althusius. The former conceives the contract by which the state is founded as an act of unconditional submission on the part of the community to the ruler, the latter conceives it merely as the issue of a (revocable) commission: in the view of the one, the sovereignty of the people is entirely alienated, "transferred," in that of the other, administrative authority alone is granted, "conceded," while the sovereign prerogatives remain with the people. Bodin is the founder of the theory of absolutism, to which Grotius and the school of Pufendorf adhere, though in a more moderate form, and which Hobbes develops to the last extreme. Althusius, on the other hand, by his systematic development of the doctrine of social contract and the inalienable sovereignty of the people, became the forerunner of Locke[1] and Rousseau.

[Footnote 1: Ulrich Huber (1674) may be called the first representative of constitutionalism, and so the intermediate link between Althusius and Locke. Cf. Gierke, *Althusius*, p. 290.]

The first independent political philosopher of the modern period was Nicolo Machiavelli of Florence (1469-1527). Patriotism was the soul of his thinking, questions of practical politics its subject, and historical fact its basis.[1] He is entirely unscholastic and unecclesiastical. The power and independence of the nation are for him of supreme importance, and the greatness and unity of Italy, the goal of his political system. He opposes the Church, the ecclesiastical state, and the papacy as the chief hindrances to the attainment of these ends, and considers the means by which help may be given to the Fatherland. In normal circumstances a republican constitution, under which Sparta, Rome, and Venice have achieved greatness, would be the best. But amid the corruption of the times, the only hope of deliverance is from the absolute rule of a strong prince, one not to be frightened back from severity and force. Should the ruler endeavor to keep within the bounds of morality, he would inevitably be ruined amid the general wickedness. Let him make himself liked, especially make himself feared, by the people; let him be fox and lion together; let him take care, when he must have recourse to bad means for the sake of the Fatherland, that they are justified by the result, and still to preserve the appearance of loyalty and honor when he is forced to act in their despite—for the populace always judges by appearance and by results. The worst thing of all is half-way measures, courses intermediate between good and evil and vacillating between reason and force. Even Moses had to kill the envious refractories, while Savonarola, the unarmed prophet, was destroyed. God is the friend of the strong, energy the chief virtue; and it is well when, as was the case with the ancient Romans, religion is associated with it without paralyzing it. The current view of Christianity as a religion of humility and sloth, which preaches only the courage of endurance and makes its followers indifferent to worldly honor, is unfavorable to the development of political vigor. The Italians have been made irreligious by the Church and the priesthood; the nearer Rome, the less pious the people. When Machiavelli, in his proposals looking toward Lorenzo (II.) dei Medici (died 1519), approves any means for restoring order, it must be remembered that he has an exceptional case in mind, that he does not consider deceit and severity just, but only unavoidable amid the anarchy and corruption of the time. But neither the loftiness of the end by which he is inspired, nor the low condition of moral views in his time, justifies his treatment of the laws as mere means to political ends, and his unscrupulous subordination of morality to calculating prudence. Machiavelli's general view of the world and of life is by no means a comforting one. Men are simple, governed by their passions and by insatiable desires, dissatisfied with what they have, and inclined to evil. They do good only of necessity;

it is hunger which makes them industrious and laws that render them good. Everything rapidly degenerates: power produces quiet, quiet, idleness, then disorder, and, finally, ruin, until men learn by misfortune, and so order and power again arise. History is a continual rising and falling, a circle of order and disorder. Governmental forms, even, enjoy no stability; monarchy, when it has run out into tyranny, is followed by aristocracy, which gradually passes over into oligarchy; this in turn is replaced by democracy, until, finally, anarchy becomes unendurable, and a prince again attains power. No state, however, is so powerful as to escape succumbing to a rival before it completes the circuit. Protection against the corruption of the state is possible only through the maintenance of its principles, and its restoration only by a return to the healthy source whence it originated. This is secured either by some external peril compelling to reflection, or internally, by wise thought, by good laws (framed in accordance with the general welfare, and not according to the ambition of a minority), and by the example of good men.

[Footnote 1: In his *Essays on the First Decade of Livy (Discorsi)*, Machiavelli investigates the conditions and the laws of the maintenance of states; while in *The Prince (Il Principe,* 1515), he gives the principles for the restoration of a ruined state. Besides these he wrote a history of Florence, and a work on the art of war, in which he recommended the establishment of national armies.]

In the interval between Machiavelli and the system of natural law of Grotius, the Netherlander (1625: *De Jure Belli et Pacis*), belong the socialistic ideal state of the Englishman, Thomas More (*De Optimo Reipublicae Statu deque Nova Insula Utopia*, 1516), the political theory of the Frenchman, Jean Bodin (*Six Livres de la République*, 1577, Latin 1584; also a philosophico-historical treatise, *Methodus ad Facilem Historiarum Cognitionem*, and the *Colloquium Heptaplomeres*, edited by Noack, 1857), and the law of war of the Italian, Albericus Gentilis, at his death professor in Oxford (*De Jure Belli*, 1588). Common to these three was the advocacy of religious tolerance, from which atheists alone were to be excepted; common, also, their ethical standpoint in opposition to Machiavelli, while they are at one with him in regard to the liberation of political and legal science from theology and the Church. With Gentilis (1551-1611) this separation assigns the first five commandments to divine, and the remainder to human law, the latter being based on the laws of human nature (especially the social impulse). In place of this derivation of law and the state from the nature of man, Jean Bodin (1530-96) insists on an historical interpretation; endeavors, though not always with success, to give sharp definitions of political concepts;[1] rejects composite state forms, and among the three pure forms, monarchy, aristocracy, and democracy, rates (hereditary) monarchy the highest, in which the subjects obey the laws of the monarch, and the latter the laws of God or of nature by respecting the freedom and the property of the citizens. So far, no one has correctly distinguished between forms of the state and modes of administration. Even a democratic state may be governed in a monarchical or aristocratic way. So far, also, there has been a failure to take into account national peculiarities and differences of situation, conditions to which legislation must be adjusted. The people of the temperate zone are inferior to those of the North in physical power and inferior to those of the South in speculative ability, but superior to both in political gifts and in the sense of justice. The nations of the North are guided by force, those of the South by religion, those between the two by reason. Mountaineers love freedom. A fruitful soil enervates men, when less fertile, it renders them temperate and industrious.

[Footnote 1: What is the state? What is sovereignty? The former is defined as the rational and supremely empowered control over a number of families and of whatever is common to them; the latter is absolute and continuous authority over the state, with the right of imposing laws without being bound by them. The prince, to whom the sovereignty has been unconditionally relinquished by the people in the contract of submission, is accountable to God alone.]

Attention has only recently been called (by O. Gierke, in the work already mentioned, Heft vii. of his *Untersuchungen zur deutschen Staats- und Rechtsgeschichte*, Breslau, 1880) to the Westphalian, Johannes Althusius (Althusen or Althaus) as a legal philosopher worthy of notice. He was born, 1557, in the Grafschaft Witgenstein; was a teacher of law in Herborn and Siegen from 1586, and Syndic in Emden from 1604 to his death in 1638. His chief legal work was the *Dicaeologica*, 1617 (a recasting of a treatise on Roman law which appeared in 1586), and his chief political work the *Politica*, 1603 (altered and enlarged 1610, and reprinted, in addition, three times before his death and thrice subsequently). Down to the beginning of the eighteenth century he was esteemed or opposed as chief among the *Monarchomachi*, so called by the Scotchman, Barclay (*De Regno et Regali Potestate*, 1600); since that time he has fallen into undeserved oblivion. The sovereign power (*majestas*) of the people is untransferable and indivisible, the authority vested in the chosen wielder of the administrative power is revocable, and the king is merely the chief functionary; individuals are subjects, it is true, but the community retains its sovereignty and has its rights represented over against the chief magistrate by a college of ephors. If the prince violates the compact, the ephors are authorized and bound to depose the tyrant, and to banish or execute him. There is but one normal state-form; monarchy and polyarchy are mere differences in administrative forms. Mention should finally be made of his valuation of the social groups which mediate between the individual and the state: the body politic is based on the narrower associations of the family, the corporation, the commune, and the province.

While with Bodin the historical, and with Gentilis the *a priori* method of treatment predominates, Hugo Grotius[1] combines both standpoints. He bases his system on the traditional distinction of two kinds of law. The origin of positive law is historical, by voluntary enactment; natural law is rooted in the nature of man, is eternal, unchangeable, and everywhere the same. He begins by distinguishing with Gentilis the *jus humanum* from the *jus divinum* given in the Scriptures. The former determines, on the one hand, the legal relations of individuals, and, on the other, those of whole nations; it is *jus personale* and *jus gentium*.[2]

[Footnote 1: Hugo de Groot lived 1583-1645. He was born in Delft, became Fiscal of Holland in 1607, and Syndic of Rotterdam and member of the States General in 1613. A leader of the aristocratic party with Oldenbarneveld, he adhered to the Arminians or Remonstrants, was thrown into prison, freed in 1621 through the address of his wife, and fled to Paris, where he lived till 1631 as a private scholar, and, from 1635, as Swedish ambassador. Here he composed his epoch-making work, *De Jure Belli et Pacis*, 1625. Previous to this had appeared his treatise, *De Veritate Religionis Christianae*, 1619, and the *Mare Liberum*, 1609, the latter a chapter from his maiden work, *De Jure Praedae*, which was not printed until 1868.]

[Footnote 2: The meaning which Grotius here gives to *jus gentium* (=international law), departs from the customary usage of the Scholastics, with whom it denotes the law uniformly acknowledged among all nations. Thomas Aquinas understands by it, in distinction to *jus naturale* proper, the sum of the conclusions deduced from this as a result of the development of human culture and its departure from primitive purity. Cf. Gierke, *Althusius*, p. 273; *Deutsches Genossenschaftsrecht*, vol. iii. p. 612. On the meaning of natural law cf. Gierke's Inaugural Address as Rector at Breslau, *Naturrecht und Deutsches Recht*, Frankfort-on-the-Main, 1883.]

The distinction between natural and conventional law which has been already mentioned, finds place within both: the positive law of persons is called *jus civile*, and the positive law of nations, *jus gentium voluntarium*. Positive law has its origin in regard for utility, while unwritten law finds its source neither in this nor (directly) in the will of God,[1] but in the rational nature of man. Man is by nature social, and, as a rational being, possesses the impulse toward ordered association. Unlawful means whatever renders such association of rational beings impossible, as the violation of promises or the taking away and retention of the property of others. In the (pre-social) state of nature, all belonged to all, but through the act of taking possession *(occupatio)* property arises (sea and air are excluded from appropriation). In the state of nature everyone has the right to defend himself against attack and to revenge himself on the evil-doer; but in the political community, founded by contract, personal revenge is replaced by punishment decreed by the civil power. The aim of punishment is not retribution, but reformation and deterrence. It belongs to God alone to punish because of sin committed, the state can punish only to prevent it. (The antithesis *quia peccatum est—ne peccetur* comes from Seneca.)

[Footnote 1: Natural law would be valid even if there were no God. With these words the alliance between the modern and the mediaeval philosophy of law is severed.]

This energetic revival of the distinction already common in the Middle Ages between "positive and natural," which Lord Herbert of Cherbury brought forward at the same period (1624) in the philosophy of religion, gave the catchword for a movement in practical philosophy whose developments extend into the nineteenth century. Not only the illumination period, but all modern philosophy down to Kant and Fichte, is under the ban of the antithesis, natural and artificial. In all fields, in ethics as well as in noëtics, men return to the primitive or storm back to it, in the hope of finding there the source of all truth and the cure for all evils. Sometimes it is called nature, sometimes reason (natural law and rational law are synonymous, as also natural religion and the religion of the reason), by which is understood that which is permanent and everywhere the same in contrast to the temporary and the changeable, that which is innate in contrast to that which has been developed, in contrast, further, to that which has been revealed. Whatever passes as law in all places and at all times is natural law, says Grotius; that which all men believe forms the content of natural religion, says Lord Herbert. Before long it comes to be said: that *alone* is genuine, true, healthy, and valuable which has eternal and universal validity; all else is not only superfluous and valueless but of evil, for it must be unnatural and corrupt. This step is taken by Deism, with the principle that whatever is not natural or rational in the sense indicated is unnatural and irrational. Parallel phenomena are not wanting, further, in the philosophy of law (Gierke, *Althusius*). But these errors must not be too harshly judged. The confidence with which they were made sprang from the real and the historical force of their underlying idea.

As already stated, the "natural" forms the antithesis to the supernatural, on the one hand, and to the historical, on the other. This combination of the revealed and the historical will not appear strange, if we remember that the mediaeval view of the world under criticism was, as Christian, historico-religious, and, moreover, that for the philosophy of religion the two in fact coincide, inasmuch as revelation is conceived as an historical event, and the historical religions assume the character of revealed. The term arbitrary, applied to both in common, was questionable, however: as revelation is a divine decree, so historical institutions are the products of human enactment, the state, the result of a contract, dogmas, inventions of the priesthood, *the results of development, artificial constructions*! It took long ages for man to free himself from the idea of the artificial and conventional in his view of history. Hegel was the first to gather the fruit whose seeds had been sown by Leibnitz, Lessing, Herder, and the historical school of law. As often, however, as an attempt was made from this standpoint of origins to show laws in the course of history, only one could be reached, a law of necessary degeneration, interrupted at times by sudden restorations—thus the Deists, thus Machiavelli and Rousseau. Everything degenerates, science itself only contributes to the fall—therefore, back to the happy beginnings of things!

If, finally, we inquire into the position of the Church in regard to the questions of legal philosophy, we may say that, among the Protestants, Luther, appealing to the Scripture text, declares rulers ordained by God and sacred, though at the same time he considers law and politics but remotely related to the inner man; that Melancthon, in his *Elements of Ethics* (1538), as in all his philosophical text-books,[1] went back to Aristotle, but found the source of natural law in the Decalogue, being followed in this by Oldendorp (1539), Hemming (1562), and B. Winkler (1615).[2]

[Footnote 1: The edition of Melancthon's works by Bretschneider and Bindseil gives the ethical treatises in vol. xvi. and the other philosophical treatises in vol. xiii. (in part also in vols. xi. and xx.).]

[Footnote 2: Cf. C.v. Kaltenborn, *Die Vorläufer des Hugo Grotius*, Leipsic, 1848.]

On the Catholic side, the Jesuits (the Order was founded in 1534, and confirmed in 1540), on the one hand, revived the Pelagian theory of freedom in opposition to the Luthero-Augustinian doctrine of the servitude of the will, and, on the other, defended the natural origin of the state in a (revocable) contract in opposition to its divine origin asserted by the Reformers, and the sovereignty of the people even to the sanctioning of tyrannicide. Bellarmin (1542-1621) taught that the prince derives his authority from the people, and as the latter have given him power, so they retain the natural right to take it back and bestow it elsewhere. The view of Juan Mariana (1537-1624; *De Rege*, 1599) is that, as the people in transferring rights to the prince retain still greater power themselves, they are entitled in given cases to call the king to account. If he corrupts the state by evil manners, and, degenerating into the tyrant, despises religion and the laws, he may, as a public enemy, be deprived by anyone of his authority and his life. It is lawful to arrest tyranny in any way, and those have always been highly esteemed who, from devotion to the public welfare, have sought to kill the tyrant.

%5. Skepticism in France.%

Toward the end of the sixteenth century, and in the very country which was to become the cradle of modern philosophy, there appeared, as a forerunner of the new thinking, a skepticism in which that was taken for complete and ultimate truth which with Descartes constitutes merely a moment or transition point in the inquiry. The earliest and the most ingenious among the representatives of this philosophy of doubt was Michel de Montaigne (1533-92), who in his *Essays*—which were the first of their kind and soon found an imitator in Bacon;

they appeared in 1580 in two volumes, with an additional volume in 1588—combined delicate observation and keen thinking, boldness and prudence, elegance and solidity. The French honor him as one of their foremost writers. The most important among these treatises or essays is considered to be the "Apology for Raymond of Sabunde" (ii. 12) with valuable excursuses on faith and knowledge. Montaigne bases his doubt on the diversity of individual views, each man's opinion differing from his fellow's, while truth must be one. There exists no certain, no universally admitted knowledge. The human reason is feeble and blind in all things, knowledge is deceptive, especially the philosophy of the day, which clings to tradition, which fills the memory with learned note-stuff, but leaves the understanding void and, instead of things, interprets interpretations only. Both sensuous and rational knowledge are untrustworthy: the former, because it cannot be ascertained whether its deliverances conform to reality, and the latter, because its premises, in order to be valid, need others in turn for their own establishment, etc., *ad infinitum*. Every advance in inquiry makes our ignorance the more evident; the doubter alone is free. But though certainty is denied us in regard to truth, it is not withheld in regard to duty. In fact, a twofold rule of practical life is set up for us: nature, or life in accordance with nature and founded on self-knowledge, and supernatural revelation, the Gospel (to be understood only by the aid of divine grace). Submission to the divine ruler and benefactor is the first duty of the rational soul. From obedience proceeds every virtue, from over-subtlety and conceit, which is the product of fancied knowledge, comes every sin. Montaigne, like all who know men, has a sharp eye for human frailty. He depicts the universal weakness of human nature and the corruption of his time with great vivacity and not without a certain pleasure in the obscene; and besides folly and passion, complains above all of the fact that so few understand the art of enjoyment, of which he, a true man of the world, was master.

The skeptico-practical standpoint of Montaigne was developed into a system by the Paris preacher, Pierre Charron (1541-1603), in his three books *On Wisdom* (1601). Doubt has a double object: to keep alive the spirit of inquiry and to lead us on to faith. From the fact that reason and experience are liable to deception and that the mind has at its disposal no means of distinguishing truth from falsehood, it follows that we are born not to possess truth but to seek it. Truth dwells alone in the bosom of God; for us doubt and investigation are the only good amid all the error and tribulation which surround us. Life is all misery. Man is capable of mediocrity alone; he can neither be entirely good nor entirely evil; he is weak in virtue, weak in vice, and the best degenerates in his hands. Even religion suffers from the universal imperfection. It is dependent on nationality and country, and each religion is based on its predecessor; the supernatural origin of which all religions boast belongs in fact to Christianity alone, which is to be accepted with humility and with submission of the reason. Charron lays chief emphasis, however, on the practical side of Christianity, the fulfillment of duty; and the "wisdom" which forms the subject of his book is synonymous with uprightness (*probité*), the way to which is opened up by self-knowledge and whose reward is repose of spirit. And yet we are not to practice it for the sake of the reward, but because nature and reason, i.e., God, absolutely (entirely apart from the pleasurable results of virtue) require us to be good. True uprightness is more than mere legality, for even when outward action is blameless, the motives may be mixed. "I desire men to be upright without paradise and hell." Religion seeks to crown morality, not to generate it; virtue is earlier and more natural than piety. In his definition of the relation between religion and ethics, his delimitation of morality from legality, and his insistence on the purity of motives (do right, because the inner rational law commands it), an anticipation of Kantian principles may be recognized.

Under Francis Sanchez (died 1632; his chief work is entitled *Quod Nihil Scitur*), a Portuguese by birth, and professor of medicine in Montpellier and Toulouse, skepticism was transformed from melancholy contemplation into a fresh, vigorous search after new problems. In the place of book-learning, which disgusts him by its smell of the closet, its continued prating of Aristotle, and its self-exhaustion in useless verbalism, Sanchez desires to substitute a knowledge of things. Perfect knowledge, it is true, can be hoped for only when subject and object correspond to each other. But how is finite man to grasp the infinite universe? Experience, the basis of all knowledge, gropes about the outer surface of things and illumines particulars only, without the ability either to penetrate to their inner nature or to comprehend the whole. We know only what we produce. Thus God knows the world which he has made, but to us is vouchsafed merely an insight into mediate or second causes, *causae secundae*. Here, however, a rich field still lies open before philosophy—only let her attack her problem with observation and experiment rather than with words.

The French nation, predisposed to skepticism by its prevailing acuteness, has never lacked representatives of skeptical philosophy. The transition from the philosophers of doubt whom we have described to the great Bayle was formed by La Mothe le Vayer (died 1672; *Five Dialogues*, 1671), the tutor of Louis XIV., and P.D. Huet(ius), Bishop of Avranches (died 1721), who agreed in holding that a recognition of the weakness of the reason is the best preparation for faith.

6. %German Mysticism%.

In a period which has given birth to a skeptical philosophy, one never looks in vain for the complementary phenomenon of mysticism. The stone offered by doubt in place of bread is incapable of satisfying the impulse after knowledge, and when the intellect grows weary and despairing, the heart starts out in the quest after truth. Then its path leads inward, the mind turns in upon itself, seeks to learn the truth by inner experience and life, by inward feeling and possession, and waits in quietude for divine illumination. The German mysticism of Eckhart[1] (about 1300), which had been continued in Suso and Tauler and had received a practical direction in the Netherlands,—Ruysbroek (about 1350) to Thomas à Kempis (about 1450),—now puts forth new branches and blossoms at the turning point of the centuries.

[Footnote 1: Master Eckhart's *Works* have been edited by F. Pfeiffer, Leipsic, 1857. The following have written on him: Jos. Bach, Vienna, 1864; Ad. Lasson, Berlin, 1868; the same, in the second part of Ueberweg's *Grundriss*, last section; Denifle, in the *Archiv für Litteratur und Kulturgeschichte des Mittelalters*. ii. 417 *seq.*; H. Siebeck, *Der Begriff des Gemuts in der deutschen Mystik (Beiträge zur Entstehungsgeschichte der neueren Psychologie*, i), Giessen Programme, 1891.]

Luther himself was originally a mystic, with a high appreciation of Tauler and Thomas à Kempis, and published in 1518 that attractive little book by an anonymous Frankfort author, the *German Theology*. When, later, he fell into literalism, it was the mysticism of German Protestantism which, in opposition to the new orthodoxy, held fast to the original principle of the Reformation, *i.e.*, to the principle that faith is not assent to historical facts, not the acceptance of dogmas, but an inner experience, a renewal of the whole man. Religion and theology must not be confounded. Religion is not doctrine, but a new birth. With Schwenckfeld, and also with Franck, mysticism is still essentially pietism; with Weigel, and by the addition of ideas from Paracelsus, it is transformed into theosophy, and as such reaches its culmination in Böhme.

Caspar Schwenckfeld sought to spiritualize the Lutheran movement and protested against its being made into a pastors' religion. Though he had been aroused by Luther's pioneer feat, he soon saw that the latter had not gone far enough; and in his *Letter on the Eucharist*, 1527, he defined the points of difference between Luther's view of the Sacrament and his own. Luther, he maintained, had fallen back to an historical view of faith, whereas the faith which saves can never consist in the outward acceptance of an historical fact. He who makes salvation dependent on preaching and the Sacrament, confuses the invisible and the visible Church, *Ecclesia interna* and *externa*. The layman is his own priest.

According to Sebastian Franck (1500-45), there are in man, as in everything else, two principles, one divine and one selfish, Christ and Adam, an inner and an outer man; if he submits himself to the former (by a timeless choice), he is spiritual, if to the latter, carnal. God is not the cause of sin, but man, who turns the divine power to good or evil. He who denies himself to live God is a Christian, whether he knows and confesses the Gospel or not. Faith does not consist in assent, but in inner transformation. The historical element in Christianity and its ceremonial observances are only the external form and garb (its "figure"), have merely a symbolic significance as media of communication, as forms of revelation for the eternal truth, proclaimed but not founded by Christ; the Bible is merely the shadow of the living Word of God.

Valentin Weigel (born in 1533, pastor in Zschopau from 1567), whose works were not printed until after his death, combines his predecessors' doctrine of inner and eternal Christianity with the microcosmos-idea of Paracelsus. God, who lacks nothing, has not created the world in order to gain, but in order to give. Man not only bears the earthly world in his body, and the heavenly world of the angels in his reason (his spirit), but by virtue of his intellect (his immortal soul) participates in the divine world also. As he is thus a microcosm and, moreover, an image of God, all his knowledge becomes self-knowledge, both sensuous perception (which is not caused by the object, but only occasioned by it), and the knowledge of God. The literalist knows not God, but he alone who bears God in himself. Man is favored above other beings with the freedom to dwell in himself or in God. When man came out from God, he was his own tempter and made himself proud and selfish. Thus evil, which had before remained hidden, was revealed, and became sin. As the separation from God is an eternal act, so also redemption and resurrection form an inner event. Christ is born in everyone who gives up the I-ness (*Ichheit*); each regenerate man is a son of God. But no vicarious suffering can save him who does not put off the old Adam, no matter how much an atheology sunk in literalism may comfort itself with the hope that man can "drink at another's cost" (that the merit of another is imputed to him).[1]

[Footnote 1: Weigel is discussed by J.O. Opel, Leipsic, 1864.]

German mysticism reaches its culmination in the Görlitz cobbler, Jacob Böhme (1575-1624; *Aurora, or the Rising Dawn*; *Mysterium Magnum, or on the First Book of Moses*, etc. The works of Böhme, collected by his apostle, Gichtel, appeared in 1682 in ten volumes, and in 1730 in six volumes; a new edition was prepared by Schiebler in 1831-47, with a second edition in 1861 *seq*.). Böhme's doctrine[1] centers about the problem of the origin of evil. He transfers this to God himself and joins therewith the leading thought of Eckhart, that God goes through a process, that he proceeds from an unrevealed to a revealed condition. At the sight of a tin vessel glistening in the sun, he conceived, as by inspiration, the idea that as the sunlight reveals itself on the dark vessel so all light needs darkness and all good evil in order to appear and to become knowable. Everything becomes perceptible through its opposite alone: gentleness through sternness, love through anger, affirmation through negation. Without evil there would be no life, no movement, no distinctions, no revelation; all would be unqualified, uniform nothingness. And as in nature nothing exists in which good and evil do not reside, so in God, besides power or the good, a contrary exists, without which he would remain unknown to himself. The theogonic process is twofold: self-knowledge on the part of God, and his revelation outward, as eternal nature, in seven moments.

[Footnote 1: Cf. Windelband's fine exposition, *Geschichte der neueren Philosophie*, vol. i. §19. The following have written on Böhme: Fr. Baader (in vols. iii. and xiii. of his *Werke*); Hamberger, Munich, 1844: H. A. Fechner, Görlitz, 1857; A. v. Harless, Berlin, 1870, new edition, Leipsic, 1882.]

At the beginning of the first development God is will without object, eternal quietude and rest, unqualified groundlessness without determinate volition. But in this divine nothingness there soon awakes the hunger after the aught (somewhat, existence), the impulse to apprehend and manifest self, and as God looks into and forms an image of himself, he divides into Father and Son. The Son is the eye with which the Father intuits himself, and the procession of this vision from the groundless is the Holy Ghost. Thus far God, who is one in three, is only understanding or wisdom, wherein the images of all the possible are contained; to the intuition of self must be added divisibility; it is only through the antithesis of the revealed God and the unrevealed groundless that the former becomes an actual trinity (in which the persons stand related as essence, power, and activity), and the latter becomes desire or nature in God.

At the creation of the world seven equally eternal qualities, source-spirits or nature-forms, are distinguished in the divine nature. First comes desire as the contractile, tart quality or pain, from which proceed hardness and heat; next comes mobility as the expansive, sweet quality, as this shows itself in water. As the nature of the first was to bind and the second was fluid, so they both are combined in the bitter quality or the pain of anxiety, the principle of sensibility. (Contraction and expansion are the conditions of perceptibility.) From these three forms fright or lightning suddenly springs forth. This fourth quality is the turning-point at which light flames up from darkness and the love of God breaks forth from out his anger; as the first three, or four, forms constitute the kingdom of wrath, so the latter three constitute the kingdom of joy. The fifth quality is called light or the warm fire of love, and has for its functions external animation and communication; the sixth, report and sound, is the principle of inner animation and intelligence; the seventh, the formative quality, corporeality, comprehends all the preceding in itself as their dwelling.

The dark fire of anger (the hard, sweet, and bitter qualities) and the light fire of love (light, report, and corporeality), separated by the lightning-fire, in which God's wrath is transformed into mercy, stand related as evil and good. The evil in God is not sin, but simply the inciting sting, the principle of movement; which, moreover, is restrained, overcome, transfigured by gentleness. Sin arises only when the creature refuses to take part in the advance from darkness to light, and obstinately remains in the fire of anger instead of forcing his way through to the fire of love. Thus that which was one in God is divided. Lucifer becomes enamored of the tart quality (the *centrum naturae* or the matrix) and will not grow into the heart of God; and it is only after such lingering behind that the kingdom of wrath become a real hell. Heaven and hell are not future conditions, but are experienced here on earth; he who instead of subduing animality becomes enamored of it, stands under the wrath of God; whereas he who abjures self dwells in the joyous kingdom of mercy. He alone truly believes who himself becomes Christ, who repeats in himself what Christ suffered and attained.

The creation of the material world is a result of Lucifer's fall. Böhme's description of it, based on the Mosaic account of creation, may be passed without notice; similarly his view of cognition, familiar from the earlier mystics, that all knowledge is derived from self-knowledge, that our destination is to comprehend God from ourselves, and the world from God. Man, whose body, spirit, and soul hold in them the earthly, the sidereal, and the heavenly, is at once a microcosm and a "little God."

Under the intractable form of Böhme's speculations and amid their riotous fancy, no one will fail to recognize their true-hearted sensibility and an unusual depth and vigor of thought. They found acceptance in England and France, and have been revived in later times in the systems of Baader and Schelling.

%7. The Foundation of Modern Physics%.

In no field has the modern period so completely broken with tradition as in physics. The correctness of the Copernican theory is proved by Kepler's laws of planetary movement, and Galileo's telescopical observations; the scientific theory of motion is created by Galileo's laws of projectiles, falling bodies, and the pendulum; astronomy and mechanics form the entrance to exact physics—Descartes ventures an attempt at a comprehensive mechanical explanation of nature. And thus an entirely new movement is at hand. Forerunners, it is true, had not been lacking. Roger Bacon (1214-94) had already sought to obtain an empirical knowledge of nature based upon mathematics; and the great painter Leonardo da Vinci (1452-1519) had discovered the principles of mechanics, though without gaining much influence over the work of his contemporaries. It was reserved for the triple star which has been mentioned to overthrow Scholasticism. The conceptions with which the Scholastic-Aristotelian philosophy of nature sought to get at phenomena—substantial forms, properties, qualitative change—are thrown aside; their place is taken by matter, forces working under law, rearrangement of parts. The inquiry into final causes is rejected as an anthropomorphosis of natural events, and deduction from efficient causes is alone accepted as scientific explanation. Size, shape, number, motion, and law are the only and the sufficient principles of explanation. For magnitudes alone are knowable; wherever it is impossible to measure and count, to determine force mathematically, there rigorous, exact science ceases. Nature a system of regularly moved particles of mass; all that takes place mechanical movement, viz., the combination, separation, dislocation, oscillation of bodies and corpuscles; mathematics the organon of natural science! Into this circle of modern scientific categories are articulated, further, Galileo's new conception of motion and the conception of atoms, which, previously employed by physicists, as Daniel Sennert (1619) and others, is now brought into general acceptance by Gassendi, while the four elements are definitively discarded (Lasswitz, *Geschichte der Atomistik*, 1890). Still another doctrine of Democritus is now revived; an evident symptom of the quantification and mechanical interpretation of natural phenomena being furnished by the doctrine of the subjectivity of sense qualities, in which, although on varying grounds, Kepler, Galileo, Descartes, Gassendi, and Hobbes agree.[1] Descartes and Hobbes will be discussed later. Here we may give a few notes on their fellow laborers in the service of the mechanical science of nature.

[Footnote 1: Cf. chapter vi. in Natorp's work on *Descartes' Erkenntnisstheorie*, Marburg, 1882, and the same author's *Analekten zur Geschichte der Philosophie*, in the *Philosophische Monatshefte*, vol. xviii. 1882, p. 572 *seq.*]

We begin with John Kepler[1] (1571-1630; chief work, *The New Astronomy or Celestial Physics, in Commentaries on the Motions of Mars*, 1609). Kepler's merit as an astronomer has long obscured his philosophical importance, although his discovery of the laws of planetary motion was the outcome of endeavors to secure an exact foundation for his theory of the world. The latter is aesthetic in character, centers about the idea of a universal world-harmony, and employs mathematics as an instrument of confirmation. For the fact that this theory satisfies the mind, and, on the whole, corresponds to our empirical impression of the order of nature, is not enough in Kepler's view to guarantee its truth; by exact methods, by means of induction and experiment, a detailed proof from empirical facts must be found for the existence not only of a general harmony, but of definitely fixed proportions. Herewith the philosophical application of mathematics loses that obscure mystical character which had clung to it since the time of Pythagoras, and had strongly manifested itself as late as in Nicolas of Cusa. Mathematical relations constitute the deepest essence of the real and the object of science. Where matter is, there is geometry; the latter is older than the world and as eternal as the divine Spirit; magnitudes are the source of things. True knowledge exists only where quanta are known; the presupposition of the capacity for knowledge is the capacity to count; the spirit cognizes sensuous relations by means of the pure, archetypal, intellectual relations born in it, which, before the advent of sense-impressions, have lain concealed behind the veil of possibility; inclination and aversion between men, their delight in beauty, the pleasant impression of a view, depend upon an unconscious and instinctive perception of proportions. This quantitative view of the world, which, with a consciousness of its novelty as well as of its scope, is opposed to the qualitative view of Aristotle;[2] the opinion that the essence of the human spirit, as well as of the divine, nay, the essence of all things, consists in activity; that, consequently, the soul is always active, being conscious of its own harmony at least in a confused way, even when not conscious of external proportions; further, the doctrine that nature loves simplicity, avoids the superfluous, and is accustomed to accomplish large results with a few principles—these remind one of Leibnitz. At the same time, the law of parsimony and the methodological conclusions concerning true hypotheses and real causes (an hypothesis must not be an artificially constructed set of fictions, forcibly adjusted to reality, but is to trace back phenomena to their real grounds), obedience to which enabled him to deduce *a priori* from causes the conclusions which Copernicus by fortunate conjecture had gathered inductively from effects—these made our thinker a forerunner of Newton. The physical method of explanation must not be corrupted either by theological conceptions (comets are entirely natural phenomena!) or by anthropomorphic views, which endow nature with spiritual powers.

[Footnote 1: See Sigwart, *Kleine Schriften*, vol. i. p. 182 *seq.*; R. Eucken, *Beiträge zur Geschichte der neueren Philosophie*, p. 54 *seq.*]

[Footnote 2: Aristotle erred when he considered qualitative distinctions (*idem* and *aliud*) ultimate. These are to be traced back to quantitative differences, and the *aliud* or *diversum* is to be replaced by *plus et minus*. There is nothing absolutely light, but only relatively. Since all things are distinguished only by "more or less," the possibility of mediating members or proportions between them is given.]

Intermediate between Bacon and Descartes, both in the order of time and in the order of fact, and a co-founder of modern philosophy, stands Galileo Galilei (1564-1641).[1] Galileo exhibits all the traits characteristic of modern thinking: the reference from words to things, from memory to perception and thought, from authority to self-ascertained principles, from chance opinion, arbitrary opinion, and the traditional doctrines of the schools, to "knowledge," that is, to one's own, well grounded, indisputable insight, from the study of human affairs to the study of nature. Study Aristotle, but do not become his slave; instead of yielding yourselves captive to his views, use your own eyes; do not believe that the mind remains unproductive unless it allies itself with the understanding of another; copy nature, not copies merely! He equals Bacon in his high estimation of sensuous experience in contrast to the often illusory conclusions of the reason, and of the value of induction; but he does not conceal from himself the fact that observation is merely the first step in the process of cognition, leaving the chief rôle for the understanding. This, supplementing the defect of experience—the impossibility of observing all cases—by its *a priori* concept of law and with its inferences overstepping the bounds of experience, first makes induction possible, brings the facts established into connection (their combination under laws is thought, not experience), reduces them to their primary, simple, unchangeable, and necessary causes by abstraction from contingent circumstances, regulates perception, corrects sense-illusions, *i. e.*, the false judgments originating in experience, and decides concerning the reality or fallaciousness of phenomena. Demonstration based on experience, a close union of observation and thought, of fact and Idea (law)—these are the requirements made by Galileo and brilliantly fulfilled in his discoveries; this, the "inductive speculation," as Dühring terms it, which derives laws of far-reaching importance from inconspicuous facts; this, as Galileo himself recognizes, the distinctive gift of the investigator. Galileo anticipates Descartes in regard to the subjective character of sense qualities and their reduction to quantitative distinctions,[2] while he shares with him the belief in the typical character of mathematics and the mechanical theory of the world. The truth of geometrical propositions and demonstrations is as unconditionally certain for man as for God, only that man learns them by a discursive process, whereas God's intuitive understanding comprehends them with a glance and knows more of them than man. The book of the universe is written in mathematical characters; motion is the fundamental phenomenon in the world of matter; our knowledge reaches as far as phenomena are measurable; the qualitative nature of force, back of its quantitative determinations, remains unknown to us. When Galileo maintains that the Copernican theory is philosophically true and not merely astronomically useful, thus interpreting it as more than a hypothesis, he is guided by the conviction that the simplest explanation is the most probable one, that truth and beauty are one, as in general he concedes a guiding though not a controlling influence in scientific work to the aesthetic demand of the mind for order, harmony, and unity in nature, to correspond to the wisdom of the Creator.

[Footnote 1: Cf. Natorp's essay on Galileo, in vol. xviii. of the *Philosophische Monatshefte*, 1882.]

[Footnote 1: This doctrine is developed by Galileo in the controversial treatise against Padre Grassi, *The Scales (Il Saggiatore*, 1623, in the Florence edition of his collected works, 1842 *seq.*, vol. iv. pp. 149-369; cf. Natorp, *Descartes' Erkenntnisstheorie*, 1882, chap. vi.). In substance, moreover, this doctrine is found, as Heussler remarks, *Baco*, p. 94, in Bacon himself, in *Valerius Terminus (Works*, Spedding, vol. iii. pp. 217-252.)]

One of the most noted and influential among the contemporaries, countrymen, and opponents of Descartes, was the priest and natural scientist, Petrus Gassendi,[1] from 1633 Provost of Digne, later for a short period professor of mathematics at Paris. His renewal of Epicureanism, to which he was impelled by temperament, by his reverence for Lucretius, and by the anti-Aristotelian tendency of his thinking, was of far more importance for modern thought than the attempts to revive the ancient systems which have been mentioned above (p. 29). Its superior influence depends on the fact that, in the conception of atoms, it offered exact inquiry a most useful point of attachment. The conflict between the Gassendists and the Cartesians, which at first was a bitter one, centered, as far as physics was concerned, around the value of the atomic hypothesis as contrasted with the corpuscular and vortex theory which Descartes had opposed to it. It soon became apparent, however, that these two thinkers followed along essentially the same lines in the philosophy of nature, sharply as they were opposed in their noëtical principles. Descartes' doctrine of body is conceived from an entirely materialistic standpoint, his anthropology, indeed, going further than the principles of his system would allow. Gassendi, on the other hand, recognizes an immaterial, immortal reason, traces the origin of the world, its marvelous arrangement, and the beginning of motion back to God, and, since the Bible so teaches, believes the earth to be at rest,—holding that, for this reason, the decision must be given in favor of Tycho Brahé and against Copernicus, although the hypothesis of the latter affords the simpler and, scientifically, the more probable explanation. Both thinkers rejoice in their agreement with the dogmas of the Church, only that with Descartes it came unsought in the natural progress of his thought, while Gassendi held to it in contradiction to his system. It is the more surprising that Gassendi's works escaped being put upon the Index, a fate which overtook those of Descartes in 1663.

[Footnote 2: Pierre Gassendi, 1592-1655: *On the Life and Character of Epicurus*, 1647; *Notes on the Tenth Book of Diogenes Laërtius, with a Survey of the Doctrine of Epicurus*, 1649. Works, Lyons, 1658, Florence, 1727. Cf. Lange, *History of Materialism*, book i. § 3, chap, 1; Natorp, *Analekten, Philosophische Monatshefte*, vol. xviii. 1882, p. 572 *seq.*]

As modern thought derives its mechanical temper equally from both these sources, and the natural science of the day has appropriated the corpuscles of Descartes under the name of molecules, as well as the atoms of Gassendi, though not without considerable modification in both conceptions (Lange, vol. i. p. 269), so we find attempts at mediation at an early period. While Père Mersenne (1588-1648), who was well versed in physics, sought an indecisive middle course between these two philosophers, the English chemist, Robert Boyle, effected a successful synthesis of both. The son of Richard Boyle, Earl of Cork, he was born at Lismore in 1626, lived in literary retirement at Oxford from 1654, and later in Cambridge, and died, 1692, in London, president of the Royal Society. His principal work, *The Sceptical Chemist (Works*, vol. i. p. 290 *seq.*), appeared in 1661, the tract, *De Ipsa Natura*, in 1682.[1] By his introduction of the atomic conception he founded an epoch in chemistry, which, now for the first, was freed from bondage to the ideas of Aristotle and the alchemists. Atomism, however, was for Boyle merely an instrument of method and not a philosophical theory of the world. A sincerely religious man,[2] he regards with disfavor both the atheism of Epicurus and his complete rejection of teleology—the world-machine points to an intelligent

Creator and a purpose in creation; motion, to a divine impulse. He defends, on the other hand, the right of free inquiry against the priesthood and the pedantry of the schools, holding that the supernatural must be sharply distinguished from the natural, and mere conjectures concerning insoluble problems from positions susceptible of experimental proof; while, in opposition to submission to authority, he remarks that the current coin of opinion must be estimated, not by the date when and the person by whom it was minted but by the value of the metal alone. Cartesian elements in Boyle are the start from doubt, the derivation of all motion from pressure and impact, and the extension of the mechanical explanation to the organic world. His inquiries relate exclusively to the world of matter so far as it was "completed on the last day but one of creation." He defends empty space against Descartes and Hobbes. He is the first to apply the mediaeval terms, primary and secondary qualities, to the antithesis between objective properties which really belong to things, and sensuous or subjective qualities present only in the feeling subject.[3]

[Footnote 1: Boyle's *Works* were published in Latin at Geneva, in 1660, in six volumes, and in 1714 in five; an edition by Birch appeared at London, 1744, in five volumes, second edition, 1772, in six. Cf. Buckle, *History of Civilization in England*, vol. i. chap. vii. pp. 265-268; Lange, *History of Materialism*, vol. i. pp. 298-306; vol. ii. p. 351 *seq.*; Georg Baku, *Der Streit über den Naturbegriff, Zeitschrift für Philosophie*, vol. xcviii., 1891, p. 162 *seq.*]

[Footnote 2: The foundation named after him had for its object to promote by means of lectures the investigation of nature on the basis of atomism, and, at the same time, to free it from the reproach of leading to atheism and to show its harmony with natural religion. Samuel Clarke's work on *The Being and Attributes of God*, 1705, originated in lectures delivered on this foundation.]

[Footnote 3: Eucken, *Geschichte der philosophischen Terminologie*, pp. 94, 196.]

%8. Philosophy in England to the Middle of the Seventeenth Century.%

%(a) Bacon's Predecessors.%—The darkness which lay over the beginnings of modern English philosophy has been but incompletely dispelled by the meritorious work of Ch. de Rémusat *(Histoire de la Philosophie en Angleterre depuis Bacon jusqu'a Locke*, 2 vols., 1878). The most recent investigations of J. Freudenthal *(Beiträge zur Geschichte der Englischen Philosophie*, in the *Archiv für Geschichte der Philosophie*, vols. iv. and v., 1891) have brought assistance in a way deserving of thanks, since they lift at important points the veil which concealed Bacon's relations to his predecessors and contemporaries, by describing the scientific tendencies and achievements of Digby and Temple. The following may be taken from his results.

Everard Digby (died 1592; chief work, *Theoria Analytica,* 1579), instructor in logic in Cambridge from 1573, who was strongly influenced by Reuchlin and who favored an Aristotelian-Alexandrian-Cabalistic eclecticism, was the first to disseminate Neoplatonic ideas in England; and, in spite of the lack of originality in his systematic presentation of theoretical philosophy, aroused the study of this branch in England into new life. His opponent, Sir William Temple [1] (1553-1626), by his defense and exposition of the doctrine of Ramus (introduced into Great Britain by George Buchanan and his pupil, Andrew Melville), made Cambridge the chief center of Ramism. He was the first who openly opposed Aristotle.

[Footnote 1: Temple was secretary to Philip Sidney, William Davison, and the Earl of Essex, and, from 1619, Provost of Trinity College, Dublin. His maiden work, *De Unica P. Rami Methodo*, which he published under the pseudonym, Mildapettus 1580, was aimed at Digby's *De Duplici Methodo*. His chief work, *P. Rami Dialectics Libri Dua Scholiis, Illustrati*, appeared in 1584.]

Bacon was undoubtedly acquainted with both these writers and took ideas from both. Digby represented the scholastic tendency, which Bacon vehemently opposed, yet without being able completely to break away from it. Temple was one of those who supplied him with weapons for this conflict. Finally, it must be mentioned that many of the English scientists of the time, especially William Gilbert (1540-1603; *De Magnete*, 1600), physician to Queen Elizabeth, used induction in their work before Bacon advanced his theory of method.

%(b) Bacon%.—The founder of the empirical philosophy of modern times was Francis Bacon (1561-1626), a contemporary of Shakespeare. Bacon began his political career by sitting in Parliament for many years under Queen Elizabeth, as whose counsel he was charged with the duty of engaging in the prosecution of his patron, the Earl of Essex, and at whose command he prepared a justification of the process. Under James I, he attained the highest offices and honors, being made Keeper of the Great Seal in 1617, Lord Chancellor and Baron Verulam in 1618, and Viscount St. Albans in 1621. In this last year came his fall. He was charged with bribery, and condemned; the king remitted the imprisonment and fine, and for the remainder of his life Bacon devoted himself to science, rejecting every suggestion toward a renewal of his political activity. The moral laxity of the times throws a mitigating light over his fault; but he cannot be aquitted of self-seeking, love of money and of display, and excessive ambition. As Macaulay says in his famous essay, he was neither malignant nor tyrannical, but he lacked warmth of affection and elevation of sentiment; there were many things which he loved more than virtue, and many which he feared more than guilt. He first gained renown as an author by his ethical, economic, and political *Essays*, after the manner of Montaigne; of these the first ten appeared in 1597, in the third edition (1625) increased to fifty-eight; the Latin translation bears the title *Sermones Fideles*. His great plan for a "restoration of the sciences" was intended to be carried out in four, or rather, in six parts. But only the first two parts of the *Instauratio Magna* were developed: the *encyclopaedia*, or division of all sciences[1], a chart of the *globus intellectualis*, on which was depicted what each science had accomplished and what still remained for each to do; and the development of the *new method*. Bacon published his survey of the circle of the sciences in the English work, the *Advancement of Learning*, 1605, a much enlarged revision of which, *De Dignitate et Augmentis Scientiarum*, appeared in Latin in 1623. In 1612 he printed as a contribution to methodology the draft, *Cogitata et Visa* (written 1607), later recast into the [first book of the] *Novum Organum*, 1620. This title, *Novum Organum*, of itself indicates opposition to Aristotle, whose logical treatises had for ages been collected under the title *Organon*. If in this work Bacon had given no connected exposition of his reforming principles, but merely a series of aphorisms, and this an incomplete one, the remaining parts are still more fragmentary, only prefaces and scattered contributions having been reduced to writing. The third part was to have been formed by a description of the world or natural *history, Historia Naturalis*, and the last,—introduced by a *Scala Intellectus* (ladder of knowledge, illustrations of the method by examples), and by *Prodromi* (preliminary results of his own inquiries),—by natural *science, Philosophia Secunda*. The best edition of Bacon's works is the London one of Spedding, Ellis & Heath, 1857 *seq.*, 7 vols., 2d ed., 1870; with 7 volumes additional of *The Letters and Life of Francis Bacon, including His Occasional Works*, and a Commentary, by J. Spedding, 1862-74. Spedding followed this further with a briefer *Account of the Life and Times of Francis Bacon*, 2 vols., 1878[2].

[Footnote 1: According to the faculties of the soul, memory, imagination, and understanding, three principal sciences are distinguished; history, poesy, and philosophy. Of the three objects of the latter, "nature strikes the mind with a direct ray, God with a refracted ray, and man himself with a reflected ray." Theology is natural or revealed. Speculative (theoretical) natural philosophy divides into physics, concerned with material and efficient causes, and metaphysics, whose mission, according to the traditional view, is to inquire into final causes, but in Bacon's own opinion, into formal causes; operative (technical) natural philosophy is mechanics and natural magic. The doctrine concerning man comprises anthropology (including logic and ethics) and politics. This division of Bacon was still retained by D'Alembert in his preliminary discourse to the *Encyclopédie*.]

[Footnote 2: Cf. on Bacon, K. Fischer, 2d ed., 1875; Chr. Sigwart, in the *Preussische Jahrbücher*, 1863 and 1864, and in vol. ii. of his *Logik*; H. Heussler, *Baco und seine geschichtliche Stellung*, Breslau, 1889. [Adamson, *Encyclopedia Britannica*, 9th. ed., vol. iii. pp. 200-222; Fowler, English Philosophers Series, 1881; Nichol, Blackwood's Philosophical Classics, 2 vols., 1888-89.—TR.]] Bacon's merit was threefold: he felt more forcibly and more clearly than previous thinkers the need of a reform in science; he set up a new and grand ideal—unbiased and methodical investigation of nature in order to mastery over nature; and he gave information and directions as to the way in which this goal was to be attained, which, in spite of their incompleteness in detail, went deep into the heart of the subject and laid the foundation for the work of centuries.[1] His faith in the omnipotence of the new method was so strong, that he thought that science for the future could almost dispense with talent. He compares his method to a compass or a ruler, with which the unpractised man is able to draw circles and straight lines better than an expert without these instruments.

[Footnote 1: His detractors are unjust when they apply the criterion of the present method of investigation and find only imperfection in an imperfect beginning.]

All science hitherto, Bacon declares, has been uncertain and unfruitful, and does not advance a step, while the mechanic arts grow daily more perfect; without a firm basis, garrulous, contentious, and lacking in content, it is of no practical value. The seeker after certain knowledge must abandon words for things, and learn the art of forcing nature to answer his questions. The seeker after fruitful knowledge must increase the number of discoveries, and transform them from matters of chance into matters of design. For discovery conditions the power, greatness, and progress of mankind. Man's power is measured by his knowledge, knowledge is power, and nature is conquered by obedience—*scientia est potentia; natura parendo vincitur*.

Bacon declares three things indispensable for the attainment of this power-giving knowledge: the mind must understand the instruments of knowledge; it must turn to experience, deriving the materials of knowledge from perception; and it must not rise from particular principles to the higher axioms too rapidly, but steadily and gradually through middle axioms. The mind can accomplish nothing when left to itself; but undirected experience alone is also insufficient (experimentation without a plan is groping in the dark), and the senses, moreover, are deceptive and not acute enough for the subtlety of nature—therefore, methodical experimentation alone, not chance observation, is worthy of confidence. Instead of the customary divorce of experience and understanding, a firm alliance, a "lawful marriage," must be effected between them. The empiricists merely collect, like the ants; the dogmatic metaphysicians spin the web of their ideas out of themselves, like the spiders; but the true philosopher must be like the bee, which by its own power transforms and digests the gathered material.

As the mind, like a dull and uneven mirror, by its own nature distorts the rays of objects, it must first of all be cleaned and polished, that is, it must be freed from all prejudices and false notions, which, deep-rooted by habit, prevent the formation of a true picture of the world. It must root out its prejudices, or, where this is impossible, at least understand them. Doubt is the first step on the way to truth. Of these Phantoms or Idols to be discarded, Bacon distinguishes four classes: Idols of the Theater, of the Market Place, of the Den, and of the Tribe. The most dangerous are the *idola theatri*, which consist in the tendency to put more trust in authority and tradition than in independent reflection, to adopt current ideas simply because they find general acceptance. Bacon's injunction concerning these is not to be deceived by stage-plays (*i.e.*, by the teachings of earlier thinkers which represent things other than they are); instead of believing others, observe for thyself! The *idola fori*, which arise from the use of language in public intercourse, depend upon the confusion of words, which are mere symbols with a conventional value and which are based on the carelessly constructed concepts of the vulgar, with things themselves. Here Bacon warns us to keep close to things. The *idola specus* are individual prepossessions which interfere with the apprehension of the true state of affairs, such as the excessive tendency of thought toward the resemblances or the differences of things, or the investigator's habit of transferring ideas current in his own department to subjects of a different kind. Such individual weaknesses are numberless, yet they may in part be corrected by comparison with the perceptions of others. The *idola tribus*, finally, are grounded in the nature of the human species. To this class belong, among others, illusions of the senses, which may in part be corrected by the use of instruments, with which we arm our organs; further, the tendency to hold fast to opinions acceptable to us in spite of contrary instances; similarly, the tendency to anthropomorphic views, including, as its most important special instance, the mistake of thinking that we perceive purposive relations everywhere and the working of final causes, after the analogy of human action, when in reality efficient causes alone are concerned. Here Bacon's injunction runs, not to interpret natural phenomena teleologically, but to explain them from mechanical causes; not to narrow the world down to the limits of the mind, but to extend the mind to the boundaries of the world, so that it shall understand it as it really is.

To these warnings there are added positive rules. When the investigator, after the removal of prejudices and habitual modes of thought, approaches experience with his senses unperverted and a purified mind, he is to advance from the phenomena given to their conditions. First of all, the facts must be established by observation and experiment, and systematically arranged,[1] then let him go on to causes and laws.[2] The true or scientific induction[3] thus inculcated is quite different from the credulous induction of common life or the unmethodical induction of Aristotle. Bacon emphasizes the fact that hitherto the importance of negative instances, which are to be employed as a kind of counter-proof, has been completely overlooked, and that a substitute for complete induction, which is never attainable, may be found, on the one hand, in the collection of as many cases as possible, and, on the other, by considering the more important or decisive cases, the "prerogative instances." Then the inductive ascent from experiment to axiom is to be followed by a deductive descent from axioms to new experiments and discoveries. Bacon rejects the syllogism on the ground that it fits one to overcome his opponent in disputation, but not to gain an active conquest over nature. In his own application of these principles of method, his procedure was that of a dilettante; the patient, assiduous labor demanded for the successful promotion of the mission of natural investigation was not his forte. His strength lay in the postulation of problems, the stimulation and direction of inquiry, the discovery of lacunae and the throwing out of suggestions; and many ideas incidentally thrown off by him surprise us by their ingenious anticipations of later discoveries. The greatest defect in his theory was his complete failure to recognize the services promised by mathematics to natural science. The charge of utilitarianism, which has been so broadly made, is, on the contrary, unjust. For no matter how strongly he emphasizes the practical value of knowledge, he is still in agreement with those who esteem the godlike condition of calm and cheerful acquaintance with truth more highly than the advantages to be expected from it; he desires science to be used, not as "a courtezan for pleasure," but "as a spouse for generation, fruit and comfort," and—leaving entirely out of view his isolated acknowledgments of the inherent value of knowledge—he conceives its utility wholly in the comprehensive and noble sense that the pursuit of science, from which as such all narrow-minded regard for direct practical application must keep aloof, is the most important lever for the advancement of human culture.

[Footnote 1: Bacon illustrates the method by the explanation of heat. The results of experimental observation are to be arranged in three tables. The table of presence contains many different cases in which heat occurs; the table of absence, those in which, under circumstances otherwise the same, it is wanting; the table of degrees or comparison enumerates phenomena whose increase and decrease accompany similar variations in the degree of heat. That which remains after the *exclusion* now to be undertaken (of that which cannot be the nature or cause of heat), yields as a preliminary result or commencement of interpretation (as a "first vintage"), the definition of heat: "a motion, expansive, restrained, and acting in its strife upon the smaller particles of bodies."]

[Footnote 2: This goal of Baconian inquiry is by no means coincident with that of exact natural science. Law does not mean to him, as to the physical scientist of to-day, a mathematically formulated statement of the course of events, but the nature of the phenomenon, to be expressed in a definition (E. König, *Entwickelung des Causalproblems bis Kant*, 1883, pp. 154-156). Bacon combines in a peculiar manner ancient and modern, Platonic and corpuscular fundamental ideas. Rejecting final causes with the atomists, yet handing over material and efficient causes (the latter of which sink with him to the level of mere changing occasional causes) to empirical physics, he assigns to metaphysics, as the true *science* of nature, the search for the "forms" and properties of things. In this he is guided by the following metaphysical presupposition: Phenomena, however manifold they may be, are at bottom composed of a few elements, namely, permanent properties, the so-called "simple natures," which form, as it were, the alphabet of nature or the colors on her palette, by the combination of which she produces her varied pictures; *e. g.*, the nature of heat and cold, of a red color, of gravity, and also of age, of death. Now the question to be investigated becomes, What, then, is heat, redness, etc.? The ground essence and law of the natures consist in certain forms, which Bacon conceives in a Platonic way as concepts and substances, but phenomenal ones, and, at the same time, with Democritus, as the grouping or motion of minute material particles. Thus the form of heat is a particular kind of motion, the form of whiteness a determinate arrangement of material particles. Cf. Natge, *Ueber F. Bacons Formenlehre*, Leipsic, 1891, in which Heussler's view is developed in more detail. [Cf. further, Fowler's *Bacon*, English Philosophers Series, 1881, chap. iv.—TR.]]

[Footnote 3: The Baconian method is to be called induction, it is true, only in the broad sense. Even before Sigwart, Apelt, *Theorie der Induction*, 1854, pp. 151, 153, declared that the question it discussed was essentially a method of abstraction. This, however, does not detract from the fame of Bacon as the founder, of the theory of inductive investigation (in later times carefully elaborated by Mill).]

Bacon intended that his reforming principles should accrue to the benefit of practical philosophy also, but gave only aphoristic hints to this end. Everything is impelled by two appetites, of which the one aims at individual welfare, the other at the welfare of the whole of which the thing is a part (*bonum suitatis—bonum communionis*). The second is not only the nobler but also the stronger; this holds of the lower creatures as well as of man, who, when not degenerate, prefers the general welfare to his individual interests. Love is the highest of the virtues, and is never, as other human endowments, exposed to the danger of excess; therefore the life of action is of more worth than the life of contemplation. By this principle of morals Bacon marked out the way for the English ethics of later times.[1] He notes the lack of a science of character, for which more material is given in ordinary discourse, in the poets and the historians, than in the works of the philosophers; he explains the power of the affections over the reason by the fact that the idea of present good fills the imagination more forcibly than the idea of good to come, and summons persuasion, habit, and morals to the aid of the latter. We must endeavor so to govern the passions (each of which combines in itself a masculine impetuosity with a feminine weakness) that they shall take the part of the reason instead of attacking it. Elsewhere Bacon gives (not entirely unquestionable) directions concerning the art of making one's way. Acute observations and ingenious remarks everywhere abound. In order to inform one's self of a man's intentions and ends, it is necessary to "keep a good mediocrity in liberty of speech, which invites a similar liberty, and in secrecy, which induces trust." "In order to get on one must have a little of the fool and not too much of the honest." "As the baggage is to an army, so is riches to virtue. It cannot be spared nor left behind, but it hindereth the march; yea, and the care of it sometimes loseth or disturbeth the victory" (impedimenta—baggage and hindrance). On envy and malevolence he says: "For men's minds will either feed upon their own good or upon others' evil; ... and whoso is out of hope to attain another's virtue will seek to come at even hand by depressing another's fortune."

[Footnote 1: Cf. Vorlaender, p. 267 *seq.*]

In ethics, as in theoretical philosophy, Bacon demands the completion of natural knowledge by revelation. The light of nature (the reason and the conscience) is able only to convince us of sin and not to give us complete information concerning our duty,—*e.g.*, the lofty moral principle, Love your enemies. Similarly, natural theology is quite sufficient to place the existence of God beyond doubt, by reasoning from the order in nature ("slight tastes of philosophy may perchance move one to atheism but fuller draughts lead back to religion"); but the doctrines of Christianity are matters of faith. Religion and science are separate fields, any confusion of which involves the danger of an heretical religion or a fabulous philosophy. The more a principle of faith contradicts the reason, the greater the obedience and the honor to God in accepting it.

%(c) Hobbes%.—Hobbes stands in sharp contrast to Bacon both in disposition and in doctrine. Bacon was a man of a wide outlook, a rich, stimulating, impulsive nature, filled with great plans, but too mobile and desultory to allow them to ripen to perfection; Hobbes is slow, tenacious, persistent, unyielding, his thought strenuous and narrow. To this corresponds a profound difference in their systems, which is by no means adequately characterized by saying that Hobbes brings into the foreground the mathematical element neglected by his predecessor, and turns his attention chiefly to politics. The dependence of Hobbes on Bacon is, in spite of their personal acquaintance, not so great as formerly was universally assumed. His guiding stars are rather the great mathematicians of the Continent, Kepler and Galileo, while Cartesian influences also are not to be denied. He finds his mission in the construction of a strictly mechanical view of the world. Mechanism applied to the world gives materialism; applied to knowledge, sensationalism of a mathematical type; applied to the will, determinism; to morality and the state, ethical and political naturalism. Nevertheless, the empirical tendency of his nation has a certain power over him; he holds fast to the position that all ideas ultimately spring from experience. With his energetic but short-breathed thinking, he did not succeed in fusing the rationalistic elements received from foreign sources with these native tendencies, so as to produce a unified system. As Grimm has correctly shown (*Zur Geschichte des Erkenntnissproblems*), there is an unreconciled contradiction between the dependence of thought on experience, which he does not give up, and the universal validity of the truths derived from pure reason, which he asserts on the basis of the mathematico-philosophical doctrines of the Continent. A similar unmediated dualism will meet us in Locke also.

Thomas Hobbes (1588-1679) was repelled while a student at Oxford by Scholastic methods in thought, with which he agreed only in their nominalistic results (there are no universals except names). During repeated sojourns in Paris, where he made the acquaintance of Gassendi, Mersenne, and Descartes, he devoted himself to the study of mathematics, and was greatly influenced by the doctrines of Galileo; while the disorders of the English revolution led him to embrace an absolutist theory of the state. His chief works were his politics, under the title *Leviathan*, 1651, and his *Elementa Philosophiae*, in three parts (*De Corpore, De Homine, De Cive*), of which the third, *De Cive*, appeared first (in Latin; in briefer form and anonymously, 1642, enlarged 1647), the first, *De Corpore*, in 1655, and the second, *De Homine*, in 1658. These had been preceded by two books [1] written, like the two last parts of the *Elements*, in English: *On Human Nature* and *De Corpore Politico*, composed 1640, printed without the author's consent in 1650. Besides these he wrote two treatises *Of Liberty and Necessity*, 1646 and 1654, and prepared, 1668, a collected edition of his works (in Latin). In Molesworth's edition, 1839-45, the Latin works occupy five volumes and the English eleven.[2]

[Footnote 1: Or rather one; the treatise *On Human Nature* consists of the first thirteen chapters of the work, *Elements of Law, Natural and Politic*, and the *De Corpore Politico* of the remainder.]

[Footnote 2: Cf. on Hobbes, G.C. Robertson (Blackwood's Philosophical Classics, vol. x.), 1886; Tönnies in the *Vierteljahrsschrift für wissenschaftliche Philosophie*, Jahrg. 3-5, 1879-81.]

Philosophy is formally defined by Hobbes as knowledge of effects from causes and causes from effects by means of legitimate rational inference. This implies the equal validity of the deductive and inductive methods,—while Bacon had proclaimed the latter the most important instrument of knowledge,—as well as the exclusion of theology based on revelation from the domain of science. Philosophy is objectively defined as the theory of body and motion: *all that exists is body; all that occurs, motion*. Everything real is corporeal; this holds of points, lines, and surfaces, which as the limits of body cannot be incorporeal, as well as of the mind and of God. The mind is merely a (for the senses too) refined body, or, as it is stated in another place, a movement in certain parts of the organic body. All events, even internal events, the feelings and passions, are movements of material parts. "Endeavor" is a diminutive motion, as the atom is the smallest of bodies; sensation and representation are changes in the perceiving body. Space is the idea of an existing thing as such, *i. e.*, merely as existing outside the perceiving subject; time, the idea of motion. All phenomena are corporeal motions, which take place with mechanical necessity. Neither formal nor final causes exist, but only efficient causes. All that happens takes its origin in the activity of an external cause, and not in itself; a body at rest (or in motion) remains at rest (or in motion) forever, unless affected by another in a contrary sense. And as bodies and their changes constitute the only objects of philosophy, so the mathematical method is the only correct method.

There are two kinds of bodies: natural bodies, which man finds in nature, and artificial bodies, which he himself produces. By the latter Hobbes refers especially to the state as a human artefact. Man stands between the two as the most perfect natural body and an element in the political body. Philosophy, therefore, besides the introductory *philosophia prima*, which discusses the underlying concepts, consists of three parts: physics, anthropology, and politics. Even the theory of the state is capable of demonstrative treatment; moral phenomena are as subject to the law of mechanical causation as physical phenomena.

The first factor in the cognitive process is an impression on a sense-organ, which, occasioned by external motion, continues onward to the heart and from this center gives rise to a reaction. The perception or sensation which thus arises is entirely subjective, a function of the knower merely, and in no way a copy of the external movement. The properties light, color, and sound, which we believe to be without us, are merely internal phenomena dependent on outer and inner motions, but with no resemblance to them. Memory consists in the lingering effects or residuary traces of perception; it is a sense or consciousness of having felt before *(sentire se sensisse meminisse est)*, and ideas are distinguished from sensations as the perfect from the present tense. Experience is the totality of perceptions retained in memory, together with a certain foresight of the future after the analogy of the past. These stages of cognition, which can yield prudence but not necessary and universal knowledge, are present in animals as well as men. The human capacity for science is dependent on the faculty of speech; words are conventional signs to facilitate the retention and communication of ideas. As the memory-images denoted by words are weaker, fainter, and less clearly discriminated than the original sensations, it comes to pass that a number of similar ideas of memory receive a common name. Thus abstract general ideas and generic concepts arise, to which nothing real corresponds, for in reality particulars alone exist. The universal is a human artefact. The combination of words into propositions, being an addition or subtraction of arbitrary symbols or marks, is called judgment; the combination of propositions into syllogisms, inference; the united body of true or demonstrated principles, science—hence mathematics is the type of all knowledge. In short, thought is nothing but calculation and the words with which we operate are mere counters; he who takes counters for coin is a fool. Animals lack reason, *i.e.*, this power of combining artificial symbols.

Hobbes's theory of the will is characterized by the same! sensationalism and mechanism as his theory of knowledge. All spiritual events originate in impressions of sense. Man responds to the action of objects by a double reaction, adding to the theoretical reaction of sensation a practical one in the feeling of pleasure or pain (according as the impression furthers or hinders the vital function), whence desire and aversion follow in respect to future experience. Further developments from the feelings experienced at the signs of honor (the acknowledgment of superior power) and the contrary, are the affections of pride, courage, anger, of shame and repentance, of hope and love, of pity, etc. Deliberation is the alternation of different appetites; the final, victorious one which immediately precedes action is called will. Freedom cannot be predicated of the will, but only of the action, and even in this case it means simply the absence of external restraints, the procedure of the action from the will of the agent; while the action is necessary nevertheless. Every motion is the inevitable result of the sum of the preceding (including cerebral) motions.

Things which we desire are termed good, and those which we shun, evil. Nothing is good *per se* or absolutely, but only relatively, for a given person, place, time, or set of circumstances. Different things are good to different men, and there is no objective, universal rule of good and evil, so long as men are considered as individuals, apart from society. A definite criterion of the good is first reached in the state: that is right which the law permits, that wrong which it forbids; good means that which is conducive to the general welfare. In the state of nature nothing is forbidden; nature gives every man a right to everything, and right is coextensive with might. What, then, induces man to abandon the state of nature and enter the state of citizenship? The opinion of Aristotle and Grotius that the state originates in the social impulse is false; for man is essentially not social, but selfish, and nothing but regard for his own interests bids him seek the protection of the state; the civil commonwealth is an artificial product of fear and prudence. The highest good is self-preservation; all other goods, as friendship, riches, wisdom, knowledge, and, above all, power, are valuable only as instruments of the former. The precondition of well-being, for which each man strives by nature, is security for life and health. This is wanting in the state of nature, in which the passions govern; for the state of nature is a state of war of everyone against everyone *(bellum omnium contra omnes)*. Each man strives for success and power, and, since he cannot trust his fellow, seeks to subdue, nay, to kill him; each looks upon his fellow as a wolf which he prefers to devour rather than submit himself to the like operation. Now, as no one is so weak as to be incapable of inflicting on his fellows that worst of evils, death, and thus the strongest is unsafe, reason, in the interest of everyone, enjoins a search after peace and the establishment of an ordered community. The conditions of peace are the "laws of nature," which relate both to politics and to morals but which do not attain their full binding authority until they become positive laws, injunctions of the sovereign power. Peace is attainable only when each man, in return for the protection vouchsafed to him, gives up his natural right to all. The compact by which each renounces his natural liberty to do what he pleases, provided all others are ready for the same renunciation,—to which are added, further, the laws of justice (sanctity of covenants), equity, gratitude, modesty, sociability, mercifulness, etc., whose opposites would bring back the state of nature,—this compact is secured against violation by the transfer of the general power and freedom to a single will (the will of an assembly or of an individual person), which then represents the general will. The civil contract includes, then, two moments: first, renunciation; second, irrevocable transference and (absolute) submission. The second unites the multitude into a civil personality, the most perfect unity being vouchsafed by absolute monarchy. The sovereign is the soul of the political body; the officials, its limbs; reward and punishment, its nerves; law and equity, its reason.

The social contract theory has often experienced democratic interpretation and application, both before and since Hobbes's time; and, in fact, it does not include *per se* the irrevocability of the transfer, the absoluteness of the sovereign power, and the monarchical head, which Hobbes considered indispensable in order to guard against the danger of anarchy. In every abridgment of the supreme power, whether by division or limitation, he sees a step toward the renewal of the state of nature; and he defends with iron rigor the omnipotence of the state and the complete lack of legal status on the part of all individuals in contrast with it. The citizen is not to obey his own conscience, which has simply the value of a private opinion, but the laws, as the public conscience; while the supreme ruler, on the contrary, is superior to the civil laws, for it is he that decrees, interprets, alters, and abrogates them. He is lord over the property, the life, and the death of the citizens, and can do no one wrong. For he alone has retained his original natural right to all, which the rest have entirely and forever renounced. He must have regard, indeed, to the welfare of the people, but he is accountable to God alone. The obligation of the subject to obey is extinguished in one case only,—when the civil power is incapable of providing him further with external and internal protection. For the rest, Hobbes declares the existing public order the lawful one, the evils of arbitrary rule much more tolerable than the universal hostility of the state of nature, and aversion to tyrants a disease inherited from the republicans of antiquity.

The sovereign, by the laws and by instruction, determines what is good and evil; he determines also what is to be believed. Religion unsanctioned by the state is superstition. The temporal ruler is also the spiritual ruler, the king, the chief pastor, and the clergy his servants. One and the same community is termed state in so far as it consists of men, and church in so far as it consists of Christian men (the ecclesiastical commonwealth). The dogmas which the law prescribes are to be received without investigation, to be swallowed like pills, without mastication.

The principle that every passion and every action is in its nature indifferent, that right and wrong exist only in the state, that the will of a despot is to determine what is moral and what immoral, has given just offense. Moreover, this was not, in fact, Hobbes's deepest conviction. Even without ascribing great importance to isolated statements,[1] it must be admitted that his doctrine was interpreted more narrowly than it was intended. He does not say that no moral distinctions whatever exist before the foundation of the state, but only that the state first supplies a fixed criterion of the good. Moral ideas have a certain currency before this, but they lack power to enforce themselves. Further, when he ascribes the origin of the state to self-interest, this does not mean that reason, conscience, generosity, and love for our fellows are entirely wanting in the state of nature, but only that they are not general enough, and, as against the passions, not strong enough to furnish a foundation for the edifice of the state. Not only exaggeration in statement but also uncouthness of thought may be forgiven the representative of a movement which is at once new and strengthened by the consciousness of agreement with a naturalistic theory of knowledge and physics; and the vigor of execution compels admiration, even though many obscurities remain to be deplored *(e. g.*, the relation of the two moral standards, the standard of the reason or natural law and the standard of positive law). And recognition must be accorded to the significant kernel of doctrine formed, on the one hand, by the endeavor to separate ethics from theology, and on the other, by the thoughts—which, it is true, were not perfectly brought out—that the moral is not founded on a natural social impulse, but on a law of the reason, and first gains a definite criterion in society, and that the interests of the individual are inseparably connected with those of the community. In any case, the attempt to form a naturalistic theory of the state would be an undertaking deserving of thanks, even if the promulgation of this theory had done no further service than to challenge refutation.

[Footnote 1: God inscribed the divine or natural law (Do not that to another, etc.) on the heart of man, when he gave him the reason to rule his actions. The laws of nature are, it is true, not always legally binding (*in foro externo*), but always and everywhere binding on the conscience (*in foro interno*). Justice is the virtue which we can measure by civil laws; love, that which we measure by the law of nature merely. The ruler *ought* to govern in accordance with the law of nature.]

%(d) Lord Herbert of Cherbury.%—Between Bacon (1605, 1620) and Hobbes (1642, 1651) stands Lord Herbert of Cherbury (1581-1648), who, by his work *De Veritate* (1624),[1] became the founder of deism, that theory of "natural religion," which, in opposition to the historical dogmatic faith of the Church theology, takes the reason, which is the same in all men, as its basis and morality for its content. Lord Herbert introduces his philosophy of religion by a theory of knowledge which makes universal consent the highest criterion of truth (*summa veritatis norma consensus universalis*), and bases knowledge on certain self-evident principles (*principia*), common to all men in virtue of a natural instinct, which gives safe guidance. These common notions (*notitiae communes*) precede all reflective inquiry, as well as all observation and experience, which would be impossible without them. The most important among them are the religious and ethical maxims of conscience.

[Footnote 1: *Tractatus de Veritate prout distinguitur a Revelatione, a Verisimili, a Possibile, et a False.* Also, *De Religione Gentilium*, 1645, complete 1663.]

This natural instinct is both an impulse toward truth and a capacity for good or impulse to self-preservation. The latter extends not only to the individual but to all things with which the individual is connected, to the species, nay, to all the rest of the world, and its final goal is eternal happiness: all natural capacities are directed toward the highest good or toward God. The sense for the divine may indeed be lulled to sleep or led astray by our free will, but not eradicated. To be rational and to be religious are inseparable; it is religion that distinguishes man from the brute, and no people can be found in which it is lacking. If atheists really exist, they are to be classed with the irrational and the insane.

The content of natural religion may be summed up in the following five articles, which all nations confess: 1. That there is a Supreme Being (*numen supremum*). 2. That he ought to be worshiped. 3. That virtue and piety are the chief elements of worship. 4. That man ought to repent of his sins. 5. That there are rewards and punishments in a future life. Besides these general principles, on the discovery of which Lord Herbert greatly prides himself, the positive religions contain arbitrary additions, which distinguish them from one another and which owe their origin, for the most part, to priestly deception, although the rhapsodies of the poets and the inventions of the philosophers have contributed their share. The essential principles of natural religion (God, virtue, faith, hope, love, and repentance) come more clearly to light in Christianity than in the religions of heathendom, where they are overgrown with myths and ceremonies.

The *Religio Medici* (1642) of Sir Thomas Browne shows similar tendencies.

%9. Preliminary Survey.%

In the line of development from the speculations of Nicolas of Cusa to the establishment of the English philosophy of nature, of religion, and of the state by Bacon, Herbert, and Hobbes, and to the physics of Galileo, modern ideas have manifested themselves with increasing clearness and freedom. Hobbes himself shows thus early the influence of Descartes's decisive step, with which the twilight gives place to the brightness of the morning. In Descartes the empiricism and sensationalism of the English is confronted by rationalism, to which the great thinkers of the Continent continue loyal. In Britain, experience, on the Continent the reason is declared to be the source of cognition; in the former, the point of departure is found in particular impressions of sense, on the latter, in general concepts and principles of the understanding; there the method of observation is inculcated and followed, here, the method of deduction. This antithesis remained decisive in the development of philosophy down to Kant, so that it has long been customary to distinguish two lines or schools, the Empirical and the Rationalistic, whose parallelism may be exhibited in the following table (when only one date is given it indicates the appearance of the philosopher's chief work):

Empiricism. Rationalism.
Bacon, 1620. (Nicolas, 1450; Bruno, 1584).
Hobbes, 1651. *Descartes*, died 1650.
Locke, 1690 (1632-1704). Spinoza, (1632-) 1677.
Berkeley, 1710. *Leibnitz*, 1710.
Hume, 1748. Wolff, died 1754.

We must not forget, indeed, the lively interchange of ideas between the schools (especially the influence of Descartes on Hobbes, and of the latter on Spinoza; further, of Descartes on Locke, and of the latter on Leibnitz) which led to reciprocal approximation and enrichment. Berkeley and Leibnitz, from opposite presuppositions, arrive at the same idealistic conclusion—there is no real world of matter, but only spirits and ideas exist. Hume and Wolff conclude the two lines of development: under the former, empiricism disintegrates into skepticism; under the latter, rationalism stiffens into a scholastic dogmatism, soon to run out into a popular eclecticism of common sense.

If we compare the mental characteristics of the three great nations which, in the period between Descartes and Kant, participated most productively in the work of philosophy,—the Italians, with their receptive temperament and so active in many fields, exerted a decisive influence on its development and progress in the transition period alone,—it will be seen that the Frenchman tends chiefly to acuteness, the Englishman to clearness and simplicity, the German to profundity of thought. France is the land of mathematical, England of practical, Germany of speculative thinkers; the first is the home of the skeptics, though of the enthusiasts as well; the second, of the realists; the third, of the idealists.

The English philosopher resembles a geographer who, with conscientious care, outlines a map of the region through which he journeys; the Frenchman, an anatomist who, with steady stroke, lays bare the nerves and muscles of the organism; the German, a mountaineer who loses in clear vision of particular objects as much as he gains in loftiness of position and extent of view. The Englishman describes the given reality, the Frenchman analyses it, the German transfigures it.

The English thinker keeps as close as possible to phenomena, and the principles which he uses in the explanation of phenomena themselves lie in the realm of concrete experience. He explains one phenomenon by another; he classifies and arranges the given material without analyzing it; he keeps constantly in touch with the popular consciousness. His reverence for reality, as this presents itself to him, and his distrust of far-reaching abstraction, are so strong that it is enough for him to take his bearings from the real, and to give a true reproduction of it, while he willingly renounces the ambition to form it anew in concepts. With this respect for concrete reality he combines a similar reverence for ethical postulates. When the development of a given line of thought threatens to bring him into conflict with practical life, he is honest enough to draw the conclusions which follow from his premises and to give them expression, but he avoids the collision by a simple compromise, shutting up the refinements of philosophy in the study and yielding in practice to the guidance of natural instinct and conscience. His support, therefore, of theories which contradict current views in morals is free from the levity in which the Frenchman indulges. Life and thought are separate fields, contradictions between them are borne in patience, and if science draws its material from life it shows itself grateful for the favor by giving life the benefit of the useful outcome of its labors, and, at the same time, shielding it from the revolutionary or disintegrating effect of its doubtful paradoxes.

While the deliberate craft of English philosophy does not willingly lose sight of the shores of the concrete world, French thought sails boldly and confidently out into the open sea of abstraction. It is not strange that it finds the way to the principles more rapidly than the way back to phenomena. A free road, a fresh start, a straight course—such is the motto of French thinking. Whatever is inconsistent with rectilinearity is ignored, or opposed as unfitting. The line drawn by Descartes through the world between matter and spirit, and that by Rousseau between nature and culture, are distinctive of the philosophical character of their countrymen. Dualism is to them entirely congenial; it satisfies their need for clearness, and with this they are content. Antithesis is in the Frenchman's blood; he thinks in it and speaks in it, in the salon or on the platform, in witty jest or in scientific earnestness of thought. Either A or not-A, and there is no middle ground. This habit of precision and sharp analysis facilitates the formation of closed parties, whereas each individual German, in philosophy as in politics, forms a party of his own. The demand for the removal of the rubbish of existing systems and the sanguine return to the sources, give French philosophy an unhistorical, radical, and revolutionary character. Minds of the second order, who are incapable of taking by themselves the step from that which is given to the sources, prove their radicalism by following down to the roots that which others have begun (so Condillac and the sensationalism of Locke). Moreover, philosophical principles are to be translated into action; the thinker has shown himself the doctrinaire in his destructive analysis of that which is given, so, also, he hopes to play the dictator by overturning existing institutions and establishing a new order of things,—only his courageous endeavor flags as soon in the region of practice as in that of theory.

The German lacks the happy faculty, which distinguishes the two nations just discussed, of isolating a problem near at hand, and he is accustomed to begin his system with Leda's egg; but, by way of compensation, he combines the lofty flight of the French with the phlegmatic endurance of the English, *i.e.*, he seeks his principles far above experience, but, instead of stopping with the establishment of points of view or when he has set the note, he carries his principles through in detail with loving industry and comprehensive architectonic skill. While common sense turns the scale with the English and analytical thought with the French, the German allows the fancy and the heart to take an important part in the discussion, though in such a way that the several faculties work together and in harmony. While in France rationalism, mysticism, and the philosophy of the heart were divided among different thinkers (Descartes, Malebranche and Pascal, Rousseau), there is in every German philosopher something of all three. The skeptical Kant provides a refuge for the postulates of thought in the sanctuary of faith; the earnest, energetic Fichte, toward the end of his life, takes his place among the mystics; Schelling thinks with the fancy and dreams with the understanding; and under the broad cloak of the Hegelian dialectic method, beside the reflection of the Critique of Reason and of the Science of Knowledge, the fancies of the Philosophy of Nature, the deep inwardness of Böhme, even the whole wealth of empirical fact, found a place. As synthesis is predominant in his view of things, so a harmonizing, conciliatory tendency asserts itself in his relations to his predecessors: the results of previous philosophers are neither discarded out of hand nor accepted in the mass, but all that appears in any way useful or akin to the new system is wrought in at its proper place, though often with considerable transformation. In this work of mediation there is considerable loss in definiteness, the just and comprehensive consideration of the most diverse interests not always making good the loss. And since such a philosophy, as we have already shown, engages the whole man, its disciple has neither impulse nor strength left for reforming labors; while, on the other hand, he perceives no external call to undertake them, since he views the world through the glasses of his system. Thus philosophy in Germany, pursued chiefly by specialists, remains a professional affair, and has not exercised a direct transforming influence on life (for Fichte, who helped to philosophize the French out of Germany, was an exception); but its influence has been the greater in the special sciences, which in Germany more than any other land are handled in a philosophic spirit.

The mental characteristics of these nations are reflected also in their methods of presentation. The style of the English philosopher is sober, comprehensible, diffuse, and slightly wearisome. The French use a fluent, elegant, lucid style which entertains and dazzles by its epigrammatic phrases, in which not infrequently the epigram rules the thought. The German expresses his solid, thoughtful positions in a form which is at once ponderous and not easily understood; each writer constructs his own terminology, with a liberal admixture of foreign expressions, and the length of his paragraphs is exceeded only by the thickness of his books. These national distinctions may be traced even in externals. The Englishman makes his divisions as they present themselves at first thought, and rather from a practical than from a logical point of view. The analytic Frenchman prefers dichotomy, while trichotomy corresponds to the synthetic, systematic character of German thinking; and Kant's naïve delight, because in each class the third category unites its two predecessors, has been often experienced by many of his countrymen at the sight of their own trichotomies.

The division of labor in the pre-Kantian philosophy among these three nationalities entirely agrees with the account given of the peculiarities of their philosophical endowment. The beginning falls to the share of France; Locke receives that tangled skein, the problem of knowledge, from the hand of Descartes, and passes it on to Leibnitz; and while the Illumination in all three countries is converting the gold inherited from Locke and Leibnitz into small coin, the solution of the riddle rings out from Königsberg.

PART I.

FROM DESCARTES TO KANT.

CHAPTER II.

DESCARTES.

The long conflict with Scholasticism, which had been carried on with ever increasing energy and ever sharper weapons, was brought by Descartes to a victorious close. The new movement, long desired, long sought, and prepared for from many directions, at length appears, ready and well-established. Descartes accomplishes everything needful with the sure simplicity of genius. He furnishes philosophy with a settled point of departure in self-consciousness, offers her a method sure to succeed in deduction from clear and distinct conceptions, and assigns her the mechanical explanation of nature as her most imperative and fruitful mission.

René Descartes was born at La Haye in Touraine, in 1596, and died at Stockholm in 1650. Of the studies taught in the Jesuit school at La Flèche, mathematics alone was able to satisfy his craving for clear and certain knowledge. The years 1613-17 he spent in Paris; then he enlisted in the military service of the Netherlands, and, in 1619, in that of Bavaria. While in winter quarters at Neuburg, he vowed a pilgrimage to Loretto if the Virgin would show him a way of escape from his tormenting doubts; and made the saving discovery of the "foundations of a wonderful science." At the end of four years this vow was fulfilled. On his return to Paris (1625), he was besought by his learned friends to give to the world his epoch-making ideas. Though, to escape the distractions of society, he kept his residence secret, as he had done during his first stay in Paris, and frequently changed it, he was still unable to secure the complete privacy and leisure for scientific work which he desired. Therefore he went to Holland in 1629, and spent twenty years of quiet productivity in Amsterdam, Franecker, Utrecht, Leeuwarden, Egmond, Harderwijk, Leyden, the palace of Endegeest, and five other places. His work here was interrupted only by a few journeys, but much disturbed in its later years by annoying controversies with the theologian Gisbert Voëtius of Utrecht, with Regius, a pupil who had deserted him, and with professors from Leyden. His correspondence with his French friends was conducted through Père Mersenne. In 1649 he yielded to pressing invitations from Queen Christina of Sweden and removed to Stockholm. There his weak constitution was not adequate to the severity of the climate, and death overtook him within a few months.

The two decades of retirement in the Netherlands were Descartes's productive period. His motive in developing and writing out his thoughts was, essentially, the desire not to disappoint the widely spread belief that he was in possession of a philosophy more certain than the common one. The work entitled *Le Monde*, begun in 1630 and almost completed, remained unprinted, as the condemnation of Galileo (1632) frightened our philosopher from publication; fragments of it only, and a brief summary, appeared after the author's death. The chief works, the *Discourse on Method*, the *Meditations on the First Philosophy*, and the *Principles of Philosophy* appeared between 1637 and 1644,—the *Discours de la Méthode* in 1637, together with three dissertations (the "Dioptrics," the "Meteors," and the "Geometry"), under the common title, *Essais Philosophiques*. To the (six) *Meditationes de Prima Philosophia*, published in 1641, and dedicated to the Paris Sorbonne, are appended the objections of various savants to whom the work had been communicated in manuscript, together with Descartes's rejoinders. He himself considered the criticisms of Arnauld, printed fourth in order, as the most important. The Third Objections are from Hobbes, the Fifth from Gassendi, the First, which were also the first received, from the theologian Caterus of Antwerp, while the Second and Sixth, collected by Mersenne, are from various theologians and mathematicians. In the second edition there were added, further, the Seventh Objections, by the Jesuit Bourdin, and the Replies of the author thereto. The four books of the *Principia Philosophiae*, published in 1644 and dedicated to Elizabeth, Countess Palatine, give a systematic presentation of the new philosophy. The *Discourse on Method* appeared, 1644, in a Latin translation, the *Meditations* and the *Principles* in French, in 1647. The *Treatise on the Passions* was published in 1650; the *Letters*, 1657-67, in French, 1668, in Latin. The *Opera Postuma*, 1701, beside the *Compendium of Music* (written in 1618) and other portions of his posthumous writings, contain the "Rules for the Direction of the Mind," supposed to have been written in 1629, and the "Search for Truth by the Light of Nature." The complete works have been often published, both in Latin and in French. The eleven volume edition of Cousin appeared in 1824-26.[1]

[Footnote 1: Of the many treatises on the philosophy of Descartes those of C. Schaarschmidt (*Descartes und Spinoza*, 1850) and J.H. Löwe, 1855, may be mentioned. Further, M. Heinze has discussed *Die Sittenlehre des Descartes*, 1872; Ed. Grimm, *Descartes' Lehre von den angeborenen Ideen*, 1873; G. Glogau, *Darlegung und Kritik des Grundgedankens der Cartesianisch. Metaphysik* (*Zeitschrift für Philosophie*, vol. lxxiii. p. 209 *seq.*), 1878; Paul Natorp, *Descartes' Erkenntnisstheorie*, 1882; and Kas. Twardowski, *Idee und Perception in Descartes*, 1892. In French, Francisque Bouillier (*Histoire de la Philosophie Cartésienne*, 1854) and E. Saisset (*Précurseurs et Disciples de Descartes*, 1862) have written on Cartesianism. [The *Method, Meditations, and Selections from the Principles* have been translated into English by John Veitch, 5th ed., 1879, and others since; and H.A.P. Torrey has published *The Philosophy of Descartes in Extracts from his Writings*, 1892 (Sneath's Modern Philosophers). The English reader may be referred, also, to Mahaffy's *Descartes*, 1880, in Blackwood's Philosophical Classics; to the article "Cartesianism," *Encyclopedia Britannica*, 9th ed., vol. v., by Edward Caird; and, for a complete discussion, to the English translation of Fischer's *Descartes and his School* by J.P. Gordy, 1887.—TR.]]

We begin our discussion with Descartes's noëtical and metaphysical principles, and then take up in order his doctrine of nature and of man.

%1. The Principles%.

That which passes nowadays for science, and is taught as such in the schools, is nothing but a mass of disconnected, uncertain, and often contradictory opinions. A principle of unity and certainty is entirely lacking. If anything permanent and irrefutable is to be accomplished in science, everything hitherto considered true must be thoroughly demolished and built up anew. For we come into the world as children and we form judgments of things, or repeat them after others, before we have come into the full possession of our intellectual powers; so that it is no wonder that we are filled with a multitude of prejudices, from which we can thoroughly escape only by considering everything doubtful which shows the least sign of uncertainty. Let us renounce, therefore, all our old views, in order later to accept better ones in their stead; or, perchance, to take the former up again after they shall have stood the test of rational criticism. The recognized precaution, never to put complete confidence in that which has once deceived us, holds of our relation to the senses as elsewhere. It is certain that they sometimes deceive us—perhaps they do so always. Again, we dream every day of things which nowhere exist, and there is no certain criterion by which to distinguish our dreams from our waking moments,—what guarantee have we, then, that we are not always dreaming? Therefore, our doubt must first of all be directed to the existence of sense-objects. Nay, even mathematics must be suspected in spite of the apparent certainty of its axioms and demonstrations, since controversy and error are found in it also.

I doubt or deny, then, that the world is what it appears to be, that there is a God, that external objects exist, that I have a body, that twice two are four. One thing, however, it is impossible for me to bring into question, namely, that I myself, who exercise this doubting function, exist. There is one single point at which doubt is forced to halt—at the doubter, at the self-existence of the thinker. I can doubt everything except that I doubt, and that, in doubting, I am. Even if a superior being sought to deceive me in all my thinking, he could not succeed unless I existed, he could not cause me not to exist so long as I thought. To be deceived means to think falsely; but that something is thought, no matter what it be, is no deception. It might be true, indeed, that nothing at all existed; but then there would be no one to conceive this non-existence. Granted that everything may be a mistake; yet the being mistaken, the thinking is not a mistake. Everything is denied, but the denier remains. The whole content of consciousness is destroyed; consciousness itself, the doubting activity, the being of the thinker, is indestructible. *Cogitatio sola a me divelli nequit*. Thus the settled point of departure required for knowledge is found in the *self-certitude of the thinking ego*. From the fact that I doubt, *i.e.*, think, it follows that I, the doubter, the thinker, am. *Cogito, ergo sum* is the first and most certain of all truths.

The principle, "I think, therefore I am," is not to be considered a deduction from the major premise, "Whatever thinks exists." It is rather true that this general proposition is derived from the particular and earlier one. I must first realize in my own experience that, as thinking, I exist, before I can reach the general conclusion that thought and existence are inseparable. This fundamental truth is thus not a syllogism, but a not further deducible, self-evident, immediate cognition, a pure intuition—*sum cogitans*. Now, if my existence is revealed by my activity of thought, if my thought is my being, and the converse, if in me thought and existence are identical, then I am a being whose essence consists in thinking. I am a spirit, an ego, a rational soul. My existence follows only from my thinking, not from any chance action. *Ambulo ergo sum* would not be valid, but *mihi videor* or *puto me ambulare, ergo sum*. If I believe I am walking, I may undoubtedly be deceived concerning the outward action (as, for instance, in dreams), but never concerning my inward belief. *Cogitatio* includes all the conscious activities of the mind, volition, emotion, and sensation, as well as representation and cognition; they are all *modi cogitandi*. The existence of the mind is therefore the most certain of all things. We know the soul better than the body. It is for the present the only certainty, and every other is dependent on this, the highest of all.

What, then, is the peculiarity of this first and most certain knowledge which renders it self-evident and independent of all proof, which makes us absolutely unable to doubt it? Its entire clearness and distinctness. Accordingly, I may conclude that everything which I perceive as clearly and distinctly as the *cogito ergo sum* is also true, and I reach this general rule, *omne est verum, quod clare et distincte percipio*. So far, then, we have gained three things: a challenge; to be inscribed over the portals of certified knowledge, *de omnibus dubitandum*; a basal truth, *sum cogitans*; a criterion of truth, *clara et distinct a perceptio*.

The doubt of Descartes is not the expression of a resigned spirit which renounces the unattainable; it is precept, not doctrine, the starting point of philosophy, not its conclusion, a methodological instrument in the hand of a strong and confident longing for truth, which makes use of doubt to find the indubitable. It is not aimed at the possibility of attaining knowledge, but at the opinion that it has already been attained, at the credulity of the age, at its excessive tendency toward historical and poly-historical study, which confuses the acquisition and handing down of information with knowledge of the truth. That knowledge alone is certain which is self-attained and self-tested—and this cannot be learned or handed down; it can only be rediscovered through examination and experience. Instead of taking one's own unsupported conjectures or the opinions of others as a guide, the secret of the search for truth is to become independent and of age, to think for one's self; and the only remedy against the dangers of self-deception and the ease of repetition is to be found in doubting everything hitherto considered true. This is the meaning of the Cartesian doubt, which is more comprehensive and more thorough than the Baconian. Descartes disputed only the certitude of the knowledge previously attained, not the possibility of knowledge—for of the latter no man is more firmly convinced than he. He is a rationalist, not a skeptic. The intellect is assured against error just as soon as, freed from hindrances, it remains true to itself, as it puts forth all its powers and lets nothing pass for truth which is not clearly and distinctly known. Descartes demands the same thing for the human understanding as Rousseau at a later period for the heart: a return to uncorrupted nature. This faith in the unartificial, the original, the natural, this radical and naturalistic tendency is characteristically French. The purification of the mind, its deliverance from the rubbish of scholastic learning, from the pressure of authority, and from inert acceptance of the thinking of others—this is all. Descartes finds the clearest proof of the mind's capacity for truth in mathematics, whose trustworthiness he never seriously questioned, but only hypothetically, in order to exhibit the still higher certainty of the "I think, therefore I am." He wants to give philosophy the stable character which had so impressed him in mathematics when he was a boy, and recommends her, therefore, not merely the evidence of mathematics as a general example, but the mathematical method for definite imitation. Metaphysics, like mathematics, must derive its conclusions by deduction from self-evident principles. Thus the geometrical method begins its rule in philosophy, a rule not always attended with beneficial results.

With this criterion of truth Descartes advances to the consideration of ideas. He distinguishes volition and judgment from ideas in the narrow sense (*imagines*), and divides the latter, according to their origin, into three classes: *ideae innatae, adventitiae, a me ipso factae*, considering the second class, the "adventitious" ideas, the most numerous, but the first, the "innate" ideas, the most important. No idea is higher or clearer than the idea of God or the most perfect being. Whence comes this idea? That every idea must have a cause, follows from the "clear and distinct" principle that nothing produces nothing. It follows from this same principle, *ex nihilo nihil fit*, however, that the cause must contain as much reality or perfection—*realitas* and *perfectio* are synonymous—as the effect, for otherwise the overplus would have come from nothing. So much ("objective," representative) reality contained in an idea, so much or more ("formal," actual) reality must be contained in its cause. The idea of God as infinite, independent, omnipotent, omniscient, and creative substance, has not come to me through the senses, nor have I formed it myself. The power to conceive a being more perfect than myself, can have only come from someone who is more perfect in reality than I. Since I know that the infinite contains more reality than the finite, I may conclude that the idea of the infinite has not been derived from the idea of the finite by abstraction and negation; it precedes the latter, and I become conscious of my defects and my finitude only by comparison with the absolute perfection of God. This idea, then, must have been implanted in me by God himself. The idea of God is an original endowment; it is as innate as the idea of myself. However incomplete it may be, it is still sufficient to give a knowledge of God's existence, although not a perfect comprehension of his being, just as a man may skirt a mountain without encircling it.

Descartes brings in the idea of God in order to escape solipsism. So long as the self-consciousness of the ego remained the only certainty, there was no conclusive basis for the assumption that anything exists beyond self, that the ideas which apparently come from without are really occasioned by external things and do not spring from the mind itself. For our natural instinct to refer them to objects without us might well be deceptive. It is only through the idea of God, and by help of the principle that the cause must contain at least as much reality as the effect, that I am taken beyond myself and assured that I am not the only thing in the world. For as this idea contains more of representative, than I of actual reality, I cannot have been its cause.

To this empirical argument, which derives God's existence from our idea of God (from the fact that we have an idea of him), Descartes joins the (modified) ontological argument of Anselm, which deduces the existence of God from the concept of God. While the ideas of all other things include only the possibility of existence, necessary existence is inseparable from the concept of the most perfect being. God cannot be thought apart from existence; he has the ground of his existence in himself; he is *a se* or *causa sui*. Finally, Descartes adds a third argument. The idea of perfections which I do not possess can only have been imparted to me by a more perfect being than I, which has bestowed on me all that I am and all that I am capable of becoming. If I had created myself, I would have bestowed upon myself these absent perfections also. And the existence of a plurality of causes is negatived by the supreme perfection which I conceive in the idea of God, the indivisible unity of his attributes. Among the attributes of God his veracity is of special importance. It is impossible that he should will to deceive us; that he should be the cause of our errors. God would be a deceiver, if he had endowed us with a reason to which error should appear true, even when it uses all its foresight in avoiding it and assents only to that which it clearly and distinctly perceives. Error is man's own fault; he falls into it only when he misuses the divine gift of knowledge, which includes its own standard. Thus Descartes finds new confirmation for his test of truth in the *veracitas dei*. Erdmann has given a better defense of Descartes than the philosopher himself against the charge that this is arguing in a circle, inasmuch as the existence of God is proved by the criterion of truth, and then the latter by the former: The criterion of certitude is the *ratio cognoscendi* of God's existence; God is the *ratio essendi* of the criterion of certitude. In the order of existence God is first, he creates the reason together with its criterion; in the order of knowledge the criterion precedes, and God's existence follows from it. Descartes himself endeavors to avoid the circle by making *intuitive* knowledge self-evident, and by not bringing in the appeal to God's veracity in *demonstrative* knowledge until, in reflective thought, we no longer have each separate link in the chain of proof present to our minds with full intuitive certainty, but only remember that we have previously understood the matter with clearness and distinctness.

Our ideas represent in part things, in part qualities. Substance is defined by the concept of independence as *res quae ita existit, ut nulla alia re indigeat ad existendum*; a pregnant definition with which the concept of substance gains the leadership in metaphysics, which it held till the time of Hume and Kant, sharing it then with the conception of cause or, rather, relinquishing it to the latter. The Spinozistic conclusion that, according to the strict meaning of this definition, there is but one substance, God, who, as *causa sui*, has absolutely no need of any other thing in order to his existence, was announced by Descartes himself. If created substances are under discussion, the term does not apply to them in the same sense (not *univoce*) as when we speak of the infinite substance; created beings require a different explanation, they are things which need for their existence only the co-operation of God, and have no need of one another. Substance is cognized through its qualities, among which one is pre-eminent from the fact that it expresses the essence or nature of the thing, and that it is conceived through itself, without the aid of the others, while they presuppose it and cannot be thought without it. The former fundamental properties are termed attributes, and these secondary ones, modes or accidents. Position, figure, motion, are contingent properties of body; they presuppose that it is extended or spatial; they are *modi extensionis*, as feeling, volition, desire, representation, and judgment are possible only in a conscious being, and hence are merely modifications of thought. Extension is the essential or constitutive attribute of body, and thought of mind. Body is never without extension, and mind never without thought—*mens semper cogitat*. Guided by the self-evident principle that the non-existent has no properties, we argue from a perceived quality to a substance as its possessor or support. Substances are distinct from one another when we can clearly and distinctly cognize one without the other. Now, we can adequately conceive mind without a corporeal attribute and body without a spiritual one; the former has nothing of extension in it, the latter nothing of thought: hence thinking substance and extended substance are entirely distinct and have nothing in common. Matter and mind are distinct *realiter*, matter and extension *idealiter* merely. Thus we attain three clear and distinct ideas, three eternal verities: *substantia infinita sive deus, substantia finita cogitans sive mens, substantia extensa sive corpus*.

By this abrupt contraposition of body and mind as reciprocally independent substances, Descartes founded that dualism, as whose typical representative he is still honored or opposed. This dualism between the material and spiritual worlds belongs to those standpoints which are valid without being ultimate truth; on the pyramid of metaphysical knowledge it takes a high, but not the highest, place. We may not rest in it, yet it retains a permanent value in opposition to subordinate theories. It is in the right against a materialism which still lacks insight into the essential distinction between mind and matter, thought and extension, consciousness and motion; it loses its validity when, with a full consideration and conservation of the distinction between these two spheres, we succeed in bridging over the gulf between them, whether this is accomplished through a philosophy of identity, like that of Spinoza and Schelling, or by an idealism, like that of Leibnitz or Fichte. In any case philosophy retains as an inalienable possession the negative conclusion, that, in view of the heterogeneity of consciousness and motion, the inner life is not reducible to material phenomena. This clear and simple distinction, which sets bounds to every confusion of spiritual and material existence, was an act of emancipation; it worked on the sultry intellectual atmosphere of the time with the purifying and illuminating power of a lightning flash. We shall find the later development of philosophy starting from the Cartesian dualism.

Descartes himself looked upon the fundamental principles which have now been discussed as merely the foundation for his life work, as the entrance portal to his cosmology. Posterity has judged otherwise; it finds his chief work in that which he considered a mere preparation for it. The start from doubt, the self-certitude of the thinking ego, the rational criterion of certitude, the question of the origin of ideas, the concept of substance, the essential distinction between conscious activity and corporeal being, and, also, the principle of thoroughgoing mechanism in the material world (from his philosophy of nature)—these are the thoughts which assure his immortality. The vestibule has brought the builder more fame, and has proved more enduring, than the temple: of the latter only the ruins remain; the former has remained undestroyed through the centuries.

%2. Nature.%

What guarantee have we for the existence of material objects affecting our senses? That the ideas of sense do not come from ourselves, is shown by the fact that it is not in our power to determine the objects which we perceive, or the character of our perception of them. The supposition that God has caused our perceptions directly, or by means of something which has no resemblance whatever to an external object extended in three dimensions and movable, is excluded by the fact that God is not a deceiver. In reliance on God's veracity we may accept as true whatever the reason declares concerning body, though not all the reports of the senses, which so often deceive us. At the instance of the senses we clearly and distinctly perceive matter distinct from our mind and from God, extended in three dimensions, length, breadth, and depth, with variously formed and variously moving parts, which occasion in us sensations of many kinds. The belief that perception makes known things as they really are is a prejudice of sense to be discarded; on the contrary, it merely informs us concerning the utility or harmfulness of objects, concerning their relation to man as a being composed of soul and body. (The body is that material thing which is very intimately joined with the mind, and occasions in the latter certain feelings, *e.g.*, pain, which as merely cogitative it would not have.) Sense qualities, as color, sound, odor, cannot constitute the essence of matter, for their variation or loss changes nothing in it; I can abstract from them without the material thing disappearing.[1] There is one property, however, extensive magnitude (*quantitas*), whose removal would imply the destruction of matter itself. Thus I perceive by pure thought that the essence of matter consists in extension, in that which constitutes the object of geometry, in that magnitude which is divisible, figurable, and movable. This thesis (*corpus = extensio sive spatium*) is next defended by Descartes against several objections. In reply to the objection drawn from the condensation and rarefaction of bodies, he urges that the apparent increase or decrease in extension is, in fact, a mere change of figure; that the rarefaction of a body depends on the increase in size of the intervals between its parts, and the entrance into them of foreign bodies, just as a sponge swells up when its pores become filled with water and, therefore, enlarged. The demand that the pores, and the bodies which force their way into them, should always be perceptible to the senses, is groundless. He meets the second point, that we call extension by itself *space*, and not body, by maintaining that the distinction between extension and corporeal substance is a distinction in thought, and not in reality; that attribute and substance, mathematical and physical bodies, are not distinct in fact but only in our thought of them. We apply the term space to extension in general, as an abstraction, and body to a given individual, determinate, limited extension. In reality, wherever extension is, there substance is also,—the non-existent has no extension,—and wherever space is, there matter is also. Empty space does not exist. When we say a vessel is empty, we mean that the bodies which fill it are imperceptible; if it were absolutely empty its sides would touch. Descartes argues against the atomic theory and against the finitude of the world, as he argues against empty space: matter, as well as space, has no smallest, indivisible parts, and the extension of the world has no end. In the identification of space and matter the former receives fullness from the latter, and the latter unlimitedness from the former, both internal unlimitedness (endless divisibility) and external (boundlessness). Hence there are not several matters but only one (homogeneous) matter, and only one (illimitable) world.

[Footnote 1: They are merely subjective states in the perceiver, and entirely unlike the motions which give rise to them, although there is a certain agreement, as the differences and variations in sensation are paralleled by those in the object.]

Matter is divisible, figurable, movable quantity. Natural science needs no other principles than these indisputably true conceptions, by which all natural phenomena may be explained, and must employ no others. The most important is motion, on which all the diversity of forms depends. Corporeal being has been shown to be extension; corporeal becoming is motion. Motion is defined as "the transporting of one part of matter, or of one body, from the vicinity of those bodies that are in immediate contact with it, or which we regard as at rest, to the vicinity of other bodies." This separation of bodies is reciprocal, hence it is a matter of choice which shall be considered at rest. Besides its own proper motion in reference to the bodies in its immediate vicinity, a body can participate in very many other motions: the traveler walking back and forth on the deck of a ship, for instance, in the motion of the vessel, of the waves, and of the earth. The common view of motion as an activity is erroneous; since it requires force not only to set in motion bodies which are at rest, but also to stop those which are in motion, it is clear that motion implies no more activity than rest. Both are simply different states of matter. Since there is no empty space, each motion spreads to a whole circle of bodies: A forces B out of its place, B drives out C, and so on, until Z takes up the position which A has left.

The ultimate cause of motion is God. He has created bodies with an original measure of motion and rest, and, in accordance with his immutable character, he preserves this quantity of motion unchanged: it remains constant in the world as a whole, though it varies in individual bodies. For with the power to create or destroy motion bodies lack, further, the power to alter their quantity of motion. By the side of God, the primary cause of motion, the laws of motion appear as secondary causes. The first of these is the one become familiar under the name, law of inertia: Everything continues of itself in the state (of motion or rest) in which it is, and changes its state only as a result of some extraneous cause. The second of these laws, which are so valuable in mechanics, runs: Every portion of matter tends to continue a motion which has been begun in the same direction, hence in a straight line, and changes its direction only under the influence of another body, as in the case of the circle above described. Descartes bases these laws on the unchangeableness of God and the simplicity of his world-conserving (*i.e.*, constantly creative) activity. The third law relates to the communication of motion; but Descartes does not recognize the equality of action and reaction as universally as the fact demands. If a body in motion meets another body, and its power (to continue its motion in a straight line) is less than the resistance of the other on which it has impinged, it retains its motion, but in a different direction: it rebounds in the opposite direction. If, on the contrary, its force is greater, it carries the other body along with it, and loses so much of its own motion as it imparts to the latter. The seven further rules added to these contain much that is erroneous. As *actio in distans* is rejected, all the phenomena of motion are traced back to pressure and impulse. The distinction between fluid and solid bodies is based on the greater or less mobility of their parts.

The leading principle in the special part of the Cartesian physics,—we can only briefly sketch it,—which embraces, first, celestial, and, then, terrestial phenomena, is the axiom that we cannot estimate God's power and goodness too highly, nor ourselves too meanly. It is presumptuous to seek to comprehend the purposes of God in creation, to consider ourselves participants in his plans, to imagine that things exist simply for our sake—there are many things which no man sees and which are of advantage to none. Nothing is to be interpreted teleologically, but all must be interpreted from clearly known attributes, hence purely mechanically. After treating of the distances of the various heavenly bodies, of the independent light of the sun and the fixed stars and the reflected light of the planets, among which the earth belongs, Descartes discusses the motion of the heavenly bodies. In reference to the motion of the earth he seeks a middle course between the theories of Copernicus and Tycho Brahé. He agrees with Copernicus in the main point, but, in reliance on his definition of motion, maintains that the earth is at rest, viz., in respect to its immediate surroundings. It is clear that the harmony of his views with those of the Church (though it was only a verbal agreement) was not unwelcome to him. According to his hypothesis,—as he suggests, perhaps an erroneous hypothesis,—the fluid matter which fills the heavenly spaces, and which may be compared to a vortex or whirlpool, circles about the sun and carries the planets along with it. Thus the planets move in relation to the sun, but are at rest in relation to the adjacent portions of the matter of the heavens. In view of the biblical doctrine, according to which the world and all that therein is was created at a stroke, he apologetically describes his attempt to explain the origin of the world from chaos under the laws of motion as a scientific fiction, intended merely to make the process more comprehensible. It is more easily conceivable, if we think of the things in the world as though they had been gradually formed from elements, as the plant develops from the seed. We now pass to the Cartesian anthropology, with its three chief objects: the body, the soul, and the union of the two.

3. %Man.%

The human body, like all organic bodies, is a machine. Artificial automata and natural bodies are distinguished only in degree. Machines fashioned by the hand of man perform their functions by means of visible and tangible instruments, while natural bodies employ organs which, for the most part, are too minute to be perceived. As the clock-maker constructs a clock from wheels and weights so that it is able to go of itself, so God has made man's body out of dust, only, being a far superior artist, he produces a work of art which is better constructed and capable of far more wonderful movements. The cause of death is the destruction of some important part of the machine, which prevents it from running longer; a corpse is a broken clock, and the departure of the soul comes only as a result of death. The common opinion that the soul generates life in the body is erroneous. It is rather true that life must be present before the soul enters into union with the body, as it is also true that life must have ended before it dissolves the bond.

The sole principles of physiology are motion and heat. The heat (vital warmth, a fire without light), which God has put in the heart as the central organ of life, has for its function the promotion of the circulation of the blood, in the description of which Descartes mentions with praise the discoveries of Harvey *(De Motu Cordis et Sanguinis in Animalibus*, 1628). From the blood are separated its finest, most fiery, and most mobile parts, called by Descartes "animal spirits" *(spiritus animales sive corporales)*, and described as a "very subtle wind" or "pure and vivid flame," which ascend into the cavities of the brain, reach the pineal gland suspended in its center *(conarion, glans pinealis, glandula)*, pass into the nerves, and, by their action on the muscles connected with the nerves, effect the motions of the limbs. These views refer to the body alone, and so are as true of animals as of men. If automata existed similar to animals in all respects, both external and internal, it would be absolutely impossible to distinguish them from real animals. If, however, they were made to resemble human bodies, two signs would indicate their unreality—we would find no communication of ideas by means of language, and also an absence of those bodily movements which take their origin in the reason (and not merely in the constitution of the body). The only thing which raises man above the brute is his rational soul, which we are on no account to consider a product of matter, but which is an express creation of God, superadded. The union of the soul or the mind *(anima sive mens)* with the body is, it is true, not so loose that the mind merely dwells in the body, like a pilot in a ship, nor, on the other hand, in view of the essential contrariety of the two substances, is it so intimate as to be more than a *unio compositionis*. Although the soul is united to the whole body, an especially active intercourse between them is developed at a single point, the pineal gland, which is distinguished by its central, protected position, above all, by the fact that it is the only cerebral organ that is not double. This gland, together with the animal spirits passing to and from it, mediates between mind and body; and as the point of union for the twofold impressions from the (right and left) eyes and ears, without which objects would be perceived double instead of single, is the seat of the soul. Here the soul exercises a direct influence on the body and is directly affected by it; here it dwells, and at will produces a slight, peculiar movement of the gland, through this a change in the course of the animal spirits (for it is not capable of generating motion, but only of changing its direction), and, finally, movements of the members; just as, on the other hand, it remarks the slightest change in the course of the *spiritus* through a corresponding movement of the gland, whose motions vary according to the sensuous properties of the object to be perceived, and responds by sensations. Although Descartes thus limits the direct interaction of soul and body to a small part of the organism, he makes an exception in the case of *memoria*, which appears to him to be more of a physical than a psychical function, and which he conjectures to be diffused through the whole brain.

In spite of the comprehensive meaning which Descartes gives to the notion *cogitatio*, it is yet too narrow to leave room for an *anima vegetativa* and an *anima sensitiva*. Whoever makes mind and soul equivalent, holds that their essence consists in conscious activity alone, and interprets sensation as a mode of thought, cannot escape the paradox of denying to animals the possession of a soul. Descartes does not shrink from such a conclusion. Animals are mere machines; they are bodies animated, but soulless; they lack conscious perception and appetition, though not the appearance of them. When a clock strikes seven it knows nothing of the fact; it does not regret that it is so late nor long soon to be able to strike eight; it wills nothing, feels nothing, perceives nothing. The lot of the brute is the same. It sees and hears nothing, it does not hunger or thirst, it does not rejoice or fear, if by these anything more than mere corporeal phenomena is to be meant; of all these it possesses merely the unconscious material basis; it moves and motion goes on in it—that is all. The psychology of Descartes, which has had important results,[1] divides *cogitationes* into two classes: *actiones* and *passiones*. Action denotes everything which takes its origin in, and is in the power of, the soul; passion, everything which the soul receives from without, in which it can make no change, which is impressed upon it. The further development of this distinction is marred by the crossing of the most diverse lines of thought, resulting in obscurities and contradictions. Descartes's simple, naïve habits of thought and speech, which were those of a man of the world rather than of a scholar, were quite incompatible with the adoption and consistent use of a finely discriminated terminology; he is very free with *sive*, and not very careful with the expressions *actio, passio, perceptio, affectio, volitio*. First he equates activity and willing, for the will springs exclusively from the soul—it is only in willing that the latter is entirely independent; while, on the other hand, passivity is made equivalent to representation and cognition, for the soul does not create its ideas, but receives them,—sensuous impressions coming to her quite evidently from the body. These equations, "*actio*—the practical, *passio* = the theoretical function," are soon limited and modified, however. The natural appetites and affections are forms of volition, it is true, but not free products of the mind, for they take their origin in its connection with the body. Further, not all perceptions have a sensuous origin; when the soul makes free use of its ideas in imagination, especially when in pure thought it dwells on itself, when without the interference of the imagination it gazes on its rational nature, it is by no means passive merely. Every act of the will, again, is accompanied by the consciousness of volition. The *volitio* is an activity, the *cogitatio volitionis* a passivity; the soul affects itself, is passively affected through its own activity, is at the same instant both active and passive.

[Footnote 1: For details cf. the able monograph of Dr. Anton Koch, 1881.]

Thus not every volition, *e.g.* sensuous desire, is action nor all perception, *e.g.* that of the pure intellect, passion. Finally, certain psychical phenomena fall indifferently under the head of perception or of volition, *e.g.*, pain, which is both an indistinct idea of something and an impulse to shun it. In accordance with these emendations, and omitting certain disturbing points of secondary importance, the matter may be thus represented:

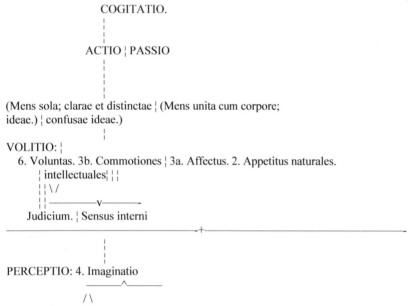

Accordingly six grades of mental function are to be distinguished: (1) The external senses. (2) The natural appetites. (3) The passions (which, together with the natural appetites, constitute the internal senses, and from which the mental emotions produced by the intellect are quite distinct). (4) The imagination with its two divisions, passive memory and active phantasy. (5) The intellect or reason. (6) The will. These various stages or faculties are, however, not distinct parts of the soul, as in the old psychology, in opposition to which Descartes emphatically defends the *unity of the soul*. It is one and the same psychical power that exercises the higher and the lower, the rational and the sensuous, the practical and the theoretical activities.

Of the mental functions, whether representative images, perceptions, or volitions, a part are referred to body (to parts of our own body, often also to external objects), and produced by the body (by the animal spirits and, generally, by the nerves as well), while the rest find both object and cause in the soul. Intermediate between the two classes stand those acts of the will which are caused by the soul, but which relate to the body, *e.g.*, when I resolve to walk or leap; and, what is more important, the *passions*, which relate to the soul itself, but which are called forth, sustained, and intensified by certain motions of the animal spirits. Since only those beings which consist of a body as well as a soul are capable of the passions, these are specifically human phenomena. These affections, though very numerous, may be reduced to a few simple or primary ones, of which the rest are mere specializations or combinations. Descartes enumerates six primitive passions (which number Spinoza afterward reduced one-half)—*admiratio, amor et odium, cupiditas (désir), gaudium et tristitia*. The first and the fourth have no opposites, the former being neither positive nor negative, and the latter both at once. Wonder, which includes under it esteem and contempt, signifies interest in an object which neither attracts us by its utility nor repels us by its hurtfulness, and yet does not leave us indifferent. It is aroused by the powerful or surprising impression made by the extraordinary, the rare, the unexpected. Love seeks to appropriate that which is profitable; hate, to ward off that which is harmful, to destroy that which is hostile. Desire or longing looks with hope or fear to the future. When that which is feared or hoped for has come to pass, joy and grief come in, which relate to existing good and evil, as desire relates to those to come.

The Cartesian theory of the passions forms the bridge over which its author passes from psychology to ethics. No soul is so weak as to be incapable of completely mastering its passions, and of so directing them that from them all there will result that joyous temper advantageous to the reason. The freedom of the will is unlimited. Although a direct influence on the passions is denied it,—it can neither annul them merely at its bidding, nor at once reduce them to silence, at least, not the more violent ones,—it still has an indirect power over them in two ways. During the continuance of the affection (e.g., fear) it is able to arrest the bodily movements to which the affection tends (flight), though not the emotion itself, and, in the intervals of quiet, it can take measures to render a new attack of the passion less dangerous. Instead of enlisting one passion against another, a plan which would mean only an appearance of freedom, but in fact a continuance in bondage, the soul should fight with its own weapons, with fixed maxims *(judicia)*, based on certain knowledge of good and evil. The will conquers the emotions by means of principles, by clear and distinct knowledge, which sees through and corrects the false values ascribed to things by the excitement of the passions. Besides this negative requirement, "subjection of the passions," Descartes' contributions to ethics—in the letters to Princess Elizabeth on human happiness, and to Queen Christina on love and the highest good— were inconsiderable. Wisdom is the carrying out of that which has been seen to be best, virtue is steadfastness, sin inconstancy therein. The goal of human endeavor is peace of conscience, which is attained only through the determination to be virtuous, i.e., to live in harmony with self.

Besides its ethical mission, the will has allotted to it the theoretical function of affirmation and negation, i.e., of judgment. If God in his veracity and goodness has bestowed on man the power to know truth, how is misuse of this power, how is error possible? Single sensations and ideas cannot be false, but only judgments—the reference of ideas to objects. Judgment or assent is a matter of the will; so that when it makes erroneous affirmations or negations, when it prefers the false judgment to the true, it alone is guilty. Our understanding is limited, our will unlimited; the latter reaches further than the former, and can assent to a judgment even before its constituent parts have attained the requisite degree of clearness. False judgment is prejudgment, for which we can hold neither God nor our own nature responsible. The possibility of error, as well as the possibility of avoiding error, resides in the will. This has the power to postpone its assent or dissent, to hold back its decision until the ideas have become entirely clear and distinct. The supreme perfection is the *libertas non errandi*. Thus knowledge itself becomes a moral function; the true and the good are in the last analysis identical. The contradiction with which Descartes has been charged, that he makes volition and cognition reciprocally determinative, that he bases moral goodness on the clearness of ideas and *vice versa*, does not exist. We must distinguish between a theoretical and a practical stadium in the will; it is true of the latter that it depends on knowledge of the right, of the former that the knowledge of the right is dependent on it. In order to the possibility of moral *action* the will must conform to clear judgment; in order to the production of the latter the will must *be* moral. It is the unit-soul, which first, by freely avoiding overhasty judgment, cognizes the truth, to exemplify it later in moral conduct.

CHAPTER III.

THE DEVELOPMENT AND TRANSFORMATION OF CARTESIANISM IN THE NETHERLANDS AND IN FRANCE.[1]

[Footnote 1: Cf. G. Monchamp, *Histoire du Cartésianisme en Belgique*, Brussels, 1886.]

%1. Occasionalism: Geulincx.%

The propagation and defense of a system of thought soon give occasion to its adherents to purify, complete, and transform it. Obscurities and contradictions are discovered, which the master has overlooked or allowed to remain, and the disciple exerts himself to remove them, while retaining the fundamental doctrines. In the system of Descartes there were two closely connected points which demanded clarification and correction, viz., his double dualism (1) between extended substance and thinking substance, (2) between created substance and the divine substance. In contrast with each other matter and mind are substances or independent beings, for the clear conception of body contains naught of consciousness, thought, representation, and that of mind nothing of extension, matter, motion. In comparison with God they are not so; apart from the creator they can neither exist nor be conceived. In every case where the attempt is made to distinguish between intrinsic and general (as here, between substance in the stricter and wider senses), an indecision betrays itself which is not permanently endured.

The substantiality of the material and spiritual worlds maintained by Descartes finds an excellent counterpart in his (entirely modern) tendency to push the *concursus dei* as far as possible into the background, to limit it to the production of the original condition of things, to give over motion, once created, to its own laws, and ideas implanted in the mind to its own independent activity; but it is hard to reconcile with it the view, popular in the Middle Ages, that the preservation of the world is a perpetual creation. In the former case the relation of God to the world is made an external relation; in the latter, an internal one. In the one the world is thought of as a clock, which once wound up runs on mechanically, in the second it is likened to a piece of music which the composer himself recites. If God preserves created things by continually recreating them they are not substances at all; if they are substances, preservation becomes an empty word, which we repeat after the theologians without giving it any real meaning.

Matter and spirit stand related in our thought only by way of exclusion; is the same true of them in reality? They can be conceived and can exist without each other; can they, further, without each other effect all that we perceive them to accomplish? There are some motions in the material world which we refer to a voluntary decision of the soul, and some among our ideas (*e.g.*, perceptions of the senses) which we refer to corporeal phenomena as their causes. If body and soul are substances, how can they be dependent on each other in certain of their activities, if they are of opposite natures, how can they affect each other? How can the incorporeal, unmoved spirit move the animal spirits and receive impulses from them? The substantiality (reciprocal independence) of body and mind, and their interaction (partial reciprocal dependence), are incompatible, one or the other is illusory and must be abandoned. The materialists (Hobbes) sacrifice the independence of mind, the idealists (Berkeley, Leibnitz), the independence of matter, the occasionalists, the interaction of the two. This forms the advance of the last beyond Descartes, who either naïvely maintains that, in spite of the contrariety of material and mental substances, an exchange of effects takes place between them as an empirical fact, or, when he realizes the difficulty of the anthropological problem,—how is the union of the two substances in man possible,—ascribes the interaction of body and mind, together with the union of the two, to the power of God, and by this abandonment of the attempt at a natural explanation, opens up the occasionalistic way of escape. Further, in his more detailed description of the intercourse between body and mind Descartes had been guilty of direct violations of his laws of natural philosophy. If the quantity of motion is declared to be invariable and a change in its direction is attributed to mechanical causes alone, we must not ascribe to the soul the power to move the pineal gland, even in the gentlest way, nor to control the direction of the animal spirits. These inconsistencies also are removed by the occasionalistic thesis.

The question concerning the substantiality of mind and matter in relation to God, is involved from the very beginning in this latter problem, "How is the appearance of interaction between the two to be explained without detriment to their substantiality in relation to each other?" The denial of the reciprocal dependence of matter and spirit leads to sharper accentuation of their common dependence upon God. Thus occasionalism forms the transition to the pantheism of Spinoza, Geulincx emphasizing the non-substantiality of spirits, and Malebranche the non-substantiality of bodies, while Spinoza combines and intensifies both. And yet history was not obliging enough to carry out this convenient and agreeable scheme of development with chronological accuracy, for she had Spinoza complete his pantheism *before* Malebranche had prepared the way. The relation which was noted in the case of Bruno and Campanella is here repeated: the earlier thinker assumes the more advanced position, while the later one seems backward in comparison; and that which, viewed from the standpoint of the question itself, may be considered a transition link, is historically to be taken as a reaction against the excessive prosecution of a line of thought which, up to a certain point, had been followed by the one who now shrinks back from its extreme consequences. The course of philosophy takes first a theological direction in the earlier occasionalists, then a metaphysical (naturalistic) trend in Spinoza, to renew finally, in Malebranche, the first of these movements in opposition to the second. The Cartesian school, as a whole, however, exhibits a tendency toward mysticism, which was concealed to a greater or less extent by the rationalistic need for clear concepts, but never entirely suppressed.

Although the real interaction of body and mind be denied, some explanation must, at least, be given for the appearance of interaction, *i.e.* for the actual correspondence of bodily and mental phenomena. Occasionalism denotes the theory of occasional causes. It is not the body that gives rise to perception, nor the mind that causes the motion of the limbs which it has determined upon—neither the one nor the other can receive influence from its fellow or exercise influence upon it; but it is God who, "on the occasion" of the physical motion (of the air and nerves); produces the sensation (of sound), and, "at the instance" of the determination of the will, produces the movement of the arms. The systematic development and marked influence of this theory, which had already been more or less clearly announced by the Cartesians Cordemoy and De la Forge,[1] was due to the talented Arnold Geulincx (1624-69), who was born at Antwerp, taught in Lyons (1646-58) and Leyden, and became a convert to Calvinism. It ultimately gained over the majority of the numerous adherents of the Cartesian philosophy in the Dutch universities,—Renery (died 1639) and Regius (van Roy; *Fundamenta Physicae*, 1646; *Philosophia Naturalis*, 1661) in Utrecht; further, Balthasar Bekker (1634-98; *The World Bewitched*, 1690), the brave opponent of the belief in angels and devils, of magic, and of prosecution for witchcraft,—in the clerical orders in France and, finally, in Germany.

[Footnote 1: Gerauld de Cordemoy, a Parisian advocate (died 1684, *Dissertations Philosophiques*, 1666), communicated his occasionalistic views orally to his friends as early as 1658 (cf. L. Stein in the *Archiv für Geschichte der Philosophie*, vol. i., 1888, p. 56). Louis de la Forge, a physician of Saumur, *Tractatus de Mente Humana*, 1666, previously published in French; cf. Seyfarth, Gotha, 1887. But the logician, Johann Clauberg, professor in Duisburg (1622-65; *Opera*, edited by Schalbruch, 1691), is, according to the investigations of Herm. Müller *(J. Clauberg und seine Stellung im Cartesianismus*, Jena, 1891), to be stricken from the list of thinkers who prepared the way for occasionalism, since in his discussion of the anthropological problem (*corporis et animae conjunctio*) he merely develops the Cartesian position, and does not go beyond it. He employs the expression *occasio*, it is true, but not in the sense of the occasionalists. According to Clauberg the bodily phenomenon becomes the stimulus or "occasion" (not for God, but) for the soul to produce from itself the corresponding mental phenomenon.]

Geulincx himself, besides two inaugural addresses at Leyden (as Lector in 1662, Professor Extraordinary in 1665), published the following treatises: *Quaestiones Quodlibeticae* (in the second edition, 1665, entitled *Saturnalia*) with an important introductory discourse; *Logica Fundamentis Suis Restituta*, 1662; *Methodus Inveniendi Argumenta* (new edition by Bontekoe, 1675); and the first part of his Ethics—*De Virtute et Primis ejus Proprietatibus, quae vulgo Virtutes Cardinales Vocantur, Tractatus Ethicus Primus*, 1665. This chief work was issued complete in all six parts with the title, *[Greek: Gnothi seauton] sive Ethica*, 1675, by Bontekoe, under the pseudonym Philaretus. The *Physics*, 1688, the *Metaphysics*, 1691, and the *Annotata Majora in Cartesii Principia Philosophiae*, 1691, were also posthumous publications, from the notes of his pupils. In view of the rarity of these volumes, and the importance of the philosopher, it is welcome news that J.P.N. Land has undertaken an edition of the collected works, in three volumes, of which the first two have already appeared.[1] The Hague, 1891-92.[2]

[Footnote 1: On vol. i. cf. Eucken, *Philosophische Monatshefte*, vol. xxviii., 1892, p,200 *seq.*]

[Footnote 2: On Geulincx see V. van der Haeghen, *Geulincx, Étude sur sa Vie, sa Philosophie, et ses Ouvrages*, Ghent, 1886, including a complete bibliography; and Land in vol. iv. of the *Archiv für Geschichte der Philosophie*, 1890. [English translation, *Mind*, vol. xvi. p. 223 *seq.*]]

Geulincx bases the *occasionalistic* position on the principle, *quod nescis, quomodo fiat, id non facis*. Unless I know how an event happens, I am not its cause. Since I have no consciousness how my decision to speak or to walk is followed by the movement of my tongue or limbs, I am not the one who effects these. Since I am just as ignorant how the sensation in my mind comes to pass as a sequel to the motion in the sense-organ; since, further, the body as an unconscious and non-rational being can effect nothing, it is neither I nor the body that causes the sensation. Both the bodily movement and the sense-impression are, rather, the effects of a higher power, of the infinite spirit. The act of my will and the sense-stimulus are only *causae occasionales* for the divine will, in an incomprehensible way, to effect, in the one case, the execution of the movement of the limbs resolved upon, and, in the other, the origin of the perception; they are (unsuitable) instruments, effective only in the hand of God; he brings it to pass that my will goes out beyond my soul, and that corporeal motion has results in it. The meaning of this doctrine is misapprehended when it is assumed,—an assumption to which the Leibnitzian account of occasionalism may mislead one,—that in it the continuity of events, alike in the material and the psychical world, is interrupted by frequent scattered interferences from without, and all becoming transformed into a series of disconnected miracles. An order of nature such as would be destroyed by God's action does not exist; God brings everything to pass; even the passage of motion from one body to another is his work. Further, Geulincx expressly says that God has imposed such *laws* on motion that it harmonizes with the soul's free volition, of which, however, it is entirely independent (similar statements occur also in De la Forge). And with this our thinker appears—as Pfleiderer[1] emphasizes—closely to approach the pre-established harmony of Leibnitz. The occasionalistic theory certainly constitutes the preliminary step to the Leibnitzian; but an essential difference separates the two. The advance does not consist in the substitution by Leibnitz of one single miracle at creation for a number of isolated and continually recurring ones, but (as Leibnitz himself remarks, in reply to the objection expressed by Father Lami, that a perpetual miracle is no miracle) in the exchange of the immediate causality of God for natural causation. With Geulincx mind and body act on each other, but not by their own power; with Leibnitz the monads do not act on one another, but they act by their own power.[2]—When Geulincx in the same connection advances to the statements that, in view of the limitedness and passivity of finite things, God is the only truly active, because the only independent, being in the world, that all activity is his activity, that the human (finite) spirit is related to the divine (infinite) spirit as the individual body to space in general, viz., as a section of it, so that, by thinking away all limitations from our mind, we find God in us and ourselves in him, it shows how nearly he verges on pantheism.

[Footnote 1: Edm. Pfleiderer, *Geulincx, als Hauptvertreter der occasionalistischen Metaphysik und Ethik*, Tübingen, 1882; the same, *Leibniz und Geulincx mit besonderer Beziehung auf ihr Uhrengleichnis*, Tübingen, 1884.]

[Footnote 2: See Ed. Zeller, *Sitzungsberichte der Berliner Akademie der Wissenschaften*, 1884, p. 673 *seq*.; Eucken, *Philosophische Monatshefte*, vol. xix., 1893, p. 525 *seq*; vol. xxiii., 1887, p. 587 *seq*.]

Geulincx's services to noëtics have been duly recognized by Ed. Grimm (Jena, 1875), although with an excessive approximation to Kant. In this field he advances many acute and suggestive thoughts, as the deduction which reappears in Lotze, that the actually existent world of figure and motion cognized by thought, though the real world, is poorer than the wonderful world of motley sensuous appearance conjured forth in our minds on the occasion of the former, that the latter is the more beautiful and more worthy of a divine author. Further, the conviction, also held by Lotze, that the fundamental activities of the mind cannot be defined, but only known through inner experience or immediate consciousness (he who loves, knows what love is; it is a *per conscientiam et intimam experientiam notissima res*); the praiseworthy attempt to give a systematic arrangement, according to their derivation from one another, to the innate mathematical concepts, which Descartes had simply co-ordinated (the concept of surface is gained from the concept of body by abstracting from the third dimension, thickness—the act of thus abstracting from certain parts of the content of thought, Geulincx terms *consideratio* in contrast to *cogitatio*, which includes the whole content); and, finally, the still more important inquiry, whether it is possible for us to reach a knowledge of things independently of the forms of the understanding, as in pure thought we strip off the fetters of sense. The possibility of this is denied; there is no higher faculty of knowledge to act as judge over the understanding, as the latter over the sensibility, and even the wisest man cannot free himself from the forms of thought (categories, *modi cogitandi*). And yet the discussion of the question is not useless: the reason should examine into the unknowable as well as the knowable; it is only in this way that we learn that it is unknowable. As the highest forms of thought Geulincx names subject (the empty concept of an existent, *ens* or *quod est*) and predicate *(modus entis)*, and derives them from two fundamental activities of the mind, a combining function *(simulsumtio, totatio)* and an abstracting function (one which removes the *nota subjecti*). Substance and accident, substantive and adjective, are expressions for subjective processes of thought and hence do not hold of things in themselves. With reference to the importance, nay, to the indispensability, of linguistic signs in the use of the understanding, the science of the forms of thought is briefly termed grammar.

The principle *ubi nihil vales, ibi nihil velis*, forms the connection between the occasionalistic metaphysics and ethics, the latter deducing the practical consequences of the former. Where thou canst do nothing, there will nothing. Since we can effect nothing in the material world, to which we are related merely as spectators, we ought also not to seek in it the motives and objects of our actions. God, does not require works, but dispositions only, for the result of our volition is beyond our power. Our moral vocation, then, consists in renunciation of the world and retirement into ourselves, and in patient faithfulness at the post assigned to us. Virtue is *amor dei ac rationis*, self-renouncing, active, obedient love to God and to the reason as the image and law of God in us. The cardinal virtues are *diligentia*, sedulous listening for the commands of the reason; *obedientia*, the execution of these *justitia*, the conforming of the whole life to what is perceived to be right; finally, *humilitas*, the recognition of our impotency and self-renunciation (*inspectio* and *despectio*, or *derelictio, neglectus, contemptus, incuria sui*). The highest of these is humility, pious submission to the divine order of things; its condition, the self-knowledge commended in the title of the Ethics; the primal evil, self-love (*Philautia—ipsissimum peccatum*). Man is unhappy because he seeks happiness. Happiness is like our shadows; it shuns us when we pursue it, it follows us when we flee from it. The joys which spring from virtue are an adornment of it, not an enticement to it; they are its result, not its aim. The ethics of Geulincx, which we cannot further trace out here, surprises one by its approximation to the views of Spinoza and of Kant. With the former it has in common the principle of love toward God, as well as numerous details; with the latter, the absoluteness of the moral law (*in rebus moralibus absolute praecipit ratio aut vetat, nulla interposita conditione*); with both the depreciation of sympathy, on the ground that it is a concealed egoistic motive.

The denial of substantiality to individual things, brought in by the occasionalists, is completed by Spinoza, who boldly and logically proclaims pantheism on the basis of Cartesianism and gives to the divine All-one a naturalistic instead of a theological character.

%2. Spinoza.%

Benedictus (originally Baruch) de Spinoza sprang from a Jewish family of Portugal or Spain, which had fled to Holland to escape persecution at home. He was born in Amsterdam in 1632; taught by the Rabbin Morteira, and, in Latin, by Van den Ende, a free-thinking physician who had enjoyed a philological training; and expelled by anathema from the Jewish communion, 1656, on account of heretical views. During the next four years he found refuge at a friend's house in the country near Amsterdam, after which he lived in Rhynsburg, and from 1664 in Voorburg, moving thence, in 1669, to The Hague, where he died in 1677. Spinoza lived in retirement and had few wants; he supported himself by grinding optical glasses; and, in 1673, declined the professorship at Heidelberg offered him by Karl Ludwig, the Elector Palatine, because of his love of quiet, and on account of the uncertainty of the freedom of thought which the Elector had assured him. Spinoza himself made but two treatises public: his dictations on the first and second parts of Descartes's *Principia Philosophiae*, which had been composed for a private pupil, with an appendix, *Cogitata Metaphysica*, 1663, and the *Tractatus Theologico-Politicus*, published anonymously in 1670, in defense of liberty of thought and the right to unprejudiced criticism of the biblical writings. The principles expressed in the latter work were condemned by all parties as sacrilegious and atheistic, and awakened concern even in the minds of his friends. When, in 1675, Spinoza journeyed to Amsterdam with the intention of giving his chief work, the *Ethics*, to the press, the clergy and the followers of Descartes applied to the government to forbid its issue. Soon after Spinoza's death it was published in the *Opera Posthuma*, 1677, which were issued under the care of Hermann Schuller,[1] with a preface by Spinoza's friend, the physician

Ludwig Meyer, and which contained, besides the chief work, three incomplete treatises (*Tractatus Politicus, Tractatus de Intellectus Emendatione, Compendium Grammatices Linguae Hebraeae*) and a collection of Letters by and to Spinoza. The *Ethica Ordine Geometrico Demonstrata*, in five parts, treats (1) of God, (2) of the nature and origin of the mind, (3) of the nature and origin of the emotions, (4) of human bondage or the strength of the passions, (5) of the power of the reason or human freedom. It has become known within recent times that Spinoza made a very early sketch of the system developed in the *Ethics*, the *Tractatus Brevis de Deo et Homine ejusque Felicitate*, of which a Dutch translation in two copies was discovered, though not the original Latin text. This treatise was published by Böhmer, 1852, in excerpts, and complete by Van Vloten, 1862, and by Schaarschmidt, 1869. It was not until our own century, and after Jacobi's *Ueber die Lehre des Spinoza in Briefen an Moses Mendelssohn* (1785) had aroused the long slumbering interest in this much misunderstood philosopher, who has been oftener despised than studied, that complete editions of his works were prepared, by Paulus 1802-03; Gfrörer, 1830; Bruder, 1843-46; Ginsberg (in Kirchmann's *Philosophische Bibliothek*, 4 vols.), 1875-82; and Van Vloten and Land,[2] 2 vols., 1882-83. B. Auerbach has worked Spinoza's life into a romantic novel, *Spinoza, ein Denkerleben*, 1837; 2d ed., 1855 [English translation by C.T. Brooks, 1882.]

[Footnote 1: See L. Stein in the *Archiv für Geschichte der Philosophie*, vol. i., 1888, p. 554 *seq.*]

[Footnote 2: For the literature on Spinoza the reader is referred to Ueberweg and to Van der Linde's *B. Spinoza, Bibliografie*, 1871; while among recent works we shall mention only Camerer's *Die Lehre Spinozas*, Stuttgart, 1877. An English translation of *The Chief Works of Spinoza* has been given by Elwes, 1883-84; a translation of the *Ethics* by White, 1883; and one of selections from the *Ethics*, with notes, by Fullerton in Sneath's Modern Philosophers, 1892. Among the various works on Spinoza, the reader may be referred to Pollock's *Spinoza, His Life and Times*, 1880 (with bibliography to same year); Martineau's *Study of Spinoza*, 1883; and J. Caird's *Spinoza*, Blackwood's Philosophical Classics, 1888.—TR.]

We shall consider Spinoza's system as a completed whole as it is given in the *Ethics*; for although it is interesting for the investigator to trace out the development of his thinking by comparing this chief work with its forerunner (that *Tractatus Brevis* "concerning God, man, and the happiness of the latter," whose dialogistical portions we may surmise to have been the earliest sketch of the Spinozistic position, and which was followed by the *Tractatus de Intellectus Emendatione*) such a procedure is not equally valuable for the student. In regard to Spinoza's relations to other thinkers it cannot be doubted, since Freudenthal's[1] proof, that he was dependent to a large degree on the predominant philosophy of the schools, *i.e.* on the later Scholasticism (Suarez[2]), especially on its Protestant side (Jacob Martini, Combachius, Scheibler, Burgersdijck, Heereboord); Descartes, it is true, felt the same influence. Joël,[3]: Schaarschmidt, Sigwart,[4] R. Avenarius,[5] and Böhmer[6] = have advanced the view that the sources of Spinoza's philosophy are not to be sought exclusively in Cartesianism, but rather that essential elements were taken from the Cabala, from the Jewish Scholasticism (Maimonides, 1190; Gersonides, died 1344; Chasdai Crescas, 1410), and from Giordano Bruno. In opposition to this Kuno Fischer has defended, and in the main successfully, the proposition that Spinoza reached, and must have reached, his fundamental pantheism by his own reflection as a development of Descartes's principles. The traces of his early Talmudic education, which have been noticed in Spinoza's works, prove no dependence of his leading ideas on Jewish theology. His pantheism is distinguished from that of the Cabalists by its rejection of the doctrine of emanation, and from Bruno's, which nevertheless may have influenced him, by its anti-teleological character. When with Greek philosophers, Jewish theologians, and the Apostle Paul he teaches the immanence of God (*Epist. 21*), when with Maimonides and Crescas he teaches love to God as the principal of morality, and with the latter of these, determinism also, it is not a necessary consequence that he derived these theories from them. That which most of all separates him from the mediaeval scholastics of his own people, is his rationalistic conviction that God can be known. His agreement with them comes out most clearly in the *Tractatus Theologico-Politicus*. But even here it holds only in regard to undertaking a general criticism of the Scriptures and to their figurative interpretation, while, on the other hand, the demand for a special historical criticism, and the object which with Spinoza was the basis of the investigation as a whole, were foreign to mediaeval Judaism—in fact, entirely modern and original. This object was to make science independent of religion, whose records and doctrines are to edify the mind and to improve the character, not to instruct the understanding. "Spinoza could not have learned the complete separation of religion and science from Jewish literature; this was a tendency which sprang from the spirit of his own time" (Windelband, *Geschichte der neueren Philosophie*, vol. i. p. 194).

[Footnote 1: J. Freudenthal, *Spinoza und die Scholastik* in the
Philosophische Aufsätze, Zeller zum 50-Jährigen Doktorjubiläum gewidmet,
Leipsic, 1887, p. 85 *seq.* Freudenthal's proof covers the *Cogitata
Metaphysica* and many of the principal propositions of the *Ethics*.]

[Footnote 2: The Spanish Jesuit, Francis Suarez, lived 1548-1617. *Works,*
Venice, 1714 Cf. Karl Werner, *Suarez und die Scholastik der letzten
Jahrhunderte*, Regensburg, 1861.]

[Footnote 3: M. Joël, *Don Chasdai Crescas' religions-philosophische Lehren in ihrem geschichtlichen Einfluss*, 1866; *Spinozas Theo.-pel. Traktat auf seine Quellen geprüft*, 1870; *Zur Genesis der Lehre Spinozas mit besonderer Berücksichtigung des kurzen Traktats*, 1871.]

[Footnote 4: *Spinozas neu entdeckter Traktat eläutert u. s. w.*, 1866; *Spinozas kurzer Traktat übersetzt mit Einleitungen und Erläuterungen,* 1870.]

[Footnote 5: *Ueber die beiden ersten Phasen des Spinozistischen
Pantheismus und das Verhältniss der zweiten zur dritten Phase*, 1868.]

[Footnote 6: *Spinozana* in Fichte's *Zeitschrift für Philosophie* vols. xxxvi., xlii., lvii., 1860-70.]

The logical presuppositions of Spinoza's philosophy lie in the fundamental ideas of Descartes, which Spinoza accentuates, transforms, and adopts. Three pairs of thoughts captivate him and incite him to think them through: first, the rationalistic belief in the power of the human spirit to possess itself of the truth by pure thought, together with confidence in the omnipotence of the mathematical method; second, the concept of substance, together with the dualism of extension and thought; finally, the fundamental mechanical position, together with the impossibility of interaction between matter and spirit, held in common with the occasionalists, but reached independently of them. Whatever new elements are added (*e. g.*, the transformation of the Deity from a mere aid to knowledge into its most important, nay, its only object; as, also, the enthusiastic, directly mystical devotion to the all-embracing world-ground) are of an essentially emotional nature, and to be referred less to historical influences than to the individuality of the thinker. The divergences from his predecessors, however, especially the extension of mechanism to mental phenomena and the denial of the freedom of the will, inseparable from this, result simply from the more consistent application of Cartesian principles. Spinoza is not an inventive, impulsive spirit, like Descartes and Leibnitz, but a systematic one; his strength does not lie in brilliant inspirations, but in the power of resolutely thinking a thing through; not in flashes of thought, but in strictly closed circles of thought. He develops, but with genius, and to the end. Nevertheless this consecutiveness of Spinoza, the praises of which have been unceasingly sung by generations since his day, has its limits. It holds for the unwavering development of certain principles derived from Descartes, but not with equal strictness for the inter-connection of the several lines of thought followed out separately. His very custom of developing a principle straight on to its ultimate consequences, without regard to the needs of the heart or to logical demands from other directions, make it impossible for the results of the various lines of thought to be themselves in harmony; his vertical consistency prevents horizontal consistency. If the original tendencies come into conflict (the consciously held theoretical principles into conflict with one another, or with hidden aesthetic or moral principles), either one gains the victory over the other or both insist on their claims; thus we have inconsistencies in the one case, and contradictions in the other (examples of which have been shown by Volkelt in his maiden work, *Pantheismus und Individualismus im Systeme Spinozas*, 1872). Science demands unified comprehension of the given, and seeks the smallest number of principles possible; but her concepts prove too narrow vessels for the rich plenitude of reality. He who asks from philosophy more than mere special inquiries finds himself confronted by two possibilities: first, starting from one standpoint, or a few such, he may follow a direct course without looking to right or left, at the risk that in his thought-calculus great spheres of life will be wholly left out of view, or, at least, will not receive due consideration; or, second, beginning from many points of departure and ascending along converging lines, he may seek a unifying conclusion. In Spinoza we possess the most brilliant example of the former one-sided, logically consecutive power of (also, no doubt, violence in) thought, while Leibnitz furnishes the type of the many-sided, harmonistic thinking. The fact that even the rigorous Spinoza is not infrequently forced out of the strict line of consistency, proves that the man was more many-sided than the thinker would have allowed himself to be.

To begin with the formal side of Spinozism: the rationalism of Descartes is heightened by Spinoza into the imposing confidence that absolutely everything is cognizable by the reason, that the intellect is able by its pure concepts and intuitions entirely to exhaust the multiform world of reality, to follow it with its light into its last refuge.[1] Spinoza is just as much in earnest in regard to the typical character of mathematics. Descartes (with the exception of an example asked for in the second of the Objections, and given as an appendix to the *Meditations*, in which he endeavors to demonstrate the existence of God and the distinction of body and spirit on the synthetic Euclidean method), had availed himself of the analytic form of presentation, on the ground that, though less cogent, it is more suited for instruction since it shows the way by which the matter has been discovered. Spinoza, on the other hand, rigorously carried out the geometrical method, even in externals. He begins with definitions, adds to these axioms (or postulates), follows with propositions or theorems as the chief thing, finally with demonstrations or proofs, which derive the later propositions from the earlier, and these in turn from the self-evident axioms. To these four principal parts are further added as less essential, deductions or corollaries immediately resulting from the theorems, and the more detailed expositions of the demonstrations or scholia. Besides these, some longer discussions are given in the form of remarks, introductions, and appendices.

[Footnote 1: Heussler's objections (*Der Rationalismus des 17 Jahrhunderts*, 1885, pp. 82-85) to this characterization of Kuno Fischer's are not convincing. The question is not so much about a principle demonstrable by definite citations as about an unconscious motive in Spinoza's thinking. Fischer's views on this point seem to us correct. Spinoza's mode of thinking is, in fact, saturated with this strong confidence in the omnipotence of the reason and the rational constitution of true reality.]

If everything is to be cognizable through mathematics, then everything must take place necessarily; even the thoughts, resolutions, and actions of man cannot be free in the sense that they might have happened otherwise. Thus there is an evident methodological motive at work for the extension of mechanism to all becoming, even spiritual becoming. But there are metaphysical reasons also. Descartes had naïvely solved the anthropological problem by the answer that the interaction of mind and body is incomprehensible but actual. The occasionalists had hesitatingly questioned these conclusions a little, the incomprehensibility as well as the actuality, only at last to leave them intact. For the explanation that there is a real influence of body on mind and *vice versa*, though not an immediate but an occasional one, one mediated by the divine will, is scarcely more than a confession that the matter is inexplicable. Spinoza, who admits neither the incognizability of anything real, nor any supernatural interferences, roundly denies both. There is no intercourse between body and soul; yet that which is erroneously considered such is both actually present and explicable. The assumed interaction is as unnecessary as it is impossible. Body and soul do not need to act on one another, because they are not two in kind at all, but constitute one being which may be looked at from two different sides. This is called body when considered under its attribute of extension, and spirit when considered under its attribute of thought. It is quite impossible for two substances to affect each other, because by their reciprocal influence, nay, by their very duality, they would lose their independence, and, with this, their substantiality. There is no plurality of substances, but only one, the infinite, the divine substance. Here we reach the center of the system. There is but one becoming and but one independent, substantial being. Material and spiritual becoming form merely the two sides of one and the same necessary world-process; particular extended beings and particular thinking beings are nothing but the changeable and transitory states *(modi)* of the enduring, eternal, unified world-ground. "Necessity in becoming and unity of being," mechanism and pantheism—these are the controlling conceptions in Spinoza's doctrine. Multiplicity, the self-dependence of particular things, free choice, ends, development, all this is illusion and error.

%(a) Substance, Attributes, and Modes%.—There is but one substance, and this is infinite (I. *prop.* 10, *schol; prop.* 14, *cor.* 1). Why, then, only one and why infinite? With Spinoza as with Descartes independence is the essence of substantiality. This is expressed in the third definition: "By substance I understand that which is in itself and is conceived by means of itself, *i.e.*, that the conception of which can be formed without the aid of the conception of any other thing." *Per substantiam intelligo id, quod in se est et per se concipitur; hoc est id, cujus conceptus non indiget conceptu alterius rei, a quo formari debeat.* An absolutely self-dependent being can neither be limited (since, in respect to its limits, it would be dependent on the limiting being), nor occur more than once in the world. Infinity follows from its self-dependence, and its uniqueness from its infinity.

Substance is the being which is dependent on nothing and on which everything depends; which, itself uncaused, effects all else; which presupposes nothing, but itself constitutes the presupposition of all that is: it is pure being, primal being, the cause of itself and of all. Thus in Spinoza the being which is without presuppositions is brought into the most intimate relation with the fullness of multiform existence, not coldly and abstractly exalted above it, as by the ancient Eleatics. Substance is the being in (not above) things, that in them which constitutes their reality, which supports and produces them. As the cause of all things Spinoza calls it God, although he is conscious that he understands by the term something quite different from the Christians. God does not mean for him a transcendent, personal spirit, but only the *ens absolute infinitum (def. sexta)*, the essential heart of things: *Deus sive substantia*.

How do things proceed from God? Neither by creation nor by emanation. He does not put them forth from himself, they do not tear themselves free from him, but they follow out of the necessary nature of God, as it follows from the nature of the triangle that the sum of its angles is equal to two right angles (I. *prop.* 17, *schol.*). They do not come out from him, but remain in him; just this fact that they are in another, in God, constitutes their lack of self-dependence (I. *prop.* 18, *dem.: nulla res, quae extra Deum in se sit*). God is their inner, indwelling cause (*causa immanens, non vero transiens.—I. prop.* 18), is not a transcendent creator, but *natura naturans*, over against the sum of finite beings, *natura naturata* (I. *prop.* 29, *schol.*): *Deus sive natura*.

Since nothing exists out of God, his actions do not follow from external necessity, are not constrained, but he is free cause, free in the sense that he does nothing except that toward which his own nature impels him, that he acts in accordance with the laws of his being (*def. septima: ea res libera dicitur, quae ex sola suae naturae necessitate existit et a se sola ad agendum determinatur; Epist.* 26). This inner necessitation is so little a defect that its direct opposite, undetermined choice and inconstancy, must rather be excluded from God as an imperfection. Freedom and (inner) necessity are identical; and antithetical, on the one side, to undetermined choice and, on the other, to (external) compulsion. Action in view of ends must also be denied of the infinite; to think of God as acting in order to the good is to make him dependent on something external to him (an aim) and lacking in that which is to be attained by the action. With God the ground of his action is the same as the ground of his existence; God's power and his essence coincide (I. *prop.* 34: *Dei potentia est ipsa ipsius essentia*). He is the cause of himself (*def. prima: per causam sui intelligo id, cujus essentia involvit existentiam, sive id, cujus natura non potest concipi nisi existens*); it would be a contradiction to hold that being was not, that God, or substance, did not exist; he cannot be thought otherwise than as existing; his concept includes his existence. To be self-caused means to exist necessarily (I. *prop.* 7). The same thing is denoted by the predicate eternal, which, according to the eighth definition, denotes "existence itself, in so far as it is conceived to follow necessarily from the mere definition of the eternal thing."

The infinite substance stands related to finite, individual things, not only as the independent to the dependent, as the cause to the caused, as the one to the many, and the whole to the parts, but also as the universal to the particular, the indeterminate to the determinate. From infinite being as pure affirmation (I. *prop.* 8, *schol.* I: *absoluta affirmatio*) everything which contains a limitation or negation, and this includes every particular determination, must be kept at a distance: *determinatio negatio est (Epist.* 50 and 41: a determination denotes nothing positive, but a deprivation, a lack of existence; relates not to the being but to the non-being of the thing). A determination states that which distinguishes one thing from another, hence what it is *not*, expresses a limitation of it. Consequently God, who is free from every negation and limitation, is to be conceived as the absolutely indeterminate. The results thus far reached run: *Substantia una infinita—Deus sive natura—causa sui (aeterna) et rerum (immanens)—libera necessitas—non determinata*. Or more briefly: Substance = God = nature. The equation of God and substance had been announced by Descartes, but not adhered to, while Bruno had approached the equation of God and nature—Spinoza decisively completes both and combines them.

A further remark may be added concerning the relation of God and the world. In calling the infinite at once the permanent essence of things and their producing cause, Spinoza raises a demand which it is not easy to fulfill, the demand to think the existence of things in substance as a following from substance, and their procession from God as a remaining in him. He refers us to mathematics: the things which make up the world are related to God as the properties of a geometrical figure to its concepts, as theorems to the axiom, as the deduction to the principle, which from eternity contains all that follows from it and retains this even while putting it forth. It cannot be doubted that such a view of causality contains error,—it has been characterized as a confusion of *ratio* and *causa*, of logical ground and real cause,—but it is just as certain that Spinoza committed it. He not only compares the dependence of the effect on its cause to the dependence of a derivative principle on that from which it is derived, but fully equates the two; he thinks that in logico-mathematical "consequences" he has grasped the essence of real "effects": for him the type of all legality, as also of real becoming, was the necessity which governs the sequence of mathematical truths, and which, on the one hand, is even and still, needing no special exertion of volitional energy, while, on the other, it is rigid and unyielding, exalted above all choice. Philosophy had sought the assistance of mathematics because of the clearness and certainty which distinguish the conclusions of the latter, and which she wished to obtain for her own. In excess of zeal she was not content with striving after this ideal of indefectible certitude, but, forgetting the diversity of the two fields, strove to imitate other qualities which are not transferable; instead of learning from mathematics she became subservient to it.

Substance does not affect us by its mere existence, but through an *Attribute*. By attribute is meant, according to the fourth definition, "that which the understanding perceives of substance as constituting the essence of it" *(quod intellectus de substantia percipit, tanquam ejusdem essentiam constituens)*. The more reality a substance contains, the more attributes it has; consequently infinite substance possesses an infinite number, each of which gives expression to its essence, but of which two only fall within our knowledge. Among the innumerable divine attributes the human mind knows those only which it finds in itself, thought and extension. Although man beholds God only as thinking and extended substance, he yet has a clear and complete; an adequate—idea of God. Since each of the two attributes is conceived without the other, hence in itself (*per se*), they are distinct from each other *realiter*, and independent. God is absolutely infinite, the attributes only in their kind (*in suo genere*).

How can the indeterminate possess properties? Are the attributes merely ascribed to substance by the understanding, or do they possess reality apart from the knowing subject? This question has given rise to much debate. According to Hegel and Ed. Erdmann the attributes are something external to substance, something brought into it by the understanding, forms of knowledge present in the beholder alone;

substance itself is neither extended nor cogitative, but merely appears to the understanding under these determinations, without which the latter would be unable to cognize it. This "formalistic" interpretation, which, relying on a passage in a letter to De Vries (*Epist*. 27), explains the attributes as mere modes of intellectual apprehension, numbers Kuno Fischer among its opponents. As the one party holds to the first half of the definition, the other places the emphasis on the second half ("that which the *understanding* perceives—as constituting the *essence* of substance"). The attributes are more than mere modes of representation—they are real properties, which substance possesses even apart from an observer, nay, in which it consists; in Spinoza, moreover, "must be conceived" is the equivalent of "to be." Although this latter "realistic" party undoubtedly has the advantage over the former, which reads into Spinoza a subjectivism foreign to his system, they ought not to forget that the difference in interpretation has for its basis a conflict among the motives which control Spinoza's thinking. The reference of the attributes to the understanding, given in the definition, is not without significance. It sprang from the wish not to mar the indeterminateness of the absolute by the opposition of the attributes, while, on the other hand, an equally pressing need for the conservation of the immanence of substance forbade a bold transfer of the attributes to the observer. The real opinion of Spinoza is neither so clear and free from contradictions, nor so one-sided, as that which his interpreters ascribe to him. Fischer's further interpretation of the attributes of God as his "powers" is tenable, so long as by *causa* and *potentia* we understand nothing more than the irresistible, but non-kinetic, force with which an original truth establishes or effects those which follow from it.

As the dualism of extension and thought is reduced from a substantial to an attributive distinction, so individual bodies and minds, motions and thoughts, are degraded a stage further. Individual things lack independence of every sort. The individual is, as a determinate finite thing, burdened with negation and limitation, for every determination includes a negation; that which is truly real in the individual is God. Finite things are *modi* of the infinite substance, mere states, variable states, of God. By themselves they are nothing, since out of God nothing exists. They possess existence only in so far as they are conceived in their connection with the infinite, that is, as transitory forms of the unchangeable substance. They are not in themselves, but in another, in God, and are conceived only in God. They are mere affections of the divine attributes, and must be considered as such.

To the two attributes correspond two classes of modes. The most important modifications of extension are rest and motion. Among the modes of thought are understanding and will. These belong in the sphere of determinate and transitory being and do not hold of the *natura naturans*: God is exalted above all modality, above will and understanding, as above motion and rest. We must not assert of the *natura naturata* (the world as the sum of all modes), as of the *natura naturans*, that its essence involves existence (I. *prop*. 24): we can conceive finite things as non-existent, as well as existent (*Epist*. 29). This constitutes their "contingency," which must by no means be interpreted as lawlessness. On the contrary, all that takes place in the world is most rigorously determined; every individual, finite, determinate thing and event is determined to its existence and action by another similarly finite and determinate thing or event, and this cause is, in turn, determined in its existence and action by a further finite mode, and so on to infinity (I. *prop*. 28). Because of this endlessness in the series there is no first or ultimate cause in the phenomenal world; all finite causes are second causes; the primary cause lies within the sphere of the infinite and is God himself. The modes are all subject to the constraint of an unbroken and endless nexus of efficient causes, which leaves room neither for chance, nor choice, nor ends. Nothing can be or happen otherwise than as it is and happens (I. *prop*. 29, 33).

The causal chain appears in two forms: a mode of extension has its producing ground in a second mode of extension; a mode of thought can be caused only by another mode of thought—each individual thing is determined by one of its own kind. The two series proceed side by side, without a member of either ever being able to interfere in the other or to effect anything in it—a motion can never produce anything but other motions, an idea can result only in other ideas; the body can never determine the mind to an idea, nor the soul the body to a movement. Since, however, extension and thought are not two substances, but attributes of one substance, this apparently double causal nexus of two series proceeding in exact correspondence is, in reality, but a single one. (III. *prop*. 2, *schol*.) viewed from different sides. That which represents a chain of motions when seen from the side of extension, bears the aspect of a series of ideas from the side of thought. *Modus extensionis et idea illius modi una cademque est res, sed duobus modis expressa* (II. *prop*. 7, *schol*.; cf. III. *prop*. 2, *schol*.). The soul is nothing but the idea of an actual body, body or motion nothing but the object or event in the sphere of extended actuality corresponding to an idea. No idea exists without something corporeal corresponding to it, no body, without at the same time existing as idea, or being conceived; in other words, everything is both body and spirit, all things are animated (II. *prop*. 13, *schol*.). Thus the famous proposition results; *Ordo et connexio idearum idem est ac ordo et connexio rerum (sive corporum; II. prop.* 7), and in application to man, "the order of the actions and passions of our body is simultaneous in nature with the order of the actions and passions of the mind" (III. *prop. 2, schol.*).

The attempt to solve the problem of the relation between the material and the mental worlds by asserting their thoroughgoing correspondence and substantial identity, was philosophically justifiable and important, though many evident objections obtrude themselves upon us. The required assumption, that there is a mental event corresponding to *every* bodily one, and *vice versa*, meets with involuntary and easily supported opposition, which Spinoza did nothing to remove. Similarly he omitted to explain how body is related to motion, mind to ideas, and both to actuality. The ascription of a materialistic tendency to Spinoza is not without foundation. Corporeality and reality appear well-nigh identical for him,—the expressions *corpora* and *res* are used synonymously,—so that there remains for minds and ideas only an existence as reflections of the real in the sphere of [an] ideality (whose degree of actuality it is difficult to determine). Moreover, individualistic impulses have been pointed out, which, in part, conflict with the monism which he consciously follows, and, in part, subserve its interests. An example of this is given in the relation of mind and idea: Spinoza treats the soul as a sum of ideas, as consisting in them. An (at least apparently substantial) bond among ideas, an ego, which possesses them, does not exist for him: the Cartesian *cogito* has become an impersonal *cogitatur* or a *Deus cogitat*. In order to the unique substantiality of the infinite, the substantiality of individual spirits must disappear. That which argues for the latter is their I-ness (*Ichheit*), the unity of self-consciousness; it is destroyed, if the mind is a congeries of ideas, a composite of them. Thus in order to relieve itself from the self-dependence of the individual mind, monism allies itself with a spiritual atomism, the most extreme which can be conceived. The mind is resolved into a mass of individual ideas.

Mention may be made in passing, also, of a strange conception, which is somewhat out of harmony with the rest of the system, and of which, moreover, little use is made. This is the conception of *infinite modes*. As such are cited, *facies totius mundi, motus et quies, intellectus absolute infinitus*. Kuno Fischer's interpretation of this difficult conception may be accepted. It denotes, according to him, the connected sum of the modes, the itself non-finite sum total of the finite—the universe meaning the totality of individual things in general (without reference to their nature as extended or cogitative); rest and motion, the totality of material being; the absolutely infinite understanding, the totality of spiritual being or the ideas. Individual spirits together constitute, as it were, the infinite intellect; our mind is a part of the divine understanding, yet not in such a sense that the whole consists of the parts, but that the part exists only through the whole. When we say, the human mind perceives this or that, it is equivalent to saying that God—not in so far as he is infinite, but as he expresses himself in this human mind and constitutes its essence—has this or that idea (II. *prop*. II, *coroll*).

The discussion of these three fundamental concepts exhausts all the chief points in Spinoza's doctrine of God. Passing over his doctrine of body (II. between *prop*. 13 and *prop*. 14) we turn at once to his discussion of mind and man.

%(b) Anthropology: Cognition and the Passions.%—Each thing is at once mind and body, representation and that which is represented, idea and ideate (object). Body and soul are the same being, only considered under different attributes. The human mind is the idea of the human body; it cognizes itself in perceiving the affections of its body; it represents all that takes place in the body, though not all adequately. As man's body is composed of very many bodies, so his soul is composed of very many ideas. To judge of the relation of the human mind to the mind of lower beings, we must consider the superiority of man's body to other bodies; the more complex a body is, and the greater the variety of the affections of which it is capable, the better and more adapted for adequate cognition, the accompanying mind.—A result of the identity of soul and body is that the acts of our will are not free (*Epist*. 62): they are, in fact, determinations of our body, only considered under the attribute of thought, and no more free than this from the constraint of the causal law (III. *prop*. 2, *schol*.).—Since the mind does nothing without at the same time knowing that it does it—since, in other words, its activity is a conscious activity, it is not merely *idea corporis humani*, but also *idea ideae corporis* or *idea mentis*.

All adherents of the Eleatic separation of the one pure being from the manifold and changing world of appearance are compelled to make a like distinction between two kinds and two organs of *knowledge*. The representation of the empirical manifold of separately existing individual things, together with the organ thereof, Spinoza terms *imaginatio*; the faculty of cognizing the true reality, the one, all-embracing substance, he calls *intellectus*. *Imaginatio* (imagination, sensuous representation) is the faculty of inadequate, confused ideas, among which are included abstract conceptions, as well as sensations and memory-images. The objects of perception are the affections of our body; and our perceptions, therefore, are not clear and distinct, because we are not completely acquainted with their causes. In the merely perceptual stage, the mind gains only a confused and mutilated idea of external objects, of the body, and of itself; it is unable to separate that in the perception (*e.g.*, heat) which is due to the external body from that which is due to its own body. An inadequate idea, however, is not in itself an error; it becomes such only when, unconscious of its defectiveness, we take it for complete and true. Prominent examples of erroneous ideas are furnished by general concepts, by the idea of ends, and the idea of the freedom of the will. The more general and abstract an idea, the more inadequate and indistinct it becomes; and this shows the lack of value in generic concepts, which are formed by the omission of differences. All cognition which is carried on by universals and their symbols, words, yields opinion and imagination merely instead of truth. Quite as valueless and harmful is the idea of ends, with its accompaniments. We think that nature has typical forms hovering before it, which it is seeking to actualize in things; when this intention is apparently fulfilled we speak of things as perfect and beautiful; when it fails, of imperfect and ugly things. Such concepts of value belong in the sphere of fictions. The same is true of the idea of the freedom of the will, which depends on our ignorance of that which constrains us. Apart from the consideration that "the will," the general conception of which comes under the rubric of unreal abstractions, is in fact merely the sum of the particular volitions, the illusion of freedom, *e.g.*, that we will and act without a cause, arises from the fact that we are conscious of our action (and also of its proximate motives), but not of its (remoter) determining causes. Thus the thirsty child believes it desires its milk of its own free will, and the timid one, that it freely chooses to run away (*Ethica, III. prop*. 2, *schol*.; I. *app*.) If the falling stone were conscious, it would, likewise, consider itself free, and its fall the result of an undetermined decision.

Two degrees are to be distinguished in the true or adequate knowledge of the intellect: rational knowledge attained through inference, and intuitive, self-evident knowledge; the latter has principles for its object, the former that which follows from them. Instead of operating with abstract concepts the reason uses common notions, *notiones communes*. Genera do not exist, but, no doubt, something common to all things. All bodies agree in being extended; all minds and ideas in being modes of thought; all beings whatever in the fact that they are modes of the divine substance and its attributes; "that which is common to all things, and which is equally in the part and in the whole, cannot but be adequately conceived." The ideas of extension, of thought, and of the eternal and infinite essence of God are adequate ideas. The adequate idea of each individual actual object involves the idea of God, since it can neither exist nor be conceived apart from God, and "all ideas, in so far as they are referred to God, are true." The ideas of substance and of the attributes are conceived through themselves, or immediately (intuitively) cognized; they are underivative, original, self-evident ideas.

There are thus three kinds, degrees, or faculties of cognition—sensuous or imaginative representation, reason, and immediate intuition. Knowledge of the second and third degrees is necessarily true, and our only means of distinguishing the true from the false. As light reveals itself and darkness, so the truth is the criterion of itself and of error. Every truth is accompanied by certainty, and is its own witness (II. *prop*. 43, *schol*.).—Adequate knowledge does not consider things as individuals, but in their necessary connection and as eternal sequences from the world-ground. The reason perceives things under the form of eternity: *sub specie aeternitatis* (II. *prop*. 44, *cor*. 2).

In his theory of the *emotions*, Spinoza is more dependent on Descartes than anywhere else; but even here he is guided by a successful endeavor after greater rigor and simplicity. He holds his predecessor's false concept of freedom responsible for the failure of his very acute inquiry. All previous writers on the passions have either derided, or bewailed, or condemned them, instead of investigating their nature. Spinoza will neither denounce nor ridicule human actions and appetites, but endeavor to comprehend them on the basis of natural laws, and to consider them as though the question concerned lines, surfaces, and bodies. He aims not to look on hate, anger, and the rest as flaws, but as necessary, though troublesome, properties of human nature, for which, as really as for heat and cold, thunder and lightning, a causal explanation is requisite.—As a determinate, finite being the mind is dependent in its existence and its activity on other finite things, and is incomprehensible without them; from its involution in the general course of nature the inadequate ideas inevitably follow, and from these the passive states or emotions; the passions thus belong to human nature, as one subject to limitation and negation.—The destruction of contingent and perishable things is effected by external causes; no one is destroyed by itself; so far as in it lies everything strives to persist in its being (III. *prop.* 4 and 6). The fundamental endeavor after self-preservation constitutes the essence of each thing (III. *prop.* 7). This endeavor *(conatus)* is termed will *(voluntas)* or desire *(cupiditas)* when it is referred to the mind alone, and appetite *(appetitus)* when referred to the mind and body together; desire or volition is conscious appetite (III. *prop.* 9, *schol.*). We call a thing good because we desire it, not desire a thing because we hold it good (cf. Hobbes, p. 75). To desire two further fundamental forms of the emotions are added, pleasure and pain. If a thing increases the power of our body to act, the idea of it increases the power of our soul to think, and is gladly imagined by it. Pleasure *(laetitia)* is the transition of a man to a greater, and pain *(tristitia)* his transition to a lesser perfection.

All other emotions are modifications or combinations of the three original ones, to which Spinoza reduces the six of Descartes (cf. p. 105). In the deduction and description of them his procedure is sometimes aridly systematic, sometimes even forced and artificial, but for the most part ingenious, appropriate, and psychologically acute. Whatever gives us pleasure augments our being, and whatever pains us diminishes it; hence we seek to preserve the causes of pleasurable emotions, and love them, to do away with the causes of painful ones, and hate them. "Love is pleasure accompanied by the idea of an external cause; hate is pain accompanied by the idea of an external cause." Since all that furthers or diminishes the being of (the cause of our pleasure) the object of our love, exercises at the same time a like influence on us, we love that which rejoices the object of our love and hate that which disturbs it; its happiness and suffering become ours also. The converse is true of the object of our hate: its good fortune provokes us and its ill fortune pleases us. If we are filled with no emotion toward things like ourselves, we sympathize in their sad or joyous feelings by involuntary imitation. Pity, from which we strive to free ourselves as from every painful affection, inclines us to benevolence or to assistance in the removal of the cause of the misery of others. Envy of those who are fortunate, and commiseration of those who are in trouble, are alike rooted in emulation. Man is by nature inclined to envy and malevolence. Hate easily leads to underestimation, love to overestimation, of the object, and self-love to pride or self-satisfaction, which are much more frequently met with than unfeigned humility. Immoderate desire for honor is termed ambition; if the desire to please others is kept within due bounds it is praised as unpretentiousness, courtesy, modesty (*modestia*). Ambition, luxury, drunkenness, avarice, and lust have no contraries, for temperance, sobriety, and chastity are not emotions (passive states), but denote the power of the soul by which the former are moderated, and which is discussed later under the name *fortitudo*. Self-abasement or humility is a feeling of pain arising from the consideration of our weakness and impotency; its opposite is self-complacency. Either of these may be accompanied by the (erroneous) belief that we have done the saddening or gladdening act of our own free will; in this case the former affection is termed repentance. Hope and fear are inconstant pleasure and pain, arising from the idea of something past or to come, concerning whose coming and whose issue we are still in doubt. There is no hope unmingled with fear, and no fear without hope; for he who still doubts imagines something which excludes the existence of that which is expected. If the cause of doubt is removed, hope is transformed into a feeling of confidence and fear into despair. There are as many kinds of emotions as there are classes among their objects or causes.

Besides the emotions to be termed "passions" in the strict sense, states of passivity, Spinoza recognizes others which relate to us as active. Only those which are of the nature of pleasure or desire belong to this class of *active* emotions; the painful affections are entirely excluded, since without exception they diminish or arrest the mind's power to think. The totality of these nobler impulses is called *fortitudo* (fortitude), and a distinction is made among them between *animositas* (vigor of soul) and *generositas* (magnanimity, noble-mindedness), according as rational desire is directed to the preservation of our own being or to aiding our fellow-men. Presence of mind and temperance are examples of the former, modesty and clemency of the latter. By this bridge, the idea of the active emotions, we may follow Spinoza into the field of ethics.

%(c) Practical Philosophy.%—Spinoza's theory of ethics is based on the equation of the three concepts, perfection, reality, activity (V. *prop.* 40, *dem.*). The more active a thing is, the more perfect it is and the more reality it possesses. It is active, however, when it is the complete or adequate cause of that which takes place within it or without it; passive when it is not at all the cause of this, or the cause only in part. A cause is termed adequate, when its effect can be clearly and distinctly perceived from it alone. The human mind, as a *modus* of thought, is active when it has adequate ideas; all its passion consists in confused ideas, among which belong the affections produced by external objects. The essence of the mind is thought; volition is not only dependent on cognition, but at bottom identical with it.

Descartes had already made the will the power of affirmation and negation. Spinoza advances a step further: the affirmation cannot be separated from the idea affirmed, it is impossible to conceive a truth without in the same act affirming it, the idea involves its own affirmation. "Will and understanding are one and the same" (II. *prop.* 49, *cor.*). For Spinoza moral activity is entirely resolved into cognitive activity. To the two stages of knowing, *imaginatio* and *intellectus*, correspond two stages of willing—desire, which is ruled by imagination, and volition, which is guided by reason. The passive emotions of sensuous desire are directed to perishable objects, the active, which spring from reason, have an eternal object—the knowledge of the truth, the intuition of God. For reason there are no distinctions of persons,—she brings men into concord and gives them a common end (IV. *prop.* 35-37,40),—and no distinctions of time (IV. *prop.* 62, 66), and in the active emotions, which are always good, no excess (IV. *prop.* 61). The passive emotions arise from confused ideas. They cease to be passions, when the confused ideas of the modifications of the body are transformed into clear ones; as soon as we have clear ideas, we become active and cease to be slaves of desire. We master the emotions by gaining a clear knowledge of them. Now, an idea is clear when we cognize its object not as an individual thing, but in its connection, as a link in the causal chain, as necessary, and as a mode of God. The more the mind conceives things in their necessity, and the emotions in their reference to God, the less it is passively subject to the emotions, the more power it attains over them: "Virtue is power" (IV. *def.* 8; *prop.* 20, *dem.*). It is true, indeed, that one emotion can be conquered only by another stronger one, a passive emotion only by an active one. The active emotion by which knowledge gains this victory over the passions is the joyous consciousness of our power (III. *prop.* 58, 59). Adequate ideas conceive their objects in union with God; thus the pleasure which proceeds from knowledge of, and victory over, the passions is accompanied by the idea of God, and, consequently (according to the definition of love), by *love toward God* (V. *prop.* 15, 32). The knowledge and love of God, together, "intellectual love toward God,"[1] is the highest good and the highest virtue (IV. *prop.* 28). Blessedness is not the reward of virtue, but virtue itself. The intellectual love of man toward God, in which the highest peace of the soul, blessedness, and freedom consist, and in virtue of which (since it, like its object and cause, true knowledge, is eternal), the soul is not included in the destruction of the body (V. *prop.* 23, 33), is a part of the infinite love with which God loves himself, and is one and the same with the love of God to man. The eternal part of the soul is reason, through which it is active; the perishable part is imagination or sensuous representation, through which it is passively affected. We are immortal only in adequate cognition and in love to God; more of the wise man's soul is immortal than of the fool's.

[Footnote 1: The conception *amor Dei intellectualis* in Spinoza is discussed in a dissertation by C. Lülmann, Jena, 1884.]

Spinoza's ethics is intellectualistic—virtue is based on knowledge.[1] It is, moreover, naturalistic—morality is a necessary sequence from human nature; it is a physical product, not a product of freedom; for the acts of the will are determined by ideas, which in their turn are the effects of earlier causes. The foundation of virtue is the effort after self-preservation: How can a man desire to act rightly unless he desires to be (IV. *prop*. 21, 22)? Since reason never enjoins that which is contrary to nature, it of necessity requires every man to love himself, to seek that which is truly useful to him, and to desire all that makes him more perfect. According to the law of nature all that is useful is allowable. The useful is that which increases our power, activity, or perfection, or that which furthers knowledge, for the life of the soul consists in thought (IV. *prop. 26; app. cap.* 5). That alone is an evil which restrains man from perfecting the reason and leading a rational life. Virtuous action is equivalent to following the guidance of the reason in self-preservation (IV. *prop*. 24).—Nowhere in Spinoza are fallacies more frequent than in his moral philosophy; nowhere is there a clearer revelation of the insufficiency of his artificially constructed concepts, which, in their undeviating abstractness, are at no point congruent with reality. He is as little true to his purpose to exclude the imperative element, and to confine himself entirely to the explanation of human actions considered as facts, as any philosopher who has adopted a similar aim. He relieves the inconsistency by clothing his injunctions under the ancient ideal of the free wise man. This, in fact, is not the only thing in Spinoza which reminds one of the customs of the Greek moralists. He renews the Platonic idea of a philosophical virtue, and the opinion of Socrates, that right action will result of itself from true insight. Arguing from himself, from his own pure and strong desire for knowledge, to mankind in general, he makes reason the essence of the soul, thought the essence of reason, and holds the direction of the impulse of self-preservation to the perfection of knowledge, which is "the better part of us," to be the natural one.

[Footnote 1: That virtue which springs from knowledge is alone genuine. The painful, hence unactive, emotions of pity and repentance may impel to actions whose accomplishment is better than their omission. Emotion caused by sympathy for others and contrition for one's own guilt, both of which increase present evil by new ones, have only the value of evils of a lesser kind. They are salutary for the irrational man, in so far as the one spurs him on to acts of assistance and the other diminishes his pride. They are harmful to the wise man, or, at least, useless; he is in no need of irrational motives to rational action. Action from insight is alone true morality.]

All men endeavor after continuance of existence (III. *prop*. 6); why not all after virtue? If all endeavor after it, why do so few reach the goal? Whence the sadly large number of the irrational, the selfish, the vicious? Whence the evil in the world? Vice is as truly an outcome of "nature" as virtue. Virtue is power, vice is weakness; the former is knowledge, the latter ignorance. Whence the powerless natures? Whence defective knowledge? Whence imperfection in general?

The concept of imperfection expresses nothing positive, nothing actual, but merely a defect, an absence of reality. It is nothing but an idea in us, a fiction which arises through the comparison of one thing with another possessing greater reality, or with an abstract generic concept, a pattern, which it seems unable to attain. That concepts of value are not properties of things themselves, but denote only their pleasurable or painful effects on us, is evident from the fact that one and the same thing may be at the same time good, bad, and indifferent: the music which is good for the melancholy man may be bad for the mourner, and neither good nor bad for the deaf. Knowledge of the bad is an abstract, inadequate idea; in God there is no idea of evil. If imperfection and error were something real, it would have to be conceded that God is the author of evil and sin. In reality everything is that which it can be, hence without defect: everything actual is, in itself considered, perfect. Even the fool and the sinner cannot be otherwise than he is; he appears imperfect only when placed beside the wise and the virtuous. Sin is thus only a lesser reality than virtue, evil a lesser good; good and bad, activity and passivity, power and weakness are merely distinctions in degree. But why is not everything absolutely perfect? Why are there lesser degrees of reality? Two answers are given. The first is found only between the lines: the imperfections in the being and action of individual things are grounded in their finitude, particularly in their involution in the chain of causality, in virtue of which they are acted on from without, and are determined in their action not by their own nature only, but also by external causes. Man sins because he is open to impressions from external things, and only superior natures are strong enough to preserve their rational self-determination in spite of this. The other answer is expressly given at the end of the first part (with an appeal to the sixteenth proposition, that everything which the divine understanding conceives as creatable has actually come into existence). "To those who ask why God did not so create all men that they should be governed only by reason, I reply only: because matter was not lacking to him for the creation of every degree of perfection from highest to lowest; or, more strictly, because the laws of his nature were so ample as so suffice for the production of everything conceivable by an infinite intellect." All possible degrees of perfection have come into being, including sin and error, which represent the lowest grade. The universe forms a chain of degrees of perfection, of which none must be wanting: particular cases of defect are justified by the perfection of the whole, which would be incomplete without the lowest degree of perfection, vice and wickedness. Here we see Spinoza following a path which Leibnitz was to broaden out into a highway in his *Theodicy*. Both favor the quantitative view of the world, which softens the antitheses, and reduces distinctions of kind to distinctions of degree. Not till Kant was the qualitative view of the world, which had been first brought into ethics by Christianity, restored to its rights. An ethics which denies freedom and evil is nothing but a physics of morals.

In his *theory of the state* Spinoza follows Hobbes pretty closely, but rejects absolutism, and declares democracy, in which each is obedient to self-imposed law, to be the form of government most in accordance with reason. (So in the *Tractatus Theologico-Politicus*, while in the later *Tractatus Politicus* he gives the preference to aristocracy.) In accordance with the supreme right of nature each man deems good, and seeks to gain, that which seems to him useful; all things belong to all, each may destroy the objects of his hate. Conflict and insecurity prevail in the state of nature as a result of the sensuous desires and emotions (*homines ex natura hostes*); and they can be done away with only through the establishment of a society, which by punitive laws compels everyone to do, and leave undone, that which the general welfare demands. Strife and breach of faith become sin only in the state; before its formation that alone was wrong which no one had the desire and power to do. Besides this mission, however, of protecting selfish interests by the prevention of aggression, the civil community has a higher one, to subserve the development of reason; it is only in the state that true morality and true freedom are possible, and the wise man will prefer to live in the state, because he finds more freedom there than in isolation. Thus the dislocation of concepts, which is perceptible in Spinoza's ethics, repeats itself in his politics. First, virtue is based on the impulse of self-preservation and the good is equated with that which is useful to the individual; then, with a transformation of mere utility into "true" utility, the rational moment is brought in (first as practical prudence, next as the impulse after knowledge, and then, with a gradual change of meaning, as moral wisdom), until, finally, in strange contrast to the naturalistic beginning, the Christian idea of virtue as purity, self-denial, love to our neighbors and love to God, is reached. In a similar way "Spinoza conceives the starting point of the state naturalistically, its culmination idealistically."[1]

[Footnote 1: C. Schindler in his dissertation *Ueber den Begriff des Guten und Nützlichen bei Spinoza*, Jena, 1885, p. 42, a work, however, which does not penetrate to the full depth of the matter. Cf. Eucken, *Lebensanschauungen*, p. 406.]

The fundamental ideas of the Spinozistic system, and those which render it important, are rationalism, pantheism, the essential identity of the material and spiritual worlds, and the uninterrupted mechanism of becoming. Besides the twisting of ethical concepts just mentioned, we may briefly note the most striking of the other difficulties and contradictions which Spinoza left unexplained. There is a break between his endeavor to exalt the absolute high above the phenomenal world of individual existence, and, at the same time, to bring the former into the closest possible conjunction with the latter, to make it dwell therein—a break between the transcendent and immanent conceptions of the idea of God. No light is vouchsafed on the relation between primary and secondary causes, between the immediate divine causality and the divine causality mediated through finite causes. The infinity of God is in conflict with his complete cognizability on the part of man; for how is a finite, transitory spirit able to conceive the Infinite and Eternal? How does the human intellect rise above modal limitations to become capable and worthy of the mystical union with God? Reference has been already made to the twofold nature of the attributes (as forms of intellectual apprehension and as real properties of substance) which invites contradictory interpretations.

3. %Pascal, Malebranche, Bayle.%

Returning from Holland to France, we find a combination of Cartesianism and mysticism similar to that which we have noticed in the former country. Under Geulincx these two forces had lived peacefully together; in Spinoza they had entered into the closest alliance; with Blaise Pascal (1623-62), the first to adopt a religious tendency, they came into a certain antithesis. Spinoza had taught: through the knowledge of God to the love of God; in Pascal the watchword becomes, God is not conceived through the reason, but felt with the heart. After attacking the Jesuits in his *Provincial Letters*, and unveiling the worthlessness of their casuistical morality, Pascal, constrained by a genuine piety, undertook to construct a philosophy of Christianity; but the attempt was ended by the early death of the author, who had always suffered under a weak constitution. Fragments of this work were published by his friends, the Jansenists, under the title, *Thoughts on Religion*, 1669, though not without mediating alterations. The Port-Royal *Logic (The Art of Thinking*, 1662), edited by Arnauld and Nicole, was based on a treatise of Pascal. His thought, which was not distinguished by clearness, but by depth and movement, and which, after the French fashion, delighted in antitheses, was influenced by Descartes, Montaigne, and Epictetus. He, too, finds in mathematics the example for all science, and holds that whatever transcends mathematics transcends the reason. By the application of mathematics to the study of nature we attain a mundane science, which is certain, no doubt, and which makes constant progress,[1] but which does not satisfy, since it reveals nothing of the infinite, of the whole, without which the parts remain unintelligible. Hence all natural philosophy together is not worth an hour's toil. Pascal consoles himself for our ignorance concerning external things by the stability of ethics.

[Footnote 1: It is this uninterrupted progress which raises the reason above the operations of nature and the instincts of animals. While the bees build their cells to-day just as they did a thousand years ago, science is continually developing. This guarantees to us our immortal destiny.]

The leading principles of his ethics are as follows: In sin the love to God created in us has left us and self-love has transgressed its limits; pride has delivered us over to selfishness and misery. Our nature is corrupted, but not beyond redemption. In his actions worthless and depraved, man is seen to be exalted and incomprehensible in his ends; in reality he is worthy of abhorrence, but great in his destination. No philosophy or religion has so taught us at once to know the greatness and the misery of man as Christianity: this bids him recognize his low condition, but at the same time to endeavor to become like God. We must humbly despise the world and renounce ourselves; in order to love God, we must hate ourselves. Moral reformation is an act of divine grace, and the merit of human volition consists only in not resisting this. God transforms the heart by a heavenly sweetness, grants it to know that spiritual pleasure is greater than bodily pleasure, and infuses into it a disgust at the allurements of sin. Virtue is finding one's greatest happiness in God or in the eternal good. As morality is a matter of feeling, not of thought, so God, so even the first principles on which the certitude of demonstration depends, are the object, not of reason, but of the heart. That which certifies to the highest indemonstrable principles is a feeling, a belief, an instinct of nature: *les principes se sentent*. As a defender of the needs and rights of the heart, Pascal is a forerunner of the great Rousseau. His depreciation of the reason to exalt faith establishes a certain relationship with the skeptics of his native land, among whom Cousin has unjustly classed him (*Études sur Pascal*, 5th ed., 1857).[1]

[Footnote 1: Of the works on Pascal we may mention that of H. Reuchlin, 1840: Havet's edition of the *Pensées*, with notes, Paris, 1866; and the *Étude* by Ed. Droz, Paris, 1886.]

Nicolas Malebranche (1638-1715), a member of the Oratory of Jesus, in Paris, which was opposed by the Jesuits, completed the development of Cartesianism in the religious direction adopted by Pascal. His thought is controlled by the endeavor to combine Cartesian metaphysics and Augustinian Christianity, those two great forces which constituted the double citadel of his order. His collected works appeared three years before his death; and a new edition in four volumes, prepared by J. Simon, in 1871. His chief work, *On the Search for Truth* (new edition by F. Bouillier, 1880), appeared in 1675, and was followed by the *Treatise on Ethics* (new edition by H. Joly, 1882) and the *Christian and Metaphysical Meditations* in 1684, the *Discussions on Metaphysics and on Religion* in 1688, and various polemic treatises. The best known among the doctrines of Malebranche is the principle that *we see all things in God (que nous voyons toutes choses en Dieu.—Recherche*, iii. 2, 6). What does this mean, and how is it established? It is intended as an answer to the question, How is it possible for the mind to cognize the body if, as Descartes has shown, mind and body are two fundamentally distinct and reciprocally independent substances?

The seeker after truth must first understand the sources of error. Of these there are two, or, more exactly, five—as many as there are faculties of the soul. Error may spring from either the cognitive or the appetitive faculty; in the first case, either from sense-perception, the imagination, or the pure understanding, and, in the latter, from the inclinations or the passions. The inclinations and the passions do not reveal the nature of things, but only express how they affect us, of what value they are to us. Further still, the senses and the imagination only reproduce the impressions which things make on us as feeling subjects, express only what they are for us, not what they are in themselves. The senses have been given us simply for the preservation of our body, and so long as we expect nothing further from them than practical information concerning the (useful or hurtful) relation of things to our body, there is no reason for mistrusting them,—here we are not deceived by sensation, but at most by the overhasty judgment of the will. "Consider the senses as false witnesses in regard to the truth, but as trustworthy counselors in relation to the interests of life!"—Sensation and imagination belong to the soul in virtue of its union with the body; apart from this it is pure spirit. The essence of the soul is thought, for this function is the only one which cannot be abstracted from it without destroying it. Hence there can be no moment in the life of the soul when it ceases to think; it thinks always (*l'âme pense toujours*), only it does not always remember the fact.

The kinds of knowledge differ with the classes of things cognized. God is known immediately and intuitively. He is necessary and unlimited being, the universal, infinite being, being absolutely; he only is known through himself. The concept of the infinite is the presupposition of the concept of the finite, and the former is earlier in us; we gain the conception of a particular thing only when we omit something from the idea of "being in general," or limit it. God is cogitative, like spirits, and extended, like bodies, but in an entirely different manner from created things. We know our own soul through consciousness or inner perception. We know its existence more certainly than that of bodies, but understand its nature less perfectly than theirs. To know that it is capable of sensations of pain, of heat, of light, we must have experienced them. For knowledge of the minds of others we are dependent upon conjecture, on analogical inferences from ourselves.

But how is the unextended soul capable of cognizing extended body? Only through the medium of *ideas*. The ideas occupy an intermediate position between objects, whose archetypes they are, and representations in the soul, whose causes they are. The ideas, after the pattern of which God has created things, and the relations among them (necessary truths), are eternal, hence uncaused; they constitute the wisdom of God and are not dependent on his will. Things are in God in archetypal form, and are cognized through these their archetypes in God. Ideas are not produced by bodies, by the emission of sensuous images,[1] nor are they originated by the soul, or possessed by it as an innate possession. But God is the cause of knowledge, although he neither imparts ideas to the soul in creation nor produces them in it on every separate occasion. The ideas or perfections of things are in God and are beheld by spirits, who likewise dwell in God as the universal reason. As space is the place of bodies, so God is the place of spirits. As bodies are modes of extension, so their ideas are modifications of the idea of extension or of "intelligible extension." The principle stated at the beginning, that things are perceived in God, is, therefore, supported in the following way: we perceive bodies (through ideas, which ideas, and we ourselves, are) in God.

[Footnote 1: Malebranche's refutation of the emanation hypothesis of the Peripatetics is acute and still worthy of attention. If bodies transmitted to the sense-organs forms like themselves, these copies, which would evidently be corporeal, must, by their departure, diminish the mass of the body from which they came away, and also, because of their impenetrability, obstruct and interfere with one another, thus destroying the possibility of clear impressions. A further point against the image theory is furnished by the increase in the size of an object, when approached. And, above all, it can never be made conceivable how motion can be transformed into sensations or ideas.]

As the knowledge of truth has been found to consist in seeing things as God sees them, so morality consists in man's loving things as God loves them, or, what amounts to the same thing, in loving them to that degree which is their due in view of their greater or less perfection. If, in the last analysis, all cognition is knowledge of God, so all volition is loving God; there is implanted in every creature a direction toward the Creator. God is not only the primordial, unlimited being, he is also the highest good, the final end of all striving. As the ideas of things are imperfect participations in, or determinations of universal being, the absolute perfection of God, so the particular desires, directed toward individual objects, are limitations of the universal will toward the good. How does it happen that the human will, so variously mistaking its fundamental direction toward God, attaches itself to perishable goods, and prefers worthless objects to those which have value, and earthly to heavenly pleasure? The soul is, on the one hand, united to God, on the other, united to the body. The possibility of error and sin rests on its union with the body, since with the ideas (as representations of the pure understanding) are associated sensuous images, which mingle with and becloud them, and passions with the inclinations (or the will of the soul, in so far as it is pure spirit). This gives, however, merely the possibility of the immoral, sensuous, God-estranged disposition, which becomes actual only through man's free act, when he fails to stand the test. For sin does not consist in having passions, but in consenting to them. The passion is not caused by the corporeal movement of which it is the sequel, but only occasioned by it; and the same is true of the movement of the limbs and the decision of the will. The one true cause of all that happens is God. It is he who produces affections in the soul, and motion in the material world. For the body possesses only the capacity of being moved; and the soul cannot be the cause of the movement, since it would then have to know how it produces the latter. In fact those who lack a medical training have no idea of the muscular and nervous processes involved. Without God we cannot even move the tongue. It is he who raises our arm, even when we use it contrary to his law.

Anxious to guard his pantheism from being identified with that of Spinoza, Malebranche points out that, according to his views, the universe is in God, not, as with Spinoza, that God is in the universe; that he teaches creation, which Spinoza denies; that he distinguishes, which Spinoza had not done, between the world in God (the ideas of things) and the world of created things, and between intelligible and corporeal extension. It may be added that he maintains the freedom of God and of man, which Spinoza rejects, and that he conceives God, who brings everything to pass, not as nature, but as omnipotent will. Nevertheless, as Kuno Fischer has shown, he approaches the naturalism of Spinoza more nearly than he is himself conscious, when he explains finite things as limitations (hence as modes) of the divine existence, posits the will of God in dependence on his wisdom (the uncreated world of ideas), thus limiting it in its omnipotence, and, which is decisive, makes God the sole author of motion, *i.e.*, a natural cause. His attempt at a Christian pantheism was consequently unsuccessful. But its failure has not shattered the well-grounded fame of its thoughtful author as the second greatest metaphysician of France.

Pierre Poiret[1] (1646-1719; for some years a preacher in Hamburg; lived later in Rhynsburg near Leyden) was rendered hostile to Cartesianism through the influence of mystical writings (among others those of Antoinette Bourignon, which he published), and through the perception of the results to which it had led in Spinoza. All cognition is taking up the form of the object. The perfection of man is based more on his passive capacities than on his active reason, which is concerned with mere ideas, unreal shadows; the mathematical spirit leads to fatalism, to the denial of freedom. The passive faculties, on the contrary, are in direct intercourse with reality, the senses with external material objects, and the arcanum of the mind, the basis of the soul, the intellect, with spiritual truths and with God, whose existence is more certain than our own. Man is not unconcerned in the development of the highest power of the mind, he must offer himself to God in sincere humility. In subordination to the passive intellect, the external faculty, the active reason, is also to be cultivated; it deserves care, like the skin. Evil consists in the absurdity that the creature, who apart from God is nothing, ascribes to himself an independent existence.

[Footnote 1: Poiret: *Cogitationes Rationates de Deo, Anima, et Malo*, 1677, the later editions including a vehement attack on the atheism of Spinoza: *L'Économie Divine*, 1682; *De Eruditione Solida, Superficiaria, et Falsa*, 1692; *Fides et Ratio Collatae*, against Locke, 1707.]

Le Vayer and Huet, who have been already mentioned (pp. 50-51), mediate between the founders of skepticism and Bayle, its most gifted representative. The latter of these two wrote a *Criticism of the Cartesian Philosophy*, 1689, besides a *Treatise on the Impotence of the Human Mind*, which did not appear until after his death. He opposes, among other things, the criterion of truth based on evidence, since there is an evidence of the false not to be distinguished from that of the true, as well as the position that God becomes a deceiver in the bestowal of a weak and blind reason—for he gives us, at the same time, the power to know its deceptive character.

As the last among those influenced by Descartes but who advanced beyond him, may be mentioned the acute Pierre Bayle (1647-1706; professor in Sedan and Rotterdam; *Works*, 1725-31[1]), who greatly excited the world of letters by his occasional and polemic treatises, and still more by the journal, *Nouvelles de la République des Lettres* from 1684, and his *Historical and Critical Dictionary*, in two volumes, 1695 and 1697. Nowhere do the most opposite antitheses dwell in such close proximity as in the mind of Bayle. Along with an ever watchful doubt he harbors a most active zeal for knowledge, with a sincere spirit of belief (which has been wrongly disputed by Lange, Zeller, and Pünjer) a demoniacal pleasure in bringing to light absurdities in the doctrines of faith, with absolute confidence in the infallibility of conscience an entirely pessimistic view of human morality. His strength lies in criticism and polemics, his work in the latter (aside from his hostility to fanaticism and the persecution of those differing in faith) being directed chiefly against optimism and the deistic religion of reason, which holds the Christian dogmas capable of proof, or, at least, faith and knowledge capable of reconciliation. The doctrines of faith are not only above reason, incomprehensible, but contrary to reason; and it is just on this that our merit in accepting them depends. The mysteries of the Gospel do not seek success before the judgment seat of thought, they demand the blind submission of the reason; nay, if they were objects of knowledge they would cease to be mysteries. Thus we must choose between religion and philosophy, for they cannot be combined. For one who is convinced of the untrustworthiness of the reason and her lack of competence in things supernatural, it is in no wise contradictory or impossible to receive as true things which she declares to be false; he will thank God for the gift of a faith which is entirely independent of the clearness of its objects and of its agreement with the axioms of philosophy. Even, when in purely scientific questions he calls attention to difficulties and shows contradictions on every hand, Bayle by no means intends to hold up principles with contradictory implications as false, but only as uncertain.[2] The reason, he says, generalizing from his own case, is capable only of destruction, not of construction; of discovering error, not of finding truth; of finding reasons and counter-reasons, of exciting doubt and controversy, not of vouchsafing certitude. So long as it contents itself with controverting that which is false, it is potent and salutary; but when, despising divine assistance, it advances beyond this, it becomes dangerous, like a caustic drug which attacks the healthy flesh after it has consumed that which was diseased.

[Footnote 1: Cf. on Bayle, L. Feuerbach. 1838, 2d ed., 1844; Eucken in the *Allgemeine Zeitung*, supplement to Nos. 251, 252, October 27, 28, 1891.]

[Footnote 2: Thus, in regard to the problem of freedom, he finds it hard to comprehend how the creatures, who are not the authors of their own existence, can be the authors of their own actions, but, at the same time, inadmissible to think of God as the cause of evil. He seeks only to show the indemonstrability and incomprehensibility of freedom, not to reject it. For he sees in it the condition of morality, and calls attention to the fact that the difficulties in which those who deny freedom involve themselves are far greater than those of their opponents. He shows himself entirely averse to the determinism and pantheism of Spinoza.]

He who seeks to refute skepticism must produce a criterion of truth. If such exists, it is certainly that advanced by Descartes, the evidence, the evident clearness of a principle. Well, then, the following principles pass for evident: That one, who does not exist, can have no responsibility for an evil action; that two things, which are identical with the same thing, are identical with each other; that I am the same man to-day that I was yesterday. Now, the revealed doctrines of original sin and of the Trinity show that the first and second of these axioms are false, and the Church doctrine of the preservation of the world as a continuous creation, that the last principle is uncertain. Thus if not even self-evidence furnishes us a criterion of truth, we must conclude that none whatever exists. Further, in regard to the origin of the world from a single principle, its creation by God, we find this supported, no doubt, both by the conclusions of the pure reason and by the consideration of nature, but controverned by the fact of evil, by the misery and wickedness of man. Is it conceivable that a holy and benevolent God has created so unhappy and wicked a being?

Bayle's motives in defending faith against reason were, on the one hand, his personal piety, on the other, his conviction of the unassailable purity of Christian ethics. All the sects agree in regard to moral principles, and it is this which assures us of the divinity of the Christian revelation. Nevertheless, he does not conceal from himself the fact that possession of the theoretical side of religion is far from being a guarantee of practice in conformity with her precepts. It is neither true that faith alone leads to morality nor that unbelief is the cause of immorality. A state composed of atheists would be not at all impossible, if only strict punishments and strict notions of honor were insisted upon.

The judgments of the natural reason in moral questions are as certain and free from error as its capacity is shown to be weak and limited in theoretical science. The idea of morality never deceives anyone; the moral law is innate in every man. Although Christianity has given the best development of our duties, yet the moral law can be understood and followed by all men, even by heathen and atheists. We do not need to be Christians in order to act virtuously; the knowledge given by conscience is not dependent upon revelation. From the knowledge of the good to the practice of it is, it is true, a long step; we may be convinced of moral truth without loving it, and God's grace alone is able to strengthen us against the power of the passions, by adding to the illumination of the mind an inclination of the heart toward the good.

Temperament, custom, self-love move the soul more strongly than general truths. As in life pleasure is far outbalanced by pain and vexation, so far more evil acts are done than good ones: history is a collection of misdeeds, with scarcely one virtuous act for a thousand crimes. It is not the external action that constitutes the ethical character of a deed, but the motive or disposition; almsgiving from motives of pride is a vice, and only when practiced out of love to one's neighbors, a virtue. God looks only at the act of the will; our highest duty, and one which admits of no exceptions, is never to act contrary to conscience.

CHAPTER IV.

LOCKE.

After the Cartesian philosophy had given decisive expression to the tendencies of modern thought, and had been developed through occasionalism to its completion in the system of Spinoza, the line of further progress consisted in two factors: Descartes's principles—one-sidedly rationalistic and abstractly scientific, as they were—were, on the one hand, to be supplemented by the addition of the empirical element which Descartes had neglected, and, on the other, to be made available for general culture by approximation to the interests of practical life. England, with its freer and happier political conditions, was the best place for the accomplishment of both ends, and Locke, a typically healthy and sober English thinker, with a distaste for extreme views, the best adapted mind. Descartes, the rationalist, had despised experience, and Bacon, the empiricist, had despised mathematics; but Locke aims to show that while the reason is the instrument of science, demonstration its form, and the realm of knowledge wider than experience, yet this instrument and this form are dependent for their content on a supply of material from the senses. The emphasis, it is true, falls chiefly on the latter half of this programme, and posterity, especially, has almost exclusively attended to the empirical side of Locke's theory of knowledge in giving judgment concerning it.

John Locke was born at Wrington, not far from Bristol, in 1632. At Oxford he busied himself with philosophy, natural science, and medicine, being repelled by the Scholastic thinkers, but strongly attracted by the writings of Descartes. In 1665 he became secretary to the English ambassador to the Court of Brandenburg. Returning thence to Oxford he made the acquaintance of Lord Anthony Ashley (from 1672 Earl of Shaftesbury; died in Holland 1683), who received him into his own household as a friend, physician, and tutor to his son (the father of Shaftesbury, the moral philosopher), and with whose varying fortunes Locke's own were henceforth to be intimately connected. Twice he became secretary to his patron (once in 1667—with an official secretaryship in 1672, when Shaftesbury became Lord Chancellor—and again in 1679, when he became President of the Council), but both times he lost his post on his friend's fall. The years 1675-79 were spent in Montpellier and Paris. In 1683 he went into voluntary exile in Holland (where Shaftesbury had died in January of the same year), and remained there until 1689, when the ascension of the throne by William of Orange made it possible for him to return to England. Here he was made Commissioner of Appeals, and, subsequently, one of the Commissioners of Trade and Plantations (till 1700). He died in 1704 at Gates, in Essex, at the house of Sir Francis Masham, whose wife was the daughter of Cudworth, the philosopher.

Locke's chief work, *An Essay concerning Human Understanding*, which had been planned as early as 1670, was published in 1689-90, a short abstract of it having previously appeared in French in Le Clerc's *Bibliothèque Universelle*, 1688. His theoretical works include, further, the two posthumous treatises, *On the Conduct of the Understanding* (originally intended for incorporation in the fourth edition of the *Essay*, which, however, appeared in 1700 without this chapter, which probably had proved too extended) and the *Elements of Natural Philosophy*. To political and politico-economic questions Locke contributed the two *Treatises on Government*, 1690, and three essays on money and the coinage. In the year 1689 appeared the first of three *Letters on Tolerance*, followed, in 1693, by *Some Thoughts on Education*, and, in 1695, by *The Reasonableness of Christianity as delivered in the Scriptures*. The collected works appeared for the first time in 1714, and in nine volumes in 1853; the philosophical works (edited by St. John) are given in Bonn's Standard Library (1867-68).[1]

[Footnote 1: Lord King and Fox Bourne have written on Locke's life, 1829 and 1876. A comparison of Locke's theory of knowledge with Leibnitz's critique was published by Hartenstein in 1865, and one by Von Benoit (prize dissertation) in 1869, and an exposition of his theory of substance by De Fries in 1879. Victor Cousin's *Philosophie de Locke* has passed through six editions. [Among more recent English discussions reference may be made to Green's Introduction to Hume's *Treatise on Human Nature*, 1874 (new ed. 1890), which is a valuable critique of the line of development, Locke, Berkeley, Hume; Fowler's *Locke*, in the English Men of Letters, 1880; and Fraser's *Locke*, in Blackwood's Philosophical Classics, 1890.—TR.]]

%(a) Theory of Knowledge.%—Locke's theory of knowledge is controlled by two tendencies, one native, furnished by the Baconian empiricism, and the other Continental, supplied by the Cartesian question concerning the origin of ideas. Bacon had demanded the closest connection with experience as the condition of fruitful inquiry. Locke supports this commendation of experience by a detailed description of the services which it renders to cognition, namely, by showing that, in simple ideas, perception supplies the material for complex ideas, and for all the cognitive work of the understanding. Descartes had divided ideas, according to their origin, into three classes: those which are self-formed, those which come from without, and those which are innate (p. 79), and had called this third class the most valuable. Locke disputes the existence of ideas in the understanding from birth, and makes it receive the elements of knowledge from the senses, that is, from without. He is a representative of sensationalism,—not in the stricter sense, first put into the term by those who subsequently continued his endeavors, that thought arises from perception, that it is transformed sensation—but in the wider sense, that thought is (free) operation with ideas, which are neither created by it nor present in it from the first, but given to it by perception, that, consequently, the cognitive process begins with sensation and so its first attitude is a passive one. From the standpoint of the Cartesian problem, which he solves in a sense opposite to Descartes, Locke supplements the empiricism of Bacon by basing it on a psychologically developed theory of knowledge. That in the course of the inquiry he introduces a new principle, which causes him to diverge from the true empirical path, will appear in the sequel.

The question "How our ideas come into the mind" receives a negative answer (in the first book of the *Essay*): "There are no innate principles in the mind"[1] The doctrine of the innate character of certain principles is based on their universal acceptance. The asserted agreement of mankind in regard to the laws of thought, the principles of morality, the existence of God, etc., is neither cogent as an argument nor correct in fact. In the first place, even if there were any principles which everyone assented to, this would not prove that they had been created in the soul; the fact of general consent would admit of a different explanation. Granted that no atheists existed, yet it would not necessarily follow that the universal conviction of the existence of God is innate, for it might have been gradually reached in each case through the use of the reason—might have been inferred, for instance, from the perception of the purposive character of the world. Second, the fact to which this theory of innate ideas appeals is not true. No moral rule can be cited which is respected by all nations. The idea of identity is entirely unknown to idiots and to children. If the laws of identity and contradiction were innate they must appear in consciousness prior to all other truths; but long before a child is conscious of the proposition "It is impossible for the same thing to be and not to be," it knows that sweet is not bitter, and that black is not white. The ideas first known are not general axioms and abstract concepts, but particular impressions of the senses. Would nature write so illegible a hand that the mind must wait a long time before becoming able to read what had been inscribed upon it? It is often said, however, that innate ideas and principles may be obscured and, finally, completely extinguished by habit, education, and other extrinsic circumstances. Then, if they gradually become corrupted and disappear, they must at least be discoverable in full purity where these disturbing influences have not yet acted; but it is especially vain to look for them in children and the ignorant. Perhaps, however, these possess such principles unconsciously; perhaps they are imprinted on the understanding, without being attended to? This would be a contradiction in terms. To be in the mind or the understanding simply means "to be understood" or to be known; no one can have an idea without being conscious of it. Finally, if the attempt be made to explain "originally in the mind" in so wide a sense that it would include all truths which man can ever attain or is capable of discovering by the right use of reason, this would make not only all mathematical principles, but all knowledge in general, all sciences, and all arts innate; there would be no ground even for the exclusion of wisdom and virtue. Therefore, either all ideas are innate or none are. This is an important alternative. While Locke decides for the second half of the proposition, Leibnitz defends the first by a delicate application of the concept of unconscious representation and of implicit knowledge, which his predecessor rejects out of hand.

[Footnote 1: According to Fox Bourne this first book was written after the others. Geil *(Ueber die Abhängigkeit Lockes von Descartes*, Strassburg, 1887, chap. iii.) has endeavored to prove that, since the arguments controverted are wanting in Descartes, the attack was not aimed at Descartes and his school, but at native defenders of innate ideas, as Lord Herbert of Cherbury and the English Platonists (Cudworth, More, Parker, Gale). That along with these the Cartesian doctrine was a second and chief object of attack is shown by Benno Erdmann in his discussion of the treatises by G. Geil and R. Sommer *(Lockes Verhältnis zu Descartes*, Berlin, 1887) in the *Archiv für Geschichte der Philosophie*, ii, pp. 99-121.]

Locke's positive answer to the question concerning the origin of ideas is given in his second book. Ideas are not present in the understanding from the beginning, nor are they originated by the understanding, but received through sensation. The understanding is like a piece of white paper on which perception inscribes its characters. All knowledge arises in experience. This is of two kinds, derived either from the external senses or the internal sense. The perception of external objects is termed Sensation, that of internal phenomena (of the states of the mind itself) Reflection. External and internal perception are the only windows through which the light of ideas penetrates into the dark chamber of the understanding. The two are not opened simultaneously, however, but one after the other; since the perceptions of the sensible qualities of bodies, unlike that of the operations of the mind itself, do not require an effort of attention, they are the earlier. The child receives ideas of sensation before those of reflection; internal perception presupposes external perception.

In this distinction between sensation and reflection, we may recognize an after-effect of the Cartesian dualism between matter and spirit. The antithesis of substances has become a duality in the faculties of perception. But while Descartes had so far forth ascribed precedence to the mind in that he held the self-certitude of the ego to be the highest and clearest of all truths and the soul to be better known than the body, in Locke the relation of the two was reversed, since he made the perception of self dependent on the precedent perception of external objects. This antithesis was made still sharper in later thinking, when Condillac made full use of the priority of sensation, which in Locke had remained without much effect; while Berkeley, on the other hand, reduced external perception to internal perception.

All original ideas are representations either of the external senses or of the internal sense, or of both. And since, in the case of ideas of sensation, there is a distinction between those which are perceived by a single one of the external senses and those which come from more than one, four classes of simple ideas result: (1) Those which come from one external sense, as colors, sounds, tastes, odors, heat, solidity, and the like. (2) Those which come from more than one external sense (sight and touch), as extension, figure, and motion. (3) Reflection on the operations of our minds yields ideas of perception or thinking (with its various modes, remembrance, judging, knowledge, faith, etc.), and of volition or willing. (4) From both external and internal perception there come into the mind the ideas of pleasure and pain, existence, power, unity, and succession. These are approximately our original ideas, which are related to knowledge as the letters to written discourse; as all Homer is composed out of only twenty-four letters, so these few simple ideas constitute all the material of knowledge. The mind can neither have more nor other simple ideas than those which are furnished to it by these two sources of experience.

Locke differs from Descartes again in regard to extension and thought. Extension does not constitute the essence of matter, nor thought the essence of mind. Extension and body are not the same; the former is presupposed by the latter as its necessary condition, but it is the former alone which yields mathematical matter. The essence of physical matter consists rather in solidity: where impenetrability is found there is body, and the converse; the two are absolutely inseparable. With space the case is different. I cannot conceive unextended matter, indeed, but I can easily conceive immaterial extension, an unfilled space Further, if the essence of the soul consisted in thought, it must be always thinking. As the Cartesians maintained, it must have ideas as soon as it begins to be, which is manifestly contrary to experience. Thinking is merely an activity of the mind, as motion is an activity of the body, and not its essential characteristic. The mind does not receive ideas until external objects occasion perception in it through impressions, which it is not able to avert. The understanding may be compared to a mirror, which, without independent activity and without being consulted, takes up the images of things. Some of the simple ideas which have been mentioned above represent the properties of things as they really are, others not. The former class includes all ideas of reflection (for we are ourselves the immediate object of the inner sense); but among the ideas of sensation those only which come from different senses, hence extension, motion and rest, number, figure, and, further, solidity, are to be accounted *primary* qualities, *i. e.*, such as are actual copies of the properties of bodies. All other ideas, on the contrary, have no resemblance to properties of bodies; they represent merely the ways in which things act, and are not copies of things. The ideas of *secondary* or derivative qualities (hard and soft, warm and cold, colors and sounds, tastes and odors) are in the last analysis caused—as are the primary—by motion, but not perceived as such. Yellow and warm are merely sensations in us, which we erroneously ascribe to objects; with equal right we might ascribe to fire, as qualities inherent in it, the changes in form and color which it produces in wax and the pain which it causes in the finger brought into proximity with it. The warmth and the brightness of the blaze, the redness, the pleasant taste, and the aromatic odor of the strawberry, exist in these bodies merely as the power to produce such sensations in us by stimulation of the skin, the eye, the palate, and the nose. If we remove the perceptions of them, they disappear as such, and their causes alone remain—the bulk, figure, number, texture, and motion of the insensible particles. The ground of the illusion lies in the fact that such qualities as color, etc., bear no resemblance to their causes, in no wise point to these, and in themselves contain naught of bulk, density, figure, and motion, and that our senses are too weak to discover the material particles and their primary qualities.—The distinction between qualities of the first and second order—first advanced by the ancient atomists, revived by Galileo and Descartes on the threshold of the modern period, retained by Locke, and still customary in the natural science of the day—forms an important link in the transition from the popular view of all sense-qualities as properties of things in themselves to Kant's position, that spatial and temporal qualities also belong to phenomena alone, and are based merely on man's subjective mode of apprehension, while the real properties of things in themselves are unknowable.

Thus far the procedure of the understanding has been purely passive. But besides the capacity for passively receiving simple ideas, it possesses the further power of variously combining and extending these original ideas which have come into it from without, of working over the material given in sensation by the combination, relation, and separation of its various elements. In this it is active, but not creative. It is not able to form new simple ideas (and just as little to destroy such as already exist), but only freely to combine the elements furnished without its assistance by perception (or, following the figure mentioned above, to combine into syllables and words the separate letters of sensation). Complex ideas arise from simple ideas through voluntary combination of the latter.

Perception is the first step toward knowledge. After perception the most indispensable faculty is retention, the prolonged consciousness of present ideas and the revival of those which have disappeared, or, as it were, have been put aside. For an idea to be "in the memory" means that the mind has the capacity to reproduce it at will, whereupon it recognizes it as previously experienced. If our ideas are not freshened up from time to time by new impressions of the same sort they gradually fade out, until finally (as the idea of color in one become blind in early life) they completely disappear. Ideas impressed upon the mind by frequent repetition are rarely entirely lost. Memory is the basis for the intellectual functions of discernment and comparison, of composition, abstraction, and naming. Since, amid the innumerable multitude of ideas, it is not possible to assign to each one a definite sign, the indispensable condition of language is found in the power of abstraction, that is, in the power of generalizing ideas, of compounding many ideas into one, and of indicating by the names of the general ideas, or of the classes and species, the particular ideas also which are contained under these. Here is the great distinction between man and the brute. The brute lacks language because he lacks (not all understanding whatever, *e.g.*, not a capacity, though an imperfect one, of comparison and composition, but) the faculty of abstraction and of forming general ideas. The object of language is simply the quick and easy communication of our thoughts to others, not to give expression to the real essence of objects. Words are not names for particular things, but signs of general ideas; and *abstracta* nothing more than an artifice for facilitating intellectual intercourse. This abbreviation, which aids in the exchange of ideas, involves the danger that the creations of the mind denoted by words will be taken for images of real general essences, of which, in fact, there are none in existence, but only particular things. In order to prevent anyone to whom I am speaking from understanding my words in a different sense from the one intended, it is necessary for me to define the complex ideas by analyzing them into their elements, and, on the other hand, to give examples in experience of the simple ideas, which do not admit of definition, or to explain them by synonyms. Thus much from Locke's philosophy of language, to which he devotes the third book of the *Essay*.

Complex ideas, which are very numerous, may be divided into three classes:
Modes, Substances, and Relations.

Modes (states, conditions) are such combinations of simple ideas which do not "contain in them the supposition of subsisting by themselves, but are considered as dependencies on, or affections of substances." They fall into two classes according as they are composed of the same simple ideas, or simple ideas of various kinds; the former are called simple, the latter mixed, modes. Under the former class belong, for example, a dozen or a score, the idea of which is composed of simple units; under the latter, running, fighting, obstinacy, printing, theft, parricide. The formation of *mixed* modes is greatly influenced by national customs. Very complicated transactions (sacrilege, triumph, ostracism), if often considered and discussed, receive for the sake of brevity comprehensive names, which cannot be rendered by a single expression in the language of other nations among whom the custom in question is not found. The elements most frequently employed in the formation of mixed modes are ideas of the two fundamental activities, thinking and motion, together with power, which is their source. Locke discusses *simple* modes in more detail, especially those derived from the ideas of space, time, unity, and power. Modifications of space are distance, figure, place, length; since any length or measure of space can be repeated to infinity, we reach the idea of immensity. As modes of time are enumerated succession (which we perceive and measure only by the flow of our ideas), duration, and lengths or measures of duration, the endless repetition of which yields the idea of eternity. From unity are developed the modes of numbers, and from the unlimitedness of these the idea of infinity. No idea, however, is richer in modes than the idea of power. A distinction must be made between active power and passive power, or mere receptivity. While bodies are not capable of originating motion, but only of communicating motion received, we notice in ourselves, as spiritual beings, the capacity of originating actions and motions. The body possesses only the passive power of being moved, the mind the active power of producing motion. This latter is termed "will." Here Locke discusses at length the freedom of the will, but not with entire clearness and freedom from contradictions (cf. below).

Modes are conditions which do not subsist of themselves, but have need of a basis or support; they are not conceivable apart from a thing whose properties or states they are. We notice that certain qualities always appear together, and habitually refer them to a substratum as the ground of their unity; in which they subsist or from which they proceed. *Substance* denotes this self-existent "we know not what," which has or bears the attributes in itself, and which arouses the ideas of them in us. It is the combination of a number of simple ideas which are presumed to belong to one thing. From the ideas of sensation the understanding composes the idea of body, and from the ideas of reflection that of mind. Each of these is just as clear and just as obscure as the other; of each we know only its effects and its sensuous properties; its essence is for us entirely unknowable. Instead of the customary names, material and immaterial substances, Locke recommends cogitative and incogitative substances, since it is not inconceivable that the Creator may have endowed some material beings with the capacity of thought. God,—the idea of whom is attained by uniting the ideas of existence, power, might, knowledge, and happiness with that of infinity,—is absolutely immaterial, because not passive, while finite spirits (which are both active and passive) are perhaps only bodies which possess the power of thinking.

While the ideas of substances are referred to a reality without the mind as their archetype, to which they are to conform and which they should image and represent, *Relations* (*e.g.*, husband, greater) are free and immanent products of the understanding. They are not copies of real things, but represent themselves alone, are their own archetypes. We do not ask whether they agree with things, but, conversely, whether things agree with them (Book iv. 4.5). The mind reaches an idea of relation by placing two things side by side and comparing them. If it perceives that a thing, or a quality, or an idea begins to exist through the operation of some other thing, it derives from this the idea of the causal relation, which is the most comprehensive of all relations, since all that is actual or possible can be brought under it. *Cause* is that which makes another thing to begin to be; *effect*, that which had its beginning from some other thing. The production of a new quality is termed alteration; of artificial things, making; of a living being, generation; of a new particle of matter, creation. Next in importance is the relation of *identity and diversity*. Since it is impossible for a thing to be in two different places at the same time and for two things to be at the same time in the same place, everything that at a given instant is in a given place is identical with itself, and, on the other hand, distinct from everything else (no matter how great the resemblance between them) that at the same moment exists in another place. Space and time therefore form the *principium individuationis*. By what marks, however, may we recognize the identity of an individual at different times and in different places? The identity of inorganic matter depends on the continuity of the mass of atoms which compose it; that of living beings upon the permanent organization of their parts (different bodies are united into *one* animal by a common life); personal identity consists in the unity of self-consciousness, not in the continuity of bodily existence (which is at once excluded by the change of matter). The identity of the person or the ego must be carefully distinguished from that of substance and of man. It would not be impossible for the person to remain the same in a change of substances, in so far as the different beings (for instance, the souls of Epicurus and Gassendi) participated in the same self-consciousness; and, conversely, for a spirit to appear in two persons by losing the consciousness of its previous existence. Consciousness is the sole condition of the self, or personal identity.—The determinations of space and time are for the most part relations. Our answers to the questions "When?" "How long?" "How large?" denote the distance of one point of time from another (*e.g.*, the birth of Christ), the relation of one duration to another (of a revolution of the sun), the relation of one extension to another well-known one taken as a standard. Many apparently positive ideas and words, as young and old, large and small, weak and strong, are in fact relative. They imply merely the relation of a given duration of life, of a given size and strength, to that which has been adopted as a standard for the class of things in question. A man of twenty is called young, but a horse of like age, old; and neither of these measures of time applies to stars or diamonds. Moral relations, which are based on a comparison of man's voluntary actions with one of the three moral laws, will be discussed below.

The inquiry now turns from the origin of ideas to their *cognitive value* or their *validity*, beginning (in the concluding chapters of the second book) with the accuracy of single ideas, and advancing (in Book iv., which is the most important in the whole work) to the truth of judgments. An idea is real when it conforms to its archetype, whether this is a thing, real or possible, or an idea of some other thing; it is adequate when the conformity is complete. The idea of a four-sided triangle or of brave cowardice is unreal or fantastical, since it is composed of incompatible elements, and the idea of a centaur, since it unites simple ideas in a way in which they do not occur in nature. The layman's ideas of law or of chemical substances are real, but inadequate, since they have a general resemblance to those of experts, and a basis in reality, but yet only imperfectly represent their archetypes. Nay, further, our ideas of substances are all inadequate, not only when they are taken for representations of the inner essences of things (since we do not know these essences), but also when they are considered merely as collections of qualities. The copy never includes all the qualities of the thing, the less so since the majority of these are powers, *i.e.*, consist in relations to other objects, and since it is impossible, even in the case of a single body, to discover all the changes which it is fitted to impart to, or to receive from, other substances. Ideas of modes and relations are all adequate, for they are their own archetypes, are not intended to represent anything other than themselves, are images without originals. An idea of this kind, however, though perfect when originally formed, may become imperfect through the use of language, when it is unsuccessfully intended to agree with the idea of some other person and denominated by a current term. In the case of mixed modes and their names, therefore, the compatibility of their elements and the possible existence of their objects are not enough to secure their reality and their complete adequacy; in order to be adequate they must, further, exactly conform to the meaning connected with their names by their author, or in common use. Simple ideas are best off, according to Locke, in regard both to reality and to adequacy. For the most part, it is true, they are not accurate copies of the real qualities of things, but only the regular effects of the powers of things. But although real qualities are thus only the causes and not the patterns of sensations, still simple ideas, by their constant correspondence with real qualities, sufficiently fulfill their divinely ordained end, to serve us as instruments of knowledge, *i.e.*, in the discrimination of things.—An unreal and inadequate idea becomes false only when it is referred to an object, whether this be the existence of a thing, or its true essence, or an idea of other things. Truth and error belong always to affirmations or negations, that is, to (it may be, tacit) propositions. Ideas uncombined, unrelated, apart from judgments, ideas, that is, as mere phenomena in the mind, are neither true nor false.

Knowledge is defined as the "perception of the connexion and agreement, or disagreement and repugnancy" of two ideas; truth, as "the right joining or separating of signs, *i.e.*, ideas or words." The object of knowledge is neither single ideas nor the relations of ideas to things, but the *relations of ideas among themselves*. This view was at once paradoxical and pregnant. If all cognition, as Locke suggests in objection to his own theory, consists in perceiving the agreement or disagreement of our ideas, are not the visions of the enthusiast and the reasonings of sober thinkers alike certain? are not the propositions, A fairy is not a centaur, and a centaur is a living being, just as true as that a circle is not a triangle, and that the sum of the angles of a triangle is equal to two right angles? The mind directly perceives nothing but its own ideas, but it seeks a knowledge of things! If this is possible it can only be indirect knowledge—the mind knows things through its ideas, and possesses criteria which show that its ideas agree with things.

Two cases must be clearly distinguished, for a considerable number of our ideas, viz., all complex ideas except those of substances, make no claim to represent things, and consequently cannot represent them falsely. For mathematical and moral ideas and principles, and the truth thereof, it is entirely immaterial whether things and conditions correspondent to them exist in nature or not. They are valid, even if nowhere actualized; they are "eternal truths," not in the sense that they are known from childhood, but in the sense that, as soon as known, they are immediately assented to.[1] The case is different, however, with simple ideas and the ideas of substances, which have their originals without the mind and which are to correspond with these. In regard to the former we may always be certain that they agree with real things, for since the mind can neither voluntarily originate them (*e.g.*, cannot produce sensations of color in the dark) nor avoid having them at will, but only receive them from without, they are not creatures of the fancy, but the natural and regular productions of external things affecting us. In regard to the latter, the ideas of substances, we may be certain at least when the simple ideas which compose them have been found so connected in experience. Perception has an external cause, whose influence the mind is not able to withstand. The mutual corroboration furnished by the reports of the different senses, the painfulness of certain sensations, the clear distinction between ideas from actual perception and those from memory, the possibility of producing and predicting new sensations of an entirely definite nature in ourselves and in others, by means of changes which we effect in the external world (e.g. by writing down a word)—these give further justification for the trust which we put in the senses. No one will be so skeptical as to doubt in earnest the existence of the things which he sees and touches, and to declare his whole life to be a deceptive dream. The certitude which perception affords concerning the existence of external objects is indeed not an absolute one, but it is sufficient for the needs of life and the government of our actions; it is "as certain as our happiness or misery, beyond which we have no concernment, either of knowing or being." In regard to the past the testimony of the senses is supplemented by memory, in which certainty [in regard to the continued existence of things previously perceived] is transformed into high probability; while in regard to the existence of other finite spirits, numberless kinds of which may be conjectured to exist, though their existence is quite beyond our powers of perception, certitude sinks into mere (though well-grounded) faith.

[Footnote 1: Thus it results that knowledge, although dependent on experience for all its materials, extends beyond experience. The understanding is completely bound in the reception of simple ideas; less so in the combination of these into complex ideas; absolutely free in the act of comparison, which it can omit at will; finally, again, completely bound in its recognition of the relation in which the ideas it has chosen to compare stand to one another. There is room for choice only in the intermediate stage of the cognitive process; at the beginning (in the reception of the simple ideas of perception, a, b, c, d), and at the end (in judging how the concepts a b c and a b d stand related to each other), the understanding is completely determined.]

More certain than our *sensitive* knowledge of the existence of external objects, are our immediate or *intuitive* knowledge of our own existence and our mediate or *demonstrative* knowledge of the existence of God. Every idea that we have, every pain, every thought assures us of our own existence. The existence of God, however, as the infinite cause of all reality, endowed with intelligence, will, and supreme power, is inferred from the existence and constitution of the world and of ourselves. Reality exists; the real world is composed of matter in motion and thinking beings, and is harmoniously ordered. Since it is impossible for any real being to be produced by nothing, and since we obtain no satisfactory answer to the question of origin until we rise to something existent from all eternity, we must assume as the cause of that which exists an Eternal Being, which possesses in a higher degree all the perfections which it has bestowed upon the creatures. As the cause of matter and motion, and as the source of all power, this Being must be omnipotent; as the cause of beauty and order in the world, and, above all, as the creator of thinking beings, it must be omniscient. But these perfections are those which we combine in the idea of God.

Intuitive knowledge is the highest of the three degrees of knowledge. It is gained when the mind perceives the agreement or disagreement of two ideas at first sight, without hesitation, and without the intervention of any third idea. This immediate knowledge is self-evident, irresistible, and exposed to no doubt. Knowledge is demonstrative when the mind perceives the agreement (or disagreement) of two ideas, not by placing them side by side and comparing them, but through the aid of other ideas. The intermediate links are called proofs; their discovery is the work of the reason, and quickness in finding them out is termed sagacity. The greater the number of the intermediate steps, the more the clearness and distinctness of the knowledge decreases, and the more the possibility of error increases. In order for an argument (*e. g.*, that a = d) to be conclusive, every particular step in it (a = b, b = c, c = d) must possess intuitive certainty. Mathematics is not the only example of demonstrative knowledge, but the most perfect one, since in mathematics, by the aid of visible symbols, the full equality and the least differences among ideas may be exactly measured and sharply determined.

Besides real existence Locke, unsystematically enough, enumerates three other sorts of agreement between ideas,—in the perception of which he makes knowledge consist,—viz., identity or diversity (blue is not yellow), relation (when equals are added to equals the results are equal), and coexistence or necessary connexion (gold is fixed). We are best off in regard to the knowledge of the first of these, "identity or diversity," for here our intuition extends as far as our ideas, since we recognize every idea, as soon as it arises, as identical with itself and different from others. We are worst off in regard to "necessary connexion." We know something, indeed, concerning the incompatibility or coexistence of certain properties (*e. g.*, that the same object cannot have two different sizes or colors at the same time; that figure cannot exist apart from extension): but it is only in regard to a few qualities and powers of bodies that we are able to discover dependence and necessary connexion by intuitive or demonstrative thought, while in most cases we are dependent on experience, which gives us information concerning particular cases only, and affords no guarantee that things are the same beyond the sphere of our observation and experiment. Since empirical inquiry furnishes no certain and universal knowledge, and since the assumption that like bodies will in the same circumstances have like effects is only a conjecture from analogy, natural science in the strict sense does not exist. Both mathematics and ethics, however, belong in the sphere of the demonstrative knowledge of relations. The principles of ethics are as capable of exact demonstration as those of arithmetic and geometry, although their underlying ideas are more complex, more involved, hence more exposed to misunderstanding, and lacking in visible symbols; though these defects can, and should, in part be made good by careful and strictly consistent definitions. Such moral principles as "where there is no property there is no injustice," or "no government allows absolute liberty," are as certain as any proposition in Euclid.

The advantage of the mathematical and moral sciences over the physical sciences consists in the fact that, in the former, the real and nominal essences of their objects coincide, while in the latter they do not; and, further, that the real essences of substances are beyond our knowledge. The true inner constitution of bodies, the root whence all their qualities, and the coexistence of these, necessarily proceed, is completely unknown to us; so that we are unable to deduce them from it. Mathematical and moral ideas, on the other hand, and their relations, are entirely accessible, for they are the products of our own voluntary operations. They are not copied from things, but are archetypal for reality and need no confirmation from experience. The connexion constituted by our understanding between the ideas crime and punishment *(e. g.*, the proposition: crime deserves punishment) is valid, even though no crime had ever been committed, and none ever punished. Existence is not at all involved in universal propositions; "general knowledge lies only in our own thoughts, and consists barely in the contemplation of our own abstract ideas" and their relations. The truths of mathematics and ethics are both universal and certain, while in natural science single observations and experiments are certain, but not general, and general propositions are only more or less probable. Both the particular experiments and the general conclusions are of great value under certain circumstances, but they do not meet the requirements of comprehensive and certain knowledge.

The *extent* of our knowledge is very limited—much less, in fact, than that of our ignorance. For our knowledge reaches no further than our ideas, and the possibility of perceiving their agreements. Many things exist of which we have no ideas—chiefly because of the fewness of our senses and their lack of acuteness—and just as many of which our ideas are only imperfect. Moreover, we are often able neither to command the ideas which we really possess, or at least might attain, nor to perceive their connexions. The ideas which are lacking, those which are undiscoverable, those which are not combined, are the causes of the narrow limits of human knowledge.

There are two ways by which knowledge may be extended: by experience, on the one hand, and, on the other, by the elevation of our ideas to a state of clearness and distinctness, together with the discovery and systematic arrangement of those intermediate ideas which exhibit the relation of other ideas, in themselves not immediately comparable. The syllogism, as an artificial form, is of little value in the perception of the agreements between these intermediate and final terms, and of none whatever in the discovery of the former. Analytical and identical propositions which merely explicate the conception of the subject, but express nothing not already known, are, in spite of their indefeasible certitude, valueless for the extension of knowledge, and when taken for more than verbal explanations, mere absurdities. Even those most general propositions, those "principles" which are so much talked of in the schools, lack the utility which is so commonly ascribed to them. Maxims are, it is true, fit instruments for the communication of knowledge already acquired, and in learned disputations may perform indispensable service in silencing opponents, or in bringing the dispute to a conclusion; but they are of little or no use in the discovery of new truth. It is a mistake to believe that special cases (as $5 = 2 + 3$, or $5 = 1 + 4$) are dependent on the truth of the abstract rule (the whole is equal to the sum of its parts), that they are confirmed by it and must be derived from it. The particular and concrete is not only as clear and certain as the general maxim, but better known than this, as well as earlier and more easily perceived. Nay, further, in cases where ideas are confused and the meanings of words doubtful, the use of axioms is dangerous, since they may easily lend the appearance of proved truth to assertions which are really contradictory.

Between the clear daylight of certain knowledge and the dark night of absolute ignorance comes the twilight of probability. We find ourselves dependent on *opinion* and presumption, or judgment based upon probability, when experience and demonstration leave us in the lurch and we are, nevertheless, challenged to a decision by vital needs which brook no delay. The judge and the historian must convince themselves from the reports of witnesses concerning events which they have not themselves observed; and everyone is compelled by the interests of life, of duty, and of eternal salvation to form conclusions concerning things which lie beyond the limits of his own perception and reflective thought, nay, which transcend all human experience and rigorous demonstration whatever. To delay decision and action until absolute certainty had been attained, would scarcely allow us to lift a single finger. In cases concerning events in the past, the future, or at a distance, we rely on the testimony of others (testing their reports by considering their credibility as witnesses and the conformity of the evidence to general experience in like cases); in regard to questions concerning that which is absolutely beyond experience, *e.g.*, higher orders of spirits, or the ultimate causes of natural phenomena, analogy is the only help we have. If the witnesses conflict among themselves, or with the usual course of nature, the grounds *pro* and *con* must be carefully balanced; frequently, however, the degree of probability attained is so great that our assent is almost equivalent to complete certainty. No one doubts,—although it is impossible for him to "know,"—that Caesar conquered Pompey, that gold is ductile in Australia as elsewhere, that iron will sink to-morrow as well as to-day. Thus opinion supplements the lack of certain knowledge, and serves as a guide for belief and action, wherever the general lot of mankind or individual circumstances prevent absolute certitude.

Although in this twilight region of opinion demonstrative proofs are replaced merely by an "occasion" for "taking" a given fact or idea "as true rather than false," yet assent is by no means an act of choice, as the Cartesians had erroneously maintained, for in knowledge it is determined by clearly discerned reasons, and in the sphere of opinion, by the balance of probability. The understanding is free only in combining ideas, not in its judgment concerning the agreement or the repugnancy of the ideas compared; it lies within its own power to decide whether it will judge at all, and what ideas it will compare, but it has no control over the result of the comparison; it is impossible for it to refuse its assent to a demonstrated truth or a preponderant probability.

In this recognition of objective and universally valid relations existing among ideas, which the thinking subject, through comparisons voluntarily instituted, discovers valid or finds given, but which it can neither alter nor demur to, Locke abandons empirical ground (cf. p. 155) and approaches the idealists of the Platonizing type. His inquiry divides into two very dissimilar parts (a psychological description of the origin of ideas and a logical determination of the possibility and the extent of knowledge), the latter of which is, in Locke's opinion, compatible with the former, but which could never have been developed from it. The rationalistic edifice contradicts the sensationalistic foundation. Locke had hoped to show the value and the limits of knowledge by an inquiry into the origin of ideas, but his estimate of this value and these limits cannot be proved from the *a posteriori* origin of ideas—it can only be maintained in despite of this, and stands in need of support from some (rationalistic) principle elsewhere obtained. Thinkers who trace back all simple ideas to outer and inner perception we expect to reject every attempt to extend knowledge beyond the sphere of experience, to declare the combinations of ideas which have their origin in sensation trustworthy, and those which are formed without regard to perception, illusory; or else, with Protagoras, to limit knowledge to the individual perceiving subject, with a consequent complete denial of its general validity. But exactly the opposite of all these is found in Locke. The remarkable spectacle is presented of a philosopher who admits no other sources of ideas than perception and the voluntary combination of perceptions, transcending the limits of experience with proofs of the divine existence, viewing with suspicion the ideas of substance formed at the instance of experience, and reducing natural science to the sphere of mere opinion; while, on the other hand, he ascribes reality and eternal validity to the combinations of ideas formed independently of perception, which are employed by mathematics and ethics, and completely abandons the individualistic position in his naïve faith in the impregnable validity of the relations of ideas, which is evident to all who turn their attention to them. The ground for the universal validity of the relations among ideas as well as of our knowledge of them, naturally lies not in their empirical origin (for my experience gives information to me alone, and that only concerning the particular case in question), but in the uniformity of man's rational constitution. If two men really have the same ideas—not merely think they have because they use similar language—it is impossible, according to Locke, that they should hold different opinions concerning the relation of their ideas. With this conviction, that the universal validity of knowledge is rooted in the uniformity of man's rational constitution, and the further one, that we attain certain knowledge only when things conform to our ideas, Locke closely approaches Kant; while his assumption of a fixed order of relations among ideas, which the individual understanding cannot refuse to recognize, and the typical character assigned to mathematics, associate him with Malebranche and Spinoza. In view of these points of contact with the rationalistic school and his manifold dependence on its founder, we may venture the paradox, that Locke may not only be termed a Baconian with Cartesian leanings, but (almost) a Cartesian influenced by Bacon. The possibility must not be forgotten, however, that rationalistic suggestions came to him also from Galileo, Hobbes, and Newton.[1]

[Footnote 1: Cf. the article by Benno Erdmann cited p. 156, note.]

Intermediate between knowledge and opinion stands faith as a form of assent which is based on testimony rather than on deductions of the reason, but whose certitude is not inferior to that of knowledge, since it is a communication from God, who can neither deceive nor be deceived. Faith and the certainty thereof depend on reason, in so far as reason alone can determine whether a divine revelation has really been made and the meaning of the words in which the revelation has come down to us. In determining the boundaries of faith and reason Locke makes use of the distinction—which has become famous—between things above reason, according to reason, and contrary to reason. Our conviction that God exists is according to reason; the belief that there are more gods than one, or that a body can be in two different places at the same time, contrary to reason; the former is a truth which can be demonstrated on rational grounds, the latter an assumption incompatible with our clear and distinct ideas. In the one case revelation confirms a proposition of which we were already certain; in the other an alleged revelation is incapable of depriving our certain knowledge of its force. Above reason are those principles whose probability and truth cannot be shown by the natural use of our faculties, as that the dead shall rise again and the account of the fall of part of the angels. Among the things which are not contrary to reason belong miracles, for they contradict opinion based on the usual course of nature, it is true, but not our certain knowledge; in spite of their supernatural character they deserve willing acceptance, and receive it, when they are well attested, whereas principles contrary to reason must be unconditionally rejected as a revelation from God. Locke's demand for the subjection of faith to rational criticism assures him an honorable place in the history of English deism. He enriched the philosophy of religion by two treatises of his own: *The Reasonableness of Christianity*, 1695, and three *Letters on Tolerance*, 1689-1692. The former transfers the center of gravity of the Christian religion from history to the doctrine of redemption; the *Letters* demand religious freedom, mutual tolerance among the different sects, and the separation of Church and State. Those sects alone are to receive no tolerance which themselves exercise none, and which endanger the well-being of society; together with atheists, who are incapable of taking oaths. In other respects it is the duty of the state to protect all confessions and to favor none.

%(b) Practical Philosophy.%—Locke contributed to practical philosophy important suggestions concerning freedom, morality, politics, and education. Freedom is the "power to begin or forbear, continue or put an end to" actions (thoughts and motions). It is not destroyed by the fact that the will is always moved by desire, more exactly, by uneasiness under present circumstances, and that the decision is determined by the judgment of the understanding. Although the result of examination is itself dependent on the unalterable relations of ideas, it is still in our power to decide whether we will consider at all, and what ideas we will take into consideration. Not the thought, not the determination of the will, is free, but the person, the mind; this has the power to suspend the prosecution of desire, and by its judgment to determine the will, even in opposition to inclination. Four stages must, consequently, be distinguished in the volitional process: desire or uneasiness; the deliberative combination of ideas; the judgment of the understanding; determination. Freedom has its place at the beginning of the second stage: it is open to me to decide whether to proceed at all to consideration and final judgment concerning a proposed action; thus to prevent desire from directly issuing in movements; and, according to the result of my examination, perhaps, to substitute for the act originally desired an opposite one. Without freedom, moral judgment and responsibility would be impossible. The above appears to us to represent the essence of Locke's often vacillating discussion of freedom (II. 21). Desire is directed to pleasure; the will obeys the understanding, which is exalted above motives of pleasure and the passions. Everything is physically good which occasions and increases pleasure in us, which removes or diminishes pain, or contributes to the attainment of some other good and the avoidance of some other evil. Actions, on the contrary, are morally good when they conform to a rule by which they are judged. Whoever earnestly meditates on his welfare will prefer moral or rational good to sensuous good, since the former alone vouchsafes true happiness. God has most intimately united virtue and general happiness, since he has made the preservation of human society dependent on the exercise of virtue.

The mark of a law for free beings is the fact that it apportions reward for obedience and punishment for disobedience. The laws to which an action must conform in order to deserve the predicate "good" are three in number (II. 28): by the divine law "men judge whether their actions are sins or duties"; by the civil law, "whether they be criminal or innocent" (deserving of punishment or not); by the law of opinion or reputation, "whether they be virtues or vices." The first of these laws threatens immorality with future misery; the second, with legal punishments; the third, with the disapproval of our fellow-men.

The third law, the law of opinion or reputation, called also philosophical, coincides on the whole, though not throughout, with the first, the divine law of nature, which is best expressed in Christianity, and which is the true touchstone of the moral character of actions. While Locke, in his polemic against innate ideas, had emphasized the diversity of moral judgments among individuals and nations (as a result of which an action is condemned in one place and praised as virtuous in another), he here gives prominence to the fact of general agreement in essentials, since it is only natural that each should encourage by praise and esteem that which is to his advantage, while virtue evidently conduces to the good of all who come into contact with the virtuous. Amid the greatest diversity of moral judgments virtue and praise, vice and blame, go together, while in general that is praised which is really praiseworthy—even the vicious man approves the right and condemns that which is faulty, at least in others. Locke was the first to call attention to general approval as an external mark of moral action, a hint which the Scottish moralists subsequently exploited. The objection that he reduced morality to the level of the conventional is unjust, for the law of opinion and reputation did not mean for him the true principle of morality, but only that which controls the majority of mankind—If anyone is inclined to doubt that commendation and disgrace are sufficient motives to action, he does not understand mankind; there is hardly one in ten thousand insensible enough to endure in quiet the constant disapproval of society. Even if the lawbreaker hopes to escape punishment at the hands of the state, and puts out of mind the thought of future retribution, he can never escape the disapproval of his misdeeds on the part of his fellows. In entire harmony with these views is Locke's advice to educators, that they should early cultivate the love of esteem in their pupils.

Of the four principles of morals which Locke employs side by side, and in alternation, without determining their exact relations—the reason, the will of God, the general good (and, deduced from this, the approval of our fellow-men), self-love—the latter two possess only an accessory significance, while the former two co-operate in such a way that the one determines the content of the good and the other confirms it and gives it binding authority. The Christian religion does the reason a threefold service—it gives her information concerning our duty, which she could have reached herself, indeed, without the help of revelation, but not with the same certitude and rapidity; it invests the good with the majesty of absolute obligation by proclaiming it as the command of God; it increases the motives to morality by its doctrines of immortality and future retribution. Although Locke thus intimately joins virtue with earthly joy and eternal happiness, and although he finds in the expectation of heaven or hell a welcome support for the will in its conflict with the passions, we must remember that he values this regard for the results and rewards of virtue only as a subsidiary motive, and does not esteem it as in itself ethical: eternal happiness forms, as it were, the "dowry" of virtue, which adds to its true value in the eyes of fools and the weak, though it constitutes neither its essence nor its basis. Virtue seems to the wise man beautiful and valuable enough even without this, and yet the commendations of philosophers gain for her but few wooers. The crowd is attracted to her only when it is made clear to it that virtue is the "best policy."

In politics Locke is an opponent of both forms of absolutism, the despotic absolutism of Hobbes and the patriarchal absolutism of Filmer (died 1647; his *Patriarcha* declared hereditary monarchy a divine institution), and a moderate exponent of the liberal tendencies of Milton (1608-74) and Algernon Sidney (died 1683; *Discourses concerning Government*). The two *Treatises on Civil Government*, 1690, develop, the first negatively, the second positively, the constitutional theory with direct reference to the political condition of England at the time. All men are born free and with like capacities and rights. Each is to preserve his own interests, without injuring those of others. The right to be treated by every man as a rational being holds even prior to the founding of the state; but then there is no authoritative power to decide conflicts. The state of nature is not in itself a state of war, but it would lead to this, if each man should himself attempt to exercise the right of self-protection against injury. In order to prevent acts of violence there is needed a civil community, based on a free contract, to which each individual member shall transfer his freedom and power. Submission to the authority of the state is a free act, and, by the contract made, natural rights are guarded, not destroyed; political freedom is obedience to self-imposed law, subordination to the common will expressing itself in the majority. The political power is neither tyrannical, for arbitrary rule is no better than the state of nature, nor paternal, for rulers and subjects are on an equality in the use of the reason, which is not the case with parents and children. The supreme power is the legislative, intrusted by the community to its chosen representatives—the laws should aim at the general good. Subordinate to the legislative power, and to be kept separate from it, come the two executing powers, which are best united in a single hand (the king), viz., the executive power (administrative and judicial), which carries the laws into effect, and the federative power, which defends the community against external foes. The ruler is subject to the law. If the government, through violation of the law, has become unworthy of the power intrusted to it, and has forfeited it, sovereign authority reverts to the source whence it was derived, that is, to the people. The people decides whether its representatives and the monarch have deserved the confidence placed in them, and has the right to depose them, if they exceed their authority. As the sworn obedience (of the subjects) is to the law alone, the ruler who acts contrary to law has lost the right to govern, has put himself in a state of hostility to the people, and revolution becomes merely necessary defense against aggression.

Montesquieu made these political ideas of Locke the common property of Europe.[1] Rousseau did a like service for Locke's pedagogical views, given in the modest but important *Thoughts concerning Education*, 1693. The aim of education should not be to instill anything into the pupil, but to develop everything from him; it should guide and not master him, should develop his capacities in a natural way, should rouse him to independence, not drill him into a scholar. In order to these ends thorough and affectionate consideration of his individuality is requisite, and private instruction is, therefore, to be preferred to public instruction. Since it is the business of education to make men useful members of society, it must not neglect their physical development. Learning through play and object teaching make the child's task a delight; modern languages are to be learned more by practice than by systematic study. The chief difference between Locke and Rousseau is that the former sets great value on arousing the sense of esteem, while the latter entirely rejects this as an educational instrument.

[Footnote 1: Cf. Theod. Pietsch, *Ueber das Verhältniss der politischen Theorien Lockes zu Montesquieus Lehre von der Teilung der Gewalten* Berlin dissertation, Breslau, 1887.]

CHAPTER V.

ENGLISH PHILOSOPHY IN THE EIGHTEENTH CENTURY.

Besides the theory of knowledge, which forms the central doctrine in his system, Locke had discussed the remaining branches of philosophy, though in less detail, and, by his many-sided stimulation, had posited problems for the Illumination movement in England and in France. Now the several disciplines take different courses, but the after-influence of his powerful mind is felt on every hand. The development of deism from Toland on is under the direct influence of his "rational Christianity"; the ethics of Shaftesbury stands in polemic relation to his denial of everything innate; and while Berkeley and Hume are deducing the consequences of his theory of knowledge, Hartley derives the impulse to a new form of psychology from his chapter on the association of ideas.

%1. Natural Philosophy and Psychology.%

In Locke's famous countryman, Isaac Newton (1642-1727),[1] the modern investigation of nature attains the level toward which it had striven, at first by wishes and demands, gradually, also, in knowledge and achievement, since the end of the mediaeval period. Mankind was not able to discard at a stroke its accustomed Aristotelian view of nature, which animated things with inner, spirit-like forces. A full century intervened between Telesius and Newton, the concept of natural law requiring so long a time to break out of its shell. A tremendous revolution in opinion had to be effected before Newton could calmly promulgate his great principle, "Abandon substantial forms and occult qualities and reduce natural phenomena to mathematical laws," before he could crown the discoveries of Galileo and Kepler with his own. For this successful union of Bacon's experimental induction with the mathematical deduction of Descartes, this combination of the analytic and the synthetic methods, which was shown in the demand for, and the establishment of, mathematically formulated natural laws, presupposes that nature is deprived of all inner life [2] and all qualitative distinctions, that all that exists is compounded of uniformly acting parts, and that all that takes place is conceived as motion. With this Hobbes's programme of a mechanical science of nature is fulfilled. The heavens and the earth are made subject to the same law of gravitation. How far Newton himself adhered to the narrow meaning of mechanism (motion from pressure and impulse), is evident from the fact that, though he is often honored as the creator of the dynamical view of nature, he rejected *actio in distans* as absurd, and deemed it indispensable to assume some "cause" of gravity (consisting, probably, in the impact of imponderable material particles). It was his disciples who first ventured to proclaim gravity as the universal force of matter, as the "primary quality of all bodies" (so Roger Cotes in the preface to the second edition of the *Principia*, 1713).

[Footnote 1: 1669-95 professor of mathematics in Cambridge, later resident in London; 1672, member, and, 1703, president of the Royal Society. Chief work, *Philosophic Naturalis Principia Mathematica*, 1687. Works, 1779 *seq*. On Newton cf. K. Snell, 1843; Durdik, *Leibniz und Newton*, 1869; Lange, *History of Materialism*, vol. i. p. 306 *seq*.]

[Footnote 2: That the mathematical view of nature, since it leaves room for quantitative distinctions alone, is equivalent to an examination of nature had been clearly recognized by Poiret. As he significantly remarked: The principles of the Cartesian physics relate merely to the "cadaver" of nature *(Erud.*, p. 260).]

Newton resembles Boyle in uniting profound piety with the rigor of scientific thought. He finds the most certain proof for the existence of an intelligent creator in the wonderful arrangement of the world-machine, which does not need after-adjustment at the hands of its creator, and whose adaptation he praises as enthusiastically as he unconditionally rejects the mingling of teleological considerations in the explanation of physical phenomena. By this "physico-theological" argument he furnishes a welcome support to deism. While the finite mind perceives in the sensorium of the brain the images of objects which come to it from the senses, God has all things in himself, is immediately present in all, and cognizes them without sense-organs, the expanse of the universe forming his sensorium.

* * * * *

The transfer of mechanical views to psychical phenomena was also accompanied by the conviction that no danger to faith in God would result therefrom, but rather that it would aid in its support. The chief representatives of this movement, which followed the example of Gay, were the physician, David Hartley[1] (1704-57), and his pupil, Joseph Priestley,[2] a dissenting minister and natural scientist (born 1733, died in Philadelphia 1804; the discoverer of oxygen gas, 1774).

The fundamental position of these psychologists is expressed in two principles: (1) all cognitive and motive life is based on the mechanism of psychical elements, the highest and most complex inner phenomena (thoughts, feelings, volitions) are produced by the combination of simple ideas, that is, they arise through the "association of ideas"; (2) all inner phenomena, the complex as well as the simple, are accompanied by, or rather depend on, more or less complicated physical phenomena, viz., nervous processes and brain vibrations. Although Hartley and Priestley are agreed in their demand for an associational and physiological treatment of psychology, and in the attempt to give one, they differ in this, that Hartley cautiously speaks only of a parallelism, a correspondence between mental and cerebral processes, and rejects the materialistic interpretation of inner phenomena, pointing out that the heterogeneity of motion and ideas forbids the reduction of the latter to the former, and that psychological analysis never reaches corporeal but only psychical elements. Moreover, it is only with reluctance that, conscious of the critical character of the conclusion, he admits the dependence of brain vibrations on the mechanical laws of the material world and the thoroughgoing determinateness of the human will, consoling himself with the belief that moral responsibility nevertheless remains intact. Priestley, on the contrary, boldly avows the materialistic and deterministic consequences of his position, holds that psychical phenomena are not merely accompanied by material motions but consist in them (thought is a function of the brain), and makes psychology, as the physics of the nerves, a part of physiology. The denial of immortality and the divine origin of the world is, however, by no means to follow from materialism. Priestley not only combated the atheism of Holbach, but also entered the deistic ranks with works of his own on Natural Religion and the Corruptions of Christianity.

[Footnote 1: Hartley, *Observations on Man, his Frame, his Duties, his Expectations*. 1749.]

[Footnote 2: Priestley, *Hartley's Theory of the Human Mind on the Principles of the Association of Ideas*, 1775; *Disquisitions relating to Matter and Spirit*, 1777; *The Doctrine of Philosophical Necessity*, 1777; *Free Discussions of the Doctrines of Materialism*, 1778 (against Richard Price's *Letters on Materialism and Philosophical Necessity*). Cf. on both Schoenlank's dissertation, *Hartley und Priestley, die Begründer des Assoziationismus in England*, 1882.]

As early as in Hartley[1] the principle, which is so important for ethics, appears that things and actions (*e.g.*, promotion of the good of others) which at first are sought and done because they are means to our own enjoyment, in time come to have a direct worth of their own, apart from the original egoistic end. James Mill (1829) has repeated this thought in later times. As fame becomes an immediate object of desire to the ambitious man, and gold to the miser, so, through association, the impulse toward that which will secure approval may be transformed into the endeavor after that which deserves approval.

[Footnote 1: Cf. Jodl, *Geschichte der Ethik*, vol. i. p. 197 *seq*.]

Among later representatives of the Associational school we may mention Erasmus Darwin *(Zoönomia, or the Laws of Organic Life*, 1794-96).

%2. Deism%.

As Bacon and Descartes had freed natural science, Hobbes, the state, and Grotius, law from the authority of the Church and had placed them on an independent basis, *i.e.*, the basis of nature and reason, so deism[1] seeks to free religion from Church dogma and blind historical faith, and to deduce it from natural knowledge. In so far as deism finds both the source and the test of true religion in reason, it is rationalism; in so far as it appeals from the supernatural light of revelation and inspiration to the natural light of reason, it is naturalism; in so far as revelation and its records are not only not allowed to restrict rational criticism, but are made the chief object of criticism, its adherents are freethinkers.

[Footnote 1: Cf. Lechler's *Geschichte des Englischen Deismus*, 1841, which is rigorously drawn from the sources. [Hunt, *History of Religious Thought in England*, 1871-73 [1884]; Leslie Stephen, *History of English Thought in the Eighteenth Century*, 1876 [1880]; Cairns, *Unbelief in the Eighteenth Century*, 1881.]]

The general principles of deism may be compressed into a few theses. There is a natural religion, whose essential content is morality; this comprises not much more than the two maxims, Believe in God and Do your duty.

Positive religions are to be judged by this standard. The elements in them which are added to natural religion, or conflict with it, are superfluous and harmful additions, arbitrary decrees of men, the work of cunning rulers and deceitful priests. Christianity, which in its original form was the perfect expression of the true religion of reason, has experienced great corruptions in its ecclesiastical development, from which it must now be purified.

These principles are supported by the following arguments: Truth is one and there is but one true religion. If the happiness of men depends on the fulfilment of her commands, these must be comprehensible to every man and must have been communicated to him; and since a special revelation and legislation could not come to the knowledge of all, they can be no other than the laws of duty inscribed on the human heart. In order to salvation, then, we need only to know God as creator and judge, and to fulfill his commands, *i.e.*. to live a moral life. The one true religion has been communicated to man in two forms, through the inner natural revelation of reason, and the outer historical revelation of the Gospel. Since both have come from God they cannot be contradictory. Accordingly natural religion and the true one among the positive religions do not differ in their content, but only in the manner of their promulgation. Reason tries historical religion by the standard furnished by natural religion, and distinguishes actual from asserted revelation by the harmony of its contents with reason: the deist believes in the Bible because of the reasonableness of its teachings; he does not hold these teachings true because they are found in the Bible. If a positive religion contains less than natural religion it is incomplete; if it contains more it is tyrannical, since it imposes unnecessary requirements. The authority of reason to exercise the office of a judge in regard to the credibility of revelation is beyond doubt; indeed, apart from it there is no means of attaining truth, and the acceptance of an external revelation as genuine, and not merely as alleged to be such, is possible only for those who have already been convinced of God's existence by the inner light of reason.

To these logical considerations is added an historical position, which, though only cursorily indicated at the beginning, is evidenced in increasing detail as the deistic movement continues on its course. Natural religion is always and everywhere the same, is universal and necessary, is perfect, eternal, and original. As original, it is the earliest religion, and as old as the world; as perfect, it is not capable of improvement, but only of corruption and restoration. Twice it has existed in perfect purity, as the religion of the first men and as the religion of Christ. Twice it has been corrupted, in the pre-Christian period by idolatry, which proceeded from the Egyptian worship of the dead, in the period after Christ by the love of miracle and blind reverence for authority. In both cases the corruption has come from power-loving priests, who have sought to frighten and control the people by incomprehensible dogmas and ostentations, mysterious ceremonies, and found their advantage in the superstition of the multitude,—each new divinity, each new mystery meaning a gain for them. As they had corrupted the primitive religion into polytheism, so Christianity was corrupted by conforming it to the prejudices of those to be converted, in whose eyes the simplicity of the new doctrine would have been no recommendation for it. The Jew sought in it an echo of the Law, the heathen longed for his festivals and his occult philosophy; so it was burdened with unprofitable ceremonial observances and needless profundity, it was Judaized and heathenized. It was inevitable that the doctrines of original sin, of satisfaction and atonement should prove especially objectionable to the purely rational temper of the deists. Neither the guilt of others (the sin of our ancestors) nor the atonement of others (Christ's death on the cross) can be imputed to us; Christ can be called the Savior only by way of metaphor, only in so far as the example of his death leads us on to faith and obedience for ourselves. The name atheism, which, it is true, orthodoxy held ready for every belief incorrect according to its standard, was on the contrary undeserved. The deists did not attack Christian revelation, still less belief in God. They considered the atheist bereft of reason, and they by no means esteemed historical revelation superfluous. The end of the latter was to stir the mind to move men to reflection and conversion, to transform morals, and if anyone declared it unnecessary because it contains nothing but natural truths, he was referred to the works of Euclid, which certainly contain nothing which is not founded in the reason, but which no one but a fool will consider unnecessary in the study of mathematics.

That which we have here summarized as the general position of deism, gained gradual expression through the regular development and specialization of deistic ideas in individual representatives of the movement. The chief points and epochs were marked by Toland's *Christianity not Mysterious*, 1696; Collins's *Discourse of Freethinking*, 1713; Tindal's *Christianity as Old as the Creation*, 1730; and Chubb's *True Gospel of Jesus Christ*, 1738. The first of these demands a critique of revelation, the second defends the right of free investigation, the third declares the religion of Christ, which is merely a revived natural religion, to be the oldest religion, the fourth reduces it entirely to moral life.

The deistic movement was called into life by Lord Herbert of Cherbury (pp. 79-80) and continued by Locke, in so far as the latter had intrusted to reason the discrimination of true from false revelation, and had admitted in Christianity elements above reason, though not things contrary to reason. Following Locke, John Toland (1670-1722) goes a step further with the proof that the Gospel not only contains nothing contrary to reason, but also nothing above reason, and that no Christian doctrine is to be called mysterious. To the demand that we should worship what we do not comprehend, he answers that reason is the only basis of certitude, and alone decides on the divinity of the Scriptures, by a consideration of their contents. The motive which impels us to assent to a truth must lie in reason, not in revelation, which, like all authority and experience, is merely the way by which we attain the knowledge of the truth; it is a means of instruction, not a ground of conviction. All faith has knowledge and understanding for its conditions, and is rational conviction. Before we can put our trust in the Scriptures, we must be convinced that they were in fact written by the authors to whom they are ascribed, and must consider whether these men, their deeds, and their works, were worthy of God. The fact that God's inmost being is for us inscrutable does not make him a mystery, for even the common things of nature are known to us only by their properties. Miracles are also in themselves nothing incomprehensible; they are simply enhancements of natural laws beyond their ordinary operations, by supernatural assistance, which God vouchsafes but rarely and only for extraordinary ends. Toland explains the mysteries smuggled into the ethical religion of Christianity as due to the toleration of Jewish and heathen customs, to the entrance of learned speculation, and to the selfish inventions of the clergy and the rulers. The Reformation itself had not entirely restored the original purity and simplicity.

Thus far Toland the deist. In his later writings, the five *Letters to Serena*, 1704, addressed to the Prussian queen, Sophia Charlotte, and the *Pantheisticon* (Cosmopoli, 1720), he advances toward a hylozoistic pantheism.

The first of the Letters discusses the prejudices of mankind; the second, the heathen doctrine of immortality; the third, the origin of idolatry; while the fourth and fifth are devoted to Spinoza, the chief defect in whose philosophy is declared to be the absence of an explanation of motion. Motion belongs to the notion of matter as necessarily as extension and impenetrability. Matter is always in motion; rest is only the reciprocal interference of two moving forces. The differences of things depend on the various movements of the particles of matter, so that it is motion which individualizes matter in general into particular things. As the Letters ascribe the purposive construction of organic beings to a divine reason, so the *Pantheisticon* also stops short before it reaches the extreme of naked materialism. Everything is from the whole; the whole is infinite, one, eternal, all-rational. God is the force of the whole, the soul of the world, the law of nature. The treatise includes a liturgy of the pantheistic society with many quotations from the ancient poets.

Anthony Collins (1676-1729), in his *Discourse of Free-thinking*, shows the right of free thought *(i. e.,* of judgment on rational grounds) in general, from the principle that no truth is forbidden to us, and that there is no other way by which we can attain truth and free ourselves from superstition, and the right to apply it to God and the Bible in particular, from the fact that the clergy differ concerning the most important matters. The fear that the differences of opinion which spring from freethinking may endanger the peace of society lacks foundation; on the contrary, it is only restriction of the freedom of thought which leads to disorders, by weakening moral zeal. The clergy are the only ones who condemn liberty of thought. It is sacrilege to hold that error can be beneficial and truth harmful. As a proof that freethinking by no means corrupts character, Collins gives in conclusion a list of noble freethinkers from Socrates down to Locke and Tillotson. Among the replies to the views of Collins we may mention the calmly objective Boyle Lectures by Ibbot, and the sharp and witty letter of Richard Bentley, the philologist. Neither of these attacks Collins's leading principle, both fully admitting the right to employ the reason, even in religious questions; but they dispute the implication that freethinking is equivalent to contentious opposition. On the one hand, they maintain that Collins's thinking is too free, that is, unbridled, hasty, presumptuous, and paradoxical; on the other, that it is not free enough (from prejudice).

After Shaftesbury had based morality on a natural instinct for the beautiful and had made it independent of religion, as well as served the cause of free thought by a keenly ironical campaign against enthusiasm and orthodoxy, and Clarke had furnished the representatives of natural religion a useful principle of morals in the objective rationality of things, the debate concerning prophecy and miracles[1] threatened to dissipate the deistic movement into scattered theological skirmishes. At this juncture Matthew Tindal (1657-1733) led it back to the main question. His *Christianity as Old as the Creation* is the doomsday book of deism. It contains all that has been given above as the core of this view of religion. Christ came not to bring in a new doctrine, but to exhort to repentance and atonement, and to restore the law of nature, which is as old as the creation, as universal as reason, and as unchangeable as God, human nature, and the relations of things, which we should respect in our actions. Religion is morality; more exactly, it is the free, constant disposition to do as much good as possible, and thereby to promote the glory of God and our own welfare. For the harmony of our conduct with the rules of reason constitutes our perfection, and on this depends our happiness. Since God is infinitely blessed and self-sufficient his purpose in the moral law is man's happiness alone. Whatever a positive religion contains beyond the moral law is superstition, which puts emphasis on worthless trivialities. The true religion occupies the happy mean between miserable unfaith, on the one hand, and timorous superstition, wild fanaticism, and pietistical zeal on the other. In proclaiming the sovereignty of reason in the sphere of religion as well as elsewhere, we are only openly demanding what our opponents have tacitly acknowledged in practice *(e. g.>* in allegorical interpretation) from time immemorial. God has endowed us with reason in order that we should by it distinguish truth from falsehood.

[Footnote 1: The chief combatant in the conflict over the argument from prophecy, which was called forth by Whiston's corruption hypothesis, was Collins *(A Discourse of the Grounds and Reasons of the Christian Religion*, 1724). Christianity is based on Judaism; its fundamental article is that Jesus is the prophesied Messiah of the Jews, its chief proof the argument from Old Testament prophecy, which, it is true, depends on the typical or allegorical interpretation of the passages in question. Whoever rejects this cuts away the ground from under the Christian revelation, which is only the allegorical import of the revelation of the Jews.—The second proof of revelation, the argument from miracles, was shaken by Thomas Woolston *(Six Discourses on the Miracles of our Saviour*, 1727-30), by his extension of the allegorical interpretation to these also. He supported himself in this by the authority of the Church Fathers, and, above all, by the argument that the accounts of the miracles, if taken literally, contradict all sense and understanding. The unavoidable doubts which arise concerning the literal interpretation of the resurrection of the dead, the healing of the sick, the driving out of devils, and the other miracles, prove that these were intended only as symbolic representations of the mysterious and wonderful effects which Jesus was to accomplish. Thus Jairus's daughter means the Jewish Church, which is to be revived at the second coming of Christ; Lazarus typifies humanity, which will be raised again at the last day; the account of the bodily resurrection of Jesus is a symbol of his spiritual resurrection from his grave in the letter of Scripture. Sherlock, whose *Trial of the Witnesses of the Resurrection of Jesus* was long considered a cogent answer to the attacks of Woolston, was opposed by Peter Annet, who, without leaving the refuge of figurative interpretation open, proceeded still more regardlessly in the discovery of contradictory and incredible elements in the Gospel reports, and declared all the scriptural writers together to be liars and falsifiers. If a man believes in miracles as supernatural interferences with the regular course of nature (and they must be so taken if they are to certify to the divine origin of the Scriptures), he makes God mutable, and natural laws imperfect arrangements which stand in need of correction. The truth of religion is independent of all history.]

Thomas Chubb (1679-1747), a man of the people (he was a glove maker and tallow-chandler), and from 1715 on a participant in deistic literature and concerned to adapt the new ideas to the men of his class, preached in *The True Gospel of Jesus Christ* an honorable working-man's Christianity., Faith means obedience to the law of reason inculcated by Christ, not the acceptance of the facts reported about him. The gospel of Christ was preached to the poor before his death and his asserted resurrection and ascension. It is probable that Christ really lived, because of the great effect of his message; but he was a man like other men. His gospel is his teaching, not his history, his own teaching, not that of his followers—the reflections of the apostles are private opinions. Christ's teaching amounts, in effect, to these three fundamental principles: (1) Conform to the rational law of love to God and one's neighbor; this is the only ground of divine acceptance. (2) After transgression of the law, repentance and reformation are the only grounds of divine grace and forgiveness. (3) At the last day every one will be rewarded according to his works. By proclaiming these doctrines, by carrying them out in his own pure life and typical death, and by founding religio-ethical associations on the principle of brotherly equality, Christ selected the means best fitted for the attainment of his purpose, the salvation of human souls. His aim was to assure men of future happiness (and of the earthly happiness connected therewith), and to make them worthy of it; and this happiness can only be attained when from free conviction we submit ourselves to the natural moral law, which is grounded on the moral fitness of things. Everything which leads to the illusion that the favor of God is attainable by any other means than by righteousness and repentance, is pernicious; as, also, the confusion of Christian societies with legal and civil societies, which pursue entirely different aims.

Thomas Morgan *(The Moral Philosopher, a Dialogue between the Christian Deist, Philalethes, and the Christian Jew, Theophanes, 1737 seq*.) stands on the same ground as his predecessors, by holding that the moral truth of things is the criterion of the divinity of a doctrine, that the Christian religion is merely a restoration of natural religion, and that the apostles were not infallible. Peculiar to him are the application of the first of these principles to the Mosaic law, with the conclusion that this was not a revelation; the complete separation of the New Testament from the Old (the Church of Christ and the expected kingdom of the Jewish Messiah are as opposed to each other as heaven and earth); and the endeavor to give a more exact explanation of the origin of superstition, the pre-Christian manifestations of which he traces back to the fall of the angels, and those since Christ to the intermixture of Jewish elements. He seeks to solve his problem by a detailed critique of Israelitish history, which is lacking in sympathy but not in spirit, and in which, introducing modern relations into the earliest times, he explains the Old Testament miracles in part as myths, in part as natural phenomena, and deprives the heroes of the Jews of their moral renown. The Jewish historians are ranked among the poets; the God of Israel is reduced to a subordinate, local tutelary divinity; the moral law of Moses is characterized as a civil code limited to external conduct, to national and mundane affairs, with merely temporal sanctions, and the ceremonial law as an act of worldly statecraft; David is declared a gifted poet, musician, hypocrite, and coward; the prophets are made professors of theology and moral philosophy; and Paul is praised as the greatest freethinker of his time, who defended reason against authority and rejected the Jewish ritual law as indifferent. Whatever is spurious in Christianity is a remnant of Judaism, all its mysteries are misunderstood and falsely (*i.e.* literally) applied allegories. Out of regard for Jewish prejudices Christ's death was figuratively described as sacrificial, as in earlier times Moses had been forced to yield to the Egyptian superstitions of his people. Morgan looks for the final victory of the rational morality of the pure, Pauline, or deistic Christianity over the Jewish Christianity of orthodoxy. Among the works of his opponents the following deserve mention: William Warburton's *Divine Legation of Moses, and* Samuel Chandler's *Vindication of the History of the Old Testament*.

It maybe doubted whether Bolingbroke (died 1751; cf. p. 203) is to be classed among the deists or among their opponents. On the one hand, he finds in monotheism the original true religion, which has degenerated into superstition through priestly cunning and fantastical philosophy; in primitive Christianity, the system of natural religion, which has been transformed into a complicated and contentious science by its weak, foolish, or deceitful adherents; in theology, the corruption of religion; in Bacon, Descartes, and Locke, types of untrammeled investigation. On the other hand, he seeks to protect revelation from the reason whose cultivation he has just commended, and to keep faith and knowledge distinct, while he demands that the Bible, with all the undemonstrable and absurd elements which it contains, be accepted on its own authority. Religion is an instrument indispensable to the government for keeping the people in subjection. Only the fear of a higher power, not the reason, holds the masses in check; and the freethinkers do wrong in taking a bit out of the mouth of the sensual multitude, when it were better to add to those already there.

As Hume, the skeptic, leads empiricism to its fall, so Hume, the philosopher of religion (see below), leads deism toward dissolution. Among those who defended revealed Christianity against the deistical attacks we may mention the names of Conybeare (1732) and Joseph Butler (1736). The former argues from the imperfection and mutability of our reason to like characteristics in natural religion. Butler (cf. p. 206) does not admit that natural and revealed religion are mutually exclusive. Christian revelation lends a higher authority to natural religion, in which she finds her foundation, and adapts it to the given relations and needs of mankind, adding, however, to the rational law of virtue new duties toward God the Son and God the Holy Ghost. It is evident that in order to be able to deal with their opponents, the apologetes are forced to accommodate themselves to the deistic principle of a rational criticism of revelation.

Notwithstanding the fear which this principle inspired in the men of the time, it soon penetrated the thought even of its opponents, and found its way into the popular mind through the channels of the Illumination.

Although it was often defended and applied with violence and with a superfluous hatred of the clergy, it forms the justifiable element in the endeavors of the deists. It is a commonplace to-day that everything which claims to be true and valid must justify itself before the criticism of reason; but then this principle, together with the distinction between natural and positive religion based upon it, exerted an enlightening and liberating influence. The real flaw in the deistical theory, which was scarcely felt as such, even by its opponents, was its lack of religious feeling and all historical sense, a lack which rendered the idea acceptable that religions could be "made," and priestly falsehoods become world-moving forces. Hume was the first to seek to rise above this unspeakable shallowness. There was a remarkable conflict between the ascription to man, on the one hand, of an assured treasure of religious knowledge in the reason, and the abandonment of him, on the other, to the juggling of cunning priests and despots. Thus the deists had no sense either for the peculiarities of an inward religious feeling, which, in happy prescience, rises above the earthly circle of moral duties to the world beyond, or for the involuntary, historically necessary origin and growth of the particular forms of religion. Here, again, we find that turning away from will and feeling to thought, from history to nature, from the oppressive complexity of that which has been developed to the simplicity of that which is original, which we have noted as one of the most prominent characteristics of the modern period.

%3. Moral Philosophy.%

The watchword of deism was "independence in religion"; that of modern ethical philosophy is "independence in morals." Hobbes had given this out in opposition to the mediaeval dependence of ethics on theology; now it was turned against himself, for he had delivered morality from ecclesiastical bondage only to subject it to the no less oppressive and unworthy yoke of the civil power. Selfish consideration, so he had taught, leads men to transfer by contract all power to the ruler. Right is that which the sovereign enjoins, wrong that which he forbids. Thus morality was conceived in a purely negative way as justice, and based on interest and agreement. Cumberland, recognizing the one-sidedness of the first of these positions, announces the principle of universal benevolence, at which Bacon had hinted before him, and in which he is followed by the school of Shaftesbury. Opposition to the foundation of ethics on self-love and convention, again, springs up in three forms, one idealistic, one logical, and one aesthetic. Ethical ideas have not arisen artificially through shrewd calculation and agreement, but have a natural origin. Cudworth, returning to Plato and Descartes, assumes an innate idea of the good. Clarke and Woolston base moral distinctions on the rational order of things, and characterize the ethically good action as a logical truth translated into practice. Shaftesbury derives ethical ideas and actions from a natural instinct for judging the good and the beautiful. Moreover, Hobbes's ethics of interest experiences, first, correction at the hands of Locke (who, along with a complete recognition of the "legal" character of the good, distinguishes the sphere of morality from that of mere law, and brings it under the law of "reputation," hence of a "tacit" agreement), and then a frivolous intensification under Mandeville and Bolingbroke. A preliminary conclusion is reached in the ethical labors of Hume and Smith.

Richard Cumberland *(De Legibus Naturae,* 1672) turns to experience with the questions, In what does morality consist? Whence does it arise? and What is the nature of moral obligation? and finds these answers: Those actions are good, or in conformity to the moral law of nature, which promote the common good *(commune bonum summa lex).* Individual welfare must be subordinated to the good of all, of which it forms only a part. The psychological roots of virtuous action are the social and disinterested affections, which nature has implanted in all beings, especially in those endowed with reason. There is nothing in man more pleasing to God than love. We recognize our obligation to the virtue of benevolence, or that God commands it, from the rewards and punishments which we perceive to follow the fulfillment or non-fulfillment of the law,—the subordination of individual to universal good is the only means of attaining true happiness and contentment. Men are dependent on mutual benevolence. He who labors for the good of the whole system of rational beings furthers thereby the welfare of the individual parts, among whom he himself is one; individual happiness cannot be separated from general happiness. All duties are implied in the supreme one: Give to others, and preserve thyself. This principle of benevolence, advanced by Cumberland with homely simplicity, received in the later development of English ethics, for which it pointed out the way, a more careful foundation.

The series of emancipations of morality begins with the Intellectual System of Ralph Cud worth *(The Intellectual System of the Universe,* 1678; *A Treatise concerning Eternal and Immutable Morality,* 1731). Ethical ideas come neither from experience nor from civil legislation nor from the will of God, but are necessary ideas in the divine and the human reason. Because of their simplicity, universality, and immutability, it is impossible for them to arise from experience, which never yields anything but that which is particular and mutable. It is just as impossible that they should spring from political constitutions, which have a temporal origin, which are transitory, and which differ from one another. For if obedience to positive law is right and disobedience wrong, then moral distinctions must have existed before the law; if, on the other hand, obedience to the civil law is morally indifferent, then more than ever is it impossible that this should be the basis of the moral distinctions in question. A law can bind us only in virtue of that which is necessarily, absolutely, or *per se* right; therefore the good is independent, also, of the will of God. The absolutely good is an eternal truth which God does not create by an act of his will, but which he finds present in his reason, and which, like the other ideas, he impresses on created spirits. On the *a priori* ideas depends the possibility of science, for knowledge is the perception of necessary truth.

In agreement with Cudworth that the moral law is dependent neither on human compact nor on the divine will, Samuel Clarke (died 1729) finds the eternal principles of justice, goodness, and truth, which God observes in his government of the universe, and which should also be the guide of human action, embodied in the nature of things or in their properties, powers, and relations, in virtue of which certain things, relations, and modes of action are suited to one another, and others not. Morality is the subjective conformity of conduct to this objective fitness of things; the good is the fitting. Moral rules, to which we are bound by conscience and by rational insight, are valid independently of the command of God and of all hope or fear in reference to the life to come, although the principles of religion furnish them an effective support, and one which is almost indispensable in view of the weakness of human nature. They are not universally observed, indeed, but universally acknowledged; even the vicious man cannot refrain from praising virtue in others. He who is induced by the voice of passion to act contrary to the eternal relations or harmony of things, contradicts his own reason in thus undertaking to disturb the order of the universe; he commits the absurdity of willing that things should be that which they are not. Injustice is in practice that which falsity and contradiction are in theoretical affairs. In his well-known controversy with Leibnitz, Clarke defends the freedom of the will against the determinism of the German philosopher.

In William Wollaston (died 1724), with whom the logical point of view becomes still more apparent, Clarke found a thinker who shared his convictions that the subjective moral principle of interest was insufficient, and, hence, an objective principle to be sought; that morality consists in the suitableness of the action to the nature and destination of the object, and that, in the last analysis, it is coincident with truth. The highest destination of man is, on the one hand, to know the truth, and, on the other, to express it in actions. That act is good whose execution includes the affirmation (and its omission the negation) of a truth. According to the law of nature, a rational being ought so to conduct himself that he shall never contradict a truth by his actions, *i. e.,* to treat each thing for what it is. Every immoral action is a false judgment; the violation of a contract is a practical denial of it. The man who is cruel to animals declares by his act that the creature maltreated is something which in fact it is not, a being devoid of feeling. The murderer acts as though he were able to restore life to his victim. He who, in disobedience toward God, deals with things in a way contrary to their nature, behaves as though he were mightier than the author of nature. To this equation of truth and morality happiness is added as a third identical member. The truer the pleasures of a being the happier it is; and a pleasure is untrue whenever more (of pain) is given for it than it is worth. A rational being contradicts itself when it pursues an irrational pleasure.—The course of moral philosophy has passed over the logical ethics of Clarke and Wollaston as an abstract and unfruitful idiosyncrasy, and it is certain that with both of these thinkers their plans were greater than their performances. But the search for an ethical norm which should be universally valid and superior to the individual will, did not lack justification in contrast to the subjectivism of the other two schools of the time—the school of interest and the school of benevolence, which made virtue a matter of calculation or of feeling.

* * * * *

The English ethics of the period culminates in Shaftesbury (1671-1713), who, reared on the principles of his grandfather's friend Locke, formed his artistic sense on the models of classical antiquity, to recall to the memory of his age the Greek ideal of a beautiful humanity. Philosophy, as the knowledge of ourselves and that which is truly good, a guide to morality and happiness; the world and virtue, a harmony; the good, the beautiful as well; the whole, a controlling force in the particular—these views, and his tasteful style of exposition, make Shaftesbury a modern Greek; it is only his bitterness against Christianity which betrays the son of the new era. Among the studies collected under the title *Characteristics of Men, Manners, Opinions, Times*, 1711, the most important are those on Enthusiasm, on Wit and Humor, on Virtue and Merit, and the Moralists.[1]

[Footnote 1: Georg v. Gizycki has written on Shaftesbury's philosophy, 1876. [Cf. Fowler's *Shaftesbury and Hutchison*, English Philosophers Series, 1882.—TR.]]

Shaftesbury's fundamental metaphysical concept is aesthetic: unity in variety is for him the all-pervasive law of the world. In every case where parts work in mutual dependence toward a common result, there rules a central unity, uniting and animating the members. The lowest of these substantial unities is the ego, the common source of our thoughts and feelings. But as the parts of the organism are governed and held together by the soul, so individuals are joined with one another into species and genera by higher unities. Each individual being is a member in a system of creatures, which a common nature binds together. Moreover, since order and harmony are spread throughout the world, and no one thing exists out of relation to all others and to the whole, the universe must be conceived as animated by a formative power which works purposively; this all-ruling unity is the soul of the world, the universal mind, the Deity. The finality and beauty of those parts of the world which we can know justifies the inference to a like constitution of those which are unapproachable, so that we may be certain that the numerous evils which we find in the details, work for the good of a system superior to them, and that all apparent imperfections contribute to the perfection of the whole. As our philosopher makes use of the idea of the world-harmony to support theism and the theodicy, so, further, he derives the content of morality from it, thus giving ethics a natural basis independent of self-interest and conventional fancies.

A being is good when its impulses toward the preservation and welfare of the species is strong, and those directed to its own good not too strong. The virtue of a rational being is distinguished from the goodness of a merely "sensible creature" by the fact that man not only possesses impulses, but reflects upon them, that he approves or disapproves his own conduct and that of others, and thus makes his affections the object of a higher, reflective, judging affection. This faculty of moral distinctions, the sense for right and wrong, or, which amounts to the same thing, for beauty and ugliness, is innate; we approve virtue and condemn vice by nature, not as the result of a compact, and from this natural feeling for good and evil exercise develops a cultivated moral taste or tact. And when, further, the reason, by means of this faculty of judgment, gains control over the passions, man becomes an ethical artist, a moral virtuoso.

Virtue pleases by its own worth and beauty, not because of any external advantage. We must not corrupt the love of the good for its own sake by mixing with it the hope of future reward, which at the best is admissible only as a counter-weight against evil passions. When Shaftesbury speaks of future bliss, his highest conception of the heavenly life is uninterrupted friendship, magnanimity, and nobility, as a continual rewarding of virtue by new virtue.

The good is the beautiful, and the beautiful is the harmonious, the symmetrical; hence the essence of virtue consists in the balance of the affections and passions. Of the three classes into which Shaftesbury divides the passions, one, including the "unnatural" or unsocial affections, as malevolence, envy, and cruelty, which aim neither at the good of the individual nor that of others, is always and entirely evil.

The two other classes, the social (or "natural") affections and the "self-affections," may be virtuous or vicious, according to their degree, *i. e.*, according to the relation of their strength to that of the other affections. In itself a benevolent impulse is never too strong; it can become so only in comparison with self-love, or in respect to the constitution of the individual in question, and conversely. Commonly the social impulses do not attain the normal standard, while the selfish exceed it; but the opposite case also occurs. Excessive parental tenderness, the pity which enervates and makes useless for aid, religious zeal for making converts, passionate partisanship, are examples of too violent social affections which interfere with the activity of the other inclinations. Just as erroneous, on the other side, is the neglect of one's own good. For although the possession of selfish inclinations does not make a man virtuous, yet the lack of them is a moral defect, since they are indispensable to the general good. No one can be useful to others who does not keep himself in a condition for service. The impulse to care for private welfare is good and necessary in so far as it comports with the general welfare or contributes to this. The due proportion between the social passions, which constitute the direct source of good, and those of self-love, consists in subordinating the latter to the former. The kinship of this ethics of harmony with the ethical views of antiquity is evident. It is completed by the eudemonistic conclusion of the system.

As the harmony of impulses constitutes the essence of virtue, so also it is the way to true happiness. Experience shows that unsocial, unsympathetic, vicious men are miserable; that love to society is the richest source of happiness; that even pity for the suffering of others occasions more pleasure than pain. Virtue secures us the love and respect of others, secures us, above all, the approval of our own conscience, and true happiness consists in satisfaction with ourselves. The search after this pure, constant, spiritual pleasure in the good, which is never accompanied by satiety and disgust, should not be called self-seeking; he alone takes pleasure in the good who is already good himself.

Shaftesbury is not well disposed toward positive Christianity, holding that it has made virtue mercenary by its promises of heavenly rewards, removed moral questions entirely out of this world into the world to come, and taught men most piously to torment one another out of pure supernatural brotherly love. In opposition to such transcendental positions Shaftesbury, a priest of the modern view of the world, gives virtue a home on earth, seeks the hand of Providence in the present world, and teaches men to reach faith in God by inspiring contemplation of the well-ordered universe. Virtue without piety is possible, indeed, though not complete. But morality is first and fixed, hence it is the condition and the criterion of genuine religion. Revelation does not need to fear free rational criticism, for the Scriptures are accredited by their contents. Besides reason, banter is with Shaftesbury a second means for distinguishing the genuine from the spurious: ridicule is the test of truth, and wit and humor the only cure for enthusiasm. With these he scourges the over-pious as religious parasites, who for safety's sake prefer to believe too much rather than too little.

Before Shaftesbury's theory of the moral sense and the disinterested affections had gained adherents and developers, the danger, which indeed had not always been escaped, that man might content himself with the satisfaction of possessing noble impulses, without taking much care to realize them in useful actions, called forth by way of reaction, a paradoxical attempt at an apology for vice. Mandeville, a London physician of French extraction, and born in Holland, had aroused attention by his poem, *The Grumbling Hive; or Knaves Turned Honest*, 1706, and in response to vehement attacks upon his work, had added a commentary to the second edition, *The Fable of the Bees; or Private Vices Public Benefits*, 1714. The moral of the fable is that the welfare of a society depends on the industry of its members, and this, in turn, on their passions and vices. Greed, extravagance, envy, ambition, and rivalry are the roots of the acquisitive impulse, and contribute more to the public good than benevolence and the control of desire. Virtue is good for the individual, it is true, since it makes him contented with himself and acceptable to God and man, but great states require stronger motives to labor and industry in order to be prosperous. A people among whom frugality, self-denial, and quietness of spirit were the rule would remain poor and ignorant. Besides holding that virtue furthers the happiness of society, Shaftesbury makes a second mistake in assuming that human nature includes unselfish inclinations. It is not innate love and goodness that make us social, but our passions and weaknesses (above all, fear); man is by nature self-seeking. All actions, including the so-called virtues, spring from vanity and egoism; thus it has always been, thus it is in every grade of society. In social life, indeed, we dare not display all these desires openly, nor satisfy them at will. Shrewd lawgivers have taught men to conceal their natural passions and to limit them by artificial ones, persuading them that renunciation is true happiness, on the ground that through it we attain the supreme good—reputation among, and the esteem of our fellows. Since then honor and shame have become the strongest motives and have incited men to that which is called virtue, *i.e.*, to actions which apparently imply the sacrifice of selfish inclinations for the good of society, while they are really done out of pride and self-love. By constantly feigning noble sentiments before others man comes, finally, to deceive himself, believing himself a being whose happiness consists in the renunciation of self and all that is earthly, and in the thought of his moral excellence.—The crass assumptions in Mandeville's reasoning are evident at a glance. After analyzing virtue into the suppression of desire, after labeling the impulse after moral approbation vanity, lawful self-love egoism, and rational acquisitiveness avarice, it was easy for him to prove that it is vice which makes the individual industrious and the state prosperous, that virtue is seldom found, and that if it were universal it would become injurious to society.

With different shading and with less one-sidedness, Bolingbroke (cf. p. 193) defended the standpoint of naturalism. God has created us for happiness in common; we are destined to assist one another. Happiness is attainable in society alone, and society cannot exist without justice and benevolence. He who exercises virtue, *i.e.*, promotes the good of the species, promotes at the same time his own good. All actions spring from self-love, which, guided at first by an immediate instinct, and later, by reason developed through experience, extends itself over ever widening spheres. We love ourselves in our relatives, in our friends, further still, in our country, finally, in humanity, so that self-love and social love coincide, and we are impelled to virtue by the combined motives of interest and duty. This is an ethic of common sense from the standpoint of the cultured man of the world—which at the proper time has the right, no doubt, to gain itself a hearing.

Meanwhile Shaftesbury's ideas had impressed Hutcheson and Butler, according to the peculiarities of each. Both of these writers deem it necessary to explain and correct the distinction between the selfish and the benevolent affections by additions, which were of influence on the ethics of Hume; both devote their zeal to the new doctrine of feelings of reflection or moral taste, in which the former gives more prominence to the aesthetic, merely judging factor, the latter to the active or mandatory one.

Francis Hutcheson[1] (died 1747), professor at Glasgow, in his posthumous *System of Moral Philosophy*, 1755, which had been preceded by an *Inquiry concerning the Original of our Ideas of Beauty and Virtue*, 1725, pursues the double aim of showing against Hobbes and Locke the originality and disinterestedness both of benevolence and of moral approval. Virtue is not exercised because it brings advantage to the agent, nor approved on account of advantage to the observer.

[Footnote 1: Cf. Fowler's treatise, cited above—TR.]

(1) The benevolent affections are entirely independent of self-love and regard for the rewards of God and of man, nay, independent even of the lofty satisfaction afforded by self-approbation. This last, indeed, is vouchsafed to us only when we seek the good of others without personal aims: the joy of inward approval is the result of virtue, not the motive to it. If love were in reality a concealed egoism, it would yield to control in cases where it promises advantage, which, as experience shows, is not the fact. Benevolence is entirely natural and as universal in the moral world as gravitation in the corporeal; and like gravitation further in that its intensity increases with propinquity—the nearer the persons, the greater the love. Benevolence is more widespread than malevolence; even the criminal does more innocent and kind acts in his life than criminal ones—the rarity of the latter is the reason why so much is said about them.

(2) Moral judgment is also entirely uninfluenced by consideration of the advantageous or disadvantageous results for the agent or the spectator. The beauty of a good deed arouses immediate satisfaction. Through the moral sense we feel pleasure at observing a virtuous action, and aversion when we perceive an ignoble one, feelings which are independent of all thought of the rewards and punishments promised by God, as well as of the utility or harm for ourselves. Hutcheson argues a complete distinction between moral approval and the perception of the agreeable and the useful, from the facts that we judge a benevolent action which is forced, or done from motives of personal advantage, quite differently from one inspired by love; that we pay esteem to high-minded characters whether their fortunes be good or ill; and that we are moved with equal force by fictitious actions, as, for instance, on the stage, and by those which really take place.

(3) A few further particulars may be emphasized from the comprehensive systematization which Hutcheson industriously and thoughtfully gave to Shaftesbury's ideas. Two points reveal the forerunner of Hume. First, the rôle assigned to the reason in moral affairs is merely subsidiary. Our motive to action is never the knowledge of a true proposition, but always simply a wish, affection, or impulse. Ultimate ends are given by the feelings alone; the reason can only discover the means thereto. Secondly, the turbulent, blind, rapidly passing passions are distinguished from the calm, permanent affections, which are mediated by cognition. The latter are the nobler; among

them, in turn, the highest place is occupied by those conducive to the general good, whose worth is still further determined by the extent of their objects. From this is derived the law that a kind affection receives the more lively approval, the more calm and deliberate it is, the higher the degree of happiness experienced by the object of the action, and the greater the number of persons affected by it. Patriotism and love of mankind in general are higher virtues than affection for friends and children. As the goal of the self-regarding affections, perfection makes its appearance—for the first time in English ethics—by the side of happiness.

Joseph Butler[1] (1692-1752; *Sermons on Human Nature*, 1726; cf. p. 194) maintains still more strictly than Hutcheson the immediateness both of the affections and the moral estimation of them. He declares that even the self-regarding impulses as such are un-egoistic, and makes moral judgment leave out of view all consequences, either foreseen or present, whereas his predecessor had resolved the goodness of the action into its advantageous effects (not for the agent and the spectator, but for its object and) for society. The conscience—so Butler terms the moral sense—directly approves or disapproves characters and actions in themselves, no matter what good or ill they occasion in the world. We judge a mode of action good, not because it is useful to society, but because it corresponds to the demands of the conscience. This must be unconditionally obeyed, whatever be the issue. We must not act contrary to truth and justice, even if it should seem to bring about more happiness than misery.—Butler, too, furnishes material for the ethics of Hume, by his revival of the separation, previously defended by the Stoics, of desire and passion from self-love or interest. Self-love desires a thing because it expects pleasure from it, but the natural impulses impel us toward their objects immediately, *i. e.*, without a representation of the pleasure to be gained; and repetition is necessary before the artificial motive of egoistic pleasure-seeking can be added to the natural motive of inborn desire. Self-love always presupposes original, immediate affections.

[Footnote 1: Cf. Collins's *Butler*, Blackwood's Philosophical Classics. 1881.—TR.]

The English moral science of the century is brought to a conclusion by Adam Smith[1] (1723-90), the celebrated founder of political economy.[2] Smith not only takes into consideration—like his greater friend, Hume—all the problems proposed by his predecessors, but, further (in his *Theory of Moral Sentiments*, 1759, published while he was professor at Glasgow), combines the various attempts at their solution, not by eclectic co-ordination but by working them over for himself, and arranges them on a uniform principle, thus accomplishing a work which has not yet received due recognition beyond the limits of his native land. He reached this comprehensive moral principle by recognizing the full bearing of a thought which Hume had incidentally expressed, that moral judgment depends on participation in the feelings of the agent, and by following out with fine psychological observation this sympathy of men into its first and last manifestations. In this way a twofold kind of morality was revealed to him: mere propriety of behavior and real merit in action. On the one hand, that is, the sympathy of the spectator—as Hume has one-sidedly emphasized—is directed to the utility of the consequences (or to the "merit") of the action, and, on the other, to the fitness of the motives (or their "propriety"). An action is proper when the impartial spectator is able to sympathize with its motive, and meritorious if he can sympathize also with its end or effect; *i.e.*, if, in the first case, the feelings are suitable to their objects (neither too strong nor too weak), and, in the second case, the consequences of the act are advantageous to others. Merit = propriety + utility. The main conclusion is this: Sympathy is that by means of which virtue is recognized and approved, as well as that which is approved as virtue; it is *ratio cognoscendi* as well as *ratio essendi*, the criterion as well as the source of morality. Thus Smith endeavors to solve the two principal problems of English ethics—the criterion and the origin of virtue—with a common answer.

[Footnote 1: Cf. Farrer's *Adam Smith*, English Philosophers Series, 1880.—TR.]

[Footnote 2: The epoch-making work, with which he called economic science into existence, *The Wealth of Nations* appeared in 1776. Cf. Wilhelm Hassbach, *Untersuchungen über Adam Smith*, Leipsic, 1891.]

"Sympathy" denotes primarily nothing more than the innate and purely formal power of imitating to a certain degree the feelings of others. From this modest germ is developed by a progressive growth the wide-spreading tree of morality: moral judgment, the moral imperative with its religious sanction, and ethical character. Accordingly we may distinguish different stages in the development of sympathy—the psychological stage of mere fellow-feeling, the aesthetic stage of moral appreciation, the imperative stage of moral precepts, which further on are construed as commands of God (the famous Kantian definition of religion was announced in Glasgow a generation earlier than in Königsberg), finally, the concluding stage wherein these laws of duty are taken up into the disposition. Besides these, there results from the mechanism of the sympathetic feelings a series of phenomena, which, although they do not entirely conform to the ethical standard, yet exercise a salutary effect on the permanence of society; *e.g.*, our exceptional judgment of the deeds of the great, the rich, and the fortunate, as also the higher worth ascribed to good (and, conversely, the greater guilt to bad) intentions when successfully carried out into action, in comparison with those which fall short of their result.

The first, the purely psychological stage, includes three cases. The spectator sympathizes (1) with the feelings of the agent; (2) with the gratitude or anger of the person affected by the action; (3) the person observed sympathizes in return with the imitative and judging feelings of the spectator.

The fundamental laws of sympathy are as follows: We are roused to imitate the feeling of another by the perception either of its signs (its natural consequences or its natural expression in visible and audible motions), or of its causes (the circumstances and experiences which occasion it), the latter exercising a more potent influence than the former. The wooden leg of the beggar is more effective in exciting our pity than his anxious air; the sight of dental instruments is more eloquent than the plaints of the sufferer from toothache. In order to be able to imitate vividly the feelings of a person, we must know the causes of them.—The feeling of the spectator is, on the average, less intense than that of the person observed, so long as the latter does not control and repress his emotions in view of the calmness of the former. The difference of intensity between the original and the sympathetic feelings differs widely with the various classes of emotions. It is difficult to take part in feelings which arise from bodily conditions, but easy to share those in the production of which the imagination is concerned—hence easier to share in hope and fear than in pleasure and pain.—We sympathize more readily with feelings which are agreeable to the observer, the observed, and other participants than with such as are not so; more willingly, therefore, with cheerfulness, love, benevolence than with grief, hatred, malevolence. This is not only true of temporary affections, but especially of those general dispositions which depend on a more or less happy situation in life; we sympathize more vividly with the fortunes of the rich and noble, because we consider them happier than the poor and lowly. Wealth and high rank are objects of general desire chiefly because their possessor enjoys the advantage of knowing that whatever gives him joy or sorrow always arouses similar feelings in countless other men. The root of all ambition is the wish to rule over the hearts of our fellows by compelling them to make our feelings their own; the central nerve of all happiness consists in seeing our own sensations shared by those about us and reflected back, as it were, from manifold mirrors. Small annoyances often have a diverting effect on the spectator; great success easily excites his envy; great sorrows and minor joys, on the contrary, are always sure of our sympathy. Hence the morose man, to whom everything is an occasion of ill-humor, is nowhere welcome, and the man of cheerful disposition, who rejoices in each little event and whose good spirits are contagious, everywhere.

Not less admirable than the fine gift of observation which guides Smith in his discovery of the primary manifestations and the laws of sympathy is the skill with which he deduces moral phenomena, from the simplest to the most complex—moral judgment, the moral law, its application to one's own conduct, the conscience—from the interchange of sympathetic feelings. From involuntary comparison of the representative feeling of the spectator with its original in the person observed arises an agreeable or disagreeable feeling of judgment, a judgment of value, approbating or rejecting the latter. This is approving when the intensity of the original harmonizes with that of the copy, disapproving when the former exceeds or fails to attain the latter. In the one case the emotion is judged suitable to the object which causes it; in the other, too violent or too weak. It is always a certain mean of passion which, as "proper," receives approval (esteem, love, or admiration). In the case of the social passions excess is more readily condoned, in the case of the unsocial and selfish ones, defect; hence we judge the over-sensitive more leniently than the over-vengeful. Anger must be well-grounded and must express itself with great moderation to arouse in the spectator a like degree of sympathetic resentment. For here the sympathy of the spectator is divided between two parties, and fellow-feeling with the angry one is weakened by fear for the person menaced by him, whereas, in the case of kind affections, sympathy is increased by doubling. While our judgment of propriety or decorum rests on simple participation in the sentiments of the agent, our judgment of merit and demerit is based, in addition, on sympathy with the feelings of gratitude or resentment experienced by the person on whom the action terminates. An act is meritorious if it appears to us to deserve thanks and reward, ill-deserving if it seems to merit resentment and punishment. Nature has inscribed on the heart, apart from all reflection on the utility of punishment, an independent, immediate, and instinctive approbation of the sacred law of retribution. This is the point at which a hitherto purely contemplative sympathy passes over into an active impulse, which prepares us to support the victim of attack and insult in his defense and revenge.

This participation in the circumstances and feelings of others is a reciprocal phenomenon. The spectator takes pains to share the sentiments of the person observed; and the latter, on his part, endeavors to reduce the emotions which move him to a degree which will render participation in them possible for the former. In these reciprocal efforts we have the beginnings of the two classes of virtues—the gentle, amiable virtues of sympathy and sensibility, and the exalted, estimable virtues of self-denial and self-command. Both of these conditions of mind, however, are considered virtues only when they are manifested in unusual intensity: humanity is a remarkably delicate fellow-feeling, greatness of soul a rare degree of self-command. (The consideration for those about one which is ethically demanded is given, moreover, to a certain extent involuntarily. The man in trouble and the merry man alike restrain themselves in the company of persons who are indifferent, or in an opposite mood, while they give rein to their emotions when with those similarly affected. Joy is enhanced by sympathy, and grief mitigated.) Thus the perfection of human nature and the divinely willed harmony among the feelings of men are dependent on every man feeling little for himself and much for others; on his holding his selfish inclinations in check and giving free course to his benevolent ones. This is the injunction of Christianity as well as of nature. And as, on the one hand, the content of the moral law is thus deduced from sympathy, so, on the other, this yields the formal criterion of good: Look upon thy sentiments and actions in the light in which the impartial spectator would see them. Conscience is the spectator taken up into our own breast. It remains to consider the origin of this third, imperative stage.

From daily experience of the fact that we judge the conduct of others, and they ours, and from the wish to gain their approval, arises the habit of subjecting our own actions to criticism. We learn to look at ourselves through the eyes of others, we assign the spectator and judge a place in our own heart, we make his calm objective judgment our own, and hear the man within calling to us: Thou art responsible for thy acts and intentions. In this way we are placed in a position to overcome two great delusions, one of passion, which overestimates the present at the expense of the future, and one of self-love, which overestimates the individual at the expense of other men; delusions from which the impartial spectator is free, for the pleasure of the moment seems to him no more desirable than pleasure to come, and one person is just the same to him as another. Through comparison of like cases in the exercise of self-examination certain rules or principles are formed concerning what is right and good. Reverence for these general rules of living is called the sense of duty. The last step in the process consists in our enhancement of the binding authority of moral rules by looking on them as commands of God. Here Smith adds subtle discussions of the question, in what cases actions ought to be done simply out of regard for these abstract maxims, and in what others we welcome the co-operation of a natural impulse or passion. We ought to be angry and to punish with reluctance, merely because reason enjoins it, but, on the other hand, we should be benevolent and grateful from affection; she is not a model wife who performs her duties merely from a sense of duty, and not from inclination also. Further, in all cases where the rules cannot be formulated with perfect exactness and definiteness (as they can in the case of justice), and are not absolutely valid without exception, reverence for them must be assisted by a natural taste for modifying and supplementing the general maxims to suit particular instances.

In this sketch of the course of Smith's moral philosophy much that is fine and much that is of importance has of necessity been passed over—his excellent analysis of the relations of benevolence and justice, and numerous descriptions of traits of character, *e. g.*, his ingenious parallel between pride and vanity. We may briefly mention, in conclusion, his observations on the irregularities of moral judgment. Prosperity and success exert an influence on this, which, though hurtful to its purity, must, on the whole, be considered advantageous to mankind. Our lenience toward the defects of princes, the great, and the rich, and our over-praise for their excellent qualities are, from the moral standpoint, an injustice, but one which has this advantage, that it encourages ambition and industry, and maintains social distinctions intact, which without loyalty and respect toward superiors would be broken down. For most men the road to fortune coincides with the path to virtue. Again, it is a beneficent provision of nature that we put a higher estimate on a successfully executed act of benevolence, and reward it more, than a kind intention which fails of execution; that we judge and punish the purposed crime which is not carried out more leniently than the one which is completed; that we even ascribe a certain degree of accountability to an unintentional act of good or evil—

although in these cases the moralist is compelled to see an ethically unjustifiable corruption of the judgment by external success or failure beyond the control of the agent. The first of these irregularities does not allow the man of good intentions to content himself with noble desires merely, but spurs him on to greater endeavors to carry them out—man is created for action; the second protects us from the inquisitorial questioning of motives, for it is easy for the most innocent to fall under grave suspicion. To this inconsistency of feeling we owe the necessary legal principle that deeds only, not intentions, are punishable. God has reserved for himself judgment concerning dispositions. The third irregularity, that he who inflicts unintentional injury is not guilty, even in his own eyes, but yet seems bound to make atonement and reparation, is useful in so far as it warns everyone to be prudent, while the corresponding illusion, in virtue of which we are grateful to an involuntary benefactor—for instance, the bearer of good tidings—and reward him, is at least not harmful, for any reason appears sufficient for the bestowal of kind intentions and actions.

It is impossible to explain in brief the relation of Smith's ethical theory to his political economy. His merit in the former consists in his comprehensive and characteristic combination of the results reached by his predecessors, and in his preparation for Kantian views, so far as this was possible from the empirical standpoint of the English. His impartial spectator was the forerunner of the categorical imperative.

English ethics after Smith may, almost without exception, be termed eclecticism. This is true of Ferguson *(Institutes of Moral Philosophy*, 1769); of Paley (1785); of the Scottish School (Dugald Stewart, 1793). Bentham's utilitarianism was the first to bring in a new phase.

%4. Theory of Knowledge.%

(a) %Berkeley%.—George Berkeley, a native of Ireland, Bishop of Cloyne (1685-1753; *An Essay toward a New Theory of Vision*, 1709; *A Treatise concerning the Principles of Human Knowledge*, 1710; *Three Dialogues between Hylas and Philonous*, 1713; *Alciphron, or the Minute Philosopher*, 1732, against the freethinkers; *Works*, 1784. Fraser's edition of the Collected Works appeared in 1871, in four volumes),[1] is related to Locke as Spinoza to Descartes. He notices blemishes and contradictions allowed by his predecessor to remain, and, recognizing that the difficulty is not to be remedied by minor corrections and artificial hypotheses, goes back to the fundamental principles, takes these more earnestly than their author, and, by carrying them out more strictly, arrives at a new view of the world. The points in Locke's doctrines which invited a further advance were the following: Locke proclaims that our knowledge extends no further than our ideas, and that truth consists in the agreement of ideas among themselves, not in the agreement of ideas with things. But this principle had scarcely been announced before it was violated. In spite of his limitation of knowledge to ideas, Locke maintains that we know (if not the inner constitution, yet) the qualities and powers of things without us, and have a "sensitive" certainty of their existence. Against this, it is to be said that there are no primary qualities, that is, qualities which exist without as well as within us. Extension, motion, solidity, which are cited as such, are just as purely subjective states in us as color, heat, and sweetness. Impenetrability is nothing more than the feeling of resistance, an idea, therefore, which self-evidently can be nowhere else than in the mind experiencing it. Extension, size, distance, and motion are not even sensations (we see colors only, not quantitative determinations), but relations which we in thinking add to the sense-qualities (secondary qualities), and which we are not able to represent apart from them; their relativity alone would forbid us to consider them objective. And material substances, the "support" of qualities invented by the philosophers, are not only unknown, but entirely non-existent. Abstract matter is a phrase without meaning, and individual things are collections of ideas in us, nothing more. If we take away all sense-qualities from a thing, absolutely nothing remains. Our ideas are not merely the only; objects of knowledge, but also the only existing things—*nothing exists except minds and their ideas*. Spirits alone are active beings, they only are indivisible substances, and have real existence, while the being of bodies (as dependent, inert, variable beings, which are in a constant process of becoming) consists alone in their appearance to spirits and their being perceived by them. Incogitative, hence passive, beings are neither substances, nor capable of producing ideas in us. Those ideas which we do not ourselves produce are the effects of a spirit which is mightier than we. With this a second inconsistency was removed which had been overlooked by Locke, who had ascribed active power to spirits alone and denied it to matter, but at the same time had made the former affected by the latter. If external sense is to mean the capacity for having ideas occasioned by the action of external material things, then there is no external sense. A third point wherein Locke had not gone far enough for his successor, concerned the favorite English doctrine of nominalism. Locke, with his predecessors, had maintained that all reality is individual, and that universals exist only in the abstracting understanding. From this point Berkeley advances a step further, the last, indeed, which was possible in this direction, by bringing into question the possibility even of abstract ideas. As all beings are particular things, so all ideas are particular ideas.

[Footnote 1: Cf. also Fraser's *Berkeley* (Blackwood's Philosophical
Classics) 1881; Eraser's *Selections from Berkeley*, 4th ed., 1891; and
Krauth's edition of the *Principles*, 1874, with notes from several
sources, especially those translated from Ueberweg.—TR.]

Berkeley looks on the refutation of these two fundamental mistakes—the assumption of general ideas in the mind, and the belief in the existence of a material world outside it—as his life work, holding them the chief sources of atheism, doubt, and philosophical discord. The first of these errors arises from the use of language. Because we employ words which denote more than one object, we have believed ourselves warranted in concluding that we have ideas which correspond to the extension of the words in question, and which contain only those characteristics which are uniformly found in all objects so named. This, however, is not the case.[1] We speak of many things which we cannot represent: names do not always stand for ideas. The definition of the word triangle as a three-sided figure bounded by straight lines, makes demands upon us which our faculties of imagination are never fully able to meet; for the triangle that we represent to ourselves is always either right-angled or oblique-angled, and not—as we must demand from the abstract conception of the figure—both and neither at once. The name "man" includes men and women, children and the aged, but we are never able to represent a man except as an individual of a definite age and sex. Nevertheless we are in a position to make a safe use of these non-presentative but useful abbreviations, and by means of a particular idea to develop truths of wider application. This takes place when, in the demonstration, those qualities are not considered which distinguish the idea from others with a like name. In this case the given idea stands for all others which are known by the same name; the representative idea is not universal, but serves as such. Thus when I have demonstrated the proposition, the sum of all the angles of a triangle is equal to two right angles, for a given triangle, I do not need to prove it for every triangle thereafter. For not only the color and size of the triangle are indifferent, but its other peculiarities as well; the question whether it is right-angled or obtuse-angled, whether it has equal sides, whether it has equal or unequal angles, is not mentioned in the demonstration, and has no influence upon it. *Abstracta* exist only in this sense. In considering the individual Paul I can attend exclusively to those characteristics which he has in common with all men or with all living beings, but it is impossible for me to represent this complex of common qualities apart from his individual peculiarities. Self-observation shows that we have no general concepts; reason, that we can have none, for the combination of opposite elements in one idea would be a contradiction in terms. Motion in general, neither swift nor slow, extension in general, at once great and small, abstract matter without sensuous determinations—these can neither exist nor be perceived.

[Footnote 1: Against the Berkeleyan denial of abstract notions the popular philosopher, Joh. Jak. Engel, directed an essay, *Ueber die Realität allgemeiner Begriffe* (Engel's *Schriften*, vol. x.), to which attention has been called by O. Liebmann, *Analysis tier Wirklichkeit*, 2d ed., p. 473.]

The "materialistic" hypothesis—so Berkeley terms the assumption that a material world exists apart from perceiving mind, and independently of being perceived—is, first, unnecessary, for the facts which it is to explain can be explained as well, or even better, without it; and, second, false, since it is a contradiction to suppose that an object can exist unperceived, and that a sensation or idea is the copy of anything itself not a sensation or idea. Ideas are the only objects of the understanding. Sensible qualities (white, sweet) are subjective states of the soul; sense objects (sugar), sensation-complexes. If sensations need a substantial support, this is the soul which perceives them, not an external thing which can neither perceive nor be perceived. Single ideas, and those combined into objects, can exist nowhere else than in the mind; the being of sense objects consists in their being perceived (*esse est percipi*). I see light and feel heat, and combine these sensations of sight and touch into the substance fire, because I know from experience that they constantly accompany and suggest each other.[1] The assumption of an "object" apart from the idea is as useless as its existence would be. Why should God create a world of real things without the mind, when these can neither enter into the mind, nor (because unperceived) be copied by its ideas, nor (because they themselves lack perception and power) produce ideas in it? Ideas signify nothing but themselves, *i. e.*, affections of the subject.

[Footnote 1: The fire that I see is not the cause of the pain which I experience in approaching it, but the visual image of the flame is only a sign which warns me not to go too near. If I look through a microscope I see a different object from the one perceived with the naked eye. Two persons never see the same object, they merely have like sensations.]

The further question arises, What is the origin of ideas? Men have been led into this erroneous belief in the reality of the material world by the fact that certain ideas are not subject to our will, while others are. Sensations are distinguished from the ideas of imagination, which we can excite and alter at pleasure, by their greater strength, liveliness, and distinctness, by their steadiness, regular order, and coherence, and by the fact that they arise without our aid and whether we will or no. Unless these ideas are self-originated they must have an external cause. This, however, can be nothing else than a willing, thinking Being; for without will it could not be active and act upon me, and without ideas of its own it could not communicate ideas to me. Because of the manifoldness and regularity of our sensations the Being which produces them must, further, possess infinite power and intelligence. The ideas of imagination are produced by ourselves, real perceptions are produced by God. The connected whole of divinely produced ideas we call nature, and the constant regularity in their succession, the laws of nature. The invariableness of the divine working and the purposive harmony of creation reveal the wisdom and goodness of the Almighty more clearly than "astonishing and exceptional events." When we hear a man speak we reason from this activity to his existence. How much less are we entitled to doubt the existence of God, who speaks to us in the thousandfold works of nature.

The natural or created ideas which God impresses on us are copies of the eternal ideas which he himself perceives, not, indeed, by passive sensation, but through his creative reason. Accordingly when it was maintained that things do not exist independently of perception, the reference was not to the individual spirit, but to all spirits. When I turn my eyes away from an object it continues to exist, indeed, after my perception has ended—in the minds of other men and in that of the Omnipresent One. The pantheistic conclusion of these principles, in the sense of Geulincx and Malebranche,[1] which one expects, was really suggested by Berkeley. Everything exists only in virtue of its participation in the one, permanent, all-comprehensive spirit; individual spirits are of the same nature with the universal reason, only they are less perfect, limited, and not pure activity, while God is passionless intelligence. But if, in the last analysis, God is the cause of all, this does not hold of the free actions of men, least of all of wicked ones. The freedom of the will must not be rejected because of the contradictions which its acceptance involves; motion, also, and mathematical infinity imply incomprehensible elements. In the philosophy of nature Berkeley prefers the teleological to the mechanical view, since the latter is able to discover the laws of phenomena only, but not their efficient and final causes. Sense and experience acquaint us merely with the course of phenomenal effects; the reason, which opens up to us the realm of causation, of the spiritual, is the only sure guide to science and truth. The understanding does not feel, the senses do not know. We have no (sensuous) idea of other spirits, but only a notion of them; instead of themselves we perceive their activities merely, from which we argue to souls like ourselves, while we know our own mind by immediate self-consciousness.[2]

[Footnote 1: The example of Arthur Collier shows that the same results which Berkeley reaches empirically can be obtained from the standpoint of rationalism. Following Malebranche, and developing further the idealistic tendencies of the latter, Collier had, independently of Berkeley, conceived the doctrine of the "non-existence or impossibility of an external world "; but had not worked it out in his *Clavis Universalis*, 1713, until after the appearance of Berkeley's chief work, and not without consideration of this. The general point of view and the arguments are the same: Existence is equivalent to being perceived by God; the creation of a real world of matter apart from the ideal world in God and from sensuous perceptions in us would have been a superfluous device, etc.]

[Footnote 2: It should be remembered, however, that this immediate knowledge of ourselves is also "not after the manner of an idea or sensation." Our knowledge of spirits is always mediated by "notions" not by "ideas" in the strict sense, that is, not by "images." Cf. *Principles*, §§ 27, 135 *seq*., especially in the second edition.—TR.]

In contrast to the fearlessness with which Berkeley propounds his spiritualism, his anxious endeavors to take away the appearance of paradox from his immaterialistic doctrine, and to show its complete agreement with common sense, excite surprise. Even the common man, he argues, desires nothing more than that his perceptions be real; the distinction between idea and object is an invention of philosophers.

Here Berkeley cannot be acquitted of a certain sophistical play upon the term "idea," which, in fact, is ambiguous. He understands by it *that which* the soul perceives (its immediate, inner object), but the popular mind, *that through which* the soul perceives an object. The reality of an idea in us is different from the idea of a real thing, or from the reality of that which is perceived without us by means of the idea, and it is just this last meaning which common sense affirms and Berkeley denies. In any case it was a work of great merit to have transferred the existence of objects beyond our ideas, of things-in-themselves, out of the region of the self-evident into the region of the problematical. We never get beyond the circle of our ideas, and if we posit a thing-in-itself as the ground and object of the idea, this also is simply a thought, an idea. For us there is no being except that of the perceiver and the perceived. Later we shall meet two other forms of idealism, in Leibnitz and Fichte. Both of these agree with Berkeley that spiritual beings alone are active, and active beings alone real, and that the being of the inactive consists in their being perceived. But while in Berkeley the objective ideas are impressed upon finite spirits by the Infinite Spirit from without and singly, with Leibnitz they appear as a fullness of germs, which God implanted together in the monads at the beginning, and which the individual develops into consciousness, and with Fichte they become the unconscious productions of the Absolute Ego acting in the individual egos. For the two former as many worlds exist as there are individual spirits, their harmony being guaranteed, in the one case, by the consistency of God's working, and, in the other, by his foresight. For Fichte, on the other hand, there is but one world, for the absolute is not outside the individual spirits, but the uniformly working force within them.

(b) Hume.—David Hume was born in Edinburgh in 1711, and died in the same city, 1776. His position as librarian, which he held in the place of his birth, 1752-57, gave the opportunity for his *History of England* (1754-62). His chief work, the *Treatise on Human Nature*, which, however, found few readers, was composed during his first residence in France in 1734-37. Later he worked over the first book of this work into his *Enquiry concerning Human Understanding* (1748); the second book into *A Dissertation on the Passions*; and the third into *An Enquiry concerning the Principles of Morals*. These, and others of his essays, found so much favor that, during his second sojourn in France, as secretary to Lord Hertford, in 1763-66, he was already honored as a philosopher of world-wide renown. Then, after serving for some time as Under-Secretary of State, he retired to private life at home (1769).

The three books of the *Treatise on Human Nature*, which appeared in 1739-40, are entitled *Of the Understanding, Of the Passions, Of Morals*. Of the five volumes of the Essays, the first contains the *Essays Moral, Political, and Literary*, 1741-42; the second, the *Enquiry concerning Human Understanding*, 1748; the third, the *Enquiry concerning the Principles of Morals*, 1751; the fourth, the *Political Discourses*, 1752; the fifth, 1757, the *Four Dissertations*, including that *On the Passions* and the *Natural History of Religion*. After Hume's death appeared the *Autobiography*, 1777; the *Dialogues concerning Natural Religion*, 1779; and the two small essays on *Suicide* and the *Immortality of the Soul*, 1783.[1] The *Philosophical Works* were published in 1827, and frequently afterward.[2]

[Footnote 1: Or 1777, cf. Green and Grose's edition, vol. iii. p. 67 *seq*.—Tr.]

[Footnote 2: Among the works on Hume we may mention Jodl's prize treatise, 1872, and Huxley's *Hume* (English Men of Letters), 1879. [The reader may be referred also to Knight's *Hume* (Blackwood's Philosophical Classics), 1886; to T.H. Green's "Introductions" in Green and Grose's edition of the collected works in four volumes, 1874 (new ed. 1889-90), which is now standard; and to Selby-Bigge's reprint of the original edition of the *Treatise*, I vol., 1888, with a valuable Analytical Index.]]

Hume's object, like that of Berkeley, is the improvement of Locke's doctrine of knowledge. In several respects he does not go so far as Berkeley, in others very much farther. In agreement with Berkeley's ultra-nominalism, which combats even the possibility of abstract ideas, he yet does not follow him to the extent of denying external reality. On the other hand, he carries out more consistently Berkeley's hint that immediate sensation includes less than is ascribed to it (*e.g.*, that by vision we perceive colors only, and not distance, etc.), as well as his principle—destructive to the certainty of our knowledge of nature—that there is no causality among phenomena; and brings the question of substance to, the negative conclusion, that there is no need whatever for a support for groups of qualities, and, therefore, that substantiality is to be denied to immaterial as well as to material beings. The points in Locke's philosophy which seemed to Hume to need completion were different from those at which Berkeley had struck in. The antithesis of rational and empirical knowledge is more sharply conceived; the combination of ideas is not left to the choice of the understanding but placed under the dominion of psychological laws; and to the distinction between outer and inner experience (to the former of which priority is conceded, on the ground that we must have had an external sensation before we can, through reflection, be conscious of it as an internal phenomenon), there is added a second, as important as the other and crossing it, between impressions and ideas, of which the former are likewise made prior to the latter.

Everyone will acknowledge the considerable difference between a sensation actually present (of heat, for instance) and the mere idea of one previously experienced, or shortly to come. This consists in the greater force, liveliness, and vividness of the former. Although these two classes of states (the idea of a landscape described by a poet and the perception of a real one, anger and the thought of anger) are only quantitatively distinct, they are scarcely ever in danger of being confused—the most lively idea is always less so than the weakest perception. The actual, outer or inner, sensations may be termed impressions; the weaker images of memory or imagination, which they leave behind them, ideas. Since nothing can gain entrance to the soul except through the two portals of outer and inner experience, there is no idea which has not arisen from an impression or several such; every idea is the image and copy of an impression. But as the understanding and imagination variously combine, separate, and transpose the elements furnished by the senses and lingering in memory, the possibility of error arises. A hidden, and, therefore more dangerous source of error consists in the reference of an idea to a different impression than the one of which it is the copy. The concepts substance and causality are examples of such false reference.

The combination of ideas takes place without freedom, in a purely mechanical, way according to fixed rules, which in the last analysis reduce to three fundamental laws of association: Ideas are associated (1) according to their resemblance and contrast; (2) according to their contiguity in space and time; (3) according to their causal connection. Mathematics is based on the operation of the first of these laws, on the immediate or mediate knowledge of the resemblance, contrariety, and quantitative relations of ideas; the descriptive and experimental part of the sciences of nature and of man on the second; religion, metaphysics, and that part of physical and moral science which goes beyond mere observation on the third. The theory of knowledge has to determine the boundaries of human understanding and the degree of credibility to which these sciences are entitled.

The objects of human thought and inquiry are either relations of ideas or matters of fact. To the former class belong the objects of mathematics, the truths of which, since they are analytic (*i. e.*, merely explicate in the predicate the characteristics already contained in the subject, and add nothing new to this), and since they concern possible relations only, not reality, possess intuitive or demonstrative certainty. It is only propositions concerning quantity and number that are discoverable *a priori* by the mere operation of thought, without dependence on real existence, and that can be proved from the impossibility of their opposites—mathematics is the only demonstrative science.

We reach certainty in matters of fact by direct perception, or by inferences from other facts, when they transcend the testimony of our senses and memory. These arguments from experience are of an entirely different sort from the rational demonstrations of mathematics; as the contrary of a fact is always thinkable (the proposition that the sun will not rise to-morrow implies no logical contradiction), they yield, strictly speaking, probability only, no matter how strong our conviction of their accuracy may be. Nevertheless it is advisable to separate this species of inferences from experience—whose certainty is not doubted except by the philosophers—from uncertain probabilities, as a class intermediate between the latter and demonstrative truth (demonstrations—proofs—probabilities). All reasonings concerning matters of fact are based on the relation of cause and effect. Whence, then, do we obtain the knowledge of cause and effect? Not by *a priori* thought. Pure reason is able only to analyze concepts into their elements, not to connect new predicates with them. All its judgments are analytic, while synthetic judgments rest on experience. Judgments concerning causation belong in this latter class, for effects are entirely distinct from causes; the effect is not contained in the cause, nor the latter in the former. In the case of a phenomenon previously unknown we cannot tell from what causes it has proceeded, nor what its effect will be. We argue that fire will warm us, and bread afford nourishment, because we have often perceived these causal pairs closely connected in space and time. But even experience does not vouchsafe all that we desire. It shows nothing more than the coexistence and succession of phenomena and events; while the judgment itself, *e. g.*, that the motion of one body stands in causal connection with that of another, asserts more than mere contiguity in space and time, it affirms not merely that the one precedes the other, but that it produces it—not merely that the second follows the first, but that it results from it. The bond which connects the two events, the force that puts forth the second from the first, the necessary connection between the two is not perceived, but added to perception by thought, construed into it.[1] What, then, is the occasion and what the warrant for transforming perceived succession in time into causal succession, for substituting *must* for *is*, for interpreting the observed connection of fact into a necessary connection which always eludes observation?

[Footnote 1: The weakness of the concept of cause had been recognized before Hume by the skeptic, J. Glanvil (1636-80). Causality itself cannot be perceived; we infer it from the constant succession of two phenomena, without being able to show warrant for the transformation of *thereafter* into *thereby*.]

We do not causally connect every chance pair of successive events, but those only which have been repeatedly observed together. The wonder is, then, that through oft-repeated observation of certain objects we come to believe that we know something about the behavior of other like objects, and the further behavior of these same ones. From the fact that I have seen a given apple fall ten times to the ground, I infer that all the apples in the world do the same when loosened, instead of flying upward, which, in itself, is quite as thinkable; I infer further that this has always been the case, and will continue to be so to all eternity. Where is the intermediate link between the proposition, "I have found that such an object has always been attended with such an effect," and this other, "I foresee that other objects which are, in appearance, similar, will be attended with similar effects"? This postulate, that the future will be like the past, and that like causes will have like effects, rests on a purely psychological basis. In virtue of the laws of association the sight of an object or event vividly recalls the image of a second, often observed in connection with the former, and leads us involuntarily to expect its appearance anew. The idea of causal connection is based on feeling (the feeling of inner determination to pass from one idea to a second), not upon insight; it is a product of the imagination, not of the understanding. From the habitual perception of two events in connection (sunshine and heat) arises the mental determination to think of the second when we perceive the first, and, anticipating the senses, to count on its appearance. It is now possible to state of what impression the idea of the causal nexus is the copy: the impression on which it is based is the habitual transition from the idea of a thing to its customary attendant. Hence the idea of causality has a purely subjective significance, not the objective one which we ascribe to it. It is impossible to determine whether there is a real necessity of becoming corresponding to the felt necessity of thought. In life we never doubt the fact, but for science our conviction of the uniformity of nature remains a merely probable (though a very highly probable) conviction. Complete certainty is vouchsafed only by rational demonstration and immediate experience. The necessary bond which we postulate between cause and effect can neither be demonstrated nor felt.

If all experiential reasonings depend on the idea of causality, and this has no other support than subjective mental habit, it follows that all knowledge of nature which goes beyond mere observed fact is not knowledge (neither demonstrative knowledge nor knowledge of fact), but belief.[1] The probability of our belief in the regularity of natural phenomena increases, indeed, with every new verification of the assumptions based thereon; but, as has been shown, it never rises to absolute certainty. Nevertheless inferences from experience are trustworthy and entirely sufficient for practical life, and the aim of the above skeptical deliverances was not to shake belief—only a fool or a lunatic can doubt in earnest the immutability of nature—but only to make it clear that it is mere belief, and not, as hitherto held, demonstrative or factual knowledge. Our doubt is intended to define the boundary between knowledge and belief, and to destroy that absolute confidence which is a hindrance rather than a help to investigation. We should recognize it as a wise provision of nature that the regulation of our thoughts and the belief in the objective validity of our anticipation of future events have not been confided to the weak, inconstant, inert, and fallacious reason, but to a powerful instinct. In life and action we are governed by this natural impulse, in spite of all the scruples of the skeptical reason.

[Footnote 1: Hume distinguishes belief as a form of knowledge from religious faith, both in fact and in name. In the *Treatise*—the passage is wanting in the *Enquiry*—our conviction of the external existence of the objects of perception is also ascribed to the former, which later formed Jacobi's point of departure. Religious faith is referred to revelation.]

In Hume's earlier work his destructive critique of the idea of cause is accompanied by a deliverance in a similar strain on the concept of substance, which is not included in the shorter revision. Substances are not perceived through impressions, but only qualities and powers. The unknown something which is supposed to have qualities, or in which these are supposed to inhere, is an unnecessary fiction of the imagination. A permanent similarity of attributes by no means requires a self-identical support for these. A thing is nothing more than a collection of qualities, to which we give a special name because they are always found together. The idea of substance, like the idea of cause, is founded in a subjective habit which we erroneously objectify. The impression from which it has arisen is our inner perception that our thought remains constant in the repeated experience of the same group of qualities (whenever I see sugar, *I do the same thing*, that is, I combine the qualities white color, sweet taste, hardness, etc., with one another), or the impression of a uniform combination of ideas. The idea of substance becomes erroneous through the fact that we refer it not to the inner activity of representation, to which it rightly belongs, but to the external group of qualities, and make it a real, permanent substratum for the latter. Mental substances disappear along with material substances. The soul or mind is, in reality, nothing more than the sum of our inner states, a collection of ideas which flow on in a continuous and regular stream; it is like a stage, across which feelings, perceptions, thoughts, and volitions are passing while it does not itself come into sight. A permanent self or ego, as a substratum of ideas, is not perceived; there is no invariable, permanent impression. That which leads to the assumption of personal identity is only the frequent repetition of similar trains of ideas, and the gradual succession of our ideas, which is easily confused with constancy. Thus robbed of its substantiality, the soul has no further claims to immateriality and immortality, and suicide ceases to be a crime.[1]

[Footnote 1: Cf. the essays on *Suicide* and the *Immortality of the Soul*, 1783, whose authorship by Hume, however, is not absolutely established [of. Green and Grose, as above, p. 221, note first.—TR.]]

Is Hume roundly to be called a skeptic? [1] He never impugned the validity of mathematical reasonings, nor experimental truths concerning matters of fact; in regard to the former his thought is rationalistic, in regard to the latter it is empirical or, more accurately, sensationalistic. His attitude toward the empirical sciences of nature and of mind is that of a semi-skeptic or probabilist, in so far as they go beyond the establishment of facts to the proof of connections under law and to inferences concerning the future. Habit is for him a safe guide for life, although it does not go beyond probabilities; absolute knowledge is unattainable for us, but not indispensable. Toward metaphysics, as an alleged science of the suprasensible, he takes up an entirely negative attitude. If an argument from experience is to be assured of merely that degree of probability which is sufficient for belief, it must not only have a well-established fact (an impression or memory-image) for its starting point, but, together with its conclusion, it must keep within the limits of possible experience. The limits of possible experience are also the limits of the knowable; inferences to the continued existence of the soul after death and to the being of God are vain sophistry and illusion. According to the famous conclusion of the *Essay*, all volumes which contain anything other than "abstract reasonings concerning quantity or number" or "experimental reasonings concerning matter of fact and existence" deserve to be committed to the flames. In view of this limitation of knowledge to that which is capable of exact measurement and that which is present in experience, as well of the principle that the elements added by thought are to be sharply distinguished from the positively given (the immediate facts of perception), we must agree with those who call Hume the father of modern positivism.[2]

[Footnote 1: In the *Essay*, Hume describes his own standpoint as mitigated or academical skepticism in antithesis to the Cartesian, which from doubt and through doubt hopes to reach the indubitable, and to the excessive skepticism of Pyrrhonism, which cripples the impulse to inquiry. This moderate skepticism asks us only, after resisting the tendency to unreflecting conclusions, to make a duty of deliberation and caution in judging, and to restrain inquiry within those fields which are accessible to our knowledge, *i.e.*, the fields of mathematics and empirical fact. In the *Treatise* Hume had favored a sharper skepticism and extended his doubt more widely, *e.g.*, even to the trustworthiness of geometry. Cf. on this point Ed. Grimm, *Zur Geschichte des Erkenntnissproblems*, 1890, p, 559 *seq.*]

[Footnote 2: So Volkelt, *Erfahrung und Denken*, 1886, p. 105.]

* * * * *

As a philosopher of religion Hume is the finisher and destroyer of deism. Of the three principles of the deists—religion, its origin and its truth are objects of scientific investigation; religion has its origin in the reason and the consciousness of duty; natural religion is the oldest, the positive religions are degenerate or revived forms of natural religion—he accepts the first, while rejecting the other two. Religion may correspond to reason or contradict it, but not proceed from it. Religion has its basis in human nature, yet not in its rational but its sensuous side; not in the speculative desire for knowledge, but in practical needs; not in the contemplation of nature, but in looking forward with fear or joy to the changing events of human life. Anxiety and hope concerning future events lead us to posit unseen powers as directing our destiny, and to seek their favor. The capriciousness of fortune points to a plurality of gods; the tendency to conceive all things like ourselves gives them human characteristics; the powerful impression made by all that comes within the sphere of the senses incites us to connect the divine power with visible objects; the allegorical laudation and deification of eminent men leads to a completed polytheism. That this and not (mono-) theism was the original form of religion, Hume assumes to be a fact for historical times, and a well-founded conjecture for prehistoric ages. Those who hold that humanity began with a perfect religion find it difficult to explain the obscuration of the truth, endow immature ages with a developed use of the reason which they can scarcely have possessed, make error grow worse with increasing culture, and contradict the historical progress upward which is everywhere else observed. The philosophical knowledge of God is a very late product of mature reflection; even monotheism, as a popular religion, did not arise from rational reflection, although its chief principle is in agreement with the results of philosophy, but from the same irrational motives as polytheism. Its origin from polytheism is accomplished by the transformation of the leading god (the king of the gods or the tutelary deity of the nation) through the fear and emulous flattery of his votaries into the one, infinite, spiritual ruler of the world. Amid the folly of the superstitious herd, however, this refined idea is not long preserved in its purity; the more exalted the conception entertained of the supreme deity, the more imperatively the need makes itself felt for the interpolation between this being and mankind of mediators and demi-gods, partaking more of the human nature of the worshipers and more familiar to them. Later a new purification takes place, so that the history of religion shows a continuous alternation of the lower and higher forms.

After depriving theism of its prerogative of originality, Hume further takes away from it its fame as in every respect the best religion. It is disadvantageously distinguished from polytheism by the fact that it is more intolerant, makes its followers pusillanimous, and, by its incomprehensible dogmas, puts their faith to severer tests; while it is on a level with polytheism in that most of its adherents exalt belief in foolish mysteries, fanaticism, and the observance of useless customs above the practice of virtue.

The *Natural History of Religion*, which far outbids the conclusions of the deists by its endeavors to explain religion, not on rational, but on historical and psychological grounds, and to separate it entirely from knowledge by relegating it to the sphere of practice, leaves the possibility of a philosophical knowledge of God an open question. The *Dialogues concerning Natural Religion* greatly diminish this hope. The most cogent argument for the intelligence of the world-ground, the teleological argument, is a hypothesis which has grave weaknesses, and one to which many other equally probable hypotheses may be opposed. The finite world, with its defects and abounding misery amid all its order and adaptation, can never yield an inference to an infinite, perfect unit-cause, to an all-powerful, all-wise, and benevolent deity. To this the eleventh section of the *Enquiry* adds the argument, that it is inadmissible to ascribe to the inferred cause other properties than those which are necessary to explain the observed effect. The tenth section of the same *Essay* argues that there is no miracle supported by a sufficient number of witnesses credible because of their intelligence and honesty, and free from a preponderance of contradictory experiences and testimony of greater probability. In short, the reason is neither capable of reaching the existence of God by well-grounded inference nor of comprehending the truth of the Christian religion with its accompanying miracles. That which transcends experience cannot be proven and known, but only believed in. Whoever is moved by faith to give assent to things which contradict all custom and experience, is conscious of a continued miracle in his own person.

Hume never denied the existence of God, never directly impugned revelation. His final word is doubt and uncertainty. It is certain that his counsel not to follow the leadership of the reason in religious matters, but to submit ourselves to the power of instinct and common opinion, was less earnest and less in harmony with the nature of the philosopher than his other advice, to take refuge from the strife of the various forms of superstition in the more quiet, though dimmer regions of—naturally, the skeptical—philosophy. Hume's originality and greatness in this field consist in his genetic view of the historical religions. They are for him errors, but natural ones, grounded in the nature of man, "sick men's dreams," whose origin and course he searches out with frightful cold-bloodedness, with the dispassionate interest of the dissector.

* * * * *

In his moral philosophy[1] Hume shows himself the empiricist only, not the skeptic. The laws of human nature are capable of just as exact empirical investigation as those of external nature; observation and analysis promise even more brilliant success in this most important, and yet hitherto so badly neglected, branch of science than in physics. As knowledge and opinion have been found reducible to the associative play of ideas, and the store of ideas, again, to original impressions and shown derivable from these; so man's volition and action present themselves as results of the mechanical working of the passions, which, in turn, point further back to more primitive principles. The ultimate motives of all action are pleasure and pain, to which we owe our ideas of good and evil. The direct passions, desire and aversion, joy and sorrow, hope and fear, are the immediate effects of these original elements. From the direct arise in certain circumstances the indirect passions, pride and humility, love and hatred (together with respect and contempt); the first two, if the objects which excite feeling are immediately connected with ourselves, the latter, when pleasure and pain are aroused by the accomplishments or the defects of others. While love and hate are always conjoined with a readiness for action, with benevolence or anger, pride and humility are pure, self-centered, inactive emotions.

[Footnote 1: Cf. G. von Gizycki, *Die Ethik David Humes*, 1878.]

All moral phenomena, will, moral judgment, conscience, virtue, are not simple and original data, but of a composite or derivative nature. They are without exception products of the regular interaction of the passions. With such views there can be, of course, no question of a freedom of the will. If anyone objects to determinism, that virtues and vices, if they are involuntary and necessary, are not praise-or blame-worthy, he is to be referred to the applause paid to beauty and talent, which are considered meritorious, although they are not dependent upon our choice. The legal attitude of theology and law first caused all desert to be based upon freedom, whereas the ancient philosophers spoke unhesitatingly of intellectual virtues.

Hume does not, like nearly all his predecessors and contemporaries, find the determining grounds of volition in ideas, but in the feelings. After curtailing the rights of the reason in the theoretical field in favor of custom and instinct, he dispossesses her also in the sphere of practice. Impassive reason, judging only of truth and falsehood, is an inactive faculty, which of itself can never inspire us with inclination and desire toward an object, can never itself become a motive. It is only capable of influencing the will indirectly, through the aid of some affection. Abstract relations of ideas, and facts as well, leave us entirely indifferent so long as they fail to acquire an emotional value through their relation to our state of mind. When we speak of a victory of reason over passion it is nothing but a conquest of one passion by another, *i. e.*, of a violent passion by a calm one. That which is commonly called reason here is nothing but one of those general and calm affections *(e. g.*, the love of life) which direct the will to a distant good, without exciting any sensible emotion in the mind; by passion we commonly understand the violent passions only, which engender a marked disturbance in the soul and the production of which requires a certain propinquity of the object. A man is said to be industrious "from reason," when a calm desire for money makes him laborious. It is a mistake to consider all violent passions powerful, and all calm ones weak. The prevalence of calm affections constitutes the essence of strength of mind.

As reason is thus degraded from a governor of the will to a "slave of the passions," so, further, judgment concerning right and wrong is taken away from her. Moral distinctions are determined by our sense of the agreeable and the disagreeable. We pass an immediate judgment of taste on the actions of our fellow-men; the good pleases, evil displeases. The sight of virtue gives us satisfaction; that of vice repels us. Accordingly an action or trait of mind is virtuous when it calls forth in the observer an agreeable, disinterested sentiment of approbation.

What, then, are the actions which receive such general approval, and how is the praise to be explained which the spectator bestows on them? We approve such traits of character as are immediately agreeable or useful, either to the person himself or to others. This yields four classes of praiseworthy qualities. The first class, those which are agreeable to the possessor (quite apart from any utility to himself or to others), includes cheerfulness, greatness of mind, courage, tranquillity, and benevolence; the second, those immediately agreeable to others, modesty, good manners, politeness, and wit; the third, those useful to ourselves, strength of will, industry, frugality, strength of body, intelligence and other mental gifts. The fourth class comprises the highest virtues, the qualities useful to others, benevolence and justice.

Pleasure and utility are in all cases the criterion of merit. The monkish virtues of humility and mortification of the flesh, which bring no pleasure or advantage either to their possessor or to society, are considered meritorious by no one who understands the subject.

If the moral value of actions is thus made to depend on their effects, we cannot dispense with the assistance of reason in judging moral questions, since it alone can inform us concerning these results of action. Reason, however, is not sufficient to determine us to praise or blame. Nothing but a sentiment can induce us to give the preference to beneficial and useful tendencies over pernicious ones. This feeling is evidently no other than satisfaction in the happiness of men and uneasiness in view of their misery—in short, it is sympathy. By means of the imagination we enter into the experiences of others and participate in their joy and sorrow. Whatever depresses or rejoices them, whatever inspires them with pride, fills us with similar emotions. From the habit of sympathetically passing moral judgment on the actions of others, and of seeing our own judged by them, is developed the further one of keeping a constant watch over ourselves and of considering our dispositions and deeds from the standpoint of the good of others. This custom is called conscience. Allied to this is the love of reputation, which continually leads us to ask, How will our behavior appear in the eyes of those with whom we associate?

Within the fourth and most important class, the social virtues, Hume distinguishes between the natural virtues of humanity and benevolence and the artificial virtues of justice and fidelity. The former proceed from our inborn sympathy with the good of others, while the latter, on the other hand, are not to be derived from a natural passion, an instinctive love of humanity, but are the product of reflection and art, and take their origin in a social convention.

In order that an action may gain the approval of the spectator two other things are required besides its salutary effects: it must be a mark of character, of a permanent disposition, and it must proceed from disinterested motives. Hume is obliged by this latter position to show that disinterested benevolence actually exists, that the unselfish affections do not secretly spring from self-love. To cite only one of the thousand examples of benevolence in which no discernible interest is concerned, we desire happiness for our friends even when we have no expectation of participating in it. The accounts of human selfishness are greatly overdrawn, and those who deduce all actions from it make the mistake of taking the inevitable consequences of virtue—the pleasure of self-approval and of being esteemed by others—for the only motives to virtue. Because virtue, in the outcome, produces inner satisfaction and is praised by others, it does not follow that it is practiced merely for the sake of these agreeable consequences. Self-love is a secondary impulse, whose appearance at all presupposes primary impulses. Only after we have experienced the pleasure which comes from the satisfaction of such an original impulse (*e. g.*, ambition), can this become the object of a conscious reflective search after pleasure, or of egoism. Power brings no enjoyment to the man by nature devoid of ambition, and he who is naturally ambitious does not desire fame because it affords him pleasure, but conversely, fame affords him pleasure because he desires it. The natural propensity which terminates directly on the object, without knowledge or foresight of the pleasurable results, comes first, and egoistic reflection directed toward the hoped-for enjoyment can develop only after this has been satisfied. The case is the same with benevolence as with the love of fame. It is implanted in the constitution of our minds as an original impulse immediately directed toward the happiness of other men. After it has been exercised and its exercise rewarded by self-satisfaction, admiration, thanks, and reciprocation, it is indeed possible for the expectation of such agreeable consequences to lead us to the repetition of beneficent acts. But the original motive is not an egoistic, regard for useful consequences. If, from the force of the passion alone, vengeance may be so eagerly pursued that every consideration of personal quiet and security is silenced, it may also be conceded that humanity causes us to forget our own interests. Nay, further, the social affections, as Shaftesbury has proven, are the strongest of all, and the man will rarely be found in whom the sum of the benevolent impulses will not outweigh that of the selfish ones.

In the section on justice Hume attacks the contract theory. Law, property, and the sacredness of contracts exist first in society, but not first in the state. The obligation to observe contracts is, indeed, made stronger by the civil law and civil authority, but not created by them. Law arises from convention, *i. e.*, not from a formal contract, but a tacit agreement, a sense of common interest, and this agreement, in turn, proceeds from an original propensity to enter into social relations. The unsocial and lawless state of nature is a philosophical fiction which has never existed; men have always been social. They have all at least been born into the society of the family, and they know no-more terrible punishment than isolation. States are not created, however, by a voluntary act, but have their roots in history. The question at issue between Hobbes and Hume was thus adjusted at a later period by Kant: the state, it is true, has not historically arisen from a contract, yet it is allowable and useful to consider it under the aspect of a contract as a regulative idea.

Only once since David Hume, in Herbert Spencer, has the English nation produced a mind of like comprehensive power. Hume and Locke form the culminating points of English thought. They are national types, in that in them the two fundamental tendencies of English thinking, clearness of understanding and practical sense, were manifested in equal force. In Locke these worked together in harmonious co-operation. In Hume the friendly alliance is broken, the common labor ceases; each of the two demands its full rights; a painful breach opens up between science and life. Reason leads inevitably to doubt, to insight into its own weakness, while life demands conviction. The doubter cannot act, the agent cannot know. It is true that a substitute is found for defective knowledge in belief based upon instinct and custom; but this is a makeshift, not a solution of the problem, an acknowledgment of the evil, not a cure for it. Further, Hume's greatness does not consist in the fact that he preached modesty to the contending parties, that he banished the doubting reason into the study and restricted life to belief in probabilities, but in the mental strength which enabled him to endure sharp contradictions, and, instead of an overhasty and easy reconciliation, to suspend the one impulse until the other had made its demands thoroughly, completely, and regardlessly heard. Though he is distinguished from other skeptics by the fact that he not only shows the fundamental conceptions of our knowledge of nature and the principles of religion uncertain and erroneous, but finds *necessary* errors in them and acutely uncovers their origin in the lawful workings of our inner life, yet his historical influence essentially rests on his skepticism. In his own country it roused in the "Scottish School" the reaction of common sense, while in Germany it helped to wake a kindred but greater spirit from the bonds of his dogmatic slumbers, and to fortify him for his critical achievements.

(c) %The Scottish School%.—Priestley's associational psychology, Berkeley's idealism, and Hume's skepticism are legitimate deductions from Locke's assumption that the immediate objects of thought are not things but ideas, and that judgment or knowledge arises from the combination of ideas originally separate. The absurdity of the consequences shows the falsity of the premises. The true philosophy must not contradict common sense. It is not correct to look upon the mind as a sheet of white paper on which experience inscribes single characters, and then to make the understanding combine these originally disconnected elements into judgments by means of comparison, and the belief in the existence of the object come in as a later result added to the ideas by reflection. It is rather true that the elements discovered by the analysis of the cognitive processes are far from being the originals from which these arise. It is not isolated ideas that come first, but judgments, self-evident axioms of the understanding, which form part of the mental constitution with which God has endowed us; and sensation is accompanied by an immediate belief in the reality of the object. Sensation guarantees the presence of an external thing possessing a certain character, although it is not an image of this property, but merely a sign for something in no wise resembling itself.

This is the standpoint of the founder[1] of the Scottish School, Thomas Reid (1710-96, professor in Aberdeen and Glasgow; *An Inquiry into the Human Mind on the Principles of Common Sense*, 1764; *Essays on the Intellectual Powers of Man*, 1785, *Essays on the Active Powers*, 1788, together under the title, *Essays on the Powers of the Human Mind. Collected Works*, 1804, and often since, especially the edition by Hamilton, with valuable notes and dissertations, 7th ed., 2 vols., 1872). We may recognize in it a revival of the common notions of Herbert, as well as a transfer of the innate faculty of judgment inculcated by the ethical and aesthetic writers from the practical to the theoretical field; the "common sense" of Reid is an original sense for truth, as the "taste" of Shaftesbury and Hutcheson was a natural sense for the good and the beautiful. Like Jacobi at a later period, Reid points out that mediate, reasoned knowledge presupposes a knowledge which is immediate, and all inference and demonstration, fixed, undemonstrable, immediately certain fundamental truths. The fundamental judgments or principles of common sense, which are true for us, even if [possibly] not true in themselves, are discoverable by observation (empirical rationalism). In the enumeration of them two dangers are to be avoided: we must neither raise contingent principles to the position of axioms, nor, from an exaggerated endeavor after unity, underestimate the number of these self-evident principles. Reid himself is always more sparing with them than his disciples. He distinguishes two classes: first principles of necessary truth, and first principles of contingent truth or truth of fact. As first principles of necessary truth he cites, besides the axioms of logic and mathematics, grammatical, aesthetic, moral, and metaphysical principles (among the last belong the principles: "That the qualities which we perceive by our senses must have a subject, which we call body, and that the thoughts we are conscious of must have a subject, which we call mind"; "that whatever begins to exist, must have a cause which produced it"). He lays down twelve principles as the basis of our knowledge of matters of fact, in which his reference to the doubt of Berkeley and Hume is evident. The most important of these are: "The existence of everything of which I am conscious"; "that the thoughts of which I am conscious, are the thoughts of a being which I call myself, my mind, my person"; "our own personal identity and continued existence, as far back as we remember anything distinctly"; "that those things do really exist which we distinctly perceive by our senses, and are what we perceive them to be"; "that we have some degree of power over our actions, and the determinations of our will"; "that there is life and intelligence in our fellow-men"; "that there is a certain regard due… to human authority in matters of opinion"; "that, in the phenomena of nature, what is to be, will probably be like what has been in similar circumstances."

[Footnote 1: In the sense of "chief founder"; cf. McCosh's *Scottish Philosophy*, 1875, pp. 36, 68 *seq.*, which is the standard authority on the school as a whole.—TR.]

The widespread and lasting favor experienced by this theory, with its invitation to forget all earnest work in the problems of philosophy by taking refuge in common sense, shows that a general relaxation had succeeded the energetic endeavors which Hume had demanded of himself and of his readers. With this declaration of the infallibility of common consciousness, the theory of knowledge, which had been so successfully begun, was incontinently thrust aside, although, indeed, empirical psychology gained by the industrious investigation of the inner life by means of self-observation. James Beattie continued the attack on Hume in his *Essay on the Nature and Immutability of Truth in Opposition to Sophistry and Skepticism*, 1770, on the principle that wisdom must never contradict nature, and that whatever our nature compels us to believe, hence whatever all agree in, is true. In his briefer dissertations Beattie discussed Memory and Imagination, Fable and Romance, the Effects of

Poetry and Music, Laughter, the Sublime, etc. While Beattie had given the preference to psychological and aesthetic questions, James Oswald (1772) appealed to common sense in matters of religion, describing it as an instinctive faculty of judgment concerning truth and falsehood. The most eminent among the followers of Reid was Dugald Stewart (professor in Edinburgh; *Elements of the Philosophy of the Human Mind*, 1792-1827; *Collected Works*, edited by Hamilton, 1854-58), who developed the doctrines of the master and in some points modified them. Thomas Brown (1778-1820), who is highly esteemed by Mill, Spencer, and Bain, approximated the teachings of Reid and Stewart to those of Hume. The philosophy of the Scottish School was long in favor both in England and in France, where it was employed as a weapon against materialism.

By way of appendix we may mention the beginnings of a psychological aesthetics in Henry Home (Lord Kames, 1696-1782), and Edmund Burke (1728-97).[1] Home, in ethics a follower of Hutcheson, is fond of supporting his aesthetic views by examples from Shakespeare. Beauty (chap. iii.) appears to belong to the object itself, but in reality it is only an effect, a "secondary quality," of the object; like color, it is nothing but an idea in the mind, "for an object is said to be beautiful for no other reason but that it appears so to the spectator." It arises from regularity, proportion, order, simplicity—properties which belong to sublimity as well (chap, iv.), but to which they are by no means so essential, since it is satisfied with a less degree of them. While the beautiful excites emotions of sweetness and gayety, the sublime rouses feelings which are agreable, it is true, but which are not sweet and gay, but strong and more serious. Burke's explanation goes deeper. He derives the antithesis of the sublime and the beautiful from the two fundamental impulses of human nature, the instinct of self-preservation and the social impulse. Whatever is contrary to the former makes a strong and terrible impression on the soul; whatever favors the latter makes a weak but agreeable one. The terrible delights us (first depressing and then exalting us), when we merely contemplate it, without being ourselves affected by the danger or the pain—this is the sublime. On the other hand, that is beautiful which inspires us with tenderness and affection without our desiring to possess it. Sublimity implies a certain greatness, beauty, a certain smallness. Delight in both is based on bodily phenomena. Terror moderated exercises a beneficent influence on the nerves by stimulating them and giving them tension; the gentle impression of beauty exerts a quieting effect upon them. The disturbances caused by the former, and the recovery induced by the latter, are both conducive to health, and hence, experienced as pleasures.

[Footnote 1: Home, *Elements of Criticism*, 1762. Burke, *A Philosophical Inquiry info the Origin of our Ideas of the Sublime and the Beautiful*, 1756.]

CHAPTER VI.

THE FRENCH ILLUMINATION.

In the last decade of the seventeenth century France had yielded the leadership in philosophy to England. Whereas Hobbes had in Paris imbibed the spirit of the Galilean and Cartesian inquiry, while Bacon, Locke, and even Hume had also visited France with advantage, now French thinkers take the watchword from the English. Montesquieu and Voltaire, returning from England in the same year (1729), acquaint their countrymen with the ideas of Locke and his contemporaries. These are eagerly caught up; are, step by step, and with the logical courage characteristic of the French mind, developed to their extreme conclusions; and, at the same time, spread abroad in this heightened form among the people beyond the circles of the learned, nay, even beyond the educated classes. The English temperament is favorable neither to this advance to extreme revolutionary inferences nor to this propagandist tendency. Locke combines a rationalistic ethics with his semi-sensational theory of knowledge; Newton is far from finding in his mechanical physics a danger for religious beliefs; the deists treat the additions of positive religion rather as superfluous ballast than as hateful unreason; Bolingbroke wishes at least to conceal from the people the illuminating principles which he offers to the higher classes. Such halting where farther progress threatens to become dangerous to moral interests does more honor to the moral, than to the logical, character of the philosopher. But with the transfer of these ideas to France, the wall of separation is broken down between the theory of knowledge and the theory of ethics, between natural philosophy and the philosophy of religion; sensationalism forces its way from the region of theory into the sphere of practice, and the mechanical theory is transformed from a principal of physical interpretation into a metaphysical view of the world of an atheistical character. Naturalism is everywhere determined to have its own: if knowledge comes from the senses, then morality must be rooted in self-interest; whoever confines natural science to the search for mechanical causes must not postulate an intelligent Power working from design, even to explain the origin of things and the beginning of motion—has no right to speak of a free will, an immortal soul, and a deity who has created the world. Further, as Bayle's proof that the dogmas of the Church were in all points contradictory to reason had, contrary to its author's own wishes, exerted an influence hostile to religion, and as, moreover, the political and social conditions of the time incited to revolt and to a break with all existing institutions, the philosophical ideas from over the Channel and the condition of things at home alike pressed toward a revolutionary intensification of modern principles, which found comprehensive expression in the atheists' Bible, the *System of Nature* of Baron Holbach, 1770. The movement begins in the middle of the thirties, when Montesquieu commences to naturalize Locke's political views in France, and Voltaire does the same service for Locke's theory of knowledge, and Newton's natural philosophy, which had already been commended by Maupertuis. The year 1748, the year also of Hume's *Essay*, brings Montesquieu's chief work and La Mettrie's *Man a Machine*. While the *Encyclopedia*, the herald of the Illumination, begun in 1751, is advancing to its completion (1772, or rather 1780), Condillac (1754) and Bonnet (1755) develop theoretical sensationalism, and Helvetius (*On Mind*, 1758; in the same year, D'Alembert's *Elements of Philosophy*) practical sensationalism. Rousseau, engaged in authorship from 1751 and a contributor to the *Encyclopedia* until 1757 comes into prominence, 1762, with his two chief works, *Emile* and the *Social Contract*. Parallel with these we find interesting phenomena in the field of political economy: Morelly's communistic *Code of Nature* (1755), the works of Quesnay (1758), the leader of the physiocrats, and those of Turgot, 1774.

Our discussion takes up, first, the introduction and popularization of English ideas; then, the further development of these into a consistent sensationalism, into the morality of interest, and into materialism; finally, the reaction against the illumination of the understanding in Rousseau's philosophy of feeling.[1]

[Footnote 1: On the whole chapter cf. Damiron, *Mémoires pour Servir à l'Histoire de la Philosophie au XVIII. Siécle*, 3 vols., 1858-64; and John Morley's *Voltaire*, 1872 [1886], *Rousseau*, 1873 [1886], and *Diderot and the Encyclopedists*, 1878 [new ed., 1886].]

1. %The Entrance of English Doctrines%.

Montesquieu[1] (1689-1755) made Locke's doctrine of constitutional monarchy and the division of powers (pp. 179-180), with which he joins the historical point of view of Bodin and the naturalistic positions of the time, the common property of the cultivated world. Laws must be adapted to the character and spirit of the nation; the spirit of the people, again, is the result of nature, of the past, of manners, of religion, and of political institutions. Nature has bestowed many gifts on the Southern peoples, but few on those of the North; hence the latter need freedom, while the former readily dispense with it. Warm climates produce greater sensibility and passionateness, cold ones, muscular vigor and industry; in the temperate zones nations are less constant in their habits, their vices, and their virtues. The laws of religion concern man as man, those of the state concern him as a citizen; the former have for their object the moral good of the individual, the latter, the welfare of society; the first aim at immutable, the second at mutable good. Laws and manners are closely interrelated. Right is older than the state, and the law of justice holds even in the state of nature; but in order to assure peace positive right is required in three forms, international, political, and civil.

[Footnote 1: Montesquieu, *Persian Letters*, 1721; *Considerations on the Causes of the Greatness of the Romans and of their Decadence*, 1734; *Spirit of Laws*, 1748.]

Each of the four political forms has a passion for its underlying principle: despotism has fear; monarchy, honor (personal and class prejudice); aristocracy, the moderation of the nobility; democracy, political virtue, which subordinates personal to general welfare, and especially the inclination to equality and frugality. While republics are destroyed by extravagance, lust, and self-seeking, a monarchy can dispense with civil virtue, patriotism, and moral disinterestedness, since in it false honor, luxury, and wantonness subserve the public good. Great states tend toward despotism; smaller ones toward aristocracy, or a democratic republicanism; for those of medium size monarchy, which is intermediate between the two former, is the best form of constitution. Although Montesquieu, in his *Lettres Persanes*, shows himself enthusiastic for the federal republics of Switzerland and the Netherlands, his opinions are different after his return from England, and in his *Esprit des Lois* he praises the English form of government as the ideal of civil liberty.

Political freedom consists in liberty to do (not what we wish, but) what we ought, or in doing that which the laws allow. Such lawful freedom is possible only where the constitution of the state and criminal legislation inspire the citizen with a sense of security. In order to prevent misuse of the supreme power, the different authorities in the state must be divided so that they shall hold one another in check. In particular Montesquieu demands for the judicial power absolute independence of the executive power (which Locke had termed the federative) as well as of the legislative power. The last belongs to parliament, which includes in its two houses an aristocratic and a democratic element.

Voltaire[1] (1694-1778)—he himself had made this anagram from his name, Arouet l(e) j(eune)—seemed by his many-sided receptivity almost made to be the interpreter of English ideas; in the words of Windelband, he "combines Newton's mechanical philosophy of nature, Locke's noëtical empiricism, and Shaftesbury's moral philosophy under the deistic point of view." The same qualities which made him the first journalist, enabled him to free philosophy from its scholastic garb, and, by concentrating it on the problems which press most upon the lay mind (God, freedom, immortality), to make it a living force among the people. His superficiality, as Erdmann acutely remarks, was his strength. True religion, so reason teaches us, consists in loving God and in being just and forbearing to our fellow-men as to our brothers; morality is so natural and necessary that it is no wonder that all philosophers since Zoroaster have inculcated the same principles. The less of dogma the better the religion; atheism is not so bad as superstition, which teaches men to commit crimes with an easy conscience. He considered it the chief mission of his life to destroy these two miserable errors. He endeavored to controvert atheism by rational arguments, while with passionate hatred and contemptuous wit he attacked positive Christianity and his persecutors, the priesthood. The existence of God is for him not merely a moral postulate, but a result of scientific reasoning. One of his famous sayings was: "If God did not exist it would be necessary to invent him; but all nature cries out to us that he exists." He defends immortality in spite of theoretical difficulties, because of its practical necessity; his attitude toward the freedom of the will, which he had energetically defended in the beginning, grows constantly more skeptical with increasing age. His position in regard to the question of evil experiences a similar change—the Lisbon earthquake made him an opponent of optimism, though he had previously favored it.

[Footnote 1: David Friedrich Strauss, *Voltaire, sechs Vorträge*, 1870.]

%2. Theoretical and Practical Sensationalism.%

We turn next from the popular introduction and dissemination of Locke's doctrines, which left their contents unchanged, to their principiant development by the French sensationalists. Condillac (1715-80) always thinks of his work as a completion of Locke's, whose *Essay* he held not to have gone down to the final root of the cognitive process. Locke did not go far enough, Condillac thinks, in his rejection of innate elements; he failed to trace out the origin of perception, reflection, cognition, and volition, as also the relation between the external senses, the internal sense, and the combining intellect, which he discussed as separate sources, the two former of particular, and the last of complex, ideas; in short, he omitted to inquire into the origin of the first function of the soul. Berkeley was right in feeling that a simplification was needed here; but by erroneously reducing outer perception to inner perception, he reached the absurd conclusion of denying the external world. The true course is just the opposite of this—the one already taken by the Bishop of Cork, Peter Browne (died 1735; *The Procedure, Extent, and Limits of the Human Understanding*, 1728): understanding and reflection must be reduced to sensation. All psychical functions are transformed sensations. The soul has only one original faculty, that of sensation; all the others, theoretical and practical alike, are acquired, *i.e.*, they have gradually developed from the former. Condillac is related to Locke as Fichte to Kant; in the former case the transition is mediated by Browne, in the latter by Reinhold. Each crowns the work of his predecessor with a unifying conclusion; each demands and offers a genetic psychology which finds the origin of all the spiritual functions—from sensation and feelings of pleasure and pain up to rational cognition and moral will—in a single fundamental power of the soul. But there is a great difference, materially as well as formally, between these kindred undertakings, a difference corresponding to that between Locke's empiricism and Kant's idealism. The idea of ends, which controls the course of thought in Fichte as in Leibnitz, is entirely lacking in Condillac; that which is first in time, sensation, is for the Science of Knowledge and the Monadology only the beginning, not the essence, of psychical activity, while Condillac makes no distinction between beginning and ground, but expressly identifies *principe* and *commencement*. With Fichte and Leibnitz sensation is immature thought, with Condillac thought is refined sensation. The former teach a teleological, the latter a mechanical mono-dynamism. The Science of Knowledge, moreover, makes a very serious task of the deduction of the particular psychical functions from the original power, while Condillac takes it extraordinarily easy. Good illustrations of his way of effacing distinctions instead of explaining them are given by such monotonously recurring phrases as memory is "nothing but" modified sensation; comparison and simultaneous attention to two ideas "are the same thing"; sensation "gradually becomes" comparison and judgment; reflection is "in its origin" attention itself; speech, thought, and the formation of general notions are "at bottom the same"; the passions are "only" various kinds of desire; understanding and will spring "from one root," etc.

The demand for a single fundamental psychical power comes from Descartes, and Condillac does not hesitate to retain the word *penser* itself as a general designation for all mental functions. Similarly he holds fast to the dualism between extension and sensation as reciprocally incompatible properties, opposes the soul as the "simple" subject of thought to "divisible" matter, and sees in the affections of the bodily organs merely the "occasions" on which the soul of itself alone exercises its sensitive activity. Even freedom—the supremacy of thought over the passions—is maintained, in striking contrast to the whole tendency of his doctrine and to the openly announced principle, that pleasure controls the attention and governs all our actions. He has just as little intention of doubting the existence of God. All is dependent on God. He is our lawgiver; it is in virtue of his wisdom that from small beginnings—perception and need—the most splendid results, science and morality, are developed under the hands of man. Whoever undertakes to complain that He has concealed from us the nature of things and granted us to know relations alone, forgets that we need no more than this. We do not exist in order to know; to live is to enjoy.

The theme of the *Treatise on the Sensations*, 1754, is: Memory, comparison, judgment, abstraction, and reflection (in a word, cognition) are nothing but different forms of attention; similarly the emotions, the appetites, and the will, nothing but modifications of desire; while both alike take their origin in sensation. Sensation is the sole source and the sole content of the life of the mind as a whole. To prove these positions Condillac makes use of the fiction of a statue, in which one sense awakes after another, first the lowest of the senses, smell, and last the most valuable, the sense of touch, which compels us (by its perception of density or resistance) to project our sensations, and thus wakes in us the idea of an external world. In themselves sensations are merely subjective states, modes of our own being; without the sense of touch we would ascribe odor, sound, and color to ourselves. Condillac distinguishes between sensation and *ideas* in a twofold sense, as mere ideas (the memory or imagination of something not present), and as ideas of objective things (the image, representative of a body); this latter sense is meant when he says, touch sensations only are also ideas.

For the details of the deduction, which often makes very happy use of a rich store of psychological material, the reader must be referred to the more extended expositions. Here we can only cite as examples the chief among the genetic definitions. Perceptions (impressions) and consciousness are the same thing under different names. A lively sensation, in which the mind is entirely occupied, becomes attention, without the necessity of assuming an additional special faculty in the mind. Attention, by its retentive effect on the sensation, becomes memory. Double attention—to a new sensation, and to the lingering trace of the previous one—is comparison; the recognition of a relation (resemblance or difference) between two ideas is judgment; the separation of an idea from another naturally connected with it, by the aid of voluntary linguistic symbols, is abstraction; a series of judgments is reflection; and the sum total of inner phenomena, that wherein ideas succeed one another, the ego or person. All truths concern relations among ideas. The tactual idea of solidity accustoms us to project the sensations of the other senses also, to transfer them thither where they are not; hence arise the ideas of our body, of external objects, and of space. If we perceive several such projected qualities together, we refer them to a substratum—substance, which we know to exist, although not what it is. By force we mean the unknown, but indubitably existent, cause of motion.

There are no indifferent mental states; every sensation is accompanied by pleasure or pain. Joy and pain give the determining law for the operation of our faculties. The soul dwells longer on agreeable sensations; without interest, ideas would pass away like shadows. The remembrance of past impressions more agreeable than the present ones is need; from this springs desire (*désir*) then the emotions of love, hate, hope, fear, and astonishment; finally, the will as an unconditional desire accompanied by the thought of its possible fulfillment. All inclinations, good and bad alike, spring from self-love. The predicates "good" and "beautiful" denote the pleasure-giving qualities of things, the former, that which is agreeable to smell and taste (and the passions), the latter, that which pleases sight, hearing, feeling (and the intellect). Morality is the conformity of our actions to laws, which men have established by convention with mutual obligations. In this way the good, which at first was the servant of the passions, becomes their lord.

Man's superiority to the brute depends on the greater perfection of his sense of touch; on the greater variety of his wants and his associations of ideas; on the idea of death, which leads him to seek not merely the avoidance of pain but also self-preservation; and the possession of language. Without denomination no abstractions, no thought, no handing down of knowledge. Although all that is mental has its origin, in the last analysis, in simple sensations, its development requires emancipation from the sensuous, and language is the means for freeing ourselves from the pressure of sensations by the generalization and combination of ideas.

A more moderate representative of sensationalism was Charles Bonnet, who later exercised a considerable influence in Germany, especially until Tetens (1720-93; *Essay in Psychology, or Considerations on the Operations of the Soul*, 1755; *Analytical Essay on the Faculties of the Soul*, 1760; *Philosophical Palingenesis, or Ideas on the Past and the Future of Living Beings*, 1769, including a defense of Christianity; *Collected Works*, 1779). Sensations, to which he, too, reduces all mental life, are, in his view, reactions of the immaterial soul to sense stimuli, which operate merely as occasional causes. On the other hand, he emphasizes more strongly than Condillac the dependence of psychical phenomena on physiological conditions, and endeavors to show definite brain vibrations as the basis not only of habit, memory, and the association of ideas, but also of the higher mental operations. In harmony with these views he adheres to determinism, and finds the motive of all endeavor: in self-love, and its ultimate aim in happiness. To the latter the hope of immortality is indispensable. The link between Bonnet's theory of the thoroughgoing dependence of the soul on the body and his orthodox convictions, is formed by his idea of an imperishable ethereal body, which enables the soul in the life to come to remember its life on earth and, after the dissolution of the present material body, to acquire a new one. Animals as well as men share in the continuance of existence and the transition to a higher stage.

The material earnestness of these thinkers is in sharp contrast to the superficial and frivolous manner in which Helvetius (1715-71) carries out sensationalism in the sphere of ethics. His chief work, *On Mind*, came out in 1758; and a year after his death, the work *On Man, his Intellectual Faculties and his Education*. The search for pleasure or self-love is, as Helvetius thinks he has discovered for the first time,[1] the only motive of action; the laws of interest reign in the moral world as the laws of motion in the physical world; justice and love for our neighbors are based on utility; we seek friends in order to be amused, aided, and, in misfortune, compassionated by them; the philanthropist and the monster both seek only their own pleasure.

[Footnote 1: In reality not only English moralists, but also some among his countrymen, had anticipated him in the position that all actions proceed from selfishness, and that virtue is merely a refined egoism. Thus La Rochefoucauld in his *Maxims (Réflexions, ou Sentences et Maximes Morales*, 1665), La Bruyère *(Les Charactères et les Moeurs de ce Siécle*, 1687), and La Mettrie (of. pp, 251-253).]

Helvetius draws the proof for these positions from Condillac. Recollection and judgment are sensation. The soul is originally nothing more than the capacity for sensation; it receives the stimulus to its development from self-love, *i.e.*, from powerful passions such as the love of fame, on the one hand, and, on the other, from hatred of *ennui*, which induces man to overcome the indolence natural to him and to submit himself to the irksome effort of attention—without passion he would remain stupid. The sum of ideas collected in him is called intellect. All distinctions among men are acquired, and concern the intellect only, not the soul: that which is innate—sensibility and self-love—is the same in all; differences arise only through external circumstances, through education. Man is the pupil of all that environs him, of his situation and his chance experience. The most important instrument in education is the law; the function of the lawgiver is to connect public and personal welfare by means of rewards and punishments, and thus to elevate morality. A man is called virtuous when his stronger passions harmonize with the general interest. Unfortunately the virtues of prejudice, which do not contribute to the public good, are more honored among most nations than the political virtues, to which alone real merit belongs. And self-interest is always the one motive to just and generous action; we serve only our own interests in furthering the welfare of the community. As the promulgator of these doctrines was himself a kind and generous man, Rousseau could make to him the apt reply: You endeavor in vain to degrade yourself below your own level; your spirit gives evidence against your principles; your benevolent heart discredits your doctrines.

The morality of enlightened self-love or "intelligent self-interest" appears in a milder form in Maupertuis (*Works*, 1752), and Frederick the Great,[1] to the latter of whom D'Alembert objected by letter that interest could never generate the sense of duty and reverence for the law.

[Footnote 1: *Essay on Self-love as a Principle of Morals*, 1770, printed in the proceedings of the Academy of Sciences. Cf. on Frederick, Ed. Zeller, 1886.]

%3. Skepticism and Materialism.%

The ideas thus far developed move in a direction whose further pursuit inevitably issues in materialism. Diderot, the editor of the *Encyclopedia of the Sciences, Arts, and Trades* (1751-72), which gathered all the currents of the Illumination into one great stream and carried them to the open sea of popular culture, reflects in his intellectual development the dialectical movement from deism through skepticism to atheism and materialism, and was a co-laborer in the work which brought the whole movement to a conclusion, Holbach's *System of Nature*. Two decades, however, before the latter work, the outcome of a long development of thought, appeared, the physician La Mettrie[1] (1709-51) had promulgated materialism, though rather in an anthropological form than as a world-system, and with cynical satisfaction in the violation of traditional beliefs—in his *Natural History of the Soul*, 1745, in a disguised form, and, undisguised, in his *Man a Machine*, 1748—and at the same time (*Anti-Seneca, or Discourse on Happiness*, 1748) had sketched out for Helvetius the outlines of the sensationalistic morality of interest. While ill with a violent fever he observed the influence of the heightened circulation of the blood on his mental tone, and inferred that thought is the result of the bodily organization. The soul can only be known from the body. The senses, the best philosophers, teach us that matter is never without form and motion; and whether all matter is sentient or not, certainly all that is sentient is material, and every part of the organism contains a vital principle (the heart of a frog beats for an hour after its removal from the body; the parts of cut-up polyps grow into perfect animals). All ideas come from without, from the senses; without sense-impressions no ideas, without education, few ideas, the mind of a man grown up in isolation remains entirely undeveloped; and since the soul is entirely dependent on the bodily organs, along with which it originates, grows, and declines, it is subject to mortality. Not only animals, as Descartes has shown, but men, who differ from the brutes only in degree, are mere machines; by the soul we mean that part of the body which thinks, and the brain has fine muscles for thinking as the leg its coarse ones for walking.

[Footnote 1: La Mettrie was born at St. Malo, and educated in Paris, and in Leyden under Boerhave; he died in Berlin, whither Frederick the Great had called him after he had been driven out of his native land and from Holland. On La Mettrie cf. Lange, *History of Materialism*, vol. ii. pp. 49-91; and DuBois-Reymond's Address, 1875.]

If man is nothing but body, there is no other pleasure than that of the body. There is a difference, however, between sensuous pleasure, which is intense and brief, and intellectual pleasure, which is calm and lasting. The educated man will prefer the latter, and find in it a higher and more noble happiness; but nature has been just enough to grant the common multitude, in the coarser pleasures, a more easily attainable happiness. Enjoy the moment, till the farce of life is ended! Virtue exists only in society, which restrains from evil by its laws, and incites to good by rousing the love of honor. The good man, who subordinates his own welfare to that of society, acts under the same necessity as the evil-doer; hence repentance and pangs of conscience, which increase the amount of pain in the world, but are incapable of effecting amendment, are useless and reprehensible: the criminal is an ill man, and must not be more harshly punished than the safety of society requires. Materialism humanizes and exercises a tranquilizing influence on the mind, as the religious view of the world, with its incitement to hatred, disturbs it; materialism frees us from the sense of guilt and responsibility, and from the fear of future suffering. A state composed of atheists, is not only possible, as Bayle argued, but it would be the happiest of all states.

Among the editors of the *Encyclopedia*, the mathematician D'Alembert *(Elements of Philosophy*, 1758) remained loyal to skeptical views. Neither matter nor spirit is in its essence knowable; the world is probably quite different from our sensuous conception of it. As Diderot (1713-84), and the *Encyclopedia* with him, advanced from skepticism to materialism, D'Alembert retired from the editorial board (1757), after Rousseau, also, had separated himself from the Encyclopedists. Diderot[1] was the leading spirit in the second half of the eighteenth century, as Voltaire in the first half. His lively and many-sided receptivity, active industry, clever and combative eloquence, and enthusiastic disposition qualified him for this rôle beyond all his contemporaries, who testify that they owe even more to his stimulating conversation than to his writings. He commenced by bringing Shaftesbury's *Inquiry into Virtue and Merit* to the notice of his countrymen; and then turned his sword, on the one hand, against the atheists, to refute whom, he thought, a single glance into the microscope was sufficient, and, on the other, against the traditional belief in a God of anger and revenge, who takes pleasure in bathing in the tears of mankind. Then followed a period of skepticism, which is well illustrated by the prayer in the *Thoughts on the Interpretation of Nature*, 1754: O God! I do not know whether thou art, but I will guide my thoughts and actions as though thou didst see me think and act, etc. Under the influence of Holbach's circle he finally reached (in the *Conversation between D'Alembert and Diderot*, and *D'Alembert's Dream*, written in 1769, but not published until 1830, in vol. iv. of the *Mémoires, Correspondance, et Ouvrages Inédits de Diderot*) the position of naturalistic monism—there exists but one great individual, the All. Though he had formerly distinguished thinking substance from material substance, and had based the immortality of the soul on the unity of sensation and the unity of the ego, he now makes sensation a universal and essential property of matter (*la pierre sent*), declares the talk about the simplicity of the soul metaphysico-theological nonsense, calls the brain a self-playing instrument, ridicules self-esteem, shame, and repentance as the absurd folly of a being that imputes to itself merit or demerit for necessary actions, and recognizes no other immortality than that of posthumous fame. But even amid these extreme conclusions, his enthusiasm for virtue remains too intense to allow him to assent to the audacious theories of La Mettrie and Helvetius.

[Footnote 1: *Works* in twenty-two vols., Paris, Brière, 1821; latest edition, 1875 *seq*. Cf. on Diderot the fine work by Karl Rosenkranz, *Diderots Leben und Werke*, 1866.]

French natural science also tended toward materialism. Buffon *(Natural History*, 1749 *seq*) endeavors to facilitate the mechanical explanation of the phenomena of life by the assumption of living molecules, from which visible organisms are built up. Robinet (*On Nature*, 1761 *seq*.), availing himself of Spinozistic and Leibnitzian conceptions, goes still further, in that he endows every particle of matter with sensation, looks on the whole world as a succession of living beings with increasing mentality, and subjects the interaction of the material and psychical sides of the individual, as well as the relation of pleasure and pain in the universe, to a law of harmonious compensation.

The *System of Nature*, 1770, which bore on its title page the name of Mirabaud, who had died 1760, proceeded from the company of freethinkers accustomed to meet in the hospitable house of Baron von Holbach (died 1789), a native of the Palatinate. Its real author was Holbach himself, although his friends Diderot, Naigeon, Lagrange, the mathematician, and the clever Grimm (died 1807) seem to have co-operated in the preparation of certain sections. The cumbrous seriousness and the dry tone of this systematic combination of the radical ideas which the century had produced, were no doubt the chief causes of its unsympathetic reception by the public. Similarly unsuccessful was the popular account of materialism with which Holbach followed it, in 1772, and Helvetius's excerpts from the *System of Nature*, 1774.

Holbach applies himself to the despiritualization of nature and the destruction of religious prejudices with sincere faith in the sacred mission of unbelief—the happiness of humanity depends on atheism. "O Nature, sovereign of all beings, and ye her daughters, Virtue, Reason, and Truth, be forever our only divinities." What has made virtue so difficult and so rare? Religion, which divides men instead of uniting them. What has so long delayed the illumination of the reason, and the discovery of truth? Religion with its mischievous errors, God, spirit, freedom, immortality. Immortality exists only in the memory of later generations; man is the creature of a day; nothing is permanent but the great whole of nature and the eternal law of universal change. Can a clock broken into a thousand pieces continue to mark the hours? The senseless doctrine of freedom was invented only to solve the senseless problem of the justification of God in view of the existence of evil. Man is at every moment of his life a passive instrument in the hands of necessity; the universe is an immeasurable and uninterrupted chain of actions and reactions, an eternal round of interchanging motions, ruled by laws, a change in which would at once alter the nature of all things. The most fatal error is the idea of human and divine spirits, which has been advanced by philosophers and adopted with applause by fools. The opinion that man is divided into two substances is based on the fact that, of the changes in our body, we directly perceive only the external molar movements, while, on the other hand, the inner motions of the invisible molecules are known only by their effects. These latter have been ascribed to the mind, which, moreover, we have adorned with properties whose emptiness is manifested by the fact that they are all mere negations of that which we know. Experience reveals to us only the extended, the corporeal, the divisible—but the mind is to be the opposite of all three, yet at the same time to possess the power (how, no man can tell) of acting on that which is material and of being acted upon by it. In thus dividing himself into body and soul, man has in reality only distinguished between his brain and himself. Man is a purely physical being. All so-called spiritual phenomena are functions of the brain, special cases of the operation of the universal forces of nature. Thought and volition are sensation, sensation is motion. The moving forces in the moral world are the same as those in the physical world; in the latter they are called attraction and repulsion, in the former, love and hate; that which the moralist terms self-love is the same instinct of self-preservation which is familiar in physics as the force of inertia.

As man has doubled himself, so also he has doubled nature. Evil gave the first impulse to the formation of the idea of God, pain and ignorance have been the parents of superstition; our sufferings were ascribed to unknown powers, of which we were in fear, but which, at the same time, we hoped to propitiate by prayer and sacrifice. The wise turned with their worship and reverence toward a more worthy object, to the great All; and, in fact, if we seek to give the word God a tenable meaning, it signifies active nature. The error lay in the dualistic view, in the distinction between nature and itself, *i.e.* its activity, and in the belief that the explanation of motion required a separate immaterial Mover. This assumption is, in the first place, false, for since the All is the complex of all that exists there can be nothing outside it; motion follows from the existence of the universe as necessarily as its other properties; the world does not receive it from without, but imparts it to itself by its own power. In the second place the assumption is useless; it explains nothing, but confuses the problems of natural science to the point of insolubility. In the third place it is self-contradictory, for after theology has removed the Deity as far away from man as possible, by means of the negative metaphysical predicates, it finds itself necessitated to bring the two together again through the moral attributes—which are neither compatible with one another nor with the meta-physical—and crowns the absurdity by the assurance that we can please God by believing that which is incomprehensible. Finally, the assumption is dangerous; it draws men away from the present, disturbs their peace and enjoyment, stirs up hatred, and thus makes happiness and morality impossible. If, then, utility is the criterion of truth, theism—even in the mild form of deism—is proven erroneous by its disastrous consequences. All error is bane.

Matter and motion are alike eternal. Nature is an active, self-moving, living whole, an endless chain of causes and effects. All is in unceasing motion, all is cause (nothing is dead, nothing rests), all is effect (there is no spontaneous motion, none directed to an end). Order and disorder are not in nature, but only in our understanding; they are abstract ideas to denote that which is conformable to our nature and that which is contrary to it. The end of the All is itself alone, is life, activity; the universal goal of particular beings, like that of the universe, is the conservation of being.

Anthropology is for Holbach essentially reduced to two problems, the deduction of thought from motion, and of morality from the physical tendency to self-preservation. The forces of the soul are no other than those of the body. All mental faculties develop from sensation; sensations are motions in the brain which reveal to us motions without the brain. All the passions may be reduced to love and hate, desire and aversion, and depend upon temperament, on the individual mixture of the fluid parts. Virtue is the equilibrium of the fluids. All human actions proceed from interest. Good and bad men are distinguished only by their organizations, and by the ideas they form concerning happiness. With the same necessity as that of the act itself, follow the love or contempt of fellow-men, the pleasure of self-esteem and the pain of repentance (regret for evil consequences, hence no evidence of freedom). Neither responsibility nor punishment is done away with by this necessity—have we not the right to protect ourselves against the stream which damages our fields, by building dikes and altering its course? The end of endeavor is permanent happiness, and this can be attained through virtue alone. The passions which are useful to society compel the affection and approval of our fellows. In order to interest others in our welfare we must interest ourselves in theirs—nothing is more indispensable to man than man. The clever man acts morally, interest binds us to the good; love for others means love for the means to our own happiness. Virtue is the art of making ourselves happy through the happiness of others. Nature itself chastises immorality, since she makes the intemperate unhappy. Religion has hindered the recognition of these rules, has misunderstood the diseases of the soul, and applied false and ineffective remedies; the renunciation which she requires is opposed to human nature. The true moralist recognizes in medicine the key to the human heart; he will cure the mind through the body, control the passions and hold them in check by other passions instead of by sermons, and will teach men that the surest road to personal ends is to labor for the public good. Illumination is the way to virtue and to happiness.

Volney (Chasseboeuf, died 1820; *Catechism of the French Citizen*, 1793, later under the title *Natural Law or Physical Principles of Morals deduced front the Organization of Man and of the Universe*; further, *The Ruins; Complete Works*, 1821) belongs among the moralists of self-love, although, besides the egoistic interests, he takes account of the natural sympathetic impulses also. This is still more the case with Condorcet (*Sketch of an Historical View of the Progress of the Human Mind*, 1794), who was influenced alike by Condillac and by Turgot, and who defends a tendency toward universal perfection both in the individual and in the race. Besides the selfish affections, which are directed as much to the injury as to the support of others, there lies in the organization of man a force which steadily tends toward the good, in the form of underived feelings of sympathy and benevolence, from which moral self-judgment is developed by the aid of reflection. The aim of true ethics and social art is not to make the "great" virtues universal, but to make them needless; the nearer the nations approximate to mental and moral perfection, the less they stand in need of these—happy the people in which good deeds are so customary that scarcely an opportunity is left for heroism. The chief instrument for the moral cultivation of the people is the development of the reason, the conscience, and the benevolent affections. Habituation to deeds of kindness is a source of pure and inexhaustible happiness. Sympathy with the good of others must be so cultivated that the sacrifice of personal enjoyment will be a sweeter joy than the pleasure itself. Let the child early learn to enjoy the delight of loving and of being loved. We must, finally, strive toward the gradual diminution of the inequalities of capacity, of property, and between ruler and ruled, for to abolish them is impossible.

Of the remaining philosophers of the revolutionary period mention may be made of the physician Cabanis *(Relations of the Physical and the Moral in Man, 1799)*, and Destutt de Tracy *(Elements of Ideology, 1801 seq.)*. The former is a materialist in psychology (the nerves are the man, ideas are secretions of the brain), considers consciousness a property of organic matter (the soul is not a being, but a faculty), and makes moral sympathy develop out of the animal instincts of preservation and nourishment. De Tracy, also, derives all psychical activity from organization and sensation. His doctrine of the will, though but briefly sketched, is interesting. The desires have a passive and an active side (corresponding to the twofold action of the nerves, on themselves and on the muscles); on the one hand, they are feelings of pleasure or pain, and on the other, they lead us to action—will is need, and, at the same time, the source of the means for satisfying this need. Both these feelings and the external movements are probably based upon unconscious organic motions. The will is rightly identified with the personality, it is the ego itself, the totality of the physico-psychical life of man attaining to self-consciousness. The inner or organic life consists in the self-preserving functions of the individual, the outer or animal life, in the functions of relation (of sense, of motion, of speech, of reproduction); individual interests are rooted in the former, sympathy in the latter. The primal good is freedom, or the power to do what we will; the highest thing in life is love. In order to be happy we must avoid punishment, blame, and pangs of conscience.

%4. Rousseau's Conflict with the Illumination.%

The Genevese, Jean Jacques Rousseau[1] (1712-78), stands in a similar relation of opposition to the French Illumination as the Scottish School to the English, and Herder and Jacobi to the German. He points us away from the cold sophistical inferences of the understanding to the immediate conviction of feeling; from the imaginations of science to the unerring voice of the heart and the conscience; from the artificial conditions of culture to healthy nature. The vaunted Illumination is not the lever of progress, but the source of all degeneration; morality does not rest on the shrewd calculation of self-interest, but on original social and sympathetic instincts (love for the good is just as natural to the human heart as self-love; enthusiasm for virtue has nothing to do with our interest; what would it mean to give up one's life for the sake of advantage?); the truths of religion are not objects of thought, but of pious feeling.

[Footnote 1: Cf. Brockerhoff, Leipsic, 1863-74; L. Moreau, Paris, 1870.]

Rousseau commenced his career as an author with the *Discourse on the Sciences and the Arts*, 1750 (the discussion of a prize question, crowned by the Academy of Dijon), which he describes as entirely pernicious, and the *Discourse on the Origin and the Bases of the Inequality among Men*, 1753. By nature man is innocent and good, becoming evil only in society. Reflection, civilization, and egoism are unnatural. In the happy state of nature pity and innocent self-love (*amour de soi*) ruled, and the latter was first corrupted by the reason into the artificial feeling of selfishness (*amour propre*) in the course of social development—thinking man is a degenerate animal. Property has divided men into rich and poor; the magistracy, into strong and weak; arbitrary power, into masters and slaves. Wealth generated luxury with its artificial delights of science and the theater, which make us more unhappy and evil than we otherwise are; science, the child of vice, becomes in turn the mother of new vices. All nature, all that is characteristic, all that is good, has disappeared with advancing culture; the only relief from the universal degeneracy is to be hoped for from a return to nature on the part of the individual and society alike—from education and a state conformed to nature. The novel *Emile* is devoted to the pedagogical, and the *Social Contract, or the Principles of Political Law*, to the political problem. Both appeared in 1762, followed two years later by the *Letters from the Mountain*, a defense against the attacks of the clergy. In these later writings Rousseau's naturalistic hatred of reason appears essentially softened.

Social order is a sacred right, which forms the basis of all others. It does not proceed, however, from nature—no man has natural power over his fellows, and might confers no right—consequently it rests on a contract. Not, however, on a contract between ruler and people. The act by which the people chooses a king is preceded by the act in virtue of which it is a people. In the social contract each devotes himself with his powers and his goods to the community, in order to gain the protection of the latter. With this act the spiritual body politic comes into being, and attains its unity, its ego, its will. The sum of the members is called the people; each member, as a participant in the sovereignty, citizen, and, as bound to obedience to the law, subject. The individual loses his natural freedom, receiving in exchange the liberty of a citizen, which is limited by the general will, and, in addition, property rights in all that he possesses, equality before the law, and moral freedom, which first really makes him master of himself. The impulse of mere desire is slavery, obedience to self-imposed law, freedom. The sovereign is the people, law the general popular will directed to the common good, the supreme goods, "freedom and equality," the chief objects of legislation. The lawgiving power is the moral will of the body politic, the government (magistracy, prince) its executive physical power; the former is its heart, the latter its brain. Rousseau calls the government the middle term between the head of the state and the individual, or between the citizen as lawgiver and as subject—the sovereign (the people) commands, the government executes, the subject obeys. The act by which the people submits itself to its head is not a contract, but merely a mandate; whenever it chooses it can limit, alter, or entirely recall the delegated power. In order to security against illegal encroachments on the part of the government, Rousseau recommends regular assemblies of the people, in which, under suspension of governmental authority, the confirmation, abrogation, or alteration of the constitution shall be determined upon. Even the establishment of the articles of social belief falls to the sovereign people. The essential difference between Rousseau's theory of the state and that of Locke and Montesquieu consists in his rejection of the division of powers and of representation by delegates, hence in its unlimited democratic character. A generation after it was given to the world, the French Revolution made the attempt to translate it into practice. "The masses carried out what Rousseau himself had thought, it is true, but never willed" (Windelband).

Rousseau's theory of education is closely allied to Locke's (cf. above), whose leading idea—the development of individuality—was entirely in harmony with the subjectivism of the philosopher of feeling. Posterity has not found it a difficult task to free the sound kernel therein from the husks of exaggeration and idiosyncrasy which surrounded it. Among the latter belong the preference of bodily over intellectual development, and the unlimited faith in the goodness of human nature. Exercise the body, the organs, the senses of the pupil, and keep his soul unemployed as long as possible; for the first, take care only that his mind be kept free from error and his heart from vice. In order to secure complete freedom from disturbance in this development, it is advisable to isolate the child from society, nay, even from the family, and to bring him up in retirement under the guidance of a private tutor.

As the Swiss republican spoke in Rousseau's politics, so his religious theories[1] betray the Genevan Calvinist. "The Savoyard Vicar's Profession of Faith" (in *Emile*) proclaims deism as a religion of feeling. The rational proofs brought forward for the existence of God—from the motion of matter in itself at rest, and from the finality of the world—are only designed, as he declares by letter, to confute the materialists, and derive their impregnability entirely from the inner evidence of feeling, which amid the vacillation of the reason *pro* and *con* gives the final decision.

[Footnote 1: Cf. Ch. Borgeaud, *Rousseaus Religionsphilosophie*, Geneva and Leipsic, 1883.]

If we limit our inquiry to that which is alone of importance for us, and rely on the evidence of feeling, it cannot be doubted that I myself exist and feel; that there exists an external world which affects me; that thought, comparison or judgment concerning relations is different from sensation or the perception of objects—for the latter is a passive, but the former an active process; that I myself produce the activity of attention or consideration; that, consequently, I am not merely a sensitive or passive, but also an active or intelligent being. The freedom of my thought and action guarantees to me the immateriality of my soul, and is that which distinguishes me from the brute. The life of the soul after the decay of the body is assured to me by the fact that in this world the wicked triumphs, while the good are oppressed. The favored position which man occupies in the scale of beings—he is able to look over the universe and to reverence its author, to recognize order and beauty, to love the good and to do it; and shall he, then, compare himself to the brute?—fills me with emotion and gratitude to the benevolent Creator, who existed before all things, and who will exist when they all shall have vanished away, to whom all truths are one single idea, all places a point, all times a moment. The *how* of freedom, of eternity, of creation, of the action of my will upon matter, etc., is, indeed, incomprehensible to me, but *that* these are so, my feeling makes me certain. The worthiest employment of my reason is to annihilate itself before God. "The more I strive to contemplate his infinite essence the less do I conceive it. But it is, and that suffices me. The less I conceive it, the more I adore."

In the depths of my heart I find the rules for my conduct engraved by nature in ineffaceable characters. Everything is good that I feel to be so. The conscience is the most enlightened of all philosophers, and as safe a guide for the soul as instinct for the body. The infallibility of its judgment is evidenced by the agreement of different peoples; amid the surprising differences of manners you will everywhere find the same ideas of justice, the same notions of good and evil. Show me a land where it is a crime to keep one's word, to be merciful, benevolent, magnanimous, where the upright man is despised and the faithless honored! Conscience enjoins the limitation of our desires to the degree to which we are capable of satisfying them, but not their complete suppression—all passions are good when we control them, all evil when they control us.

In the second part of the "Profession du Foi du Vicaire Savoyard" Rousseau turns from his attacks on sensationalism, materialism, atheism, and the morality of interest, to the criticism of revelation. Why, in addition to natural religion, with its three fundamental doctrines, God, freedom, and immortality, should other special doctrines be necessary, which rather confuse than clear up our ideas of the Great Being, which exact from us the acceptance of absurdities, and make men proud, intolerant, and cruel—whereas God requires from us no other service than that of the heart? Every religion is good in which men serve God in a befitting manner. If God had prescribed one single religion for us, he would have provided it with infallible marks of its unique authenticity. The authority of the fathers and the priesthood is not decisive, for every religion claims to be revealed and alone true; the Mohammedan has the same right as the Christian to adhere to the religion of his fathers. Since all revelation comes down to us by human tradition, reason alone can be the judge of its divinity. The careful examination of the documents, which are written in ancient languages, would require an amount of learning which could not possibly be a condition of salvation and acceptance with God. Miracles and prophecy are not conclusive, for how are we to distinguish the true among them from the false? If we turn from the external to the internal criteria of the doctrines themselves, even here no decision can be reached between the reasons *pro* and *con* (the author puts the former into the mouth of a believer, and the latter into that of a rationalist); even if the former outweighed the latter, the difficulty would still remain of reconciling it with God's goodness and justice that the gospel has not reached so many of mankind, and of explaining how those to whom the divinity of Christ is now proclaimed can convince themselves of it, while his contemporaries misjudged and crucified him. In my opinion, I am incapable of fathoming the truth of the Christian religion and its value to those who confess it. The investigation of the reason ends in "reverential doubt": I neither accept revelation nor reject it, but I reject the obligation to accept it. My heart, however, judges otherwise than the reflection of my intellect; for this the sacred majesty and exalted simplicity of the Scriptures are a most cogent proof that they are more than human, and that He whose history they contain is more than man. The touching grace and profound wisdom of his words, the gentleness of his conduct, the loftiness of his maxims, his mastery over his passions, abundantly prove that he was neither an enthusiast nor an ambitious sectary. Socrates lived and died like a philosopher, Jesus like a God. The virtues of justice, patriotism, and moderation taught by Socrates, had been exercised by the great men of Greece before he inculcated them. But whence could Jesus derive in his time and country that lofty morality which he alone taught and exemplified? Things of this sort are not invented. The inventor of such deeds would be more wonderful than the doer of them. Thus again, in the question of revealed religion, the voice of the heart triumphs over the doubts of the reason, as, in the question of natural religion, it had done over the objections of opponents. It is true, however, that this enthusiasm is paid not to the current Christianity of the priests, but to I the real Christianity of the gospel.

Rousseau was the conscience of France, which rebelled against the negations and the bald emptiness of the materialistic and atheistic doctrines. By vindicating with fervid eloquence the participation of the whole man in the highest questions, in opposition to the one-sided illumination of the understanding, he became a pre-Kantian defender of the faith of practical reason. His emphatic summons aroused a loud and lasting echo, especially in Germany, in the hearts of Goethe, Kant, and Fichte.

CHAPTER VII.

LEIBNITZ.

In the contemporaries Spinoza and Locke, the two schools of modern philosophy, the Continental, starting from Descartes, and the English, which followed Bacon, had reached the extreme of divergence and opposition, Spinoza was a rationalistic pantheist, Locke, an empirical individualist. With Leibnitz a twofold approximation begins. As a rationalist he sides with Spinoza against Locke, as an individualist with Locke against Spinoza. But he not only separated rationalism from pantheism, but also qualified it by the recognition (which his historical tendencies had of themselves suggested to him) of a relative justification for empiricism, since he distinguished the factual truths of experience from the necessary truths of reason, gave to the former a noëtical principle of their own, the principle of sufficient reason, and made sensation an indispensable step to thought.

To the tendencies thus manifested toward a just estimation and peaceful reconciliation of opposing standpoints, Leibnitz remained true in all the fields to which he devoted his activity. Thus, in the sphere of religion, he took an active part in the negotiations looking toward the reunion of the Protestant and Catholic Churches, as well as in those concerning the union of the Lutheran and the Reformed. Himself a stimulating man, he yet needed stimulation from without. He was an astonishingly wide reader, and declared that he had never found a book that did not contain something of value. With a ready adaptability to the ideas of others he combined a remarkable power of transformative appropriation; he read into books more than stood written in them. The versatility of his genius was unlimited: jurist, historian, diplomat, mathematician, physical scientist, and philosopher, and in addition almost a theologian and a philologist—he is not only at home in all these departments, because versed in them, but everywhere contributes to their advancement by original ideas and plans. In such a combination of productive genius and wealth of knowledge Aristotle and Leibnitz are unapproached.

Gottfried Wilhelm Leibnitz was born in 1646 at Leipsic, where his father (Friederich Leibnitz, died 1652) was professor of moral philosophy; in his fifteenth year he entered the university of his native city, with law as his principal subject. Besides law, he devoted himself with quite as much of ardor to philosophy under Jacob Thomasius (died 1684, the father of Christian Thomasius), and to mathematics under E. Weigel in Jena. In 1663 (with a dissertation entitled *De Principio Individui*) he became Bachelor, in 1664 Master of Philosophy, and in 1666, at Altdorf, Doctor of Laws, and then declined the professorship extraordinary offered him in the latter place. Having made the acquaintance of the former minister of the Elector of Mayence, Freiherr von Boineburg, in Nuremberg, he went, after a short stay at Frankfort-on-the-Main, to the court of the Elector at Mayence, at whose request he devoted himself to the reform of legal procedure, besides writing, while there, on the most diverse subjects. In 1672 he went to Paris, where he remained during four years with the exception of a short stay in London. The special purpose of the journey to Paris—to persuade Louis XIV to undertake a campaign in Egypt, in order to divert him from his designs upon Germany—was not successful; but Leibnitz was captivated by the society of the Parisian scholars, among them the mathematician, Huygens. From the end of 1676 until his death in 1716 Leibnitz lived in Hanover, whither he had been called by Johann Friedrich, as court councillor and librarian. The successor of this prince, Ernst August, who, with his wife Sophie, and his daughter Sophie Charlotte, showed great kindness to the philosopher, wished him to write a history of the princely house of Brunswick; and a journey which he made in order to study for this purpose was extended as far as Vienna and Rome. Upon his return he took charge of the Wolfenbüttel library in addition to his other engagements.

The marriage of the Princess Sophie Charlotte with Frederick of Brandenburg, the first king of Prussia, brought Leibnitz into close relations with Berlin. At his suggestion the Academy (Society) of Sciences was founded there in 1700, and he himself became its first president. In Charlottenburg he worked on his principal work, the *New Essays concerning the Human Understanding*, which was aimed at Locke, but the publication of which was deferred on account of the death of the latter in the interim (1704), and did not take place until 1765, in Raspe's collective edition. The death of the Prussian queen in 1705 interrupted for several years the *Theodicy*, which had been undertaken at her request, and which did not appear until 1710. In Vienna, where he resided in 1713-14, Leibnitz composed a short statement of his system for Prince Eugen; this, according to Gerhardt, was not the sketch in ninety paragraphs, familiar under the title *Monadology*, which was first published in the original by J.E. Erdmann in his excellent *Complete Edition of the Philosophical Works of Leibnitz*, 1840, but the *Principles of Nature and of Grace*, which appeared two years after the author's death in *L'Europe Savante*. While Ernst August, as well as the German emperor and Peter the Great, distinguished the philosopher, who was not indifferent to such honors, by the bestowal of titles and preferments, his relations with the Hanoverian court, which until then had been so cordial, grew cold after the Elector Georg Ludwig ascended the English throne as George I. The letters which Leibnitz interchanged with his daughter-in-law, gave rise to the correspondence, continued to his death, with Clarke, who defended the theology of Newton against him. The contest for priority between Leibnitz and Newton concerning the invention of the differential calculus was later settled by the decision that Newton invented his method of fluxions first, but that Leibnitz published his differential calculus earlier and in a more perfect form. The variety of pursuits in which Leibnitz was engaged was unfavorable to the development and influence of his philosophy, in that it hindered him from working out his original ideas in systematic form, and left him leisure only for the composition of shorter essays. Besides the two larger works mentioned above, the *New Essays* and the *Theodicy*, we have of philosophical works by Leibnitz only a series of private letters, and articles for the scientific journals (the *Journal des Savants* in Paris, and the *Acta Eruditorum* in Leipsic, etc.), among which may be mentioned as specially important the *New System of Nature, and of the Interaction of Substances as well as of the Union which exists between the Soul and the Body*, 1695, which was followed during the next year by three explanations of it, and the paper *De Ipsa Natura*, 1698. Previous to

Erdmann (1840) the following had deserved credit for their editions of Leibnitz: Feller, Kortholt, Gruber, Raspe, Dutens, Feder, Guhrauer (the German works), and since Erdmann, Pertz, Foucher de Careil, Onno Klopp, and especially J.C. Gerhardt. The last named published the mathematical works in seven volumes in 1849-63, and recently, Berlin, 1875-90, the philosophical treatises, also in seven volumes.[1] In our account of the philosophy of Leibnitz we begin with the fundamental metaphysical concepts, pass next to his theory of living beings and of man (theory of knowledge and ethics), and close with his inquiries into the philosophy of religion.

[Footnote 1: We have a life of Leibnitz by G.E. Guhrauer, jubilee edition, Breslau, 1846 [Mackie's *Life*, Boston, 1845 is based on Guhrauer]. Among recent works on Leibnitz, we note the little work by Merz, Blackwood's Philosophical Classics, 1884, and Ludwig Stein's *Leibniz und Spinoza*, Berlin, 1890, in which with the aid of previously unedited material the relations of Leibnitz to Spinoza (whom he visited at The Hague on his return journey from Paris) are discussed, and the attempt is made to trace the development of the theory of monads, down to 1697. The new exposition of the Leibnitzian monadology by Ed. Dillman, which has just appeared, we have not yet been able to examine [The English reader may be referred further to Dewey's *Leibniz* in Griggs's Philosophical Classics, 1888, and Duncan's *Philosophical Works of Leibnitz* (selections translated, with notes), New Haven, 1890, as well as to the work of Merz already mentioned.—TR.]]

%1. Metaphysics: the Monads, Representation, the Pre-established Harmony; the Laws of Thought and of the World.%

Leibnitz develops his new concept of substance, the monad,[1] in conjunction with, yet in opposition to, the Cartesian and the atomistic conceptions. The Cartesians are right when they make the concept of substance the cardinal point in metaphysics and explain it by the concept of independence. But they are wrong in their further definition of this second concept. If we take independence in the sense of unlimitedness and aseity, we can speak, as the example of Spinoza shows, of only one, the divine substance. If the Spinozistic result is to be avoided, we must substitute independent action for independent existence, self-activity for self-existence. Substance is not that which exists through itself (otherwise there would be no finite substances), but that which acts through itself, or that which contains in itself the ground of its changing states. Substance is to be defined by active force,[2] by which we mean something different from and better than the bare possibility or capacity of the Scholastics. The *potentia sive facultas*, in order to issue into action, requires positive stimulation from without, while the *vis activa* (like an elastic body) sets itself in motion whenever no external hindrance opposes. Substance is a being capable of action (*la substance est un être capable d'action*). With the equation of activity and existence (*quod non agit, non existit*) the substantiality which Spinoza had taken away from individual things is restored to them: they are active, consequently, in spite of their limitedness, substantial beings (*quod agit, est substantia singularis*). Because of its inner activity every existing thing is a determinate individual, and different from every other being. Substance is an individual being endowed with force.

[Footnote 1: According to L. Stein's conjecture, Leibnitz took the expression Monad, which he employs after 1696, from the younger (Franc. Mercurius) van Helmont.]

[Footnote 2: Francis Glisson (1596-1677, professor of medicine in Cambridge and London) had as early as 1671, conceived substances as forces in his treatise *De Natura Substantiae Energetica*. That Glisson influenced Leibnitz, as maintained by H. Marion (Paris, 1880), has not been proven; cf. L. Stein, p. 184.]

The atomists are right when they postulate for the explanation of phenomenal bodies simple, indivisible, eternal units, for every composite consists of simple parts. But they are wrong when they regard these invisible, minute corpuscles, which are intended to subserve this purpose as indivisible: everything that is material, however small it be, is divisible to infinity, nay, is in fact endlessly divided. If we are to find indivisible units, we must pass over into the realm of the immaterial and come to the conclusion that bodies are composed of immaterial constituents. Physical points, the atoms, are physical, but not points; mathematical points are indivisible, but not real; metaphysical or substantial points, the incorporeal, soul-like units, alone combine in themselves indivisibility and reality—the monads are the true atoms. Together with indivisibility they possess immortality; as it is impossible for them to arise and perish through the combination and separation of parts, they cannot come into being or pass out of it in any natural way whatever, but only by creation or annihilation. Their non-spatial or punctual character implies the impossibility of all external influence, the monad develops its states from its own inner nature, has need of no other thing, is sufficient unto itself, and therefore deserves the Aristotelian name, entelechy.

Thus two lines of thought combine in the concept of the monad. Gratefully recognizing the suggestions from both sides, Leibnitz called Cartesianism the antechamber of the true philosophy, and atomism the preparation for the theory of monads. From the first it followed that the substances were self-acting forces; from the second, that they were immaterial units. Through the combination of both determinations we gain information concerning the kind of force or activity which constitutes the being of the monad: the monads are representative forces. There is nothing truly real in the world save the monads and their representations [ideas, perceptions].

In discussing the representation in which the being and activity of the monads consist, we must not think directly of the conscious activity of the human soul. Representation has in Leibnitz a wider meaning than that usually associated with the word. The distinction, which has become of the first importance for psychology, between mere representation and conscious representation, or between perception and apperception, may be best explained by the example of the sound of the waves. The roar which we perceive in the vicinity of the sea-beach is composed of the numerous sounds of the single waves. Each single sound is of itself too small to be heard; nevertheless it must make an impression on us, if only a small one, since otherwise their total—as a sum of mere nothings—could not be heard. The sensation which the motion of the single wave causes is a weak, confused, unconscious, infinitesimal perception (*petite, insensible perception*), which must be combined with many similar minute sensations in order to become strong and distinct, or to rise above the threshold of consciousness. The sound of the single wave is felt, but not distinguished, is perceived, but not apperceived. These obscure states of unconscious representation, which are present in the mind of man along with states of clear consciousness, make up, in the lowest grade of existence, the whole life of the monad. There are beings which never rise above the condition of deep sleep or stupor.

In conformity with this more inclusive meaning, perception is defined as the representation of the external in the internal, of multiplicity in unity (*representatio multitudinis in unitate*). The representing being, without prejudice to its simplicity, bears in itself a multitude of relations to external things. What now is the manifold, which is expressed, perceived, or represented, in the unit, the monad? It is the whole world. Every monad represents all others in itself, is a concentrated all, the universe in miniature. Each individual contains an infinity in itself *(substantia infinitas actiones simul exercet)* and a supreme intelligence, for which every obscure idea would at once become distinct, would be able to read in a single monad the whole universe and its history—all that is, has been, or will be; for the past has left its traces behind it, and the future will bring nothing not founded in the present: the monad is freighted with the past and bears the future in its bosom. Every monad is thus a mirror of the universe,[1] but a living mirror *(miror vivant de l'univers)*, which generates the images of things by its own activity or develops them from inner germs, without experiencing influences from without. The monad has no windows through which anything could pass in or out, but in its action is dependent only on God and on itself.

[Footnote 1: The objection has been made against Leibnitz, and not without reason, that strictly speaking there is no content for the representation of the monads, although he appears to offer them the richest of all contents, the whole world. The "All" which he makes them represent is itself nothing but a sum of beings, also representative. The objects of representation are merely representing subjects; the monad A represents the monads from B to Z, while these in turn do nothing more than represent one another. The monad mirrors mirrors—where is the thing that is mirrored? The essence of substance consists in being related to others, which themselves are only points of relation; amid mere relativities we never reach a real. That which prevented Leibnitz himself from recognizing this empty formalism was, no doubt, the fact that for him the mere form of representation was at once filled with a manifold experiential content, with the whole wealth of spiritual life, and that the quantitative differences in representation, which for him meant also degrees of feeling, desire, action, and progress, imperceptibly took on the qualitative vividness of individual characteristics. Moreover, it must not be overlooked that the spiritual beings represent not merely the universe but the Deity as well, hence a very rich object.]

All monads represent the same universe, but each one represents it differently, that is, from its particular point of view—represents that which is near at hand distinctly, and that which is distant confusedly. Since they all reflect the same content or object, their difference consists only in the energy or degree of clearness in their representations. So far then, as their action consists in representation, distinct representation evidently coincides with complete, unhindered activity, confused representation with arrested activity, or passivity. The clearer the representations of a monad the more active it is. To have clear and distinct perceptions only is the prerogative of God; to the Omnipresent everything is alike near. He alone is pure activity; all finite beings are passive as well, that is, so far as their perceptions are not clear and distinct. Retaining the Aristotelian-Scholastic terminology, Leibnitz calls the active principle form, the passive matter, and makes the monad, since it is not, like God, *purus actus* and pure form, consist of form (entelechy, soul) and matter. This matter, as a constituent of the monad, does not mean corporeality, but only the ground for the arrest of its activity. The *materia prima* (the principle of passivity in the monad) is the ground, the *materia secunda* (the phenomenon of corporeal mass) the result of the indistinctness of the representations. For a group of monads appears as a body when it is indistinctly perceived. Whoever deprives the monad of activity falls into the error of Spinoza; whoever takes away its passivity or matter falls into the opposite error, for he deifies individual beings.

No monad represents the common universe and its individual parts just as well as the others, but either better or worse. There are as many different degrees of clearness and distinctness as there are monads.

Nevertheless certain classes may be distinguished. By distinguishing between clear and obscure perceptions, and in the former class between distinct and confused ones—a perception is clear when it is sufficiently distinguished from others, distinct when its component parts are thus distinguished—Leibnitz reaches three principal grades. Lowest stand the simple or naked monads, which never rise above obscure and unconscious perception and, so to speak, pass their lives in a swoon or sleep. If perception rises into conscious feeling, accompanied by memory, then the monad deserves the name of soul. And if the soul rises to self-consciousness and to reason or the knowledge of universal truth, it is called spirit. Each higher stage comprehends the lower, since even in spirits many perceptions remain obscure and confused. Hence it was an error when the Cartesians made thought or conscious activity—by which, it is true, the spirit is differentiated from the lower beings—to such a degree the essence of spirit that they believed it necessary to deny to it all unconscious perceptions.

From perception arises appetition, not as independent activity, but as a modification of perception; it is nothing but the tendency to pass from one perception to another *(l'appetit est la tendance d'une perception à une autre)*; impulse is perception in process of becoming. Where the perceptions are conscious and rational appetition rises into will. All monads are self-active or act spontaneously, but only the thinking ones are free. Freedom is the spontaneity of spirits. Freedom does not consist in undetermined choice, but in action without external compulsion according to the laws of one's own being. The monad develops its representations out of itself, from the germs which form its nature. The correspondence of the different pictures of the world, however, is grounded in a divine arrangement, through which the natures of the monads have from the beginning been so adapted to one another that the changes in their states, although they take place in each according to immanent laws and without external influence, follow an exactly parallel course, and the result is the same as though there were a constant mutual interaction. This general idea of a *pre-established harmony* finds special application in the problem of the interaction between body and soul. Body and soul are like two clocks so excellently constructed that, without needing to be regulated by each other, they show exactly the same time. Over the numberless lesser miracles with which occasionalism burdened the Deity, the one great miracle of the pre-established harmony has an undeniable advantage. As one great miracle it is more worthy of the divine wisdom than the many lesser ones, nay, it is really no miracle at all, since the harmony does not interfere with natural laws, but yields them. This idea may even be freed from its theological investiture and reduced to the purely metaphysical expression, that the natures of the monads, by which the succession of their representations is determined in conformity with law, consist in nothing else than the sum of relations in which this individual thing stands to all other parts of the world, wherein each member takes account of all others and at the same time is considered by them, and thus exerts influence as well as suffers it. In this way the external idea of an artificial adaptation is avoided. The essence of each thing is simply the position which it occupies in the organic whole of the universe; each member is related to every other and shares actively and passively in the life of all the rest. The history of the universe is a single great process in numberless reflections.

The metaphysics of Leibnitz begins with the concept of representation and ends with the harmony of the universe. The representations were multiplicity (the endless plurality of the represented) in unity (the unity of the representing monad); the harmony is unity (order, congruity of the world-image) in multiplicity (the infinitely manifold degrees of clearness in the representations). All monads represent the same universe; each one mirrors it differently. The unity, as well as the difference, could not be greater than it is; every possible degree of distinctness of representation is present in each single monad, and yet there is a single harmonic accord in which the unnumbered tones unite. Now order amid diversity, unity in variety make up the concept of beauty and perfection. If, then, this world shows, as it does, the greatest unity in the greatest multiplicity, so that there is nothing wanting and nothing superfluous, it is the most perfect, the best of all possible worlds. Even the lowest grades contribute to the perfection of the whole; their disappearance would mean a hiatus; and if the unclear and confused representations appear imperfect when considered in themselves, yet they are not so in reference to the whole; for just on this fact, that the monad is arrested in its representation or is passive, *i.e.*, conforms itself to the others and subordinates itself to them, rest the order and connection of the world. Thus the idea of harmony forms the bridge between the Monadology and optimism.

As in regard to the harmony of the universe we found it possible to distinguish between a half-mythical, narrative form of presentation and a purely abstract conception, so we may make a similar distinction in the doctrine of creation. This actual world has been chosen by God as the best among many other conceivable worlds. Through the will of God the monads of which the world consists attained their reality; as possibilities or ideas they were present in the mind of God (as it were, prior to their actualization), present, too, with all the distinctive properties and perfections that they now exhibit in a state of realization, so that their merely possible or conceivable being had the same content as their actual being, and their essence is not altered or increased by their existence. Now, since the impulse toward actualization dwells in every possible essence, and is the more justifiable the more perfect the essence, a competition goes on before God, in which, first, those monad-possibilities unite which are mutually compatible or compossible, and, then, among the different conceivable combinations of monads or worlds that one is ordained for entrance into existence which shows the greatest possible sum of perfection. It was, therefore, not the perfection of the single monad, but the perfection of the system of which it forms a necessary part, that was decisive as to its admission into existence. The best world was known through God's wisdom, chosen through his goodness, and realized through his power.[1] The choice was by no means arbitrary, but wholly determined by the law of fitness or of the best (*principe du meilleur*); God's will must realize that which his understanding recognizes as most perfect. It is at once evident that in the competition of the possible worlds the victory of the best was assured by the *lex melioris*, apart from the divine decision.

[Footnote 1: In regard to the dependence of the world on God, there is a certain conflict noticeable in Leibnitz between the metaphysical interests involved in the substantiality of individual beings, together with the moral interests involved in guarding against fatalism, and the opposing interests of religion. On the one side, creation is for him only an actualization of finished, unchangeable possibilities, on the other, he teaches with the mediaeval philosophers that this was not accomplished by a single act of realization, that the world has need of conservation, *i.e.*, of continuous creation.]

This law is the special expression of a more general one, the principle of sufficient reason, which Leibnitz added, as of equal authority, to the Aristotelian laws of thought. Things or events are real (and assertions true) when there is a sufficient reason for their existence, and for their determinate existence. The *principium rationis sufficientis* governs our empirical knowledge of contingent truths or truths of fact, while, on the other hand, the pure rational knowledge of necessary or eternal (mathematical and metaphysical) truths rests on the *principium contradictionis*. The principle of contradiction asserts, that is, whatever contains a contradiction is false or impossible; whatever contains no contradiction is possible; that whose opposite contains a contradiction is necessary. Or positively formulated as the principle of identity, everything and every representative content is identical with itself.[2] Upon this antithesis between the rational laws of contradiction and sufficient reason—which, however, is such only for us men, while the divine spirit, which cognizes all things *a priori*, is able to reduce even the truths of fact to the eternal truths—Leibnitz bases his distinction between two kinds of necessity. That is metaphysically necessary whose opposite involves a contradiction; that is morally necessary or contingent which, on account of its fitness, is preferred by God to its (equally conceivable) opposite. To the latter class belongs, further, the physically necessary: the necessity of the laws of nature is only a conditional necessity (conditioned by the choice of the best); they are contingent truths or truths of fact. The principle of sufficient reason holds for efficient as well as for final causes, and between the two realms there is, according to Leibnitz, the most complete correspondence. In the material world every particular must be explained in a purely mechanical way, but the totality of the laws of nature, the universal mechanism itself, cannot in turn be mechanically explained, but only on the basis of finality, so that the mechanical point of view is comprehended in, and subordinated to, the teleological. Thus it becomes clear how Leibnitz in the *ratio sufficiens* has final causes chiefly in mind.

[Footnote 2: Within the knowledge of reason, as well as in experiential knowledge, a further distinction is made between primary truths (which need no proof) and derived truths. The highest truths of reason are the identical principles, which are self-evident; from these intuitive truths all others are to be derived by demonstration—proof is analysis and, as free from contradictions, demonstration. The primitive truths of experience are the immediate facts of consciousness; whatever is inferred from them is less certain than demonstrative knowledge. Nevertheless experience is not to be estimated at a low value; it is through it alone that we can assure ourselves of the reality of the objects of thought, while necessary truths guarantee only that a predicate must be ascribed to a subject (*e.g.*, a circle), but make no deliverance as to whether this subject exists or not.]

To the broad and comprehensive tendency which is characteristic of Leibnitz's thinking, philosophy owes a further series of general laws, which all stand in the closest relation to one another and to his monadological and harmonistic principles, viz., the law of continuity, the law of analogy, the law of the universal dissimilarity of things or of the identity of indiscernibles, and, finally, the law of the conservation of force.

The most fundamental of these laws is the *lex continui*. On the one hand, it forbids every leap, on the other, all repetition in the series of beings and the series of events. Member must follow member without a break and without superfluous duplication; in the scale of creatures, as in the course of events, absolute continuity is the rule. Just as in the monad one state continually develops from another, the present one giving birth to the future, as it has itself grown out of the past, just as nothing persists, as nothing makes its entrance suddenly or without the way being prepared for it, and as all extremes are bound together by connecting links and gradual transitions,—so the monad itself stands in a continuous gradation of beings, each of which is related to and different from each. Since the beings and events form a single uninterrupted series, there are no distinctions of kind in the world, but only distinctions in degree. Rest and motion are not opposites, for rest may be considered as infinitely minute motion; the ellipse and the parabola are not qualitatively different, for the laws which hold for the one may be applied to the other. Likeness is vanishing unlikeness, passivity arrested activity, evil a lesser good, confused ideas simply less distinct ones, animals men with infinitely little reason, plants animals with vanishing consciousness, fluidity a lower degree of solidity, etc. In the whole world similarity and correspondence rule, and it is everywhere the same as here—between apparent opposites there is a distinction in degree merely, and hence, analogy. In the macrocosm of the universe things go on as in the microcosm of the monad; every later state of the world is prefigured in the earlier, etc. If, on the one side, the law of analogy follows as a consequence from the law of continuity, on the other, we have the *principium (identitatis) indiscernibilium*. As nature abhors gaps, so also it avoids the superfluous. Every grade in the series must be represented, but none more than once. There are no two things, no two events which are entirely alike. If they were exactly alike they would not be two, but one. The distinction between them is never merely numerical, nor merely local and temporal, but always an intrinsic difference: each thing is distinguished from every other by its peculiar nature. This law holds both for the truly real (the monads) and for the phenomenal world—you will never find two leaves exactly alike. By the law of the conservation of force, Leibnitz corrects the Cartesian doctrine of the conservation of motion, and approaches the point of view of the present day. According to Descartes it is the sum of actual motions, which remains constant; according to Leibnitz, the sum of the active forces; while, according to the modern theory, it is the sum of the active and the latent or potential forces—a distinction, moreover, of which Leibnitz himself made use.

We now turn from the formal framework of general laws, to the actual, to that which, obeying these laws, constitutes the living content of the world.

%2. The Organic World.%

A living being is a machine composed of an infinite number of organs. The natural machines formed by God differ from the artificial machines made by the hand of man, in that, down to their smallest parts, they consist of machines. Organisms are complexes of monads, of which one, the soul, is supreme, while the rest, which serve it, form its body. The dominant monad is distinguished from those which surround it as its body by the greater distinctness of its ideas. The supremacy of the soul-monad consists in this one superior quality, that it is more active and more perfect, and clearly reflects that which the body-monads represent but obscurely. A direct interaction between soul and body does not take place; there is only a complete correspondence, instituted by God. He foresaw that the soul at such and such a moment would have the sensation of warmth, or would wish an arm-motion executed, and has so ordered the development of the body-monads that, at the same instant, they appear to cause this sensation and to obey this impulse to move. Now, since God in this foreknowledge and accommodation naturally paid more regard to the perfect beings, to the more active and more distinctly perceiving monads than to the less perfect ones, and subordinated the latter, as means and conditions, to the former as ends, the soul, prior to creation, actually exercised an ideal influence—through the mind of God—upon its body. Its activity is the reason why in less perfect monads a definite change, a passion takes place, since the action was attainable only in this way, "compossible" with this alone.[1] The monads which constitute the body are the first and direct object of the soul; it perceives them more distinctly than it perceives, through them, the rest of the external world. In view of the close connection of the elements of the organism thus postulated, Leibnitz, in the discussions with Father Des Bosses concerning the compatibility of the Monadology with the doctrine of the Church, especially with the real presence of the body of Christ in the Supper, consented, in favor of the dogma, to depart from the assumption that the simple alone could be substantial and to admit the possibility of composite substances, and of a "substantial bond" connecting the parts of living beings. It appears least in contradiction with the other principles of the philosopher to assign the rôle of this *vinculum substantiate* to the soul or central monad itself.

[Footnote 1: Cf. Gustav Class, *Die metaphysischen Voraussetzungen des Leibnizischen Determinismus*, Tübingen, 1874.]

Everything in nature is organized; there are no soulless bodies, no dead matter. The smallest particle of dust is peopled with a multitude of living beings and the tiniest drop of water swarms with organisms: every portion of matter may be compared to a pond filled with fish or a garden full of plants. This denial of the inorganic does not release our philosopher from the duty of explaining its apparent existence. If we thoughtfully consider bodies, we perceive that there is nothing lifeless and non-representative. But the phenomenon of extended mass arises for our confused sensuous perception, which perceives the monads composing a body together and regards them as a continuous unity. Body exists only as a confused idea in the feeling subject; since, nevertheless, a reality without the mind, namely, an immaterial monad-aggregate, corresponds to it, the phenomenon of body is a well-founded one *(phenomenon bene fundatum)*. As matter is merely something present in sensation or confused representation, so space and time are also nothing real, neither substances nor properties, but only ideal things—the former the order of coexistences, the latter the order of successions.

If there are no soulless bodies, there are also no bodiless souls; the soul is always joined with an aggregate of subordinate monads, though not always with the same ones. Single monads are constantly passing into its body, or into its service, while others are passing out; it is involved in a continuous process of bodily transformation. Usually the change goes on slowly and with a constant replacement of the parts thrown off. If it takes place quickly men call it birth or death. Actual death there is as little as there is an actual genesis; not the soul only, but every living thing is imperishable. Death is decrease and involution, birth increase and evolution. The dying creature loses only a portion of its bodily machine and so returns to the slumberous or germinal condition of "involution", in which it existed before birth, and from which it was aroused through conception to development. Pre-existence as well as post-existence must be conceded both to animals and to men. Leuwenhoek's discovery of the spermatozoa furnished a welcome confirmation for this doctrine, that all individuals have existed since the beginning of the world, at least as preformed germs. The immortality of man, conformably to his superior dignity, differs from the continued existence of all monads, in that after his death he retains memory and the consciousness of his moral personality.

%3. Man: Cognition and Volition.%

In reason man possesses reflection or self-consciousness as well as the knowledge of God, of the universal, and of the eternal truths or *a priori* knowledge, while the animal is limited in its perception to experience, and in its reasoning to the connection of perceptions in accordance with memory. Man differs from higher beings in that the majority of his ideas are confused. Under confused ideas Leibnitz includes both sense-perceptions—anyone who has distinct ideas alone, as God, has no sense-perceptions—and the feelings which mediate between the former and the perfectly distinct ideas of rational thought. The delight of music depends, in his opinion, on an unconscious numbering and measuring of the harmonic and rhythmic relations of tones, aesthetic enjoyment of the beautiful in general, and even sensuous pleasure, on the confused perception of a perfection, order, or harmony.

The application of the *lex continui* to the inner life has a very wide range. The principal results are: (1) the mind always thinks; (2) every present idea postulates a previous one from which it has arisen; (3) sensation and thought differ only in degree; (4) in the order of time, the ideas of sense precede those of reason. We are never wholly without ideas, only we are often not conscious of them. If thought ceased in deep sleep, we could have no ideas on awakening, since every representation proceeds from a preceding one, even though it be unconscious.

In the thoughtful *New Essays concerning the Human Understanding* Leibnitz develops his theory of knowledge in the form of a polemical commentary to Locke's chief work.[1] According to Descartes some ideas (the pure concepts) are innate, according to Locke none, according to Leibnitz all. Or: according to Descartes some ideas (sensuous perceptions) come from without, according to Locke all do so, according to Leibnitz none. Leibnitz agrees with Descartes against Locke in the position that the mind originally possesses ideas; he agrees with Locke against Descartes, that thought is later than sensation and the knowledge of universals later than that of particulars. The originality which Leibnitz attributes to intellectual ideas is different from that which Descartes had ascribed and Locke denied to them. They are original in that they do not come into the soul and are not impressed upon it from without; they are not original in that they can develop only from previously given sense-ideas; again, they are original in that they can be developed from confused ideas only because they are contained in them *implicite* or as pre-dispositions. Thus Leibnitz is able to agree with both his predecessors up to a certain point: with the one, that the pure concepts have their origin within the mind; with the other, that they are not the earliest knowledge, but are conditioned by sensations. This synthesis, however, was possible only because Leibnitz looked on sensation differently from both the others. If sensation is to be the mother of thought, and the latter at the same time to preserve its character as original, *i.e.*, as something not obtained from without, sensation must, first, include an unconscious thinking in itself, and, secondly, must itself receive a title to originality and spontaneity. As the Catholic dogma added the immaculate conception of the mother to that of the Son, so Leibnitz transfers the (virginal) origin of rational concepts, independent of external influence, to sensations. The monad has no windows. It bears germinally in itself all that it is to experience, and nothing is impressed on it from without. The intellect should not be compared to a blank tablet, but to a block of marble in whose veins the outlines of the statue are prefigured. Ideas can only arise from ideas, never from external impressions or movements of corporeal parts. Thus *all* ideas are innate in the sense that they grow from inner germs; we possess them from the beginning, not developed (*explicite*), but potentially, that is, we have the capacity to produce them. The old Scholastic principle that "there is nothing in the understanding which was not previously in sense" is entirely correct, only one must add, except the understanding itself, that is, the faculty of developing our knowledge out of ourselves. Thought lies already dormant in perception. With the mechanical position (sensuous representation precedes and conditions rational thought) is joined the teleological position (sensuous representations exist, in order to render the origin of thoughts possible), and with this purposive determination, sensation attains a higher dignity: it is more than has been seen in it before, for it includes in itself the future concept of the understanding in an unconscious form, nay, it is itself an imperfect thought, a thought in process of becoming. Sensation and thought are not different in kind, and if the former is called a passive state, still passivity is nothing other than diminished activity. Both are spontaneous; thought is merely spontaneous in a higher degree.

[Footnote 1: A careful comparison of Locke's theory of knowledge with that of Leibnitz is given by G. Hartenstein, *Abhandlungen der k. sächs. Gesellschaft der Wissenschaften*, Leipsic, 1865, included in Hartenstein's *Historisch-philosophische Abhandlungen*, 1870.]

By making sensation and feeling the preliminary step to thought, Leibnitz became the founder of that intellectualism which, in the system of Hegel, extended itself far beyond the psychological into the cosmical field, and endeavored to conceive not only all psychical phenomena but all reality whatsoever as a development of the Idea toward itself. This conception, which may be characterized as intellectualistic in its content, presents itself on its formal side as a quantitative way of looking at the world, which sacrifices all qualitative antitheses in order to arrange the totality of being and becoming in a single series with no distinctions but those of degree. If Leibnitz here appears as the representative of a view of the world which found in Kant a powerful and victorious opponent, yet, on the other hand, he prepared the way by his conception of innate ideas for the Critique of Reason. By his theory of knowledge he forms the transition link between Descartes and Kant, since he interprets necessary truths not as dwelling in the mind complete and explicit from the start, but as produced or raised into consciousness only on the occasion of sensuous experience. It must be admitted, moreover, that this in reality was only a restoration of Descartes's original position, *i.e.*, a deliverance of it from the misinterpretations and perversions which it had suffered at the hands of adherents and opponents alike, but which Descartes, it is true, had failed to render impossible from the start by conclusive explanations. The author of the theory of innate ideas certainly did not mean what Locke foists upon him, that the child in the cradle already possesses the ideas of God, of thought, and of extension in full clearness. But whether Leibnitz improved or only restored Descartes, it was in any case an important advance when experience and thought were brought into more definite relation, and the productive force in rational concepts was secured to the latter and the occasion of their production to the former.

The unconscious or minute ideas, which in noëtics had served to break the force of Locke's objections against the innateness of the principles of reason, are in ethics brought into the field against indeterminism. They are involved whenever we believe ourselves to act without cause, from pure choice, or contrary to the motives present. In this last case, a motive which is very strong in itself is overcome by the united power of many in themselves weaken The will is always determined, and that by an idea (of ends), which generally is of a very complex nature, and in which the stronger side decides the issue. An absolute equilibrium of motives is impossible: the world cannot be divided into two entirely similar parts (this in opposition to "Buridan's ass"). A spirit capable of looking us through and through would be able to calculate all our volitions and actions beforehand.

In spite of this admitted inevitableness of our resolutions and actions, the predicate of freedom really belongs to them, and this on two grounds. First, they are only physically or morally, not metaphysically, necessary; as a matter of fact, it is true, they cannot happen otherwise, but their opposite involves no logical contradiction and remains conceivable. To express this thought the formula, often repeated since, that our motives only impel, incite, or stimulate the will, but do not compel it (*inclinant, non necessitant*), was chosen, but not very happily. Secondly, the determination of the will is an inner necessitation, grounded in the being's own nature, not an external compulsion. The agent determines himself in accordance with his own nature, and for this each bears the responsibility himself, for God, when he brought the monads out of possibility into actuality, left their natures as they had existed before the creation in the form of eternal ideas in His understanding. Though Leibnitz thus draws a distinction between his deterministic doctrine and the "fatalism" of Spinoza, he recognizes a second concept of freedom, which completely corresponds to Spinoza's. A decision is the more free the more distinct the ideas which determine it, and a man the more free the more he withdraws his will from the influence of the passions, *i.e.*, confused ideas, and subordinates it to that of reason. God alone is absolutely free, because he has no ideas which are not distinct. The bridge between the two conceptions of freedom is established by the principle that reason constitutes the peculiar nature of man in a higher degree than the sum of his ideas; for it is reason which distinguishes him from the lower beings. According to the first meaning of freedom man is free, according to the second, which coincides with activity, perfection, and morality, he should become free.

Morality is the result of the natural development of the individual. Every being strives after perfection or increased activity, *i.e.*, after more distinct ideas. Parallel to this theoretical advance runs a practical advance in a twofold form: the increasing distinctness of ideas, or enlightenment, or wisdom, raises the impulse to transitory, sensuous pleasure into an impulse to permanent delight in our spiritual perfection, or toward happiness, while, further, it opens up an insight into the connection of all beings and the harmony of the world, in virtue of which the virtuous man will seek to promote the perfection and happiness of others as well as his own, *i.e.*, will *love* them, for to love is to find pleasure in the happiness of others. To promote the good of all, again, is the same as to contribute one's share to the world-harmony and to co-operate in the fulfillment of God's purposes. Probity and piety are the same. They form the highest of the three grades of natural right, which Leibnitz distinguishes as *jus strictum* (mere right, with the principle: Injure no one), *aequitas* (equity or charity, with the maxim: To each his due), and *probitas sive pietas* (honorableness joined with religion, according to the command: Lead an upright and morally pure life). They may also be designated as commutative, distributive, and universal justice. Belief in God and immortality is a condition of the last.

%4. Theology and Theodicy.%

God is the ground and the end of the world. All beings strive toward him, as all came out from him. In man the general striving toward the most perfect Being rises into conscious love to God, which is conditioned by the knowledge of God and produces virtuous action as its effect. Enlightenment and virtue are the essential constituents of religion; all else, as cultus and dogma, have only a derivative value. Religious ceremonies are an imperfect expression of the practical element in piety, as the doctrines of faith are a weak imitation of the theoretical. It is a direct contradiction of the intention of the Divine Teacher when occult formulas and ceremonies, which have no connection with virtue, are made the chief thing. The points in which the creeds agree are more important than those by which they are differentiated. Natural religion has found its most perfect expression in Christianity, although paganism and Judaism had also grasped portions of the truth. Salvation is not denied to the heathen, for moral purity is sufficient to make one a partaker of the grace of God. The religion of the Jews elevated monotheism, which, it is true, made its appearance among the heathen in isolated philosophers, but was never the popular religion, into a law; but it lacked the belief in immortality. Christianity made the religion of the sage the religion of the people.

Whatever of positive doctrine revelation has added to natural religion transcends the reason, it is true, but does not contradict it. It contains no principles contrary to reason (whose opposite can be proved), but, no doubt, principles above reason, *i.e.*, such as the reason could not have found without help from without, and which it cannot fully comprehend, though it is able approximately to understand them and to defend them against objections. Hence Leibnitz defended the Trinity, which he interpreted as God's power, understanding, and will, the eternity of the torments of hell (which brought him the commendation of Lessing), and other dogmas. Miracles also belong among the things the how and why of which we are not in a position to comprehend, but only the that and what. Since the laws of nature are only physically or conditionally necessary, *i.e.* have been enacted only because of their fitness for the purposes of God, they may be suspended in special cases when a higher end requires it.

While the positive doctrines of faith cannot be proved—as, on the other hand, they cannot be refuted—the principles of natural religion admit of strict demonstration. The usual arguments for the existence of God are useful, but need amendment. The ontological argument of Descartes, that from the concept of a most perfect Being his existence follows, is correct so soon as the idea of God is shown to be possible or free from contradiction. The cosmological proof runs: Contingent beings point to a necessary, self-existent Being, the eternal truths especially presuppose an eternal intelligence in which they exist. If we ask why anything whatever, or why just this world exists, this ultimate ground of things cannot be found within the world. Every contingent thing or event has its cause in another. However far we follow out the series of conditions, we never reach an ultimate, unconditioned cause. Consequently the sufficient reason for the series must be situated without the world, and, as is evident from the harmony of things, can only be an infinitely wise and good Being. Here the teleological proof comes in: From the finality of the world we reason to the existence of a Being, as the author of the world, who works in view of ends and who wills and carries out that which is best,—to the supreme intelligence, goodness, and power of the Creator. A special inferential value accrues to this position from the system of pre-established harmony—it is manifest that the complete correspondence of the manifold substances in the world, which are not connected with one another by any direct interaction, can proceed only from a common cause endowed with infinite intelligence and power.

The possibility of proving the existence of one omnipotent and all-beneficent God, and the impossibility of refuting the positive dogmas, save the harmony of faith and reason, which Bayle had denied. The conclusion of the *New Essays* and the opening of the *Theodicy* are devoted to this theme. The second part gives, also against Bayle, the justification of God in view of the evil in the world. *Si Deus est, unde malum*? Optimism has to reckon with the facts of experience, and to show that this world, in spite of its undeniable imperfections, is still the best world. God could certainly have brought into actuality a world in which there would have been less imperfection than in ours, but it would at the same time have contained fewer perfections. No world whatever can exist entirely free from evil, entirely without limitation—whoever forbids God to create imperfect beings forbids him to create a world at all. Certain evils—in general terms, the evil of finitude—are entirely inseparable from the concept of created beings; imperfection attaches to every created thing as such. Other evils God has permitted because it was only through them that certain higher goods, which ought not to be renounced, could be brought to pass. Think of the lofty feelings, noble resolves, and great deeds which war occasions, think of national enthusiasm, readiness for sacrifice, and defiance of death—all these would be given over, if war should be taken out of the world on account of the suffering which it also brings in its train.

If we turn from the general principles to their application in detail, we find a separate proof for the inevitableness or salutary nature of each of the three kinds of evil—the metaphysical evil of created existence, the physical evil of suffering (and punishment), and the moral evil of sin. Metaphysical evil is absolutely unavoidable, if a world is to exist at all; created beings without imperfection, finiteness, limitation, are entirely inconceivable—something besides gods must exist. The physical evil of misery finds its justification in that it makes for good. First of all, the amount of suffering is not so great as it appears to discontented spirits to be. Life is usually quite tolerable, and vouchsafes more joy and pleasure than grief and hardship; in balancing the good and the evil we must especially remember to reckon on the positive side the goods of activity, of health, and all that which affords us, perchance, no perceptible pleasure, but the removal of which would be felt as an evil (*Theodicy*, ii. § 251). Most evils serve to secure us a much greater good, or to ward off a still greater evil. Would a brave general, if given the choice of leaving the battle unwounded, but also without the victory, or of winning the victory at the cost of a wound, hesitate an instant to choose the latter? Other troubles, again, must be regarded as punishment for sins and as means of reformation; the man who is resigned to God's will may be certain that the sufferings which come to him will turn out for his good.

Especially if we consider the world as a whole, it is evident that the sum of evil vanishes before the sum of good. It is wrong to look upon the happiness of man as the end of the world. Certainly God had the happiness of rational beings in mind, but not this exclusively, for they form only a part of the world, even if it be the highest part. God's purpose has reference rather to the perfection of the whole system of the universe. Now the harmony of the universe requires that all possible grades of reality be represented, that there should be indistinct ideas, sense, and corporeality, not merely a realm of spirits, and with these, conditions of imperfection, feelings of pain, and theoretical and moral errors are inevitably given. The connection and the order of the world demands a material element in the monad, but happiness without alloy can never be the lot of a spirit joined to a body. Thirdly, in regard to moral evil also we receive the assurance that the sum of the bad is much less than that of the good. Then, moral evil is connected with metaphysical evil: created beings cannot be absolutely perfect, hence, also, not morally perfect or sinless. But, in return for this, there is no being that is absolutely imperfect, none only and entirely evil. With this is joined the well-known principle of the earlier thinkers, that evil is nothing actual, but merely deprivation, absence of good, lack of clear reason and force of will. That which is real in the evil action, the power to act, is perfect and good, and, as force, comes from God—the negative or evil element in it comes from the agent himself; just as in the case of two ships of the same size, but unequally laden, which drift with the current, the speed comes from the stream and the retardation from the load of the vessels themselves. God is not responsible for sin, for he has only permitted it, not willed it directly, and man was already evil before he was created. The fact that God foresaw that man would sin does not constrain the latter to commit the evil deed, but this follows from his own (eternal) being, which God left unaltered when he granted him existence. The guilt and the responsibility fall wholly on the sinner himself. The permission of evil is explained by the predominantly good results which follow from it (not, as in physical evil, for the sufferer himself, but for others)—from the crime of Sextus Tarquinius sprang a great kingdom with great men (of. the beautiful myth in connection with a dialogue of Laurentius Valla, *Theodicy,* iii. 413-416). Finally, reference is made again to the contribution which evil makes to the perfection of the whole. Evil has the same function in the world as the discords in a piece of music, or the shadows in a painting—the beauty is heightened by the contrast. The good needs a foil in order to come out distinctly and to be felt in all its excellence.

In the Leibnitzian theodicy the least satisfactory part is the justification of moral evil. We miss the view defended in such grand outlines by Hegel, and so ingeniously by Fechner, that the good is not the flower of a quiet, unmolested development, but the fruit of energetic labor; that it has need of its opposite; that it not merely must approve itself in the battle against evil without and within the acting subject, but that it is only through this conflict that it is attainable at all. Virtue implies force of will as well as purity, and force develops only by resistance. Although he does not appreciate the full depth of the significance of pain, Leibnitz's view of suffering deserves more approval than his questionable application to the ethical sphere of the quantitative view of the world, with its interpretation of evil as merely undeveloped good. But, in any case, the compassionate contempt of the pessimism of the day for the "shallow" Leibnitz is most unjustifiable.

CHAPTER VIII.

THE GERMAN ILLUMINATION.

%1. The Contemporaries of Leibnitz.%

The period between Kepler and Leibnitz in Germany was very poor in noteworthy philosophical phenomena. The physicist, Christoph Sturm[1] of Altdorf (died 1703), was a follower of Descartes, Joachim Jungius[2] (died 1657) a follower of Bacon, though not denying with the latter the value of the mathematical method in natural science. Hieronymus Hirnhaym, Abbot at Prague (*The Plague of the Human Race, or the Vanity of Human Learning*, 1676), declared the thirst for knowledge of his age a dangerous disease, knowledge uncertain, since no reliance can be placed on sense-perception and the principles of thought contradict the doctrines of faith, and harmful, since it contributes nothing to salvation, but makes its possessors proud and draws them away from piety. He maintained, further, that divine authority is the only refuge for man, and moral life the true science. Side by side with such skepticism Hirnhaym's contemporary, the poet Angelus Silesius (Joh. Scheffler, died 1667), defended mysticism. The teacher of natural law, Samuel Pufendorf[3] (1632-94, professor in Heidelberg and Lund, died in Berlin), aimed to mediate between Grotius and Hobbes. Natural law is demonstrable, its real ground is the will of God, its noëtical ground (not revelation, but) reason and observation of the (social) nature of man, and the fundamental law the promotion of universal good. The individual must not violate the interests of society in satisfying his impulse to self-preservation, because his own interests require social existence, and, consequently, respect for its conditions.

[Footnote 1: Chr. Sturm: *Physica Conciliatrix*, 1687; *Physica Electiva*, vol. i. 1697, vol. ii. with preface by Chr. Wolff, 1722; *Compendium Universalium seu Metaphysica Euclidea*.]

[Footnote 2: J. Jung *Logica Hamburgiensis*, 1638; cf. Guhrauer, 1859.]

[Footnote 3: Pufendorf: *Elementa Juris Universalis*, 1660; *De Statu Imperii Germanici*, 1667, under the pseudonym Monzambano; *De Jure Naturæ et Gentium* 1672, and an abstract of this, *De Officio Hominis et Civis*, 1673.]

Pufendorf was followed by Christian Thomasius[1] (1655-1728; professor of law at the University of Halle from its foundation in 1694). He was the first instructor who ventured to deliver lectures in the German language—in Leipsic from 1687—and at the same time was the editor of the first learned journal in German (*Teutsche Monate, Geschichte der Weisheit und Thorheit*). In Thomasius the characteristic features of the German Illumination first came out in full distinctness, namely, the avoidance of scholasticism in expression and argument, the direct relation of knowledge to life, sober rationality in thinking, heedless eclecticism, and the demand for religious tolerance. Philosophy must be generally intelligible, and practically useful, knowledge of the world (not of God); its form, free and tasteful ratiocination; its object, man and morals; its first duty, culture, not learning; its highest aim, happiness; its organ and the criterion of every truth, common sense. He alone gains true knowledge who frees his understanding from prejudice and judges only after examining for himself; the joy of mental peace is given to no one who does not free his heart from foolish desires and vehement passions, and devote it to virtue, to "rational love." The positive doctrines of Thomasius have less interest than this general standpoint, which prefigured the succeeding period. He divides practical philosophy into natural law which treats of the *justum*, politics which treats of the *decorum*, and ethics which treats of the *honestum*. Justice bids us, Do not to others what you would not that others should do to you; decorum, Do to others as you would that they should do to you; and morality, Do to yourself as you would that others should do to themselves. The first two laws relate to external, the third to internal, peace; legal duties may be enforced by compulsion, moral duties not.

[Footnote 1: Thomasius: *Institutionum Jurisprudentiae Divinae Libri Tres*, 1688; *Fundamenta Juris Naturae et Gentium*, 1705, both in Latin; in German, appeared in 1691-96 the *Introduction and Application of Rational and Moral Philosophy*.]

If Thomasius was the leader of those popular philosophers who, unconcerned about systematic continuity, discussed every question separately before the tribunal of common sense, and found in their lack of allegiance to any philosophical sect a sufficient guarantee of the unprejudicedness and impartiality of their reflections, Count Walter von Tschirnhausen (1651-1708; *Medecina Mentis sive Artis Inveniendi Praecepta Generalia*, 1687), a friend of Spinoza and Leibnitz, became the prototype of another group of the philosophers of the Illumination. This group favored eclecticism of a more scientific kind, by starting from considerations of method and seeking to overcome the antithesis between rationalism and empiricism. While fully persuaded of the validity and necessity of the mathematical method in philosophical investigations, as well as elsewhere, Tschirnhausen still holds it indispensable that the deductions, on the one hand, start from empirical facts, and, on the other, that they be confirmed by experiments. Inner experience gives us four primal facts, of which the chief is the certainty of self-consciousness. The second, that many things affect us agreeably and many disagreeably, is the basis of morals; the third, that some things are comprehensible to us and others not, the basis of logic; the fourth, that through the senses we passively receive impressions from without, the basis of the empirical sciences, in particular, of physics. Consequently consciousness, will, understanding, and sensuous representation *(imaginatio)*, together with corporeality, are our fundamental concepts. Not perception *(perceptio)*, but conception *(conceptio)* alone gives science; that which we can "conceive" is true; the understanding as such cannot err, but undoubtedly the imagination can lead us to confuse the merely perceived with that which is conceived. The method of science is geometrical demonstration, which starts from (genetic) definitions, and from their analysis obtains axioms, from their combination, theorems. That which is thus proved *a priori* must, as already remarked, be confirmed *a posteriori*. The highest of all sciences is natural philosophy, since it considers not sense-objects only, not (like mathematics) the objects of reason only, but the actual itself in its true character. Hence it is the divine science, while the human sciences busy themselves only with our ideas or the relations of things to us.

%2. Christian Wolff.%

Christian Wolff was born at Breslau in 1679, studied theology at Jena, and in addition mathematics and philosophy, habilitated at Leipsic in 1703, and obtained, through the instrumentality of Leibnitz, a professorship of mathematics at Halle, in 1706. His lectures, which soon extended themselves over all philosophical disciplines, met with great success. This popularity, as well as the rationalistic tendency of his thinking, aroused the disfavor of the pietists, Francke and Lange, who succeeded, in 1723, in securing from King Frederick William I. his removal from his chair and his expulsion from the kingdom. Finding a refuge in Marburg, he was called back to Halle by Frederick the Great a short time after the latter's ascension of the throne. Here he taught and wrote zealously until his death in 1754. In his lectures, as well as in half of his writings,[1] he followed the example of Thomasius in using the German language, which he prepared in a most praiseworthy manner for the expression of philosophical ideas and furnished with a large part of the technical terms current to-day. Thus the terms *Verhältniss* (relation), *Vorstellung* (representation, idea), *Bewusstsein* (consciousness), *stetig (continuus)*, come from Wolff, as well as the distinction between *Kraft* (power) and *Vermögen* (faculty), and between *Grund* (ground) and *Ursache* (cause),[2] Another great service consisted in the reduction of the philosophy of Leibnitz to a systematic form, by which he secured a dissemination for it which otherwise it would scarcely have obtained. But he did not possess sufficient originality to contribute anything remarkable of his own, and it showed little self-knowledge when he became indignant at the designation Leibnitzio-Wolffian philosophy, which was first used by his pupil, Bilfinger. The alterations which he made in the doctrines of Leibnitz are far from being improvements, and the parts which he rejected are just the most characteristic and thoughtful of all. Such at least is the opinion of thinkers to-day, though this mutilation and leveling down of the most daring of Leibnitz's hypotheses was perhaps entirely advantageous for Wolff's impression on his contemporaries; what appeared questionable to him would no doubt have repelled them also. Leibnitz's two leading ideas, the theory of monads and the pre-established harmony, were most of all affected by this process of toning down. Wolff weakens the former by attributing a representative power only to actual souls, which are capable of consciousness, although he holds that bodies are compounded of simple beings and that the latter are endowed with (a not further defined) force. He limits the application of the pre-established harmony to the relation of body and soul, which to Leibnitz was only a case especially favorable for the illustration of the hypothesis. By such trifling the real meaning of both these ideas is sacrificed and their bloom rubbed off.—While depth is lacking in Wolff's thinking, he is remarkable for his power of systematization, his persevering diligence, and his logical earnestness, so that the praise bestowed on him by Kant, that he was the author of the spirit of thoroughness in Germany, was well deserved. He, too, finds the end of philosophy in the enlightenment of the understanding, the improvement of the heart, and, ultimately, in the promotion of the happiness of mankind. But while Thomasius demanded as a condition of such universal intelligibility and usefulness that, discarding the scholastic garb, philosophy should appear in the form of easy ratiocination, Wolff, on the other hand, regards methodical procedure and certainty in results as indispensable to its usefulness, and, in order to this certainty, insists on distinctness of conception and cogency of proof. He demands a *philosophia et certa et utilis*. If, finally, his methodical deliberateness, especially in his later works, leads him into wearisome diffuseness, this pedantry is made good by his genuinely German, honest spirit, which manifests itself agreeably in his judgment on practical questions.

[Footnote 1: *Reasonable Thoughts on the Powers of the Human Understanding*, 1712; *Reasonable Thoughts on God, the World, and the Soul of Man, also on All Things in General*, 1719 (*Notes* to this 1724); *Reasonable Thoughts on the Conduct of Man*, 1720; *Reasonable Thoughts on the Social Life of Man*, 1721; *Reasonable Thoughts on the Operations of Nature*, 1723; *Reasonable Thoughts on the Purposes of Natural Things*, 1724; *Reasonable Thoughts on the Parts of Man, Animals, and Plants*, 1725, all in German. Besides these there are extensive Latin treatises (1728-53) on Logic, Ontology, Cosmology, Empirical and Rational Psychology, Natural Theology, and all branches of Practical Philosophy. Detailed extracts may be found in Erdmann's *Versuch einer wissenschaftlichen Darstellung*, ii. 2. The best account of the Wolffian philosophy has been given by Zeller (pp. 211-273).]

[Footnote 2: Eucken, *Geschichte der Terminologie^* pp. 133-134.]

Wolff reaches his division of the sciences by combining the two psychological antitheses—the higher (rational) and lower (sensuous) faculties of cognition and appetite. On the first is based the distinction between the rational and the empirical or historical method of treatment. The latter concerns itself with the actual, the former with the possible and necessary, or the grounds of the actual; the one observes and describes, the other deduces. The antithesis of cognition and appetite gives the basis for the division into theoretical and practical philosophy. The former, called metaphysics, is divided into a general part, which treats of being in general whether it be of a corporeal or a spiritual nature, and three special parts, according to their principal subjects, the world, the soul, and God,—hence into ontology, cosmology, psychology, and theology. The science which establishes rules for action and regards man as an individual being, as a citizen, and as the head or member of a family, is divided (after Aristotle) into ethics, politics, and economics, which are preceded by practical philosophy in general, and by natural law. The introduction to the two principal parts is furnished by formal logic.

Philosophy is the science of the possible, *i.e.*, of that which contains no contradiction; it is science from concepts, its principle, the law of identity, its form, demonstration, and its instrument, analysis, which in the predicate explicates the determinations contained in the concept of the subject. In order to confirm that which has been deduced from pure concepts by the facts of experience, *psychologia rationalis* is supplemented by *psychologia empirica*, rational cosmology by empirical physics, and speculative theology by an experimental doctrine of God (teleology). Wolff gives no explanation how it comes about that the deliverances of the reason agree so beautifully with the facts of experience; in his naïve, unquestioning belief in the infallibility of the reason he is a typical dogmatist.

A closer examination of the Wolffian philosophy seems unnecessary, since its most essential portions have already been discussed under Leibnitz and since it will be necessary to recur to certain points in our chapter on Kant. Therefore, referring the reader to the detailed accounts in Erdmann and Zeller, we shall only note that Wolff's ethics opposes the principle of perfection to the English principle of happiness (that is good which perfects man's condition, and this is life in conformity with nature or reason, with which happiness is necessarily connected); that he makes the will determined by the understanding, and assigns ignorance as the cause of sin; that his philosophy of religion, which argues for a natural religion in addition to revealed religion (experiential and rational proofs for the existence of God, and a deduction of his attributes), and sets up certain tests for the genuineness of revelation, favors a rationalism which was flexible enough to allow his pupils either to take part in orthodox movements or to advance to a deism hostile to the Church.

Among the followers of Wolff, Alexander Baumgarten (1714-62) deserves the first place, as the founder of German aesthetics (*Aesthetica*, 1750 *seq.*). He perceives a gap in the system of the philosophical sciences. This contains in ethics a guide to right volition, and in logic a guide to correct thinking, but there are no directions for correct feeling, no aesthetic. The beautiful would form the subject of this discipline. For the perfection (the harmonious unity of a manifold, which is pleasant to the spectator), which manifests itself to the will as the good and to the clear thinking of the understanding as the true, appears—according to Leibnitz—to confused sensuous perception as beauty. From this on the name aesthetics was established for the theory of the beautiful, though in Kant's great work it is used in its literal meaning as the doctrine of sense, of the faculty of sensations or intuitions. Baumgarten's pupils and followers, the aesthetic writer G.F. Meier at Halle, Baumeister, and others, contributed like himself to the dissemination of the Wolffian system by their manuals on different branches of philosophy. To this school belong also the following: Thümmig (*Institutiones Philosophia Wolfianae*, 1725-26); the theologian Siegmund Baumgarten at Halle, the elder brother of the aesthete; the mathematician Martin Knutzen, Kant's teacher;[1] the literary historian Gottsched [2] at Leipsic; and G. Ploucquet, who in his *Methodus Calculandi in Logicis*, with a *Commentatio de Arte Characteristica Universali* appended to his *Principia de Substantiis et Phaenomenis*, 1753, took up again Leibnitz's cherished plan for a logical calculus and a universal symbolic language. The psychologist Kasimir von Creuz (*Essay on the Soul*, in two parts, 1753-54), and J.H. Lambert,[3] whom Kant deemed worthy of a detailed correspondence, take up a more independent position, both demanding that the Wolffian rationalism be supplemented by the empiricism of Locke, and the latter, moreover, in anticipation of the Critique of Reason, pointing very definitely to the distinction between content and form as the salient point in the theory of knowledge.

[Footnote 1: Benno Erdmann, *M. Knutzen und seine Zeit*, 1876.]

[Footnote 2: Th. W. Danzel, *Gottsched und seine Zeit*, 1848.]

[Footnote 3: Lambert: *Cosmological Letters*, 1761; *New Organon*, 1764; *Groundwork of Architectonics*, 1771. Bernoulli edited some of Lambert's papers and his correspondence.]

Among the opponents of the Wolffian philosophy, all of whom favor eclecticism, A. Rüdiger[1] and Chr. Aug. Crusius,[2] who was influenced by Rüdiger, and, like him, a professor at Leipsic, are the most important. Rüdiger divides philosophy according to its objects, "wisdom, justice, prudence," into three parts—the science of nature (which must avoid one-sided mechanical views, and employ ether, air, and spirit as principles of explanation); the science of duty (which, as metaphysics, treats of duties toward God, as natural law, of duties to our neighbor, and deduces both from the primary duty of obedience to the will of God); and the science of the good (in which Rüdiger follows the treatise of the Spaniard, Gracian, on practical wisdom). Crusius agrees with Rüdiger that mathematics is the science of the possible, and philosophy the science of the actual, and that the latter, instead of imitating to its own disadvantage the deductive-analytical method of geometry, must, with the aid of experience and with attention to the probability of its conclusions, rise to the highest principles synthetically. Besides its deduction the determinism of the Wolffian philosophy gave offense, for it was believed to endanger morals, justice, and religion. The will, the special fundamental power of the soul (consisting of the impulses to perfection, love, and knowledge), is far from being determined by ideas; it is rather they which depend on the will. The application of the principle of sufficient reason, which is wrongly held to admit of no exception, must be restricted in favor of freedom. For the rest, we may note concerning Crusius that he derives the principle of sufficient reason (everything which is now, and before was not, has a cause) and the principle of contingency from the principles of contradiction, inseparability, and incompatibility, and these latter from the principle of conceivability; that he rejects the ontological argument, and makes the ground of obligation in morality consist in obedience toward God, and its content in perfection. Among the other opponents of the Wolffian philosophy, we may mention the theologian Budde(us)[3] *(Institutiones Philosophiae Eclecticae*, 1705); Darjes (who taught in Jena and Frankfort-on-the-Oder; *The Way to Truth*, 1755); and Crousaz (1744).

[Footnote 1: Rüdiger: *Disputatio de eo quod Omnes Idea Oriantur a Sensione*, 1704; *Philosophia Synthetica*, 1707; *Physica Divina*, 1716; *Philosophia Pragmatica*, 1723.]

[Footnote 2: Crusius: *De Usu et Limitibus Principii Rationis*, 1743; *Directions how to Live a Rational Life* (theory of the will and of ethics), 1744; *A Sketch of the Necessary Truths of Reason*, 1745; *Way to the Certainty and Trustworthiness of Human Knowledge*, 1747.]

[Footnote 3: J.J. Brucker *(Historia Critica Philosophiae*, 5 vols., 1742-44; 2d ed., 6 vols., 1766-67) was a pupil of Budde.]

%3. The Illumination as Scientific and as Popular Philosophy.%

After a demand for the union of Leibnitz and Locke, of rationalism and empiricism, had been raised within the Wolffian school itself, and still more directly in the camp of its opponents, under the increasing influence of the empirical philosophy of England,[1] eclecticism in the spirit of Thomasius took full possession of the stage in the Illumination period. There was the less hesitation in combining principles derived from entirely different postulates without regard to their systematic connection, as the interest in scholastic investigation gave place more and more to the interest in practical and reassuring results. Metaphysics, noëtics, and natural philosophy were laid aside as useless subtleties, and, as in the period succeeding Aristotle, man as an individual and whatever directly relates to his welfare—the constitution of his inner nature, his duties, the immortality of the soul, and the existence of God—became the exclusive subjects of reflection. The fact that, besides ethics and religion, psychology was chosen as a favorite field, is in complete harmony with the general temper of an age for which self-observation and the enjoyment of tender and elevated feelings in long, delightfully friendly letters and sentimental diaries had become a favorite habit. Hand in hand with this narrowing of the content of philosophy went a change in the form of presentation. As thinkers now addressed themselves to all cultivated people, intelligibility and agreeableness were made the prime requisites; the style became light and flowing, the method of treatment facile and often superficial. This is true not only of the popular philosophers proper—who, as Windelband pertinently remarks (vol. i. p. 563), did not seek after the truth, but believed that they already possessed it, and desired only to disseminate it; who did not aim at the promotion of investigation, but the instruction of the public—but to a certain extent, also, of those who were conscious of laboring in the service of science. Among the representatives of the more polite tendency belong, Moses Mendelssohn[2] (1729-86); Thomas Abbt (*On Death for the Fatherland*, 1761; *On Merit*, 1765); J.J. Engel (*The philosopher for the World*, 1775); G.S. Steinbart (*The Christian Doctrine of Happiness*, 1778); Ernst Platner (*Philosophical Aphorisms*, 1776, 1782; on Platner cf. M. Heinze, 1880); G.C. Lichtenberg (died 1799; *Miscellaneous Writings*, 1800 *seq*.; a selection is given in *Reclam's Bibliothek*); Christian Garve (died 1798; *Essays*, 1792 *seq.; Translations from the Ethical Works of Aristotle, Cicero, and Ferguson*); and Friedrich Nicolai[3] (died 1811). Eberhard, Feder, and Meiners will be mentioned later among the opponents of the Kantian philosophy.

[Footnote 1: The influence of the English philosophers on the German philosophy of the eighteenth century is discussed by Gustav Zart, 1881.]

[Footnote 2: Mendelssohn: *Letters on the Sensations*, 1755; *On Evidence in the Metaphysical Sciences*, a prize essay crowned by the Academy, 1764; *Phaedo, or on Immortality*, 1767; *Jerusalem*, 1783; *Morning Hours, or on the Existence of God*, 1785; *To the Friends of Lessing* (against Jacobi), 1786; *Works*, 1843-44. Cf. on Mendelssohn, Kayserling, 1856, 1862, 1883.]

[Footnote 3: Nicolai: *Library of Belles Lettres*, from 1757; *Letters on the Most Recent German Literature*, from 1759; *Universal German Library*, from 1765; *New Universal German Library*, 1793-1805.]

Among the psychologists J.N. Tetens, whose *Philosophical Essays on Human Nature*, 1776-77, show a remarkable similarity to the views of Kant,[1] takes the first rank. The two thinkers evidently influenced each other. The three fold division of the activities of the soul, "knowing, feeling, and willing," which has now become popular and which appears to us self-evident, is to be referred to Tetens, from whom Kant took it; in opposition to the twofold division of Aristotle and Wolff into "cognition and appetition," he established the equal rights of the faculty of feeling—which had previously been defended by Sulzer (1751), the aesthetic writer, and by Mendelssohn (1755, 1763, 1785). Besides Tetens, the following should be mentioned among the psychologists: Tetens's opponent, Johann Lossius (1775), an adherent of Bonnet; D. Tiedemann (*Inquiries concerning Man*, from 1777), who was estimable also as a historian of philosophy (*Spirit of Speculative Philosophy*, 1791-97); Von Irwing (1772 *seq*.; 2d ed., 1777); and K. Ph. Moriz (*Magazin zur Erfahrungsseelenlehre*, from 1785). Basedow (died 1790), Campe (died 1818), and J.H. Pestalozzi (1745-1827) did valuable work in pedagogics.

[Footnote 1: Sensation gives the content, and the understanding spontaneously produces the form, of knowledge. The only objectivity of knowledge which we can attain consists in the subjective necessity of the forms of thought or the ideas of relation. Perception enables us to cognize phenomena only, not the true essence of things and of ourselves, etc.]

One of the clearest and most acute minds among the philosophers of the Illumination was the deist Hermann Samuel Reimarus[1] (1694-1768), from 1728 professor in Hamburg. He attacks atheism, in whatever form it may present itself, with as much zeal and conviction as he shows in breaking down the belief in revelation by his inexorable criticism (in his *Defense*, communicated in manuscript to a few friends only). He obtains his weapons for this double battle from the Wolffian philosophy. The existence of an extramundane deity is proved by the purposive arrangement of the world, especially of organisms, which aims at the good—not merely of man, as the majority of the physico-theologists have believed, but—of all living creatures. To believe in a special revelation, *i.e.*, a miracle, in addition to such a revelation of God as this, which is granted to all men, and is alone necessary to salvation, is to deny the perfection of God, and to do violence to the immutability of his providence. To these general considerations against the credibility of positive revelation are to be added, as special arguments against the Jewish and Christian revelations, the untrustworthiness of human testimony in general, the contradictions in the biblical writings, the uncertainty of their meaning, and the moral character of the persons regarded as messengers of God, whose teachings, precepts, and deeds in no wise correspond to their high mission. Jewish history is a "tissue of sheer follies, shameful deeds, deceptions, and cruelties, the chief motives of which were self-interest and lust for power." The New Testament is also the work of man; all talk of divine inspiration, an idle delusion, the resurrection of Christ, a fabrication of the disciples; and the Protestant system, with its dogmas of the Trinity, the fall of man, original sin, the incarnation, vicarious atonement, and eternal punishment, contrary to reason. The advance of Reimarus beyond Wolff consists in the consistent application of the criteria for the divine character of revelation, which Wolff had set up without making a positive, not to speak of a negative, use of them. His weakness[2] consists in the fact that, on the one hand, he contented himself with a rationalistic interpretation of the biblical narratives, instead of pushing on—as Semler did after him at Halle (1725-91)—to a historical criticism of the sources, and, on the other, held fast to the alternative common to all the deists, "Either divine or human, either an actual event or a fabrication," without any suspicion of that great intermediate region of religious myth, of the involuntary and pregnant inventions of the popular fancy.

[Footnote 1: H.S. Reimarus: *Discussions on the Chief Truths of Natural Religion*, 1754; *General Consideration of the Instincts of Animals*, 1762; *Apology or Defense for the Rational Worshipers of God*. Fragments of the last of these works, which was kept secret during its author's life, were published by Lessing (the well-known "Wolffenbüttel Fragments," from 1774). A detailed table of contents is to be found in *Reimarus und seine Schutzschrift*, 1862, by D. Fr. Strauss, included in the fifth volume of his *Gesammelte Schriften*.]

[Footnote 2: Cf. O. Pfleiderer, *Philosophy of Religion*, vol. i. p. 102, p. 106 *seq*.]

The philosophico-religious standpoint of G.E. Lessing (1729-81), in whom the Illumination reached its best fruitage, was less one-sided. Apart from the important aesthetic impulses which flowed from the *Laocoon* (1766) and the *Hamburg Dramaturgy* (1767-69), his philosophical significance rests on two ideas, which have had important consequences for the religious conceptions of the nineteenth century: the speculative interpretation of certain dogmas (the Trinity, etc.), and the application of the Leibnitzian idea of development to the history of the positive religions. By both of these he prepared the way for Hegel. In regard to his relation to his predecessors, Lessing sought to mediate between the pantheism of Spinoza and the individualism of Leibnitz; and in his comprehension of the latter showed himself far superior to the Wolffians. He can be called a Spinozist only by those who, like Jacobi, have this title ready for everyone who expresses himself against a transcendent, personal God, and the unconditional freedom of the will. Moreover, in view of his critical and dialectical, rather than systematic, method of thinking, we must guard against laying too great stress on isolated statements by him.[1]

[Footnote 1: A caution which Gideon Spicker (*Lessings Weltanschauung*, 1883) counsels us not to forget, even in view of the oft cited avowal of determinism, "I thank God that I must, and that I must the best." Among the numerous treatises on Lessing we may note those by G.E. Schwarz (1854), and Zeller (in Sybel's *Historische Zeitschrift*, 1870, incorporated in the second collection of Zeller's *Vorträge und Abhandlungen*, 1877); and on his theological position, that of K. Fischer on Lessing's *Nathan der Weise*, 1864, as well as J.H. Witte's *Philosophie unserer Dichterheroen*, vol. i. *(Lessing and Herder)*, 1880. [Cf. in English, Sime, 2 vols., 1877, and *Encyclopedia Britannica*, vol. xiv. pp, 478-482.—TR.]]

Lessing conceives the Deity as the supreme, all-comprehensive, living unity, which excludes neither a certain kind of plurality nor even a certain kind of change; without life and action, without the experience of changing states, the life of God would be miserably wearisome. Things are not out of, but in him; nevertheless (as "contingent") they are distinct from him. The Trinity must be understood in the sense of immanent distinctions. God has conceived himself, or his perfections, in a twofold manner: he conceived them as united and himself as their sum, and he conceived them as single. Now God's thinking is creation, his ideas actualities. By conceiving his perfections united he created his eternal image, the Son of God; the bond between God representing and God represented, between Father and Son, is the Holy Spirit. But when he conceived his perfections singly he created the world, in which these manifest themselves divided among a continuous series of particular beings. Every individual is an isolated divine perfection; the things in the world are limited gods, all living, all with souls, and of a spiritual nature, though in different degrees. Development is everywhere; at present the soul has five senses, but very probably it once had less than five, and in the future it will have more. At first the actions of men were guided by obscure instinct; gradually the reason obtained influence over the will, and one day will govern it completely through its clear and distinct cognitions. Thus freedom is attained in the course of history—the rational and virtuous man consciously obeys the divine order of the world, while he who is unfree obeys unconsciously.

Lessing shares with the deistic Illumination the belief in a religion of reason, whose basis and essential content are formed by morality; but he rises far above this level in that he regards the religion of reason not as the beginning but as the goal of the development, and the positive religions as necessary transition stages in its attainment. As natural religion differs in each individual according to his feelings and powers, without positive enactments there would be no unity and community in religious matters. Nevertheless the statutory and historical element is not a graft from without, but a shell organically grown around natural religion, indispensable for its development, and to be removed but gradually and by layers—when the inclosed kernel has become ripe and firm. The history of religions is an *education of the human race through divine revelation*; so teaches his small but thoughtful treatise of 1780.[1] As the education of the individual man puts nothing extraneous into him, but only gives him more quickly and easily that which he could have reached of himself, so human reason is illuminated by revelation concerning things to which it could have itself attained, only that without God's help the process would have been longer and more difficult—perhaps it would have wandered about for many millions of years in the errors of polytheism, if God had not been pleased by a single stroke (his revelation to Moses) to give it a better direction. And as the teacher does not impart everything to the pupil at once, but considers the state of development reached by him at each given period, so God in his revelation observes a certain order and measure. To the rude Jewish people he revealed himself first as a national God, as the God of their fathers; they had to wait for the Persians to teach them that the God whom they had hitherto worshiped as the most powerful among other gods was the only one. Although this lowest stage in the development of religion lacked the belief in immortality, yet it must not be lightly valued; let us acknowledge that it was an heroic obedience for men to observe the laws of God simply because they are the laws of God, and not because of temporal or future rewards! The first practical teacher of immortality was Christ; with him the second age of religion begins: the first good book of elementary instruction, the Old Testament, from which man had hitherto learned, was followed by the second, better one, the New Testament. As we now can dispense with the first primer in regard to the doctrine of the unity of God, and as we gradually begin to be able to dispense with the second in regard to the doctrine of the immortality of the soul, so this New Testament may easily contain still further truths, which for the present we wonder at as revelations, until the reason shall learn to derive them from other truths already established.

Lessing himself makes an attempt at a philosophical interpretation of the dogmas of the Trinity (see above), of original sin, and of atonement. Such an advance from faith to knowledge, such a development of revealed truths into proved truths of reason, is absolutely necessary. We cannot dispense with the truths of revelation, but we must not remain content with simply believing them, but must endeavor to comprehend them; for they have been revealed in order that they may become rational. They are, as it were, the sum which the teacher of arithmetic tells his pupils beforehand so that they may guide themselves by it; but if they content themselves with this solution—which was given merely as a guide—they would never learn to calculate. Hand in hand with the advance of the understanding goes the progress of the will. Future recompenses, which the New Testament promises as rewards of virtue, are means of education, and will gradually fall into disuse: in the highest stage, the stage of purity of heart, virtue will be loved and practiced for its own sake, and no longer for the sake of heavenly rewards. Slowly but surely, along devious paths which are yet salutary, we are being led toward that great goal. It will surely come, the time of consummation, when man will do the good because it is good, this time of the new, eternal Gospel, this third age, this "Christianity of reason." Continue, Eternal Providence, thine imperceptible march; let me not despair of thee because it is imperceptible, not even when to me thy steps seem to lead backward. It is not true that the straight line is always the shortest.

[Footnote 1: *Die Erziehung des Menschengeschlects.*]

With the thought that every individual must traverse the same course as that by which the race attains its perfection, Lessing connects the idea of the transmigration of souls. Why may not the individual man have been present in this world more than once? Is this hypothesis so ridiculous because it is the oldest?

If Lessing abandoned the ranks of the deists by his recognition of the fact that the positive religions contain truth in a gradual process of purification, by his free criticism, on the other hand, he broke with the orthodox, whose idolatrous reverence for the Bible was to him an abomination. The letter is not the spirit, the Bible is not religion, nor yet its foundation, but only its records. Contingent historical truths can never serve as a proof of the necessary truths of reason. Christianity is older than the New Testament.

Already, in the case of Lessing, we may doubt, in view of his historical temper and of certain speculative tendencies, whether he is to be included among the Illuminati. In the case of Kant a decided protest must be raised against such a classification. When Hegel numbers him among the philosophers of the Illumination, on account of his lack of rational intuition, and some theologians on account of his religious rationalism, the answer to the former is that Kant did not lack the speculative gift, but only that it was surpassed by his gift of reflection, and, to the latter, that in regard to the positive element in religion he judged very differently from the deists and appreciated the historical element more justly than they—if not to the same extent as Lessing and Herder. We do not need to lay great stress on the fact that Kant had a lively consciousness that he was making a contribution to thought, and that the Illumination contemplated this new doctrine without comprehending it, in order to recognize that the difference between his efforts and achievements and those of the Illumination is far greater than their kinship. For although Kant is upon common ground with it, in so far as he adheres to its motto, "Have courage to use thine own understanding, become a man, cease to trust thyself to the guidance of others, and free thyself in all fields from the yoke of authority," and, although besides such formal injunctions to freedom of thought, he also shares in certain material tendencies and convictions (the turning from the world to man, the attempt at a synthesis of reason and experience, and the belief in a religion of reason); yet in method and results, he stands like a giant among a race of dwarfs, like one instructed, who judges from principles, among men of opinion, who merely stick results together, a methodical systematizer among well-meaning but impotent eclectics. The philosophy of the Illumination is related to that of Kant as argument to science, as halting mediation to principiant resolution, as patchwork to creation out of full resources, yet at the same time as wish to deed and as negative preparation to positive achievement. It was undeniably of great value to the Kantian criticism that the Illumination had created a point of intersection for the various tendencies of thought, and had brought about the approximation and mutual contact of the opposing systems which then existed, while, at the same time, it had crumbled them to pieces, and thus awakened the need for a new, more firmly and more deeply founded system.

%4. The Faith Philosophy.%

The philosophers of feeling or faith stand in the same relation to the German Illumination as Rousseau to the French. Here also the rights of feeling are vindicated against those of the knowing reason. Among the distinguished representatives of this anti-rationalistic tendency Hamann led the way, Herder was the most prolific, and Jacobi the clearest. That the fountain of certitude is to be sought not in discriminating thought, but in intuition, experience, revelation, and tradition; that the highest truths can be felt only and not proved; that all existing things are incomprehensible, because individual—these are convictions which, before Jacobi defended them as based on scientific principles, had been vehemently proclaimed by that singular man, J.G. Hamann (died 1788) of Königsberg. From an unprinted review by Hamann, Herder drew the objections which his "Metacritique" raises against Kant's Critique of Reason—that the division of matter and form, of sensibility and understanding, is inadmissible; that Kant misunderstood the significance of language, which is just where sensibility and understanding unite, etc.

In Herder[1] (1744-1803: after 1776 Superintendent-General in Weimar) the philosophy of feeling gained a finer, more perspicuous and harmonious nature, who shared Lessing's interest in history and his tendency to hold fast equally to pantheism and to individualism. God is the all-one, infinite, spiritual (non-personal) primal force, which wholly reveals itself in each thing *(God: Dialogues on the System of Spinoza*, 1787). To the life, power, wisdom, and goodness of God correspond the life and perfection of the universe and of individual creatures, each of which possesses its own irreplaceable value and bears in itself its future in germ. Everywhere, one and the same life in an ascending series of powers and forms with imperceptible transitions. Always, an inner and an outer together; no power without organ, no spirit without a body. As thought is only a higher stage of sensation, which develops from the lower by means of language—reason, like sense, is not a productive but a receptive faculty of knowing, perceiving ("*Vernehmen*")—so the free process of history is only the continuation and completion of the nature-process (*Ideas for the Philosophy of the History of Mankind*, 1784 *seq.*). Man, the last child of nature and her first freedman, is the nodal point where the physical series of events changes into the ethical; the last member of the organisms of earth is at the same time the first in the spiritual development. The mission of history is the unfolding of all the powers which nature has concentrated in man as the compendium of the world; its law, that everywhere on our earth everything be realized that can be realized there; its end, humanity and the harmonious development of all our capacities. As nature forms a single great organism, and from the stone to man describes a connected development, so humanity is a one great individual which passes through its several ages, from infancy (the Orient), through boyhood (Eygpt and Phoenicia), youth (Greece), and manhood (Rome), to old age (the Christian world). The spirit stands in the closest dependence upon nature, and nature is concerned in history throughout. The finer organization of his brain, the possession of hands, above all, his erect position, make man, man and endow him with reason. Similarly it is natural conditions, climate, the character of the soil, the surrounding animal and vegetable life, etc., that play an essential part in determining the manners, the characters, and the destinies of nations. The connection of nature with history by means of the concept of development and through the idea that the two merely represent different stages of the same fundamental process, made Herder the forerunner of Schelling.

[Footnote 1: On Herder cf. the biography by R. Haym, 2 vols., 1877, 1885; and the work by Witte which has been referred to above (p. 306, note).]

His polemic against Kant in the *Metacritique*, 1799 (against the *Critique of Pure Reason*), and the dialogue *Calligone*, 1800 (against the *Critique of Judgment*), is less pleasing. These are neither dignified in tone nor essentially of much importance. In the former the distinction between sensibility and reason is censured, and in the latter the separation of the beautiful from the true and the good, but Kant's theory of aesthetics is for the most part grossly misunderstood. The "disinterested" satisfaction Herder makes a cold satisfaction; the harmonious activity of the cognitive powers, a tedious, apish sport; the satisfaction "without a concept," judgment without ground or cause. The positive elements in his own views are more valuable. Pleasure in mere form, without a concept, and without the idea of an end, is impossible. All beauty must mean or express something, must be a symbol of inner life; its ground is perfection or adaptation. Beauty is that symmetrical union of the parts of a being, in virtue of which it feels well itself and gives pleasure to the observer, who sympathetically shares in this well-being. The charm and value of the *Calligone* lie more in the warmth and clearness with which the expressive beauty of single natural phenomena is described than in the abstract discussion.

Friedrich Heinrich Jacobi (1743-1819) gave the most detailed statement of the position of the philosophy of feeling, and the most careful proof of it. He was born in Düsseldorf, the son of a manufacturer; until 1794 he lived in his native place and at his country residence in Pempelfort; later he resided in Holstein, and, from 1805, in Munich, where, in 1807-13, he was president of the Academy of Sciences. Of his works, collected in five volumes, 1812-25, we are here chiefly concerned with the letters *On the Doctrine of Spinoza*, 1785; *David Hume on Faith, or Idealism and Realism*, 1787; and the treatise *On Divine Things*, 1811, which called out Schelling's merciless response, *Memorial of Jacobi*. Besides Hume and Spinoza, the sensationalism of Bonnet and the criticism of Kant had made the most lasting impression on Jacobi. His relation to Kant is neither that of an opponent nor of a supporter and popularizer. He declares himself in accord with Kant's critique of the understanding (the understanding is merely a formal function, one which forms and combines concepts only, but does not guarantee reality, one to which the material of thought must be given from elsewhere and for which the suprasensible remains unattainable); in regard to the critique of reason he raises the objection that it; makes the Ideas mere postulates, which possess no guarantee for their reality. The critique of sensibility appears to him still more unsatisfactory, as it does not explain the origin of sensations. Without the concept of the "thing-in-itself" one cannot enter the Kantian philosophy, and with it one cannot remain there. Fichte has drawn the correct conclusion from the Kantian premises; idealism is the unavoidable result of the Critique of Reason and foretold by; it as the Messiah was foretold by John the Baptist. And by the evil fruit we know the evil root: the idealistic theory is philosophical nihilism, for it denies the reality of the external world, as the materialism of Spinoza denies a transcendent God and the freedom of the will. Reality slips away from both these systems—they are the only consistent ones there are—material reality escaping from the former and suprasensible reality from the latter; and this must be so, because reality, of whatever kind it be, cannot be known, but only believed and felt. The actual, the existence of the noumenal as well as of the external world, even the existence of our own body, makes itself known to us through revelation alone; the understanding comprehends relations only; the certainty that a thing exists is attained only through experience and faith. Sense and reason are the organs of faith, and hence the true sources of knowledge; the former apprehends the natural, the latter, the supernatural, while for the understanding is left only the analysis and combination of given intuitions.

Philosophy as a science from concepts must necessarily prove atheistic and fatalistic. Conception and proof mean deduction from conditions. How shall that which has no cause from which to explain it, the unconditioned, God, and freedom, be comprehended and proved? Demonstration rises along the chain of causes to the universe alone, not to a transcendent Creator; mediate knowledge is confined to the sphere of conditioned being and mechanical becoming. The intuitive knowledge of feeling alone leads us beyond this, and along with the wonderful, the inconceivable power of freedom in ourselves, which is above all nature, shows us the primal source of all wonders, the transcendent God above us. The inference from our own spiritual, self-conscious, free personality to that of God is no unauthorized anthropomorphism—in the knowledge of God we may fearlessly deify our human existence, because God, when he created man, gave his divine nature human form. Reason and freedom are the same: the former is theoretical, the latter practical elevation to the suprasensible. Nevertheless virtue is not based upon an inflexible, despotic, abstractly, formal law, but upon an instinct, which, however, does not aim at happiness. Thus Jacobi attempts to mediate between the ethics of the Illumination and the ethics of Kant, by agreeing with the former in regard to the origin of virtue (it arises from a natural impulse), and with the latter in regard to its nature (it consists in disinterestedness). Hence with the Illumination he rejects the imperative form, and with Kant the eudemonistic end. At the same time he endeavors to introduce Herder's idea of individuality into ethics, by demanding that morality assume a special form in each man. Schiller and the romantic school take from Jacobi their ideal of the "beautiful soul," which from natural impulse realizes in its action, and still more in its being, the good in an individual way.

PART II. FROM KANT TO THE PRESENT TIME.%

CHAPTER IX.

KANT.

The suit between empiricism and rationalism had continued for centuries, but still awaited final decision. Are all our ideas the result of experience, or are they (wholly or in part) an original possession of the mind? Are they received from without (by perception), or produced from within (by self-activity)? Is knowledge a product of sensation or of pure thought? All who had thus far taken part in this discussion had resembled partisans or advocates rather than disinterested judges. They had given less attention to investigation than to the defense of the traditional theses of their schools; they had not endeavored to obtain results, but to establish results already determined; and, along with real arguments, popular appeals had not been despised. Each of the opposing schools had given variations on a definite theme, and whenever timid attempts had been made to bring the two melodies into harmony they had met with no approval. The proceedings thus far had at least made it evident to the unbiased hearer that each of the two parties made extravagant claims, and, in the end, fell into self-contradiction. If the claim of empiricism is true, that all our concepts arise from perception, then not only the science of the suprasensible, which it denies, but also the science of the objects of experience, about which it concerns itself, is impossible. For perception informs us concerning single cases merely, it can never comprehend all cases, it yields no necessary and universal truth; but knowledge which is not apodictically valid for every reasoning being and for all cases is not worthy the name. The very reasons which were intended to prove the possibility of knowledge give a direct inference to its impossibility. The empirical philosophy destroys itself, ending with Hume in skepticism and probabilism. Rationalism is overtaken by a different, and yet an analogous fate—it breaks up into a popular eclecticism. It believes that it has discovered an infallible criterion of truth in the clearness and distinctness of ideas, and a sure example for philosophical method in the method of mathematics. In both points it is wrong. The criterion of truth is insufficient, for Spinoza and Leibnitz built up their opposing theories—the pantheism of the one and the monadology of the other—from equally clear and distinct conceptions; tried by this standard individualism is just as true as pantheism. Mathematics, again, does not owe its unquestioned acceptance and cogent force to the clearness and distinctness of its conceptions, but to the fact that these are capable of construction in intuition. The distinction between mathematics and metaphysics was overlooked, namely, that mathematical thought can transform its conceptions into intuitions, can generate its objects or sensuously present them, which philosophical thought is not in a position to do. The objects of the latter must be given to it, and to the human mind they are given in no other way than through sensuous intuition. Metaphysics seeks to be a science of the real, but it is impossible to conjure being out of thought; reality cannot be proved from concepts, it can only be felt. In making the unperceivable and suprasensible (the real nature of things, the totality of the world, the Deity, and immortality) the special object of philosophy, rationalism looked on the understanding as a faculty of knowledge by which objects are given. In reality objects can never be given through concepts; these only render it possible to think objects given in some other way (by intuition). It is true that concepts of the suprasensible exist, but nothing can be known through them, there is nothing intuitively given to be subsumed under them.

With this failure to perceive the intuitive element in mathematics was joined the mistake of overlooking its synthetic character. The syllogistic method of presentation employed in the Euclidean geometry led to the belief that the more special theorems had been derived from the simpler ones, and these from the axioms, by a process of conceptual analysis; while the fact is that in mathematics all progress is by intuition alone, the syllogism serving merely to formulate and explain truths already attained, but not to supply new ones. Following the example of mathematics thus misunderstood, the mission of philosophy was made to consist in the development of the truths slumbering in pregnant first principles by means of logical analysis. If only there were metaphysical axioms! If we only did not demand, and were not compelled to demand, of true science that it increase our knowledge, and not merely give an analytical explanation of knowledge. When once the clearness and distinctness of conceptions had been taken in so purely formal a sense, it was inevitable that in the end, as productivity became less, the principle should be weakened down to a mere demand for the explanation and elucidation of the metaphysical ideas present in popular consciousness. Thus the rationalistic current lost itself in the shallow waters of the Illumination, which soon gave as ready a welcome to the empirical theories—since these also were able to legitimate themselves by clear and distinct conceptions—as it had given to the results of the rationalistic systems.

It was thus easy to see that each of the contending parties had been guilty of one-sidedness, and that in order to escape this a certain mean must be assumed between the two extremes; but it was a much more difficult matter to discover the due middle ground. Neither of the opposing standpoints is so correct as its defenders believe, and neither so false as its opponents maintain. Where, then, on either side, does the mistaken narrowness begin, and how far does the justification of each extend?

The conflict centers, first, about the question concerning the origin of human knowledge and the sphere of its validity. Rationalism is justified when it asserts that some ideas do not come from the senses. If knowledge is to be possible, some concepts cannot originate in perception, those, namely, by which knowledge is constituted, for if they should, it would lack universality and necessity. The sole organ of universally valid knowledge is reason. Empiricism, on the other hand, is justified when it asserts that the experiential alone is knowable. Whatever is to be knowable must be given as a real in sensuous intuition. The only organ of reality is sensibility. Rationalism judges correctly concerning the origin of the most important classes of ideas; empiricism concerning the sphere of their validity. The two may be thus combined: some concepts (those which produce knowledge) take their origin in reason or are *a priori*, but they are valid for objects of experience alone. The conflict concerns, secondly, the use of the deductive (syllogistic) or the inductive method. Empiricism, through its founder Bacon, had recommended induction in place of the barren syllogistic method, as the only method which would lead to new discoveries. It demands, above all things, the extension of knowledge. Rationalism, on the contrary, held fast to the deductive method, because the syllogism alone, in its view, furnishes knowledge valid for all rational beings. It demands, first of all, universality and necessity in knowledge. Induction has the advantage of increasing knowledge, but it leads only to empirical and comparative, not to strict universality. The syllogism has the advantage of yielding universal and necessary truth, but it can only explicate and establish knowledge, not increase it. May it not be possible so to do justice to the demands of both that the advantages which they seek shall be combined, and the disadvantages which have been feared, avoided? Are there not cognitions which increase our knowledge (are *synthetic*) without being empirical, which are universally and necessarily valid (*a priori*) without being analytic? From these considerations arises the main question of the *Critique of Pure Reason*: How are synthetic judgments *a priori* possible?

The philosophy of experience had overestimated sense and underestimated the understanding, when it found the source of all knowledge in the faculty of perception and degraded the faculty of thought to an almost wholly inactive recipient of messages coming to it from without. From the standpoint of empiricism concepts (Ideas) deserve confidence only in so far as they can legitimate themselves by their origin in sensations (impressions). It overlooks the *active* character of all knowing. Among the rationalists, on the other hand, we find an underestimation of the senses and an overestimation of the understanding. They believe that sense reveals only the deceptive exterior of things, while reason gives their true non-sensuous essence. That which the mind perceives of things is deceptive, but that which it thinks concerning them is true. The former power is the faculty of confused, the latter the faculty of distinct knowledge. Sense is the enemy rather than the servant of true knowledge, which consists in the development and explication of pregnant innate conceptions and principles. These philosophers forget that we can never reach reality by conceptual analysis; and that the senses have a far greater importance for knowledge than merely to give it an impulse; that it is they which supply the understanding with real objects, and so with the content of knowledge. Beside the (formal) activity (of the understanding), cognition implies a passive factor, a reception of impressions. Neither sense alone nor the understanding alone produces knowledge, but both cognitive powers are necessary, the active and the passive, the conceptual and the intuitive. Here the question arises, How do concept and intuition, sensuous and rational knowledge, differ, and what is the basis of their congruence? Notwithstanding their different points of departure and their variant results, the two main tendencies of modern philosophy agree in certain points. If the conflict between the two schools and their one-sidedness suggested the idea of supplementing the conclusions of the one by those of the other, the recognition of the incorrectness of their common convictions furnished the occasion to go beyond them and to establish a new, a higher point of view above them both, as also above the eclecticism which sought to unite the opposing principles. The errors common to both concern, in the first place, the nature of judgment and the difference between sensibility and understanding. Neither side had recognized that the peculiar character of judgment consists in *active connection*. The rationalists made judgment an active function, it is true, but a mere activity of conscious development, of elucidation and analytical inference, which does not advance knowledge a single step. The empiricists described it as a process of comparison and discrimination, as the mere perception and recognition of the relations and connections already existing between ideas; while in reality judgment does not discover the relations and connections of representations, but itself establishes them. In the former case the synthetic moment is ignored, in the latter the active moment. The imperfect view of judgment was one of the reasons for the appearance of extreme theories concerning the origin of ideas in reason or in perception. Rationalism regards even those concepts which have a content as innate, whereas it is only formal concepts which are so. Empiricism regards all, even the highest formal concepts (the categories), as abstracted from experience, whereas experience furnishes only the content of knowledge, and not the synthesis which is necessary to it. On the one hand too much, and on the other too little, is regarded as the original possession of the understanding. The question "What concepts are innate?" can be decided only by answering the further question, What are the concepts through which the faculty of judgment connects the representations obtained from experience? These connective concepts, these formal instruments of synthesis are *a priori*. The agreement of the two schools is still greater in regard to the relation of sense and understanding, notwithstanding the apparently sharp contrast between them. The empiricist considers thought transformed, sublimated perception, while the rationalist sees in perception only confused and less distinct thought. For the former concepts are faded images of sensations, for the latter sensations are concepts which have not yet become clear; the difference is scarcely greater than if the one should call ice frozen water, and the other should prefer to call water melted ice. Both arrange intuition and thought in a single series, and derive the one from the other by enhancement or attenuation. Both make the mistake of recognizing only a difference in degree where a difference in kind exists. In such a case only an energetic dualism can afford help. Sense and understanding are not one and the same cognitive power at different stages, but two heterogeneous faculties. Sensation and thought are not different in degree, but in kind. As Descartes began with the metaphysical dualism of extension and thought, so Kant begins with the noëtical dualism of intuition and thought.

Much more serious, however, than any of the mistakes yet mentioned was a sin of omission of which the two schools were alike guilty, and the recognition and avoidance of which constituted in Kant's own eyes the distinctive character of his philosophy and its principiant-advance beyond preceding systems. The pre-Kantian thinker had proceeded to the discussion of knowledge without raising *the question of the possibility of knowledge*. He had approached things in the full confidence that the human mind was capable of cognizing them, and with a naïve trust in the power of reason to possess itself of the truth. His trust was naïve and ingenuous, because the idea that it could deceive him had never entered his mind. Now no matter whether this belief in man's capacity for knowledge and in the possibility of knowing things is justifiable or not, and no matter how far it may be justifiable, it was in any case untested; so that when the skeptic approached with his objections the dogmatist was defenseless. All previous philosophy, so far as it had not been skeptical, had been, according to Kant's expression, dogmatic; that is, it had held as an article of faith, and without precedent inquiry, that we possess the power of cognizing objects. It had not asked *how* this is possible; it had not even asked what knowledge is, what may and must be demanded of it, and by what means our reason is in a position to satisfy such demands. It had left human intelligence and its extent uninvestigated. The skeptic, on the other hand, had been no more thorough. He had doubted and denied man's capacity for knowledge just as uncritically as the dogmatist had believed and presupposed it. He had directed his ingenuity against the theories of dogmatic philosophy, instead of toward the fundamental question of the possibility of knowledge. Human intelligence, which the dogmatist had approached with unreasoned trust and the skeptic with just as unreasoned distrust, is subjected, according to the plan of the critical philosopher, to a searching examination. For this reason Kant termed his standpoint "criticism," and his undertaking a "Critique of Reason." Instead of asserting and denying, he investigates how knowledge arises, of what factors it is composed, and how far it extends. He inquires into the origin and extent of knowledge, into its sources and its limits, into the grounds of its existence and of its legitimacy. The Critique of Reason finds itself confronted by two problems, the second of which cannot be solved until after the solution of the first. The investigation of the sources of knowledge must precede the inquiry into the extent of knowledge. Only after the conditions of knowledge have been established can it be ascertained what objects are attainable by it. Its sphere cannot be determined except from its origin.

Whether the critical philosopher stands nearer to the skeptic or to the dogmatist is rather an idle question. He is specifically distinct from both, in that he summons and guides the reason to self-contemplation, to a methodical examination of its capacity for knowledge. Where the one had blindly trusted and the other suspected and denied, he investigates; they overlook, he raises the question of the possibility of knowledge. The critical problem does not mean, Does a faculty of knowledge exist? but, Of what powers is it composed? are all objects knowable which have been so regarded? Kant does not ask whether, but how and by what means, knowledge is possible. Everyone who gives himself to scientific reflection must postulate that knowledge is possible, and the demand of the noëtical theorists of the day for a philosophy absolutely without assumptions is quite incapable of fulfillment. Nay, in order to be able to begin his inquiry at all, it was necessary for Kant to assume still more special postulates; for that a cognition of cognition is possible, that there is a critical, self-investigating reason could, at first, be only a matter of belief. This would not have excluded a supplementary detailed statement concerning the *how* of this self-knowledge, concerning the organ of the critical philosophy. But Kant never gave one, and the omission subsequently led to a sharp debate concerning the character and method of the Critique of Reason. On this point, if we may so express it, Kant remained a dogmatist.

Kant felt himself to be the finisher of skepticism; but this was chiefly because he had received the strongest impulse to the development of his critique of knowledge from Hume's inquiries concerning causation. Brought up in the dogmatic rationalism of the Wolffian school, to which he remained true for a considerable period as a teacher and writer (till about 1760), although at the same time he was inquiring with an independent spirit, Kant was gradually won over through the influence of the English philosophy to the side of empirical skepticism. Then—as the result, no doubt, of reading the *Nouveaux Essais* of Leibnitz, published in 1765—he returned to rationalistic principles, until finally, after a renewal of empirical influences,[1] he took the position crystallized in the *Critique of Pure Reason*, 1781, which, however, experienced still other, though less considerable, changes in the sequel, just as in itself it shows the traces of previous transformations.

[Footnote 1: Cf. H. Vaihinger's *Kommentar zu Kants Kritik der reinen Vernunft*, vol. i., 1881, pp. 48-49. This is a work marked by acuteness, great industry, and an objective point of view which merits respect. The second volume, which treats of the Transcendental Aesthetic, appeared in 1892.]

It would be a most interesting task to trace in the writings which belong to Kant's pre-critical period the growth and development of the fundamental critical positions. Here, however, we can only mention in passing the subjects of his reflection and some of the most striking anticipations and beginnings of his epoch-making position. Even his maiden work, *Thoughts on the True Estimation of Vis Viva*, 1747, betokens the mediating nature of its author. In this it is argued that when men of profound and penetrating minds maintain exactly opposite opinions, attention must be chiefly directed to some intermediate principle to a certain degree compatible with the correctness of both parties. The question under discussion was whether the measure of *vis viva* is equal, as the Cartesians thought, to the product of the mass into the velocity, or, according to the Leibnitzians, to the product of the mass into the square of the velocity. Kant's unsatisfactory solution of the problem—the law of Descartes holds for dead, and that of Leibnitz for living forces—drew upon him the derision of Lessing, who said that he had endeavored to estimate living forces without having tested his own. A similar tendency toward compromise—this time it is a synthesis of Leibnitz and Newton—is seen in his *Habilitationsschrift, Principiorum Primorum Cognitionis Metaphysicae Nova Dilucidatio*, 1755, and in the dissertation *Monadologia Physica*, 1756. The former distinguishes between *ratio essendi* and *ratio cognoscendi*, rejects the ontological argument, and defends determinism against Crusius on Leibnitzian grounds. In the *Physical Monadology* Kant gives his adherence to dynamism (matter the product of attraction and repulsion), and makes the monads or elements of body fill space without prejudice to their simplicity. A series of treatises is devoted to subjects in natural science: The Effect of the Tides in retarding the Earth's Rotation; The Obsolescence of the Earth; Fire (Inaugural Dissertation), Earthquakes, and the Theory of the Winds. The most important of these, the *General Natural History and Theory of the Heavens*, 1755, which for a long time remained unnoticed, and which was dedicated to Frederick II., developed the hypothesis (carried out forty years later by Laplace in ignorance of Kant's work) of the mechanical origin of the universe and of the motion of the planets. It presupposes merely the two forces of matter, attraction and repulsion, and its primitive chaotic condition, a world-mist with elements of different density. It is noticeable that Kant acknowledges the failure of the mechanical theory at two points: it is brought to a halt at the origin of the organic world and at the origin of matter. The mechanical cosmogony is far from denying creation; on the contrary, the proof that this well-ordered and purposive world necessarily arose from the regular action of material forces under law and without divine intervention, can only serve to support our assumption of a Supreme Intelligence as the author of matter and its laws; the belief is necessary, just because nature, even in its chaotic condition, can act only in an orderly and regular way.

The empirical phase of Kant's development is represented by the writings of the 60's. *The False Subtlety of the Four Syllogistic Figures*, 1762, asserts that the first figure is the only natural one, and that the others are superfluous and need reduction to the first. In the *Only Possible Foundation for a Demonstration of the Existence of God*, 1763, which, in the seventh Reflection of the Second Division, recapitulates the cosmogony advanced in the *Natural History of the Heavens*, the discussions concerning being ("existence" is absolute position, not a predicate which increases the sum of the qualities but is posited in a merely relative way), and the conclusion, prophetical of his later point of view, "It is altogether necessary that we should be *convinced* of the existence of God, but not so necessary that his existence should be *demonstrated*" are more noteworthy than the argument itself. This runs: All possibility presupposes something actual wherein and whereby all that is conceivable is given as a determination or a consequence. That actuality the destruction of which would destroy all possibility is absolutely necessary. Therefore there exists an absolutely necessary Being as the ultimate real ground of all possibility; this Being is one, simple, unchangeable, eternal, the *ens realissimum* and a spirit. The *Attempt to introduce the Notion of Negative Quantities into Philosophy*, 1763, distinguishes—contrary to Crusius—between logical opposition, contradiction or mere negation (*a* and *not-a*, pleasure and the absence of pleasure, power and lack of power), and real opposition, which cannot be explained by logic (+*a* and -*a*, pleasure and pain, capital and debts, attraction and repulsion; in real opposition both determinations are positive, but in opposite directions). Parallel with this it distinguishes, also, between logical ground and real ground. The prize essay, *Inquiry concerning the Clearness* (Evidence) *of the Principles of Natural Theology and Ethics*, 1764, draws a sharp distinction between mathematical and metaphysical knowledge, and warns philosophy against the hurtful imitation of the geometrical method, in place of which it should rather take as an example the method which Newton introduced into natural science. Quantity constitutes the object of mathematics, qualities, the object of philosophy; the former is easy and simple, the latter difficult and complicated—how much more comprehensible the conception of a trillion is than the philosophical idea of freedom, which the philosophers thus far have been unable to make intelligible. In mathematics the general is considered under symbols *in concrete*, in philosophy, by means of symbols *in abstracto*; the former constructs its object in sensuous intuition, while the object of the latter is given to it, and that as a confused concept to be decomposed. Mathematics, therefore, may well begin with definitions, since the conception which is to be explained is first brought into being through the definition, while philosophy must begin by seeking her conceptions. In the former the definition is first in order, and in the latter almost always last; in the one case the method is synthetic, in the other it is analytic. It is the function of mathematics to connect and compare clear and certain concepts of quantity in order to draw conclusions from them; the function of philosophy is to analyze concepts given in a confused state, and to make them detailed and definite. Philosophy has also this disadvantage, that it possesses very many undecomposable concepts and undemonstrable propositions, while mathematics has only a few such. "Philosophical truths are like meteors, whose brightness gives no assurance of their permanence. They vanish, but mathematics remains. Metaphysics is without doubt the most difficult of all human sciences *(Einsichten)*, but a metaphysic has never yet been written"; for one cannot be so kind as to "apply the term philosophy to all that is contained in the books which bear this title." In the closing paragraphs, on the ultimate bases of ethics, the stern features of the categorical imperative are already seen, veiled by the English theory of moral sense, while the attractive *Observations on the Feeling of the Beautiful and the Sublime*, which appeared in the same year, still naïvely follow the empirical road.

The empirical phase reaches its skeptical termination in the satire *Dreams of a Ghost-seer explained by the Dreams of Metaphysics*, 1766, which pours out its ingenious sarcasm impartially on spiritualism and on the assumed knowledge of the suprasensible. Here Kant is already clearly conscious of his new problem, a theory of the limits of human reason, conscious also that the attack on this problem is to be begun by a discussion of the question of space. This second question had been for many years a frequent subject of his reflections;[1] and it was this part of the general critical problem that first received definitive solution. In the Latin dissertation *On the Form and Principles of the Sensible and Intelligible World*, 1770, which concludes the pre-critical period, and which was written on the occasion of his assumption of his chair as ordinary professor, the critique of sensibility, the new theory of space and time, is set forth in approximately the same form as in the *Critique of Pure Reason*, while the critique of the understanding and of reason, the theory of the categories and the Ideas and of the sphere of their validity, required for its completion the intellectual labor of several more years. For this essay, *De Mundi Sensibilis atque Intelligibilis Forma et Principiis*, leaves unchallenged the possibility of a knowledge of things in themselves and of God, thus showing that its author has abandoned the skepticism maintained in the *Dreams of a Ghost-seer*, and has turned anew to dogmatic rationalism, whose final overthrow required another swing in the direction of skeptical empiricism. In regard to the progress of this latter phase of opinion, the letters to M. Herz are almost the only, though not very valuable, source of information.

[Footnote 1: *New Theory of Motion and Rest*, 1758; *On the First Ground of the Distinction of Positions in Space*, 1768; besides several of the works mentioned above.]

The *Critique of Pure Reason* appeared in 1781, much later than Kant had hoped when he began a work on "The Limits of Sensibility and Reason," and a second, altered edition in 1787.[1] After the *Prolegomena to every Future Metaphysic which may present itself as Science*, 1783, had given a popular form to the critical doctrine of knowledge, it was followed by the critical philosophy of ethics in the *Foundation of the Metaphysics of Ethics*, 1785, and the *Critique of Practical Reason*, 1788; by the critical aesthetics and teleology in the *Critique of Judgment*, 1790; and by the critical philosophy of religion in *Religion within the Limits of Reason Only*, 1793[2] (consisting of four essays, of which the first, "Of Radical Evil," had already appeared in the *Berliner Monatsschrift* in 1792). The *Metaphysical Elements of Natural Science*, 1786, and the *Metaphysics of Ethics*, 1797 (in two parts, "Metaphysical Elements of the Theory of Right," and "Metaphysical Elements of the Theory of Virtue "), are devoted to the development of the system. The year 1798 brought two more larger works, the *Conflict of the Faculties* and the *Anthropology*. Of the reviews, that on Herder's *Ideen* maybe mentioned, and among the minor essays, the following: *Idea for a Universal History in a Cosmopolitan Sense, Answer to the Question: What is Illumination* f both in 1784; *What does it mean to Orient oneself in Thought?* 1786; *On the Use of Teleological Principles in Philosophy*, 1788; *On a Discovery according to which all Recent Criticism of Pure Reason is to be superseded by a Previous One*, 1790; *On the Progress of Metaphysics since the Time of Wolff; On Philosophy in General, The End of all Things*, 1794; *On Everlasting Peace*, 1795. Kant's *Logic* was published by Jäsche in 1800; his *Physical Geography* and his *Observations on Pedagogics* by F.T. Rink in 1803; his lectures on the *Philosophical Theory of Religion* (1817; 2d. ed., 1830) and on *Metaphysics* (1821; cf. Benno Erdmann in the *Philosophische Monatshefte*, vol. xix. 1883, p. 129 *seq*., and vol. xx. 1884, p. 65 *seq*.) by Pölitz. If we may judge by the specimens given by Reicke in the *Altpreussische Monatsschrift*, 1882-84, and by Krause himself,[3] the promised publication of a manuscript of Kant's last years, now in possession of the Hamburg pastor, Albrecht Krause, and which discusses the transition from the metaphysical elements of natural science to physics, will hardly meet the expectations which some have cherished concerning it. Benno Erdmann has issued *Nachträge zu Kants Kritik der reinen Vernunft aus Kants Nachlass*, 1881, and *Reflexionen Kants zur kritischen Philosophie aus handschriftlichen Aufzeichnungen*—the first volume first Heft *(Reflexionen zur Anthropologie)* appearing in 1882, the second volume *(Reflexionen zur Kritik der reinen Vernunft, aus Kants Handexemplar von Baumgartens Metaphysica)* in 1884. Max Müller has made an English translation of the *Critique of Pure Reason*, 2 vols., 1881.[4]

[Footnote 1: There has been much discussion and much has been written concerning the relation of the two editions. In opposition to Schopenhauer and Kuno Fischer it must be maintained that the alterations in the second edition consist in giving greater prominence to realistic elements, which in the first edition remained in the background, though present even there.]

[Footnote 2: This publication was the occasion of a conflict between Kant and the censorship concerning the right of free religious inquiry; cf. Dilthey in the *Archiv für Geschichte der Philosophie*, vol. in. 1890, pp. 418-450.]

[Footnote 3: A. Krause: *I. Kant wider K. Fischer, zum ersten Male mit Hülfe des verloren gewesenen Kantischen Hauptwerkes vertheidigt*, 1884 (in reply, K. Fischer, *Das Streber- und Gründerthum in der Litteratur*, 1884); also, *Das nachgelassene Werk I. Kants, mit Belegen populär-wissenschaftlich dargestellt*, 1888.]

[Footnote 4: Besides this (centenary) translation the English reader may be referred to the earlier version of Meiklejohn in Bonn's Library; to the versions of the *Prolegomena* by Bax (also in Bonn's Library, and including the *Metaphysical Elements of Natural Science*), and Mahaffy and Bernard, new ed., 1889; to Abbot's *Kant's Theory of Ethics*, 4th ed., 1889, containing the *Foundation of the Metaphysics of Ethics* and the *Critique of Practical Reason* entire, with portions of the *Metaphysics of Ethics* and *Religion within the Limits of Reason Only*; to Bernard's translation of the *Kritik of Judgment*, 1892; and to Watson's *Selections from Kant*, 2d ed., 1888 (in Sneath's Modern Philosophers, 1892).—TR.]

The best complete edition of the works of Kant is the second edition of Hartenstein, in eight volumes, 1867-68, which is chronologically arranged and excellently gotten up. Simultaneously with the first edition of Hartenstein in ten volumes, in 1838 *seq.*, appeared the edition in twelve volumes by K. Rosenkranz and F.W. Schubert (containing in the last volumes a biography of Kant by Schubert, and a history of the Kantian philosophy by Rosenkranz, 1842). Kehrbach's edition of the principal works in Reclam's *Universal-Bibliothek*, with the pagination of the original and collective editions (1877 *seq.*), is more valuable than Von Kirchmann's edition of the complete works in his *Philosophische Bibliothek*.

Among the works on Kant those of Kuno Fischer (vols. iii.-iv. of the *Geschichte der neueren Philosophie*, 3d ed., 1882; also Kant's *Leben und die Grundlagen seiner Lehre*, 1860) take the first place. The writings of Liebmann, Cohen, Stadler, Riehl, Volkelt, and others will be mentioned later, in connection with the neo-Kantian movement; here we may give some of the more important monographs and essays, selected from the enormously developed Kantian literature:

Ad. Böhringer, *Kants erkenntnisstheoretischer Idealismus*, 1888; K. Dieterich, *Die Kantische Philosophie in ihrer inneren Entwickelungsgeschichte*, 2 parts, 1885 (first published separately, *Kant und Newton*, 1877; *Kant und Rousseau*, 1878); W. Dilthey, *Aus den Rostocker Kanthandschriften* in the *Archiv für Geschichte der Philosophie*, vols. ii.-iii. 1889-90; M.W. Drobisch, *Kants Ding an sich und sein Erfahrungsbegriff*, 1885; B. Erdmann, *Kants Kritizismus in der I. und II. Auflage der Kritik der reinen Vernunft*, 1878; the same, *Kants Prolegomena herausgegeben und erläutert*, 1878, Introduction (in reply Emil Arnoldt, *Kants Prolegomena nicht doppelt redigiert*, 1879; cf. also H. Vaihinger, *Die Erdmann-Arnoldtsche Kontroverse* in the *Philosophische Monatshefte*, vol. xvi. 1880); Franz Erhardt, *Kritik der Kantischen Antinomienlehre*, 1888; R. Eucken, *Ueber Bilder und Gleichnisse bei Kant, Zeitschrift für Philosophie*, vol. lxxxiii. 1883, reprinted in his *Beiträge zur Geschichte der neueren Philosophie*, 1886; F. Frederichs, *Der phänomenale Idealismus Berkeleys und Kants*, 1871; the same, *Kants Prinzip der Ethik*, 1879; Ed. von Hartmann, *Das Ding an sich und seine Beschaffenheit*, 1871, in the 2d ed., 1875, and the 3d, 1885, entitled *Kritische Grundlegung des transzendentalen Realismus*; C. Hebler, *Kantiana*, in his *Philosophische Aufsätze*, 1869; Alfred Hegler, *Die Psychologie in Kants Ethik*, 1891; A. Hölder, *Darstellung der Kantischen Erkenntnisstheorie*, 1873 J. Jacobson, *Die Auffindung des Apriori*, 1876; the same, *Ueber die Beziehungen zwischen Kategorien und Urtheilsformen*, 1877; Wilhelm Koppelmann, *Kants Lehre vom analytischen Urtheil, Philosoph. Monatshefte*, vol. xxi, 1885; the same, *Lotzes Stellung zu Kants Kritizismus, Zeitschrift für Philosophie*, vol. lxxxviii, 1886; the same, *Kants Lehre vom kategorischen Imperativ*, 1888; the same, *Kant und die Grundlagen der Christlichen Religion*, 1890; E. Laas, *Kants Analogien der Erfahrung*, 1876; the same, *Einige Bemerkungen zur Transzendentalphilosophie*, Strassburg *Abhandlungen*, 1884; J. Mainzer, *Die kritische Epoche in der Lehre von der Einbildungskraft*, 1881; J.B. Meyer, *Kants Psychologie*, 1870; F. Paulsen, *Was Kant uns sein kann, Vierteljahrsschrift für wissenschaftliche Philosophie*, 1881; B. Pünjer, *Die Religionslehre Kants*, 1874; R. Quaebicker, *Kants und Herbarts metaphysische Grundansichten über das Wesen der Seele*, 1870; J. Rehmke, *Physiologie und Kantianismus*, address in Eisenach, 1883; Rud. Reicke, *Lose Blätter aus Kants Nachlass*, 1889 (on this H. Vaihinger in the *Zeitschrift für Philosophie*, vol. xcvi. 1889); O. Riedel, *Die monadologischen Bestimmungen in Kants Lehre vom Ding an sich*, dissertation at Kiel, 1884; O. Schneider, *Die psychologische Entwickelung des Apriori*, 1883; the same, *Transzendentalpsychologie*, 1891; F. Staudinger, *Noumena*, 1884; M. Steckelmacher, *Die formale Logik Kants*, Breslau Prize Essay, 1879; A. Stern, *Die Beziehung Garves zu Kant, nebst ungedruckten Briefen*, 1884; C. Stumpf, *Psychologie und Erkenntnisstheorie, Abhandlungen der bayerischen Akademie der Wissenschaften*, 1891; G. Thiele, *Kants intellectuelle Anschauung als Grundbegriff seines Kritizismus*, 1876; the same, *Die Philosophie Kants nach ihrem systematischen Zusammenhange und ihrer logischhistorischen Entwickelung*, I. (1) *Kants vorkritische Naturphilosophie*, 1882; (2) *Kants vorkritische Erkenntnisstheorie*, 1887; Ad. Trendelenburg, *Ueber eine Lücke in Kants Beweis von der ausschliessenden Subjectivität des Raumes und der Zeit* in vol. iii. of his *Historische Beiträge zur Philosophie*, 1867; Ueberhorst, *Kants Lehre von dem Verhältnisse der Kategorien zu der Erfahrung*, 1878; H. Vaihinger, *Eine Blattversetzung in Kants Prolegomena, Philosoph. Monatshefte*, vol. xv. 1879; the same, *Zu Kants Widerlegung des Idealismus*, Strassburg *Abhandlungen*, 1884; J. Walter, *Zum Gedächtniss Kants, Festrede*, 1881; Th. Weber, *Zur Kritik der Kantischen Erkenntnisstheorie* (from the *Zeitschrift für Philosophie*), 1882; W. Windelband, *Ueber die verschiedenen Phasen der Kantischen Lehre vom Ding an sich, Vierteljahrsschrift für wissenschaftliche Philosophie*, 1877 (cf. the same author's *Geschichte der neueren Philosophie*, § 58); J. Witte, *Beiträge zum Verständniss Kants*, 1874; the same, *Kantischer Kritizismus gegenüber unkritischem Dilettantismus* (against A. Stöhr), 1885; Wohlrabe, *Kants Lehre vom Gewissen*, 1889; E. Zeller, *Ueber das Kantische Moralprinzip*, 1880; R. Zimmermann, *Ueber Kants Widerlegung des Idealismus von Berkeley*, 1871; the same, *Ueber Kants mathematisches Vorurtheil und dessen Folgen*, 1871.

Popular expositions have been given by the following: K. Fortlage (in his *Philos. Vorträge*, 1869); E. Last, *Mehr Licht! Die Haupsätze Kants und Schopenhauers*, 1879; the same, *Die realistische und die idealistische Anschauung entwickelt an Kants Idealität von Raum und Zeit*, 1884; H. Romundt, *Antaeus, neuer Aufbau der Lehre Kants über Seele, Freiheit, und Gott*, 1882; the same, *Grundlegung zur Reform der Philosophie, vereinfachte und erweiterte Darstellung von Kants Kritik der reinen Vernunft*, 1885; the same, *Die Vollendung des Socrates, Kants Grundlegung zur Reform der Sittenlehre*; the same, *Ein neuer Paulus, Kants Grundlegung zu einer sicheren Lehre von der Religion*, 1886; the same, *Die drei Fragen Kants*, 1887; A. Krause, *Populäre Darstellung von Kants Kritik der reinen Vernunft*, 1881; K. Lasswitz, *Die Lehre Kants von der Idealität des Raumes und der Zeit*, 1883; Wilhelm Münz, *Die Grundlagen der Kantischen Erkenntnisstheorie*, 2d ed., 1885.

Among foreigners Villers, Cousin, Nolen, Desdouits, Cantoni, E. Caird [*A Critical Account of the Philosophy of Kant*, 1877; *The Critical Philosophy of Immanuel Kant*, 2 vols., 1889], Adamson [*On the Philosophy of Kant*, 1879, and a valuable article in the *Encyclopedia Britannica*, 9th ed., vol. xiii.], Stirling [*Text-book to Kant*, 1881], [Watson, *Kant and his English Critics*, 1881], Morris *Kant's Critique of Pure Reason*, Griggs's Philosophical Classics, 1882, [Wallace, *Kant*, Blackwood's Philosophical Classics, 1882; Porter, *Kant's Ethics*, Griggs's Philosophical Classics, 1886; Green, *Lectures*, Works, vol. ii., 1886.—Tr.], have among others made contributions to Kantian literature. Of the older works we may mention the dictionaries of E. Schmid, 1788, and Mellin (in six volumes), 1797 *seq.*, the critique of the Kantian philosophy in the first volume of Schopenhauer's chief work, 1819, and the essay of C.H. Weisse, *In welchem Sinne hat sich die deutsche Philosophie jetzt wieder an Kant zu orientieren*, 1847.

Kant's outward life was less eventful and less changeful than his philosophical development.[1] Born in Königsberg in 1724, the son of J.G. Cant, a saddler of Scottish descent, his home and school training were both strict and of a markedly religious type. He was educated at the university of his native city, and for nine years, from 1746 on, filled the place of a private tutor. In 1755 he became *Docent*, in 1770 ordinary professor in Königsberg, serving also for six years of this time as under-librarian. He seldom left his native city and never the province. The clearness which marked his extremely popular lectures on physical geography and anthropology was due to his diligent study of works of travel, and to an unusually acute gift of observation, which enabled him to draw from his surroundings a comprehensive knowledge of the world and of man. He ceased lecturing in 1797, and in 1804 old age ended a life which had always, even in minute detail, been governed by rule. A man of extreme devotion to duty, particularity, and love of truth, and an amiable, bright, and witty companion, Kant belongs to the acute rather than to the profound thinkers. Among his manifold endowments the tendency to combination and the faculty of intuition (as the *Critique of Judgment* especially shows) are present to a noticeable degree, yet not so markedly as the power of strict analysis and subtle discrimination. So that, although a mediating tendency is rightly regarded as the distinguishing characteristic of the Kantian thinking, it must also be remembered that synthesis is everywhere preceded by a mighty work of analysis, and that this still exerts its power even after the adjustment is complete. Thus Kant became the energetic defender of a qualitative view of the world in opposition to the quantitative view of Leibnitz, for which antitheses (*e.g.*, sensation and thought, feeling and cognition, good and evil, duty and inclination) fade into mere differences of degree.

[Footnote 1: The following have done especially valuable service in the investigation of the development of Kant's doctrine: Paulsen (*Versuch einer Entwickelungsgeschichte der Kantischen Erkenntnisstheorie*, 1875), B. Erdmann, Vaihinger, and Windelband. Besides Hume and Leibnitz, Newton, Locke, Shaftesbury, Rousseau, and Wolff exercised an important influence on Kant.]

In the beginning of this chapter we have indicated how the new ideal of knowledge, under whose banner Kant brought about a reform of philosophy, grew out of the conflict between the rationalistic (dogmatic) and the empirical (skeptical) systems. This combines the Baconian ideal of the extension of knowledge with the Cartesian ideal of certainty in knowledge. It is synthetic judgments alone which extend knowledge, while analytic judgments are explicative merely.[1] *A priori* judgments alone are perfectly certain, absolutely universal, and necessarily valid; while *a posteriori* judgments are subjectively valid merely, lack necessity, and, at best, yield only relative universality.[2] All analytic judgments are *a priori*, all empirical or *a posteriori* judgments are synthetic. Between the two lies the object of Kant's search. Do *synthetic judgments a priori* exist, and how are they possible?

[Footnote 1: "All bodies are extended" is an analytic judgment; "all bodies possess weight," a synthetic judgment. The former explicates the concept of the subject by bringing into notice an idea already contained in it and belonging to the definition as a part thereof; it is based on the law of contradiction: an unextended body is a self-contradictory concept. The latter, on the contrary, goes beyond the concept of the subject and adds a predicate which had not been thought therein. It is experience which teaches us that weight is joined to matter, a fact which cannot be derived from the concept of matter. Almost all mathematical principles are synthetic, and here, as will be shown, it is not experience but "pure intuition" which permits us to go beyond the concept and add a new mark to it.]

[Footnote 2: The Scholastics applied the term *a priori* to knowledge from causes (from that which precedes), and *a posteriori* to knowledge from effects. Kant, following Leibnitz and Lambert, uses the terms to designate the antithesis, knowledge from reason and knowledge from experience. An *a priori* judgment is a judgment obtained without the aid of experience. When the principle from which it is derived is also independent of experience it is absolutely *a priori*, otherwise it is relatively *a priori*.]

Two sciences discuss the *how*, and a third the *if* of such judgments, which, at the same time, are ampliative and absolutely universal and necessary. The first two sciences are pure mathematics and pure natural science, of which the former is protected against doubt concerning its legitimacy by its evident character, and the latter, by the constant possibility of verification in experience; each, moreover, can point to the continuous course of its development. All this is absent in the third science, metaphysics, as science of the suprasensible, and to its great disadvantage. Experiential verification is in the nature of things denied to a presumptive knowledge of that which is beyond experience; it lacks evidence to such an extent that there is scarcely a principle to be found to which all metaphysicians assent, much less a metaphysical text-book to compare with Euclid; there is so little continuous advance that it is rather true that the later comers are likely to overthrow all that their predecessors have taught. In metaphysics, therefore, which, it must be confessed, is actual as a natural tendency, the question is not, as in the other two sciences, concerning the grounds of its legitimacy, but concerning this legitimacy itself. Mathematics and pure physics form synthetic judgments *a priori*, and metaphysics does the same. But the principles of the two former are unchallenged, while those of the third are not. In the former case the subject for investigation is, Whence this authority? in the latter case, Is she thus authorized?

Thus the main question, How are synthetic judgments *a priori* possible? divides into the subordinate questions, How is pure mathematics possible? How is pure natural science possible, and, How is metaphysics (in two senses: metaphysics in general, and metaphysics as science) possible? The Transcendental *Aesthetic* (the critique of sensibility or the faculty of intuition) answers the first of these questions; the Transcendental *Analytic* (the critique of the understanding), the second; and the Transcendental *Dialectic* (the critique of "reason" in the narrower sense) and the Transcendental *Doctrine of Method (Methodenlehre)*, the third. The Analytic and the Dialectic are the two parts of the Transcendental "Logic" (critique of the faculty of thought), which, together with the Aesthetic, forms the Transcendental "Doctrine of Elements" *(Elementarlehre)*, in contrast to the Doctrine of Method. The *Critique of Pure Reason* follows this scheme of subordinate division, while the *Prolegomena* co-ordinates all four parts in the manner first mentioned.

Let us anticipate the answers. Pure mathematics is possible, because there are pure or *a priori intuitions* (space and time), and pure natural science or the metaphysics of phenomena, because there are *a priori concepts* (categories) *and principles* of the pure understanding. Metaphysics as a presumptive science of the suprasensible has been possible in the form of unsuccessful attempts, because there are *Ideas* or concepts of reason which point beyond experience and look as though knowable objects were given through them; but as real science it is not possible, because the application of the categories is restricted to the limits of experience, while the objects thought through the Ideas cannot be sensuously given, and all assumed knowledge of them becomes involved in irresolvable contradictions (antinomies). On the other hand, a science is possible and necessary to teach the correct use of the categories, which may be applied to phenomena alone, and of the Ideas, which may be applied only to our knowledge of things (and our volition), and to determine the origin and the limits of our knowledge—that is to say, a transcendental philosophy. In regard to metaphysics (knowledge from pure reason), then, this is the conclusion reached: Rejection of transcendent metaphysics (that which goes beyond experience), recognition and development of immanent metaphysics (that which remains within the limits of possible experience). It is not possible as a metaphysic of things in themselves; it is possible as a metaphysic of nature (of the totality of phenomena), and as a metaphysic of knowledge (critique of reason).

The interests of the reason are not exhausted, however, by the question, What can we know? but include two further questions, What ought we to do? and, What may we hope? Thus to the metaphysics of nature there is added a metaphysics of morals, and to the critique of theoretical reason, a critique of practical reason or of the will, together with a critique of religious belief. For even if a "knowledge" of the suprasensible is denied to us, yet "practical" grounds are not wanting for a sufficiently certain "conviction" concerning God, freedom, and immortality.

After carrying the question of the possibility of synthetic judgments *a priori* from the knowledge of nature over to the knowledge of our duty, Kant raises it, in the third place, in regard to our judgment concerning the subjective and objective purposiveness of things, or concerning their beauty and their perfection, and adds to his critique of the intellect and the will a critique of the faculty of aesthetic and teleological *judgment*.

The Kantian philosophy accordingly falls into three parts, one theoretical, one practical (and religious), one aesthetic and teleological.

* * * * *

Before advancing to our account of the first of these parts, a few preliminary remarks are indispensable concerning the presuppositions involved in Kant's critical work and on the method which he pursues. The presuppositions are partly psychological, partly (as the classification of the forms of judgment and inference, and the twofold division of judgments) logical, either in the formal or the transcendental sense, and partly metaphysical (as the thing in itself). Kant takes the first of these from the psychology of his time, by combining the Wolffian classification of the faculties with that of Tetens, and thus obtains six different faculties: lower (sensuous) and higher (intellectual) faculties of cognition, of feeling, and of appetition; or sensibility (the capacity for receiving representations through the way in which we are affected by objects), understanding (the faculty of producing representations spontaneously and of connecting them); the sensuous feelings of pleasure and pain, taste; desire, and will. The understanding in the wide sense is equivalent to the higher faculty of cognition, and divides further into understanding in the stricter sense (faculty of concepts), judgment (faculty of judging), and reason (faculty of inference). Of these the first gives laws to the faculty of cognition or to nature, the second laws to taste, and the third laws to the will.

The most important of the fundamental assumptions concerns the relation, the nature, and the mission of the two faculties of cognition. These do not differ in degree, through the possession of greater or less distinctness—for there are sensuous representations which are distinct and intellectual ones which are not so—but specifically: Sensibility is the faculty of intuitions, understanding the faculty of concepts. Intuitions are particular, concepts general representations. The former relate to objects directly, the latter only indirectly (through the mediation of other representations). In intuition the mind is receptive, in conception it acts spontaneously. "Through intuitions objects are *given* to us; through concepts they are *thought*." It results from this that neither of the two faculties is of itself sufficient for the attainment of knowledge, for cognition is objective thinking, the determination of objects, the unifying combination or elaboration of a given manifold, the forming of a material content. Rationalists and empiricists alike have been deceived in regard to the necessity for co-operation between the senses and the understanding. Sensibility furnishes the material manifold, which of itself it is not able to form, while the understanding gives the unifying form, to which of itself it cannot furnish a content. "Intuitions without concepts are *blind*" (formless, unintelligible), "concepts without intuitions are *empty*" (without content). In the one case, form and order are wanting; in the other, the material to be formed. The two faculties are thrown back on each other, and knowledge can arise only from their union.

A certain degree of form is attained in sense, it is true, since the chaos of sensations is ordered under the "forms of intuition," space and time, which are an original possession of the intuiting subject, but this is not sufficient, without the aid of the understanding, for the genesis of knowledge. In view of the *a priori* nature of space and time, though without detraction from their intuitive character (they are immediate particular representations), we may assign pure sensibility to the higher faculty of cognition and speak of an intuiting reason.

The forms of intuition and of thought come from within, they lie ready in the mind *a priori*, though not as completed representations. They are functions, necessary actions of the soul, for the execution of which a stimulus from without, through sensations, is necessary, but which, when once this is given, the soul brings forth spontaneously. The external impulse merely gives the soul the occasion for such productive acts, while their grounds and laws are found in its own nature. In this sense Kant terms them "originally acquired," and in the Introduction to the *Critique of Pure Reason* declares that although it is indubitable that "all our knowledge begins *with* experience (impressions of sense), yet it does not all arise *from* experience." That a representation or cognition is *a priori*[1] does not mean that it precedes experience in time, but that (apart from the merely exciting, non-productive stimulation through impressions already mentioned) it is independent of all experience, that it is not derived or borrowed from experience.

[Footnote 1: The terms *a priori* representation and pure representation (concept, intuition) are equivalent; but in judgments, on the other hand, there is a distinction. A judgment is *a priori* when the connection takes place independently of experience, no matter whether the concepts connected are *a priori* or not. If the former is the case the *a priori* judgment is pure (mixed with nothing empirical); if the latter, it is mixed.]

The material of intuition and thought is given to the soul, received by it; it arises through the action of objects upon the senses, and is always empirical. Intuition is the only organ of reality; in sensation the presence of a real object as the cause of the sensation is directly revealed. When Kant's transcendental idealism was placed by a reviewer on a level with the empirical idealism of Berkeley, which denies the existence of the external world, he distinctly asserted that it had never entered his mind to question the reality of external things. Further, after the existence of real things affecting the senses had been transformed in his mind from a basis of the investigation into an object of inquiry, he endeavored to defend this assumption (which at first he had naïvely borrowed from the realism of pre-scientific thought) by arguments, but without any satisfactory result.[1]

[Footnote 1: The task of confirming the existence of things in themselves changes under his hands into another, that of proving the existence of external phenomena. "That external objects are real as representations" Berkeley had never disputed.]

On the basis of the inseparability of sensibility and understanding the ideal of knowledge—an extension of knowledge to be attained by *a priori* means (p. 333)—experiences a remarkable addition in the position that the rational synthesis thus obtained must be a knowledge of reality, must be applied to matter given in intuition. To the question, "How are synthetic judgments *a priori possible*?" is joined a second equally legitimate inquiry, "How do they become *objectively valid*, or applicable to objects of experience?" The principle from which their validity is proved—they are applicable to objects of experience because *without them experience would not be possible*, because they are *conditions of experience*—like the criterion of apriority (strict universality and necessity), is one of the noëtic assumptions of the critical theory.[1]

[Footnote 1: Cf. Vaihinger, *Kommentar*, i. pp. 425-430.]

Inasmuch as its investigation relates to the conditions of experience the Kantian criticism follows a method which it itself terms *transcendental*. Heretofore, when the metaphysical method had been adopted, the object had been the suprasensible; and when knowledge had been made the object of investigation, the method followed had been empirical, psychological. Kant had the right to consider himself the creator of noëtics, for he showed it the transcendental point of view. Knowledge is an object of experience, but its conditions are not. The object is to explain knowledge, not merely to describe it psychologically,—to establish a new science of knowledge from principles, from pure reason. That which lies beyond experience is sealed from our thought; that which lies on this side of it is still uninvestigated, though capable and worthy of investigation, and in extreme need thereof. Criticism forbids the *transcendent* use of reason (transcending experience); it permits, demands, and itself exercises the *transcendental*[1] use of it, which explains an experiential object, knowledge, from its conditions, which are not empirically given.

[Footnote A: Kant applies the term *transcendental* to the knowledge (the discovery, the proof) of the *a priori* factor and its relation to objects of experience. Unfortunately he often uses the same word not only to designate the *a priori* element itself, but also as a synonym for transcendent. In all three cases its opposite is *empirical*, namely, empirico-psychological investigation by observation in distinction from noëtical investigation from principles; empirical origin in distinction from an origin in pure reason, and empirical use in distinction from application beyond the limits of experience.]

There is, apparently, a contradiction between the empiristic result of the Critique of Reason (the limitation of knowledge to objects of experience) and its rationalistic proofs (which proceed metaphysically, not empirically), and, in fact, a considerable degree of opposition really exists. Kant argues in a metaphysical way that there can be no metaphysics. This contradiction is solved by the distinction which has been mentioned between that which is beyond, and that which lies within, the boundary of experience. That metaphysic is forbidden which on the objective side soars beyond experience, but that pure rational knowledge is permissible and necessary which develops from principles the grounds of experiential knowledge existing in the subject. In the Kantian school, however, these complementary elements,—empirical result, transcendental or metaphysical, properly speaking, pro-physical method,—were divorced, and the one emphasized, favored, and further developed at the expense of the other. The empiricists hold to the result, while they either weaken or completely misunderstand the rationalism of the method: the *a priori* factor, says Fries, was not reached by *a priori*, but by *a posteriori*, means, and there is no other way by which it could have been reached. The constructive thinkers, Fichte and his successors, adopt and continue the metaphysical method, but reject the empirical result. Fichte's aim is directed to a system of necessary, unconscious processes of reason, among which, rejecting the thing in itself, he includes sensation. According to Schelling nature itself is *a priori*, a condition of consciousness. This discrepancy between foundation and result continues in an altered form even among contemporary thinkers—as a discussion whether the "main purpose" of Criticism is to be found in the limitation of knowledge to possible experience, or the establishment of *a priori* elements—though many, in adherence to Kant's own view, maintain that the metaphysics of knowledge and of phenomena (immanent rationalism) is the only legitimate metaphysics.

%1. Theory of Knowledge.

(a) The Pure Intuitions (Transcendental Aesthetic).%—The first part of the Critique of Reason, the Transcendental Aesthetic, lays down the position that *space and time* are not independent existences, not real beings, and not properties or relations which would belong to things in themselves though they were not intuited, but *forms of our intuition*, which have their basis in the subjective constitution of our, the human, mind. If we separate from sensuous intuition all that the understanding thinks in it through its concepts, and all that belongs to sensation, these two forms of intuition remain, which may be termed pure intuitions, since they can be considered apart from all sensation. As subjective *conditions* (lying in the nature of the subject) through which alone a thing can become an object of intuition for us, they precede all empirical intuitions or are *a priori*.

Space and time are neither substantial receptacles which contain all that is real nor orders inhering in things in themselves, but forms of intuition. Now all our representations are either pure or empirical in their origin, and either intuitive or conceptual in character. Kant advances four proofs for the position that space and time are not empirical and not concepts, but pure intuitions: (1) Time is not an empirical concept which has been abstracted from experience. For the coexistence or succession of phenomena, *i.e.*, their existence at the same time or at different times (from which, as many believe, the representation of time is abstracted), itself presupposes time—a coexistence or succession is possible only in time. It is no less false that space is abstracted from the empirical space relations of external phenomena, their existence outside and beside one another, or in different places, for it is impossible to represent relative situation except in space. Therefore experience does not make space and time possible; but space and time first of all make experience possible, the one outer, the other inner experience. They are postulates of perception, not abstractions from it. (2) Time is a necessary representation *a priori*. We can easily think all phenomena away from it, but we cannot remove time itself in view of phenomena in general; we can think time without phenomena, but not phenomena without time. The same is true of space in reference to external objects. Both are conditions of the possibility of phenomena. (3) Time is not a discursive or general concept. For there is but one time. And different times do not precede the one time as the constituent parts of which it is made up, but are mere limitations of it; the part is possible only through the whole. In the same way the various spaces are only parts of one and the same space, and can be thought in it alone. But a representation which can be given only by a single object is a particular representation or an intuition. Because, therefore, of the oneness of space and time, the representation of each is an intuition. The *a priori*, immediate intuition of the one space is entirely different from the empirical, general conception of space, which is abstracted from the various spaces. (4) Determinate periods of time arise by limitation of the one, fundamental time. Consequently this original time must be unlimited or infinite, and the representation of it must be an intuition, not a concept. Time contains in itself an endless number of representations (its parts, times), but this is never the case with a generic concept, which, indeed, is contained as a partial representation in an endless number of representations (those of the individuals having the same name), and, consequently, comprehends them all under itself, but which never contains them in itself. The general concept horse is contained in each particular representation of a horse as a general characteristic, and that of justice in each representation of a definite just act; time, however, is not contained in the different times, but they are contained in it. Similarly the relation of infinite space to the finite spaces is not the logical relation of a concept to examples of it, but the intuitive relation of an unlimited whole to its limited parts.

The *Prolegomena* employs as a fifth proof for the intuitive character of space, an argument which had already appeared in the essay *On the Ultimate Ground of the Distinction of Positions in Space*. There are certain spatial distinctions which can be grasped by intuition alone, and which are absolutely incapable of comprehension through the understanding—for example, those of right and left, above and below, before and behind. No logical marks can be given for the distinction between the object and its image in the mirror, or between the right ear and the left. The complete description of a right hand must, in all respects (quality, proportionate position of parts, size of the whole), hold for the left as well; but, despite the complete similarity, the one hand cannot be exactly super-imposed on the other; the glove of the one cannot be worn on the other. This difference in direction, which has significance only when viewed from a definite point, and the impossibility mentioned of a congruence between an object (right hand) and its reflected image (left hand) can be understood only by intuition; they must be seen and felt, and cannot be made clear through concepts, and, consequently, can never be explained to a being which lacks the intuition of space.

In the "transcendental" exposition of space and time Kant follows this "metaphysical" exposition, which had to prove their non-empirical, and non-discursive, hence their *a priori* and intuitive, character, with the proof that only such an explanation of space and time could make it conceivable how synthetic cognitions *a priori* can arise from them. The principles of mathematics are of this kind. The synthetic character of geometrical truths is explained by the intuitive nature of space, their apodictic character by its apriority, and their objective reality or applicability to empirical objects by the fact that space is the condition of (external) perception. The like is true of arithmetic and time.

If space were a mere concept, no proposition could be derived from it which should go beyond the concept and extend our knowledge of its properties. The possibility of such extension or synthesis in mathematics depends on the fact that spatial concepts can always be presented or "constructed" in intuition. The geometrical axiom that in the triangle the sum of two sides is greater than the third is derived from intuition, by describing the triangle in imagination or, actually, on the board. Here the object is given through the cognition and not before it.—If space and time were empirical representations the knowledge obtained from them would lack necessity, which, as a matter of fact, it possesses in a marked degree. While experience teaches us only that something is thus or so, and not that it could not be otherwise, the axioms, (space has only three dimensions, time only one; only one straight line is possible between two points), nay, all the propositions of mathematics are strictly universal and apodictically certain: we are entirely relieved from the necessity of measuring all triangles in the world in order to find out whether the sum of their angles is equal to two right angles, and we do not need, as in the case of judgments of experience, to add the limitation, so far as it is yet known there are no exceptions to this rule. The apriority is the *ratio essendi* of the strict necessity involved in the "it must be so" (*des Soseinmüssens*), while the latter is the *ratio cognoscendi* of the former. Now since the necessity of mathematical judgments can only be explained through the ideality of space, this doctrine is perfectly certain, not merely a probable hypothesis.—The validity of mathematical principles for all objects of perception, finally, is based on the fact that they are rules under which alone experience is possible for us. It should be mentioned, further, that the conceptions of change and motion (change of place) are possible only through and in the representation of time. No concept could make intelligible the possibility of change, that is, of the connection of contradictory predicates in one and the same thing, but the intuition of succession easily succeeds in accomplishing it.

The argument is followed by conclusions and explanations based upon it; (1) Space is the form of the outer, time of the inner, sense. Through the outer sense external objects are given to us, and through the inner sense our own inner states. But since all representations, whether they have external things for their objects or not, belong in themselves, as mental determinations, to our inner state, time is the formal condition of all phenomena in general, directly of internal (psychical) phenomena, and, thereby, indirectly of external phenomena also. (2) The validity of the relations of space and time cognizable *a priori* is established for all objects of possible experience, but is limited to these. They are valid for *all phenomena* (for all things which at any time may be given to our senses), but only for these, not for things as they are *in themselves*. They have "empirical reality, but, at the same time, transcendental ideality." As external phenomena all things are beside one another in space, and all phenomena whatever are in time and of necessity under temporal relations; in regard to all things which can occur in our experience, and in so far as they can occur, space and time are objectively, therefore empirically, real. But they do not possess absolute reality (neither subsistent reality nor the reality of inherence); for if we abstract from our sensuous intuition both vanish, and, apart from the subject (*N.B.*, the transcendental subject, concerning which more below), they are naught. It is only from man's point of view that we can speak of space, and of extended, moveable, changeable things; for we can know nothing concerning the intuitions of other thinking beings, we have no means of discovering whether they are bound by the same conditions which limit our intuitions, and which for us are universally valid. (3) Nothing which is intuited in space is a thing in itself. What we call external objects are nothing but mere representations of our sensibility, whose true correlative, the *thing in itself*, cannot be known by ever so deep penetration into the phenomenon; such properties as belong to things in themselves can never be given to us through the senses. Similarly nothing that is intuited in time is a thing in itself, so that we intuit ourselves only as we appear to ourselves, and not as we are.

The merely empirical reality of space and time, the limitation of their validity to phenomena, leaves the certainty of knowledge within the limits of experience intact; for we are equally certain of it, whether these forms necessarily belong to things in themselves, or only to our intuitions of things. The assertion of their absolute reality, on the other hand, involves us in sheer absurdities (that is, it necessitates the assumption of two infinite nonentities which exist, but without being anything real, merely in order to comprehend all reality, and on one of which even our own existence would be dependent), in view of which the origin of so peculiar a theory as the idealism of Berkeley appears intelligible. The critical theory of space and time is so far from being identical with, or akin to, the theory of Berkeley, that it furnishes the best and only defense against the latter. If anyone assumes the absolute or transcendental reality of these forms, it is impossible for him to prevent everything, including even our own existence, from being changed thereby into mere illusion. But the critical philosopher is far from degrading bodies to mere illusion; external phenomena are just as real for him as internal phenomena, though only as phenomena, it is true, as (possible) representations.

Phenomenon and illusion are not the same. The transcendental distinction between phenomena and things in themselves must not be confused with the distinction common to ordinary life and to physics, in accordance with which we call the rainbow a mere appearance (better, illusion), but the combination of sun and rain which gives rise to this illusion the thing in itself, as that which in universal experience and in all different positions with respect to the senses, is thus and not otherwise determined in intuition, or that which essentially belongs to the intuition of the object, and is valid for every human sensibility (in antithesis to that which only contingently belongs to it, and is valid only for a special position or organization of this or that sense). Similarly an object always appears to grow smaller as its distance increases, while in itself it is and remains of some fixed size. And this use of words is perfectly correct, in the *physical or empirical* sense of "in itself"; but in the *transcendental* sense the raindrops, also, together with their form and size, are themselves mere phenomena, the "in itself" of which remains entirely unknown to us. Kant, moreover, does not wish to see the subjectivity of the forms of intuition placed on a level with the subjectivity of sensations or explained by this, though he accepts it as a fact long established. The sensations of color, of tone, of temperature are, no doubt, like the representation of space in that they belong only to the subjective constitution of the sensibility, and can be attributed to objects only in relation to our senses. But the great difference between the two is that these sense qualities may be different in different persons (the color of the rose may seem different to each eye), or may fail to harmonize with any human sense; that they are not *a priori* in the same strict sense as space and time, and consequently afford no knowledge of the objects of possible experience independently of perception; and that they are connected with the phenomenon only as the contingently added effects of a particular organization, while space, as the condition of external objects, necessarily belongs to the phenomenon or intuition of them. *It is through space alone that it is possible for things to be external objects for us*. The subjectivity of sensation is individual, while that of space and time is general or universal to mankind; the former is empirical, individually different, and contingent, the latter *a priori* and necessary. Space alone, not sensation, is a *conditio sine qua non* of external perception. Space and time are the sole *a priori* elements of the sensibility; all other sensuous concepts, even motion and change, presuppose perception; the movable in space and the succession of properties in an existing thing are empirical data.

In confirmation of the theory that all objects of the senses are mere phenomena, the fact is adduced that (with the exception of the will and the feelings, which are not cognitions) nothing is given us through the senses but representations of relations, while a thing in itself cannot be known by mere relations. The phenomenon is a sum total of mere relations. In regard to matter we know only extension, motion, and the laws of this motion or forces (attraction, repulsion, impenetrability), but all these are merely relations of the thing to something, else, that is, external relations. Where is the inner side which underlies this exterior, and which belongs to the object in itself? This is never to be found in the phenomenon, and no matter how far the observation and analysis of nature may advance (a work with unlimited horizons!) they reach nothing but portions of space occupied by matter and effects which matter exercises, that is, nothing beyond that which is comparatively internal, and which, in its turn, consists of external relations. The absolutely inner side of matter is a mere fancy; and if the complaint that the "inner side" of things is concealed from us is to mean that we do not comprehend what the things which appear to us may be in themselves, it is unjust and irrational, for it demands that we should be able to intuit without senses, in other words, that we should be other than men. The transcendent questions concerning the noumenon of things are unanswerable; we know ourselves, even, only as phenomena! A phenomenon consists in nothing but the relation of something in general to the senses.

It is indubitable *that* something corresponds to phenomena, which, by affecting our sensibility, occasions sensations in us, and thereby phenomena. The very word, the very concept, "phenomenon", indicates a relation to something which is not phenomenon, to an object not dependent on the sensibility. *What* this may be continues hidden from us, for knowledge is impossible without intuition. Things in themselves are unknowable. Nevertheless the idea (it must be confessed, the entirely empty idea) of this "transcendental object", as an indeterminate somewhat $= x$ which underlies phenomena, is not only allowable, but, as a limiting concept, unavoidable in order to confine the pretensions of sense to the only field which is accessible to it, that is, to the field of phenomena.

The inference "space and time are nothing but representations and representations are in us, therefore space and time as well as all phenomena in them, bodies with their forces and motions, are in us," does not accurately express Kant's position, for he might justly reply that, according to him, bodies as phenomena are in different parts in space from that which we assign to ourselves, and thus without us; that space is the form of external intuition, and through it external objects arise for us from sensations; but that, in regard to the things in themselves which affect us, we are entirely ignorant whether they are within or without us.

It can easily be shown by literal quotations that there were distinct tendencies in Kant, especially in the first edition of his principal work, toward a radical idealism which doubts or denies not merely the cognizability, but also the existence of objects external to the subject and its representations, and which degrades the thing in itself to a mere thought in us, or completely does away with it (*e.g.*, "The representation of an object as a thing in general is not only insufficient, but, ... independently of empirical conditions, in itself contradictory "). But these expressions indicate only a momentary inclination toward such a view, not a binding avowal of it, and they are outweighed by those in which idealism is more or less energetically rejected. That which according to Kant *exists outside the representation of the individual* is twofold: (1) the unknown things in themselves with their problematical characteristics, as the ground of phenomena; (2) the phenomena "themselves" with their knowable immanent laws, and their relations in space and time, as possible representations. When I turn my glance away from the rose its redness vanishes, since this predicate belongs to it only in so far and so long as it acts in the light on my visual apparatus. What, then, is left? That thing in itself, of course, which, when it appears to me, calls forth in me the intuition of the rose. But there is still something else remaining—the phenomenon of the rose, with its size, its form, and its motion in the wind. For these are predicates which must be attributed to the phenomenon itself as the object of my representation. If the rose, as determined in space and time, vanished when I turned my head away, it could not, unless intuited by a subject, experience or exert effects in space and time, could not lose its leaves in the wind and strew the ground with its petals. Perception and thought inform me not merely concerning events of which I am a witness, but also of others which have occurred, or which will occur, in my absence. The process of stripping the leaves from the rose has actually taken place as a phenomenon and does not first become real by my subsequent representation of it or inference to it. The things and events of the phenomenal world exist both before and after my perception, and are something distinct from my subjective and momentary representations of them. The space and time, however, in which they exist and happen are not furnished by the intuiting individual, but by the supra-individual, *transcendental consciousness* or generic reason of the race. The phenomenon thus stands midway between its objective ground (the absolute thing in itself) and the subject, whose common product it is, as a relative thing in itself, as a reality which is independent of the contingent and changing representation of the individual, empirical subject, which is dependent for its form on the transcendental subject, and which is the only reality accessible to us, yet entirely valid for us. The phenomenal world is not a contingent and individual phenomenon, but one necessary for all beings organized as we are, a phenomenon for humanity. My representations are not the phenomena themselves, but images and signs through which I cognize phenomena, *i.e.*, real things as they are for me and for every man (not as they are in themselves). The reality of phenomena consists in the fact that they can be perceived by men, and the objective validity of my knowledge of them in the fact that every man must agree in it. The laws which the understanding (not the individual understanding!) imposes upon nature hold for phenomena, because they hold for every man. Objectivity is universal validity. If the world of phenomena which is intuited and known by us wears a different appearance from the world of things in themselves, this does not justify us in declaring it to be mere seeming and dreaming; a dream which all dream together, and which all must dream, is not a dream, but reality. As we must represent the world> so it is, though for us, of course, and not in itself.

Many places in Kant's works seem to argue against the intermediate position here ascribed to the world of phenomena—according to which it is less than things in themselves and more than subjective representation—which, since they explain the phenomenon as a mere representation, leave room for only two factors (on the one hand, the thing in itself = that in the thing which cannot be represented; on the other, the thing for me = my representation of the thing). In fact, the distinction between the phenomenon "itself" and the representation which the individual now has of it and now does not have, is far from being everywhere adhered to with desirable clearness; and wherever it is impossible to substitute that which has been represented and that which may be represented or possible intuitions for "mere representations in me," we must acknowledge that there is a departure from the standpoint which is assumed in some places with the greatest distinctness. The latter finds unequivocal expression, among other places, in the "Analogies of Experience" and the "Deduction of the Pure Concepts of the Understanding," § 2, No. 4 (first edition). The second of these passages speaks of one and the same universal experience, in which all perceptions are represented in thoroughgoing and regular connection, and of the thoroughgoing affinity of phenomena as the basis of the possibility of the association of representations. This affinity is ascribed to the objects of the senses, not to the representations, whose association is rather the result of the affinity, and not to the things in themselves, in regard to which the understanding has no legislative power.

The relation between the thing in itself and the phenomenon is also variable. Now they are regarded as entirely heterogeneous (that which can never be intuited exists in a mode opposed to that of the intuited and intuitable), and now as analogous to each other (non-intuitable properties of the thing in itself correspond to the intuitable characteristics of the phenomenon). The former is the case when it is said that phenomena are in space and time, while things in themselves are not; that in the first of these classes natural causation rules, and in the second freedom; that in the one-conditioned existence alone is found, in the other unconditioned.[1] But just as often things in themselves and phenomena are conceived as similar to one another, as two sides of the same object,[2] of which one, like the counter-earth of the Pythagoreans, always remains turned away from us, while the other is turned toward us, but does not reveal the true being of the object. According to this each particular thing, state, relation, and event in the world of phenomena would have its real counterpart in the noumenal sphere: un-extended roses in themselves would lie back of extended roses, certain non-temporal processes back of their growth and decay, intelligible relations back of their relations in space. This is approximately the relation of the two conceptions as in part taught by Lotze himself, in part represented by him as taught by Kant. Herbart's principle, "So much seeming, so much indication of being" (*wie viel Schein so viel Hindeutung aufs Sein*), might also be cited in this connection. That which continually impelled Kant, in spite of his proclamation of the unknowableness of things in themselves, to form ideas about their character, was the moral interest, but this sometimes threw its influence in favor of their commensurability with phenomena and sometimes in the opposite scale. For in his ethics Kant needs the intelligible character or man as noumenon, and must assume as many men in themselves (to be consistent, then, in general, as many beings in themselves) as there are in the world of phenomena. But for practical reasons, again, the causality of the man in himself must be thought of as entirely different from, and opposed to, the mechanical causality of the sense world. Kant's judgment is, also, no more stable concerning the value of the knowledge of the suprasensible, which is denied to us. "I do not *need* to know what things in themselves may be, because a thing can never be presented to me otherwise than as a phenomenon." And yet a natural and ineradicable need of the reason to obtain some conviction in regard to the other world is said to underlie the abortive attempts of metaphysics; and Kant himself uses all his efforts to secure to the practical reason the satisfaction of this need, though he has denied it to the speculative reason, and to make good the gap in knowledge by faith. From the theoretical standpoint an extension of knowledge beyond the limits of phenomena appears impossible, but unnecessary; from the practical standpoint it is, to a certain extent, possible and indispensable.

[Footnote 1: Kant's conjectures concerning a common ground of material and mental phenomena, and those concerning the common root of sensibility and understanding, show the same tendency. On the one hand, duality, on the other, unity.]

[Footnote 2: "Phenomenon, which always has *two sides*, the one when the object in itself is considered (apart from the way in which it is intuited, and just because of which fact its character always remains problematical), the other when we regard the form of the intuition of this object, which must be sought not in the object in itself, but in the subject to whom the object appears, while it nevertheless actually and necessarily belongs to the phenomenon of *this object*." "This predicate "—*sc.*, spatial quality, extension—"is attributed to things only in so far as *they* appear to us."]

There is, then, a threefold distinction to be made: (1) *Things in themselves*, which can never be the object of our knowledge, because our forms of intuition are not valid for them. (2) *Phenomena*, things for us, nature or the totality of that which either is or, at least, may be the object of our knowledge (here belong the possible inhabitants of the moon, the magnetic matter which pervades all bodies, and the forces of attraction and repulsion, though the first have never been observed, and the second is not perceptible on account of the coarseness of our senses, and the last, because forces in general are not perceptible; nature comprehends everything whose existence "is connected with our perceptions in a possible experience"[1]). (3) *Our representations* of phenomena, *i.e.*, that of the latter which actually enters into the consciousness of the empirical individual. In the realm of things in themselves there is no motion whatever, but at most an intelligible correlate of this relation; in the world of phenomena, the world of physics, the earth moves around the sun; in the sphere of representation the sun moves around the earth. It is true, as has been said, that Kant sometimes ignores the distinction between phenomena as related to noumena and phenomena as related to representations; and, as a result of this, that the phenomenon is either completely volatilized into the representation[2] or split up into an objective half independent of us and a representative half dependent on us, of which the former falls into the thing in itself,[3] while the latter is resolved into subjective states of the ego.

[Footnote 1: "Nothing is actually given to us but the perception and the empirical progress from this to other possible perceptions." "To call a phenomenon a real thing antecedent to perception, means … that in the *progress of experience* we must meet with such a perception."]

[Footnote 2: Phenomena "are altogether in me," "exist only in our sensibility as a modification of it." "There is nothing in space but that which is actually represented in it." Phenomena are "mere representations, which, if they are not given in us (in perception) nowhere exist."]

[Footnote 3: Here Kant is guilty of the fault which he himself has censured, of confusing the physical and transcendental meanings of "in itself." He forgets that the thing, if it is momentarily not intuited or represented by me, and therefore is not immediately given for me as an individual, is nevertheless still present for me as man, is mediately given, that is, is discoverable by future search. That which is without my present consciousness is not for this reason without all human consciousness. In fact, Kant often overlooks the distinction between actual and possible intuition, so that for him the "objects" of the latter slip out of space and time and into the thing in itself. To the "transcendental object we may ascribe the extent and connection of our possible perceptions, and say that it is given in itself before all experience." In it "the real things of the past are given."]

After the possibility and the legitimacy of synthetic judgments *a priori* have been proved for pure mathematics upon the basis of the pure intuitions, there emerges, in the second place, the problem of the possibility of *a priori* syntheses in pure natural science, or the question, Do pure concepts exist? And after this has been answered in the affirmative, the further questions come up, Is the application of these, first, to phenomena, and second, to things in themselves, possible and legitimate, and how far?

%(b) The Concepts and Principles of the Pure Understanding (Transcendental Analytic).%—Sensations, in order to become "intuition" or the perception of a phenomenon, needed to be ordered in space and time; in order to become "experience" or a unified knowledge of objects, intuitions need a synthesis through concepts. In order to objective knowledge the manifold of intuition (already ordered by its arrangement in space and time) must be connected in the unity of the concept. Sensibility gives the manifold to be connected, the understanding the connecting unity. The former is able to intuit only, the latter only to think; knowledge can arise only as the result of their union. Intuitions depend on affections, concepts on functions, that is, on unifying acts of the understanding.

To discover the pure forms of thought it is necessary to isolate the understanding, just as an isolation of the sensibility was necessary above in order to the discovery of the pure forms of intuition. We obtain the elements of the pure knowledge of the understanding by rejecting all that is intuitive and empirical. These elements must be pure, must be concepts, further, not derivative or composite, but fundamental concepts, and their number must be complete. This completeness is guaranteed only when the pure concepts or *categories* are sought according to some common principle, which assigns to each its position in the connection of the whole, and not (as with Aristotle) collected by occasional, unsystematic inquiries undertaken at random. The table of the forms of judgment will serve as a guide for the discovery of the categories. Thought is knowledge through concepts; the understanding can make no other use of concepts than to judge by means of them. Hence, since the understanding is the faculty of judging, the various kinds of connection in judgment must yield the various pure "connective-concepts" (*Verknüpfungsbegriffe*.—K. Fischer) or categories.

In regard to quantity, every judgment is universal, particular, or singular; in regard to quality, affirmative, negative, or infinite; in regard to relation, categorical, hypothetical, or disjunctive; and in regard to modality, problematical, assertory, or apodictic. To these twelve forms of judgment correspond as many categories, viz., I., Unity, Plurality, Totality; II., Reality, Negation, Limitation; III., Subsistence and Inherence (Substance and Accident), Causality and Dependence (Cause and Effect), Community (Reciprocity between the Active and the Passive); IV., Possibility—Impossibility, Existence—Non-existence, Necessity—Contingency.

The first six of these fundamental concepts, which have no correlatives, constitute the mathematical, the second six, which appear in pairs, the dynamical categories. The former relate to objects of (pure or of empirical) intuition, the latter to the existence of these objects (in relation to one another or to the understanding). Although all other *a priori* division though concepts must be dichotomous, each of the four heads includes three categories, the third of which in each case arises from the combination of the second and first,[1] but, nevertheless, is an original (not a derivative) concept, since this combination requires a special *actus* of the understanding. Universality or totality is plurality regarded as unity, limitation is reality combined with negation, community is the reciprocal causality of substances, and necessity is the actuality given by possibility itself. Kant omits, as unnecessary here, the useful, easy, and not unpleasant task of noting the great number of derivative concepts *a priori* (predicables) which spring from the combination of these twelve original concepts (predicaments = categories) with one another, or with the modes of pure sensibility,—the concepts force, action, passion, would belong as subsumptions under causality, presence and resistance under community, origin, extinction, and change under modality,—since his object is not a system, but only the principles of one. His liking or even love for this division according to quantity, quality, relation, and modality, which he always has ready as though it were a universal key for philosophical problems, reveals a very strong architectonic impulse, against which even his ever active skeptical tendency is not able to keep up the battle.

[Footnote 1: Concerning this "neat observation," Kant remarked that it might "perhaps have important consequences in regard to the scientific form of all knowledge of reason." This prophecy was fulfilled, although in a different sense from that which floated before his mind. Fichte and Hegel composed their "thought-symphonies" in the three-four time given by Kant.]

In view of the derivation of the forms of thought from the forms of judgment Kant does not stop to give a detailed proof that the categories are concepts, and that they are pure. Their discursive (not intuitive) character is evident from the fact that their reference to the object is mediate only (and not, as in the case of intuition, immediate), and their *a priori* origin, from the necessity which they carry with them, and which would be impossible if their origin were empirical. Here Kant starts from Hume's criticism of the idea of cause. The Scottish skeptic had said that the necessary bond between cause and effect can neither be perceived nor logically demonstrated; that, therefore, the relation of causality is an idea which we—with what right?—add to perceived succession in time. This doubt (without the hasty conclusions), says Kant, must be generalized, must be extended to the category of substance (which had been already done by Hume, pp. 226-7, though the author of the Critique of Reason was not aware of the fact), and to all other pure concepts of the understanding. Then we may hope to kindle a torch at the spark which Hume struck out. The problem "It is impossible to see why, because something exists, something else must necessarily exist," is the starting point alike of Hume's skepticism and Kant's criticism. The former recognized that the principle of causality is neither empirical nor analytic, and therefore concluded that it is an invention of reason, which confuses subjective with objective necessity. The latter shows that in spite of its subjective origin it has an objective value; that it is a truth which is independent of all experience, and yet valid for all who have experience, and for all that can be experienced.

Of the two questions, "How can the concepts which spring from our understanding possess objective validity?" and, "How (through what means or media) does their application to objects of experience take place?" the first is answered in the Deduction of the Pure Concepts of the Understanding, and the second in the chapter on their Schematism.

The *Deduction*, the most difficult portion of the Critique, shows that the objective validity of the categories, as concepts of objects in general, depends on the fact that *through them alone experience* as far as regards the form of thought _is possible, *i.e.*, it is only through them that any object whatever can be thought. All knowledge consists in judgments; all judgments contain a connection of representations; all connection—whether it be conscious or not, whether it relates to concepts or to pure or empirical intuitions—is an *act of the understanding*; it cannot be given by objects, but only spontaneously performed by the subject itself. We cannot represent anything as connected in the object unless we have ourselves first connected it. The connection includes three conceptions: that of the manifold to be connected (which is given by intuition), that of the act of synthesis, and that of the unity; this last is two-fold, an objective unity (the conception of an object in general in which the manifold is united), and a subjective unity (the unity of consciousness under which or, rather, through which the connection is effected). The categories represent the different kinds of combination, each one of these, again, being completed in three stages, which are termed the Synthesis of Apprehension in Intuition, the Synthesis of Reproduction in Imagination, and the Synthesis of Recognition in Concepts. If I wish to think the time from one noon to the next, I must (1) grasp (apprehend) the manifold representations (portions of time) in succession; (2) retain or renew (reproduce) in thought those which have preceded in passing to those which follow; (3) be conscious that that which is now thought is the same with that thought before, or know again (recognize) the reproduced representation as the one previously experienced. If the mind did not exercise such synthetic activity the manifold of representation would not constitute a whole, would lack the unity which consciousness alone can impart to it. Without this *one* consciousness, concepts and knowledge of objects would be wholly impossible. The unity of pure self-consciousness or of "transcendental apperception" is the postulate of all use of the understanding. In the flux of internal phenomena there is no constant or abiding self, but the unchangeable consciousness here demanded is a precedent condition of all experience, and gives to phenomena a connection according to laws which determine an object for intuition, *i.e.*, the conception of something in which they are necessarily connected.[1] Reference to an object is nothing other than the necessary unity of consciousness. The connective activity of the understanding, and with it experience, is possible only through "the synthetic unity of pure apperception," the "I think," which must be able to accompany all my representations, and through which they first become *mine*.

[Footnote 1: Object is "that which opposes the random or arbitrary determination of our cognitions," and which causes "them to be determined in a certain way *a priori*."]

Experience (in the strict sense) is distinguished from perception (experience in the wide sense) by its objectivity or universal validity. A judgment of perception (the sun shines upon the stone and the stone becomes warm) is only subjectively valid; while, on the other hand, a judgment of experience (the sun warms the stone) aims to be valid not only for me and my present condition, but always, for me and for everyone else. If the former is to become the latter, an *a priori* concept must be added to the perception (in the above case, the concept of cause), under which the perception is subsumed. The category determines the perceptions in view of the form of the judgment, gives to the judgment its reference to an object, and thus gives to the percepts, or rather, concepts (sunshine and warmth), necessary and universally valid connection. The "reason why the judgments of others" must "agree with mine" is "the unity of the object to which they all relate, with which they agree, and hence must also all agree with one another."

Though the categories take their origin in the nature of the subject, they are objective and valid for objects of experience, because experience is possible alone through them. They are not the product, but the ground of experience. The second difficulty concerns their applicability to phenomena, which are wholly disparate. By what means is the gulf between the categories, which are concepts and *a priori*, and perceptions, which are intuitous and empirical, bridged over? The connecting link is supplied by the imagination, as the faculty which mediates between sensibility and understanding to provide a concept with its image, and consists in the intuition of time, which, in common with the categories, has an *a priori* character, and, in common with perceptions, an intuitive character, so that it is at once pure and sensuous. The subsumption of phenomena or empirical intuitions under the category is effected through the *Schemata*[1] of the concepts of the understanding, *i.e.*, through *a priori* determinations of time according to rules, which relate to time-*series*, time-*content*, time-*order*, and time-*comprehension*, and indicate whether I have to apply this or that category to a given object.

[Footnote 1: The schema is not an empirical image, but stands midway between this (the particular intuition of a definite triangle or dog) and the unintuitable concept, as a general intuition (of a triangle or a dog in general, which holds alike for right- and oblique-angled triangles, for poodles and pugs), or as a rule for determining our intuition in accordance with a concept.]

Each category has its own schema. The schema of quantity is number, as comprehending the successive addition of homogeneous parts. Filled time (being in time) is the schema of reality, empty time (not-being in time) the schema of negation, and more or less filled time (the intensity of sensation, indicating the degree of reality) the schema of limitation. Permanence in time is the sign for the application of the category of substance;[1] regular succession, for the application of the concept of cause; the coexistence of the determinations of one substance with those of another, the signal for their subsumption under the concept of reciprocity. The schemata of possibility, actuality, and necessity, finally, are existence at any time whatever (whensoever), existence at a definite time, and existence at all times. By such schematic syntheses the pure concept is brought near to the empirical intuition, and the way is prepared for an application of the former to the latter, or, what is the same thing, for the subsumption of the latter under the former.

[Footnote 1: This determination is important for psychology. Since the inner sense shows nothing constant, but everything in a continual flux,—for the permanent subject of our thoughts is an identical activity of the understanding, not an intuitable object,—the concept of substance is not applicable to psychical phenomena. Representations of a permanent (material substances) exist, indeed, but not permanent representations. The abiding self (ego, soul) which we posit back of internal phenomena is, as the Dialectic will show, a mere Idea, which, or, rather, the object of which, maybe "thought" as substance, it is true, but cannot be "given" in intuition, hence cannot be "known."]

As a result of the fact that the schematism permits a presentation of the categories in time intuition antecedent to all experience, the possibility is given of synthetic judgments *a priori* concerning objects of possible experience. Such judgments, in so far as they are not based on higher and more general cognitions, are termed "principles," and the system of them—to be given, with the table of the categories as a guide, in the *Analytic of Principles* or the Doctrine of the Faculty of Judgment—furnishes the outlines of "pure natural science." When thus the rules of the subsumption to be effected have been found in the pure concepts, and the conditions and criteria of the subsumption in the schemata, it remains to indicate the principles which the understanding, through the aid of the schemata, actually produces *a priori* from its concepts.

The principle of quantity is the *Axiom of Intuition*, the principle of quality the *Anticipation of Perception*; the principles of relation are termed *Analogies of Experience*, those of modality *Postulates of Empirical Thought in General*. The first runs, "All intuitions are extensive quantities"; the second, "In all phenomena sensation, and the real which corresponds to it in the object, has an intensive quantity, i.e., a degree." The principle of the "Analogies" is, "All phenomena, as far as their existence is concerned, are subject *a priori* to rules, determining their mutual relation in time" (in the second edition this is stated as follows: "Experience is possible only through the representation of a necessary connection of perceptions"). As there are three modes of time, there result three "Analogies," the principles of permanence, of succession (production), and of coexistence. These are: (1) "In all changes of phenomena the substance is permanent, and its quantum is neither increased nor diminished in nature." (2) "All changes take place according to the law of connection between cause and effect"; or, "Everything that happens (begins to be) presupposes something on which it follows according to a rule." (3) "All substances, in so far as they are coexistent, stand in complete community, that is, reciprocity, one to another." And, finally, the three "Postulates": "That which agrees with the formal conditions of experience (in intuition and in concepts) is possible," "That which is connected with the material conditions of experience (sensation) is actual" (perception is the only criterion of actuality). "That which, in its connection with the actual, is determined by universal conditions of experience, is (exists as) necessary."

As the categories of substance and causality are specially preferred to the others by Kant and the Kantians, and are even proclaimed by some as the only fundamental concepts, so also the principles of relation have an established reputation for special importance. The leading ideas in the proofs of the "Analogies of Experience"—for in spite of their underivative character the principles require, and are capable of, proof—may next be noted.

The time determinations of phenomena, the knowledge of their duration, their succession, and their coexistence, form an indispensable part of our experience, not only of scientific experience, but of everyday experience as well. How is the objective time-determination of things and events possible? If the matter in hand is the determination of the particulars of a fight with a bloody ending, the witnesses are questioned and testify: We heard and saw how A began the quarrel by insulting B, and the latter answered the insult with a blow, whereupon A drew his knife and wounded his opponent. Here the succession of perceptions on the part of the persons present is accepted as a true reproduction of the succession of the actual events. But the succession of perceptions is not always the sure indication of an actual succession: the trees along an avenue are perceived one after the other, while they are in reality coexistent. We might now propose the following statement: The representation of the manifold of phenomena is always successive, I apprehend one part after another. I can decide whether these parts succeed one another in the object also, or whether they are coexistent, by the fact that, in the second case, the series of my perceptions is reversible, while in the first it is not. I can, if I choose, direct my glance along the avenue in such a way that I shall begin the second time with the tree at which I left off the first time; if I wish to assure myself that the parts of a house are coexistent, I cause my eye to wander from the upper to the lower portions, from the right side to the left, and then to perform the same motions in the opposite direction. On the other hand, it is not left to my choice to hear the thunder either before or after I see the lightning, or to see a passing wagon now here, now there, but in these cases I am bound in the succession of my sensuous representations. The possibility of interchange in the series of perceptions proves an objective coexistence, the impossibility of this, an objective succession. But this criterion is limited to the immediate present, and fails us when a time relation between unobserved phenomena is to be established. If I go at evening into the dining room and see a vessel of bubbling water, which is to be used in making tea, over a burning spirit lamp, whence do I derive the knowledge that the water began, and could begin, to boil only after the alcohol had been lighted, and not before? Because I have often seen the flame precede the boiling of the water, and in this the irreversibility of the two perceptions has guaranteed to me the succession of the events perceived? Then I may only assume that it is very probable, not that it is certain, that in this case also the order of the two events has been the same as I have observed several times before. As a matter of fact, however, we all assert that the water could not have come into a boiling condition unless the generation of heat had preceded; that in every case the fire must be there before the boiling of the water can commence. Whence do we derive this *must*? Simply and alone from the thought of a causal connection between the two events. Every phenomenon *must* follow in time that phenomenon of which it is the effect, and must precede that of which it is the cause. It is through the relation of causality, and through this alone, that the objective time relation of phenomena is determined. If nothing preceded an event on which it must follow according to a rule,[1] then all succession in perception would be subjective merely, and nothing whatever would be objectively determined by it as to what was the antecedent and what the consequent in the phenomenon itself. We should then have a mere play of representations without significance for the real succession of events. Only the thought of a rule, according to which the antecedent state contains the necessary condition of the consequent state, justifies us in transferring the time order of our representations to phenomena.[2] Nay, even the distinction between the phenomenon itself, as the object of our representations, and our representations of it, is effected only by subjecting the phenomenon to this rule, which assigns to it its definite position in time after another phenomenon by which it is caused, and thus forbids the inversion of the perceptions. We can derive the rule of the understanding which produces the objective time order of the manifold from experience, only because we have put it into experience, and have first brought experience into being by means of the rule. We recapitulate in Kant's own words: The objective (time) relation of phenomena remains undetermined by mere perception (the mere succession in my apprehension, if it is not determined by means of a rule in relation to an antecedent, does not guarantee any succession in the object). In order that this may be known as determined, the relation between the two states must be so conceived (through the understanding's concept of causality) that it is thereby determined with necessity which of them must be taken as coming first, and which second, and not conversely. Thus it is only by subjecting the succession of phenomena to the law of causality that empirical knowledge of them is possible. Without the concept of cause no objective time determination, and hence, without it, no experience.

[Footnote 1: "A reality following on an empty time, that is, a beginning of existence preceded by no state of things, can as little be apprehended as empty time itself."]

[Footnote 2: "If phenomena were things in themselves no one would be able, from the succession of the representations of their manifold, to tell how this is connected in the object."]

That which the relation of cause and effect does for the succession[1] of phenomena, the relation of reciprocity does for their coexistence, and that of substance and accident for their duration. Since absolute time is not an object of perception, the position of phenomena in time cannot be directly determined, but only through a concept of the understanding. When I conclude that two objects (the earth and the moon) must be coexistent, because perceptions of them can follow upon one another in both ways, I do this on the presupposition that the objects themselves reciprocally determine their position in time, hence are not isolated, but stand in causal community or a relation of reciprocal influence. It is only on the condition of reciprocity between phenomena, through which they form a whole, that I can represent them as coexistent.

[Footnote 1: Against the objection that cause and effect are frequently, indeed in most cases, simultaneous (*e.g.* the heated stove and the warmth of the room), Kant remarks that the question concerns the order of time merely, and not the lapse of time. The ball lying on a soft cushion is simultaneous, it is true, with its effect, the depression in the cushion. "But I, nevertheless, distinguish the two by the time relation of dynamical connection. For if I place the ball on the cushion, its previously smooth surface is followed by a depression, but if there is a depression in the cushion (I know not whence) a leaden ball does not follow from it."]

Coexistence and succession can be represented only in a permanent substratum; they are merely the modes in which the permanent exists. Since time (in which all change takes place, but which itself abides and does not change) in itself cannot be perceived, the substratum of simultaneity and succession must exist in phenomena themselves: the permanent in relation to which alone all the time relations of phenomena can be determined, is substance; that which alters is its determinations, accidents, or special modes of existing. Alteration, *i.e.*, origin and extinction, is true of states only, which can begin and cease to be, and not of substances, which change (*sich verändern*), i.e., pass from one mode of existence into another, but do not alter (*wechseln*), i.e., pass from non-existence into existence, or the reverse. It is the permanent alone that changes, and its states alone that begin and cease to be. The origin and extinction of substances, or the increase and diminution of their quantum, would remove the sole condition of the empirical unity of time; for the time relations of the coexistent and the successive can be perceived only in an identical substratum, in a permanent, which exists always. The law "From nothing nothing comes, and nothing can return to nothing," is everywhere assumed and has been frequently advanced, but never yet proved, for, indeed, it is impossible to prove it dogmatically. Here the only possible proof for it, the critical proof, is given: the principle of permanence is a necessary condition of experience. The same argument establishes the principle of sufficient reason, and the principle of the community of substances, together with the unity of the world to be inferred from this. The three Analogies together assert: "All phenomena exist in one nature and must so exist, because without such a unity *a priori* no unity of experience, and therefore no determination of objects in experience, would be possible."—In connection with the Postulates the same transcendental proof is given for a series of other laws of nature *a priori*, viz., that in the course of the changes in the world—for the causal principle holds only for effects in nature, not for the existence of things as substances—there can be neither blind chance nor a blind necessity (but only a conditional, hence an intelligible, necessity); and, further, that in the series of phenomena, there can be neither leap, nor gap, nor break, and hence no void—*in mundo non datur casus, non datur fatum, non datur saltus, non datur hiatus*.

While the dynamical principles have to do with the relation of phenomena, whether it be to one another (Analogies), or to our faculty of cognition (Postulates), the mathematical relate to the quantity of intuitions and sensations, and furnish the basis for the application of mathematics to natural science.[1] An extensive quantity is one in which the representation of the parts makes the representation of the whole possible, and so precedes it. I cannot represent a line without drawing it in thought, i.e., without producing all parts of it one after the other, starting from a point. All phenomena are intuited as aggregates or as collections of previously given parts. That which geometry asserts of pure intuition (i.e., the infinite divisibility of lines) holds also of empirical intuition. An intensive quantity is one which is apprehended only as unity, and in which plurality can be represented only by approximation to negation = 0. Every sensation, consequently every reality in phenomena, has a degree, which, however small it may be, is never the smallest, but can always be still more diminished; and between reality and negation there exists a continuous connection of possible smaller intermediate sensations, or an infinite series of ever decreasing degrees. The property of quantities, according to which no part in them is the smallest possible part, and no part is simple, is termed their continuity. All phenomena are continuous quantities, i.e., all their parts are in turn (further divisible) quantities. Hence it follows, first, that a proof for an empty space or empty time can never be drawn from experience, and secondly, that all change is also continuous. "It is remarkable," so Kant ends his proof of the Anticipation, "that of quantities in general we can know one *quality* only *a priori*, namely, their continuity, while with regard to quality (the real of phenomena) nothing is known to us *a priori* but their intensive *quantity*, that is, that they must have a degree. Everything else is left to experience."

[Footnote 1: In each particular science of nature, science proper (i.e., apodictically certain science) is found only to the extent in which mathematics can be applied therein. For this reason chemistry can never be anything more than a systematic art or experimental doctrine; and psychology not even this, but only a natural history of the inner sense or natural description of the soul. That which Kant's *Metaphysical Elements of Natural Science*, 1786—in four chapters, Phoronomy, Dynamics, Mechanics, and Phenomenology—advances as pure physics or the metaphysics of corporeal nature, is a doctrine of motion. The fundamental determination of matter (of a somewhat which is to be the object of the external senses) is motion, for it is only through motion that these senses can be affected, and the understanding itself reduces all other predicates of matter to this. The second and most valuable part of the work defines matter as the movable, that which fills space by its moving force, and recognizes two original forces, repulsive, expansive superficial force or force of contact, by which a body resists the entrance of other bodies into its own space, and attractive, penetrative force or the force which works at a distance, in virtue of which all particles of matter attract one another. In order to a determinate filling of space the co-operation of both fundamental forces is required. In opposition to the mechanical theory of the atomists, which explains forces from matter and makes them inhere in it, Kant holds fast to the dynamical view which he had early adopted (cf. p. 324), according to which forces are the primary factor and matter is constituted by them.]

The outcome of the Analytic of Principles sounds bold enough. *The understanding is the lawgiver of nature*: "It does not draw its laws *a priori* from nature, but prescribes them to it"; the principles of the pure understanding are the most universal laws of nature, the empirical laws of nature only particular determinations of these. All order and regularity take their origin in the spirit, and are put into objects by this. Universal and necessary knowledge remained inexplicable so long as it was assumed that the understanding must conform itself to objects; it is at once explained if, conversely, we make objects conform themselves to the understanding. This is a reversal of philosophical opinion which may justly be compared to the Copernican revolution in astronomy; it is just as paradoxical as the latter, but just as incontestably true, and just as rich in results. The sequel will show that this strangely sounding principle, that things conform themselves to our representations and the laws of nature are dependent on the understanding, is calculated to make us humble rather than proud. Our understanding is lawgiver within the limits of its knowledge, no doubt, but it knows only within the limits of its legislative authority; nature, to which it dictates laws, is nothing but a totality of phenomena; beyond the limits of the phenomenal, where its commands become of no effect, its wishes also find no hearing.

In the second edition the Analytic of Principles contains as a supplement a "Refutation of Idealism," which, in opposition to Descartes's position that the only immediate experience is inner experience, from which we reach outer experience by inference alone, argues that, conversely, it is only through outer experience, which is immediate experience proper, that inner experience—as the consciousness of my own existence in time—is possible. For all time determination presupposes something permanent in perception, and this permanent something cannot be in me (the mere representation of an external thing), but only actually existing things which I perceive without me. There is, further, a chapter on the "Ground of the Distinction of all Objects in general into Phenomena and Noumena," with an appendix on the Amphiboly (ambiguity) of the Concepts of Reflection. The latter shows that the concepts of comparison: identity and difference, agreement and opposition, the internal and the external, matter and form, acquire entirely different meanings when they relate to phenomena and to things in themselves (in other words, to things in their relation to the sensibility, and in relation to the understanding merely); and further, in a criticism of the philosophy of Leibnitz, reproaches him with having intellectualized phenomena, while Locke is said to have sensationalized the concepts of the understanding.

The chapter on the distinction between phenomena and noumena very much lessens the hopes, aroused, perchance, by the establishment of the non-empirical origin of the categories, for an application of these not confined to any experience. Although the categories, that is, are in their origin entirely independent of all experience (so much so that they first make experience possible), they are yet confined in their application within the bounds of possible experience. They "serve only to spell phenomena, that we may be able to read them as experience," and when applied to things in themselves lose all significance.[1] Similarly the principles which spring from them are "nothing more than principles of possible experience," and can be referred to phenomena alone, beyond which they are arbitrary combinations without objective reality. Things in themselves may be thought, but they can never be known; for knowledge, besides the empty thought of an object, implies intuitions which must be subsumed under it or by which the object must be determined. In themselves the pure concepts relate to all that is thinkable, not merely to that which can be experienced, but the schemata, which assures their applicability in the field of experience, at the same time limit them to this sphere. The schematism makes the immanent use of the categories, and thus a metaphysics of phenomena, possible, but the transcendent use of them, and consequently the metaphysics of the suprasensible, impossible. The case would be different if our intuition were intellectual instead of sensuous, or, which is the same thing, if our understanding were intuitive instead of discursive; then the objects which we think would not need to be given us from another source (through sensuous intuition), but would be themselves produced in the act by which we thought them. The divine spirit may be such an archetypal, creative understanding (*intellectus archetypus*), which generates objects by its thought; the human spirit is not such, and therefore is confined, with its knowledge, within the circle of possible perception.—The conception of "intellectual intuition" leads to a distinction in regard to things in themselves: in its negative meaning noumenon denotes a thing in so far as it is *not* the object of our *sensuous* intuition, in its positive meaning a thing which is the object of a *non-sensuous* intuition. The positive thing in itself is a problematical concept; its possibility depends on the existence of an intuitive understanding, something about which we are ignorant. The negative thing in itself cannot be known, indeed, but it can be thought; and the representation of it is a possible concept, one which is not self-contradictory[2] (a principle which is of great importance for practical philosophy). Still further, it is an indispensable concept, which shows that the boundary where our intuition ends is not the boundary of the thinkable as well; and even if it affords no positive extension of knowledge[3] it is, nevertheless, very useful, since it sets bounds to the use of the understanding, and thus, as it were, negatively extends our knowledge. That which lies beyond the boundary, the "how are they possible" *(Wiemöglichkeit)* of things in themselves is shrouded in darkness, but the boundary itself, *i.e.*, the "that they are possible" *(Dassmöglichkeit)*, of things in themselves, and the unknowableness of their nature, belongs to that which is within the boundary and lies in the light. In this way Kant believed that the categories of causality and substance might be applied to the relation of things in themselves to phenomena without offending against the prohibition of their transcendent use, since here the boundary appeared only to be touched, and not overstepped.

[Footnote 1: "A pure use of the categories is no doubt possible, that is, not self-contradictory, but it has no kind of objective validity, because it refers to no intuition to which it is meant to impart the unity of an object. The categories remain forever mere functions of thought by which no object can be given to me, but by which I can only think whatever may be given to me in intuition" (*Critique of Pure Reason*, Max Müller's translation, vol. ii. p. 220). Without the condition of sensuous intuition, for which they supply the synthesis, the categories have no relation to any definite object; for without this condition they contain nothing but the logical function, or the form of the concept, by means of which alone nothing can be known and distinguished as to any object belonging to it (*Ibid.*, pp. 213, 214).]

[Footnote 2: The thing in itself denotes the object in so far as it can be thought by us, but not intuited, and consequently not determined by intuitions, *i.e.*, cannot be known. It is only through the schematism that the categories are limited to phenomena. O. Liebmann (*Kant und die Epigonen*, p. 27, and *passim*) overlooks or ignores this when he says: Kant here allows himself to "recognize an object emancipated from the forms of knowledge, therefore an irrational object, *i.e.*, to represent something which is not representable—wooden iron." The thing in itself is insensible, but not irrational, and the forms of intuition and forms of thought joined by Liebmann under the title forms of knowledge have in Kant a by no means equal rank.]

[Footnote 3: A category by itself, freed from all conditions of intuition (*e.g.*, the representation of a substance which is thought without permanence in time, or of a cause which should not act in time), can yield no definite concept of an object.]

Though the concepts of the understanding possess a cognitive value in the sphere of phenomena alone, the hope still remains of gaining an entrance into the suprasensible sphere through the concepts of reason. It is indubitable that our spirit is conscious of a far higher need than that for the mere connection of phenomena into experience; it is that which cannot be experienced, the Ideas God, freedom, and immortality, which form the real end of its inquiry. Can this need be satisfied, and how? Can this end be attained, and reality be given to the Ideas? This is the third question of the Critique of Reason.

%(c) The Reason's Ideas of the Unconditioned (Transcendental Dialectic).%—"All our knowledge begins with the senses, proceeds thence to the understanding, and ends with reason." The understanding is the faculty of rules, reason the faculty of principles. The categories of the understanding are necessary concepts which make experience possible, and which, therefore, can always be given in experience; the Ideas of reason are necessary concepts to which no corresponding object can be given. Each of the Ideas gives expression to an unconditioned. How does the concept of the unconditioned arise, and what service does it perform for knowledge?

As perceptions are connected by the categories in the unity of the understanding, and thus are elevated into experience, so the manifold knowledge of experience needs a higher unity, the unity of reason, in order to form a connected system. This is supplied to it by the Ideas— which, consequently, do not relate directly to the objects of intuition, but only to the understanding and its judgments—in order, through the concept of the unconditioned, to give completion to the knowledge of the understanding, which always moves in the sphere of the conditioned, *i.e.*, to give it the greatest possible unity together with the greatest possible extension. The concept of the absolute grows out of the logical task which is incumbent on reason, *i.e.*, inference, and it may be best explained from this as a starting point. In the syllogism the judgment asserted in the conclusion is derived from a general rule, the major premise. The validity of this general proposition is, however, itself conditional, dependent on higher conditions. Then, as reason seeks the condition for each conditioned moment, and always commands a further advance in the series of conditions, it acts under the Idea of *the totality of conditions*, which, nevertheless, since it can never be given in experience, does not denote an object, but only an heuristic maxim for knowledge, the maxim, namely, never to stop with any one condition as ultimate, but always to continue the search further. The Idea of the unconditioned or of the completeness of conditions is a goal which we never attain, but which we are continually to approach. The categories and the principles of the understanding were *constitutive* principles, the Ideas are *regulative* merely; their function is to guide the understanding, to give it a direction helpful for the connection of knowledge, not to inform it concerning the actual character of things.

Since reason is the faculty of inference (as the understanding was found to be the faculty of judgment), the forms of the syllogism perform the same service for us in our search for the Ideas as the forms of judgment in the discovery of the categories. To the categorical, hypothetical, and disjunctive syllogisms correspond the three concepts of reason, the soul or the thinking subject, the world or the totality of phenomena, and God, the original being or the supreme condition of the possibility of all that can be thought. By means of these we refer all inner phenomena to the ego as their (unknown) common subject, think all beings and events in nature as ordered under the comprehensive system of the (never to be experienced) universe, and regard all things as the work of a supreme (unknowable) intelligence. These Ideas are necessary concepts; not accidental products nor mere fancies, but concepts sprung from the nature of reason; their use is legitimate so long as we remember that we can have a problematical concept of objects corresponding to them, but no knowledge of these; that they are problems and rules for knowledge, never objects and instruments of it. Nevertheless the temptation to regard these regulative principles as constitutive and these problems as knowable objects is almost irresistible; for the ground of the involuntary confusion of the required with the given absolute lies not so much in the carelessness of the individual as in the nature of our cognitive faculty. The Ideas carry with them an unavoidable illusion of objective reality, and the sophistical inferences which spring from them are not sophistications of men, but of pure reason itself, are natural misunderstandings from which even the wisest cannot free himself. At best we can succeed in avoiding the error, not in doing away with the transcendental illusion from which it proceeds. We can see through the illusion and avoid the erroneous conclusions built upon it, not shake off the illusion itself.

On this erroneous objective use of the Ideas three so-called sciences are based: speculative psychology, speculative cosmology, and speculative theology, which, together with ontology, constitute the stately structure of the (Wolffian) metaphysics. The Critique of Reason completes its work of destruction when, as Dialectic (Logic cf. Illusion), it follows the refutation of dogmatic ontology—developed in the Analytic—which believed that it knew things in themselves through the concepts of the understanding, with a refutation of rational psychology, rational cosmology, and rational theology. It shows that the first is founded on paralogisms, and the second entangled in irreconcilable contradictions, while the third makes vain efforts to prove the existence of the Supreme Being.

(i) *The Paralogisms of Rational Psychology*. The transcendental self-consciousness or pure ego which accompanies and connects all my representations, the subject of all judgments which I form, is, as the Analytic recognized, the presupposition of all knowing (pp. 358-359), but as such it can never become an object of knowledge. We must not make a given object out of the subject which never can be a predicate, nor substitute a real thinking substance for the logical subject of thought, nor revamp the unity of self-consciousness into the simplicity and identical personality of the soul. The rational psychology of the Wolffian school is guilty of this error, and whatever of proof it advances for the substantiality, simplicity, and personality of the soul, and, by way of deduction, for its immateriality and immortality as well as for its relation to the body, is based upon this substitution, this ambiguity of the middle term, and therefore upon a *quaternio terminorum*,—all its conclusions are fallacious. It is allowable and unavoidable to add in thought an absolute subject, the unity of the ego, to inner phenomena;[1] it is inadmissible to treat the Idea of the soul as a knowable thing. In order to be able to apply the category of substance to it, we would have to lay hold of a permanent in intuition such as cannot be found in the inner sense. Empirical psychology, then, alone remains for the extension of our knowledge of mental life, while rational psychology shrivels up from a doctrine into a mere discipline, which watches that the limits of experience are not overstepped. But even as a mere limiting determination it has great value. For, along with the hope of proving the immateriality and immortality of the soul, the fear of seeing them *disproved* is also dissipated; materialism is just as unfounded as spiritualism, and if the conclusions of the latter concerning the soul as a simple, immaterial substance which survives the death of the body, cannot be proved, yet we need not, for that reason, regard them as erroneous, for the opposite is as little susceptible of demonstration. The whole question belongs not in the forum of knowledge, but in the forum of faith, and that which we gain by the proof that nothing can be determined concerning it by theoretical reasoning (viz., assurance against materialistic objections) is far more valuable than what we lose.

[Footnote 1: The rational concept of the soul as a simple, independent intelligence does not signify an actual being, but only expresses certain principles of systematic unity in the explanation of psychical phenomena, viz., "To regard all determinations as existing in one subject, all powers, as far as possible, as derived from, one fundamental power, all change as belonging to the states of one and the same permanent being, and to represent all phenomena in space as totally distinct from acts of thought."]

(2) *The Antinomies of Rational Cosmology*. If in its endeavor to spin metaphysical knowledge concerning the nature of the spirit and the existence of the soul after death out of the concept of the thinking ego the reason falls into the snare of an ambiguous *terminus medius*, the difficulties which frustrate its attempts to use the Idea of the world in the extension of its knowledge *a priori* are of quite a different character. Here the formal correctness of the method of inference is not open to attack. It may be proved with absolute strictness (and in the apagogical or indirect form, from the impossibility of the contrary) that the world has a beginning in time, and also that it is *limited* in space; that every compound substance consists of *simple* parts; that, besides the causality according to the laws of nature, there is a causality through *freedom*, and that an *absolutely necessary Being* exists, either as a part of the world or as the cause of it. But the contrary may be proved with equal stringency (and indirectly, as before): The world is infinite in space and time; there is nothing simple in the world; there is no freedom, but everything in the world takes place entirely according to the laws of nature; and there exists no absolutely necessary Being either within the world or without it. This is the famous doctrine of the conflict of the four cosmological theses and antitheses or of the Antinomy of Pure Reason, the discovery of which indubitably exercised a determining influence upon the whole course of the Kantian Critique of Reason, and which forms one of its poles. The transcendental idealism, the distinction between phenomena and noumena, and the limitation of knowledge to phenomena, all receive significant confirmation from the Antithetic. Without the critical idealism (that which is intuited in space and time, and known through the categories, is merely the phenomenon of things, whose "in itself" is unknowable), the antinomies would be insoluble. How is reason to act in view of the conflict? The grounds for the antitheses are just as conclusive as those for the theses; on neither side is there a preponderance which could decide the result. Ought reason to agree with both parties or with neither?

The solution distinguishes the first two antinomies, as the mathematical, from the second two, as the dynamical antinomies; in the former, since it is a question of the composition and division of quanta, the conditions may be homogeneous with the conditioned, in the latter, heterogeneous. In the former, thesis and antithesis are alike *false*, since both start from the inadmissible assumption that the universe (the complete series of phenomena) is given, while in fact it is only required of us (is an Idea). The world does not exist in itself, but only in the empirical regress of phenomenal conditions, in which we never can reach infinity and never the limitation of the world by an empty space or an antecedent empty time, for infinite space, like empty space (and the same holds in regard to time), is not perceivable. Consequently the quantity of the world is neither finite nor infinite. The question of the quantity of the world is unanswerable, because the concept of a sense-world existing by itself *(before* the regress) is self-contradictory. Similarly the problem whether the composite consists of simple elements is insoluble, because the assumption that the phenomenon of body is a thing in itself, which, antecedent to all experience, contains all the parts that can be reached in experience—in other words, that representations exist outside of the representative faculty—is absurd. Matter is infinitely divisible, no doubt, yet it does not consist of infinitely numerous parts, and just as little of a definite number of simple parts, but the parts exist merely in the representation of them, in the division (decomposition), and this goes as far as possible experience extends. The case is different with the dynamical antinomies, where thesis and antithesis can both be *true*, in so far as the former is referred to things in themselves and the latter to phenomena. The contradiction vanishes if we take that which the thesis asserts and the antithesis denies in different senses. The fact that in the world of phenomena the causal nexus proceeds without interruption and without end, so that there is no room in it either for an absolutely necessary Being or for freedom, does not conflict with this other, that beyond the world of sense there may exist an omnipotent, omniscient cause of the world, and an intelligible freedom as the ground of our empirically necessary actions. "May exist," since for the critical philosopher, who has learned that every extension of knowledge beyond the limits of experience is impossible, the question can concern only the conceivability of the world-ground and of freedom. This possibility is amply sufficient to give a support for faith, as, on the other hand, it is indispensable in order to satisfy at once the demands of the understanding and of reason, especially to satisfy their practical interests. For if it were not possible to resolve the apparent contradiction, and to show its members capable of reconciliation, it would be all over either with the possibility of experiential knowledge or with the basis of ethics and religion. Without unbroken causal connection, no nature; without freedom, no morality; and without a Deity, no religion. Of special interest is the solution of the third antinomy, which is accomplished by means of the valuable (though in the form in which it is given by Kant, untenable) conception of the *intelligible character*.[1] Man is a citizen of two worlds. As a being of the senses (phenomenon) he is subject in his volition and action to the control of natural necessity, while as a being of reason (thing in itself) he is free. For science his acts are the inevitable results of precedent phenomena, which, in turn, are themselves empirically caused; nevertheless moral judgment holds him responsible for his acts. In the one case, they are referred to his empirical character, in the other, to his intelligible character. Man cannot act otherwise than he does act, if he be what he is, but he need not be as he is; the moral constitution of the intelligible character, which reflects itself in the empirical character, is his own work, and its radical transformation (moral regeneration) his duty, the fulfillment of which is demanded, and, hence, of necessity possible.

[Footnote 1: On the difficulties in the way of this theory and the possibility of their removal cf. R. Falckenberg, *Ueber den intelligiblen Character, zur Kritik der Kantischen Freiheitslehre* (from the *Zeitschrift für Philosophie*, vol. lxxv.), Halle, 1879.]

(3) *Speculative Theology*. The principle of complete determination, according to which of all the possible predicates of things, as compared with their opposites, one must belong to each thing, relates the thing to be determined to the sum of all possible predicates or the *Idea of an ens realissimum*, which, since it is the representation of a single being, may be called the *Ideal* of pure reason. From this prototype things, as its imperfect copies, derive the material of their possibility; all their manifold determinations are simply so many modes of limiting the concept of the highest reality, which is their common substratum, just as all figures are possible only as different ways of limiting infinite space. Or better: the derivative beings are not related to the ideal of the original Being as limitations to the sum of the highest reality (on which view the Supreme Being would be conceived as an aggregate consisting of the derivative beings, whereas these presuppose it, and hence cannot constitute it), but as consequences to a ground. But reason does not remain content with this entirely legitimate thought of the dependence of finite things on the ideal of the Being of all beings, as a relation of concepts to the Idea, but, dazzled by an irresistible illusion, proceeds to realize, to hypostatize, and to personify this ideal, and, since she herself is dimly conscious of the illegitimacy of such a transformation of the mere Idea into a given object, devises *arguments for the existence of God*. Reason, moreover, would scarcely be induced to regard a mere creation of its thought as a real being, if it were not compelled from another direction to seek a resting place somewhere in the regress of conditions, and to think the empirical reality of the contingent world as founded upon the rock of something absolutely necessary. There is no being, however, which appears more fit for the prerogative of absolute necessity than that one the concept of which contains the therefore to every wherefore, and is in no respect defective; in other words, rational theology joins the rational ideal of the most perfect Being with the fourth cosmological Idea of the absolutely necessary Being.

The proof of the existence of God may be attempted in three ways: we may argue the existence of a supreme cause either by starting from a definite experience (the special constitution and order of the sense-world, that is, its purposiveness), or from an indefinite experience (any existence whatever), or, finally, abstracting from all experience, from mere concepts *a priori*. But neither the empirical nor the transcendent nor the intermediate line of thought leads to the goal. The most impressive and popular of the proofs is the *physico-theological* argument. But even if we gratuitously admit the analogy of natural products with the works of human art (for the argument is not able to prove that the purposive arrangement of the things in the world, which we observe with admiration, is contingent, and could only have been produced by an ordering, rational principle, not self-produced by their own nature according to general mechanical laws), this can yield an inference only to an intelligent author of the purposive form of the world, and not to an author of its matter, only, therefore, to a world-architect, not to a world-creator. Further, since the cause must be proportionate to the effect, this argument can prove only a very wise and wonderfully powerful, but not an omniscient and omnipotent, designer, and so cannot give any definite concept of the supreme cause of the world. In leaping from the contingency of the purposive order of the world to the existence of something absolutely necessary and thence to an all-comprehensive reality, the teleological argument abandons the ground of experience and passes over into the *cosmological argument*, which in its turn is merely a concealed ontological argument (these two differ only in the fact that the cosmological proof argues from the antecedently given absolute necessity of a being to its unlimited reality, and the ontological, conversely, from supreme reality to necessary existence). The weaknesses of the cosmological argument in its first half consist in the fact that, in the inference from the contingent to a cause for it, it oversteps the boundary of the sense-world, and, in the inference from the impossibility of an infinite series of conditions to a first cause, it employs the subjective principle of investigation—to assume hypothetically a necessary ultimate ground in behalf of the systematic unity of knowledge—as an objective principle applying to things in themselves. The *ontological argument*, finally, which the two nominally empirical arguments hoped to avoid, but in which in the end they were forced to take refuge, goes to wreck on the impossibility of dragging out of an idea the existence of the object corresponding to it. Existence denotes nothing further than the position of the subject with all the marks which are thought in its concept—that is, its relation to our knowledge, but does not itself belong to the predicates of the concept, and hence cannot be analytically derived from the latter. The content of the concept is not enriched by the addition of being; a hundred real dollars do not contain a penny more than a hundred conceived dollars. All existential propositions are synthetic; hence the existence of God cannot be demonstrated from the concept of God. It is a contradiction, to be sure, to say that God is not almighty, just as it is a contradiction to deny that a triangle has three angles: *if* I posit the concept I must not remove the predicate which necessarily belongs to it. If I remove the subject, however, together with its predicate (the almighty God is not), no contradiction arises, for in that case nothing remains to be contradicted.

Thus all the proofs for the existence of a necessary being are shown to be illusory, and the basis of speculative theology uncertain. Nevertheless the idea of God retains its validity, and the perception of the inability of reason to demonstrate its objective reality on theoretical grounds has great value. For though the existence of God cannot be proved, it is true, by way of recompense, that it cannot be disproved; the same grounds which show us that the assertion of his existence is based on a weak foundation suffice also to prove every contrary assertion unfounded. And should practical motives present themselves to turn the scale in favor of the assumption of a supreme and all-sufficient Being, reason would be obliged to take sides and to follow these grounds, which, it is true, are not objectively sufficient,[1] but still preponderant, and than which we know none better. After, however, the objective reality of the idea of God is guaranteed from the standpoint of ethics, there remains for transcendental theology the important negative duty ("censorship," Censor) of exactly determining the concept of the most perfect Being (as a being which through understanding and freedom contains the first ground of all other things), of removing from it all impure elements, and of putting an end to all opposite assertions, whether atheistic, deistic (deism maintains the possibility of knowing the existence of an original being, but declares all further determination of this being impossible), or (in the dogmatic sense) anthropomorphic. Theism is entirely possible apart from a mistaken anthropomorphism, in so far as through the predicates which we take from inner experience (understanding and will) we do not determine the concept of God as he is in himself, but only *analogically*[2] in his relation to the world. That concept serves only to aid us in our contemplation of the world,[3] not as a means of knowing the Supreme Being himself. For speculative purposes it remains a mere ideal, yet a perfectly faultless one, which completes and crowns the whole of human knowledge.

[Footnote 1: "They need favor to supply their lack of legitimate claims." Of themselves alone, therefore, they are unable to yield any theological knowledge, but they are fitted to prepare the understanding for it, and to give emphasis to other possible (moral) proofs.]

[Footnote 2: We halt *at* the boundary of the legitimate use of reason, without overstepping it, when we limit our judgment to the relation of the world to the Supreme Being, and in this allow ourselves a symbolical anthropomorphism only, which in reality has reference to our language alone and not to the object.]

[Footnote 3: We are compelled to *look on* the world *as if* it were the work of a supreme intelligence and will. "We may confidently derive the phenomena of the world and their existence from other (phenomena), as if no necessary being existed, and yet unceasingly strive after completeness in the derivation, as though such a being were presupposed as a supreme ground." In short, physical (mechanical) *explanation*, and a theistic point of view or teleological *judgment*.]

Thus the value of the Ideas is twofold. By showing the untenable ness of atheism, fatalism, and naturalism, they I clear the way for the objects of faith. By providing natural science with the standpoint of a systematical unity through teleological connection, they make an extension of the use of the understanding possible within the realm of experience,[1] though not beyond it. The systematic development of the Kantian teleology, which is here indicated in general outlines only, is found in the second part of the *Critique of Judgment*; while the practical philosophy, which furnishes the only possible proof, the moral proof, for the reality of the Ideas, erects on the site left free by the removal of the airy summer-houses of dogmatic metaphysics the solid mansion of critical metaphysics, that is, the metaphysics of duties and of hopes. "I was obliged to destroy knowledge in order to make room for faith." The transition from the impossible theoretical or speculative knowledge of things in themselves to the possible "practical knowledge" of them (the belief that there is a God and a future world) is given in the *Doctrine of Method*, which is divided into four parts (the Discipline, the Canon, the Architectonic, and the History of Pure Reason), in its second chapter. There, in the ideal of the *Summum Bonum*, the proof is brought forward for the validity of the Ideas God, freedom, and immortality, as postulates inseparable from moral obligation; and by a cautious investigation of the three stages of assent (opinion, knowledge, and belief) both doctrinal and moral belief are assigned their places in the system of the kinds of knowledge.

[Footnote 1: The principle to regard all order in the world (*e.g.*, the shape of the earth, mountains, and seas, the members of animal bodies) as if it proceeded from the design of a supreme reason leads the investigator on to various discoveries.]

We may now sum up the results of the three parts of Kant's theoretical philosophy. The pure intuitions, the categories, and the Ideas are functions of the spirit, and afford non-empirical *(erfahrungsfreie)* knowledge concerning the objects of possible experience (and concerning the possibility of knowledge). The first make universal and necessary knowledge possible in relation to the forms under which objects can be given to us; the second make a similarly apodictic knowledge possible in relation to the forms under which phenomena must be thought; the third make possible a judgment of phenomena differing from this knowledge, yet not in conflict with it. The categories and the Ideas, moreover, yield problematical concepts of objects which are not given to us in intuition, but which may exist outside of space and time: things in themselves cannot be known, it is true, but they can be thought, a fact of importance in case we should be assured of their existence in some other way than by sensuous intuition.

The determination of the limits of speculative reason is finished. All knowing and all demonstration is limited to phenomena or possible experience. But the boundary of that which can be experienced is not the boundary of that which is, still less of that which ought to be; the boundary of theoretical reason is not the boundary of practical reason. We *ought* to act morally; in order to be able to do this we must ascribe to ourselves the power to initiate a series of events; and, in general, we are warranted in assuming everything the non-assumption of which makes moral action impossible. If we were merely theoretical, merely experiential beings, we should lack all occasion to suppose a second, intelligible world behind and above the world of phenomena; but we are volitional and active beings under laws of reason, and though we are unable to know things in themselves, yet we may and must *postulate* them—our freedom, God, and immortality. For not only that which is a condition of experience is true and necessary, but that, also, which is a condition of morality. The discovery of the laws and conditions of morality is the mission of practical philosophy.

%2. Theory of Ethics.%

The investigation now turns from the laws of nature, which express a "must," to the laws of will, in which an "ought" is expressed, and by which certain actions are not compelled, but prescribed. (If we were merely rational, and not at the same time sensuous beings, the moral law would determine the will in the form of a natural law; since, however, the constant possibility of deviation is given in the sensibility, or, rather, the moral standpoint can only be attained by conquering the sensuous impulses, therefore the moral law speaks to us in the form of an "ought," of an imperative.) Among the laws of the will or imperatives, also, there are some which possess the character of absolute necessity and universality, and which, consequently, are *a priori*. As the understanding dictates laws to the phenomenal world, so practical reason gives a law to itself, is *autonomous*; and as the *a priori* laws of nature relate only to the form of the objects of experience, so the moral law determines not the content, but only the form of volition: "Act only on that maxim whereby thou canst at the same time will that it should become a universal law." The law of practical reason is a "categorical imperative." What does this designation mean, and what is the basis of the formula of the moral law which has just been given?

Practical principles are either subjectively valid, in which case they are termed maxims (volitional principles of the individual), or objectively valid, when they are called imperatives or precepts. The latter are either valid under certain conditions (If you wish to become a clergyman you must study theology; he who would prosper as a merchant must not cheat his customers), or unconditionally valid (Thou shalt not lie). All prudential or technical rules are hypothetical imperatives, the moral law is a categorical imperative. The injunction to be truthful is not connected with the condition that we intend to act morally, but this general purpose, together with all the special purposes belonging to it, to avoid lying, etc., is demanded unconditionally and of everyone—as surely as we are rational beings we are under moral obligation, not in order to reputation here below and happiness above, but without all "ifs" and "in order to's." Thou shalt unconditionally, whatever be the outcome. And as the moral law is independent of every end to be attained, so it suffers neither increase nor diminution in its binding force, whether men obey it or not. It has absolute authority, no matter whether it is fulfilled frequently or seldom, nay, whether it is fulfilled anywhere or at any time whatsoever in the world!

There is an important difference between the good which we are under obligation to do and the evil which we are under obligation not to do, and the goods and ills which we seek and avoid. The goods are always relatively good only, *good for something*—as means to ends—and a bad use can be made of all that nature and fortune give us as well as a good one. That which duty commands is an end in itself, in itself good, absolutely worthful, and no misuse of it is possible. It might be supposed that pleasure, that happiness is an ultimate end. But men have very different opinions in regard to what is pleasant, one holding one thing pleasurable and another another. It is impossible to discover by empirical methods what duty demands of all men alike and under all circumstances; the appeal is to our reason, not to our sensibility. If happiness were the end of rational beings, then nature had endowed us but poorly for it, since instead of an unfailing instinct she has given us the weak and deceitful reason as a guide, which, with its train, culture, science, art, and luxury, has brought more trouble than satisfaction to mankind. Man has a destiny other than well-being, and a higher one—the formation of good dispositions: here we have the only thing in the whole world that can never be used for evil, the only thing that does not borrow its value from a higher end, but itself originally and inalienably contains it, and that gives value to all else that merits esteem. "Nothing can possibly be conceived in the world, or even out of it, which can be called good without qualification, except a *good will*." Understanding, courage, moderation, and whatever other mental gifts or praiseworthy qualities of temperament may be cited, as also the gifts of fortune, "are undoubtedly good and desirable in many respects, but they may also become extremely evil and mischievous, if the will which is to make use of them is not good." These are the classic words with which Kant commences the *Foundation of the Metaphysics of Ethics*.

When does the will deserve the predicate "good"? Let us listen to the popular moral consciousness, which distinguishes three grades of moral recognition. He who refrains from that which is contrary to duty, no matter from what motives—as, for example, the shopkeeper who does not cheat because he knows that honesty is the best policy—receives moderate praise for irreproachable outward behavior. We bestow warmer praise and encouragement on him whom ambition impels to industry, kind feeling to beneficence, and pity to render assistance. But he alone earns our esteem who does his duty for duty's sake. Only in this third case, where not merely the external action, nor merely the impulse of a happy disposition, but the will itself, the maxim, is in harmony with the moral law, where the good is done for the sake of the good, do we find true morality, that unconditioned, self-grounded worth. The man who does that which is in accordance with duty out of reflection on its advantages, and he who does it from immediate—always unreliable—inclination, acts *legally*; he alone acts *morally* who, without listening to advantage and inclination, takes up the law into his disposition, and does his duty because it is duty. The sole moral motive is the consciousness of duty, *respect for the moral lazy*[1]

[Footnote 1: The respect or reverence which the law, and, derivatively, the person in whom it is realized, compel from us, is, as self-produced through a concept of reason and as the only feeling which can be known *a priori*, specifically different from all feelings of inclination or fear awakened by sensuous influences. As it strengthens and raises our rational nature, the consciousness of our freedom and of our high destination, but, at the same time, humbles our sensibility, there is mingled with the joy of exaltation a certain pain, which permits no intimate affection for the stern and sublime law. It is not quite willingly that we pay our respect—just because of the depressing effect which this feeling exerts on our self-love.]

Here Kant is threatened by a danger which he does not succeed in escaping. The moral law demands perfect purity in our maxims; only the idea of duty, not an inclination, is to determine the will. Quite right. Further, the one judging is himself never absolutely certain, even when his own volition is concerned, that no motives of pleasure have mingled with the feeling of duty in contributing to the right action, unless that which was morally demanded has been contrary to all his inclinations. When a person who is not in need and who is free from cupidity leaves the money-box intrusted to his care untouched, or when a man who loves life overcomes thoughts of suicide, I may assume that the former was sufficiently protected against the temptation by his moderation, and the other by his cheerful disposition, and I rate their behavior as merely legal. When, on the other hand, an official inclined to extravagance faithfully manages the funds intrusted to him, or one who is oppressed by hopeless misery preserves his life, although he does not love it, then I may ascribe the abstinence from wrongdoing to moral principles. This, too, may be admitted. We are certain of the morality of a resolution only when it can be shown that no inclination was involved along with the maxim. The cases where the right action is performed in opposition to inclination are the only ones in which we may be certain that the moral quality of the action is unmixed—are they, then, the only ones in which a moral disposition is present? Kant rightly maintains that the admixture of egoistic motives beclouds the purity of the disposition, and consequently diminishes its moral worth. With equal correctness he draws attention to the possibility that, even when we believe that we are acting from pure principles, a hidden sensuous impulse may be involved. But he leaves unconsidered the possibility that, even when the inclinations are favorable to right action, the action may be performed, not from inclination, but because of the consciousness of duty. Given that a man is naturally industrious, does this happy predisposition protect him from fits of idleness? And if he resists them, must it always be his inclination to activity and never moral principle which overcomes the temptation? In yielding to the danger of confounding the limits of our certain knowledge of the purity of motives with the limits of moral action, and in admitting true morality only where action proceeds from principle in opposition to the inclinations, Kant really deserves the reproach of rigorism or exaggerated purism—sometimes groundlessly extended to the justifiable strictness of his views—and the ridicule of the well-known lines of Schiller ("Scruples of Conscience" and "Decision" at the conclusion of his distich-group "The Philosophers"):

"The friends whom I love I gladly would serve, but to this inclination
    incites me;
And so I am forced from virtue to swerve since my act, through affection,
    delights me.
The friends whom thou lovest thou must first seek to scorn, for to no
    other way can I guide thee;

'Tis alone with disgust thou canst rightly perform the acts to which
  duty would lead thee."

If we return from this necessary limitation of a groundless inference (that true morality is present only when duty is performed against our inclinations, when it is difficult for us, when a conflict with sensuous motives has preceded), to the development of the fundamental ethical conceptions, we find that important conclusions concerning the origin and content of the moral law result from the principle obtained by the analysis of moral judgment: this law commands with *unconditional authority*—for every rational being and under all circumstances—what has *unconditioned worth*—the disposition which corresponds to it. The universality and necessity (*unconditionalness*) of the categorical imperative proves that it springs from no other source than reason itself. Those who derive the moral law from the will of God subject it to a condition, viz., the immutability of the divine will. Those who find the source of moral legislation in the pursuit of happiness make rational will dependent on a natural law of the sensibility; it would be folly to enjoin by a moral law that which everyone does of himself, and does superabundantly. Moreover, the theories of the social inclinations and of moral sense fail of their purpose, since they base morality on the uncertain ground of feeling. Even the principle of perfection proves insufficient, inasmuch as it limits the individual to himself, and, in the end, like those which have preceded, amounts to a refined self-love. Theonomic ethics, egoistic ethics, the ethics of sympathy, and the ethics of perfection are all eudemonistic, and hence heteronomic. The practical reason[1] receives the law neither from the will of God nor from natural impulse, but draws it out of its own depths; it binds itself.

[Footnote 1: Will and practical reason are identical. The definition runs: Will is the faculty of acting in accordance with the representation of laws.]

The grounds which establish the derivation of the moral law from the will or reason itself exclude at the same time every material determination of it. If the categorical imperative posited definite ends for the will, if it prescribed a direction to definite objects, it could neither be known *a priori* nor be valid for all rational beings: its apodictic character forbids the admission of empirical elements of every sort.[1] If we think away all content from the law we retain the form of universal legality,[2] and gain the formula: "Act so that the maxim of thy will can always at the same time hold good as a principle of universal legislation." The possibility of conceiving the principle of volition as a universal law of nature is the criterion of morality. If you are in doubt concerning the moral character of an action or motive simply ask yourself the question, What would become of humanity if everyone were to act according to the same principle? If no one could trust the word of another, or count on aid from others, or be sure of his property and his life, then no social life would be possible. Even a band of robbers cannot exist unless certain laws are respected as inviolable duties.

[Footnote 1: The moral law, therefore, is independent of all experience in three respects, as to its origin, its content, and its validity. It springs from reason, it contains a formal precept only, and its validity is not concerned, whether it meets with obedience or not. It declares what ought to be done, even though this never should be done.]

[Footnote 2: The "formal principle" of the Kantian ethics has met very varied criticism. Among others Edmund Pfleiderer (*Kantischer Kritizismus und Englische Philosophie*, 1881) and Zeller express themselves unfavorably, Fortlage and Liebmann (*Zur Analysis der Wirklichkeit*, 2d ed., 1880, p. 671) favorably.]

It was indispensable to free the supreme formula of the moral law from all material determinations, *i.e.*, limitations. This does not prevent us, however, from afterward giving the abstract outline a more concrete coloring. First of all, the concept of the dignity of persons in contrast to the utility of things offers itself as an aid to explanation and specialization. Things are means whose worth is always relative, consisting in the useful or pleasant effects which they exercise, in the satisfaction of a need or of the taste, they can be replaced by other means, which fulfill the same purpose, and they have a (market or fancy) *value*; while that which is above all value and admits of no equivalent has an ultimate worth or *dignity*, and is an object of respect. The legislation which determines all worth, and with this the disposition which corresponds to it, has a dignity, an unconditioned, incomparable worth, and lends its subjects, rational beings framed for morality, the advantage of being ends in themselves. "Therefore morality, and humanity so far as it is capable of morality, is that which alone possesses dignity." Accordingly the following formulation of the moral law may be held equivalent to the first: "So act as to treat humanity, whether in thine own person or in that of any other, in every case as an end, never as a means only."

A further addition to the abstract formula of the categorical imperative results from the discussion of the question, What universal ends admit of subsumption under it, *i.e.*, stand the test of fitness to be principles of a universal legislation? Here again Kant stands forth as an arbiter between the contending parties, and, with a firm grasp, combines the useful elements from both sides after winnowing them out from the worthless principles. The majority of the eudemonistic systems, along with the promotion of private welfare, prescribe the furtherance of universal good without being able to indicate at what point the pursuit of personal welfare should give way to regard for the good of others, while in the perfectionist systems the social element is wanting or retreats unduly into the background. The principle of happiness represents moral empiricism, the principle of perfection moral rationalism. Kant resolves the antithesis by restricting the theses of the respective parties within their proper limits: "Make *thine own perfection* and *the happiness of others* the end of thy actions;" these are the only ends which are at the same time duties. The perfection of others is excluded by the fact that I cannot impart to anyone a good disposition, for everyone must acquire it for himself; personal happiness by the fact that everyone seeks it naturally.

This antithesis (which is crossed by the further distinction between perfect, *i.e.*, indispensable, and imperfect duties) serves as a basis for the division of moral duties into duties toward ourselves and duties toward other men.[1] The former enjoin the preservation and development of our natural and moral powers, the latter are duties of obligation (of respect) or of merit (of love). Since no one can obligate me to feel, we are to understand by love not the pathological love of complacency, but only the active love of benevolence or practical sympathy. Since it is just as impossible that the increase of the evils in the world should be a duty, the enervating and useless excitation of pity, which adds to the pain of the sufferer the sympathetic pain of the spectator, is to be struck off the list of virtues, and active readiness to aid put in its place. In friendship love and respect unite in exact equipoise. Veracity is one of the duties toward self; lying is an abandonment of human dignity and under no conditions allowable, not even if life depends on it.

[Footnote 1: All duties are toward men, not toward supra-human or infra-human beings. That which we commonly term duties toward animals, likewise the so-called duties toward God, are in reality duties toward ourselves. Cruelty to animals is immoral, because our sympathies are blunted by it. To have religion is a duty to ourselves, because the view of moral laws as laws of God is an aid to morality.]

After it has been settled what the categorical imperative enjoins, the further problem awaits us of explaining how it is possible. The categorical imperative is possible only on I the presupposition of our *freedom*. Only a free being gives laws to itself, just as an autonomous being alone is free. In theoretical philosophy the pure self-consciousness, the "I think," denoted a point where the thing in itself manifests to us not its nature, indeed, but its existence. The same holds true in practical philosophy of the moral law. The incontestable fact of the moral law empowers me to rank myself in a higher order of things than the merely phenomenal order, and in another causal relation than that of the merely necessary (mechanical) causation of nature, to regard myself as a legislative member of an intelligible world, and one independent of sensuous impulses—in short, to regard myself as free. Freedom is the *ratio essendi* of the self-given moral law, the latter the *ratio cognoscendi* of freedom. The law would have no meaning if we did not possess the power to obey it: I can *because* I ought. It is true that freedom is a mere Idea, whose object can never be given to me in an experience, and whose reality, consequently, cannot be objectively known and proved, but nevertheless, is required with satisfactory subjective necessity as the condition of the moral law and of the possibility of its fulfillment. I may not say it is certain, but, with safety, I am certain that I am free. Freedom is not a dogmatic proposition of theoretical reason, but a *postulate* of practical reason; and the latter holds the *primacy* over the former to this extent, that it can require the former to show that certain transcendent Ideas of the suprasensible, which are most intimately connected with moral obligation, are compatible with the principles of the understanding. It was just in view of the practical interests involved in the rational concepts God, freedom, immortality, that it was so important to establish, at least, their possibility (their conceivability without contradiction). That, therefore, which the Dialectic recognized as possible is in the Ethics shown to be real: Whoever seeks to fulfill his moral destiny—and this is the duty of every man—must not doubt concerning the conditions of its possible fulfillment, must, in spite of their incomprehensibility, *believe* in freedom and a suprasensible world. They are both postulates of practical reason, *i.e.*, assumptions concerning that which is in behalf of that which ought to be. Naturally the interests of the understanding must not be infringed upon by those of the will. The principle of the complete causal determination of events retains its validity unimpeached for the sphere of the knowledge of the understanding, that is, for the realm of phenomena; while, on the other hand, it remains permissible for us to postulate another kind of causality for the realm of things in themselves, although we can have no idea of its *how*, and to ascribe to ourselves a free intelligible character.

While the Idea of freedom can be derived directly from the moral law as a postulate thereof, the proof of the reality of the two other Ideas is effected indirectly by means of the concept of the "highest good," in which reason conceives a union of perfect virtue and perfect happiness. The moral law requires absolute correspondence between the disposition and the commands of reason, or holiness of will. But besides this supreme good (*bonum supremum*) of completed morality, the highest good (*bonum consummatum*) further contains a degree of happiness corresponding to the degree of virtue. Everyone agrees in the judgment that, by rights, things should go well with the virtuous and ill with the wicked, though this must not imply any deduction from the principle previously announced that the least impulse of self-interest causes the maxim to forfeit its worth: the motive of the will must never be happiness, but always the being worthy of happiness. The first element in the highest good yields the argument for *immortality*, and the second the argument for the *existence of God*. (1) Perfect correspondence between the will and the law never occurs in this life, because the sensibility never allows us to attain a permanently good disposition, armed against every temptation; our will can never be holy, but at best virtuous, and our lawful disposition never escape the consciousness of a constant tendency to transgression, or at least of impurity. Since, nevertheless, the demands of the (Christian) moral law continue in their unrelenting stringency to be the standard, we are justified in the hope of an unlimited continuation of our existence, in order that by constant progress in goodness we may draw nearer *in infinitum* to the ideal of holiness. (2) The establishment of a rational proportion between happiness and virtue is also not to be expected until the future life, for too often on earth it is the evil man who prospers, while the good man suffers. A justly proportioned distribution of rewards and punishment can only be expected from an infinite power, wisdom, and goodness, which rules the moral world even as it has created the natural world. Deity alone is able to bring the physical and moral realms into harmony, and to establish the due relation between well-being and right action. This, the moral argument, is the only possible proof for the existence of God. Theology is not possible as speculative, but only as moral theology. The certitude of faith, moreover, is only different from, not less than, the certainty of knowledge, in so far as it brings with it not an objective, but a subjective, although universally valid, necessity. Hence it is better to speak of belief in God as a need of the reason than as a duty; while a logical error, not a moral one, should be charged against the atheist. The atheist is blind to the intimate connection which exists between the highest good and the Ideas of the reason; he does not see that God, freedom, and immortality are the indispensable conditions of the realization of this ideal.

Thus faith is based upon duty without being itself duty: ethics is the *basis of religion*, which consists in our regarding moral laws as (*instar*, as if they were) divine commands. They are not valid or obligatory because God has given them (this would be heteronomy), but they should be regarded as divine because they are necessary laws of reason. Religion differs from ethics only in its form, not in its content, in that it adds to the conception of duty the idea of God as a moral lawgiver, and thus increases the influence of this conception on the will; it is simply a means for the promotion of morality. Since, however, besides natural religion or the pure faith of reason (the moral law and the moral postulates), the historical religions contain statutory determinations or a doctrinal faith, it becomes the duty of the critical philosopher to inquire how much of this positive admixture can be justified at the bar of reason. In this investigation the question of the divine revelation of dogma and ceremonial laws is neither supra-rationalistically affirmed nor naturalistically derived, but rationalistically treated as an open question.

The four essays combined under the title *Religion within the Limits of Reason Only* treat of the Radical Evil in Human Nature, the Conflict of the Good Principle with the Evil for the Mastery over Man, the Victory of the Good Principle over the Evil and the Founding of a Kingdom of God upon Earth, and, finally, Service and False Service under the Dominion of the

Good Principle, or Religion and Priestcraft; or more briefly, the fall, the atonement (the Christ-idea), the Church, and true and false service of God.

(1) The individual evil deeds of the empirical character point to an original fault of the intelligible character, a *propensity to evil* dwelling in man and not further deducible. This, although it is self-incurred, may be called natural and innate, and consists (not in the sensibility merely, but) in a freely chosen reversal of the moral order of our maxims, in virtue of which the maxim of duty or morality is subordinated to that of well-being or self-love instead of being placed above it, and that which should be the supreme condition of all satisfaction is degraded into a mere means thereto. Morality is therefore a *conversion* from the evil to the good, and requires a complete revolution in the disposition, the putting on of a new man, a "new birth," which, an act out of time, can manifest itself in the temporal world of phenomena only as a gradual transformation in conduct, as a continuous advance, but which, we may hope, is judged by him who knows the heart, who regards the disposition instead of particular imperfect actions, as a completed unity.

(2) By the eternal Son of God, for whose sake God created all things, we are to understand the ideal of the perfect man, which in truth forms the end of creation, and is come down from heaven, etc. To believe in Christ means to resolve to realize in one's self the ideal of human nature which is well pleasing to God, or to make the divine disposition of the Son of God our own, not to believe that this ideal has appeared on earth as an actual man, in the person of Jesus of Nazareth. The only saving faith is the belief of reason in the ideal which Christ represents, and not the historical belief in his person. The vicarious atonement of the ideal man for those who believe on him is to be interpreted to mean that the sufferings and sacrifices (crucifixion of the flesh) imposed by moral conversion, which are due to the sinful man as punishment, are assumed by the regenerate man: the new Adam bears the sufferings of the old. In the same way as that in which Kant handles the history of Christ and the doctrine of justification, all biblical narratives and ecclesiastical doctrines are in public instruction (from the pulpit) to be interpreted morally, even where the authors themselves had no such meaning in mind.

(3) The Church is a society based upon the laws of virtue, an ethical community or a people of God, whose members confirm each other in the performance of duty by example and by the profession of a common moral conviction; we are all brothers, the children of one father. Ideally there is only one (the universal, invisible) Church, and its foundation the pure faith of reason; but in consequence of a weakness peculiar to human nature the foundation of an actual church required the addition of a statutory historical faith, with claims to a divine origin, from which a multitude of visible churches and the antithesis of orthodox and heretics have sprung. The history of the Church since the establishment of Christianity represents the conflict between the historical faith and the faith of reason; its goal is the submission of the former to the latter, as, indeed, we have already begun to perceive that God does not require a special service beyond the practice of virtue.

(4) The true service of God consists in a moral disposition and its manifestation: "All that man supposes himself able to do in order to please God, beyond living a good life, is *false service*" False service is the false subordination of the pure faith of reason to the statutory faith, by which the attainment of the goal of religious development is hindered and the laity are brought into dangerous dependence upon the clergy. Priestcraft, hypocrisy, and fanaticism enter in the train of fetich service. The church-faith is destined little by little to make itself superfluous. It has been necessary as a vehicle, as a means for the introduction and extension of the pure religion of morality, and it still remains useful for a time, until humanity shall become of age; with man's entrance on the period of youth and manhood, however, the leading-string of holy traditions, which in its time did good service, becomes unnecessary, nay, finally, a fetter. (This relative appreciation of the positive element in religion, in antithesis to the unthinking rejection of it by the Illumination, resembles the view of Lessing; cf. pp. 306-309.) Moreover, since it is a duty to be a co-worker in the transition from the historical to the pure religious faith, the clergy must be free as scientific theologians, as scholars and authors to examine the doctrines of faith and to give expression to dissenting opinions, while, as preachers in the pulpit, speaking under commission, they are bound to the creeds. To decide the articles of belief unalterable would be a crime against human nature, whose primal destination is just this—to progress. To renounce illumination means to trample upon the divine rights of reason.

The "General Observations" appended to each division add to the four principle discussions as many collateral inquiries concerning Operations of Grace, Miracles, Mysteries, and Means of Grace, objects of transcendent ideas, which do not properly belong in the sphere of religion within pure reason itself, but which yet border on it. (1) We are entirely incapable of calling forth works of grace, nay, even of indicating the marks by which actual divine illuminations are distinguished from imaginary ones; the supposed experience of heavenly influences belongs in the region of superstitious religious illusion. But their impossibility is just as little susceptible of proof as their reality. Nothing further can be said on the question, save that works of grace may exist, and perhaps must exist in order to supplement our imperfect efforts after virtue; and that everyone, instead of waiting for divine assistance, should do for his own amendment all that is in his power. (2) Kant judges more sharply in regard to the belief in miracles, which contradict the laws of experience without in the least furthering the performance of our duties. In practical life no one regards miracles as possible; and their limitation to the past and to rare instances does not make them more credible. (3) In so far as the Christian mysteries actually represent impenetrable secrets they have no bearing on moral conduct; so far as they are morally valuable they admit of rational interpretation and thus cease to be mysteries. The Trinity signifies the three moral qualities or powers united in the head of the moral state: the one God as holy lawgiver, gracious governor, and just judge. (4) The services of the Church have worth as ethical ceremonies, as emblems of the moral disposition (prayer) and of moral fellowship (church attendance, baptism, and the Lord's Supper); but to find in these symbolic ceremonies means of grace and to seek to purchase the favor of God by them, is an error of the same kind as sorcery and fetichism. The right way leads from virtue to grace, not in the opposite direction; piety without morality is worthless.

The Kantian theory of religion is rationalistic and moralistic. The fact that religion is based on morality should never be assailed. But the foundation is not the building, the origin not the content and essence of the thing itself. As far as the nature of religion is concerned, the Kantian view does not exclude completion in the direction of Schleiermacher's theory of feeling, just as by its speculative interpretation of the Christian dogmas and its appreciation of the history of religion as a gradual transformation of historical faith into a faith of reason, it points out the path afterward followed by Hegel. The philosophy of religion of the future must be, as some recent attempts aim to be (O. Pfleiderer, Biedermann, Lipsius), a synthesis of Kant, Schleiermacher, and Hegel.

While the moral law requires rightness not only of the action, but also of the disposition, the law of right is satisfied when the act enjoined is performed, no matter from what motives. Legal right, as the sum of the conditions under which the will of the one can consist with the will of others according to a universal law, relates only to enforceable actions, without concerning itself about motives. Private right includes right in things or property, personal right or right of contract, and real-personal right (marriage right); public right is divided into the right of states, of nations, and of citizens of the world. Kant's theory of punishment is original and important. He bases it not upon prudential regard for the protection of society, or the deterrence or reformation of the criminal, but upon the exalted idea of retaliation (*jus talionis*), which demands that everyone should meet with what his deeds deserve: Eye for eye, life for life. In *politics* Kant favors democratic theories, though less decidedly than Rousseau and Fichte. As he followed with interest the efforts after freedom manifested in the American and French Revolutions, so he opposed an hereditary nobility as a hindrance to the natural equality of rights, and demanded freedom for the public expression of opinion as the surest means of guarding against revolutions. The only legitimate form of the state is the republican, *i.e.*, that in which the executive power is separated from the legislative power, in contrast to despotism, where they are united in one hand. The best guaranty for just government and civil liberty is offered by constitutional monarchy, in which the people through its representatives exercises the legislative power, the sovereign the executive power, and judges chosen by the people the judicial power. The contract from which we may conceive the state to have arisen is not to be regarded as an historical fact, but as a rational idea or rule, by which we may judge whether the laws are just or not: that which the people as a whole cannot prescribe for itself, this cannot be prescribed for it by the ruler (cf. p. 235). That there is a constant progress—not only of individuals, but—of the race, not merely in technical and intellectual, but also in moral respects, is supported both by rational grounds (without faith in such progress we could not fulfill our duty as co-laborers in it) and by experiential grounds (above all, the unselfish sympathy which all the world gave to the French Revolution); and the never-ending complaint that the times are growing worse proves only that mankind is continually setting up stricter standards for itself. The beginning of *history* is to be placed at the point where man passes out of the condition of innocence, in which instinct rules, and begins to subdue nature, which hitherto he has obeyed. The goal of history, again, is the establishment of the perfect form of the state. Nature itself co-operates with freedom in the gradual transformation of the state based on necessity *(Notstaat)* into a rational state, inasmuch as selfish competition and the commercial spirit require peace, order, and justice for their own security and help to bring them about. And so, further, we need not doubt that humanity will constantly draw nearer to the ideal condition of everlasting peace among the nations (guaranteed by a league of states which shall as a mediator settle disputes between individual states), however impracticable the idea may at present appear.

If the bold declaration of Fortlage, that in Kant the system of absolute truth appeared, is true of any one part of his philosophy, it is true of the practical part, in which Christian morality has found its scientific expression. If we may justly complain that on the basis of his sharp distinction between legality and morality, between legal duty and virtue-duty, Kant took into account only the legal side of the institutions of marriage and of the state, overlooking the fact that besides these they have a moral importance and purpose, if we may demand a social ethic as a supplement to his ethics, which is directed to the duties of the individual alone, yet these and other well-founded desiderata may be attained by slight corrections and by the addition of another story to the Kantian edifice, while the foundations are still retained. The bases are immovable. Autonomy, absolute oughtness, the formal character of the law of reason, and the incomparable worth of the pure, disinterested disposition—these are the corner stones of the Kantian, nay, of all morals.

%3. Theory of the Beautiful and of Ends in Nature.%

We now know the laws which the understanding imposes upon nature and those which reason imposes upon the will. If there is a field in which to be (*Sein*) and ought to be (*Sollen*), nature and freedom, which we have thus far been forced to consider antithetical, are reconciled—and that there is such a field is already deducible from the doctrine of the religious postulates (as practical truths or assumptions concerning what is, in behalf of what ought to be), and from the hints concerning a progress in history (in which both powers co-operate toward a common goal)—then the source of its laws is evidently to be sought in that faculty which mediates alike between understanding and reason and between knowing and feeling: in *Judgment*, as the higher faculty of feeling. Judgment, in the general sense, is the faculty of thinking a particular as contained in a universal, and exercises a twofold function: as "determinant" judgment it subsumes the particular under a given universal (a law), as "reflective" it seeks the universal for a given particular. Since the former coincides with the understanding, we are here concerned only with the reflective judgment, judgment in the narrower sense, which does not cognize objects, but judges them, and this according to the principle of purposiveness.[1]

[Footnote 1: The universal laws springing from the understanding, to which every nature must conform to become an object of experience for us, determine nothing concerning the particular form of the given reality; we cannot deduce the special laws of nature from them. Nevertheless the nature of our cognitive faculty does not allow us to accept the empirical manifoldness of our world as contingent, but impels us to regard it as purposive or adapted to our knowledge, and to look upon these special laws as if an intelligence had given them in order to make a system of experience possible.]

This, in turn, is of two kinds. An object is really or *objectively* purposive (perfect) when it corresponds to its nature or its determination, formally or *subjectively* purposive (beautiful) when it is conformed to the nature of our cognitive faculty. The perception of purpose is always accompanied by a feeling of pleasure; in the first case, where the pleasure is based on a concept of the object, it is a logical satisfaction, in the second, where it springs only from the harmony of the object with our cognitive powers, aesthetic satisfaction. The objects of the teleological and the aesthetic judgment, the purposive and the beautiful products of nature and art, constitute the desired intermediate field between nature and freedom; and here again the critical question comes up, How, in relation to these, synthetic judgments *a priori* are possible?

%(a) Esthetic Judgment.%—The formula holds of Kant's aesthetics as well as of his theoretical and practical philosophy, that his aim is to overcome the opposition between the empirical and the rationalistic theories, and to find a middle course of his own between the two extremes. Neither Burke nor Baumgarten satisfied him. The English aesthetics was sensational, the German, *i.e.*, that of the Wolffian school, rationalistic. The former identified the beautiful with the agreeable, the latter identified it with the perfect or with the conformity of the object to its concept; in the one case, aesthetic appreciation is treated as sensuous pleasure, in the other, it is treated as a lower, confused kind of knowledge, its peculiar nature being in both cases overlooked. In opposition to the sensualization of aesthetic appreciation, its character as judgment must be maintained; and in opposition to its rationalization, its character as feeling. This relation of the Kantian aesthetics to that of his predecessors explains both its fundamental tendency and the elements in it which appear defective and erroneous. In any case, Kant shows himself in this field also an unapproachable master of careful analysis.

The first task of aesthetics is the careful distinction of its object from related phenomena. The beautiful has points of contact with the agreeable, the good, the perfect, the useful, and the true. It is distinguished from the true by the fact that it is not an object of knowledge, but of satisfaction. If we inquire further into the difference between the satisfaction in the beautiful and the satisfaction in the agreeable, in the good (in itself), and in the (good for something, as a means, or in the) useful, which latter three have this in common, that they are objects of appetition—of sensuous want, of moral will, of prudential desire—it becomes evident that the beautiful pleases through its mere representation (that is, independently of the real existence of the object), and that the delight in the beautiful is a contemplative pleasure. It is for contemplation only, not to be sensuously enjoyed nor put to practical use; and, further, its production is not a universal duty. Sensuous, prudential, or moral appetition has always an "interest" in the actual existence of the object; the beautiful, on the other hand, calls forth a disinterested satisfaction.

According to quality the beautiful is the object of a disinterested, free (bound by no interest), and sportive satisfaction. According to quantity and modality the judgment of taste claims universal and necessary validity, without this being based upon concepts. This posits further differences between the beautiful and the agreeable and the good. The good also pleases universally, but it pleases through concepts; the agreeable as well as the beautiful pleases without a concept, but it does not please universally.

That which pleases the reason through the concept is good; that which pleases the senses in sensation is agreeable. That which pleases *universally and necessarily without a concept* is beautiful. Moral judgment demands the assent of all, and its universal validity is demonstrable. The judgment concerning the agreeable is not capable of demonstration, but neither does it pretend to possess universal validity; we readily acknowledge that what is pleasant to one need not be so to every other man. In regard to the beautiful, on the contrary, we do not content ourselves with saying that tastes differ, but we expect it to please all. We expect everyone to assent to our judgment of taste, although it is able to support itself by no proofs.

Here there is a difficulty: since the judgment of taste does not express a characteristic of the object, but a state of mind in the observer, a feeling, a satisfaction, it is purely subjective; and yet it puts forth a claim to be universally communicable. The difficulty can be removed only on the assumption of a common aesthetic sense, of a corresponding organization of the powers of representation in all men, which yields the common standard for the pleasurableness of the impression. The agreeable appeals to that in man which is different in different individuals, the beautiful to that which functions alike in all; the former addresses itself to the passive sensibility, the latter to the active judgment. The agreeable—because of the non-calculable differences in our sensuous inclinations, which are in part conditioned by bodily states—possesses no universality whatever, the good possesses an objective, and the beautiful a subjective universality. The judgment concerning the agreeable has an empirical, that concerning the beautiful an *a priori*, determining ground: in the former case, the judgment follows the feeling, in the latter, it precedes it.

An object is considered beautiful (for, strictly speaking, we may say only this, not that it is beautiful) when its form puts the powers of the human mind in a state of harmony, brings the intuitive and rational faculties into concordant activity, and produces an agreeable proportion between the imagination and the understanding. In giving the occasion for an harmonious play of the cognitive activities (that is, for an easy combination of the manifold into unity) the beautiful object is purposive for us, for our function of apprehension; it is—here we obtain a determination of the judgment of taste from the standpoint of relation—*purposive without a definite purpose*. We know perfectly well that a landscape which attracts us has not been specially arranged for the purpose of delighting us, and we do not wish to find in a work of art anything of an intention to please. An object is perfect when it is purposive for itself (corresponds to its concept); useful when it is purposive for our desire (corresponds to a practical intention of man); beautiful when the arrangement of its parts is purposive for the relation between the fancy and understanding of the beholder (corresponds in an unusual degree to the conditions of our apprehension). Perfection is internal (real, objective) purposiveness, and utility is external purposiveness, both for a definite purpose; beauty, on the other hand, is purposiveness without a purpose, formal, subjective purposiveness. The beautiful pleases by its mere form. The satisfaction in the perfect is of a conceptual or intellectual kind, the satisfaction in the beautiful, emotional or aesthetic in character.

The combination of these four determinations yields an exhaustive definition of the beautiful: The beautiful is that which universally and necessarily arouses disinterested satisfaction by its mere form (purposiveness without the representation of a purpose).

Since the pleasurableness of the beautiful rests on the fact that it establishes a pleasing harmony between the imagination and the understanding, hence between sensuous and intellectual apprehension, the aesthetic attitude is possible only in sensuous-rational beings. The agreeable exists for the animal as well, and the good is an object of approval for pure spirits; but the beautiful exists for humanity alone. Kant succeeded in giving very delicate and felicitous verbal expression to these distinctions: the agreeable gratifies *(vergnügt)* and excites inclination *(Neigung)*; the good is approved *(gebilligt)* and arouses respect *(Achtung)*; the beautiful "pleases" *(gefällt)* and finds "favor" *(Gunst)*.

In the progress of the investigation the principle that beauty depends on the form alone, and that the concept, the purpose, the nature of the object is not taken into account at all in aesthetic judgment, experiences limitation. In its full strictness this applies only to a definite and, in fact, a subordinate division of the beautiful, which Kant marks off under the name of pure or *free* beauty. With this he contrasts *adherent* beauty, as that which presupposes a generic concept to which its form must correspond and which it must adequately present. Too much a purist not to mark the coming in of an intellectual pleasure as a beclouding of the "purity" of the aesthetic satisfaction, he is still just enough to admit the higher worth of adherent beauty. For almost the whole of artificial beauty and a considerable part of natural beauty belong to this latter division, which we to-day term ideal and characteristic beauty. Examples of free or purely formal beauty are tapestry patterns, arabesques, fountains, flowers, and landscapes, the pleasurableness of which rests simply on the proportion of their form and relations, and not upon their conformity to a presupposed significance and determination of the thing. A building, on the contrary—a dwelling, a summer-house, a temple—is considered beautiful only when we perceive in it not merely harmonious relations of the parts one to another, but also an agreement between the form and the purpose or generic concept: a church must not look like a chalet. Here the external form is compared with an inner nature, and harmony is required between form and content. Adherent beauty is significant and expressive beauty, which, although the satisfaction in it is not "purely" aesthetic, nevertheless stands higher than pure beauty, because it gives to the understanding also something to think, and hence busies the whole spirit.

The analytical investigations concerning the nature of the beautiful receive a valuable supplement in the classical definition of genius. Kant gives two definitions of productive talent, one formal and one genetic.

Natural beauty is a beautiful thing; artificial beauty, a beautiful representation of a thing. The gift of agreeably presenting a thing which in itself, perhaps, is ugly, is called taste. To judge of the beautiful it is sufficient to possess taste, but for its production there is still another talent needed, spirit or genius. For an art product can fulfill the demands of taste and yet not aesthetically satisfy; while formally faultless, it may be spiritless.

While beautiful nature looks as though it were art (as though it were calculated for our enjoyment), beautiful art should resemble nature, must not appear to be intentional though, no doubt, it is so, must show a careful but not an overnice adherence to rules (*i.e.*, not one which fetters the powers of the artist). This is the case when the artist bears the rule in himself, that is, when he is gifted. Genius is the innate disposition (through) which (nature) gives rules to art; its characteristics are originality, exemplariness, and unreflectiveness. It does not produce according to definite rules which can be learned, but it is a law in itself, it is original. It creates instinctively without consciousness of the rule, and cannot describe how it produces its results. It creates typical works which impel others to follow, not to imitate. It is only in art that there are geniuses, *i.e.*, spirits who produce that which absolutely cannot be learned, while the great men of science differ only in degree, not in kind, from their imitators and pupils, and that which they discover can be learned by rule.

This establishes the criteria by which genius may be recognized. If we ask by what psychological factors it is produced the answer is as follows: Genius presupposes a certain favorable relation between imagination and reason. Genius is the faculty of aesthetic Ideas, but an aesthetic Idea is a representation of the imagination which animates the mind, which adds to a concept of the understanding much of ineffable thought, much that belongs to the concept but which cannot be comprehended in a definite concept. With the aid of this idea Kant solves the antinomy of the aesthetic judgment. The thesis is: The judgment of taste is not based upon concepts; for otherwise it would admit of controversy (would be determinable by proofs). The antithesis is: It is based upon concepts; for otherwise we could not contend about it (endeavor to obtain assent). The two principles are reconcilable, for "concept" is understood differently in the two cases. That which the thesis rightly seeks to exclude from the judgment of beauty is the determinate concept of the understanding; that which the antithesis with equal justice pronounces indispensable is the indeterminate concept, the aesthetic Idea.

The freest play is afforded the imagination by poetry, the highest of all arts, which, with rhetoric ("insidious," on account of its earnest intention to deceive), forms the group termed arts of speech. To the class of formative arts belong architecture, sculpture, and painting as the art of design. A third group, the art of the beautiful play of sensations, includes painting as the art of color, and music, which as a "fine" art is placed immediately after poetry, as an "agreeable" art at the very foot of the list, and as the play of tone in the vicinity of the entertaining play of fortune [games of chance] and the witty play of thought. The explanation of the comic (the ludicrous is based, according to Kant, on a sudden transformation of strained expectation into nothing) lays great (indeed exaggerated) weight on the resulting physiological phenomena, the bodily shock which heightens vital feeling and favors health, and which accompanies the alternating tension and relaxation of the mind.

Besides free and adherent beauty, there is still a third kind of aesthetic effect, the Sublime. The beautiful pleases by its bounded form. But also the boundless and formless can exert aesthetic effect: that which is great beyond all comparison we judge sublime. Now this magnitude is either extensive in space and time or intensive greatness of force or power; accordingly there are two forms of the sublime. That phenomenon which mocks the power of comprehension possessed by the human imagination or surpasses every measure of our intuition, as the ocean and the starry heavens, is mathematically sublime. That which overcomes all conceivable resistance, as the terrible forces of nature, conflagrations, floods, earthquakes, hurricanes, thunderstorms, is dynamically sublime or mighty. The former is relative to the cognitive, the latter to the appetitive faculty. The beautiful brings the imagination and the understanding into accord; by the sublime the fancy is brought into a certain favorable relation, not directly to be termed harmony, with reason. In the one case there arose a restful, positively pleasurable mood; here a shock is produced, an indirect and negative pleasure proceeding from pain. Since the sublime exceeds the functional capability of our sensuous representations and does violence to the imagination, we first feel small at the sight of the absolutely great, and incapable of compassing it with our sensuous glance. The sensibility is not equal to the impression; this at first seems contrary to purpose and violent. This humiliating impression, however, is quickly followed by a reaction, and the vital forces, which were at first checked, are stimulated to the more lively activity. Moreover, it is the sensuous part of man which is humbled and the spiritual part that is exalted: the overthrow of sensibility becomes a triumph for reason. The sight of the sublime, that is, awakens the *Idea of the unconditioned, of the infinite*. This Idea can never be adequately presented by an intuition, but can be aroused only by the inadequacy of all that is sensuous to present it; the infinite is presented through the impossibility of presenting it. We cannot intuit the infinite, but we can think it. In comparison with reason (as the faculty of Ideas, the faculty of thinking the infinite) even the greatest thing that can be given in the sense-world appears small; reason is the absolutely great. "That is sublime the mere ability to think which proves a faculty of the mind surpassing every standard of sense." "That is sublime which pleases immediately through its opposition to the interest of the senses." The conflict between phantasy and reason, the insufficiency of the former for the attainment of the rational Idea, makes us conscious of the superiority of reason. Just because we feel small as sensuous beings we feel great as rational beings. The pleasure (related to the moral feeling of respect and, like this, mingled with a certain pain) which accompanies this consciousness of inner greatness is explained by the fact that the imagination, in acknowledging reason superior, places itself in the appropriate and purposive relation of subordination. It is evident from the foregoing that the truly sublime is reason, the moral nature of man, his predisposition and destination, which point beyond the present world. Schiller declares that "in space the sublime does not dwell," and Kant says, "Sublimity is contained in none of the things of nature, but only in our mind, in so far as we are conscious of being superior to nature within us and without us." Nevertheless, since in this contemplation we fix our thoughts entirely on the object without reflecting on ourselves, we transfer the admiration of right due to the reason and its Idea of the infinite by subreption to the object by which the Idea is occasioned, and call the object itself sublime, instead of the mood which it wakes in us.

If the sublime marks the point where the aesthetic touches on the boundary of the moral, the beautiful is also not without some relation to the good. By showing the agreement of sensibility and reason, which is demanded by the moral law, realized in aesthetic intuition (as a voluntary yielding of the imagination to the legitimacy of the understanding), it gives us the inspiring consciousness that the antithesis is reconcilable, that the rational can be presented in the sensuous, and so becomes a "symbol of the good."

%(b) Teleological Judgment.%—Teleological judgment is not knowledge, but a way of looking at things which comes into play where the causal or mechanical explanation fails us. This is not the case if the purposiveness is external, relative to its utility for something else. The fact that the sand of the sea-shore furnishes a good soil for the pine neither furthers nor prevents a causal knowledge of it. Only inner purposiveness, as it is manifested in the products of organic nature, brings the mechanical explanation to a halt. Organisms are distinguished above inorganic forms by the fact that of themselves they are at once cause and effect, that they are self-productive and this both as a species (the oak springs from the acorn, and in its turn bears acorns) and as individuals (self-preservation, growth, and the replacement of dying parts by new ones), and also by the fact that the reciprocally productive parts are in their form and their existence all conditioned by the whole. This latter fact, that the whole is the determining ground for the parts, is perfectly obvious in the products of human art. For here it is the representation of the whole (the idea of the work desired) which as the ground precedes the existence and the form of the parts (of the machine). But where is the subject to construct organisms according to its representations of ends? We may neither conceive nature itself as endowed with forces acting in view of ends, nor a praetermundane intelligence interfering in the course of nature. Either of these suppositions would be the death of natural philosophy: the hylozoist endows matter with a property which conflicts with its nature, and the theist oversteps the boundary of possible experience. Above all, the analogy of the products of organic nature with the products of human technique is destroyed by the fact that machines do not reproduce themselves and their parts cannot produce one another, while the organism organizes itself.

For our discursive understanding an interaction between the whole and the parts is completely incomprehensible. We understand when the parts precede the whole (mechanically) or the representation of the whole precedes the parts (teleologically); but to think the whole itself (not the Idea thereof) as the ground of the parts, which is demanded by organic life, is impossible for us. It would have been otherwise if an intuitive understanding had been bestowed upon us. For a being possessing intellectual intuition the antithesis between possibility and actuality, between necessity and contingency, between mechanism and teleology, would disappear along with that between thought and intuition. For such a being everything possible (all that it thinks) would be at the same time actual (present for intuition), and all that appears to us contingent—intentionally selected from several possibilities and in order to an end—would be necessary as well; with the whole would be given the parts corresponding thereto, and consequently natural mechanism and purposive connection would be identical, while for us, to whom the intuitive understanding is denied, the two divide. Hence the teleological view is a mere form of human representation, a subjective principle. We may not say that a mechanical origin of living beings is impossible, but only that we are unable to understand it. If we knew how a blade of grass or a frog sprang from mechanical forces, we would also be in a position to produce them.

The antinomy of the teleological judgment—thesis: all production of material things and their forms must be judged to be possible according to merely mechanical laws; antithesis: some products of material nature cannot be judged to be possible according to merely mechanical laws, but to judge them requires the causality of final causes—is insoluble so long as both propositions are taken for constitutive principles; but it is soluble when they are taken as regulative principles or standpoints for judgment. For it is in no wise contradictory, on the one hand, to continue the search for mechanical causes as far as this is in any way possible, and, on the other, clearly to recognize that, at last, this will still leave a remainder which we cannot make intelligible without calling to our aid the concept of ends. Assuming that it were possible to carry the explanation of life from life, from ancestral organisms (for the *generatio aequivoca* is an absurd theory) so far that the whole organic world should represent one great family descended from one primitive form as the common mother, even then the concept of final causes would only be pushed further back, not eliminated: the origin of the first organization will always resist mechanical explanation. Besides this mission of putting limits to causal derivation and of filling the gap in knowledge by a necessary, although subjective, way of looking at things, the Idea of ends has still another, the direct promotion of knowledge from efficient causes through the discovery of new causal problems. Thus, for example, physiology owes the impulse to the discovery of previously unnoticed mechanical connections (cf. also p. 382 note) to the question concerning the purpose of organs. As doctrines mechanism and teleology are irreconcilable and impossible; as rules or maxims of inquiry they are compatible, and the one as indispensable as the other.

After the problem of life, which is insoluble by means of the mechanical explanation, has necessitated the application of the concept of ends, the teleological principle must, at least by way of experiment, be extended to the whole of nature. This consideration culminates in the position that man, as the subject of morality, must be held to be the final aim of the world, for it is only in regard to a moral being that no further inquiry can be raised as to the purpose of its existence. It also repeats the moral argument for the existence of a supreme reason, thus supplementing physico-theology, which is inadequate to the demonstration of one absolutely perfect Deity; so that the third *Critique*, like the two preceding, concludes with the Idea of God as an object of practical faith.

* * * * *

There are three original and pregnant pairs of thoughts which cause Kant's name to shine in the philosophical sky as a star of the first magnitude: the demand for a critique of knowledge and the proof of *a priori* forms of knowledge; the moral autonomy and the categorical imperative; the regulative validity of the Ideas of reason and the practical knowledge of the transcendent world. No philosophical theory, no scientific hypothesis can henceforth avoid the duty of examining the value and legitimacy of its conclusions, as to whether they keep within the limits of the competency of human reason; whether Kant's determination of the origin and the limits of knowledge may count on continued favor or not, the fundamental critical idea, that reflection upon the nature and range of our cognitive faculty is indispensable, retains its validity for all cases and makes an end of all philosophizing at random.[1] No ethical system will with impunity pass by the autonomous legislation of reason and the unconditional imperative (the admonition of conscience translated into conceptual language): the nature and worth of moral will will be everywhere sought in vain if they are not recognized where Kant has found them—in the unselfish disposition, in that maxim which is fitted to become a general law for all rational beings. The doctrine of the Ideas, finally, reveals to us, beyond the daylight of phenomenal knowledge, the starlit landscape of another mode of looking at things,[2] in which satisfaction is afforded for the hitherto unmet wishes of the heart and demands of the reason.

[Footnote 1: "*Reason* consists just in this, that we are able to give account of all our concepts, opinions, and assertions, either on objective or subjective grounds."]

[Footnote 2: Those who regard all future metaphysics as refuted by the Critique of Reason are to be referred to the positive side of the Kantian doctrine of Ideas. Kant admits that the mechanical explanation does not satisfy reason, and that, besides it, a judgment according to Ideas is legitimate. When, therefore, the speculation of the constructive school gives an ideal interpretation of the world, it may be regarded as an extended application of "regulative principles," which exceeds its authority only when it professes to be "objective knowledge."]

The effect of the three *Critiques* upon the public was very varied. The first great work excited alarm by the sharpness of its negations and its destruction of dogmatic metaphysics, which to its earliest readers appeared to be the core of the matter; Kant was for them the universal destroyer. Then the Science of Knowledge brought into prominence the positive, boldly conquering side, the investigation of the conditions of empirical knowledge. In later times the endeavor has been made to do justice to both sides, but, in opposition to the overbold procedure of the constructive thinkers, who had fallen into a revived dogmatism, more in the spirit of caution and resignation. The second great work aroused glowing enthusiasm: "Kant is no mundane luminary," writes Jean Paul in regard to the *Critique of Practical Reason*, "but a whole solar system shining at once." The third, because of its subject and by its purpose of synthetic reconciliation between fields heretofore sharply separated, gained the sympathy of our poet-heroes Schiller and Goethe, and awakened in a young, speculative spirit Ideas for a Philosophy of Nature. Schelling reclaimed the intuitive understanding, which Kant had problematically attributed to the primal spirit, as the property of the philosopher, after Fichte had drawn attention to the fact that the consciousness of the categorical imperative, which Kant had not thoroughly investigated, could be nothing else than intellectual intuition, because in it knowing and doing coincide. Fichte, however, does not derive the material for his system from the *Critique of Judgment*, though he also had a high appreciation of it, but from the two earlier *Critiques*, the fundamental conceptions of which he—following the hint that practical and theoretical reason are only different applications of one and the same reason—brings into the closest connection. He unites the central idea of the practical philosophy, the freedom and autonomous legislation of the will, with the leading principle of the theoretical philosophy, the spontaneity of the understanding, under the original synthesis of the pure ego, in order to deduce from the activity of the ego not only the *a priori* forms of knowledge, but also, rejecting the thing in itself, the whole content of empirical consciousness. The thought which intervenes between the Kantian Critique of Reason and the development of thoroughgoing idealism by Fichte, with its criticisms of and additions to the former and its preparation for the latter, may be glanced at in a few supplementary pages.

%4. From Kant to Fichte.%

To begin with the works which aided in the extension and recognition of the Kantian philosophy, besides Kant's *Prolegomena*, the following stand in the front rank: *Exposition of the Critique of Pure Reason*, by the Königsberg court preacher, Johannes Schulz, 1784; the flowing *Letters concerning the Kantian Philosophy*, by K.L. Reinhold in Wieland's *Deutscher Merkur*, 1786-87; and the *Allgemeine Litteraturzeitung*, in Jena, founded in 1785, and edited by the philologist Schütz and the jurist Hufeland, which offered itself as the organ of the new doctrine. Jena became the home and principal stronghold of Kantianism; while by the beginning of the nineteenth century almost all German chairs belonged to it, and the non-philosophical sciences as well received from it stimulation and guiding ideas.

In the camp of the enemy there was no less of activity. The Wolffian, Eberhard of Halle, founded a special journal for the purpose of opposing the Kantian philosophy: the *Philosophisches Magazin*, 1789, continued from 1792 as the *Philosophisches Archiv*. The Illumination collected its forces in the *Philosophische Bibliothek*, edited by Feder and Meiners. Nicolai waved the banner of common sense in the *Allgemeine deutsche Bibliothek*, and in satirical romances, and was handled as he deserved by the heroes of poetry and philosophy (cf. the *Xenien* of Goethe and Schiller, Kant's *Letter on Bookmaking*, and Fichte's cutting disposal of him, *Nicolai's Life and Peculiar Opinions*). The attacks of the faith-philosophers have been already noticed (pp. 310-314).

The advance from Kant to Fichte was preparing alike among friends and enemies, and this in two points. The demand was in part for a formal complement (a first principle from which the Kantian results could be deduced, and by which the dualism of sense and understanding could be overcome), in part for material correction (the removal of the thing in itself) and development (to radical idealism). Karl Leonhard Reinhold (born at Vienna in 1758; fled from a college of the St. Barnabite order, 1783; in 1787-94 professor in Jena, and then as the successor of Tetens in Kiel, where he died in 1823) undertook the former task in his *Attempt at a New Theory of the Human Faculty of Representation*, 1789. Kant's classical theory of the faculty of cognition requires for its foundation a theory of the faculty of representation, or an elementary philosophy, which shall take for its object the deduction of the several functions of reason (intuition, concept, Idea) from the original activity of representation. The Kantian philosophy lacks a first principle, which, as first, cannot be demonstrable, but only a fact immediately evident and admitted by everyone. The primal fact, which we seek, is consciousness. No one can dispute that every representation contains three things: the subject, the object, and, between the two, the activity of representation. Accordingly the principle of consciousness runs: "The representation is distinguished in consciousness from the represented [object] and the representing [subject], and is referred to both." From this first principle Reinhold endeavors to deduce the well-known principles of the material manifold given by the action of objects, and the forms of representation spontaneously produced by the subject, which combine this manifold into unity. When, a few years later, Fichte's Science of Knowledge brilliantly succeeded in bridging the gap between sense and understanding by means of a first principle, thus accomplishing what Reinhold had attempted, the latter became one of his adherents, only to attach himself subsequently to Jacobi, and then to Bardili (*Outlines of Logic*, 1800), and to end with a verbal philosophy lacking both in influence and permanence.

In Reinhold's elementary philosophy the thing in itself was changed from a problematical, negative, merely limiting concept into a positive element of doctrine. Objections were raised against Kantianism, as thus dogmatically modified in the direction of realism, by Schulze, Maimon, and Beck—by the first for purposes of attack, by the second in order to further development, and by the third with an exegetical purpose. Gottlob Ernst Schulze, professor in Helmstädt, and from 1810 in Göttingen, in his *Aenesidemus* (1792, published anonymously), which was followed later by psychological works, defended the skeptical position in opposition to the Critique of Reason. Hume's skepticism remains unrefuted by Kant and Reinhold. The thing in itself, which is to produce the material of representation by affecting the senses, is a self-contradictory idea. The application of the category of cause to things in themselves violates the doctrine that the latter are unknowable and that the use of the pure concepts of the understanding beyond the sphere of experience is inadmissible. The transcendental philosophy has never proved that the ground of the material of representation cannot, just as the form thereof, reside in the subject itself.

Side by side with the anti-critical skepticism of Aenesidemus-Schulze, Salomon Maimon (died 1800; cf. Witte, 1876), who was highly esteemed by the greatest philosophers of his time, represents critical skepticism. With Reinhold he holds consciousness (as the combination of a manifold into objective unity) to be the common root of sensibility and understanding, and with Schulze, the concept of the thing in itself to be an imaginary or irrational quantity, a thought that cannot be carried out; it is not only unknowable, but unthinkable. That alone is knowable which we ourselves produce, hence only the form of representation. The matter of representation is "given," but this does not mean that it arises from the action of the thing in itself, but only that we do not know its origin. Understanding and sense, or spontaneity and receptivity, do not differ generically, but only in degree, viz., as complete and incomplete consciousness. Sensation is an incomplete consciousness, because we do not know how its object arises.

By the removal of the thing in itself Aenesidemus-Schulze sought to refute the Kantian theory and Maimon to improve it. Sigismund Beck (1761-1840), in his *Only Possible Standpoint from which the Critical Philosophy must be Judged*, 1796,[1] seeks by it to elucidate the Kantian theory, holding up idealism as its true meaning. In opposition to the usual opinion that a representation is true when it agrees with its object, he points to the impossibility of comparing the one with the other. Of objects out of consciousness we can know nothing; after the removal of all that is subjective there is nothing positive left of the representation. Everything in it is produced by us; the matter arises together with the form through the "original synthesis."

[Footnote 1: This book forms the third volume of his *Expository Abridgment of the Critical Writings of Professor Kant*; in the same year appeared the *Outlines of the Critical Philosophy*. Cf. on Beck, Dilthey in the *Archiv für Geschichte der Philosophie*, vol. ii., 1889, pp. 592-650.]

The last mentioned attempts to develop the Kantian philosophy were so far surpassed by Fichte's great achievement that they have received from their own age and from posterity a less grateful appreciation and remembrance than was essentially their due. A phenomenon of a different sort, which is also to be placed at the threshold between Kant and Fichte, but which forms rather a supplement to the noëtics and ethics of the latter than a link in the transition to them, has, on the contrary, gained an honorable position in the memory of the German people, viz., Schiller's aesthetics.[1] In its center stand the Kantian antithesis of sensibility and reason and the reconciliation of the two sides of human nature brought about by its occupation with the beautiful. Artistic activity or the play-impulse mediates between the lower, sensuous matter-impulse and the higher, rational form-impulse, and unites the, two in harmonious co-operation. Where appetite seeks after satisfaction, and where the strict idea of duty rules, there only half the man is occupied; neither lust nor moral worth is beautiful. In order that beauty and grace may arise, the matter-impulse and the form-impulse, or sensibility and reason, must manifest themselves uniformly and in harmony. Only when he "plays" is man wholly and entirely man; only through art is the development of humanity possible. The discernment of the fact that the beautiful brings into equilibrium the two fundamental impulses, one or the other of which preponderates in sensuous desire and in moral volition, does not of itself decide the relative rank of artistic and moral activity. The recognition of this mediating position of art may be connected with the view that it forms a transitional stage toward and a means of education for morality, as well as with the other, that in it human nature attains its completion. Evidence of both views can be found in Schiller's writings. At first he favors the Kantian moralism, which admits nothing higher than the good will, and sets art the task of educating men up to morality by ennobling their natural impulses. Gradually, however, aesthetic activity changes in his view from a preparation for morality into the ultimate goal of human endeavor. Peaceful reconciliation is of more worth than the spirit's hardly gained victory in the conflict with the sensibility; fine feeling is more than rational volition; the highest ideal is the beautiful soul, in which inclination not merely obeys the command of duty, but anticipates it.

[Footnote 1: The most important of Schiller's aesthetic essays are those *On Grace and Dignity*, 1793; *On Naïve and Sentimental Poetry*, 1795-96; and the *Letters on Aesthetic Education*, intermediate between them. Cf. Kuno Fischer, *Schiller als Philosoph*, 1858, 2d ed. (*Schillerschriften*, iii., iv.) 1891-92.]

CHAPTER X.

FICHTE.

Fichte is a Kantian in about the same sense that Plato was a Socratic. Instead of taking up and developing particular critical problems he makes the vivifying kernel, the soul of criticism, his own. With the self-activity of reason (as a real force and as a problem) for his fundamental idea, he outlines with magnificent boldness a new view of the world, in which the idealism concealed in Kant's philosophy under the shell of cautious limitations was roused into vigorous life, and the great Königsberger's noble words on the freedom, the position, and the power of the spirit translated from the language of sober foresight into that of vigorous enthusiasm. The world can be understood only from the standpoint of spirit, the spirit only from the will. The ego is pure activity, and all reality its product. Fichte's system is all life and action: its aim is not to mediate knowledge, but to summon the hearer and reader to the production of a new and pregnant fundamental view, in which the will is as much a participant as the understanding; it begins not with a concept or a proposition, but with a demand for action (posit thyself; do consciously what thou hast done unconsciously so often as thou hast called thyself I; analyze, then, the act of self-consciousness, and cognize in their elements the forces from which all reality proceeds); its God is not a completed absolute substance, but a self-realizing world-order. This inner vivacity of the Fichtean principle, which recalls the pure actuality of Aristotle's [Greek: nous] and the ceaseless becoming of Heraclitus, finds its complete parallel in the fact that, although he was wanting neither in logical consecutiveness nor in the talent for luminous and popular exposition, Fichte felt continually driven to express his ideas in new forms, and, just when he seemed to have succeeded in saying what he meant with the greatest clearness, again unsatisfied, to seek still more exact and evident renderings for his fundamental position, which proved so difficult to formulate.

The author of the *Wissenschaftslehre* was the son of a poor ribbon maker, and was born at Rammenau in Lusatia in 1762. The talents of the boy induced the Freiherr von Miltiz to give him the advantage of a good education. Fichte attended school in Meissen and in Pforta, and was a student of theology at the universities of Jena and Leipsic. While a tutor in Zurich he made the acquaintance of Lavater and Pestalozzi, as well as of his future wife, Johanna Rahn, a niece of Klopstock. Returning to Leipsic, his whole mode of thought was revolutionized by the Kantian philosophy, in which it was his duty to instruct a pupil. This gives to the mind, as his letters confess, an inconceivable elevation above all earthly things. "I have adopted a nobler morality, and, instead of occupying myself with things without me, have been occupied more with myself." "I now believe with all my heart in human freedom, and am convinced that only on this supposition duty and virtue of any kind are possible." "I live in a new world since I have read the *Critique of Practical Reason*. Things which I believed never could be proved to me, *e.g.*, the idea of an absolute freedom and duty, have been proved, and I feel the happier for it. It is inconceivable what reverence for humanity, what power this philosophy gives us, what a blessing it is for an age in which the citadels of morality had been destroyed, and the idea of duty blotted out from all the dictionaries!" A journey to Warsaw, whither he had been attracted by the expectation of securing a position as a private tutor, soon afforded him the opportunity of visiting at Königsberg the author of the system which had effected so radical a transformation in his convictions. His rapidly written treatise, *Essay toward a Critique of All Revelation*, attained the end to which its inception was due by gaining for its author a favorable reception from the honored master. Kant secured for Fichte a tutor's position in Dantzic, and a publisher for his maiden work. When this appeared, at Easter, 1792, the name of its author was by oversight omitted from the title page, together with the preface, which had been furnished after the rest of the book; and as the anonymous work was universally ascribed to Kant (whose religious philosophy was at this time eagerly looked for), the young writer became famous at a stroke as soon as the error was explained. A second edition was issued as early as the following year.

After his marriage in Zurich, where he had completed several political treatises (the address, *Reclamation of the Freedom of Thought from the Princes of Europe, who have hitherto suppressed it, Heliopolis in the Last Year of the Old Darkness*, and the two *Hefte, Contributions toward the Correction of the Public Judgment on the French Revolution*, 1793), Fichte accepted, in 1794, a call to Jena, in place of Reinhold, who had gone to Kiel, and whose popularity was soon exceeded by his own. The same year saw the birth of the *Wissenschaftslehre*. His stay in Jena was embittered by conflicts with the clergy, who took offense at his ethical lectures (*On the Vocation of the Scholar*) held on Sunday mornings (though not at an hour which interfered with church service), and with the students, who, after they had been untrue to their decision—which they had formed as a result of these lectures—to dissolve their societies or orders, gave vent to their spite by repeatedly smashing the windows of Fichte's residence. Accordingly he took leave of absence, and spent the summer of 1795 in Osmannstädt. The years 1796-98, in which, besides the two *Introductions to the Science of Knowledge*, the *Natural Right* and the *Science of Ethics* (one of the most all important works in German philosophical literature) appeared, mark the culmination of Fichte's famous labors. The so-called atheistic controversy[1] resulted in Fichte's departure from Jena. The *Philosophisches Journal*, which since 1797 had been edited by Fichte in association with Niethammer, had published an article by Magister Forberg, rector at Saalfeld, entitled "The Development of the Concept of Religion," and as a conciliating introduction to this a short essay by Fichte, "On the Ground of our Belief in a Divine Government of the World."[2] For this it was confiscated by the Dresden government on the charge of containing atheistical matter, while other courts were summoned to take like action. In Weimar hopes were entertained of an amicable adjustment of the matter. But when Fichte, after publishing two vindications[3] couched in vehement language, had in a private letter uttered the threat that he would answer with his resignation any censure proceeding from the University Senate, not only was censure for indiscretion actually imposed, but his (threatened) resignation accepted.

[Footnote 1: Cf. Karl August Hase, *Jenaisches Fichtebüchlein*, 1856.]

[Footnote 2: It is a mistake, Fichte writes here, referring to the conclusion of Forberg's article ("Is there a God? It is and remains uncertain," etc.), to say that it is doubtful whether there is a God or not. That there is a moral order of the world, which assigns to each rational individual his determined place and counts on his work, is most certain, nay, it is the ground of all other certitude. The living and operative moral order *(ordo ordinans)* is itself God; we need no other God, and can conceive no other. There is no ground in reason for going beyond this world order to postulate a particular being as its cause. Whoever ascribes personality and consciousness to this particular being makes it finite; consciousness belongs only to the individual, limited ego. And it is allowable to state this frankly and to beat down the prattle of the schools, in order that the true religion of joyous well-doing may lift up its head.]

[Footnote 3: *Appeal to the Public*, and *Formal Defense against the Charge of Atheism*, 1799. The first of these maintains that Fichte's standpoint and that of his opponents are related as duty and advantage, sensible and suprasensible, and that the substantial God of his accusers, to be derived from the sensibility, is, as personified fate, as the distributer of all happiness and unhappiness to finite beings, a miserable fetich.]

Going to Berlin, Fichte found a friendly government, a numerous public for his lectures, and a stimulating circle of friends in the romanticists, the brothers Schlegel, Tieck, Schleiermacher, etc. In the first years of his Berlin residence there appeared *The Vocation of Man. The Exclusive Commercial State*, 1800; *The Sun-clear Report to the Larger Public on the Essential Nature of the New Philosophy*, and the *Answer to Reinhold*, 1801. Three works, which were the outcome of his lectures and were published in the year 1806 (*Characteristics of the Present Age, The Nature of the Scholar, Way to the Blessed Life or Doctrine of Religion*), form a connected whole. In the summer of 1805 Fichte filled a professorship at Erlangen, and later, after the outbreak of the war, he occupied for a short time a chair at Königsberg, finding a permanent university position at the foundation of the University of Berlin in 1810. His glowing *Addresses to the German Nation*, 1808, which essentially aided in arousing the national spirit, have caused his name to live as one of the greatest of orators and most ardent of patriots in circles of the German people where his philosophical importance cannot be understood. His death in 1814 was also a result of unselfish labor in the service of the Fatherland. He succumbed to a nervous fever contracted from his wife, who, with self-sacrifice equal to his own, had shared in the care of the wounded, and who had brought the contagion back with her from the hospital. On his monument is inscribed the beautiful text, "The teachers shall shine as the brightness of the firmament, and they that turn many to righteousness as the stars that shine forever and ever." Forberg in his journal records this estimate: The leading trait in Fichte's character is his absolute integrity. All his words are weighty and important. His principles are stern and little modified by affability. The spirit of his philosophy is proud and courageous, one which does not so much lead as possess us and carry us along. His philosophemes are inquiries in which we see the truth arise before our eyes, and which just for this reason lay the foundations of science and conviction.

The philosopher's son, Immanuel Hermann Fichte (his own name was Johann Gottlieb), wrote a biography of his father (1830; 2d ed., 1862), and supervised the publication of both the *Posthumous Works* (1834-35, 3 vols.) and the *Collected Works* (1845-46, 8 vols.). The simple and luminous *Facts of Consciousness* of 1811, or 1817 (not the lecture of 1813 with the same title), is especially valuable as an introduction to the system. Among the many redactions of the *Wissenschaftslehre*, the epoch-making *Foundation of the whole Science of Knowledge*, 1794, with the two *Introductions to the Science of Knowledge*, 1797, takes the first rank, while of the practical works the most important are the *Foundation of Natural Right according to the Principles of the Science of Knowledge*, 1796, and the *System of the Science of Ethics according to the Principles of the Science of Knowledge*, 1798, and next to these the *Lectures on the Theory of the State*, 1820 (delivered in 1813).[1]

[Footnote 1: At the same time as J.H. Löwe's book *Die Philosophie Fichtes*, 1862, there appeared in celebration of the centenary of Fichte's birthyear, or birthday, a large number of minor essays and addresses by Friedrich Harms, A.L. Kym, Trendelenburg, Franz Hoffman, Karl Heyder, F.C. Lott, Karl Köstlin, J.B. Meyer, and others (cf. Reichlin-Meldegg in vol. xlii. of the *Zeitschrift für Philosophie*). Lasson has written, 1863, on Fichte's relation to Church and state, Zeller on Fichte as a political thinker (*Vorträge und Abhandlungen*, 1865), and F. Zimmer on his philosophy of religion. Among foreign works we may note Adamson's *Fichte*, 1881, and the English translations of several of Fichte's works by Kroeger [*Science of Knowledge*, 1868; *Science of Rights*, 1869—both also, 1889] and William Smith [*Popular Writings*, 4th ed., 1889; also Everett's *Fichte's Science of Knowledge* (Griggs's Philosophical Classics, 1884), and several translations in the *Journal of Speculative Philosophy*, including one of *The Facts of Consciousness*.—TR.]]

%1. The Science of Knowledge.%

%(a) The Problem.%—In Fichte's judgment Kant did not succeed in carrying through the transformation in thought which it was his aim to effect, because the age did not understand the spirit of his philosophy. This spirit, and with it the great service of Kant, consists in *transcendental idealism*, which by the doctrine that objects conform themselves to representations, not representations to objects, draws philosophy away from external objects and leads it back into ourselves. We have followed the letter, he thinks, instead of the spirit of Kant, and because of a few passages with a dogmatic ring, whose references to a given matter, the thing in itself, and the like, were intended only as preliminary, have overlooked the numberless others in which the contrary is distinctly maintained. Thus the interpreters of Kant, using their own prejudices as a criterion, have read into him exactly that which he sought to refute, and have made the destroyer of all dogmatism himself a dogmatist; thus in the Kantianism of the Kantians there has sprung up a marvelous combination of crude dogmatism and uncompromising idealism. Though such an absurd mingling of entirely heterogeneous elements may be excused in the case of interpreters and successors, who have had to construct for themselves the guiding principle of the whole from their study of the critical writings, yet we cannot assume it in the author of the system, unless we believe the *Critique of Pure Reason* the result of the strangest chance, and not the work of intellect. Two men only, Beck, the teacher of the Standpoint, and Jacobi, the clearest mind of the century, are to be mentioned with respect as having risen above the confusion of the time to the perception that Kant teaches idealism, that, according to him, the object is not given, but made.

Besides the perspicuity which would have prevented these misunderstandings, Fichte misses something further in Kant's work. Considered as a system Kant's expositions were incomplete; and, on his own confession, his aim was not to furnish the science itself, but only the foundation and the materials for it. Therefore, although the Kantian philosophy is established as far as its inner content is concerned, there is still need of earnest work to systematize the fragments and results which he gives into a firmly connected and impregnable whole. The *Wissenschaftslehre* takes this completion of idealism for its mission. It cannot solve the problem by a commentary on the Kantian writings, nor by the correction and addition of particulars, but only by restoring the whole at a stroke. He alone finds the truth who new creates it in himself, independently and in his own way. Thus Fichte's system contains the same view of the matter as the critical system—the author is aware, runs the preface to the programme, *On the Concept of the Science of Knowledge*, 1794, "that he never will be able to say anything at which Kant has not hinted, immediately or mediately, more or less clearly, before him,"—but in his procedure he is entirely independent of the Kantian exposition. We shall first raise the question, What in the Kantian philosophy is in need of completion? and, secondly, What method must be adopted in completing it?

Kant discusses the laws of intelligence when they are already applied to objects, without enlightening us concerning the ground of these laws. He derived the pure concepts (the laws of substantiality, of causality, etc.) from (logic, and thus mediately from) experience instead of deducing them from the nature of intelligence; similarly he never furnished this deduction for the forms of intuition, space and time. In order to understand that intelligence, and why intelligence, must act in just this way (must think just by means of these categories), we must prove, and not merely, with Kant, assert, that these functions or forms are really laws of thought—or, what amounts to the same thing, that they are conditions of self-consciousness. Again, even if it be granted that Kant has explained the properties and relations of things (that they appear in space and time, and that their accidents must be referred to substances), the question still remains unanswered, Whence comes the matter which is taken up into these forms? So long as the whole object is not made to arise before the eyes of the thinker, dogmatism is not driven out of its last corner. The thing in itself is, like the rest, only a thought in the ego. If thus the antithesis between the form and the matter of cognition undergoes modification, so, further, the allied distinction between understanding and sensibility must, as Reinhold accurately recognized, be reduced to a common principle and receptivity be conceived as self-limiting spontaneity. In his practical philosophy also Kant left much unfinished. The categorical imperative is susceptible of further deduction, it is not the principle itself, but a conclusion from the true principle, from the injunction to absolute *self-dependence on the part of reason*; moreover, the nature of our consciousness of the moral law must be more thoroughly discussed, and in order to gain a real, instead of a merely formal, ethics the relation of this law to natural impulse. Finally, Kant never discussed the foundation of philosophy as a whole, but always separated its theoretical from its practical side, and Reinhold also did nothing to remove this dualism. In short, some things that Kant only asserted or presupposed can and must be proved, some that he kept distinct must be united. In what way are both to be accomplished?

Since correct inferences from correct premises yield correct results, and correct inference is easy to secure, everything depends on the correct point of departure. If we neglect this and consider only the process and the results of inference, there are two consistent systems: the dogmatic or realistic course of thought, which seeks to derive representations from things; and the idealistic, which, conversely, seeks to derive being from thought. Now, no matter how consistently dogmatism may proceed (and when it does so it becomes, like the system of

Spinoza, materialism and fatalism or determinism, maintaining that all is nature, and all goes on mechanically; treats the spirit as a thing among others, and denies its metaphysical and moral independence, its immateriality and freedom), it may be shown to be false, because it starts from a false principle. Thought can never be derived from being, because it is not contained therein; from being only being can proceed, and never representation. Being, however, can be derived from thought, for consciousness is also being; nay, it is more than this, it is conscious being. And as consciousness contains both being and a knowledge of this being, idealism is superior to realism, because idealism includes the latter as a moment in itself, and hence can explain it, though it is not explicable by it. Dogmatism makes the mistake of going beyond consciousness or the ego, and working with empty, merely formal concepts. A concept is empty when nothing actual corresponds to it, or no intuition can be subsumed under it (here it is to be noted that, besides sensuous intuition, there is an intellectual intuition also; an example is found in the ego as a self-intuiting being). Philosophy, indeed, may abstract and must abstract, must rise above that which is given—for how could she explain life and particular knowledge if she assumed no higher standpoint than her object?—but true abstraction is nothing other than the separation of factors which in experience always present themselves together; it analyzes empirical consciousness in order to reconstruct it from its elements, it causes empirical consciousness to arise before our eyes, it is a pragmatic *history of consciousness*. Such abstraction, undertaken in order to a genetic consideration of the ego, does not go beyond experience, but penetrates into the depths of experience, is not transcendent, but transcendental, and, since it remains in close touch with that which is intuitable, yields a real philosophy in contrast to all merely formal philosophy.

These theoretical advantages of idealism are supplemented by momentous reasons of a practical kind, which determine the choice between the two systems, besides which none other is possible. The moral law says: Thou shalt be self-dependent. If I ought to be so I must be able to be so; but if I were matter I would not be able. Thus idealism proves itself to be the ethical mode of thought, while the opposite mode shows that those who favor it have not raised themselves to that independence of all that is external which is morally enjoined, for in order to be able to know ourselves free we must have made ourselves free.[1] Thus the philosophy which a man chooses depends on what sort of a man he is. If, on the other hand, the categorical imperative calls for belief in the reality of the external world and of other minds, this is nothing against idealism. For idealism does not deny the realism of life, but explains it as a necessary, though not a final, mode of intuition. The dogmatic mode of thought is merely an explanation from the standpoint of common consciousness, and for idealism, as the only view which is both scientifically and practically satisfactory, this explanation itself needs explaining. Realism and idealism, like natural impulse and moral will in the sphere of action, are both grounded in reason. But idealism is the true standpoint, because it is able to comprehend and explain the opposing theory, while the converse is not the case.

[Footnote 1: Cf. O. Liebmann (*Ueber den individuellen Beweis für die Freiheit des Willens p, 131. 1866*) "Here we discover the noteworthy point where theoretical and practical philosophy actually pass over into each other. For this principle results: In order to carry out the individual proof for the freedom of the will, I must do my duty."]

The nature, the goal, and the methods of the Science of Knowledge have now been determined. It is genuine, thoroughgoing idealism, which raises the Kantian philosophy to the rank of an evident science by deducing its premises from a first principle which is immediately certain, and by removing the twofold dualism of intuition and thought, of knowledge and volition, viz., by proving both contraries acts of one and the same ego. While Reinhold had sought a supreme truth as a fundamental principle of unity, without which the doctrine of knowledge would lack the systematic form essential to science, while Beck had interpreted the spirit of the Kantian philosophy in an idealistic sense, and Jacobi had demanded the elimination of the thing in itself, all these desires combined are fulfilled in Fichte's doctrine, and at the same time the results of the Critique of Reason are given that evidence which Aenesidemus-Schulze had missed in them. As an answer to the question, "How is knowledge brought about?" (as well the knowledge of common sense as that given in the particular sciences), "how is experience possible?", and as a construction of common consciousness as this manifests itself in life and in the particular sciences, Fichteanism adopts the name *Science of Knowledge*, being distinguished from the particular sciences by the fact that they discuss the voluntary, and it the necessary, representations or actions of the spirit. (The representation of a triangle or a circle is a free one, it may be omitted; the representation of space in general is a necessary one, from which it is impossible for us to abstract.) How does intelligence come to have sensations, to intuit space and time, and to form just such categories (thing and property, cause and effect, and not others quite different)? While Kant correctly described these functions of the intuiting and thinking spirit, and showed them actual, they must further be proven, be shown necessary or deduced. Deduced whence? From the "deed-acts" (*Thathandlungen*) of the ego which lie at the basis of all consciousness, and the highest of which are formulated in three principles.

%(b) The Three Principles.%—At the portal of the Science of Knowledge we are met not by an assertion, but by a summons—a summons to self-contemplation. Think anything whatever and observe what thou dost, and of necessity must do, in thinking. Thou wilt discover that thou dost never think an object without thinking thyself therewith, that it is absolutely impossible for thee to abstract from thine ego. And second, consider what thou dost when thou dost think thine "ego." This means to affirm or posit one's self, to be a subject-object. The nature of self-consciousness is the identity of the representing [subject] and the represented [object]. The pure ego is not a fact, but an original doing, the act of being for self (*Fürsichsein*), and the (philosophical, or—as seems to be the case according to some passages—even the common) consciousness of this doing an intellectual intuition; through this we become conscious of the deed-act which is ever (though unconsciously) performing. This is the meaning of the first of the principles: "The *ego* posits originally and absolutely its own being," or, more briefly: The ego posits itself; more briefly still: I am. The nature of the ego consists in positing itself as existing.[1] Since, besides this self-cogitation of the ego, an op-position is found among the facts of empirical consciousness (think only of the principle of contradiction), and yet, besides the ego, there is nothing which could be opposed, we must assume as a second principle: To the ego there is absolutely opposed a *non-ego*. These two principles must be united, and this can be accomplished only by positing the contraries (ego and non-ego), since they are both in the ego, as reciprocally limiting or partially sublating one another, that is, each as *divisible* (capable of quantitative determination). Accordingly the third principle runs: "The ego opposes in the ego a divisible non-ego to the divisible ego." From these principles Fichte deduces the three laws of thought, identity, contradiction, and sufficient reason, and the three categories of quality—reality, negation, and limitation or determination. Instead of following him in these labors, we may emphasize the significance of his view of the ego as pure activity without an underlying substratum, with which he carries dynamism over from the Kantian philosophy of nature to metaphysics. We must not conceive the ego as something which must exist before it can put forth its activities. Doing is not a property or consequence of being, but being is an accident and effect of doing. All substantiality is derivative, activity is primal; *being arises from doing*. The ego is nothing more than self-position; it exists not only for itself (*für sich*), but also through itself (*durch sich*).

[Footnote 1: The ego spoken of in the first of the principles, the ego as the object of intellectual intuition and as the ground and creator of all being, is, as the second *Introduction to the Science of Knowledge* clearly announces, not the individual, but the I-ness *(Ichheit)* (which is to be presupposed as the prius of the manifold of representation, and which is exalted above the opposition of subject and object), mentality in general, eternal reason, which is common to all and the same in all, which is present in all thinking and at the basis thereof, and to which particular persons stand related merely as accidents, as instruments, as special expressions, destined more and more to lose themselves in the universal form of reason. But, further still, a distinction must be made between the absolute ego as intuition (as the form of I-ness), from which the Science of Knowledge starts, and the ego as Idea (as the supreme goal of practical endeavor) with which it ends. In neither is the ego conceived as individual; in the former the I-ness is not yet determined to the point of individuality, in the latter individuality has disappeared, Fichte is right when he thinks it remarkable that "a system whose beginning and end and whole nature is aimed at forgetfulness of individuality in the theoretical sphere and denial of it in the practical sphere" should be "called egoism." And yet not only opponents, but even adherents of Fichte, as is shown by *Friedrich Schlegel's* philosophy of genius, have, by confusing the pure and the empirical ego, been guilty of the mistake thus censured. On the philosophy of the romanticists cf. Erdmann's *History*, vol. ii. §§ 314, 315; Zeller, p. 562 *seq*.; and R. Haym, *Die Romantische Schule*, 1870.]

The actions expressed in the three principles are never found pure in experience, nor do they represent isolated acts of the ego. Intelligence can think nothing without thinking itself therewith; it is equally impossible for it to think "I am" without at the same time thinking something else which is not itself; subject and object are inseparable. It is rather true that the acts of position described are one single, all-inclusive act, which forms only the first member in a connected system of pre-conscious actions, through which consciousness is produced, and the complete investigation of whose members constitutes the further business of the Science of Knowledge as a theory of the nature of reason. In this the Science of Knowledge employs a method which, by its rhythm of analysis and synthesis, development and reconciliation of opposites, became the model of Hegel's dialectic method. The synthesis described in the third principle, although it balances thesis and antithesis and unites them in itself, still contains contrary elements, in order to whose combination a new synthesis must be sought. In this, in turn, the analytic discovery and the synthetic adjustment of a contrariety is repeated, etc., etc. The original synthesis, moreover, prescribes a division of the inquiry into two parts, one theoretical and the other practical. For it contains the following principles: The ego posits itself as limited by the non-ego—it functions cognitively; and: The ego posits itself as determining the non-ego—it functions volitionally and actively.

%(c) The Theoretical Ego.%—In positing itself as determined by the non-ego, the ego is at once passive (affected by something other than itself) and active (it posits its own limitation). This is possible only as it posits reality in itself only in part, and transfers to the non-ego so much as it does not posit in itself. Passivity is diminished activity, negation of the totality of reality. From reflection on this relation between ego and non-ego spring the categories of reciprocal determination, of causality (the non-ego as the cause of the passion of the ego), and substantiality (this passion merely the self-limitation of the ego). The conflict between the causality of the non-ego (by which the ego is affected) and the substantiality of the ego (in which and the activity of which all reality is contained) is resolved only by the assumption of two activities (or, rather, of two opposite directions of one activity) in the ego, one of which (centrifugal, expansive) strives infinitely outward while the other (centripetal or contractile) sets a bound to the former, and drives the ego back into itself, whereupon another excursus follows, and a new limitation and return, etc. With every repetition of this double act of production and reflection a special class of representations arises. Through the first limitation of the in itself unlimited activity "sensation" arises (as a product of the "productive imagination"). Because the ego produces this unconsciously, it appears to be given, brought about by influence from without. The second stage, "intuition," is reached when the ego reflects on sensation, when it opposes to itself something foreign which limits it. Thirdly, by reflection on intuition an "image" of that which is intuited is constructed, and, as such, distinguished from a real thing to which the image corresponds; at this point the categories and the forms of intuition, space and time, appear, which thus arise along with the object.[1] The fourth stadium is "understanding," which steadies the fluctuating intuition into a concept, realizes the object, and looks upon it as the cause of the intuition. Fifthly, "judgment" makes its appearance as the faculty of free reflection and abstraction, or the power to consider a definite content or to abstract from it. As judgment is itself the condition of the bound reflection of the understanding, so it points in turn to its condition, to the sixth and highest stage of intelligence, "reason," by means of which we are able to abstract from all objects whatever, while reason itself, pure self-consciousness, is that from which abstraction is never possible. It is only in the highest stage that consciousness or a representation of representation takes place. And at the culmination of the theoretical ego the point of transition to the practical ego appears. Here the ego becomes aware that in positing itself as determined by the non-ego it has only limited itself, and therefore is itself the ground of the whole content of consciousness; here it apprehends itself as determining the non-ego or as acting, and recognizes as its chief mission to impress the form of the ego as far as possible on the non-ego, and ever to extend the boundary further.

[Footnote 1: The object is a product of the ego only for the observer, not for the observed ego itself, to which, from this standpoint of imagination, it appears rather as a thing in itself independent of the ego and affecting it. Further, it must so appear, because the ego, in its after reflection on its productive activity, and just by this reflection, transforms the productive action considered into a fixed and independent product found existing.]

The "deduction of representation" whose outline has just been given was the first example (often imitated in the school of Schelling and Hegel) of a *constructive psychology*, which, from the mission or the concept of the soul—in this case from the nature of self-consciousness—deduces the various psychical functions as a system of actions, each of which is in its place implied by the rest, as it in turn presupposes them. This is distinguished from the sensationalistic psychology, which is also genetic (cf. pp. 245-250), as well as from the mechanical or associational psychology, which likewise excludes the idea of an isolated coexistence of mental faculties, by the fact that it demands a new manifestation of the soul-ground in order to the ascent from one member of the series to the next higher. It is also distinguished from sensationalism by its teleological point of view. For no matter how much Fichte, too, may speak of the mechanism of consciousness, it is plain to the reader of the theoretical part of his system not only that he makes this mechanism work in the service of an end, but also that he finds its origin in purposive activity of the ego; while the practical part gives further and decisive confirmation of the fact. The danger and the defect of such a constructive treatment of psychology—as we may at once remark for all later attempts—lies in imagining that the task of mental science has been accomplished and all its problems solved when each particular activity of the ego has been assigned its mission and work for the whole, and its place in the system, without any indication of the means through which this destination can be fulfilled.

%(d) The Practical Ego.%—The deduction of representation has shown how (through what unconscious acts of the ego) the different stages of cognition, the three sensuous and the three intellectual functions of representation, come into being. It has proved incapable, however, of giving any account of the way in which the ego comes at one point to arrest its activity, which tends infinitely outward, and to turn it back upon itself. We know, indeed, that this first limitation, through which sensation arises, and on which as a basis the understanding, by continued reflection constructs the objective world, was necessary in order that consciousness and knowledge might arise. If the ego did not limit its infinite activity neither representation nor an objective world would exist. But why, then, are there such things as consciousness, representation, and a world? From the standpoint of the theoretical ego this problem, "Whence the original non-ego or opposition (*Anstoss*), which impels the ego back upon itself?" cannot be solved, since it is only through the opposition that it itself arises. The "deduction of the opposition," which the theoretical part of the Science of Knowledge did not furnish, is to be looked for from the practical part. The primacy of practical reason, already emphasized by Kant, gives us the answer: *The ego* limits itself and *is theoretical, in order to be practical.* The whole machinery of representation and the represented world exists only to furnish us the possibility of fulfilling our duty. We are intelligence in order that we may be able to be will.

Action, action—that is the end of our existence. Action is giving form to matter, it is the alteration or elaboration of an object, the conquest of an impediment, of a limitation. We cannot act unless we have something in, on, and against which to act. The world of sensation and intuition is nothing but a means for attaining our ethical destiny, it is "the material of our duty under the form of sense." The theoretical ego posits an object (*Gegenstand*) that the practical ego may experience resistance (*Widerstand*). No action is possible without a world as the object of action; no world is possible without a consciousness which represents it; no consciousness possible without reflection of the ego on itself; no reflection without limitation, without an opposition or non-ego. The *Anstoss* is deduced. The ego posits a limit (is theoretical) in order (as practical) to overcome it. Our duty is the only *per se (Ansich)* of the phenomenal world, the only truly real element in it: "Things are in themselves that which we ought to make of them." Objectivity exists only to be more and more sublated, that is, to be so worked up that the activity of the ego may in it become evident.—The same ground of explanation which reveals the necessity of an external nature enables us to understand why the one infinite ego (the universal life or the Deity, as Fichte puts it in his later works) divides into the many empirical egos or individuals, why it does not carry out its plan immediately, but through finite spirits as its organs. Action is possible only under the form of the individual, only in individuals are consciousness and morality possible. Without resistance, no action; without conflict, no morality. Individuality, it is true, is to be overcome and destroyed in moral endeavor; but in order to this it must have existed. Virtue is a conquest over external *and internal* nature.

A gradation of practical functions corresponding to the series of theoretical activities leads from feeling and striving (longing and desire) through the system of impulses (the impulse to representation or reflection, to production, to satisfaction) up to moral will or the impulse to harmony with self, which stands opposed to the natural impulses as the categorical imperative. The practical ego mediates between the theoretical and the absolute ego. The ego ought to be infinite and self-dependent, but finds itself finite and dependent on a non-ego—a contradiction which is resolved by the ego becoming practical, by the fact that in ever increasing measure it subdues nature to itself, and by such increasing extension of the boundary draws nearer and ever nearer to the realization of its destination, to become absolute ego.

%2. The Science of Ethics and of Right.%

The moral law demands the control of the sensuous impulse by the pure impulse. If the former aims at comfortable ease and enjoyment, the latter is directed toward satisfaction with one's self, to endeavor and self-dependence. (Enjoyment is inevitable, it is true, as satisfaction where any impulse whatever is carried out; only it must not form the end of action.) Morality is activity for its own sake, the radical evil—from which only a miracle can deliver us, but a miracle which we must ourselves perform—is inertness, lack of will to rise above the natural determinateness of the impulse of self-preservation to the clear consciousness of duty and of freedom. For the moral man there is no resting; each end attained becomes for him the impulse to renewed endeavor, each task fulfilled leads him to a fresh one. Become self-dependent, act autonomously, make thyself free; let every action have a place in a series, in the continuation of which the ego must become independent. To this formal and universal norm, again, there is added a special injunction for each individual. Each individual spirit has its definite mission assigned to it by the world-order: each ought to do that which it alone should and can do. Always fulfill thy moral vocation, thy special destination.[1] Or both in popular combination: Never act contrary to conscience.

[Footnote 1: Although Fichte was justly charged with surpassing even the abstractness of the Kantian ethics with his bald moral principle, the self-dependence of the ego, he deserves praise for having given ethics a concrete content of indisputable soundness and utility by his introduction of Jacobi's idea of purified individuality.]

The elevation to freedom is accomplished gradually. At first freedom consists only in the consciousness of the natural impulse, then follows a breaking away from this by means of maxims, which in the beginning are maxims of individual happiness. Later on a blind enthusiasm for self-dependence arises and produces an heroic spirit, which would rather be generous than just, which bestows sympathy more readily than respect; true morality, however, does not arise until, with constant attention to the law and continued watchfulness of self, duty is done for its own sake. No man is for a moment secure of his morality without continued endeavor. In order to deliverance from the original sin of inertness and its train, cowardice and falsity, men stand in need of examples, such as have been given them in the founders of religions, to construe for them the riddle of freedom. The necessary enlightenment concerning moral conviction is given by the Church, whose symbols are not to be looked upon as dogmatic propositions, but only as means for the proclamation of the eternal verities, and which, like the state (for both are institutions based on necessity), has for its object to make itself unnecessary as time goes on.

The system of duties distinguishes four classes of duties on the basis of the twofold opposition of universal (non-transferable) and particular (transferable) duties, and of unconditional duties (directed to the whole) and conditional duties (directed toward self). These four classes are the duties of self-preservation, of class, of non-interference with others, and of vocation. The lower calling includes the producers, artisans, and tradesmen, whose action terminates directly on nature; and the higher, the scholars, teachers of the people or clergy, artists, and government officials, who work directly on the community of rational beings. Fichte's thoughtful and sympathetically written discussion of marriage is in pleasant contrast to the bald, purely legal view of this relation adopted by Kant.

Natural right is for Fichte, as for Kant, whose theory of right, moreover, appeared later than Fichte's, entirely independent of ethics, and distinguished from the latter by its exclusive reference to external conduct instead of to the disposition and the will. The rule of right gains from the moral law, it is true, new sanction for conscience, but cannot be derived from the law.—The concept of right is to be deduced as a necessary act of the ego, *i.e.*, to be shown a condition of self-consciousness. The ego must posit itself as an individual, and can accomplish this only by positing itself in a relation of right to other finite rational beings; without a thou, no I. A finite rational being cannot posit itself without ascribing to itself a free activity in an external sense-world; and it cannot effect this latter unless (1) it ascribes free activity to other beings as well, hence not without assuming other finite rational beings outside itself, and positing itself as standing in *the relation of right* to them; and unless (2) it ascribes to itself a material body and posits this as standing under the influence of a person outside it. But, further, Fichte considers it possible to deduce the particular constitution both of the external world and of the human body (as the sphere of all free actions possible to the person). In the former there must be present a tough, durable matter capable of resistance, and light and air in order to the possibility of intercourse between spirits; while the latter must be an organized, articulated nature-product, furnished with senses, capable of infinite determination, and adapted to all conceivable motions.

If a community of free beings, such as has been shown the condition of individual self-consciousness, is to be possible, the following must hold as the law of right: So limit thy freedom that others may be free along with thee. This law is conditioned on the lawful behavior of others. Where this is lacking, where my fellow does not recognize and treat me as a free, rational being, the right of coercion comes in; coercion, however, is not to be exercised by the individual himself—since then there would be no guaranty either for its successful exercise or for the non-violation of the legal limit—but devolves upon the state. The state takes its origin in the common will of all to unite for the safeguarding of their rights, and determines by positive laws (intermediate between the law of right and legal judgments) what shall be considered rights. Thus there result three subjects for natural right: original rights or the sum of that which pertains to freedom or personality (inviolability of the body and of property), the right of coercion, and political right. The aim of punishment is the reform of the evil doer and the deterrence of others. Fichte is in agreement with Kant concerning the principle of popular sovereignty (Rousseau) and the exercise of the political power through representatives; but not so concerning the guaranties against the violation of the fundamental law of the state. Instead of the division of powers recommended by Kant he demands supervision of the rulers of the state by ephors, who, themselves without any legislative or executive authority, shall suspend the rulers in case they violate the law, and call them to account before the community. Every constitution in which the rulers are not responsible is despotic. Fichte did not continue loyal to this principle, that the state is merely a legal institution. He not only demands a state organization of labor by which everyone shall be placed in a position to live from his work, in the *Natural Right* and the *Exclusive Commercial State*, but, in his posthumous *Theory of Right*, 1812, he makes it the chief duty of the state to lead men, by the moral and intellectual training of the people, to do from insight what they have hitherto done from traditional belief. Through the education of the people the empirical state is gradually to transform itself into the rational state.

%3. Fichte's Second Period: his View of History and his Theory of Religion.%

Fichte's transfer to Berlin brought him into more intimate contact with the world, and along with new experiences and new emotions gave him new problems. While a vigorously developing religious sentiment turned his speculation to the relation of the individual ego to the primal source of spiritual life, empirical reality also acquired greater significance for him, and the intellectual, moral, and political situation of the time especially attracted his attention. The last required philosophical interpretation, demanded at once inquiry into its historical conditions and a consideration of the means by which the glaring contradiction between the condition of the nation at the time and the ideals of reason could be diminished. The *Addresses to the German Nation* outlined a plan for a moral reformation of the world, to start with the education of the German people;[1] while the *Characteristics of the Present Age*, which had preceded the *Addresses*, defined the place of the age in the general development of humanity. The scheme of historical periods given in the *Characteristics* and similarly in the *Theory of the State* (innocence—sin—supremacy of reason, with intermediate stages between each two) is interesting as a forerunner of Hegel's undertaking.

[Footnote 1: "Among all nations you are the one in whom the germ of human perfection is most decidedly present." The spiritual regeneration of mankind must proceed from the German people, for they are the one original or primitive people of the new age, the only one which has preserved its living language—French is a dead tongue—and has raised itself to true creative poetry and free science. The ground of distinction between Germanism and the foreign spirit lies in the question, whether we believe in an original element in man, in the freedom, infinite perfectibility, and eternal progress of our race, or put no faith in all these.]

History is produced through the interaction of the two principles, faith and understanding, which are related to each other as law and freedom, and strives toward a condition in which these two shall be so reconciled that faith shall have entirely passed over into the form of understanding, shall have been transformed into insight, and understanding shall have taken up the content of faith into itself. History begins with the coming together of two original and primitive races, one of order or faith, and one of freedom or understanding, neither of which would attain to an historical development apart from the other. From the legal race the free race learns respect for the law, as in turn it arouses in the former the impulse toward freedom. The course of history divides into five periods. In the state of "innocence" or of rational instinct that which is rational is done unconsciously, out of natural impulse; in the state of "commencing sin" the instinct for the good changes into an external compulsory authority, the law of reason appears as a ruling power from without, which can be disobeyed as well as obeyed. We ourselves live in the period of "completed sinfulness," of absolute license and indifference to all truth, of unlimited caprice and selfishness. But however far removed from the moral ideal this age appears, in which the individual, freed from all restraints, heeds naught except his egoistic desire, and in his care for his own welfare forgets to labor for the universal, yet this ultimate goal, this doing from free insight that which in the beginning was done out of blind faith, cannot be attained unless authority shall have first been shaken off and the individual become self-dependent. A few signs already betoken the dawn of the fourth era, that of rational science or of "commencing justification," in which truth shall be acknowledged supreme, and the individual ego, at least as cognitive, shall submit itself to the generic reason. Finally, with the era of rational art, or the state of "completed justification and sanctification," wherein the will of the individual shall entirely merge in life for the race, the end of the life of humanity on earth—the free determination of all its relations according to reason—will be fulfilled.

In the Jena period the religious life of the ego simply coincided for Fichte with its practical life; piety coincided with moral conduct; the Deity with the absolute ego, with the moral law, with the moral order of the world. A change subsequently took place in his views on this point. He experienced feelings which, at least in quality, were distinct from readiness for moral action, no matter how intimately they are intertwined with this, and no matter how little they can actually be separated from it; *religion* is possible neither without a metaphysical belief in a suprasensible world, nor without obedience to the moral law, yet in itself it is not that belief nor this action, but the inner spirit which pervades and animates all our thought and action—it is life, love, blessedness. And as quiet blessedness is here distinguished from ceaseless action, so for our thinker the inactive Deity, the self-identical life of the absolute, separates from the active universal reason, which in its individual organs advances from task to task. The earlier undivided and unique principle, the absolute ego, divides into the *Ichheit* (moral law, world-order), and an absolute as the ground thereof. "The spirit (the ego, or, as Fichte now prefers to say, knowledge) an image of God, the world an image of the spirit." The active order of the world (the moral law which realizes itself in individuals) the immediate, and objective reality the mediate, revelation of the absolute!

Does this view of religion, which Fichte incorporates also in the later expositions of the Science of Knowledge, indicate an abandonment and denial of the earlier standpoint? The philosophy of Fichte's second period is a new system—so judge the majority of the historians of philosophy. It is not a transformation, but a completion of the earlier system; the doctrine promulgated in Berlin continues to be idealistic, as that advanced in Jena had itself been pantheistic—this is the opinion of Fortlage and Harms, in agreement with the philosopher himself and with his son. Kuno Fischer, also, who shows a constant advance in the development of Fichteanism, a gradual transition "without a break," may be counted among the minority who hold that throughout his life Fichte taught but one system. We believe it our duty to adhere to this latter view. The Science of Knowledge (the world a product of the ego) enters as it is into the later form of the Fichtean philosophy; the latter gives up none of the fundamental positions of the former, but only adds to it a culmination, by which the appearance of the building is altered, it is true, but not the edifice itself. In the discussion of the question the following three have been emphasized as the most important points of distinction between the two periods: In the earlier system God is made equivalent to the absolute ego and the moral order of the world, in the later he is separated from these and removed beyond them; in the former the nature of God is described as activity, in the latter, as being; in the one, action is designated as the highest mission of man, in the other, blessed devotion to God. All three variations of the later doctrine from the earlier may be admitted without giving up the position that the former is only an extension of the latter and not an essential modification of it (*i.e.*, in its teachings concerning the relation of the ego and the world). Fichte experienced religious feelings the philosophical outcome of which he worked into his system. He now knows a first thing (the Deity as distinct from the absolute ego) and a last thing (the inwardness of religious devotion to the world-ground), which he had before not overlooked, much less denied, but combined in one with the second (the absolute ego or the moral order of the world) and the one before the last (moral action). It is incorrect to say that, in his later doctrine, Fichte substituted the inactive absolute in place of the active absolute ego, and the quiet blessedness of contemplation in place of ceaseless action. Not in place of these, but beyond them, while all else remains as it was. The categorical imperative, the absolute ego or knowledge is no longer God himself, but the first manifestation of God, though a necessary revelation of him. Religion had previously been included for Fichte in moral action; now fellowship with God goes beyond this, though morality remains its indispensable condition and inseparable companion. Finally, how to construe the previously avoided predicate, being, in relation to the Deity, is shown by the no less frequent designation of the absolute as the "Universal Life." The expression being, which it must be confessed is ambiguous, here signifies in our opinion only the quiet, self-identical activity of the absolute, in opposition to the unresting, changeful activity of the world-order and its finite organs, not that inert and dead being posited by the ego, the ascription of which to the Deity Fichte had forbidden in his essay which had been charged with atheism, not to speak of the existence-mode of a particular self-conscious and personal being. Instead of speaking of a conversion of Fichte to the position of his opponents, we might rather venture the paradoxical assertion, that, when he characterizes the absolute as the only true being, he intends to produce the same view in the mind of the reader as in his earlier years, when he expressed himself against the application of the concepts existence, substance, and conscious personality to God, on the ground that they are categories of sense. The chief thing, at least, remains unaltered: the opposition to a view of religion which transforms the sublime and sacred teaching of Christianity "into an enervating doctrine of happiness."

CHAPTER XI.

SCHELLING.

Friedrich Wilhelm Joseph (von) Schelling was born January 27, 1775, at Leonberg (in Würtemberg), and died August 20, 1854, at the baths of Ragatz (in Switzerland). In 1790-95 he attended the seminary at Tübingen, in company with Hölderlin and Hegel, who were five years older than himself; at seventeen he published a dissertation on the Fall of Man, and a year later an essay on Religious Myths; and was called in 1798 from Leipsic—where, after several treatises[1] in explanation of the Science of Knowledge, he had issued, in 1797, the *Ideas for a Philosophy of Nature*—to Jena. In the latter place he became acquainted with his future wife, Caroline,[2] *née* Michaëlis (1763-1809), widow of Böhmer and at this time the brilliant wife of August Wilhelm Schlegel. From 1803 to 1806 he served as professor in Würzburg; then followed two residences of fourteen years each in Munich, separated by seven years in Erlangen: 1806-20 as Member of the Academy of Sciences and General Secretary of the Academy of the Plastic Arts (he received this latter position after delivering on the king's birthday his celebrated address on "The Relation of the Plastic Arts to Nature," 1807); and 1827-41 as professor in the newly established university, and President of the Academy of Sciences. In 1812 Schelling married his second wife, Pauline Gotter. Besides various journals[3] and the works to be noticed later, two polemic treatises should be mentioned, the *Exposition of the True Relation of the Philosophy of Nature to the Improved Doctrine of Fichte*, 1806, in which his former friend is charged with plagiarism, and the *Memorial of the Treatise on Divine Things by Herr Jacobi*, 1812, which answers a bitter attack of Jacobi still more bitterly. From this on our philosopher, once so fond of writing, becomes silent.[4] The often promised issue of the positive philosophy, which had already been twice commenced in print (*The*

Ages of the World, 1815; *Mythological Lectures*, 1830), was both times suspended. Being called to the Berlin Academy by Frederick William IV., in order to counterbalance the prevailing Hegelianism, Schelling delivered lectures in the university also (on Mythology and Revelation), which he ceased, however, when notes taken by his hearers were printed without his consent.[5] His collected works were published in fourteen volumes (1856-61) under the care of his son, K.E.A. Schelling.[6]

[Footnote 1: *On the Possibility of a Form of Philosophy in General, On the Ego as Principle of Philosophy*, both in 1795; *Letters on Dogmatism and Criticism*, 1796; *Essays in Explanation of the Science of Knowledge*, 1797.]

[Footnote 2: *Karoline*, Letters, edited by G. Waitz, 1871.]

[Footnote 3: *Kritisches Journal der Philosophie* (with Hegel), 1802; *Zeitschrift für spekulative Physik*, 1800 (continued as *Neue Zeitschrift für spekulative Physik*); *Jahrbücher der Medizin als Wissenschaft* (with Marcus), 1806-08; *Allgemeine Zeitschrift von Deutschen für Deutsche*, 1813.]

[Footnote 4: Besides a supplement to *Die Weltalter* and his inaugural lecture at Berlin, he published only two prefaces, one to *Viktor Cousin über französische und deutsche Philosophie*, done into German by Hubert Beckers, 1834, and one to Steffens's *Nachgelassene Schriften*, 1846.]

[Footnote 5: Paulus, *Die endlich offenbar gewordene positive Philosophie der Offenbarung*, 1843. Frauenstädt had previously published a sketch from this later doctrine, 1842.]

[Footnote 6: On Schelling cf. the Lectures by K. Rosenkranz, 1843; the articles by Heyder in vol. xiii. of Herzog's *Realencyclopädie für protestantische Theologie*, 1860, and Jodl in the *Allgemeine deutsche Biographie*; R. Haym, *Die romantische Schule*, 1870; *Aus Schellings Leben, in Briefen*, edited by Plitt, 3 vols., 1869-70. [Cf. also Watson's *Schelling's Transcendental Idealism* (Griggs's Philosophical Classics, 1882); and several translations from Schelling in the *Journal of Speculative Philosophy*.—TR.]]

The leading motive in Schelling's thinking is an unusually powerful fancy, which gives to his philosophy a lively, stimulating, and attractive character, without making it to a like degree logically satisfactory. If the systems of Fichte and Hegel, which in their content are closely related to Schelling's, impress us by their logical severity, Schelling chains us by his lively intuition and his suggestive power of feeling his way into the inner nature of things. With him analogies outweigh reasons; he is more concerned about the rich content of concepts than about their sharp definition; and in the endeavor to show the unity of the universe, both in the great and in the little, especially to show the unity of nature and spirit, he dwells longer on the relationship of objects than on their antitheses, which he is glad to reduce to mere quantitative and temporary differences. He adds to this an astonishing mobility of thought, in virtue of which every offered suggestion is at once seized and worked into his own system, though in this the previous standpoint is unconsciously exchanged for a somewhat altered one. Schelling's philosophy is, therefore, in a continual state of flux, nearly every work shows it in a new form, and it is always ideas from without whose incorporation has caused the transition. Besides Leibnitz, Kant, and Fichte, who were already familiar to Schelling as a pupil at Tübingen, it was first Herder, then Spinoza and Bruno, who exerted a transforming influence on his system, to be followed later by Neoplatonism and Böhme's mysticism, and, finally, by Aristotle and the Gnostics, not to speak of his intercourse with his contemporaries Kielmeyer, Steffens, Baader, Eschenmayer, and others. Omitting his early adherence to Fichte, at least three periods must be distinguished in Schelling's thinking. The first period (1797-1800) includes the epoch-making feat of his youth, the *philosophy of nature*, and, as an equally legitimate second part of his system, the philosophy of spirit or *transcendental philosophy*. The latter is a supplementary recasting of Fichte's Science of Knowledge, while in the former Schelling follows Kant and Herder. The second period, from 1801, adds to these two co-ordinate parts, the philosophy of nature and the philosophy of spirit, and as a fundamental discipline, a science of the absolute, the *philosophy of identity*, which may be characterized as Spinozism revived on a Fichtean basis. Besides the example of Spinoza, Giordano Bruno had most influence on this form of Schelling's philosophy. With the year 1809, after the signs of a new phase had become perceptible from 1804 on, his system enters on its third, the theosophical, period, the period of the *positive philosophy*, in which we shall distinguish a mystical and a scholastic stage. The former is represented by the doctrine of freedom inspired by Jacob Böhme; the latter, by the philosophy of mythology and revelation, which goes back to Aristotle and the Gnostics. In the first period the absolute for Schelling is creative nature; in the second, the identity of opposites; in the third it is an antemundane process which advances from the not-yet-present of the contraries to their overcoming. In neither of these advances is it Schelling's intention to break with his previous teachings, but in each case only to add a supplement. That which has hitherto been the whole is retained as a part. The philosophy of nature takes its place beside the completed Fichtean transcendental philosophy, with equal rights, though with a reversed procedure; then the theory of identity assumes a place above both; finally, a positive (existential) philosophy is added to the previous negative (rational) philosophy.

%1a. Philosophy of Nature.%

Schelling agrees with Fichte that philosophy is transcendental science, the doctrine of the conditions of consciousness, and has to answer the question, What must take place in order that knowledge may arise? They agree, further, that these conditions of knowledge are necessary acts, outgoings of an active original ground which is not yet conscious self, but seeks to become such, and that the material world is the product of these actions. Nature exists in order that the ego may develop. But while Fichte correctly understood the purpose of nature, to help intelligence into being, he failed to recognize the dignity of nature, for he deprived it of all self-dependence, all life of its own, all generative power, and treated it merely as a dead tool, as a passive, merely posited non-ego. Nature is not a board which the original ego nails up before itself in order, striking against it, to be driven back upon itself, to be compelled to reflection, and thereby to become theoretical ego; in order, further, working over the non-ego, and transforming it, to exercise its practical activity: but it is a ladder on which spirit rises to itself. Spirit develops out of nature; nature itself has a spiritual element in it; it is undeveloped, slumbering, unconscious, benumbed intelligence. By transferring to nature the power of self-position or of being subject, Schelling exalts the drudge of the Science of Knowledge to the throne. The threefold division, "infinite original activity—nature or object—individual ego or subject," remains as in Fichte, only that the first member is not termed pure ego, but nature, yet creative nature, *natura naturans*. Schelling's aim is to show how from the object a subject arises, from the existent something represented, from the representable a representer, from nature an ego. He could only hope to solve this problem if he conceived natural objects—in the highest of which, man, he makes conscious spirit break forth or nature intuit itself—as themselves the products of an original subject, of a creative ground striving toward consciousness. For him also doing is more original than being. It would not be exact, therefore, to define the difference between Fichte and Schelling by saying that, with the former, nature proceeds from the ego, and with the latter the ego, from nature. It is rather true that with them both nature and spirit are alike the products of a third and higher term, which seeks to become spirit, and can accomplish this only by positing nature. In the Science of Knowledge, it is true, this higher ground is conceived as an ethical, in the Philosophy of Nature as a physical, power, although one framed for intelligence; in the former, moreover, the *natura naturata* appears as the position once for all of a non-spiritual, in the latter as a progressive articulated construction, with gradually increasing intelligence. In the unconscious products of nature, nature's aim to reflect upon itself, to become intelligence, fails, in man it succeeds. Nature is the embryonic life of spirit. Nature and spirit are essentially identical: "That which is posited *out of* consciousness is in its essence the same as that which is posited *in* consciousness also." Therefore "the knowable must itself bear the impress of the knower." Nature the preliminary stage, not the antithesis, of spirit; history, a continuation of physical becoming; the parallelism between the ideal and the real development-series—these are ideas from Herder which Schelling introduces into the transcendental philosophy. The Kantio-Fichtean moralism, with its sharp contraposition of nature and spirit, is limited in the *Naturphilosophie* by Herder's physicism.

"Nature *is a priori*" (everything individual in it is pre-determined by the whole, by the Idea of a nature in general); hence the forms of nature can be deduced from the concept of nature. The philosopher creates nature anew, he constructs it. Speculative physics considers nature as *subject*, becoming, productivity (not, like empirical science, as object, being, product), and for this purpose it needs, instead of individualizing reflection, an intuition directed to the whole. To this productive nature, as to the absolute ego of Fichte, are ascribed two opposite activities, one expansive or repulsive, and one attractive, and on these is based the universal law of *polarity*. The absolute productivity strives toward an infinite product, which it never attains, because apart from arrest no product exists. At definite points a check must be given it in order that something knowable may arise. Thus every product in nature is the result of a positive, centrifugal, accelerating, universalizing force, and a negative, limiting, retarding, individualizing one. The endlessness of the creative activity manifests itself in various ways: in the striving for development on the part of every product, in the preservation of the genus amid the disappearance of individuals, in the endlessness of the series of products. Nature's creative impulse is inexhaustible, it transcends every product. Qualities are points of arrest in the one universal force of nature; all nature is a connected development. Because of the opposition in the nature-ground between the stimulating and the retarding activity, the law of duality everywhere rules. To these two forces, however, still a third factor must be added as their copula, which determines the relation or measure of their connection. This is the source of the threefold division of the Philosophy of Nature. The magnet with its union of opposite polar forces is the type of all configuration in nature.

With Fichte's synthetic method and Herder's naturalistic principles Schelling combines Kantian ideas, especially Kant's dynamism (matter is a force-product),[1] and his view of the organic (organisms are self-productive beings, and are regarded by us as ends in themselves, because of the interaction between their members and the whole). The three organic functions sensibility, irritability, and reproduction, on the other hand, Schelling took from Kielmeyer, whose address *On the Relations of the Organic Forces*, 1793, excited great attention. The concept of life is dominant in Schelling's theory of nature. The organic is more original than the inorganic; the latter must be explained from the former; that which is dead must be considered as a product of departing life. No less erroneous than the theory of a magic vital force is the mechanical interpretation, which looks on life merely as a chemical phenomenon. The dead, mechanical and chemical, forces are merely the negative conditions of life; to them there must be added as a positive force a vital stimulus external to the individual, which continually rekindles the conflict between the opposing activities on which the vital process depends. Life consists, that is, in the perpetual prevention of the equilibrium which is the object of the chemical process. This constant disturbance proceeds from "universal nature," which, as the common principle of organic and inorganic nature, as that which determines them for each other, which founds a pre-established harmony between them, deserves the name of the world-soul. Schelling thus recognizes a threefold nature: organized, inorganic, and universal organizing (according to Harms, cosmical) nature, of which the two former arise from the third and are brought by it into connection and harmony. (As Schelling here takes an independent middle course between the mechanical explanation of life and the assumption of a specific vital force, so in all the burning physical questions of the time he seeks to rise above the contending parties by means of mediating solutions. Thus, in the question of "single or double electricity," he ranges himself neither on the side of Franklin nor on that of his opponents; in regard to the problem of light, endeavors to overcome the antithesis between Newton's emanation theory and the undulation theory of Euler; and, in his chapter on combustion, attacks the defenders of phlogiston as well as those who deny it).

[Footnote 1: Schelling terms his philosophy of nature dynamic atomism, since it posits pure intensities as the simple (atoms), from which qualities are to be explained.]

Schelling's philosophy of nature[1] proposes to itself three chief problems: the construction of general, indeterminate, homogeneous matter, with differences in density alone, of determinate, qualitatively differentiated matter and its phenomena of motion or the dynamical process, and of the organic process. For each of these departments of nature an original force in universal nature is assumed—gravity, light, and their copula, universal life. Gravity—this does not mean that which as the force of attraction falls within the view of sensation, for it is the union of attraction and repulsion—is the principle of corporeality, and produces in the visible world the different conditions of aggregation in solids, fluids, and gases. Light—this, too, is not to be confounded with actual light, of which it is the cause—is the principle of the soul (from it proceeds all intelligence, it is a spiritual potency, the "first subject" in nature), and produces in the visible world the dynamical processes magnetism, electricity, and chemism. The higher unity of gravity and light is the copula or life, the principle of the organic, of animated corporeality or the processes of growth and reproduction, irritability, and sensibility.

[Footnote 1: This is contained in the following treatises: *Ideas for a Philosophy of Nature, 1797; On the World-soul, 1798; First Sketch of a System of the Philosophy of Nature, 1799; Universal Deduction of the Dynamical Process or the Categories of Physics* (in the *Zeitschrift für spekulative Physik*) 1800. In the above exposition, however, the modified philosophy of nature of the second period has also been taken into account.]

General *matter* or the filling of space, arises from the co-operation of three forces: the centrifugal, which manifests itself as repulsion (first dimension), the centripetal, manifested as attraction (second dimension), and the synthesis of the two, manifested as gravity (third dimension). These forces are raised by light to a higher potency, and then make their appearance as the causes of the *dynamical* process or of the specific differences of matter. The linear function of magnetism is the condition of coherence; the surface force of electricity, the basis of the qualities perceivable by sense; the tri-dimensional force of the chemical process, in which the two former are united, produces the chemical qualities. Galvanism forms the transition to living nature, in which through the operation of the "copula" these three dynamical categories are raised to *organic* categories. To magnetism as the most general, and hence the lowest force, corresponds reproduction (the formative impulse, as nutrition, growth, and production, including the artistic impulse); electricity develops into irritability or excitability; the higher analogue to the chemical process as the most individual and highest stage is sensibility or the capacity of feeling. (Such at least is Schelling's doctrine after Steffens had convinced him of the higher dignity of that which is individual, whereas at first he had made sensibility parallel with magnetism, and reproduction with chemism, because the former two appear most seldom, and the latter most frequently. Electricity and irritability always maintained their intermediate position.) With the awakening of feeling nature has attained its goal—intelligence. As inorganic substances are distinguished only by relative degrees of repulsion and attraction, so the differentiation of organisms is conditioned by the relation of the three vital functions: in the lower forms reproduction predominates, then irritability gradually increases, while in the highest forms both of these are subordinated to sensibility. All species, however, are connected by a common life, all the stages are but arrests of the same fundamental force. This accentuation of the unity of nature, which establishes a certain kinship between Schelling's philosophy of nature and Darwinism, was a great idea, which deserves the thanks of posterity in spite of such defects as its often sportive, often heedlessly bold reasoning in details.

The parallelism of the potencies of nature, as we have developed it by leaving out of account the numerous differences between the various expositions of the *Naturphilosophie*, may be shown by a table:

I. UNIVERSAL NATURE. II. INORGANIC NATURE III. ORGANIC NATURE.
(ORGANIZING)
3. Copula 3. Organization
 or Life. |
 ___^___ /Chemical \ G | /Sensi- Man.
/ \ |Process (3d| a | |bility. __^__
2. Light 2.*Dynamical*|Dimen- | 1 | | / \
 (Soul). *Process*. < sion) | v | |Irritabi- Male
b. At- \ (Determi- |Electri- | a |_|lity. (=Light) traction.| nate |city (2d Di->n |Animal. >1. Gra- matter.) | mension.) | i | | vity 1. Indeter-
|Magnetism | s |Repro- Female a. Re- | (Body) minate |(1st Di- | m |duction (-Gravity) pulsion / *matter*. \ mension.) / \ Plant.

%1b. Transcendental Philosophy.%

The philosophy of nature explained the products of nature teleologically, deduced them from the concept or the mission of nature, by ignoring the mechanical origin of physical phenomena and inquiring into the significance of each stage in nature in view of this ideal meaning of the whole. It asks what is the outcome of the chemical process for the whole of nature, what is given by electricity, by magnetism, etc.—what part of the general aim of nature is attained, is realized through this or that group of phenomena. The philosophy of spirit given in the *System of Transcendental Idealism*, 1800, finds itself confronted by corresponding questions concerning the phenomena of intelligence, of morals, and of art. Here again Schelling does not trace out the mechanics of the soul-life, but is interested only in the meaning, in the teleological significance of the psychical functions. His aim is a constructive psychology in the Fichtean sense, a history of consciousness, and the execution of his design as well closely follows the example of the *Wissenschaftslehre*.

Since truth is the agreement of thought and its object, every cognition necessarily implies the coming together of a subjective and an objective factor. The problem of this coming together may be treated in two ways. With the philosophy of nature we may start from the object and observe how intelligence is added to nature. The transcendental philosophy takes the opposite course, it takes its position with the subject, and asks, How is there added to intelligence an object corresponding to it? The transcendental philosopher has need of intellectual intuition in order to recognize the original object-positing actions of the ego, which remain concealed from common consciousness, sunk in the outcome of these acts. The *theoretical* part of the system explains the representation of objective reality (the feeling connected with certain representations that we are compelled to have them), from pure self-consciousness, whose opposing moments, a real and an ideal force, limit each other by degrees,—and follows the development of spirit in three periods ("epochs"). The first of these extends from sensation, in which the ego finds itself limited, to productive intuition, in which a thing in itself is posited over against the ego and the phenomenon between the two; the second, from this point to reflection (feeling of self, outer and inner intuition together with space and time, the categories of relation as the original categories); the third, finally, through judgment, wherein intuition and concept are separated as well as united, up to the absolute act of will. Willing is the continuation and completion of intuition;[1] intuition was unconscious production, willing is conscious production. It is only through action that the world becomes objective for us, only through interaction with other active intelligences that the ego attains to the consciousness of a real external world, and to the consciousness of its freedom. The *practical* part follows the will from impulse (the feeling of contradiction between the ideal and the object) through the division into moral law and resistant natural impulse up to arbitrary will. Observations on legal order, on the state, and on history are added as "supplements." The law of right, by which unlawful action is directed against itself, is not a moral, but a natural order, which operates with blind necessity. The state, like law, is a product of the genus, and not of individuals. The ideal of a cosmopolitan legal condition is the goal of *history*, in which caprice and conformity to law are one, in so far as the conscious free action of individuals subserves an unconscious end prescribed by the world-spirit. History is the never completed revelation of the absolute (of the unity of the conscious and the unconscious) through human freedom. We are co-authors in the historical world-drama, and invent our own parts. Not until the third (the religious) period, in which he reveals himself as "providence," will God *be*; in the past (the tragical) period, in which the divine power was felt as "fate," and in the present (the mechanical) period, in which he appears as the "plan of nature," God is not, but is only *becoming*.

[Footnote 1: With this transformation of the antithesis between knowledge and volition into a mere difference in degree, Schelling sinks back to the standpoint of Leibnitz. In all the idealistic thinkers who start from Kant we find the endeavor to overcome the Critical dualism of understanding and will, as also that between intellect and sensibility. Schiller brings the contrary impulses of the ego into ultimate harmonious union in artistic activity. Fichte traces them back to a common ground; Schelling combines both these methods by extolling art as a restoration of the original identity. Hegel reduces volition to thought, Schopenhauer makes intellect proceed from will.]

An interesting supplement to the Fichtean philosophy is furnished by the third, the *aesthetic*, part of the transcendental idealism, which makes use of Kant's theory of the beautiful in a way similar to that in which the philosophy of nature had availed itself of his theory of the organic. Art is the higher third in which the opposition between theoretical and practical action, the antithesis of subject and object, is removed; in which cognition and action, conscious and unconscious activity, freedom and necessity, the impulse of genius and reflective deliberation are united. The beautiful, as the manifestation of the infinite in the finite, shows the problem of philosophy, the identity of the real and the ideal, solved in sensuous appearance. Art is the true organon and warrant of philosophy; she opens up to philosophy the holy of holies, is for philosophy the supreme thing, the revelation of all mysteries. Poesy and philosophy (the aesthetic intuition of the artist and the intellectual intuition of the thinker) are most intimately related; they were united in the old mythology—why should not this repeat itself in the future?

%2. System of Identity.%

The assertion which had already been made in the first period that "nature and spirit are fundamentally the same," is intensified in the second into the proposition, "The ground of nature and spirit, the absolute, is the identity of the real and the ideal," and in this form is elevated into a principle. As the absolute is no longer employed as a mere ground of explanation, but is itself made the object of philosophy, the doctrine of identity is added to the two co-ordinate disciplines, the philosophy of nature and the philosophy of spirit, as a higher third, which serves as a basis for them, and in Schelling's exposition of which several phases must be distinguished.[1]

[Footnote 1: The philosophy of identity is given in the following treatises: *Exposition of my System of Philosophy*, 1801; *Further Expositions of the System of Philosophy*, 1802; *Bruno, or on the Divine and Natural Principle of Things*, 1803; *Lectures on the Method of Academical Study*, 1803; *Aphorisms by way of Introduction to the Philosophy of Nature, Aphorisms on the Philosophy of Nature* (both in the *Jahrbücher für Medizin)*, 1806. Besides these the following also bear on this doctrine: the additions to the second edition of the *Ideas*, 1803, and the *Exposition*, against Fichte, 1806.]

Following Spinoza, whom he at first imitated even in the geometrical method of proof, Schelling teaches that there are two kinds of knowledge, the philosophical knowledge of the reason and the confused knowledge of the imagination, and, as objects of these, two forms of existence, the infinite, undivided existence of the absolute, and the finite existence of individual things, split up into multiplicity and becoming. The manifold and self-developing things of the phenomenal world owe their existence to isolating thought alone; they possess as such no true reality, and speculation proves them void. While things appear particular to inadequate representation, the philosopher views them *sub specie aeterni*, in their *per se*, in their totality, in the identity, as Ideas. To construe things is to present them as they are in God. But in God all things are one; in the absolute all is absolute, eternal, infinitude itself. (Accord-to Hegel's parody, the absolute is the night, in which all cows are black.)

The world-ground appears as nature and spirit; yet in itself it is neither the one nor the other, but the unity of both which is raised above all contrariety, the indifference of objective and subjective. Although amid the finitude of the things of the world the self-identity of the absolute breaks up into a plurality of self-developing individual existences, yet even in the phenomenal world of individuals the unity of the ground is not entirely lost: each particular existence is a definite expression of the absolute, and to it as such the character of identity belongs, though in a diminished degree and mingled with difference (Bruno's "monads"). The world-ground is absolute, the individual thing is relative, identity and totality; nothing exists which is merely objective or merely subjective; everything is both, only that one or other of these two factors always predominates. This Schelling terms quantitative difference: the phenomena of nature, like the phenomena of spirit, are a unity of the real and the ideal, only that in the former there is a preponderance of the real, in the latter a preponderance of the ideal.

At first Schelling, in Neoplatonic fashion, maintained the existence of another intermediate region between the spheres of the infinite and the finite: absolute knowing or the self-knowledge of the identity. In this, as the "form" of the absolute, the objective and the subjective are not absolutely one, as they are in the being or "essence" of the absolute, but ideally (potentially) opposed, though one *realiter*. Later he does away with this distinction also, as existing for reflection alone, not for rational intuition, and outbids his earlier determinations concerning the simplicity of the absolute with the principle, that it is not only the unity of opposites, but also the unity of the unity and the opposition or the identity of the identity, in which fanciful description the dialogue *Bruno* pours itself forth. A further alteration is brought in by characterizing the absolute as the identity of the finite and the infinite, and by equating the finite with the real or being, the infinite with the ideal or knowing. With this there is joined a philosophical interpretation of the Trinity akin to Lessing's. In the absolute or eternal the finite and the infinite are alike absolute. God the Father is the eternal, or the unity of the finite and the infinite; the Son is the finite in God (before the falling away); the Spirit is the infinite or the return of the finite into the eternal.

In the construction of the real series Schelling proceeds still more schematically and analogically than in the *Naturphilosophie* of the first period, the contents of which are here essentially reproduced. With this is closely connected his endeavor, in correspondence with the principles of the theory of identity, to show in every phenomenon the operation of all three moments of the absolute. In each natural product all three "potencies" or stages, gravity A^1, light A^2, and organization A^3, are present, only in subordination to one of their number. Since the third potency is never lacking, all is organic; that which appears to us as inorganic matter is only the residuum left over from organization, that which could become neither plant nor animal. New here is the cohesion-series of Steffens (the phenomenon of magnetism), in which nitrogen forms the south pole, carbon the north pole, and iron the point of indifference, while oxygen, hydrogen, and water represent the east pole, west pole, and indifference point in electrical polarity. In the organic world plants represent the carbon pole, animals the nitrogen pole; the former is the north pole, the latter the south. Moreover, the points of indifference reappear: the plant corresponds to water, the animal to iron. Schelling was far outdone in fantastic analogies of this kind by his pupils, especially by Oken, who in his *Sketch of the Philosophy of Nature*, 1805, compares the sense of hearing, for example, to the parabola, to a metal, to a bone, to the bird, to the mouse, and to the horse. As nature was the imaging of the infinite (unity or essence) into the finite (plurality or form), so spirit is the taking up of the finite into the infinite. In the spiritual realm also all three divine original potencies are every, where active, though in such a way that one is dominant. In intuition (sensation, consciousness, intuition, each in turn thrice divided) the infinite and the eternal are subordinated to the finite; in thought or understanding (concept, judgment, inference, each in three kinds) the finite and the eternal are subordinated to the infinite; in reason (which comprehends all under the form of the absolute) the finite and the infinite are subordinated to the eternal. Intuition is finite cognition, thought infinite cognition, reason eternal cognition. The forms of the understanding do not suffice for the knowledge of reason; common logic with its law of contradiction has no binding authority for speculation, which starts with the equalization of opposites. In the *Aphorisms by way of Introduction* science, religion, and art figure as stages of the ideal all, in correspondence with the potencies of the real all—matter, motion, and organization. Nature culminates in man, history in the state. Reason, philosophy, is the re-establishment of identity, the return of the absolute to itself.

Unconditioned knowledge, as Schelling maintains in his encyclopedia, *i.e.*, his *Lectures on the Method of Academical Study*, is the presupposition of all particular knowledge. The function of universities is to maintain intact the connection between particular knowledge and absolute knowledge. The three higher faculties correspond to the three potencies in the absolute: Natural Science and Medicine to the real or finite; History and Law to the ideal or infinite; Theology to the eternal or the copula. There is further a faculty of arts, the so-called Philosophical Faculty, which imparts whatever in philosophy is teachable. The two lectures on theology (viii. and ix.) are especially important. There are two forms of religion, one of which discovers God in nature, while the other finds him in history; the former culminates in the Greek religion, the latter in the Christian, and with the founding of this the third period of history (which Schelling had previously postponed into the future), the period of providence begins. In Christianity mythology is based on religion, not religion on mythology, as was the case in heathenism. The speculative kernel of Christianity is the incarnation of God, already taught by the Indian sages; this, however, is not to be understood as a single event in time, but as eternal. It has been a hindrance to the development of Christianity that the Bible, whose value is far below that of the sacred books of India, has been more highly prized than that which the patristic thinking succeeded in making out of its meager contents.

If, finally, we compare Schelling's system of identity with its model, the system of Spinoza, two essential differences become apparent. Although both thinkers start from a principiant equal valuation of the two phenomenal manifestations of the absolute, nature and spirit, Spinoza tends to posit thought in dependence on extension (the soul represents what the body is), while in Schelling, conversely, the Fichtean preference of spirit is still potent (the state and art stand nearer to the absolute identity than the organism, although, principiantly considered, the greatest possible approximation to the equilibrium of the real and the ideal is as much attained in the one as in the other). The second difference lies in the fact that the idea of development is entirely lacking in Spinoza, while in Schelling it is everywhere dominant. It reminds one of Lessing and Herder, who also attempted to combine Spinozistic and Leibnitzian elements.

%3a. Doctrine of Freedom.%

The system of identity had, with Spinoza, distinguished two worlds, the real world of absolute identity and the imagined world of differentiated and changeable individual things; it had traced back the latter to the former as its ground, but had not deduced it from the former. Whence, then, the imagination which, instead of the unchangeable unity, shows us the changing manifold? Whence the imperfections of the finite, whence evil? The pantheism of Spinoza is inseparably connected with determinism, which denies evil without explaining it. Evil and finitude demand explanation, not denial, and this without the abandonment of pantheism. But explanation by what? By the absolute, for besides the absolute there is naught. How, then, must the pantheistic doctrine of the absolute be transformed in order that the fact of evil and the separate existence of the finite may become comprehensible? To this task are devoted the *Inquiries into the Nature of Human Freedom (Philosophical Works*, vol. i., 1809, with which should be compared the *Memorial of Jacobi*, 1812, and the *Answer to Eschenmayer*, 1813).

As early as in the *Bruno*, the problem occasionally emerges why matters do not rest with the original infinite unity of the absolute, why the finite breaks away from the identical primal ground. The possibility of the separation, it is answered, lies in the fact that the finite is like the infinite *realiter*, and yet, ideally, is different from it; the actuality of the coming forth, however, lies in the non-deducible self-will of the finite. Then after Eschenmayer[1] *(Philosophy in its Transition to Not-philosophy*, 1803) had characterized the procession of the Ideas out of the Godhead as an impenetrable mystery for thought, before which philosophy must yield to faith, Schelling, in the essay *Religion and Philosophy*, 1804, goes more deeply into the problem. The origin of the sense-world is conceivable only as a breaking away, a spring, a *falling away*, which consists in the soul's grasping itself in its selfhood, in its subordination of the infinite in itself to the finite, and in its thus ceasing to be in God. The procession of the world from the infinite is a free act, a fact which can only be described, not deduced as necessary. The counterpart of this attainment of independence on the part of things or creation is history as the return of the world to its source. They are related to each other as the fall to redemption. Both the dismission of the world and its reception back, together with the intervening development, are, however, events needed by God himself in order to become actual God: He develops through the world. (A similar thought was not unknown in the Middle Ages: if God is to give a complete revelation of himself he must make known his grace; and this presupposes sin. As the occasion of divine grace, the fall is a happy, saving fault; without it God could not have revealed himself as gracious, as forgiving, hence not completely.) Schelling's study of Jacob Böhme, to which he was led by Baader, essentially contributed to the concentration of his thought on this point. *The Exposition of the True Relation*, etc., already distinctly betrays the influence of this mystic. In correspondence with Böhme's doctrine that God is living God only through his inclusion of negation in himself, it is here maintained: A being can manifest itself only when it is not merely one, but has another, an opposition (the many), in itself, whereby it is revealed to itself as unity. With the addition of certain Kantian ideas, in particular the idea of transcendental freedom and the intelligible character, Schelling's theosophy now assumes the following form:

The only way to guard against the determinism and the lifeless God of Spinoza is to assume something in God which is not God himself, to distinguish between God as existent and that which is merely the ground of his existence or "nature in God." In God also the perfect proceeds from the imperfect, he too develops and realizes himself. The actual, perfect God, who is intelligence, wisdom, goodness, is preceded by something which is merely the possibility of all this, an obscure, unconscious impulse toward self-representation. For in the last analysis there is no being but willing; to willing alone belong the predicates of the primal being, groundlessness, eternity, independence of time, self-affirmation. This "ground of existence" is an obscure "longing" to give birth to self, an unconscious impulse to become conscious; the goal of this longing is the "understanding," the Logos, the Word, wherein God becomes revealed to self. By the self-subordination of this longing to the understanding as its matter and instrument, God becomes actual God, becomes spirit and love. The operation of the light understanding on the dark nature-will consists in a separation of forces, whence the visible world proceeds. Whatever in the latter is perfect, rational, harmonious, and purposive is the work of the understanding; the irrational remainder, on the other hand, conflict and lawlessness, abortion, sickness and death, originates in the dark ground. Each thing has two principles in it: its self-will it receives from nature in God, yet, at the same time, as coming from the divine understanding, it is the instrument of the universal will. In God the light and dark principles stand in indissoluble unity, in man they are separable. The freedom of man's will makes him independent of both principles; going over from truth to falsehood, he may strive to make his selfhood supreme and to reduce the spiritual in him to the level of a means, or—with divine assistance—continuing in the center, he may endeavor to subordinate the particular will to the will of love. Good consists in overcoming resistance, for in every case a thing can be revealed only through its opposite. If man yields to temptation it is his own guilty choice. Evil is not merely defect, privation, but something positive, selfhood breaking away, the reversal of the rightful order between the particular and the universal will. The possibility of a separation of the two wills lies in the divine ground (it is "permitted" in order that by overmastering the self-will the will of love may approve itself), the actuality of evil is the free act of the creature. Freedom is to be conceived, in the Kantian sense, as equally far removed from chance or caprice and from compulsion: Man chooses his own non-temporal, intelligible nature; he predestinates himself in the first creation, *i.e.*, from eternity, and is responsible for his actions in the sense-world, which are the necessary results of that free primal act.

[Footnote 1: K. Ad. Eschenmayer was originally a physician, then, 1811-36, professor of philosophy in Tübingen, and died in 1852 at Kirchheim unter Teck.]

As in nature and in the individual, so also in the history of mankind, the two original grounds of things do battle with one another. The golden age of innocence, of happy indecision and unconsciousness concerning sin, when neither good nor evil yet was, was followed by a period of the omnipotence of nature, in which the dark ground of existence ruled alone, although it did not make itself felt as actual evil until, in Christianity, the spiritual light was born in personal form. The subsequent conflict of good against evil, in which God reveals himself as spirit, leads toward a state wherein evil will be reduced to the position of a potency and everything subordinated to spirit, and thus the complete identity of the ground of existence and the existing God be brought about.

Besides this after-reconciliation of the two divine moments, Schelling recognizes another, original unity of the two. The not yet unfolded unity of the beginning (God as Alpha) he terms *indifference* or groundlessness; the more valuable unity of the end, attained by unfolding (God as Omega) is called *identity* or spirit. In the former the contraries are not yet present; in the latter they are present no longer. The groundless divides into two equally eternal beginnings, nature and light, or longing and understanding, in order that the two may become one in love, and thereby the absolute develop into the personal God. In this way Schelling endeavors to overcome the antithesis between naturalism and theism, between dualism and pantheism, and to remove the difficulties which arise for pantheism from the fact of evil, as well as from the concepts of personality and of freedom.

In the two moments of the absolute (nature in God—personal spirit) we recognize at once the antithesis of the real and ideal which was given in the philosophy of identity. The chief difference between the mystical period and the preceding one consists in the fact that the absolute itself is now made to develop (from indifference to identity, from the neither-nor to the as-well-as of the antithesis), and that there is conceded to the sense-world a reality which is more than apparent, more than merely present for imagination. That which facilitated this rapid, almost unceasing change of position for Schelling, and which at the same time concealed the fact from him, was, above all, the ambiguous and variable meaning of his leading concepts. The "objective," for example, now signifies unconscious being, becoming, and production, now represented reality, now the real, in so far as it is not represented, but only *is*. "God" sometimes means the whole absolute, sometimes only the infinite, spiritual moment in the absolute. Scarcely a single term is sharply defined, much less consistently used in a single meaning.

%3b. Philosophy of Mythology and Revelation.%

Once again Schelling is ready with a new statement of the problem. Philosophy is the science of the existent. In this, however, a distinction is to be made between the *what (quid sit)* and the *that (quod sit)*, or between essence and existence. The apprehension of the essence, of the concept, is the work of reason, but this does not go as far as actual being. Rational philosophy cognizes only the universal, the possible, the necessary truths (whose contradictory is unthinkable), but not the particular and factual. This philosophy can only assert: If anything exists it must conform to these laws; existence is not given with the *what*. Hegel has ignored this distinction between the logical and the actual, has confused the rational and the real. Even the system of identity was merely rational, *i.e., negative*, philosophy, to which there must be added, as a second part, a positive or existential philosophy, which does not, like the former, rise to the highest principle, to God, but starts from this supreme Idea and shows its actuality.

The content of this phase of Schelling's thought[1] was so unfruitful, and its influence so small, that brief hints concerning it must here suffice. First of all, the doctrine of the divine potencies and of creation is repeated in altered form, and then there is given a philosophy of the history of religion as a reflection of the theogonic process in human consciousness.

[Footnote 1: On Schelling's negative and positive philosophy, published in the four volumes of the second division of the *Works*, cf. Karl Groos, *Die reine Vernunftwissenschaft, systematische Darstellung von Schellings negativer Philosophie*, 1889; Konstantin Frantz, *Schellings positive Philosophie*, in three parts, 1879-80; Ed. von Hartmann, *Gesammelte Studien und Aufsätze*, 1876, p. 650 *seq.*; Ad. Planck, *Schellings nachgelassene Werke*, 1858; also the essay by Heyder, referred to above].

The potencies are now called the infinite ability to be (inactive will, subject), pure being (being without potentiality, object), and spirit, which is free from the one-sidednesses of mere potentiality and of mere being, and master of itself (subject-object); to these is added, further—not as a fourth, but as that which has the three predicates and is wholly in each—the absolute proper, as the cause and support of these attributes. The original unity of the three forms is dissolved, as the first raises itself out of the condition of a mere potency and withdraws itself from pure being in order to exist for itself; the tension extends itself to the two others—the second now comes out from its selflessness, subdues the first, and so leads the third back to unity. In creation the three potencies stand related as the unlimited Can-be, the limiting Must-be, and the Ought-to-be, or operate as material, formal, and final causes, all held in undivided combination by the soul. It was not until the end of creation that they became personalities. Man, in whom the potencies come to rest, can divide their unity again; his fall calls forth a new tension, and thereby the world becomes a world outside of God. History, the process o progressive reconciliation between the God-estranged world and God, passes through two periods—heathenism, in which the second person works as a natural potency, and Christianity, in which it works with freedom. In the discussion of these positive philosophy becomes a *philosophy of mythology and revelation*. The irresistible force of mythological ideas is explained by the fact that the gods are not creations of the fancy, but real powers, namely, these potencies, which form the substance of human conciousness.

The history of religion has for its starting-point the relative monotheism of humanity in its original unity, and for its goal the absolute monotheism of Christianity. With the separation into nations polytheism arises. This is partly simultaneous polytheism (a plurality of gods under a chief god), partly successive polytheism (an actual plurality of divinities, changing dynasties of several chief gods), and develops from star worship or Sabeism up to the religion of the Greeks. The Greek mysteries form the transition from mythology to revelation. While in the mythological process one or other of the divine potencies (Ground, Son, Spirit) was always predominant, in Christianity they return into unity. The true monotheism of revelation shows God as an articulated unity, in which the opposites are contained, as being overcome. The person of Christ constitutes the content of Christianity, who, in his incarnation and sacrificial death, yields up the independence out of God which had come to him through the fall of man. The three periods in the development of the Church (real, substantial unity—ideality or freedom—the reconciliation of the two) were foreshadowed in the chief apostles: Peter, with his leaning toward the past, represents the Papal Church; Paul the thinker the Protestant Church; and the gentle John the Church of the future.

CHAPTER XII.

SCHELLING'S CO-WORKERS.

In his period of vigorous creation Schelling was the center of an animated philosophical activity. Each phase of his philosophy found a circle of enthusiastic fellow-laborers, whom we must hesitate to term disciples because of their independence and of their reaction on Schelling himself. Only G.M. Klein (1776-1820, professor in Würzburg), Stutzmann (died 1816 in Erlangen; *Philosophy of the Universe*, 1806; *Philosophy of History*, 1808), and the historians of philosophy Ast and Rixner can be called disciples of Schelling. Prominent among his co-workers in the philosophy of nature were Steffens, Oken, Schubert, and Carus; besides these the physiologist Burdach, the pathologist Kieser, the plant physiologist Nees von Esenbeck, and the medical thinker Schelver (*Philosophy of Medicine*, 1809) deserve mention. Besides Hegel, J.J. Wagner and Friedrich Krause distinguished themselves as independent founders of systems of identity; Troxler, Suabedissen, and Berger are also to be assigned to this group. Baader and Schleiermacher were competitors of Schelling in the philosophy of religion, and Solger in aesthetics. Finally Fr. J. Stahl (died 1861; *Philosophy of Right*, 1830 seq..), was also influenced by Schelling. There is a wide divergence in Schelling's school, as J.E. Erdmann accurately remarks, between the naturalistic pantheist Oken and the mystical theosophist Baader, in whom elements which had been united in Schelling appear divided.

%1. The Philosophers of Nature.%

Henrik Steffens[1] (a Norwegian, 1773-1845; professor in Halle, Breslau, and Berlin) makes individual development the goal of nature—which is first completely attained in man and in his peculiarity or talent—and holds that the catastrophes of the spirit are reflected in the history of the earth. Lorenz Oken[2] (1779-1851; professor in Jena 1807-27, then in Munich and Zurich) identifies God and the universe, which comes to self-consciousness in man, the most perfect animal; teaches the development of organisms from an original slime (a mass of organic elements, infusoria, or cells); and looks on the animal kingdom as man anatomized, in that the animal world contains in isolated development that which man possesses collected in minute organs—the worm is the feeling animal, the insect the light animal, the snail the touch animal, the bird the hearing animal, the fish the smelling animal, the amphibian the taste animal, the mammal the animal of all senses.

[Footnote 1: Steffens, *Contributions to the Inner Natural History of the Earth*, 1801; *Caricatures of the Holiest*, 1819-21; *Anthropology*, 1822.]

[Footnote 2: Oken: *On the Significance of the Bones of the Skull*, 1807; *Text-book of the Philosophy of Nature*, 1809-11, 2d ed. 1831, 3d ed. 1843; the journal *Isis*, from 1817. On Oken cf. C. Güttler, 1885.]

While in Steffens geological interests predominate, and in Oken biological interests, Schubert, Carus, and Ennemoser are the psychologists of the school. Gotthilf Heinrich Schubert[1] (1780-1860; professor in Erlangen and Munich) brings the human soul into intimate relation with the world-soul, whose phantasy gives form to all that is corporeal, and delights to dwell on the abnormal and mysterious phenomena of the inner life, the border-land between the physical and the psychical, on the unconscious and the half-conscious, on presentiments and clairvoyance, as from another direction also Schelling's philosophy was brought into perilous connection with somnambulism. A second predominantly contemplative thinker was Karl Gustav Carus[2] (1789-1869; at his death in Dresden physician to the king; *Lectures on Psychology*, 1831; *Psyche*, 1846; *Physis*, 1851), greatly distinguished for his services to comparative anatomy. Carus endows the cell with unconscious psychical life,—a memory for the past shows itself in the inheritance of dispositions and talents, just as the formation of milk in the breasts of the pregnant and the formation of lungs in the embryo betray a prevision of the future,—and points out that with the higher development of organic and spiritual life the antitheses constantly become more articulate: individual differences are greater among men than among women, among adults than among children, among Europeans than among negroes.

[Footnote 1: G.H. Schubert: *Views of the Dark Side of Natural Science*, 1808; *The Primeval World and the Fixed Stars*, 1822; *History of the Soul*, 1830 (in briefer form, *Text-book of the Science of Man and of the Soul*, 1838).]

[Footnote 2: Not to be confused with Friedrich August Carus (1770-1807; professor in Leipsic), whose *History of Psychology*, 1808, forms the third part of his posthumous works.]

%2. The Philosophers of Identity.%

It has been said of the Dane Johann Erich von Berger (1772-1833; from 1814 professor in Kiel; *Universal Outlines of Science*, 1817-27) that he adopted a middle course between Fichte and Schelling. The same may be asserted of Karl Ferdinand Solger (1780-1819; at his death professor in Berlin; *Erwin, Four Dialogues on Beauty and Art*, 1815; *Lectures on Aesthetics*, edited by Heyse, 1829), who points out the womb of the beautiful in the fancy, and introduces into aesthetics the concept of irony, that spirit of sadness at the vanity of the finite, though this is needed by the Idea in order to its manifestation.

In Johann Jacob Wagner[1] (1775-1841; professor in Würzburg) and in J.P.V. Troxler[2] (1780-1866) we find, as in Steffens, a fourfold division instead of Schelling's triads. Both Wagner and Troxler find an exact correspondence between the laws of the universe and those of the human mind. Wagner (in conformity to the categories essence and form, opposition and reconciliation) makes all becoming and cognition advance from unity to quadruplicity, and finds the four stages of knowledge in representation, perception, judgment, and Idea. Troxler shares with Fries the anthropological standpoint, (philosophy is anthropology, knowledge of the world is self-knowledge), and distinguishes, besides the emotional nature or the unity of human nature, four constituents thereof, spirit, higher soul, lower soul (body, *Leib*), and body *(Körper)*, and four corresponding kinds of knowledge, in reverse order, sensuous perception, experience, reason, and spiritual intuition, of which the middle two are mediate or reflective in character, while the first and last are intuitive. For D. Th. A. Suabedissen also (1773-1835; professor in Marburg; *Examination of Man*, 1815-18) philosophy is the science of man, and self-knowledge its starting point.

[Footnote 1: J.J. Wagner: *Ideal Philosophy*, 1804; *Mathematical Philosophy*, 1811; *Organon of Human Knowledge*, 1830, in three parts, System of the World, of Knowledge, and of Language. On Wagner cf. L. Rabus, 1862.]

[Footnote 2: Troxler: *Glances into the Nature of Man*, 1812; *Metaphysics*, 1828; *Logic*, 1830.]

The relatively limited reputation enjoyed in his own time and to-day by Friedrich Krause[1] (born in Eisenberg 1781; habilitated in Jena 1802; lived privately in Dresden; became a *Privatdocent* in Göttingen from 1824; and died at Munich 1832; *Prototype of Humanity*, 1812, and numerous other works) has been due, on the one hand, to the appearance of his more gifted contemporary Hegel, and, on the other, to his peculiar terminology. He not only Germanized all foreign words in a spirit of exaggerated purism, but also coined new verbal roots, *(Mäl, Ant, Or, Om)* and from these formed the most extraordinary combinations (*Vereinselbganzweseninnesein, Oromlebselbstschauen*). His most important pupil, Ahrens (professor in Leipsic, died 1874; *Course of Philosophy*, 1836-38; *Natural Right*, 1852), helped Krause's doctrine to gain recognition in France and Belgium by his fine translations into French; while it was introduced into Spain by J.S. del Rio of Madrid (died 1869).—Since the finite is a negative, the infinite a positive concept, and hence the knowledge of the infinite primal, the principle of philosophy is the absolute, and philosophy itself knowledge of God or the theory of essence. The Subjective Analytic Course leads from the self-viewing of the ego up to the vision of God; the Synthetic Course starts from the fundamental Idea, God, and deduces from this the partial Ideas, or presents the world as the revelation of God. For his attempted reconciliation of theism and pantheism Krause invented the name panentheism, meaning thereby that God neither is the world nor stands outside the world, but has the world in himself and extends beyond it. He is absolute identity, nature and reason are relative identity, viz., the identity of the real and ideal, the former with the character of reality, the latter with the character of ideality. Or, the absolute considered from the side of its wholeness (infinity) is nature, considered from the side of its selfhood (unconditionality) is reason; God is the common root of both. Above nature and reason is humanity, which combines in itself the highest products of both, the most perfect animal body and self-consciousness. The humanity of earth, the humanity known to us, is but a very small portion of the humanity of the universe, which in the multitude of its members, which cannot be increased, constitutes the divine state. Krause's most important work is his philosophy of right and of history, with its marks of a highly keyed idealism. He treats human right as an effluence of divine right; besides the state or legal union, he recognizes many other associations—the science and the art union, the religious society, the league of virtue or ethical union. His philosophy of history (*General Theory of Life*, edited by Von Leonhardi, 1843) follows the Fichteo-Hegelian rhythm, unity, division, and reunion, and correlates the several ages with these. The first stage is germinal life; the second, youth; the third, maturity. The culmination is followed by a reverse movement from counter-maturity, through counter-youth, to counter-childhood, whereupon the development recommences—without cessation. It is to be regretted that this noble-minded man joined to his warm-hearted disposition, broad outlook, and rigorous method a heated fancy, which, crippling the operation of these advantageous qualities, led his thought quite too far away from reality. Ahrens, Von Leonhardi, Lindemann, and Roeder may be mentioned as followers of Krause.

[Footnote 1: On Krause cf. P. Hohlfeld, *Die Krausesche Philosophic*, 1879; B. Martin, 1881; R. Eucken, *Zur Erinnerung an Krause, Festrede*, 1881. From his posthumous works Hohlfeld and Wünsche have published the *Lectures on Aesthetics*, the *System of Aesthetics* (both 1882), and numerous other treatises.]

%3. The Philosophers of Religion.%

Franz (von) Baader, the son of a physician, was born in Munich in 1765, resided there as superintendent of mines, and, from 1826, as professor of speculative dogmatics, and died there also in 1841. His works, which consisted only of a series of brief treatises, were collected (16 vols., 1851-60) by his most important adherent, Franz Hoffman[1] (at his death in 1881 professor in Würzburg). Baader may be characterized as a mediaeval thinker who has worked through the critical philosophy, and who, a believing, yet liberal Catholic, endeavors to solve with the instruments of modern speculation the old Scholastic problem of the reconciliation of faith and knowledge. His themes are, on the one hand, the development of God, and, on the other, the fall and redemption, which mean for him, however, not merely inner phenomena, but world-events. He is in sympathy with the Neoplatonists, with Augustine, with Thomas Aquinas, with Eckhart, with Paracelsus, above all, with Jacob Böhme, and Böhme's follower Louis Claude St. Martin (1743-1804), but does not overlook the value of the modern German philosophy. With Kant he begins the inquiry with the problem of knowledge; with Fichte he finds in self-consciousness the essence, and not merely a property, of spirit; with Hegel he looks on God or the absolute spirit not only as the object, but also as the subject of knowledge. He rejects, however, the autonomy of the will and the spontaneity of thought; and though he criticises the

Cartesian separation between the thought of the creator and that of the creature, he as little approves the pantheistic identification of the two—human cognition participates in the divine, without constituting a part of it.

[Footnote 1: Besides Hoffman, Lutterbeck and Hamberger have described and expounded Baader's system. See also Baumann's paper in the *Philosophische Monatshefte*, vol. xiv., 1878, p. 321 *seq*.]

In accordance with its three principal objects, "God, Nature, and Man," philosophy divides into fundamental science (logic or the theory of knowledge and theology), the philosophy of nature (cosmology or the theory of creation and physics), and the philosophy of spirit (ethics and sociology). In all its parts it must receive religious treatment. Without God we cannot know God. In our cognition of God he is at once knower and known; our being and all being is a being known by him; our self-consciousness is a consciousness of being known by God: *cogitor, ergo cogito et sum*; my being and thinking are based on my being thought by God. Conscience is a joint knowing with God's knowing (*conscientia*). The relation between the known and the knower is threefold. Cognition is incomplete and lacks the free co-operation of the knower when God merely pervades (*durchwohnt*) the creature, as is the case with the devil's timorous and reluctant knowledge of God. A higher stage is reached when the known is present to the knower and dwells with him (*beiwohnt*). Cognition becomes really free and perfect when God dwells in (*inwohnt*) the creature, in which case the finite reason yields itself freely and in admiration to the divine reason, lets the latter speak in itself, and feels its rule, not as foreign, but as its own. (Baader maintains a like threefoldness in the practical sphere: the creature is either the object or, rather, the passive recipient, or the organ, or the representative of the divine action, i.e., in the first case, God alone works; in the second, he co-operates with the creature; in the third, the creature works with the forces and in the name of God. Joyful obedience, conscious of its grounds, is the highest freedom). Knowing and loving, thought and volition, knowledge and faith, philosophy and dogma are as little to be abstractly divided as thing and self, being and thought, object and subject. True freedom and genuine speculation are neither blind traditional belief nor doubting, God-estranged thinking, but the free recognition of authority, and self-attained conviction of the truth of the Church doctrine.

Baader distinguishes a twofold creation of the world and a double process of development (an esoteric and an exoteric revelation) of God himself. The creation of the ideal world, as a free act of love, is a non-deducible fact; the theogonic process, on the contrary, is a necessary event by which God becomes a unity returning from division to itself, and so a living God. The eternal self-generation of God is a twofold birth: in the immanent or logical process the unsearchable will (Father) gives birth to the comprehensible will (Son) to unite with it as Spirit; the place of this self-revelation is wisdom or the Idea. In the emanent or real process, since desire or nature is added to the Idea and is overcome by it, these three moments become actual persons. In the creation of the—at first immaterial—world, in which God unites, not with his essence, but with his image only, the same two powers, desire and wisdom, operate as the principles of matter and form. The materialization of the world is a consequence of the fall. Evil consists in the elevation of selfhood, which springs from desire, into self-seeking. Lucifer fell because of pride, and man, yielding to Lucifer's temptation, from baseness, by falling in love with nature beneath him. By the creation of matter God has out of pity preserved the world, which was corrupted by the fall, from the descent into hell, and at the same time has given man occasion for moral endeavor. The appearance of Christ, the personification of the moral law, is the beginning of reconciliation, which man appropriates through the sacrament. Nature participates in the redemption, as in the corruption.

Friedrich Daniel Ernst Schleiermacher was born in 1768 at Breslau, and died in 1834 in Berlin, where he had become preacher at Trinity church in 1809, professor of theology in 1810, member of the philosophical section of the Academy in 1811, and its secretary in 1814. Reared in the Moravian schools at Niesky and Barby, he studied at Halle; and, between 1794 and 1804, was a preacher in Landsberg on the Warthe, in Berlin (at the Charité Hospital), and in Stolpe, then professor in Halle. He first attracted attention by the often republished *Discourses on Religion addressed to the Educated among those who despise it*, 1799 (critical edition by Pünjer, 1879), which was followed in the succeeding year by the *Monologues*, and the anonymous *Confidential Letters on Lucinde* (*Lucinde* was the work of his friend Fr. Schlegel). Besides several collections of sermons, mention must further be made of his *Outlines of a Critique of Previous Ethics*, 1803; *The Celebration of Christmas*, 1806; and his chief theological work, *The Christian Faith*, 1822, new edition 1830. In the third (the philosophical) division of his *Collected Works* (1835-64) the second and third volumes contain the essays on the history of philosophy, on ethical, and on academic subjects; vols. vi. to ix., the Lectures on Psychology, Esthetics, the Theory of the State, and Education, edited by George, Lommatsch, Brandis, and Platz; and the first part of vol. iv., the *History of Philosophy* (to Spinoza), edited by Ritter. The *Monologues* and *The Celebration of Christmas* have appeared in *Reclam's Bibliothek*.

Schleiermacher's philosophy is a rendezvous for the most diverse systems. Side by side with ideas from Kant, Fichte, and Schelling we meet Platonic, Spinozistic, and Leibnitzian elements; even Jacobi and the Romanticists have contributed their mite. Schleiermacher is an eclectic, but one who, amid the fusion of the most diverse ideas, knows how to make his own individuality felt. In spite of manifold echoes of the philosophemes of earlier and of contemporary thinkers, his system is not a conglomeration of unrelated lines of thought, but resembles a plant, which in its own way works over and assimilates the nutritive elements taken up from the soil. Schleiermacher is attractive rather than impressive; he is less a discoverer than a critic and systematizer. His fine critical sense works in the service of a positive aim, subserves a harmonizing tendency; he takes no pleasure in breaking to pieces, but in adjusting, limiting, and combining. There is no one of the given views which entirely satisfies him, none which simply repels him; each contains elements which seem to him worthy of transformation and adoption. When he finds himself confronted by a sharp conflict of opinion, he seeks by careful mediation to construct a whole out of the two "half truths," though this, it is true, does not always give a result more satisfactory than the partial views which he wishes to reconcile. A single example may be given of this conciliatory tendency: space, time, and the categories are not only subjective forms of knowledge, but at the same time objective forms of reality. "Not only" is the watchword of his philosophy, which became the prototype of the numberless "ideal realisms" with which Germany was flooded after Hegel's death. If the skeptical and eclectic movements, which constantly make their appearance together, are elsewhere divided among different thinkers, they here come together in one mind in the form of a mediating criticism, which, although it argues logically, is yet in the end always guided by the invisible cords of a *feeling* of justice in matters scientific. In its weaker portions Schleiermacher's philosophy is marked by lack of grasp, pettiness, and sportiveness. It lacks courage and force, and the rare delicacy of the thought is not entirely able to compensate for this defect. In its fear of one-sidedness it takes refuge in the arms of an often faint-hearted policy of reconciliation.

We shall not discuss the specifically theological achievements of this many-sided man, nor his great services in behalf of the philological knowledge of the history of philosophy—through his translation of Plato, 1804-28, and a series of valuable essays on Greek thinkers—but shall confine our attention to the leading principles of his theory of knowledge, of religion, and of ethics.

The *Dialectic*[1] (edited by Jonas, 1839), treats in a transcendental part and a technical or formal part of the concept and the forms of knowledge. *Knowledge* is thought. What distinguishes that thought which we call knowledge from that other thought which does not deserve this honorable title, from mere opinion? Two criteria: its agreement with the thought of other thinkers (its universality and necessity), and its agreement with the being which is thought in it. That thought alone is knowledge which is represented as necessarily valid for all who are capable of thought, and as corresponding to a being or reproducing it. These two agreements (among thinkers, and of thought with the being which is thought) are the criteria of knowledge—let us turn now to its factors. These are essentially the two brought forward by Kant, sensibility and understanding; Schleiermacher calls them the organic function and the intellectual function. The organic activity of the senses furnishes us, in sensations, the unordered, manifold material of knowledge, which is formed and unified by the activity of reason. If we except two concepts which limit our knowledge, chaos and God—absolute formlessness or chaos is an idea just as incapable of realization as absolute unity or deity—every actual cognition is a product of both factors, of the sensuous organization and of reason. But these two do not play equal parts in every cognitive act. When the organic function is predominant we have perception; when the intellectual function predominates we have thought in the strict sense. A perfect balance of the two would be intuition, which, however, constitutes the goal of knowledge, never fully to be realized. These two kinds of knowledge, therefore, are not specifically, but only relatively, different: in all perception reason is also active, and in all thought sensibility, only to a less degree than the opposite function. Moreover, perception and thought, or sensibility and reason, are by no means to relate to different objects. They have the same object, only that the organic activity represents it as an indefinite, chaotic manifold, while the activity of reason (whose work consists in discrimination and combination), represents it as a well-ordered multiplicity and unity. It is the same being which is represented by perception in the form of an "image," and by thought in the form of a "concept." In the former case we have the world as chaos; in the latter, we have it as cosmos. Inasmuch as the two factors in knowledge represent the same object in relatively different ways, it may be said of them that they are opposed to each other, and yet identical. The same is true of the two modes of being which Schleiermacher posits as real and ideal over against the two factors in thought. The real is that which corresponds to the organic function, the ideal that which corresponds to the activity of reason. These forms of being also are opposed, and yet identical. Our self-consciousness gives clear proof of the fact that *thought and being* can be *identical*; in it, as thinking being, we have the identity of the real and the ideal, of being and thought immediately given. As the ego, in which the subject of thought and the object of thought are one, is the undivided ground of its several activities, so God is the primal unity, which lies at the basis of the totality of the world. As in Schelling, the absolute is described as self-identical, absolute unity, exalted above the antithesis of real and ideal, nay, above all antitheses. God is the negation of opposites, the world the totality of them. If there were an adequate knowledge of the absolute identity it would be an absolute knowledge. This is denied, however, to us men, who are never able to rise above the opposition of sensuous and intellectual cognition. The unity of thought and being is presupposed in all thinking, but can never actually be thought. As an Idea this identity is indispensable, but to think it definitely, either by conception or judgment, is impossible. The concepts supreme power (God or creative nature) and supreme cause (fate or providence) do not attain to that which we seek to think in them: that which has in it no opposition is an idea incapable of realization by man, but, nevertheless, a necessary ideal, the presupposition of all cognition (and volition), and the ground of all certitude. All knowledge must be related to the absolute unity and be accompanied by it. Since, then, the absolute identity cannot be presented, but ever sought for only, and absolute knowledge exists only as an ideal, dialectic is not so much a science as a technique of thought and proof, an introduction to philosophic thinking or (since knowledge is thought in common) to discussion in conformity with the rules of the art. With this name dialectic returns to its original Platonic meaning.

[Footnote 1: Cf. Quaebicker, *Ueber Schleiermachers erkeuntnisstheoretische Grundansicht*, 1871, and the *Inquiries* by Bruno Weiss in the *Zeitschrift für Philosophie*, vols. lxxiii.-lxxv., 1878-79.]

The popular ideas of God ill stand examination by the standard furnished by the principle of identity. The plurality of attributes which we are accustomed to ascribe to God agree but poorly with his unity free from all contrariety. In reality God does not possess these manifold attributes; they first arise in the religious consciousness, in which his unconditioned and undivided working is variously reflected and, as it were, divided. They are only the various reflections of his undivided nature in the mind of the observer. In God ability and performance, intelligence and will, his thought of self and his thought of the world coincide in one. Even the concept of personality must not be ascribed to God, since it is a limitation of the infinite and belongs to mythology; while the idea of life, on the contrary, is allowable as a protection against atheism and fatalism. When Schleiermacher, further, equates the activity of God and the causality of nature he ranges himself on the pantheistic side in regard to the question of the "immanence or transcendence of God," without being willing to acknowledge it. It sounds Spinozistic enough when he says: God never was without the world, he exists neither before nor outside it, we know him only *in* us and in things. Besides that which he actually brings forth, God could not produce anything further, and just as little does he miraculously interfere in the course of the world as regulated by natural law. Everything takes place necessarily, and man is distinguished above other beings neither by freedom (if by freedom we understand anything more than inner necessitation) nor by eternal existence. Like all individual beings, so we are but changing states in the life of the universe, which, as they have arisen, will disappear again. The common representations of immortality, with their hope of future compensation, are far from pious. The true immortality of religion is this—amid finitude to become one with the infinite, and in one moment to be eternal.

Schleiermacher's optimism well harmonizes with this view of the relation between God and the world. If the universe is the phenomenon of the divine activity, then considered as a whole it is perfect; whatever of imperfection we find in it, is merely the inevitable result of finitude. The bad is merely the less perfect; everything is as good as it can be; the world is the best possible; everything is in its right place; even the meanest thing is indispensable; even the mistakes of men are to be treated with consideration. All is good and divine. In this way Schleiermacher weds ideas from Spinoza to Leibnitzian conceptions. From the former he appropriates pantheism, from the latter optimism and the concept of individuality; he shares determinism with both: all events, even the decisions of the will, are subject to the law of necessity.

In the *philosophy of religion* Schleiermacher created a new epoch by his separation between religion and related departments with which it had often been identified before his time, as it has been since. In its origin and essence religion is not a matter of knowing, further, not a matter of willing, but a matter of the heart. It lies quite outside the sphere of speculation and of practice, coincides neither with metaphysics nor with ethics, is not knowledge and not volition, but an intermediate third: it has its own province in the emotional nature, where it reigns without limitation; its essence is intuition and feeling in undivided unity. In *feeling* is revealed the presence of the infinite; in feeling we become immediately aware of the Deity. The absolute, which in cognition and volition we only presuppose and demand, but never attain, is actually given in feeling alone as the relative identity and the common ground of cognition and volition. Religion is *piety*, an affective, not an objective, consciousness. And if certain religious ideas and actions ally themselves with the pious state of mind, these are not essential constituents of religion, but derivative elements, which possess a religious significance only in so far as they immediately develop from piety and exert an influence upon it. That which makes an act religious is always feeling as a point of indifference between knowing and doing, between receptive and forthgoing activity, as the center and junction of all the powers of the soul, as the very focus of personality. And as feeling in general is the middle point in the life of the soul, so, again, the religious feeling is the root of all genuine feeling. What sort of a feeling, then, is piety? Schleiermacher answers: A feeling of *absolute dependence*. Dependence on what? On the universe, on God. Religion grows out of the longing after the infinite, it is the sense and taste for the All, the direction toward the eternal, the impulse toward the absolute unity, immediate experience of the world harmony; like art, religion is the immediate apprehension of a whole. In and before God all that is individual disappears, the religious man sees one and the same thing in all that is particular. To represent all events in the world as actions of a God, to see God in all and all in God, to feel one's self one with the eternal,—this is religion. As we look on all being within us and without as proceeding from the world-ground, as determined by an ultimate cause, we feel ourselves dependent on the divine causality. Like all that is finite, we also are the effect of the absolute Power. While we stand in a relation of interaction with the individual parts of the world, and feel ourselves partially free in relation to them, we can only receive effects from God without answering them; even our self-activity we have from him. Nevertheless the feeling of dependence is not to be depressing, not humbling merely, but the joyous sense of an exaltation and broadening of life. In our devotion to the universe we participate in the life of the universe; by leaning on the infinite we supplement our finitude—religion makes up for the needy condition of man by bringing him into relation with the absolute, and teaching him to know and to feel himself a part of the whole.

From this elevating influence of religion, which Schleiermacher eloquently depicts, it is at once evident that his definition of it as a feeling of absolute dependence is only half correct. It needs to be supplemented by the feeling of freedom, which exalts us by the consciousness of the oneness of the human reason and the divine. It is only to this side of religion, neglected by Schleiermacher, that we can ascribe its inspiring influence, which he in vain endeavors to derive from the feeling of dependence. Power can never spring from humility as such. This defect, however, does not detract from Schleiermacher's merit in assigning to religion a special field of spiritual activity. While Kant treats religion as an appendix to ethics, and Hegel, with a one-sidedness which is still worse, reduces it to an undeveloped form of knowledge, Schleiermacher recognizes that it is not a mere concomitant phenomenon—whether an incidental result or a preliminary stage—of morality or cognition, but something independent, co-ordinate with volition and cognition, and of equal legitimacy. The proof that religion has its habitation in feeling is the more deserving of thanks since it by no means induced Schleiermacher to overlook the connection of the God-consciousness with self-consciousness and the consciousness of the world. Schleiermacher's theory, moreover, may be held correct without ignoring the relatively legitimate elements in the views of religion which he attacked. With the view that religion has its seat in feeling, it is quite possible to combine a recognition of the fact that it has its origin in the will, and its basis in morals, and that, further, it has the significance of being (to use Schopenhauer's words) the "metaphysics of the people."

Although religion and piety be made synonymous, it must still be admitted that in a being capable of knowing and willing as well as of feeling, this devout frame will have results in the spheres of cognition and action. In regard to *cultus* Schleiermacher maintains that a religious observance which does not spring from one's own feeling and find an echo therein is superstitious, and demands that religious feeling, like a sacred melody, accompany all human action, that everything be done with religion, nothing from religion. Instead of expressing itself in single specifically religious actions, the religious feeling should uniformly pervade the whole life. Let a private room be the temple where the voice of the priest is raised. Dogmas, again, are descriptions of pious excitation, and take their origin in man's reflection on his religious feelings, in his endeavor to explain them, in his expression of them in ideas and words. The concepts and principles of theology are valid only as descriptions and presentations of feelings, not as cognitions; by their unavoidable anthropomorphic character alone they are completely unfitted for science. The dogmatic system is an envelopment which religion accepts with a smile. He who treats religious doctrines as science falls into empty mythology. Principles of faith and principles of knowledge are in no way related to one another, neither by way of opposition nor by way of agreement; they never come into contact. A theology in the sense of an actual science of God is impossible. Further, out of its dogmas the Church constructs prescriptive symbols, a step which must be deplored. It is to be hoped that some time religion will no longer have need of the Church. In view of the present condition of affairs it must be said that the more religious a man is the more secular he must become, and that the cultured man opposes the Church in order to promote religion.

So-called natural religion is nothing more than an abstraction of thought; in reality positive religions alone exist. Because of the infinity of God and the finitude of man, the one, universal, eternal religion can only manifest itself in the form of particular historical religions, which are termed revealed because founded by religious heroes, creative personalities, in whom an especially lively religious feeling is aroused by a new view of the universe, and determines (not, like artistic inspiration, single moments, but) their whole existence. Three stages are to be distinguished in the development of religion, according as the world is represented as an unordered unity (chaos), or as an indeterminate manifold of forces and elements (plurality without unity), or, finally, as an organized plurality dominated by unity (system)—fetichism with fatalism, polytheism, mono- (including pan-) theism. Among the religions of the third stadium Islam is physical or aesthetic in spirit; Judaism and Christianity, on the other hand, ethical or teleological. The Christian religion is the most perfect, because it gives the central place to the concept of redemption and reconciliation (hence to that which is essential to religion) instead of to the Jewish idea of retribution.

The concept of individuality became of the highest importance for Schleiermacher's ethics, as well as for his philosophy of religion; and by his high appreciation of it he ranges himself with Leibnitz, Herder, Goethe, and Novalis. Now two sides may be distinguished both in regard to that which the individual is and to that which he ought to accomplish. Like every particular being, man is an abbreviated, concentrated presentation of the universe; he contains everything in himself, contains all, that is, in a not yet unfolded, germinal manner, awaiting development in life in time, but yet in a form peculiar to him, which is never repeated elsewhere. This yields a twofold moral task. The individual ought to rouse into actuality the infinite fullness of content which he possesses as possibility, as slumbering germs, should harmoniously develop his capacities; yet in this he must not look upon the unique form which has been bestowed upon him as worthless. He is not to feel himself a mere specimen, an unimportant repetition of the type, but as a particular, and in this particularity a significant, expression of the absolute, whose omission would cause a gap in the world. It is surprising that the majority of the thinkers who have defended the value of individuality lay far less stress upon the micro-cosmical nature of the individual and the development of his capacities in all directions than on care for his peculiar qualities. So also Schleiermacher. Yet he gradually returned from the extreme individualism—the *Monologues* affect one almost repellently by the impulse which they give to vain self-reflection—which he at first defended.

In the *Ethics* (edited by Kirchmann, 1870; earlier editions by Schweizer, 1835, and Twesten, 1841) Schleiermacher brings the well-nigh forgotten concept of goods again into honor. The three points of view from which ethics is to be discussed, and each of which presents the whole ethical field in its own peculiar way—the good, virtue, duty—are related as resultant, force, and law of motion. Every union of reason and nature produced by the action of the former on the latter is called a *good*; the sum of these unities, the highest good. According as reason uses nature as an instrument in formation or as a symbol in cognition her action is formative or indicative; it is, further, either common or peculiar. On the crossing of these (fluctuating) distinctions of identical and individual organization and symbolization is based the division of the theory of goods:

SPHERES. RELATIONS. GOODS.
Ident. Organ.: Intercourse. Right. The State.
Individ. Organ.: Property. Free Sociability. Class, House,
Friendship.
Ident. Symbol.: Knowledge. Faith. School and
University.
Individ. Symbol.: Feeling. Revelation. The Church
(Art).

The four ethical communities, each of which represents the organic union of opposites—rulers and subjects, host and guests, teachers and pupils or scholars and the public, the clergy and the laity—have for their foundation the family and the unity of the nation. Virtue (the personal unification of reason and sensibility) is either disposition or skill, and in each case either cognitive or presentative; this yields the cardinal virtues wisdom, love, discretion, and perseverance. The division of duties into duties of right, duties of love, duties of vocation, and duties of conscience rests on the distinction between community in production and appropriation, each of which may be universal or individual. The most general laws of duty (duty is the Idea of the good in an imperative form) run: Act at every instant with all thy moral power, and aiming at thy whole moral problem; act with all virtues and in view of all goods, further, Always do that action which is most advantageous for the whole sphere of morality, in which two different factors are included: Always do that toward which thou findest thyself inwardly moved, and that to which thou findest thyself required from without. Instead of following further the wearisome schematism of Schleiermacher's ethics, we may notice, finally, a fundamental thought which our philosopher also discussed by itself: The sharp contraposition of natural and moral law, advocated by Kant, is unjustifiable; the moral law is itself a law of nature, viz., of rational will. It is true neither that the moral law is a mere "ought" nor that the law of nature is a mere "being," a universally followed "must." For, on the one hand, ethics has to do with the law which human action really follows, and, on the other, there are violations of rule in nature also. Immorality, the imperfect mastery of the sensuous impulses by rational will, has an analogue in the abnormalities—deformities and diseases—in nature, which show that here also the higher (organic) principles are not completely successful in controlling the lower processes. The higher law everywhere suffers disturbances, from the resistance of the lower forces, which cannot be entirely conquered. It is Schleiermacher's determinism which leads him, in view of the parallelism of the two legislations, to overlook their essential distinction.

Adherents of Schleiermacher are Vorländer (died 1867), George (died 1874), the theologian, Richard Rothe (died 1867; cf. Nippold, 1873 *seq.*), and the historians of philosophy, Brandis (died 1867) and H. Ritter (died 1869).[1]

[Footnote 1: W. Dilthey (born 1834), the successor of Lotze in Berlin, is publishing a life of Schleiermacher (vol. i. 1867-70). Cf. also Dilthey's briefer account in the *Allgemeine deutsche Biographie*, and Haym's *Romantische Schule*, 1870. Further, *Aus Schleiermachers Leben, in Briefen*, 4 vols., 1858-63.]

CHAPTER XIII.

HEGEL.

Georg Wilhelm Friedrich Hegel was born at Stuttgart on August 27, 1770. He attended the gymnasium of his native city, and, from 1788, the Tübingen seminary as a student of theology; while in 1793-1800 he resided as a private tutor in Berne and Frankfort-on-the-Main. In the latter city the plan of his future system was already maturing. A manuscript outline divides philosophy, following the ancient division, logic, physics, and ethics, into three parts, the first of which (the fundamental science, the doctrine of the categories and of method, combining logic and metaphysics) considers the absolute as pure Idea, while the second considers it as nature, and the third as real (ethical) spirit. Hegel habilitated in 1801 at Jena, with a Latin dissertation *On the Orbits of the Planets*, in which, ignorant of the discovery of Ceres, he maintained that on rational grounds—assuming that the number-series given in Plato's *Timaeus* is the true order of nature—no additional planet could exist between Mars and Jupiter. This dissertation gives, further, a deduction of Kepler's laws. The essay on the *Difference between the Systems of Fichte and Schelling* had appeared even previous to this. In company with Schelling he edited in 1802-03 the *Kritisches Journal der Philosophie*. The article on "Faith and Knowledge" published in this journal characterizes the standpoint of Kant, Jacobi, and Fichte as that of reflection, for which finite and infinite, being and thought form an antithesis, while true *speculation* grasps these in their identity. In the night before the battle of Jena Hegel finished the revision of his *Phenomenology of Spirit*, which was published in 1807. The extraordinary professorship given him in 1805 he was forced to resign on account of financial considerations; then he was for a year a newspaper editor in Bamberg, and in 1808 went as a gymnasial rector to Nuremberg, where he instructed the higher classes in philosophy. His lectures there are printed in the eighteenth volume of his works, under the title *Propaedeutic*. In the Nuremberg period fell his marriage and the publication of the *Logic* (vol. i. 1812, vol. ii. 1816). In 1816 he was called as professor of philosophy to Heidelberg (where the *Encyclopedia* appeared, 1817), and two years later to Berlin. The *Outlines of the Philosophy of Right*, 1821, is the only major work which was written in Berlin. The *Jahrbücher für wissenschaftliche Kritik*, founded in 1827 as an organ of the school, contained a few critiques, but for the rest he devoted his whole strength to his lectures. He fell a victim to the cholera on November 14, 1831. The collected edition of his works in eighteen volumes (1832-45) contains in vols. ii.-viii. the four major works which had been published by Hegel himself (the *Encyclopaedia* with additions from the Lectures); in vols. i., xvi., and xvii. the minor treatises; in vols. ix.-xv. the Lectures, edited by Cans, Hotho, Marheineke, and Michelet. The Letters from and to Hegel have been added as a nineteenth volume, under the editorship of Karl Hegel, 1887.[1]

[Footnote 1: Hegel's Life has been written by Karl Rosenkranz (1844), who has also defended the master (*Apologie Hegels*, 1858) against R. Haym *(Hegel und seine Zeit,* 1857), and extolled him as the national philosopher of Germany (1870; English by G.S. Hall). Cf., further, the neat popular exposition by Karl Köstlin, 1870, and the essays by Ed. von Hartmann, *Ueber die dialektische Methode*, 1868, and *Hegels Panlogismus* (1870, incorporated in the *Gesammelte Studien und Aufsätze*, 1876). [The English reader may consult E. Caird's *Hegel* in Blackwood's Philosophical Classics, 1883; Harris's *Hegel's Logic*, Morris's *Hegel's Philosophy of the State and of History*, and Kedney's *Hegel's Aesthetics* in Griggs's Philosophical Classics; and Wallace's translation of the "Logic"—from the *Encyclopaedia*—with Prolegomena, 1874, 2d. ed., Translation, 1892, Prolegomena to follow. Stirling's *Secret of Hegel, 2* vols., London, 1865, includes a translation of a part of the *Logic*, and numerous translations from different works of the master are to be found in the *Journal of Speculative Philosophy*. The *Lectures on the Philosophy of History* have been translated by J. Sibree, M.A., in Bohn's Library, 1860, and E.S. Haldane is issuing a translation of those on the *History of Philosophy*, vol. i., 1892.—TR.]]

We may preface our exposition of the parts of the system by some remarks on Hegel's standpoint in general and his scientific method.

%1. Hegel's View of the World and his Method.%

In Hegel there revives in full vigor the intellectualism which from the first had lain in the blood of German philosophy, and which Kant's moralism had only temporarily restrained. The primary of practical reason is discarded, and theory is extolled as the ground, center, and aim of human, nay, of all existence.

Leibnitz and Hegel are the classical representatives of the intellectualistic view of the world. In the former the subjective psychological point of view is dominant, in the latter, the objective cosmical position: Leibnitz argues from the representative nature of the soul to an analogous constitution of all elements of the universe; from the general mission of all that is real, to be a manifestation of reason, Hegel deduces that of the individual spirit, to realize a determinate series of stages of thought. The true reality is reason; all being is the embodiment of a pregnant thought, all becoming a movement of the concept, the world a development of thought. The absolute or the logical Idea exists first as a system of antemundane concepts, then it descends into the unconscious sphere of nature, awakens to self-consciousness in man, realizes its content in social institutions, in order, finally, in art, religion, and science to return to itself enriched and completed, *i.e.*, to attain a higher absoluteness than that of the beginning. Philosophy is the highest product and the goal of the world-process. As will, intuition, representation, and feeling are lower forms of thought, so ethics, art, and religion are preliminary stages in philosophy; for it first succeeds in that which these vainly attempt, in presenting the concept adequately, in conceptual form.

If we develop that which is contained as a constituent factor or by implication in the intellectualistic thesis, "All being is thought realized, all becoming a development of thought," we reach the following definitions: (i) The object of philosophy is formed by the Ideas of things. Its aim is to search out the concept, the purpose, the significance of phenomena, and to assign to these their corresponding positions in the world and in the system of knowledge. It is chiefly interested in discovering where in the scale of values a thing belongs according to its meaning and its destination; the procedure is teleological, valuing, aesthetic. Instead of a causal explanation of phenomena we are given an ideal interpretation of them. (So Lotze accurately describes the character of German idealism.) (2) If all that is real is a manifestation of reason and each thing a stage, a modification of thought, then thought and being are identical. (3) If the world is thought in becoming, and philosophy has to set forth this process, philosophy is a theory of development. If each thing realizes a thought, then all that is real is rational; and if the world-process attains its highest stadium in philosophy, and this in turn its completion in the system of absolute idealism, then all that is rational is real. Reason or the Idea is not merely a demand, a longed for ideal, but a world-power which accomplishes its own realization. "The rational is real and the real is rational" (Preface to the *Philosophy of Right*). Or to sum it up— Hegel's philosophy is *idealism, a system of identity, and an optimistic doctrine of development*. What, then, distinguishes Hegel from other idealists, philosophers of identity, and teachers of development? What in particular distinguishes him from his predecessor Schelling?

In Schelling nature is the subject and art the conclusion of the development; his idealism has a physical and aesthetical character, as Fichte's an ethical character. In Hegel, however, the concept is the subject and goal of the development, his philosophy is, in the words of Haym, a "*Logisierung*" of the world, a *logical idealism*.

The theory of identity is that system which looks upon nature and spirit as one in essence and as phenomenal modes of an absolute which is above them both. But while Schelling treats the real and the ideal as having equal rights, Hegel restores the Fichtean subordination of nature to spirit, without, however, sharing Fichte's contempt for nature. Nature is neither co-ordinate with spirit nor a mere instrument for spirit, but a transition stage in the development of the absolute, viz., the Idea in its other-being *(Anderssein)*. It is spirit itself that becomes nature in order to become actual, conscious spirit; before the absolute became nature it was already spirit, not, indeed, "for itself" *(für sich)*, yet "in itself" *(an sich)*, it was Idea or reason. The ideal is not merely the morning which follows the night of reality, but also the evening which precedes it. The absolute (the concept) develops from in-itself *(Ansich)* through out-of-self *(Aussersich)* or other-being to for-itself *(Fürsich)*; it exists first as reason (system of logical concepts), then as nature, finally as living spirit. Thus Hegel's philosophy of identity is distinguished from Schelling's by two factors: it subordinates nature to spirit, and conceives the absolute of the beginning not as the indifference of the real and ideal, but as ideal, as a realm of eternal thoughts.

The assertion that Hegel represents a synthesis of Fichte and Schelling is therefore justified. This is true, further, for the character of Hegel's thought as a whole, in so far as it follows a middle course between the world-estranged, rigid abstractness of Fichte's thinking and Schelling's artistico-fanciful intuition, sharing with the former its logical stringency as well as its dominant interest in the philosophy of spirit, and with the latter its wide outlook and its sense for the worth and the richness of that which is individual.

We have characterized Hegel's system, thirdly, as a philosophy of development. The point of distinction here is that Hegel carries out with logical consecutiveness and up to the point of obstinacy the principle of development which Fichte had discovered, and which Schelling also had occasionally employed,—the threefold rhythm *thesis, antithesis, synthesis*. Here we come to Hegel's *dialectic method*. He reached this as the true method of speculation through a comparison of the two forms of philosophy which he found dominant at the beginning of his career—the Illumination culminating in Kant, on the one hand, and, on the other, the doctrine of identity defended by Schelling and his circle—neither of which entirely satisfied him.

In regard to the main question he feels himself one with Schelling: philosophy is to be metaphysics, the science of the absolute and its immanence in the world, the doctrine of the identity of opposites, of the, *per se* of things, not merely of their phenomenon. But the form which Schelling had given it seems to him unscientific, unsystematic, for Schelling had based philosophical knowledge on the intuition of genius—and science from intuition is impossible. The philosophy of the Illumination impresses him, on the other hand, by the formal strictness of its inquiry; he agrees with it that philosophy must be science from concepts. Only not from abstract concepts. Kant and the Illumination stand on the platform of reflection, for which the antithesis of thought and being, finite and infinite remains insoluble, and, consequently, the absolute transcendent, and the true essence of things unknowable. Hegel wishes to combine the advantages of both sides, the depth of content of the one, and the scientific form of the other.

The intuition with which Schelling works is immediate cognition, directed to the concrete and particular. The concept of the philosophy of reflection is mediate cognition, moving in the sphere of the abstract and universal. Is it not feasible to do away with the (unscientific) immediateness of the one, and the (non-intuitive, content-lacking) abstractness of the other, to combine the concrete with the mediate or conceptual, and in this way to realize the Kantian ideal of an intuitive understanding? *A concrete concept* would be one which sought the universal not without the particular, but in it; which should not find the infinite beyond the finite, nor the absolute at an unattainable distance above the world, nor the essence hidden behind the phenomenon, but manifesting itself therein. If the philosophy of reflection, in the abstract lifelessness of its concepts, looked on opposites as incapable of sublation, and Schelling regarded them as immediately identical, if the former denied the identity of opposites, and the latter maintained it primordially given (in the absolute indifference which is to be grasped by intuition), the concrete concept secures the identity of *opposites through self-mediation*, their passing over into it; it teaches us to know the identity as the result of a process. First immediate unity, then divergence of opposites, and, finally, reconciliation of opposites—this is the universal law of all development.

The conflict between the philosophy of reflection and the philosophy of intuition, which Hegel endeavors to terminate by a speculation at once conceptual and concrete, concerns (1) the organ of thought, (2) the object of thought, (3) the nature and logical dignity of the contradiction.

The organ of the true philosophy is neither the abstract reflective understanding, which finds itself shut up within the limits of the phenomenal, nor mystical intuition, which expects by a quick leap to gain the summit of knowledge concerning the absolute, but reason as the faculty of concrete concepts. That concept is concrete which does not assume an attitude of cold repulsion toward its contrary, but seeks self-mediation with the latter, and moves from thesis through antithesis, and with it, to synthesis. Reason neither fixes the opposites nor denies them, but has them become identical. The unity of opposites is neither impossible nor present from the first, but the result of a development.

The object of philosophy is not the phenomenal world or the relative, but the absolute, and this not as passive substance, but as living subject, which divides into distinctions, and returns from them to identity, which develops through the opposites. The absolute is a process, and all that is real the manifestation of this process. If science is to correspond to reality, it also must be a process. Philosophy is thought-movement (dialectic); it is a system of concepts, each of which passes over into its successor, puts its successor forth from itself, just as it has been generated by its predecessor.

All reality is development, and the motive force in this development (of the world as well as of science) is opposition, *contradiction*. Without this there would be no movement and no life. Thus all reality is full of contradiction, and yet rational. The contradiction is not that which is entirely alogical, but it is a spur to further thinking. It must not be annulled, but "sublated" _(aufgehoben), *i.e.*, at once negated and conserved. This is effected by thinking the contradictory concepts together in a third higher, more comprehensive, and richer concept, whose moments they then form. As sublated moments they contradict each other no longer; the opposition or contradiction is overcome. But the synthesis is still not a final one; the play begins anew; again an opposition makes its appearance, which in turn seeks to be overcome, etc. Each separate concept is one-sided, defective, represents only a part of the truth, needs to be supplemented by its contrary, and, by its union with this, its complement, yields a higher concept, which comes nearer to the whole truth, but still does not quite reach it. Even the last and richest concept—the absolute Idea—is by itself alone not the full truth; the result implies the whole development through which it has been attained. It is only at the end of such a dialectic of concepts that philosophy reaches complete correspondence with the living reality, which it has to comprehend; and the speculative progress of thought is no capricious sporting with concepts on the part of the thinking subject, but the adequate expression of the movement of the matter itself. Since the world and its ground is development, it can only be known through a development of concepts. The law which this follows, in little as in great, is the advance from position to opposition, and thence to combination. The most comprehensive example of this triad—Idea, Nature, Spirit—gives the division of the system; the second—Subjective, Objective, Absolute Spirit—determines the articulation of the third part.

%2. The System.%

Hegel began with a *Phenomenology* by way of introduction, in which (not to start, like the school of Schelling, with absolute knowledge "as though shot from a pistol") he describes the genesis of philosophical cognition with an attractive mingling of psychological and philosophico-historical points of view. He makes spirit—the universal world-spirit as well as the individual consciousness, which repeats in brief the stages in the development of humanity—pass through six stadia, of which the first three (consciousness, self-consciousness, reason) correspond to the progress of the intermediate part of the Doctrine of Subjective Spirit, which is entitled *Phänomenologie*, and the others (ethical spirit, religion, and absolute knowledge) give an abbreviated presentation of that which the Doctrine of Objective and Absolute Spirit develops in richer articulation.

%(a) Logic% considers the Idea in the abstract element of thought, only as it is thought, and not yet as it is intuited, nor as it thinks itself; its content is the truth as it is without a veil in and for itself, or God in his eternal essence before the creation of the world. Unlike common logic, which is merely formal, separating form and content, speculative logic, which is at the same time ontology or metaphysics, treats the categories as real relations, the forms of thought as forms of reality: as thought and thing are the same, so logic is the theory of thought and of being in one. Its three principal divisions are entitled *Being, Essence, the Concept*. The first of these discusses quality, quantity, and measure or qualitative quantum. The second considers essence as such, appearance, and (essence appearing or) actuality, and this last, in turn, in the moments, substantiality, causality, and reciprocity. The third part is divided into the sections, subjectivity (concept, judgment, syllogism), objectivity (mechanism, chemism, teleology), and the Idea (life, cognition, the absolute Idea).

As a specimen of the way in which Hegel makes the concept pass over into its opposite and unite with this in a synthesis, it will be sufficient to cite the famous beginning of the *Logic*. How must the absolute first be thought, how first defined? Evidently as that which is absolutely without presupposition. The most general concept which remains after abstracting from every determinate content of thought, and from which no further abstraction is possible, the most indeterminate and immediate concept, is pure *being*. As without quality and content it is equivalent to *nothing*. In thinking pure being we have rather cogitated nothing; but this in turn cannot be retained as final, but passes back into being, for in being thought it exists as a something thought. Pure being and pure nothing are the same, although we mean different things by them; both are absolute indeterminateness. The transition from being to nothing and from nothing to being is *becoming*. Becoming is the unity, and hence the truth of both. When the boy is "becoming" a youth he is, and at the same time is not, a youth. Being and not-being are so mediated and sublated in becoming that they are no longer contradictory. In a similar way it is further shown that quality and quantity are reciprocally dependent and united in measure (which may be popularly illustrated thus: progressively diminishing heat becomes cold, distances cannot be measured in bushels); that essence and phenomenon are mutually inseparable, inasmuch as the latter is always the appearance of an essence, and the former is essence only as it manifests itself in the phenomenon, etc.

The significance of the Hegelian logic depends less on its ingenious and valuable explanations of particulars than on the fundamental idea, that the categories do not form an unordered heap, but a great organically connected whole, in which each member occupies its determinate position, and is related to every other by gradations of kinship and subordination. This purpose to construct a *globus* of the pure concepts was itself a mighty feat, which is assured of the continued admiration of posterity notwithstanding the failure in execution. He who shall one day take it up again will draw many a lesson from Hegel's unsuccessful attempt. Before all, the connections between the concepts are too manifold and complex for the monotonous transitions of this dialectic method (which Chalybaeus wittily called articular disease) to be capable of doing them justice. Again, the productive force of thought must not be neglected, and to it, rather than to the mobility of the categories themselves, the matter of the transition from one to the other must be transferred.

%(b) The Philosophy of Nature% shows the Idea in its other-being. Out of the realm of logical shades, wherein the souls of all reality dwell, we move into the sphere of external, sensuous existence, in which the concepts take on material form. Why does the Idea externalize itself? In order to become actual. But the actuality of nature is imperfect, unsuited to the Idea, and only the precondition of a better actuality, the actuality of spirit, which has been the aim from the beginning: reason becomes nature in order to become spirit; the Idea goes forth from itself in order—enriched—to return to itself again. Only the man who once has been in a foreign land knows his home aright.

The relation of natural objects to one another and their action upon one another is an external one: they are governed by mechanical necessity, and the contingency of influences from without arrests and disturbs their development, so that while reason is everywhere discernible in nature, it is not reason alone; and much that is illogical, contrary to purpose, lawless, painful, and unhealthy, points to the fact that the essence of nature consists in externality. This inadequacy in the realization of the Idea, however, is gradually removed by development, until, in "life," the way is prepared for the birth of spirit.

As Hegel in his philosophy of nature—which falls into three parts, mechanics, physics, and organics—follows Schelling pretty closely, and, moreover, does not show his power, it does not seem necessary to dwell longer upon it. In the next section, also, in view of the fact that its models, the constructive psychologies of Fichte and Schelling, have already been discussed in detail, a statement of the divisions and connections must suffice.

%(c) The Doctrine of Subjective Spirit% makes freedom (being with or in self) the essence and destination of spirit, and shows how spirit realizes this predisposition in increasing independence of nature. The subject of anthropology is spirit as the (natural, sensitive, and actual) "soul" of a body; here are discussed the distinctions of race, nation, sex, age, sleeping and waking, disposition and temperament, together with talents and mental diseases, in short, whatever belongs to spirit in its union with a body. Phenomenology is the science of the "ego," i.e., of spirit, in so far as it opposes itself to nature as the non-ego, and passes through the stages of (mere) consciousness, self-consciousness, and (the synthesis of the two) reason. Psychology (better pneumatology) considers "spirit" in its reconciliation with objectivity under the following divisions: Theoretical Intelligence as intuition (sensation, attention, intuition), as representation (passive memory, phantasy, memory), and (as conceiving, judging, reasoning) thought; Practical Intelligence as feeling, impulse (passion and caprice), and happiness; finally, the unity of the knowing and willing spirit, free spirit or rational will, which in turn realizes itself in right, ethics, and history.

%(d) The Doctrine of Objective Spirit%, comprehending ethics, the philosophy of right, of the state, and of history, is Hegel's most brilliant achievement. It divides as follows: (1) Right (property, contract, punishment); (2) Morality (purpose, intention and welfare, good and evil); (3) Social Morality: (a) the family; (b) civil society; (c) the state (internal and external polity, and the history of the world). In right the will or freedom attains to outer actuality, in morality it attains to inner actuality, in social morality to objective and subjective actuality at once, hence to complete actuality.

Right, as it were a second, higher nature, because a necessity posited and acknowledged by spirit, is originally a sum of prohibitions; wherever it seems to command the negative has only received a positive expression. Private right contains two things—the warrant to be a person, and the injunction to respect other persons as such. Property is the external sphere which the will gives to itself; without property no personality. Through punishment (retaliation) right is restored against un-right (*Unrecht*), and the latter shown to be a nullity. The criminal is treated according to the same maxim as that of his action—that coercion is allowable.

In the stadium of morality the good exists in the form of a requirement which can never be perfectly fulfilled, as a mere imperative; there remains an irrepressible opposition between the moral law and the individual will, between intention and execution. Here the judge of good and evil is the conscience, which is not secure against error. That which is objectively evil may seem good and a duty to subjective conviction. (According to Fichte this was impossible).

On account of the conflict between duty and will, which is at this stage irrepressible, Hegel is unable to consider morality, the sphere of the subjective disposition, supreme. He thinks he knows a higher sphere, wherein legality and morality become one: "social morality" (*Sittlichkeit*). This sphere takes its name from *Sitte*, that custom ruling in the community which is felt by the individual not as a command from without, but as his own nature. Here the good appears as the spirit of the family and of the people, pervading individuals as its substance. Marriage is neither a merely legal nor a merely sentimental relation, but an "ethical" (*sittliches*) institution. While love rules in the family, in civil society each aims at the satisfaction of his private wants, and yet, in working for himself, subserves the good of the whole. Class distinctions are based on the division of labor demanded by the variant needs of men (the agricultural, industrial, and thinking classes). Class and party honor is, in Hegel's view, among the most essential supports of general morality. Strange to say, he brings the administration of justice and the police into the same sphere.

The state, the unity of the family and civil society, is the completed actualization of freedom. Its organs are the political powers (which are to be divided, but not to be made independent): the legislative power determines the universal, the executive subsumes the particular thereunder, the power of the prince combines both into personal unity. In the will of the prince the state becomes subject. The perfect form of the state is constitutional monarchy, its establishment the goal of history, which Hegel, like Kant, considers chiefly from the political standpoint.

History is the development of the rational state; the world-spirit the guiding force in this development; its instruments the spirits of the nations and great men. A particular people is the expression of but one determinate moment of the universal spirit; and when it has fulfilled its commission it loses its legal warrant, and yields up its dominion to another, now the only authorized one: the history of the world is the judgment of the world, which is held over the nations. The world-historical characters, also, are only the instruments of a higher power, the purposes of which they execute while imagining that they are acting in their own interests—their own deed is hidden from them, and is neither their purpose nor their object. This should be called the cunning of reason, that it makes the passions work in its service.

History is progress in the consciousness of freedom. At first one only knows himself free, then several, finally all. This gives three chief periods, or rather four world-kingdoms,—Oriental despotism, the Greek (democratic) and the Roman (aristocratic) republic, and the Germanic monarchy,—in which humanity passes through its several ages. Like the sun, history moves from east to west. China and India have not advanced beyond the preliminary stages of the state; the Chinese kingdom is a family state, India a society of classes stiffened into castes. The Persian despotism is the first true state, and this in the form of a conquering military state. In the youth and manhood of humanity the sovereignty of the people replaces the sovereignty of one; but not all have yet the consciousness of freedom, the slaves have no share in the government. The principle of the Greek world, with its fresh life and delight in beauty, is individuality; hence the plurality of small states, in which Sparta is an anticipation of the Roman spirit. The Roman Republic is internally characterized by the constitutional struggle between the patricians and the plebeians, and externally by the policy of world conquest. Out of the repellent relations between the universal and the individual, which oppose one another as the abstract state and abstract personality, the unhappy imperial period develops. In the Roman Empire and Judaism the conditions were given for the appearance of Christianity. This brings with it the idea of humanity: every man is free as man, as a rational being. In the beginning this emancipation was religious; through the Germans it became political as well. The remaining divisions cannot here be detailed. Their captions run: The Elements of the Germanic Spirit (the Migrations; Mohammedanism; the Frankish Empire of Charlemagne); the Middle Ages (the Feudal System and the Hierarchy; the Crusades; the Transition from Feudal Rule to Monarchy, or the Cities); Modern Times (the Reformation; its Effect on Political Development; Illumination and Revolution).

The philosophy of history[1] is Hegel's most brilliant and most lasting achievement. His view of the state as the absolute end, the complete realization of the good, is dominated, no doubt, by the antique ideal, which cannot take root again in the humanity of modern times. But his splendid endeavor to "comprehend" history, to bring to light the laws of historical development and the interaction between the different spheres of national life, will remain an example for all time. The leading ideas of his philosophy of history have so rapidly found their way into the general scientific consciousness that the view of history which obtained in the period of the Illumination is well nigh incomprehensible to the investigator of to-day.

[Footnote 1: A well-chosen collection of aphorisms from the philosophy of history is given by M. Schasler under the title *Hegel: Populäre Gedanken aus seinen Werken*, 2d. ed., 1873.]

%(e) Absolute Spirit% is the unity of subjective and objective spirit. As such, spirit becomes perfectly free (from all contradictions) and reconciled with itself. The break between subject and object, representation and thing, thought and being, infinite and finite is done away with, and the infinite recognized as the essence of the finite. The knowledge of the reconciliation of the highest opposites or of the infinite *in* the finite presents itself in three forms: in the form of intuition (art), of feeling and representation (religion), of thought (philosophy).

(1) *Aesthetics*.—The beautiful is the absolute (the infinite in the finite) in sensuous existence, the Idea in limited manifestation. According to the relation of these moments, according as the outer form or the inner content predominates, or a balance of the two occurs, we have the symbolic form of art, in which the phenomenon predominates and the Idea is merely suggested; or the classical form, in which

Idea and intuition, or spiritual content and sensuous form, completely balance and pervade each other, in which the former of them is ceaselessly taken up into the latter; or the romantic form, in which the phenomenon retires, and the Idea, the inwardness of the spirit predominates. Classical art, in which form and content are perfectly conformed to each other, is the most beautiful, but romantic art is, nevertheless, higher and more significant.

Oriental, including Egyptian and Hebrew, art was symbolic; Greek art, classical; Christian art is romantic, bringing into art entirely new sentiments of a knightly and a religious sort—love, loyalty and honor, grief and repentance—and understanding how by careful treatment to ennoble even the petty and contingent. The sublime belongs to symbolic art; the Roman satire is the dissolution of the classical, and humor the dissolution of the romantic, ideal.

Architecture is predominantly symbolic; sculpture permits the purest expression of the classical ideal; painting, music, and poetry bear a romantic character. This does not exclude the recurrence of these three stages within each art—in architecture, for example, as monumental (the obelisk), useful (house and temple), and Gothic (the cathedral) architecture. As the plastic arts reached their culmination among the Hellenes, so the romantic arts culminate among the Christian nations. In poetry, as the most perfect and universal (or the totality of) art, uniting in itself the two contraries, the symbolic and the classical, the lyric is a repetition of the architectonic-musical, the epic, of the plastic-pictorial, the drama, the union of the lyric and the epic.

(2) *Philosophy of Religion.*—The withdrawal from outer sensibility into the inner spirit, begun in romantic art, especially in poetry, is completed in religion. In religion the nations have recorded the way in which they represent the substance of the world; in it the unity of the infinite and the finite is felt, and represented through imagination. Religion is not merely a feeling of piety, but a thought of the absolute, only not in the form of thinking. Religion and philosophy are materially the same, both have God or the truth for their object, they differ only in form—religion contains in an empirical, symbolic form the same speculative content which philosophy presents in the adequate form of the concept. Religion is developing knowledge as it gradually conquers imperfection. It appears first as definite religion in two stadia, natural religion and the religion of spiritual individuality, and finally attains the complete realization of its concept in the absolute religion of Christianity.

Natural religion, in its lowest stage magic, develops in three forms—as the religion of measure (Chinese), of phantasy (Indian or Brahmanical), and of being in self (Buddhistic). In the Persian (Zoroastrian) religion of light, the Syrian religion of pain, and the Egyptian religion of enigma, is prepared the way for the transformation into the religion of freedom. The Greek solves the riddle of the Sphinx by apprehending himself as subject, as man.

The religion of spiritual individuality or free subjectivity passes through three stadia: the Jewish religion of sublimity (unity), the Greek religion of beauty (necessity), the Roman religion of purposiveness (of the understanding). In contrast to the Jewish religion of slavish obedience, which by miracle makes known the power of the one God and the nullity of nature, which has been "created" by his will, and the prosaic severity of the Roman, which, in Jupiter and Fortuna, worships only the world-dominion of the Roman people, the more cheerful art-religion of the Hellenes reverences in the beautiful forms of the gods, the powers which man is aware of in himself—wisdom, bravery, and beauty.

The Christian or revealed religion is the religion of truth, of freedom, of spirit. Its content is the unity of the divine nature and the human, God as knowing himself in being known of man+; the knowledge of God is God's self-knowledge. Its fundamental truths are the Trinity (signifying that God differentiates and sublates the difference in love), the incarnation (as a figure of the essential unity of the infinite and finite spirit), the fall, and Christ's atoning death (this signifies that the realization of the unity between man and God presupposes the overcoming of naturality and selfishness).

(3) *Philosophy.*—Finally the task remains of clothing the absolute content given in religion in the form adequate to it, in the form of the concept. In philosophy absolute spirit attains the highest stage, its perfect self-knowledge. It is the self-thinking Idea.

Here we must not look for further detailed explanations: philosophy is just the course which has been traversed. Its systematic exposition is encyclopaedia; the consideration of its own actualization, the history of philosophy, which, as a "philosophical" discipline, has to show the conformity to law and the rationality of this historical development, to show the more than mere succession, the genetic succession, of systems, as well as their connection with the history of culture. Each system is the product and expression of its time, and as the self-reflection of each successive stage in culture cannot appear before this has reached its maturity and is about to be overcome. Not until the approach of the twilight does the owl of Minerva begin its flight.

CHAPTER XIV.

THE OPPOSITION TO CONSTRUCTIVE IDEALISM: FRIES, HERBART, SCHOPENHAUER.

In Fries, Herbart, and Schopenhauer a threefold opposition was raised against the idealistic school represented by Fichte, Schelling, and Hegel. The opposition of Fries is aimed at the method of the constructive philosophers, that of Herbart against their ontological positions, and that of Schopenhauer against their estimate of the value of existence. Fries and Beneke declare that a speculative knowledge of the suprasensible is impossible, and seek to base philosophy on empirical psychology; to the monism (panlogism) of the idealists Herbart opposes a pluralism, to their philosophy of becoming, a philosophy of being; Schopenhauer rejects their optimism, denying rationality to the world and the world-ground. Among themselves the thinkers of the opposition have little more in common than their claim to a better understanding of the Kantian philosophy, and a development of it more in harmony with the meaning of its author, than it had experienced at the hands of the idealists. Whoever fails to agree with them in this, and ascribes to the idealists whom they oppose better grounded claims to the honor of being correct interpreters and consistent developers of Kantian principles, will be ready to adopt the name *Semi-Kantians*, given by Fortlage to the members of the opposition,—a title which seems the more fitting since each of them appropriates only a definitely determinable part of Kant's views, and mingles a foreign element with it. In Fries this non-Kantian element comes from Jacobi's philosophy of faith; in Herbart it comes from the monadology of Leibnitz, and the ancient Eleatico-atomistic doctrine; in Schopenhauer, from the religion of India and (as in Beneke) from the sensationalism of the English and the French. We can only hint in passing at the parallelism which exists between the chief representatives of the idealistic school and the leaders of the opposition. Fries's theory of knowledge and faith is the empirical counterpart of Fichte's Science of Knowledge. Schopenhauer, in his doctrine of Will and Idea, in his vigorously intuitive and highly fanciful view of nature and art, and, in general, in his aesthetical mode of philosophizing, with its glad escape from the fetters of method, has so much in common with Schelling that many unhesitatingly treat his system as an offshoot of the Philosophy of Nature. The contrast between Herbart and Hegel is the more pronounced since they are at one in their confidence in the power of the concept. The most conspicuous point of comparison between the metaphysics of the two thinkers is the significance ascribed by them to the contradiction as the operative moment in the movement of philosophical thought. The attitude of hostility which Schleiermacher assumed in relation to Hegel's intellectualistic conception of religion induced Harms to give to Schleiermacher also a place in the ranks of the opposition. Following the chronological order, we begin with the campaign opened by Fries under the banner of anthropology against the main branch of the Kantian school.

%1. The Psychologists: Fries and Beneke.%

Jacob Friedrich Fries (1773-1843) was born and reared at Barby, studied at Jena, and habilitated at the same university in the year 1801; he was professor at Heidelberg in 1806-16, and at Jena from 1816 until his death. His chief work was the *New Critique of Reason*, in three volumes, 1807 (2d ed., 1828 *seq.*), which had been preceded, in 1805, by the treatise *Knowledge, Faith, and Presentiment*. Besides these he composed a *Handbook of Psychical Anthropology*, 1821 (2d ed., 1837 *seq.*), text-books of Logic, Metaphysics, the Mathematical Philosophy of Nature, and Practical Philosophy and the Philosophy of Religion, and a philosophical novel, *Julius and Evagoras, or the Beauty of the Soul*.

Fries adopts and popularizes Kant's results, while he rejects Kant's method. With Reinhold and Fichte, he thinks "transcendental prejudice" has forced its way into philosophy, a phase of thought for which Kant himself was responsible by his anxiety to demonstrate everything. That *a priori* forms of knowledge exist cannot be proved by speculation, but only by empirical methods, and discovered by inner observation; they are given facts of reason, of which we become conscious by reflection or psychological analysis. The *a priori* element cannot be demonstrated nor deduced, but only shown actually present. The question at issue[1] between Fries and the idealistic school therefore becomes, Is the discovery of the *a priori* element itself a cognition *a priori* or *a posteriori*? Is the criticism of reason a metaphysical or an empirical, that is, an anthropological inquiry? Herbart decides with the idealists: "All concepts through which we think our faculty of knowledge are themselves metaphysical concepts" (*Lehrbuch zur Einleitung*, p. 231). Fries decides: The criticism of reason is an empirico-psychological inquiry, as in general empirical psychology forms the basis of all philosophy.

[Footnote 1: Cf. Kuno Fischer's Pro-Rectoral Address, *Die beiden Kantischen Schulen in Jena*, 1862.]

With the exception of this divergence in method Fries accepts Kant's results almost unchanged, unless we must call the leveling down which they suffer at his hands a considerable alteration. Only the doctrine of the Ideas and of the knowledge of reason is transformed by the introduction and systematization of Jacobi's principle of the immediate evidence of faith. Reason, the faculty of Ideas, *i.e.*, of the indemonstrable yet indubitable principles, is fully the peer of the sensibility and the understanding. The same subjective necessity which guarantees to us the objective reality of the intuitions and the categories accompanies the Ideas as well; the faith which reveals to us the *per se* of things is no less certain than the knowledge of phenomena. The ideal view of the world is just as necessary as the natural view; through the former we cognize the same world as through the latter, only after a higher order; both spring from reason or the unity of transcendental apperception, only that in the natural view we are conscious of the fact, from which we abstract in the ideal view, that this is the condition of experience. That which necessitates us to rise from knowledge to faith is the circumstance that the empty unity-form of reason is never completely filled by sensuous cognition. The Ideas are of two kinds: the aesthetic Ideas are intuitions, which lack clear concepts corresponding to them; the logical Ideas are concepts under which no correspondent definite intuitions can be subsumed. The former are reached through combination; the latter by negation, by thinking away the limitations of empirical cognition, by removing the limits from the concepts of the understanding. By way of the negation of all limitations we reach as many Ideas as there are categories, that is, twelve, among which the Ideas of relation are the most important. These are the three axioms of faith—the eternity of the soul (its elevation above space and time, to be carefully distinguished from immortality, or its permanence in time), the freedom of the will, and the Deity. Every Idea expresses something absolute, unconditioned, perfect, and eternal.—The dualism of knowledge and faith, of nature and freedom, or of phenomenal reality and true, higher reality, is bridged over by a third and intermediate mode of apprehension, feeling or presentiment, which teaches us the reconciliation of the two realities, the union of the Idea and the phenomenon, the interpenetration of the eternal and the temporal. The beautiful is the Idea as it manifests itself in the phenomenon, or the phenomenon as it symbolizes the eternal. The aesthetico-religious judgment looks on the finite as the revelation and symbol of the infinite. In brief, "Of phenomena we have knowledge; in the true nature of things we believe; presentiment enables us to cognize the latter in the former."

Theoretical philosophy is divided into the philosophy of nature, which is to use the mathematical method, hence to give a purely mechanical explanation of all external phenomena, including those of organic life, and to leave the consideration of the world as a teleological realm to religious presentiment—and psychology. The object of the former is external nature, that of the latter internal nature. I know myself only as phenomenon, my body through outer, my ego through inner, experience. It is only a variant mode of appearing on the part of one and the same reality—so Fries remarks in opposition to the *influxus physicus* and the *harmonia praestabilata*—which now shows me my person inwardly as my spirit, and now outwardly as the life-process of my body. Practical philosophy includes ethics, the philosophy of religion, and aesthetics. In accordance with the threefold interest of our animal, sensuo-rational, and purely rational impulses, there result three ideals for the legislation of values. These are the ideal of happiness, the ideal of perfection, and the ideal of morality, or of the agreeable, the useful, and the good, the third of which alone possesses an unconditioned worth and validity as a universal and necessary law. The moral laws are deduced from faith in the equal personal dignity of men, and the ennobling of humanity set up as the highest mission of morality. The three fundamental aesthetical tempers are the idyllic and epic of enthusiasm, the dramatic of resignation, the lyric of devotion.

Fries's system is thus a union of Kantian positions with elements from Jacobi, in which the former experience deterioration, and the latter improvement, namely, more exact formulation. Among his adherents, and he has them still, the following appear deserving of mention: the botanists Schleiden and Hallier; the theologian De Wette; the philosophers Calker (of Bonn, died 1870) and Apelt (1812-59). The last made himself favorably known by his *Epochs of the History of Humanity*, 1845-46, *Theory of Induction*, 1854, and *Metaphysics*, 1857; his *Philosophy of Religion* (1860) did not appear until after his death. The Catholic theologian, Georg Hermes of Bonn (1775-1831) favored a Kantianism akin to that of Fries.

* * * * *

The psychological view founded by Fries was consistently developed by Friedrich Eduard Beneke (1798-1854). With the exception of three years of teaching in Göttingen, 1824-27, whither he had gone in consequence of a prohibition of his lectures called forth by his *Foundation of the Physics of Ethics*, 1822, he was a member of the university of his native city, Berlin, first as *Docent*, and, from 1832, after the death of Hegel, who was unfavorably disposed toward him, as professor extraordinary.[1] Besides Kant, Jacobi, and Fries, Schleiermacher, Herbart (with whom he became acquainted in 1821), and the English thinkers exerted a determining influence on the formation of his philosophy. Beneke denies the possibility of speculative knowledge even more emphatically than Fries. Kant's undertaking was aimed at the destruction of a non-experiential science from concepts, and if it has not succeeded in preventing the neo-Scholasticism of the Fichtean school, with its overdrawn attempts to revive a deductive knowledge of the absolute, this has been chiefly due to the false, non-empirical method of the great critic of reason. The root and basis of all knowledge is experience; metaphysics itself is an empirical science, it is the last in the series of philosophical disciplines. Whoever begins with metaphysics, instead of ending with it, begins the house at the roof. The point of departure for all cognition is inner experience or self-observation; hence the fundamental science is psychology, and all other branches of philosophy nothing but applied psychology. By the inner sense we perceive our ego as it really is, not merely as it appears to us; the only object whose *per se* we immediately know is our own soul; in self-consciousness being and representation are one. Thus, in opposition to Kant, Beneke stands on the side of Descartes: The soul is better known to us than the external world, to which we only transfer the existence immediately given in the soul as a result of instinctive analogical inference, so that in the descent of our knowledge from men organized like ourselves to inorganic matter the inadequacy of our representations progressively increases.

[Footnote 1: On Beneke's character cf. the fourth of Fortlage's *Acht psychologische Vorträge*, which are well worth reading.]

Psychology—we may mention of Beneke's works in this field the *Psychological Sketches*, 1825-27, and the *Text-book of Psychology*, 1833, the third and fourth (1877) editions of which, edited by Dressler, contain as an appendix a chronological table of all Beneke's works—must, as internal natural science, follow the same method, and, starting with the immediately given, employ the same instruments in the treatment of experience as external natural science, *i.e.* the explanation of facts by laws, and, further still, by hypotheses and theories. Gratefully recognizing the removal of two obstacles to psychology, the doctrine of innate ideas and the traditional theory of the faculties of the soul by Locke and Herbart, (the commonly accepted faculties—memory, understanding, feeling, will—are in fact not simple powers, but mere abstractions, hypostatized class concepts of extremely complex phenomena,) Beneke seeks to discover the simple elements from which all mental life is compounded. He finds these in the numerous elementary faculties of receiving and appropriating external stimuli, which the soul in part possesses, in part acquires in the course of its life, and which constitute its substance; each separate sense of itself includes many such faculties. Every act or product of the soul is the result of two mutually dependent factors: *stimulus and receptivity*. Their coming together gives the first of the *four fundamental processes*, that of perception. The second is the constant addition of new elementary faculties. By the third, the equilibration or reciprocal transfer of the movable elements in representations, Beneke explains the reproduction of an idea through another associated with it, and the widening of the mental horizon by emotion, *e.g.*, the astounding eloquence of the angry. Since each representation which passes out of consciousness continues to exist in the soul as an unconscious product (where we cannot tell; the soul is not in space), it is not retention, but oblivescence which needs explanation. That which persists of the representation which is passing into unconsciousness, and which makes its reappearance in consciousness possible, is called a "trace" in reference to its departed cause, and a "disposition" (*Angelegtheit*) in reference to its future results. Every such trace or germ (*Anlage*)—that which lies intermediate between perception and recollection—is a force, a striving, a tendency. The fourth of the fundamental processes (which may be traced downward into the material world, since the corporeal and the psychical differ only in degree and pass over into each other) is the combination of mental products according to the measure of their similarity, as these come to light in the formation of judgments, comparisons, witticisms, of collective images, collective feelings, and collective desires. The innate differences among men depend on the greater or lesser "powerfulness, vivacity, and receptivity" of their elementary faculties; all further differences arise gradually and are due to the external stimuli; even the distinction between the human and the animal soul, which consists in the spiritual nature of the former, is not original.

Of the five constructive forms of the soul, which result from the varying relation between stimulus and faculty, four are emotional products or products of moods. If the stimulus is too small pain (dissatisfaction, longing) arises, while pleasure springs from a marked, but not too great, fullness of stimulus. If the stimulus gradually increases to the point of excess, blunted appetite and satiety come in; when the excess is sudden it results in pain. A clear representation, a sensation arises when the stimulus is exactly proportioned to the faculty; it is in this case only that the soul assumes a theoretical attitude, that it merely perceives without any admixture of agreeable or disagreeable feelings. Desire is pleasure remembered, the ego the complex of all the representations which have ever arisen in the soul, the totality of the manifold given within me. For the immortality of the immaterial soul Beneke advances an original and attractive argument based on the principle that, in consequence of the constantly increasing traces, through which the substance of the soul is continually growing, consciousness turns more and more from the outer to the inner, until finally perception dies entirely away. At death the connection with the outer world ceases, it is true, but not the inner being of the soul, for which that which has hitherto been highest now becomes the foundation for new and still higher developments.

Like Herbart, on whom he was in many ways dependent, Beneke discussed psychology and pedagogics with greater success than logic, metaphysics, practical philosophy, and the philosophy of religion. He combats the apriorism of Kant in ethics as elsewhere. The moral law does not arise until the end of a long development. First in order are the immediately felt values of things, which we estimate according to the degree of enhancement or depression in the psychical state which they call forth. From the feelings are formed concepts, from concepts judgments; and the abstraction of the categorical imperative is a highly derivative phenomenon and a very late result, although the feeling of oughtness or of moral obligation, which accompanies the correct estimation of values and bids us prefer spiritual to sensuous delights and the general good to our own welfare, grows necessarily out of the inner nature of the human soul. There are two sources of religion: one theoretical, for the idea of God; the other practical, for the worship of God. We are impelled to the assumption of a suprasensible, an unconditioned, a providence, on the one hand, by the desire for a unitary conclusion for our fragmentary knowledge of the world; and, on the other, by moral need, by our unsatisfied longing after the good. The attributes which we ascribe to God are taken from experience, the abstract attributes from being in general, the naturalistic from the world, the spiritual from man. As an inevitable outcome of the transformation of religious feelings into representations, and one which is harmless because of the unmistakableness of their symbolic character, the anthropomorphic predicates, through which we think the Deity as personal, themselves establish the superiority of theism over pantheism. The object of religion, moreover, is accessible only to the subjective certitude of feeling which is given by faith, and not to scientific knowledge.

Feuerbach's anthropological standpoint will be discussed below. Like Friedrich Ueberweg (1826-71; professor in Königsberg; *System of Logic*, 1857, 5th ed., edited by J.B. Meyer, 1882—English translation, 1871), Karl Fortlage was strongly influenced in his psychological views by Beneke. Born in 1806 at Osnabrück, and at his death in 1881 a professor in Jena, Fortlage shared with Beneke an impersonality of character, as well as the fate of meeting with less esteem from his contemporaries than he merited by the seriousness and originality of his thinking. To his *System of Psychology*, 1855, in two volumes, he added, as it were, a third volume, his *Contributions to Psychology*, 1875, besides psychological lectures of a more popular cast (*Eight Lectures*, 1869, 2d ed., 1872; *Four Lectures*, 1874).[1] Fortlage characterizes his psychological method—in the criticism of which F.A. Lange fails to show the justice for which he is elsewhere to be commended—as observation by the inner sense. In the first place, consciousness, as the active form of representation, must be separated from that of which we are conscious, from the "content of representation," which is in itself unconscious, but capable of coming into consciousness. Next Fortlage seeks to determine the laws of these two factors. In regard to the content of representation he distinguishes more sharply than Herbart between the fusibility of the homogeneous and the capacity for complex combination possessed by the heterogeneous (the fusion of similars goes on even without aid from consciousness, while the connection of dissimilars is brought about only through the help of the latter), and adds to these two general properties of the content of representation two further ones, its revivability (its persistence in unconsciousness), and its dissolubility in the scale of size, color, etc. Consciousness, on the other hand, which for Fortlage coincides with the ego or self, is treated as the presupposition of all representations, not as their result—it is underived activity. He explains the nature of consciousness by the concept of attention, characterizes them both as "questioning activity" (*Fragethätigkeit*), and follows them out in their various degrees from expectation through observation up to reflection. The listening and watching of the hunter when waiting for the game is only a prolongation of the same consciousness which accompanies all less exciting representations. The essential element in conscious or questioning activity is the oscillation between yes and no.

As soon as the disjunction is decided by a yes, the desire which lies at its basis, and which in the condition of consciousness is arrested, passes over into activity. All consciousness is based on interest, and in its origin is "arrested impulse" (*Triebhemmung*). "The direction of impulse to an intuition to be expected only in the future is called consciousness." The rank of a being depends on its capacity for reflection: the greater the extent of its attention and the smaller the stimuli which suffice to rouse this to action, the higher it stands. Impulse—this is the fundamental idea of Fortlage's psychology, like will with Fichte, and representation with Herbart—consists of an element of representation and an element of feeling.

Pleasure + effort-image = impulse.

[Footnote 1: Among Fortlage's other works we may mention his valuable *History of Poetry*, 1839; the *Genetic History of Philosophy since Kant*, 1852; and the attractive *Six Philosophical Lectures*, 1869, 2d ed., 1872.]

In his metaphysical convictions, to which he gave expression in his *Exposition and Criticism of the Arguments for the Existence of God*, 1840, among other works, Fortlage belongs to the philosophers of identity. Originally sailing in Hegel's wake, he soon recognizes that the roots of the theory of identity go back to the Kantio-Fichtean philosophy, with which the system of absolute truth, as he holds, has come into being. He thus becomes an adherent of the Science of Knowledge, whose deductive results he finds inductively confirmed by psychological experience. Psychology is the empirical test for the metaphysical calculus of the Science of Knowledge. In regard to the absolute Fortlage is in agreement with Krause, the younger Fichte, Ulrici, etc., and calls his standpoint *transcendent pantheism*. According to this all that is good, exalted, and valuable in the world is divine in its nature; the human reason is of the same essence as the divine reason (there can be nothing higher than reason); the Godhead is the absolute ego of Fichte, which employs the empirical egos as organs, which thinks and wills in individuals, in so far as they think the truth and will the good, but at the same time as universal subject goes beyond them. If, after the example of Hegel, we give up transcendent pantheism in favor of immanence, two unphilosophical modes of representing the absolute at once result—on the one hand, materialism; on the other, popular, unphilosophical theism. If the Fichtean Science of Knowledge could be separated from its difficult method, which it is impossible ever to make comprehensible to the unphilosophical mind, it would be called to take the place of religion.[1]

[Footnote 1: Among Fortlage's posthumous manuscripts was one on the Philosophy of Religion, on which Eucken published an essay in the *Zeitschrift für Philosophie*, vol. lxxxii. 1883, p. 180 *seq.* after Lipsius had given a single chapter from it—"The Ideal of Morality according to Christianity"—in his *Jahrbücher für protestantische Theologie* (vol. ix. pp. 1-45). The journals *Im Neuen Reich*, 1881, No. 24, and *Die Gegenwart*, 1882, No. 34, contained warmly written notices of Fortlage by J. Volkelt. Leopold Schmid (in Giessen, died 1869) gives a favorable and skillfully composed outline of Fortlage's system in his *Grundzüge der Einleitung in die Philosophie mit einer Beleuchtung der von K. Ph. Fischer, Sengler, und Fortlage ermöglichten Philosophie der That*, 1860, pp. 226-357. Cf. also Moritz Brasch, *K. Fortlage, Ein philosophisches Charakterbild*, in *Unsere Zeit*, 1883, Heft II, pp. 730-756, incorporated in the same author's *Philosophie der Gegenwart*, 1888.]

%2. Realism: Herbart.%

Johann Friedrich Herbart was scientifically the most important among the philosophers of the opposition. Herbart was born at Oldenburg in 1776, the son of a councilor of justice, and had already become acquainted with the systems of Wolff and Kant before he entered the University of Jena in 1794. In 1796 he handed in to his instructor Fichte a critique of two of Schelling's treatises, in which the youthful thinker already broke away from idealism. While a private tutor in Switzerland he made the acquaintance of Pestalozzi. In 1802 he habilitated in Göttingen, where, in 1805, he was promoted to a professorship extraordinary; while in 1809 he received the professorship in Königsberg once held by Kant, and later by W. Tr. Krug (died 1842). He died in 1841 at Göttingen, whither he had been recalled in 1833. His *Collected Works* were published in twelve volumes, 1850-52 (reprinted 1883 *seq.*), by his pupil Hartenstein, who has also given an excellent exposition of his master's system in his *Probleme und Grundlehren der allgemeinen Metaphysik*, 1836, and his *Grundbegriffe der ethischen Wissenschaften*, 1844; a new edition, in chronological order, and under the editorship of K. Kehrbach, began to appear in 1882, or rather 1887, and has now advanced to the fourth volume, 1891. Herbart's chief works were written during his Königsberg residence: the *Text-book of Introduction to Philosophy*, 1813, 4th ed., 1837 (very valuable as an introduction to Herbartian modes of thought); *General Metaphysics*, 1829 (preceded in 1806 and 1808 by *The Principal Points in Metaphysics*, with a supplement, *The Principal Points in Logic); Text-book of Psychology*,[1] 1816, 2d ed., 1834; *On the Possibility and Necessity of applying Mathematics to Psychology*, 1822; *Psychology as a Science*, 1824-25. The two works on ethics, which were widely separated in time, were, on the other hand, written in Göttingen: *General Practical Philosophy*, 1808; *Analytical Examination of Natural Right and of Morals*, 1836. To these may be added a *Discourse on Evil*, 1817; *Letters on the Doctrine of the Freedom of the Human Will*, 1836; and the *Brief Encyclopaedia of Philosophy*, 1831, 2d ed., 1841. His works on education and instruction, whose influence and value perhaps exceed those of his philosophical achievements (collected editions of the pedagogical works have been prepared by O. Willmann, 1873-75, 2d ed., 1880; and by Bartholomaei), extended through his whole life. Besides pedagogics, psychology was the chief sphere of his services.

[Footnote 1: English translation by M.K. Smith, 1891.]

In antithesis to the philosophy of intuition with its imagined superiority to the standpoint of reflection, Herbart makes philosophy begin with attention to concepts, defining it as the elaboration of concepts. Philosophy, therefore, is not distinguished from other sciences by its object, but by its method, which again must adapt itself to the peculiarity of the object, to the starting point of the investigation in question—there is no universal philosophical method. There are as many divisions of philosophy as there are modes of elaborating concepts. The first requisite is the discrimination of concepts, both the discrimination of concepts from others and of the marks within each concept. This work of making concepts clear and distinct is the business of logic. With this discipline, in which Herbart essentially follows Kant, are associated two other forms of the elaboration of concepts, that of physical and that of aesthetic concepts. Both of these classes require more than a merely logical elucidation. The physical concepts, through which we apprehend the world and ourselves, contain contradictions and must be freed from them; their correction is the business of meta-physics. Metaphysics is the science of the comprehensibility of experience. The aesthetic (including the ethical) concepts are distinguished from the nature-concepts by a peculiar increment which they occasion in our representation, and which consists in a judgment of approval or disapproval. To clear up these concepts and to free them from false allied ideas is the task of aesthetics in its widest sense. This includes all concepts which are accompanied by a judgment of praise or blame; the most important among them are the ethical concepts. Thus, aside from logic, we reach two principal divisions of philosophy, which are elsewhere contrasted as theoretical and practical, but here in Herbart as metaphysics and aesthetics. Herbart maintains that these are entirely independent of each other, so that aesthetics, since it presupposes nothing of metaphysics, may be discussed before metaphysics, while the philosophy of nature and psychology depend throughout on ontological principles. Together with natural theology the two latter sciences constitute "applied" metaphysics. This in turn presupposes "general" metaphysics, which subdivides into four parts: Methodology, Ontology, Synechology, *i.e.*, the theory of the continuous ([Greek: *suneches*]), which treats of the continua, space, time, and motion, and Eidolology, *i.e.*, the theory of images or representations. The last forms the transition to psychology, while synechology forms the preparation for the philosophy of nature, whose most general problems it solves. Our exposition will not need to observe these divisions closely.

Metaphysics starts with the given, but cannot rest content with it, for it contains contradictions. In resolving these we rise above the given. What *is given*? Kant has not answered this question with entire correctness. We may, indeed, term the totality of the given "phenomena," but this presupposes something which appears. If nothing existed there would also nothing appear. As smoke points to fire, so appearance to being. So much seeming, so much indication of being. Things in themselves may be known mediately, though not immediately, by following out the indications of being contained by the given appearance. Further, not merely the unformed matter of cognition is given to us, but it is rather true that everything comes under this concept which experience so presses on us that we cannot resist it; hence not merely single sensations, but entire sensation-groups, not merely the matter, but also the forms of experience. If the latter were really subjective products, as Kant holds, it would necessarily be possible for us at will to think each perceptive-content either under the category of substance, or property, or cause—possible for us, if we chose, to see a round table quadrilateral. In reality we are bound in the application of these forms; they are given for each object in a definite way. The given forms—Herbart calls them experience-concepts—contain contradictions. How can these contradictions be removed? We may neither simply reject the concepts which are burdened with contradictions, for they are given, nor leave them as they are, for the logical *principium contradictionis* requires that the contradiction as such be rooted out. The experience-concepts are valid (they find application in experience), but they are not thinkable. Therefore we must so transform and supplement them that they shall become free from contradictions and thinkable. The method which Herbart employs to remove the contradictions is as follows: The contradiction always consists in the fact that an a should be the same as a b, but is not so. The desiderated likeness of the two is impossible so long as we think a as *one* thing. That which is unsuccessful in this case will succeed, perhaps, if in thought we break up the a into several things—[Greek: $a\ b\ g$]. Then we shall be able to explain through the "together" (*Zusammen*) of this plurality what we were unable to explain from the undecomposed a, or from the single constituents of it. The "together" is a "relation" established by thought among the elements of the real. For this reason Herbart terms his method of finding out necessary supplements to the given "the method of relations." Another name for the same thing is "the method of contingent aspects." Mechanics operates with contingent aspects when, for the sake of explanation, it resolves a given motion into several components. Such fictions and substitutions—auxiliary concepts, which are not real, but which serve only as paths for thought—may be successfully employed by metaphysics also. The abstract expression of this method runs: The contradiction is to be removed by thinking one of its members as manifold rather than as one. In order to observe the workings of this Herbartian machine we shall go over the four principal contradictions by which his acuteness is put to the test—the problems of inherence, of change, of the continuous, of the ego.

We call the given sensation-complexes "things," and ascribe "properties" to them. How can one and the same thing have different properties—how can the one be at the same time many? To say that the thing "possesses" the properties does not help the matter. The possession of the different properties is itself just as manifold and various as the properties which are possessed. Hence the concept of the thing and its properties must be so transformed that the plurality which seems to be in the thing shall be transferred without it. Instead of one thing let us assume several, each with a single definite property, from whose "together" the appearance of many qualities in one thing now arises. The appearance of manifold properties in the one thing has its ground in the "together" of many things, each of which has one simple quality. Again, it is just as impossible for a thing to have different qualities in succession, or to change, as it is for it to have them at the same time. The popular view of change, which holds that a thing takes on different forms (ice, water, steam) and yet remains the same substance, is untenable. How is it possible to become another, and yet to remain the same? The universal feeling that the concept needs correction betrays itself in the fact that everyone involuntarily adds a cause to the change in thought, and seeks a cause for it, and thus of himself undertakes a transformation of the concept, though, it is true, an inadequate one. If we think this concept through we come upon a trilemma, a threefold impossibility. Whether we endeavor to deduce the change from external or from internal causes, or (with Hegel) to think it as causeless, in each case we involve ourselves in inconceivabilities. All three ideas—change as mechanism, as self-determination or freedom, as absolute becoming—are alike absurd. We can escape these contradictions only by the bold decision to conceive the quality of the existent as unchangeable. For the truly existent there is no change whatever. It remains, however, to explain the appearance of change, in which the wand of decomposition and the "together" again proves its magic power. Supported by the motley manifoldness of phenomena, we posit real beings as qualitatively different, and view this diversity as partial contraposition; we resolve, *e.g.*, the simple quality a into the elements $x + z$, and a second quality b into $y - z$. So long as the individual things remain by themselves, the opposition of the qualities will not make itself evident. But as soon as they come together, something takes place—now the opposites ($+z$ and $-z$) seek to destroy or at least to disturb each other. The reals defend themselves against the disturbance which would follow if the opposites could destroy each other, by each conserving its simple, unchangeable quality, *i.e.*, by simply remaining self-identical. *Self-conservation against* threatened *disturbances* from without (it may be compared to resistance against pressure) is the only real change, and apparent change, the empirical changes of things, to be explained from this. That which changes is only the relations between the beings, as a thing maintains itself now against this and now against that other thing; the relations, however, and their change are something entirely contingent and indifferent to the existent. In itself the self-conservation of a real is as uniform as the quality which is conserved, but in virtue of the changing relations (the variety of the disturbing things) it can express itself for the observer in manifold ways as force. The real itself changes as little as a painting changes, for instance, when, seen near at hand, the figures in it are clearly distinguished, while for the distant observer, on the contrary, they run together into an indistinguishable chaos. Change has no meaning in the sphere of the existent.

Anyone who speaks thus has denied change, not deduced it. Among the many objections experienced by Herbart's endeavor to explain the empirical fact of change by his theory of self-conservation against threatened disturbances Lotze's is the most cogent: The unsuccessful attempt to solve the difficulties in the concept of becoming and action is still instructive, for it shows that they cannot be solved in this way—from the concept of inflexible being. If the "together," the threatened disturbance, and the reaction against the latter be taken as realities, then, in the affection by the disturber, the concept of change remains unelimitated and uncorrected; if they be taken as unreal concepts auxiliary to thought, change is relegated from the realm of being to the realm of seeming. Herbart gives to them a kind of semi-reality, less true than the unmoving ground of things (their unchangeable, permanent qualities), and more true than their contradictory exterior (the empirical appearance of change). Between being and seeming he thrusts in, as though between day and night, the twilight region of his "contingent aspects," with their relations, which are nothing to the real, their disturbances, which do not come to pass, and their self-conservations, which are nothing but undisturbed continuance in existence on the part of the real.

Besides the contradictions in the concepts of inherence, of change, and action and passion, it is the concept of being which prevents our philosopher from ascribing a living character to reality. Being, as Kant correctly perceived, contains nothing qualitative; it is absolute position. Whoever affirms that an object *is*, expresses thereby that the matter is to rest with the simple position; in which is included that it is nothing dependent, relative, or negative. (Every negation is something relative, relates to a precedent position, which is to be annulled by it.) Besides being, the existent contains something more—a quality; it consists of this absolute position and a *what*. If this *what* is separated from being we reach an "image"; united with being it yields an essence or a real. This *what* of things is not their sensuous qualities; the latter belong rather to the mere phenomenon. No one of them indicates what the object is by itself, when left alone. They depend on contingent circumstances, and apart from these they would not exist—what is color in the dark? what sound in airless space? what weight in empty space? what fusibility without fire?—they are each and all relative. Since being excludes negation of every kind, the quality of the existent must be absolutely *simple and unchangeable*; it brooks no manifoldness, no quantity, no distinctions in degree, no becoming; all this were a corruption of the purely affirmative or positive character of being. The existent is unextended and eternal. The Eleatics are to be praised because the need of escaping from the contradictions in the world of experience led them to make themselves masters of the concept of being without relation and without negation, and of the simple, homogeneous quality of the existent in its full purity. But while the Eleatics conceived the existent as one, the atomists made an advance by assuming a *plurality* of reals. The truly one never becomes a plurality; plurality is given, hence an original plurality must be postulated. Herbart characterizes his own standpoint as qualitative atomism, since his reals are differentiated by their properties, not by quantitative relations (size and figure). The idealists and the pantheists make a false use of the tendency toward unity which, no doubt, is present in our reason, when they maintain that true being must be one. There is absolutely nothing in the concept of being to forbid us to think the existent as many; while the world of phenomena, with its many things and their many properties, gives irrefragable grounds which compel us to this conclusion. Hence, according to Herbart, the true reality is a (very large, though not, it is true, an infinite[1]) plurality of supra-sensible (non-spatial and non-temporal) reals, or, according to the Leibnitzian expression, monads, which all their life have nothing further to do than to preserve intact against disturbances the simple quality in which they consist (for the existent is not distinct from its quality; it does not have the quality, but is the quality). Each thing has but one response for the most varied influences: it answers all suggestions from without by affirming its *what*, by continually repeating, as it were, the same note, which gains a varying meaning only in so far as, in accordance with the character of the disturber, it appears now as a third, now as a fifth or seventh. This picture of the world is certainly not attractive; in it all change and becoming, all life and all activity is offered up on the altar of monotonous being. Happily Herbart is inconsistent enough to enliven this comfortless waste of changeless being by the relatively real or semi-real manifoldness of the self-conservations.

The infinite divisibility of space and of matter forms the chief difficulty in the problem of the continuous. Herbart endeavors to solve it by the assumption of an intelligible space with "fixed" lines (lines formed by a definite number of points, hence finitely divisible, and not continuous). Metaphysics demands the fixed or discrete line, although common thought is incapable of conceiving it. Space is a mere form of combination in representation or for the observer, and yet it is objective, *i.e.*, it is valid for all intelligences, and not merely for human intelligence. From his complex and unproductive endeavors to derive the appearance of continuity from discontinuous reality we hurry on to the fourth, the psychological problem, which Herbart discusses with great acuteness. He considers it the chief merit of Fichte's Science of Knowledge that it called attention to this problem.

The concept of the ego, of whose reality we have so strong and immediate a conviction that, in the formula of asseveration, "as true as I exist," it is made the criterion of all other certitude, labors under various contradictions. Besides the familiar difficulty, here especially sensible, of one thing with many marks, it contains other absurdities of its own. In the ego or self-consciousness subject and object are to be identical. The identity of the representing and the represented ego is a self-contradictory idea, for the law of contradiction forbids the equation of opposites, while a subject is subject only through the fact that it is not object. But, again, self-consciousness can never be realized, because it involves a *regressus in infinitum*. The ego is defined as that which represents itself. What is this "self"? It is, in turn, the self-knower. This new explanation contains still a further self; which once more signifies the self-knower and so on to infinity. The ego represents the representation (*Vorstellen*) of its representation (*Vorstellen*), etc. The representation (*Vorstellung*) of the ego, therefore, can never be actually brought to completion. (The assumption of the freedom of the will leads to an analogous *regressus in infinitum*, in which the question, "Willst thou thy volition?" "Willst thou the willing of this volition"? is repeated to infinity.) The only escape from this tissue of absurdities is to think the ego otherwise than is done by popular consciousness. The knowing and the known ego are by no means the same, but the observing subject in self-consciousness is one group of representations, the observed subject another. Thus, for example, newly formed representations are apperceived by the existing older ones, but the highest apperceiver is not, in turn, itself apperceived. The ego is not a unit being, which represents itself in the literal meaning of the phrase, but that which is represented is a plurality. The ego is the junction of numberless series of representations, and is constantly changing its place; it dwells now in this representation, now in that. But as we distinguish the point of meeting from the series which meet there, and imagine that it is possible simultaneously to abstract from all the represented series (whereas in fact we can only abstract from each one separately), there arises the appearance of a permanent ego as the unit subject of all our representations. In reality the ego is not the source of our representations, but the final result of their combination. The representation, not the ego, is the fundamental concept of psychology, the ego constituting rather its most difficult problem.[1] It is a "result of other representations, which, however, in order to yield this result, must be together in a single substance, and must interpenetrate one another" (*Text-book of Introduction*, p. 243). In this way Herbart defends the substantiality of the soul against Kant and Fries. The soul's immortality (as also its pre-existence) goes without saying, because of the non-temporal character of the real.

[Footnote 1: On the Herbartian psychology, cf. Ribot, *German Psychology of To-day*, English Translation by Baldwin, 1886, pp. 24-67; and G.F. Stout, *Mind*, vols. xiii.-xiv.—TR.]

The soul is one of these reals which, unchangeable in themselves, enter into various relations with others, and conserve themselves against the latter. In its simple *what* as unknowable as the rest, it is yet familiar to us in its self-conservations. In the absence of a more fitting expression for the totality of psychical phenomena we call these *representations*, the phenomenal manifoldness of which is due to the variety of the disturbances and exists for the observer alone. In itself, without a plurality of dispositions and impulses, the soul is originally not a representative force, but first becomes such under certain circumstances, viz., when it is stimulated to self-conservation by other beings. The sum of the reals which stand in immediate relation to the soul is called its body; this, an aggregate of simple beings, furnishes the intermediate link of causal relation between the soul and the external world. The soul has its (movable) seat in the brain. In opposition to the physiological treatment of psychology, Herbart remarks that psychology throws much more light on physiology than she can ever receive from it.

The simplest representations are the sensations, which, amid all their variety, still group themselves into definite classes (odors, sounds, colors). They serve us as symbols of the disturbing reals, but they are not images of things, nor effects of these, but products of the soul itself: the generation of sensations is the soul's peculiar way of guarding itself against threatened disturbances. Every representation once come into being disappears again from consciousness, it is true, but not from the soul. It persists, unites with others, and stands with them in a relation of interaction—in both cases according to definite laws. These original representations are the only ones which the soul produces by its own activity; all other psychical phenomena, feeling, desire, will, attention, memory, judgment, the whole wealth of inner events, result of themselves from the interplay of the primary representations under law. Representation (more exactly sensation) is alone original; space, time, the categories, which Kant makes *a priori*, are all acquired, *i.e.*, like all the higher mental life, they are the results of a psychical *mechanism*, results whose production needs no renewed exertion on the part of the soul itself. It has been a very harmful error in psychology hitherto to ascribe each particular mental activity to a special *faculty of the soul* having a similar name, instead of deriving it from combinations of simple representations. Abstract, empty class ideas have been treated as real forces, in the belief that thus the single concrete acts had been "explained."

There is no bitterer foe of the faculty theory than Herbart. His campaign against it, if not victorious, was yet salutary, and the motives of his hostility, up to a certain point, entirely justified. Nothing is more useless than the assurance that what the soul actually does, that it must also have the power to do. Who disputes this? A faculty explains nothing so long as the laws under which its functions and its relations to other faculties remain unexplained. But although the faculty idea serves no positive end, it cannot be entirely discarded. It marks the boundary where our ability to reduce one class of psychical phenomena to another ceases. Herbart's polemic has no force against the moderate and necessary use of this idea, no matter how much it was in place in view of the impropriety of a superfluous multiplication of the faculties of the soul. The realization of the ideal of psychology, the reduction of the complex phenomena of mental life to the smallest possible number of simple elements, is limited by the heterogeneity of the original phenomena, knowing, feeling, willing, which wholly resists derivation from the combination of sensations. That which blinded Herbart to these limitations was that tendency toward unity, which, as a metaphysician and moral philosopher, he had all too willfully suppressed, and which now took revenge for this infringement of its rights by misleading the psychologist to an exaggeration which had important consequences. Nevertheless his unsuccessful attempt remains interesting and worthy of gratitude.

The discovery of the laws which govern the interaction of the psychical elements is the task of a *statics and a mechanics* of representations. The former investigates the equilibrium or the settled final state; the latter, the change, *i.e.* the movements of representations. These names of themselves betray Herbart's conviction that mathematics can and must be applied to psychology. The bright hopes, however, which Herbart formed for the attempt at a mathematical psychology, were fulfilled neither in his own endeavors nor in those of his pupils, although, as Lotze remarks, it would be asserting too much to say that the most general formulas which he set up contradict experience.—The unity of the soul forces representations to act on one another. Disparate representations, those, that is, which belong to different representative series, as the visual image of a rose and the auditory image of the word rose, or as the sensations yellow, hard, round, ringing, connected in the concept gold piece, enter into complications [complexes]. Homogeneous representations (the memory image and the perceptual image of a black poodle) fuse into a single representation. Opposed representations (red and blue) arrest one another when they are in consciousness together. The connection and graded fusion of representations is the basis of their retention and reproduction, as well as of the formation of continuous series of representations. The reproduction is in part immediate, a free rising of the representation by its own power as soon as the hindrances give way; in part mediate, a coming up through the help of others. On the *arrest* of partially or totally opposed representations Herbart bases his psychological calculus. Let there be given simultaneously in consciousness three opposed representations of different intensities, the strongest to be called *a*, the weakest *c*, the intermediate one *b*. What happens? They arrest one another, *i.e.* a part of each is forced to sink below the threshold of consciousness.[1]

What is the amount of the arrest? As much as all the weaker representations together come to—the sum of arrest or the sum of that which becomes unconscious (as it were the burden to be divided) is equal to the sum of all the representations with the exception of the strongest (hence $= b + c$), and is divided among the individual representations in the inverse ratio of their strength, consequently in such a way that the strongest (the one which most actively and successfully resists arrest) has the least, and the weakest the most, of it to bear. It may thus come to pass that a representation is entirely driven out of consciousness by two stronger ones, while it is impossible for this to happen to it from a single one, no matter how superior it be. The simplest case of all is when two equally strong representations are present, in which case each is reduced to the half of its original intensity. The sum of that which remains in consciousness is always equal to the greatest representation.

[Footnote 1: By their mutual pressure representations are transformed into a mere *tendency* to represent, which again becomes actual representation when the arrest ceases. The parts of a representation transformed into a tendency, and the residua remaining unobscured, are not pieces cut off, but the quantity denotes merely a degree of obscuration in the whole representation, or rather in the representation which actually takes place.]

As soon as a representation reaches the zero point of consciousness, or as soon as a new representation (sensation) comes in, the others begin at once to rise or sink. The Mechanics seeks to investigate the laws of these movements of representations; but we may the more readily pass over its complicated calculations since their precise formulas can never more than very roughly represent the true state of the case, which simply rebels against precision. The rock on which every immanent use of mathematics in psychology must strike, is the impossibility of exactly measuring one representation by another. We may, indeed, declare one stronger than another on the basis of the immediate impression of feeling, but we cannot say how much stronger it is, nor with reason assert that it is twice or half as intense. Herbart's mathematical psychology was wrecked by this insurmountable difficulty. The demand for exactness which it raised, but which it was unable to satisfy with the means at its disposal, has recently been renewed, and has led to assured results in psycho-physics, which works on a different basis and with ingenious methods of measurement.

Herbart endeavors, as we have seen, to deduce the various mental activities from the play of representations, Feeling and desire are not something beside representations, are not special faculties of the soul, but results of the relations of representations, changing states of representations arrested and working upward against hindrances. A representation which has been forced out of consciousness persists as a *tendency or effort* to represent, and as such exerts a pressure on the conscious representations. If a representation is suspended between counteracting forces a feeling results; desire is the rise of a representation in the face of hindrances, aversion is hesitation in sinking. If the effort is accompanied by the idea that its goal is attainable, it is termed will. The character of a man depends on the fact that definite masses of representations have become dominant, and by their strength and persistence hold opposing representations in check or suppress them. The longer the dominant mass of representations exercises its power, the firmer becomes the habit of acting in a certain way, the more fixed the will. Herbart's intellectualistic denial of self-dependence to the practical capacities of the soul leads him logically to determinism. Volition depends on insight, is determined by representations; freedom signifies nothing but the fact that the will can be determined by motives. If the individual decisions of man were undetermined he would have no character; if the character were free in the choice between two actions, then, along with the noblest resolve, there would remain the possibility of an opposite decision; freedom of choice would make pure chance the doer of our deeds. Pedagogics, above all, must reject the idea of an undetermined freedom; education, along with imputation, correction, and punishment, would be a meaningless word, if no determining influence on the will of the pupil were possible.—This last objection overlooks the fact that the pedagogical influence is always mediate, and can do no more than, by disciplining the impulses of the pupil and by supplying him with aids against immoral inclinations, to lighten his moral task. We can work on the motives only, never directly on the will itself. Otherwise it would be inexplicable that even the best pedagogical skill proves powerless in the case of many individuals.

Herbart's psychology was preceded by a philosophy of nature, which construes matter from attraction and repulsion, and declares an *actio in distans* impossible. The intermediate link between physics and psychology is formed by the science of organic life (physiology or biology); and with this natural theology is connected by the following principles: The purposiveness which we notice with admiration in men and the higher animals compels us, since it can neither come from chance nor be explained on natural grounds alone, to assume as its author a supreme artificer, an intelligence which works by ends. It is true, indeed, that the existence of the Deity is not demonstrated by the teleological argument; this is only an hypothesis, but one as highly probable as the assumption that the human bodies by which we are surrounded are inhabited by human souls—a fact which we can only assume, not perceive nor prove. The assurance of faith is different from that of logic and experience, but not inferior to it. Religion is based on humility and grateful reverence, which is favored, not injured, by the immeasurable sublimity of its object, the incompleteness of our idea of the Supreme Being, and the knowledge of our ignorance. If faith rests, on the one hand, on the teleological view of nature, it is, on the other, connected with moral need, and exercises, in addition, aesthetic influences. By comforting the suffering, setting right the erring, reclaiming and pacifying the sinner, warning, strengthening, and encouraging the morally sound, religion brings the spirit into a new and better land, shows it a higher order of things, the order of providence, which, amid all the mistakes of men, still furthers the good. The religious spirit always includes an ethical element, and the bond of the Church holds men together even where the state is destroyed. Indispensable theoretically as a supplement to our knowledge, and practically because of the moral imperfection of men, who need it to humble, warn, comfort, and lift them up, religion is, nevertheless, in its origin independent of knowledge and moral will. Faith is older than science and morals: the doctrine of religion did not wait for astronomy and cosmology, nor the erection of temples for ethics. Before the development of the moral concepts religion already existed in the form of wonder without a special object, of a gloomy awe which ascribed every sudden inner excitement to the impulse of an invisible power. Since a speculative knowledge of the nature of God is impossible, the only task which remains for metaphysics is the removal of improper determinations from that which tradition and phantasy have to say on the subject. We are to conceive God as personal, extramundane, and omnipotent, as the creator, not of the reals themselves, but of their purposive coexistence (*Zusammen*). In order, however, to rise from the idea of the original, most real, and most powerful being to that of the most excellent being we need the practical Ideas, without which the former would remain an indifferent theoretical concept. Man can pray only to a wise, holy, perfect, just, and good God.

This, in essential outline, is the content of the scattered observations on the philosophy of religion given by Herbart. Drobisch (*Fundamental Doctrines of the Philosophy of Religion*, 1840), from the standpoint of religious criticism and with a renewal of the moral argument, and Taute (1840-52) and Flügel (*Miracles and the Possibility of a Knowledge of God*, 1869) with an apologetic tendency and one toward a belief in miracles, have, among others, endeavored to make up for the lack of a detailed treatment of this discipline by Herbart—from which, moreover, much of value could hardly have been expected in view of the jejuneness of his metaphysical conceptions and the insufficiency of his appreciation of evil.

It remains only to glance at Herbart's Aesthetics. The beautiful is distinguished from the agreeable and the desirable, which, like it, are the objects of preference and rejection, by the facts, first, that it arouses an involuntary and disinterested judgment of approval; and second, that it is a predicate which is ascribed to the object or is objective. To these is added, thirdly, that while desire seeks for that which is to come, taste possesses in the present that which it judges.

That which pleases or displeases is always the form, never the matter; and further, is always a relation, for that which is entirely simple is indifferent. As in music we have succeeded in discovering the simplest relations, which please immediately and absolutely—we know not why—so this must be attempted in all branches of the theory of art. The most important among them, that which treats of moral beauty, moral philosophy, has therefore to inquire concerning the simplest relations of will, which call forth moral approval or disapproval (independently of the interest of the spectator), to inquire concerning the practical Ideas or pattern-concepts, in accordance with which moral taste, involuntarily and with unconditional evidence, judges concerning the worth or unworth of (actually happening or merely represented) volitions. Herbart enumerates five such primary Ideas or fundamental judgments of conscience.

(1) The Idea of inner freedom compares the will with the judgment, the conviction, the conscience of the agent himself. The agreement of his desire with his own judgment, with the precept of his taste, pleases, lack of agreement displeases. Since the power to determine the will according to one's own insight of itself establishes only an empty consistency and loyalty to conviction, and may also subserve immoral craft, the first Idea waits for its content from the four following.

(2) The Idea of perfection has reference to the quantitative relations of the manifold strivings of a subject, in intensity, extension, and concentration. The strong is pleasing in contrast with the weak, the greater (more extended, richer) in contrast with the smaller, the collected in contrast with the scattered; in other words, in the individual desires it is energy which pleases, in their sum variety, in the system co-operation. While the first two Ideas have compared the will of the individual man with itself, the remaining ones consider its relation to the will of other rational beings, the third to a merely represented will, and the last two to an actual one.

(3) According to the Idea of benevolence or goodness, which gives the most immediate and definite criterion of the worth of the disposition, the will pleases if it is in harmony with the (represented) will of another, *i.e.*, makes the satisfaction of the latter its aim.

(4) The Idea of right is based on the fact that strife displeases. If several wills come together at one point without ill-will (in claiming a thing), the parties ought to submit themselves to right as a rule for the avoidance of strife.

(5) In retribution and equity, also, the original element is displeasure, displeasure in an unrequited act as a disturbance of equilibrium. This last Idea demands that no deed of good or evil remain unanswered; that in reward, thanks, and punishment, a quantum of good and evil equal to that of which he has been the cause return upon the agent. The one-sided deed of good or ill is a disturbance, the removal of which demands a corresponding requital.

Herbart warns us against the attempt to derive the five original Ideas (which scientific analysis alone separates, for in life we always judge according to all of them together) from a single higher Idea, maintaining that the demand for a common principle of morals is a prejudice. From the union of several beings into one person proceed five other pattern-concepts, the derived or social Ideas of the ethical institutions in which the primary Ideas are realized. These correspond to the primary Ideas in the reverse order: The system of rewards, which regulates punishment; the legal society, which hinders strife; the system of administration, aimed at the greatest possible good of all; the system of culture, aimed at the development of the greatest possible power and virtuosity; finally, as the highest, and that which unites the others in itself, society as a person, which, when it is provided with the necessary power, is termed the state.

If we combine the totality of the original Ideas into the unity of the person the concept of virtue arises. If we reflect on the limitations which oppose the full realization of the ideal of virtue, we gain the concepts of law and duty. An ethics, like that of Kant, which exclusively emphasizes the imperative or obligatory character of the good, is one-sided; it considers morality only in arrest, a mistake which goes with its false doctrine of freedom. On the other hand, it was a great merit in Kant that he first made clear the unconditional validity of moral judgment, independent of all eudemonism. Politics and pedagogics are branches of the theory of virtue. The end of education is development in virtue, and, as a means to this, the arousing of varied interests and the production of a stable character.

In conclusion, we may sum up the points in which Herbart shows himself a follower of Kant—he calls himself a "Kantian of the year 1828." His practical philosophy takes from Kant its independence of theoretical philosophy, the disinterested character of aesthetic judgment, the absoluteness of ethical values, the non-empirical origin of the moral concepts: "The fundamental ethical relations are not drawn from experience." His metaphysics owes to Kant the critical treatment of the experience-concepts (its task is to make experience comprehensible), in which the leading idea in the Kantian doctrine of the antinomies, the inevitableness of contradictions, is generalized, extended to all the fundamental concepts of experience, and, as it were, transferred from the Dialectic to the Analytic; it owes to him, further, the conception of being as absolute position, and, finally, the dualism of phenomena and things in themselves. Herbart (with Schopenhauer) considers the renewal of the Platonic distinction between seeming and being the chief service of the great critical philosopher, and finds his greatest mistake in the *a priori* character ascribed to the forms of cognition. In the doctrine of the pure intuitions and the categories, and the Critique of Judgment, he rejects, and with full consciousness, just those parts of Kant on which the Fichtean school had built further. Finally, Herbart's method of thought, his impersonality, the at times anxious caution of his inquiry, and the neatness of his conceptions, are somewhat akin to Kant's, only that he lacked the gift of combination to a much greater degree than his great predecessor on the Königsberg rostrum. His remarkable acuteness is busier in loosening than in binding; it is more happy in the discovery of contradictions than in their resolution. Therefore he does not belong to the kings who have decided the fate of philosophy for long periods of time; he stands to one side, though it is true he is the most important figure among these who occupy such a position.

The first to give his adherence to Herbart in essential positions, and so to furnish occasion for the formation of an Herbartian school, was Drobisch (born 1802), in two critiques which appeared in 1828 and 1830. Besides Drobisch, from whom we have valuable discussions of Logic (1836, 5th ed., 1887) and Empirical Psychology (1842), and an interesting essay on *Moral Statistics and the Freedom of the Will* (1867), L. Strümpell (born 1812; *The Principal Points in Herbart's Metaphysics Critically Examined*, 1840), is a professor in Leipsic. The organ of the school, the *Zeitschrift für exakte Philosophie*, now edited by Flügel (the first volume, 1860, contained a survey of the literature of the school), was at first issued by T. Ziller, the pedagogical thinker, and Allihn. The *Zeitschrift für Völkerpsychologie und Sprachwissenschaft*, from 1859, edited by M. Lazarus (born 1824; *The Life of the Soul*, 3 vols., 1856 *seq.*, 3d ed., 1883 *seq.*) and H. Steinthal (born 1823; *The Origin of Language*, 4th ed., 1888; *Sketch of the Science of Language*, part i. 2d ed., 1881; *General Ethics*, 1885) of Berlin, also belongs to the Herbartian movement. Distinguished service has been done in psychology by Nahlowsky (*The Life of Feeling*, 1862, 2d. ed., 1884), Theodor Waitz in Marburg (1821-84; *Foundation of Psychology*, 1846; *Text-book of Psychology*, 1849), and Volkmann in Prague (1822-77; *Text-book of Psychology*, 3d. ed., by Cornelius, 1884 and 1885); while Friedrich Exner (died 1853) was formerly much spoken of as an opponent of the Hegelian psychology (1843-44). Robert Zimmermann in Vienna (born 1824) represents an extreme formalistic tendency in aesthetics (*History of Aesthetics*, 1858; *General Esthetics as Science of Form*, 1865; further, a series of thorough essays on subjects in the history of philosophy). Among historians of philosophy Thilo has given a rather one-sided representation of the Herbartian standpoint. The school's philosophers of religion have been mentioned above (p. 532). Beneke, whom we have joined with Fries on account of his anthropological standpoint, stands about midway between Herbart and Schopenhauer. He shares in the former's interest in psychology, in the latter's foundation of metaphysical knowledge on inner experience, and in the dislike felt by both for Hegel; while, on the other hand, he differs from Herbart in his empirical method, and from Schopenhauer in the priority ascribed to representation over effort.

%3. Pessimism: Schopenhauer.%

Schopenhauer is in all respects the antipodes of Herbart. If in Herbart philosophy breaks up into a number of distinct special inquiries, Schopenhauer has but one fundamental thought to communicate, in the carrying out of which, as he is convinced, each part implies the whole and is implied by the whole. The former operates with sober concepts where the latter follows the lead of gifted intuition. The one is cool, thorough, cautious, methodical to the point of pedantry; the other is passionate, ingenious, unmethodical to the point of capricious dilettantism. In the one case, philosophy is as far as possible exact science, in which the person of the thinker entirely retires behind the substance of the inquiry; in the other, philosophy consists in a sum of artistic conceptions, which derive their content and value chiefly from the individuality of the author. The history of philosophy has no other system to show which to the same degree expresses and reflects the personality of the philosopher as Schopenhauer's. This personality, notwithstanding its limitations and its whims, was important enough to give interest to Schopenhauer's views, even apart from the relative truth which they contain.

Arthur Schopenhauer (1788-1860) was the son of a merchant in Dantzic and his wife Johanna, *née* Trosiener, who subsequently became known as a novelist. His early training was gained from foreign travel, but after the death of his father he exchanged the mercantile career, which he had begun at his father's request, for that of a scholar, studying under G.E. Schulze in Göttingen, and under Fichte at Berlin. In 1813 he gained his doctor's degree in Jena with a dissertation *On the Fourfold Root of the Principle of Sufficient Reason*. Then he moved from Weimar, the residence of his mother, where he had associated considerably with Goethe and had been introduced to Indian philosophy by Fr. Mayer, to Dresden (1814-18). In the latter place he wrote the essay *On Sight and Colors* (1816; subsequently published by the author in Latin), and his chief work, *The World as Will and Idea* (1819; new edition, with a second volume, 1844). After the completion of the latter he began his first Italian journey, while his second tour fell in the interval between his two quite unsuccessful attempts (in Berlin 1820 and 1825) to propagate his philosophy from the professor's desk. From 1831 until his death he lived in learned retirement in Frankfort-on-the-Main. Here he composed the opuscule *On Will in Nature*, 1836, the prize treatises *On the Freedom of the Human Will* and *On the Foundation of Ethics* (together, *The Two Fundamental Problems of Ethics*, 1841), and the collection of minor treatises *Parerga and Paralipomena*, 2 vols., 1851 (including an essay "On Religion"). J. Frauenstädt has published a considerable amount of posthumous material (among other things the translation, *B. Gracians Handorakel der Weltklugheit*); the *Collected Works* (6 vols., 1873-74, 2d ed., 1877, with a biographical notice); *Lichtstrahlen aus Schopenhauers Werken*, 1861, 5th ed. 1885; and a *Schopenhauer Lexicon*, 2 vols., 1871.[1]

[Footnote 1: From the remaining Schopenhauer literature (F. Laban has published a chronological survey of it, 1880) we may call attention to the critiques of the first edition of the chief work by Herbart and Beneke, and that of the second edition by Fortlage (*Jenaische Litteratur Zeitung*, 1845, Nos. 146-151); J.E. Erdmann *Herbart und Schopenhauer, eine Antithese (Zeitschrift für Philosophie*, 1851); Wilh. Gwinner, *Schopenhauers Leben*, 1878 (the second edition of *Schopenhauer aus persönlichem Umgang dargestellt*, 1862); Fr. Nietzsche, *Schopenhauer als Erzieher (Unzeitgemässe Betrachtungen, Stück iii.*, 1874); O. Busch, *A. Schopenhauer*, 2d. ed., 1878; K. Peters, *Schopenhauer als Philosoph und Schriftsteller*, 1880; R. Koeber, *Die Philosophie A. Schopenhauers*, 1888. [The English reader may be referred to Haldane and Kemp's translation of *The World as Will and Idea*, 3 vols., 1883-86; the translation of *The Fourfold Root* and the *Will in Nature* in Bohn's Philosophical Library, 1889; Saunders's translations from the *Parerga and Paralipomena*, 1889 seq.; Helen Zimmern's *Arthur Schopenhauer, his Life and his Philosophy*, 1876; W. Wallace's *Schopenhauer*, Great Writers Series, 1890 (with a bibliography by Anderson, including references to numerous magazine articles, etc.); Sully's *Pessimism*, 2d ed., 1882, chap. iv.; and Royce's *Spirit of Modern Philosophy*, chap, viii., 1892.—TR.]]

In regard to subjective idealism Schopenhauer confesses himself a thoroughgoing Kantian. That sensations are merely states in us has long been known; Kant opened the eyes of the world to the fact that the forms of knowledge are also the property of the subject. I know things only as they appear to me, as I represent them in virtue of the constitution of my intellect; the world is my idea. The Kantian theory, however, is capable of simplification, the various forms of cognition may be reduced to a single one, to the category of causality or principle of sufficient reason—which was preferred by Kant himself—as the general expression of the regular connection of our representations. This principle, in correspondence with the several classes of objects, or rather of representations—viz., pure (merely formal) intuitions, empirical (complete) intuitions, acts of will, abstract concepts—has four forms: it is the *principium rationis essendi, rationis fiendi, rationis agendi, rationis cognoscendi*. The *ratio essendi* is the law which regulates the coexistence of the parts of space and the succession of the divisions of time. The *ratio fiendi* demands for every change of state another from which it regularly follows as from its cause, and a substance as its unchangeable substratum—matter. All changes take place necessarily, all that is real is material; the law of causality is valid for phenomena alone, not beyond them, and holds only for the states of substances, not for substances themselves. In inorganic nature causes work mechanically, in organic nature as stimuli (in which the reaction is not equal to the action), and in animated nature as motives. A motive is a conscious (but not therefore a free) cause; the law of motivation is the *ratio agendi*. This serial order, "mechanical cause, stimulus, and motive," denotes only distinctions in the mode of action, not in the necessity of action. Man's actions follow as inevitably from his character and the motives which influence him as a clock strikes the hours; the freedom of the will is a chimera. Finally, the *ratio cognoscendi* determines that a judgment must have a sufficient ground in order to be true. Judgment or the connection of concepts is the chief activity of the reason, which, as the faculty of abstract thought and the organ of science, constitutes the difference between man and the brute, while the possession of the understanding with its intuition of objects is common to both. In opposition to the customary overestimation of this gift of mediate representations, of language, and of reflection, Schopenhauer gives prominence to the fact that the reason is not a creative faculty like the understanding, but only a receptive power, that it clarifies and transforms the content furnished by intuition without increasing it by new representations.

Objective cognition is confined within the circle of our representations; all that is knowable is phenomenon. Space, time, and causality spread out like a triple veil between us and the *per se* of things, and prevent a vision of the true nature of the world. There is one point, however, at which we know more than mere phenomena, where of these three disturbing media only one, time-form, separates us from the thing in itself. This point is the consciousness of ourselves.

On the one hand, I appear to myself as body. My body is a temporal, spatial, material object, an object like all others, and with them subject to the laws of objectivity. But besides this objective cognition, I have, further, an immediate consciousness of myself, through which I apprehend my true being—I know myself as willing. My will is more than a mere representation, it is the original element in me, the truly real which appears to me as body. The will is related to the intellect as the primary to the secondary, as substance to accident; it is related to the body as the inner to the outer, as reality to phenomenon. The act of will is followed at once and inevitably by the movement of the body willed, nay, the two are one and the same, only given in different ways: will is the body seen from within, body the will seen from without, the will become visible, objectified. After the analogy of ourselves, again, who appear to ourselves as material objects but in truth are will, all existence is to be judged. The universe is the *mac-anthropos*; the knowledge of our own essence, the key to the knowledge of the essence of the world. Like our body, the whole world is the visibility of will. The human will is the highest stage in the development of the same principle which manifests its activity in the various forces of nature, and which properly takes its name from the highest species. To penetrate further into the inner nature of things than this is impossible. What that which presents itself as will and which still remains after the negation of the latter (see below) is in itself, is for us absolutely unknowable.

The world is *per se* will. None of the predicates are to be attributed to the primal will which we ascribe to things in consequence of our subjective forms of thought—neither determination by causes or ends, nor plurality: it stands outside the law of causality, as also outside space and time, which form the *principium individuationis*. The primal will is groundless, blind stress, unconscious impulse toward existence; it is one, the one and all, [Greek: en nai pan]. That which manifests itself as gravity, as magnetic force, as the impulse to growth, as the *vis medicatrix naturae*, is only this one world-will, whose unity (not conscious character!) shows itself in the purposiveness of its embodiments. The essence of each thing, its hidden quality, at which empirical explanation finds its limit, is its will: the essence of the stone is its will to fall; that of the lungs is the will to breathe; teeth, throat, and bowels are hunger objectified. Those qualities in which the universal will gives itself material manifestation form a series with grades of increasing perfection, a realm of unchangeable specific forms or eternal Ideas, which (with a real value difficult to determine) stand midway between the one primal will and the numberless individual beings. That the organic individual does not perfectly correspond to the ideal of its species, but only approximates this more or less closely, is grounded in the fact that the stadia in the objectification of the will, or the Ideas, contend, as it were, for matter; and whatever of force is used up in the victory of the higher Ideas over the lower is lost for the development of the examples of the former. The higher the level on which a being stands the clearer the expression of its individuality. The most general forces of nature, which constitute the raw mass, play the fundamental bass in the world-symphony, the higher stages of inorganic nature, with the vegetable and animal worlds, the harmonious middle parts, and man the guiding treble, the significant melody. With the human brain the world as idea is given at a stroke; in this organ the will has kindled a torch in order to throw light upon itself and to carry out its designs with careful deliberation; it has brought forth the intellect as its instrument, which, with the great majority of men, remains in a position of subservience to the will. Brain and thought are the same; the former is nothing other than the will to know, as the stomach is will to digest. Those only talk of an immaterial soul who import into philosophy—where such ideas do not belong—concepts taught them when they were confirmed.

Schopenhauer's philosophy is as rich in inconsistencies as his personality was self-willed and unharmonious. "He carries into his system all the contradictions and whims of his capricious nature," says Zeller. From the most radical idealism (the objective world a product of representation) he makes a sharp transition to the crassest materialism (thought a function of the brain); first matter is to be a mere idea, now thought is to be merely a material phenomenon! The third and fourth books of *The World as Will and Idea*, which develop the aesthetic and ethical standpoint of their author, stand in as sharp a contradiction to the first (poëtical) and the second (metaphysical) books as these to each other. While at first it was maintained that all representation is subject to the principle of sufficient reason, we are now told that, besides causal cognition, there is a higher knowledge, one which is free from the control of this principle, viz., aesthetic and philosophical intuition. If, before, it was said that the intellect is the creature and servant of the will, we now learn that in favored individuals it gains the power to throw off the yoke of slavery, and not only to raise itself to the blessedness of contemplation free from all desire, but even to enter on a victorious conflict with the tyrant, to slay the will. The source of this power—is not revealed. R. Haym *(A. Schopenhauer*, 1864, reprinted from the *Preussische Jahrbücher*) was not far wrong in characterizing Schopenhauer's philosophy as a clever novel, which entertains the reader by its rapid vicissitudes.

The contemplation which is free from causality and will is the essence of aesthetic life; the partial and total sublation, the quieting and negation of the will, that of ethical life. It is but seldom, and only in the artistic and philosophical genius, that the intellect succeeds in freeing itself from the supremacy of the will, and, laying aside the question of the *why* and *wherefore*, *where* and *when*, in sinking itself completely in the pure *what* of things. While with the majority of mankind, as with animals, the intellect always remains a prisoner in the service of the will to live, of self-preservation, of personal interests, in gifted men, in artists and thinkers, it strips off all that is individual, and, in disinterested vision of the Ideas, becomes pure, timeless subject, freed from the will. Art removes individuality from the subject as well as from the object; its comforting and cheering influence depends on the fact that it elevates those enjoying it to the stand-point—raised above all pain of desire—of a fixed, calm, completely objective contemplation of the unchangeable essence, of the eternal types of things. For aesthetic intuition the object is not a thing under relations of space, time, and cause, but only an expression, an exemplification, a representative of the Idea. Poetry, which presents—most perfectly in tragedy—the Idea of humanity, stands higher than the plastic arts. The highest rank, however, belongs to music, since it does not, like the other arts, represent single Ideas, but—as an unconscious metaphysic, nay, a second, ideal world above the material world—the will itself. In view of this high appreciation of their art, it is not surprising that musicians have contributed a considerable contingent to the band of Schopenhauer worshipers. A different source of attraction for the wider circle of readers was supplied by the piquant spice of pessimism.

If the purposiveness of the phenomena of nature points to the unity of the primal will, the unspeakable misery of life, which Schopenhauer sets forth with no less of eloquence, proves the blindness and irrationality of the world-ground. To live is to suffer; the world contains incomparably more pain than pleasure; it is the worst possible world. In the world of sub-animal nature aimless striving; in the animal world an insatiable impulse after enjoyment—while the will, deceiving itself with fancied happiness to come, which always remains denied it, and continually tossed to and fro between necessity and *ennui*, never attains complete satisfaction. The pleasure which it pursues is nothing but the removal of a dissatisfaction, and vanishes at once when the longing is stilled, to be replaced by fresh wants, that is, by new pains. In view of the indescribable misery in the world, to favor optimism is evidence not so much of folly and blindness as of a wanton disposition. The old saying is true: Non-existence is better than existence. The misery, however, is the just punishment for the original sin of the individual, which gave itself its particular existence by an act of intelligible freedom. Redemption from the sin and misery of existence is possible only through a second act of transcendental freedom, which, since it consists in the complete transformation of our being, and since it is supernatural in its origin, the Church is right in describing as a new birth and work of grace.

Morality presupposes pessimistic insight into the badness of the world and the fruitlessness of all desire, and pantheistic discernment of the untruth of individual existence and the identity in essence of all individuals from a metaphysical standpoint. Man is able to free himself from egoistic self-affirmation only when he perceives the two truths, that all striving is vain and the longed-for pleasure unattainable, and that all individuals are at bottom one, viz. manifestations of the same primal will. This is temporarily effected in sympathy, which, as the only counterpoise to natural selfishness, is the true moral motive and the source of all love and justice. The sympathizer sees himself in others and feels their suffering as his own. The entire negation of the will, however, inspiring examples of which have been furnished by the Christian ascetics and Oriental penitents, stands higher than the vulgar virtue of sympathy with the sufferings of others. Here knowledge, turned away from the individual and vain to the whole and genuine, ceases to be a motive for the will and becomes a means of stilling it; the intellect is transformed from a motive into a quietive, and brings him who gives himself up to the All safely out from the storm of the passions into the peace of deliverance from existence. Absence of will, resignation, is holiness and blessedness in one. For him who has slain the will in himself the motley deceptive dream of phenomena has vanished, he lives in the ether of true reality, which for our knowledge is an empty nothingness ("Nirvana"), yet (as the ultimate, incomprehensible *per se*, which remains after the annulling of the will) only a relative nothingness—relative to the phenomenon.

Schopenhauer disposes of the sense of responsibility and the reproofs of conscience, which are inconvenient facts for his determinism, by making them both refer, not to single deeds and the empirical character, but to the indivisible act of the intelligible character. Conscience does not blame me because I have acted as I must act with my character and the motives given, but for being what in these actions I reveal myself to be. *Operari sequitur esse*. My action follows from my being, my being was my own free choice, and a new act of freedom is alone capable of transforming it.

If Schopenhauer is fond of referring to the agreement of his views with the oldest and most perfect religions, the idea lies in the background that religion,—which springs from the same metaphysical needs as philosophy, and, for the great multitude, who lack the leisure and the capacity for philosophical thought, takes the place of the former,—as the metaphysics of the people, clothes the same fundamental truths which the philosopher offers in conceptual form and supports by rational grounds in the garb of myth and allegory, and places them under the protection of an external authority. When this character of religion is overlooked, and that which is intended to be symbolical is taken for literal truth (it is not the supernaturalists alone who start with this unjust demand, but the rationalists also, with their minimizing interpretations), it becomes the worst enemy of true philosophy. In Christianity the doctrines of original sin and of redemption are especially congenial to our philosopher, as well as mysticism and asceticism. He declares Mohammedanism the worst religion on account of its optimism and abstract theism, and Buddhism the best, because it is idealistic, pessimistic, and—atheistic.

It was not until after the appearance of the second edition of his chief work that Schopenhauer experienced in increasing measure the satisfaction—which his impatient ambition had expected much earlier—of seeing his philosophy seriously considered. A zealous apostle arose for him in Julius Frauenstädt (died 1878; *Letters on the Philosophy of Schopenhauer*, 1854; *New Letters on the Philosophy of Schopenhauer*, 1876), who, originally an Hegelian, endeavored to remove pessimism from the master's system. Like Eduard von Hartmann, who will be discussed below, Julius Bahnsen (died 1882; *The Contradiction in the Knowledge and Being of the World, the Principle and Particular Verification of Real-Dialectic*, 1880-81; also, interesting characterological studies) seeks to combine elements from Schopenhauer and Hegel, while K. Peters (*Will-world and World-will*, 1883) shows in another direction points of contact with the first named thinker. Of the younger members of the school we may name P. Deussen in Kiel (*The Elements of Metaphysics*, 2d ed., 1890), and Philipp Mainländer (*Philosophy of Redemption*, 2d ed., 1879). As we have mentioned above, Schopenhauer's doctrines have exercised an attractive force in artistic circles also. Richard Wagner (1813-83; *Collected Writings*, 9 vols., 1871-73, vol. x. 1883; 2d ed., 1887-88), whose earlier aesthetic writings (*The Art-work of the Future*, 1850; *Opera and Drama*, 1851) had shown the influence of Feuerbach, in his later works (*Beethoven*, 1870; *Religion and Art*, in the third volume of the *Bayreuther Blätter*, 1880) became an adherent of Schopenhauer, after, in the *Ring of the Nibelung*, he had given poetical expression to a view of the world nearly allied to Schopenhauer's, though this was previous to his acquaintance with the works of the latter.[1] One of the most thoughtful disciples of the Frankfort philosopher and the Bayreuth dramatist is Friedrich Nietzsche (born 1844). His *Unseasonable Reflections*, 1873-76,[2] is a summons to return from the errors of modern culture, which, corrupted by the seekers for gain, by the state, by the polite writers and savants, especially by the professors of philosophy, has made men cowardly and false instead of simple and honorable, mere self-satisfied "philistines of culture." In his writings since 1878[3] Nietzsche has exchanged the rôle of a German Rousseau for that of a follower of Voltaire, to arrive finally at the ideal of the man above men.[4]

[Footnote 1: Cf. on Wagner, Fr. v. Hausegger, *Wagner und Schopenhauer*, 1878. [English translation of Wagner's *Prose Works* by Ellis, vol. i., 1892.—TR.]]

[Footnote 2: "D. Strauss, the Confessor and the Author"; "On the Advantage and Disadvantage of History for Life"; "Schopenhauer as an Educator"; "R. Wagner in Bayreuth."]

[Footnote 3: *Human, All-too-human*, new ed., 1886; *The Dawn, Thoughts on Human Prejudices*, 1881; *The Merry Science*, 1882; *So spake Zarathustra*, 1883-84; *Beyond Good and Evil*, 1886; *On the Genealogy of Morals*, 1887, 2d ed., 1887; *The Wagner Affair*, 1888, 2d ed., 1892; *Götzendämmerung, or How to Philosophize with the Hammer*, 1889.]

[Footnote 4: Cf. H. Kaatz, *Die Weltanschauung Fr. Nietzsches, I. Kultur und Moral*, 1892.]

CHAPTER XV.

PHILOSOPHY OUT OF GERMANY.

%1. Italy.%

The Cartesian philosophy, which had been widely accepted in Italy, and had still been advocated, in the sense of Malebranche, by Sigismond Gerdil (1718-1802), was opposed as an unhistorical view of the world by Giambattista Vico,[1] the bold and profound creator of the philosophy of history (1668-1744; from 1697 professor of rhetoric in the University of Naples). Vico's leading ideas are as follows: Man makes himself the criterion of the universe, judges that which is unknown and remote by the known and present. The free will of the individual rests on the judgments, manners, and habits of the people, which have arisen without reflection from a universal human instinct. Uniform ideas among nations unacquainted with one another are motived in a common truth. History is the development of human nature; in it neither chance nor fate rules, but the legislative power of providence, in virtue of which men through their own freedom progressively realize the idea of human nature. The universal course of civilization is that culture transfers its abode from the forests and huts into villages, cities, and, finally, into academies; the nature of the nations is at first rude, then stern, gradually it becomes mild, nay, effeminate, and finally wanton; at first men feel only that which is necessary, later they regard the useful, the convenient, the agreeable and attractive, until the luxury sprung from the sense for the beautiful degenerates into a foolish misuse of things. Vico divides antiquity into three periods: the divine (theocracy), the heroic (aristocracy), and the human (democracy and monarchy). The same course of things repeats itself in the nations of later times: to the patriarchal dominion of the fanciful, myth-making Orient correspond the spiritual states of the migrations; to the old Greek aristocracy, the chivalry and robbery of the period of the Crusades; to the republicanism and the monarchy of later antiquity, the modern period, which gives even the citizens and peasants a share in the universal equality. If European culture had not been transplanted to America, the same three-act drama of human development would there be playing. Vico carries this threefold division into his consideration of manners, laws, languages, character, etc.

[Footnote 1: Vico: *Principles of a New Science of the Common Nature of Nations*, 1725; *Works*, in six volumes, edited by G. Ferrari, 1835-37, new ed.. 1853 *seq.* On Vico cf. K. Werner, 1877 and 1879. [Also Flint's *Vico*, Blackwood's Philosophical Classics, 1884.—TR.]]

If Vico anticipates the Hegelian view of history, Antonio Genovesi (1712-69), who also taught at the University of Naples, and while the former was still living, shows himself animated by a presentiment of the Kantian criticism.[1] Appreciating Leibnitz and Locke, and appropriating the idea of the monads from the one and the unknowableness of substance from the other, he reaches the conviction— according to statements in his letters—that sense-bodies are nothing but the appearances of intelligible unities; that each being for us is an activity, whose substratum and ground remains unknown to us; that self-consciousness and the knowledge of external impressions yield phenomena alone, through the elaboration of which we produce the intellectual worlds of the sciences. For the rest, Genovesi thus advises his friends: Study the world, devote yourselves to languages and to mathematics, think more about men than about the things above us, and leave metaphysical vagaries to the monks! His countrymen honor in him the man who first included ethics and politics in philosophical instruction, and who used the Italian language both from the desk and in his writings, holding that a nation whose scientific works are not composed in its own tongue is barbarian.

[Footnote 1: In the following account we have made use of a translation of the concluding section of Francesco Florentine's *Handbook of the History of Philosophy*, 1879-81, which was most kindly placed at our disposal by Dr. J. Mainzer. Cf. *La Filosofia Contemporanea in Italia*, 1876, by the same author; further, Bonatelli, *Die Philosophic in Italien seit*, 1815; *Zeitschrift für Philosophic und philosophische Kritik*, vol. liv. 1869, p. 134 *seq.*; and especially, K. Werner, *Die Italienische Philosophic des XIX. Jahrhunderts*, 5 vols., 1884-86. [The English reader may be referred to the appendix on Italian philosophy in vol. ii. of the English translation of Ueberweg, by Vincenzo Botta; and to Barzellotti's "Philosophy in Italy," *Mind*, vol. in. 1878.—TR.]]

The sensationalism of Condillac, starting from Parma, gained influence over Melchiore Gioja (1767-1828; *Statistical Logic*, 1803; *Ideology*, 1822) and Giandomenico Romagnosi (1761-1835; *What is the Sound Mind?* 1827), but not without experiencing essential modification from both. The importance of these men, moreover, lies more in the sphere of social philosophy than in the sphere of noëtics.

Of the three greatest Italian philosophers of this century, Galluppi, Rosmini, and Gioberti, the first named is more in sympathy with the Kantian position than he himself will confess. Pasquale Galluppi[1] (1770-1846; from 1831 professor at Naples) adheres to the principle of experience, but does not conceive experience as that which is sensuously given, but as the elaboration of this through the synthetic relations *(rapporti)* of identity and difference, which proceed from the activity of the mind. Vincenzo de Grazia (*Essay on the Reality of Human Knowledge*, 1839-42), who holds all relations to be objective, and Ottavio Colecchi (died 1847; *Philosophical Investigations*, 1843), who holds them all subjective, oppose the view of Galluppi that some are objective and others subjective. According to De Grazia judgment is observation, not connection; it finds out the relations contained in the data of sensation; it discovers, but does not produce them. Colecchi reduces the Kantian categories to two, substance and cause. Testa, Borelli (1824), and, among the younger men, Cantoni, are Kantians; Labriola is an Herbartian.

[Footnote 1: Galluppi: *Philosophical Essay on the Critique of Knowledge*, 1819 *seq.; Lectures on Logic and Metaphysics*, 1832 *seq.; Philosophy of the Will*, 1832 *seq.; On the System of Fichte, or Considerations on Transcendental Idealism and Absolute Rationalism*, 1841. By the *Letters on the History of Philosophy from Descartes to Kant*, 1827, in the later editions to Cousin, he became the founder of this discipline in his native land.]

Antonio Rosmini-Serbati[1] (born 1797 at Rovereto, died 1855 at Stresa) regards knowledge as the common product of sensibility and understanding, the former furnishing the matter, the latter the form. The form is one: the Idea of being which precedes all judgment, which does not come from myself, which is innate, and apprehensible by immediate inner perception *(essere ideale, ente universale)*. The pure concepts (substance, cause, unity, necessity) arise when the reflecting reason analyzes this general Idea of being; the mixed Ideas (space, time, motion; body, spirit), when the understanding applies it to sensuous experience. The universal Idea of being and the particular existences are in their being identical, but in their mode of existence different. In his posthumous *Theosophy*, 1859 *seq.*, Rosmini no longer makes the universal being receive its determinations from without, but produce them from its own inner nature by means of an *a priori* development. Vincenzo Gioberti[1] (born 1801 in Turin, died 1852 at Paris) has been compared as a patriot with Fichte, and in his cast of thought with Spinoza. In place of Rosmini's "psychologism," which was advanced by Descartes and which leads to skepticism, he seeks to substitute "ontologism," which is alone held capable of reconciling science and the Catholic religion. By immediate intuition (the content of which Gioberti comprehends in the formula "Being creates the existences") we cognize the absolute as the creative ground of two series, the series of thought and the series of reality. The endeavors of Rosmini and Gioberti to bring the reason into harmony with the faith of the Church were fiercely attacked by Giussepe Ferrari (1811-76) and Ausonio Franchi (1853), while Francesco Bonatelli *(Thought and Cognition*, 1864) and Terenzio Mamiani (1800-85; *Confessions of a Metaphysician*, 1865), follow a line of thought akin to the Platonizing views of the first named thinkers. The review *Filosofia delle Scuole Italiane*, called into life by Mamiani in 1870, has been continued since 1886 under the direction of L. Ferri as the *Rivista Italiana di Filosofia*.

[Footnote 1: Rosmini: *New Essay on the Origin of Ideas*, 1830 (English translation, 1883-84); *Principles of Moral Science*, 1831; *Philosophy of Right*, 1841.] [Footnote B: Gioberti: *Introduction to the Study of Philosophy*, 1840; *Philosophical Errors of A. Rosmini*, 1842; *On the Beautiful*, 1841; *On the Good*, 1842; *Protology* edited by Massari, 1857. On both cf. R. Seydel, *Zeitschrift für Philosophie*, 1859.]

The Thomistic doctrine has many adherents in Italy, among whom the Jesuit M. Liberatore (1865) may be mentioned. The Hegelian philosophy has also found favor there (especially in Naples), as well as positivism. The former is favored by Vera, Mariano, Ragnisco, and Spaventa (died 1885); the *Rivista di Filosofia Scientifica*, 1881 *seq.*, founded by Morselli, supports the latter, and E. Caporali's *La Nuova Scienza*, 1884, moves in a similar direction. Pietro Siciliani *(On the Revival of the Positive Philosophy in Italy*, 1871) makes the third, the critical, period of philosophy by which scholasticism is overthrown and the reason made authoritative, commence with Vico, and bases his doctrine on Vico's formula: The conversion (transposition) of the *verum* and the *factum*, and *vice versa*. Subsequently he inclined to positivism, which he had previously opposed, and among the representatives of which we may mention, further, R. Ardigò of Pavia *(Psychology as Positive Science*, 1870; *The Ethics of Positivism*, 1885; *Philosophical Works*, 1883 *seq.*), and Andrea Angiulli of Naples (died 1890; *Philosophy and the Schools*, 1889), who explain matter and spirit as two phenomena of the same essence; further, Giuseppe Sergi, Giovanni Cesca, and the psychiatrist, C. Lombroso, the head of the positivistic school of penal law.

%2. France.%

Among the French philosophers of this century[1] none can compare in far-reaching influence, both at home and abroad, with Auguste Comte,[2] the creator of positivism (born at Montpellier in 1798, died at Paris in 1857), whose chief work, the *Course of Positive Philosophy*, 6 vols., appeared in 1830 42. [English version, "freely translated and condensed," by Harriet Martineau, 1853.]

[Footnote 1: Accounts of French philosophy in the nineteenth century have been given by Taine (1857, 3d ed., 1867); Janet *(La Philosophie Française Contemporaine*, 2d ed., 1879); A. Franck; Ferraz (3 vols., 1880-89); Felix Ravaisson (2d ed., 1884); the Swede, J.

Borelius (*Glances at the Present Position of Philosophy in Germany and France*, German translation by Jonas, 1887); [and Ribot, *Mind*, vol. ii., 1877].]

[Footnote 2: On Comte cf. B. Pünjer, *Jahrbücher für protestantische Theologie*, 1878; R. Eucken, *Zur Würdigung Comtes und des Positivismus*, in the *Aufsätze zum Zellerjubiläum*, 1887; Maxim. Brütt, *Der Positivismus*, Programme of the *Realgymnasium des Johanneums*, Hamburg, 1889; [also, besides Mill, p. 560, John Morley, *Encyclopedia Britannica*, vol. vi. pp. 229-238, and E. Caird, *The Social Philosophy and Religion of Comte*, 1885.—Tr.]]

The positive philosophy seeks to put an end to the hoary error that anything more is open to our knowledge than given facts—phenomena and their relations. We do not know the essence of phenomena, and just as little their first causes and ultimate ends; we know—by means of observation, experiment, and comparison—only the constant relations between phenomena, the relations of succession and of similarity among facts, the uniformities of which we call their laws. All knowledge is, therefore, relative; there is no absolute knowledge, for the inmost essence of facts, and likewise their origin, the way in which they are produced, is for us impenetrable. We know only, and this by experience, that the phenomenon A is invariably connected with the phenomenon B, that the second always follows on the first, and call the constant antecedent of a phenomenon its cause. We know such causes only as are themselves phenomena. The fact that our knowledge is limited to the succession and coexistence of phenomena is not to be lamented as a defect: the only knowledge which is attainable by us is at the same time the only useful knowledge, that which lends us practical power over phenomena. When we inquire into causes we desire to hasten or hinder the effect, or to change it as we wish, or at least to anticipate it in order to make our preparations accordingly. Such foresight and control of events can be attained only through a knowledge of their laws, their order of succession, their phenomenal causes. *Savoir pour prévoir*. But, although the prevision of facts is the only knowledge which we need, men have always sought after another, an "absolute" knowledge, or have even believed that they were in possession of it; the forerunners of the positive philosophy themselves, Bacon and Descartes, have been entangled in this prejudice. A long intellectual development was required to reach the truth, that our knowledge does not extend beyond the cognition of the succession and coexistence of facts; that the same procedure must be extended to abstract speculation which the common mind itself makes use of in its single actions. On the other hand, the positive philosophy, notwithstanding its rejection of metaphysics, is far from giving its sanction to empiricism. Every isolated, empirical observation is useless and uncertain; it obtains value and usefulness only when it is defined and explained by a theory, and combined with other observations into a law—this makes the difference between the observations of the scholar and the layman.

The positive stage of a science, which begins when we learn to explain phenomena by their laws, is preceded by two others: a theological stage, which ascribes phenomena to supposed personal powers, and a metaphysical stage, which ascribes them to abstract natural forces. These three periods denote the childhood, the youth, and the manhood of science.

The earliest view of the world is the theological view, which derives the events of the world from the voluntary acts of supernatural intelligent beings. The crude view of nature sees in each individual thing a being animated like man; later man accustoms himself to think of a whole class of objects as governed by one invisible being, by a divinity; finally the multitude of divinities gives place to a single God, who creates, maintains, and rules the universe, and by extraordinary acts, by miracles, interferes in the course of events. Thus fetichism (in its highest form, astrolatry), polytheism, and monotheism are the stages in the development of the theological mode of thought. In the second, the metaphysical, period, the acts of divine volition are replaced by entities, by abstract concepts, which are regarded as realities, as the true reality back of phenomena. A force, a power, an occult property or essence is made to dwell in things; the mysterious being which directs events is no longer called God, but "Nature," and invested with certain inclinations, with a horror of a vacuum, an aversion to breaks, a tendency toward the best, a *vis medicatrix*, etc. Here belong, also, the vegetative soul of Aristotle, the vital force and the plastic impulse of modern investigators. Finally the positive stage is reached, when all such abstractions, which are even yet conceived as half personal and acting voluntarily, are abandoned, and the unalterable and universally valid laws of phenomena established by observation and experiment alone. But to explain the laws of nature themselves transcends, according to Comte, the fixed limits of human knowledge. The beginning of the world lies outside the region of the knowable, atheism is no better grounded than the theistic hypothesis, and if Comte asserts that a blindly acting mechanism is less probable than a world-plan, he is conscious that he is expressing a mere conjecture which can never be raised to the rank of a scientific theory. The origin and the end of things are insoluble problems, in answering which no progress has yet been made in spite of man's long thought about them. Only that which lies intermediate between the two inscrutable termini of the world is an object of knowledge.

It is not only the human mind in general that exhibits this advance from the theological, through the metaphysical, to the positive mode of thought, but each separate science goes through the same three periods—only that the various disciplines have developed with unequal rapidity. While some have already culminated in the positive method of treatment, others yet remain caught in the theological period of beginnings, and others still are in the metaphysical transition stage. Up to the present all three phases of development exist side by side, and even among the objects of the most highly developed sciences there are some which we continue to regard theologically; these are the ones which we do not yet understand how to calculate, as the changes of the weather or the spread of epidemics. Which science first attained the positive state, and in what order have the others followed? With this criterion Comte constructs his *classification of the sciences*, in which, however, he takes account only of those sciences which he calls abstract, that is, those which treat of "events" in distinction from "objects." The abstract sciences (as biology) investigate the most general laws of nature, valid for all phenomena, from which the particular phenomena which experience presents to us cannot be deduced, but on the basis of which an entirely different world were also possible. The concrete sciences, on the other hand (*e.g.*, botany and zoölogy), have to do with the actually given combinations of phenomena. The former follow out each separate one of the general laws through all its possible modes of operation, the latter consider only the combination of laws given in an object. Thus oaks and squirrels are the result of very many laws, inasmuch as organisms are dependent not only on biological, but also on physical, chemical, and mathematical laws.

Comte enumerates six of these abstract sciences, and arranges them in such a way that each depends on the truths of the preceding, and adds to these its own special truths, while the first (the most general and simplest) presupposes no earlier laws whatever, but is presupposed by all the later ones. According to this principle of increasing particularity and complexity the following scale results: (1) Mathematics, in which the science of number, as being absolutely without presuppositions, precedes geometry and mechanics; (2) Astronomy; (3) Physics (with five subordinate divisions, in which the first place belongs to the theory of weight, and the last to electrology, while the theory of heat, acoustics, and optics are intermediate); (4) Chemistry; (5) Biology or physiology; (6) Sociology or the science of society. This sequence, which is determined by the increasing complexity and increasing dependence of the objects of the sciences, is the order in which they have historically developed—before the special laws of the more complicated sciences can be ascertained, the general laws of the more simple ones must be accurately known. It is also advisable to follow this same order of increasing complexity and difficulty in the study of the sciences, for acquaintance with the methods of those which are elementary is the best preparation for the pursuit of the higher ones. In arithmetic and geometry we study positivity at its source; in the sociological spirit it finds its completion.

Mathematics entered on its positive stage at quite an early period, chemistry and biology only in recent times, while, in the highest and most complicated science, the metaphysical (negative, liberal, democratic, revolutionary) mode of thought is still battling with the feudalism of the theological mode. To make sociology positive is the mission of the second half of Comte's work, and to this goal his philosophical activity had been directed from the beginning. Comte rates the efforts of political economy very low, with the exception of the work of Adam Smith, and will not let them pass as a preparation for scientific sociology, holding that they are based on false abstractions. Psychology, which is absent from the above enumeration, is to form a branch of biology, and exclusively to use the objective method, especially phrenology (to the three faculties of the soul, "heart, character, and intellect," correspond three regions of the brain). Self-observation, so Comte, making an impossibility out of a difficulty, teaches, can at most inform us concerning our feelings and passions, and not at all concerning our own thinking, since reflection brings to a stop the process to which it attends, and thus destroys its object. The sole source of knowledge is external sense-perception. In his *Positive Polity* Comte subsequently added a seventh fundamental science, ethics or anthropology.

Sociology,[1] the elevation of which to the rank of a positive science is the principal aim of our philosopher, uses the same method as the natural sciences, namely, the interrogation and interpretation of experience by means of induction and deduction, only that here the usual relation of these two instruments of knowledge is reversed. Between inorganic and organic philosophy, both of which proceed from the known to the unknown, there is this difference, that in the former the advance is from the elements, as that which alone is directly accessible, to the whole which is composed of them, while in the latter the opposite is the case, since here the whole is better known than the individual parts of which it consists. Hence, in inorganic science the laws of the composite phenomena are obtained by deduction (from the laws of the simple facts inductively discovered) and confirmed by observation; in sociology, on the other hand, the laws are found through (historical) experience, and deductively verified (from the nature of man as established by biology) only in the sequel. Since the phenomena of society are determined not merely by the general laws of human nature, but, above all, by the growing influence of the past, historical studies must form the basis of sociological inquiry.

[Footnote 1: Cf. Krohn: *Beiträge zur Kenntniss und Würdigung der Soziologie, Jahrbücher für Nationalökonomie und Statistik*, New Series, vols. i. and iii., 1880 and 1881.]

Of the two parts of sociology, the Statics, which investigates the equilibrium (the conditions of the existence, the permanence, and the coexistence of social states), and Dynamics, which investigates the movement (the laws of the progress) of social phenomena, the first was in essence established by Aristotle. The fundamental concept of the Statics is the *consensus*, the harmony, solidarity, or mutual dependence of the members of the social organism. All its parts, science, art, religion, politics, industry, must be considered together; they stand in such intimate harmony and correlation that, for every important change of condition in one of these parts, we may be certain of finding corresponding changes in all the others, as its causes and effects. Besides the selfish propensities, there dwell in man an equally original, but intrinsically weaker, impulse toward association, which instinctively leads him to seek the society of his fellows without reflection on the advantages to be expected therefrom, and a moderate degree of benevolence. As altruism conflicts with egoism, so the reason, together with the impulse to get ahead, which can only be satisfied through labor, is in continual conflict with the inborn disinclination to regulated activity (especially to mental effort). The character of society depends on the strength of the nobler incentives, that is, the social inclinations and intellectual vivacity in opposition to the egoistic impulses and natural inertness. The former nourish the progressive, the latter the conservative spirit. Women are as much superior to men in the stronger development of their sympathy and sociability as they are inferior in insight and reason. Society is a group of families, not of individuals, and domestic life is the foundation, preparation, and pattern for social life, Comte praises the family, the connecting link between the individual and the species, as a school of unselfishness, and approves the strictness of the Catholic Church in regard to the indissolubility of the marriage relation. He remarks the evil consequences of the constantly increasing division of labor, which makes man egoistic and narrow-minded, since it hides rather than reveals the social significance of the employment of the individual and its connection with the welfare of the community, and seeks for a means of checking them. Besides the universal education of youth, he demands the establishment of a spiritual power to bring the general interest continually to the minds of the members of all classes and avocations, to direct education, and to enjoy the same authority in moral and intellectual matters as is conceded to the astronomer in the affairs of his department. The function of this power would be to occupy the position heretofore held by the clergy. Comte conceives it as composed of positive philosophers, entirely independent of the secular authorities, but in return cut off from political influence and from wealth. Secular authority, on the other hand, he wishes put into the hands of an aristocracy of capitalists, with the bankers at the head of these governing leaders of industry.

The Dynamics, the science of the temporal succession of social phenomena, makes use of the principle of development. The progress of society, which is to be regarded as a great individual, consists in the growing predominance of the higher, human activities over the lower and animal. The humanity in us, it is true, will never attain complete ascendency over the animality, but we can approach nearer and nearer to the ideal, and it is our duty to aid in this march of civilization. Although the law of progress holds good for all sides of mental life, for art, politics, and morals, as well as for science, nevertheless the most important factor in the evolution of the human race is the development of the intellect as the guiding power in us (though not in itself the strongest). Awakened first by the lower wants, the intellect assumes in increasing measure the guidance of human operations, and gives a determinate direction to the feelings. The passions divide men, and, without the guidance of the speculative faculty, would mutually cripple one another; that which alone unites them into a collection force is a common belief, an idea. Ideas are related to feeling—to quote a comparison from John Stuart Mill's valuable treatise *Auguste Comte and Positivism*, 3d ed., 1882, a work of which we have made considerable use—as the steersman who directs the ship is to the steam which drives it forward. Thus the history of humanity has been determined by the history of man's intellectual convictions, and this in turn by the three familiar stages in the theory of the universe. With the development from the theological to the positive mode of thought is most intimately connected, further, the transition from the military to the industrial mode of life. As the religious spirit prepares the way for the scientific spirit, so without the dominion of the military spirit industry could not have been developed. It was only in the school of war that the earliest societies could learn order; slavery was beneficial in that through it labor was imposed upon the greater part of mankind in spite of their aversion to it. The political preponderance of the legists corresponds to the intermediate, metaphysical stage. The sociological law (discovered by Comte in the year 1822) harmonizes also with the customary division which separates the ancient from the modern world by the Middle Ages.

In his philosophy of history Comte gives the further application of these principles. Here he has won commendation even from his opponents for a sense of justice which merits respect and for his comprehensive view. The outlooks and proposals for the future here interspersed were in later writings[1] worked out into a comprehensive theory of the regeneration of society; the extravagant character of which has given occasion to his critics to make a complete division between the second, "subjective or sentimental," period of his thinking, in which the philosopher is said to be transformed into the high priest of a new religion, and the first, the positivistic period, although the major part of the qualities pointed out as characteristic of the former are only intensifications of some which may be shown to have been present in the latter. Beneath the surface of the most sober inquiry mystical and dictatorial tendencies pulsate in Comte from the beginning, and science was for him simply a means to human happiness. But now he no longer demands the independent pursuit of science in order to the attainment of this end, but only the believing acceptance of its results. The intellect is to be placed under the dominion of the heart, and only such use made of it as promises a direct advantage for humanity; the determination of what problems are most important at a given time belongs to the priesthood. The systematic unity or harmony of the mind demands this dominion of the feelings over thought. The religion of positivism, which has "love for its principle, order for its basis, and progress for its end," is a religion without God, and without any other immortality than a continuance of existence in the grateful memory of posterity. The dogmas of the positivist religion are scientific principles. Its public *cultus* with nine sacraments and a large number of annual festivals, is paid to the *Grand Être* "Humanity" (which is not omnipotent, but, on account of its composite character, most dependent, yet infinitely superior to any of its parts); and, besides this, space, the earth, the universe, and great men of the past are objects of reverence. Private devotion consists in the adoration of living or dead women as our guardian angels. The *ethics* of the future declares the good of others to be the sole moral motive to action (altruism). Comte's last work, the *Philosophy of Mathematics*, 1856, indulges in a most remarkable numerical mysticism. The historical influence exercised by Comte through his later writings is extremely small in comparison with that of his chief work. Besides Blignières and Robinet, E. Littré, the well-known author of the *Dictionnaire de la Langue Française* (1863 *seq*.) who was the most eminent of Comte's disciples and the editor of his *Collected Works* (1867 *seq*.), has written on the life and work of the master. Comte's school divided into two groups—the apostates, with Littré (1801-81) at their head, who reject the subjective phase and hold fast to the earlier doctrine, and the faithful, who until 1877, when a new division between strict and liberal Comteans took place within this group, gathered about P. Laffitte (born 1823).[2] The leader of the English positivists is Frederic Harrison (born 1831). Positivistic societies exist also in Sweden, Brazil, Chili, and elsewhere. Positivism has been developed in an independent spirit by J.S. Mill and Herbert Spencer.

[Footnote 1: *Positivist Catechism*, 1852 [English translation by Congreve, 1858, 2d ed., 1883]; *System of Positive Polity*, 4 vols., 1851-54 [English translation, 1875-77]. Cf. Pünjer, *A. Comtes "Religion der Menschheit"* in the *Jahrbücher für protestantische Theologie*, 1882.]

[Footnote 2: On this division cf. E. Caro, *M. Littré et le Positivisme*, 1883, and Herm. Gruber (S.J.), *Der Positivismus vom Tode Comtes bis auf unsere Tage*, 1891.]

The following brief remarks on the course of French philosophy may also be added. Against the sensationalism of Condillac as continued by Cabanis, Destutt de Tracy (see above, pp. 259-260), and various physiologists, a twofold reaction asserted itself. One manifestation of this proceeded from the *theological school*, represented by the "traditionalists" Victor de Bonald (1818), Joseph de Maistre (1753-1821; *St. Petersburg Soirées*, 1821), and F. de Lamennais (1782-1854), who, however, after his break with the Church (*Words of a Believer*, 1834) developed in his *Sketch of a Philosophy*, 1841 *seq*., an ontological system after Italian and German models. The other came from the *spiritualistic school*, at whose head stood Maine de Biran[1] (1766-1824; *On the Foundations of Psychology*; his *Works* have been edited by Cousin, 1841, Naville, 1859, and Bertrand) and Royer Collard (1763-1845). Their pupil Victor Cousin (1792-1867; *Works*, 1846-50), who admired Hegel also, became the head of the *eclectic school*. Cousin will neither deny metaphysics with the Scotch, nor construe metaphysics *a priori* with the Germans, but with Descartes bases it on psychology. For a time an idealist of the Hegelian type (infinite and finite, God and the world, are mutually inseparable; the Ideas reveal themselves in history, in the nations, in great men), he gradually sank back to the position of common sense. His adherents, among whom Théodore Jouffroy (died 1842) was the most eminent, have done special service in the history of philosophy. From Cousin's school, which was opposed by P. Leroux and J. Reynaud, have come Ravaisson, Saisset, Jules Simon, P. Janet (born 1823),[2] and E. Caro (born 1826; *The Philosophy of Goethe*, 1866). Kant has influenced Charles Renouvier (born 1817; *Essays in General Criticism*, 4 vols., 1854-64) and E. Vacherot (born 1809; *Metaphysics and Science*, 1858, 2d ed., 1863; *Science and Consciousness*, 1872).

[Footnote 1: Cf. E. König in *Philosophische Monatshefte*, vol. xxv. 1889, p.160 *seq*.]

[Footnote 2: Janet: *History of Political Science in its Relations to Morals*, 1858, 3d ed., 1887; *German Materialism of the Present Day*, 1864, English translation by Masson, 1866: *The Family*, 1855; *The Philosophy of Happiness*, 1862; *The Brain and Thought*, 1867; *Elements of Morals*, 1869 [English translation by Corson, 1884]; *The Theory of Morals*, 1874 [English translation by Mary Chapman, 1883]; *Final Causes*, 1876 [English translation by Affleck, with a preface by Flint, new ed., 1883].]

Among other thinkers of reputation we may mention the socialist Henri de Saint-Simon (1760-1825; *Selected Works*, 1859), the physiologist Claude Bernard (1813-78), the positivist H. Taine (1828-93; *The Philosophy of Art*, English translation by Durand, 2d ed., 1873; *On Intelligence*, 1872, English translation by Haye, 1871), E. Renan (1823-92; *The Life of Jesus*, 1863, English translation by Wilbour, *Philosophical Dialogues and Fragments*—English, 1883), the writer on aesthetics and ethics J.M. Guyau (*The Problems of Contemporary Aesthetics*, 1884; *Sketch of an Ethic without Obligation or Sanction*, 1885; *The Irreligion of the Future*, 1887), Alfred

Fouillée (*The Future of Metaphysics founded on Experience*, 1889; *Morals, Art, and Religion according to Guyau*, 1889; *The Evolutionism of the Idea-Forces*, 1890), and the psychologist Th. Ribot,[1] editor of the *Revue Philosophique* (from 1876).

[Footnote 1: Ribot: *Heredity*, 2d ed., 1882 [English translation, 1875]; *The Diseases of Memory*, 1881 [English translation, 1882]; *The Diseases of the Will*, 1883 [English. 1884]; *The Diseases of Personality*, 1885 [English, 1887]; *The Psychology of Attention*, 1889 [English, 1890]; *German Psychology of To-day*, 2d ed., 1885 [English translation by Baldwin, 1886].]

%3. Great Britain and America.%

Prominent among the British philosophers of the nineteenth century[1] are Hamilton, Bentham, J.S. Mill, and Spencer. Hamilton is the leading representative of the Scottish School; Bentham is known as the advocate of utilitarianism; Mill, an exponent of the traditional empiricism of English thinking, develops the theory of induction and the principle of utility; Spencer combines an agnostic doctrine of the absolute and thoroughgoing evolution in the phenomenal world into a comprehensive philosophical system.[2] In recent years there has been a reaction against empirical doctrines on the basis of neo-Kantian and neo-Hegelian principles. Foremost among the leaders of this movement we may mention T.H. Green.

[Footnote 1: Cf. Harald Höffding, *Einleitung in die englische Philosophie unserer Zeit* (Danish, 1874), German (with alterations and additions by the author) by H. Kurella, 1889; David Masson, *Recent British Philosophy*, 1865, 3d ed., 1877; Ribot, *La Psychologie Anglaise Contemporaine*, 1870, 2d ed., 1875 [English, 1874] Guyau, *La Morale Anglaise Contemporaine*, 1879 [Morris, *British Thought and Thinkers*, 1880; Porter, "On English and American Philosophy," Ueberweg's *History*, English translation, vol. ii. pp. 348-460; O. Pfleiderer, *Development of Theology*, 1890, book iv.—TR.]]

[Footnote 2: Cf. on Mill and Spencer, Bernh. Pünjer, *Jahrbücher für protestantische Theologie*, 1878.]

The Scottish philosophy has been continued in the nineteenth century by James Mackintosh (*Dissertation on the Progress of Ethical Philosophy*, 1830, 3d ed., 1863), and William Whewell (*History of the Inductive Sciences*, 3d ed., 1857; *Philosophy of the Inductive Sciences*, 1840, 3d ed., 1858-60). Its most important representative is Sir William Hamilton[1] of Edinburgh (1788-1856), who, like Whewell, is influenced by Kant. Hamilton bases philosophy on the facts of consciousness, but, in antithesis to the associational psychology, emphasizes the mental activity of discrimination and judgment. Our knowledge is relative, and relations its only object. Consciousness can never transcend itself, it is bound to the antithesis of subject and object, and conceives the existent under relations of space and time. Hence the unconditioned is inaccessible to knowledge and attainable by faith alone. Among Hamilton's followers belong Mansel (*Metaphysics*, 3d. ed., 1875; *Limits of Religions Thought*, 5th ed., 1870) and Veitch. The Scottish doctrine was vigorously opposed by J.F. Ferrier (1808-64; *Institutes of Metaphysics*, 2d ed., 1856), who himself developed an idealistic standpoint.

[Footnote 1: Hamilton: *Discussions on Philosophy and Literature*, 1852, 3d ed., 1866; *Lectures on Metaphysics*, 2d ed., 1860, and on *Logic*, 2d ed., 1866, edited by his pupils, Mansel and Veitch; *Reid's Works*, with notes and dissertations, 1846, 7th ed., 1872. On Hamilton cf. Veitch, 1882, 1883 [Monck, 1881].]

In the United States the Scottish philosophy has exercised a wide influence. In recent times it has been strenuously advocated, chiefly in the spirit of Reid, by James McCosh (a native of Scotland, but since 1868 in America; *The Intuitions of the Mind*, 3d ed., 1872; *The Laws of Discursive Thought*, new ed., 1891; *First and Fundamental Truths*, 1889); while in Noah Porter (died 1892; *The Human Intellect*, new ed., 1876; *The Elements of Moral Science*, 1885) it appears modified by elements from German thinking.

Jeremy Bentham[1] (1748-1832) is noteworthy for his attempt to revive Epicureanism in modern form. Virtue is the surest means to pleasure, and pleasure the only self-evident good. Every man strives after happiness, but not every one in the right way. The honest man calculates correctly, the criminal falsely; hence a careful calculation of the value of the various pleasures, and a prudent use of the means to happiness, is the first condition of virtue; in this the easily attainable minor joys, whose summation amounts to a considerable quantum, must not be neglected. The value of a pleasure is measured by its intensity, duration, certainty, propinquity, fecundity in the production of further pleasure, purity or freedom from admixture of consequent pain, and extent to the greatest possible number of persons. Every virtuous action results in a balance of pleasure. Inflict no evil on thyself or others from which a balance of good will not result. The end of morality is the "greatest happiness of the greatest number," in the production of which each has first to care for his own welfare: whoever injures himself more than he serves others acts immorally, for he diminishes the sum of happiness in the world; the interest of the individual coincides with the interest of society. The two classes of virtues are prudence and benevolence. The latter is a natural, though not a disinterested affection: happiness enjoyed with others is greater than happiness enjoyed alone. Love is a pleasure-giving extension of the individual; we serve others to be served by them.

[Footnote 1: Bentham: *Introduction to the Principles of Morals and Legislation*, 1789; new ed., 1823, reprinted 1876; *Deontology*, 1834, edited by Bowring, who also edited the *Works*, 1838-43. *The Principles of Civil and Criminal Legislation*, edited in French from Bentham's manuscripts by his pupil Etienne Dumont (1801, 2d ed., 1820; English by Hildreth, 5th ed., 1887), was translated into German with notes by F.E. Beneke, 1830.]

Associationalism has been reasserted by James Mill (1773-1836; *Analysis of the Phenomena of the Human Mind*, 1829), whose influence lives on in the work of his greater son. The latter, John Stuart Mill,[1] was born in London 1806, and was from 1823 to 1858 a secretary in the India House; after the death of his wife he lived (with the exception of two years of service as a Member of Parliament) at Avignon; his death occurred in 1873. Mill's *System of Logic* appeared in 1843, 9th ed., 1875; his *Utilitarianism*, 1863, new ed., 1871; *An Examination of Sir William Hamilton's Philosophy*, 1865, 5th ed., 1878; his notes to the new edition of his father's work, *Analysis of the Phenomena of the Human Mind*, 2d ed., 1878, also deserve notice. With the phenomenalism of Hume and the (somewhat corrected) associational psychology of his father as a basis, Mill makes experience the sole source of knowledge, rejecting *a priori* and intuitive elements of every sort. Matter he defines as a "permanent possibility of sensation"; mind is resolved into "a series of feelings with a background of possibilities of feeling," even though the author is not unaware of the difficulty involved in the question how a series of feelings can be aware of itself as a series. Mathematical principles, like all others, have an experiential origin—the peculiar certitude ascribed to them by the Kantians is a fiction—and induction is the only fruitful method of scientific inquiry (even in mental science). The syllogism is itself a concealed induction.

[Footnote 1: Cf. on Mill. Taine, *Le Positivisme Anglais*, 1864 [English, by Haye]; the objections of Jevons *(Contemporary Review*, December, 1877 *seq.*, reprinted in *Pure Logic and other Minor Works*, 1890; cf. *Mind*, vol. xvi. pp. 106-110) to Mill's doctrine of the inductive character of geometry, his treatment of the relation of resemblance, and his exposition of the four methods of experimental inquiry in their relation to the law of causation; and the finely conceived essay on utilitarianism, by C. Hebler, *Philosophische Aufsätze*, 1869, pp. 35-66. [Also Mill's own *Autobiography*, 1873: Bain's *John Stuart Mill, a Criticism*, 1882; and T.H. Green, Lectures on the *Logic, Works*, vol. ii.—TR.]]

When I assert the major premise the inference proper is already made, and in the conclusion the comprehensive formula for a number of particular truths which was given in the premise is merely explicated, interpreted. Because universal judgments are for him merely brief expressions for aggregates of particular truths, Mill is able to say that all knowledge is generalization, and at the same time to argue that all inference is from particulars to particulars. Inference through a general proposition is not necessary, yet useful as a collateral security, inasmuch as the syllogistic forms enable us more easily to discover errors committed. The ground of induction, the uniformity of nature in reference both to the coexistence and the succession of phenomena, since it wholly depends on induction, is not unconditionally certain; but it may be accepted as very highly probable, until some instance of lawless action (in itself conceivable) shall have been actually proved. Like the law of causation, the principles of logic are also not *a priori*, but only the highest generalizations from all previous experience.

Mill's most brilliant achievement is his theory of experimental inquiry, for which he advances four methods: (1) The Method of Agreement: "If two or more instances of the phenomenon under investigation have only one circumstance in common, the circumstance in which alone all the instances agree is the cause (or effect) of the given phenomenon." (2) The Method of Difference: "If an instance in which the phenomenon under investigation occurs, and an instance in which it does not occur, have every circumstance in common save one, that one occurring only in the former; the circumstance in which alone the two instances differ, is the effect, or the cause, or an indispensable part of the cause, of the phenomenon," These two methods (the method of observation, and the method of artificial experiment) may also be employed in combination, and the Canon of the Joint Method of Agreement and Difference runs: "If two or more instances in which the phenomenon occurs have only one circumstance in common, while two or more instances in which it does not occur have nothing in common save the absence of that circumstance, the circumstance in which alone the two sets of instances differ is the effect, or the cause, or an indispensable part of the cause, of the phenomenon." (3) The Method of Residues: "Subduct from any phenomenon such part as is known by previous inductions to be the effect of certain antecedents, and the residue of the phenomenon is the effect of the remaining antecedents." (4) The Method of Concomitant Variations: "Whatever phenomenon varies in any manner whenever another phenomenon varies in some particular manner, is either a cause or an effect of that phenomenon, or is connected with it through some fact of causation." When the phenomena are complex the deductive method must be called in to aid: from the inductively ascertained laws of the action of single causes this deduces the laws of their combined action; and, as a final step, the results of such ratiocination are verified by the proof of their agreement with empirical facts. To explain a phenomenon means to point out its cause; the explanation of a law is its reduction to other, more general laws. In all this, however, we remain within the sphere of phenomena; the essence of nature always eludes our knowledge.

In the chapter "Of Liberty and Necessity" (book vi. chap. ii.) Mill emphasizes the position that the necessity to which human actions are subject must not be conceived, as is commonly done, as irresistible compulsion, for it denotes nothing more than the uniform order of our actions and the possibility of predicting them. This does not destroy the element in the idea of freedom which is legitimate and practically valuable: we have the power to alter our character; it is formed *by* us as well as *for* us; the desire to mould it is one of the most influential circumstances in its formation. The principle of morality is the promotion of the happiness of all sentient beings. Mill differs from Bentham, however, from whom he derives the principle of utility, in several important particulars—by his recognition of qualitative as well as of quantitative differences in pleasures, of the value of the ordinary rules of morality as intermediate principles, of the social feelings, and of the disinterested love of virtue. Opponents of the utilitarian theory have not been slow in availing themselves of the opportunities for attack thus afforded.[1] A third distinguished representative of the same general movement is Alexander Bain, the psychologist (born 1818; *The Senses and the Intellect*, 3d ed., 1868; *The Emotions and the Will*, 3d ed., 1875; *Mental and Moral Science*, 1868, 3d ed., 1872, part ii., 1872; *Mind and Body*, 3d ed., 1874).

[Footnote 1: On the relation of Bentham and Mill cf. Höffding, p. 68:
Sidgwick's *Outlines*, chap. iv. § 16; and John Grote's *Examination of the
Utilitarian Philosophy*, 1870, chap. i.]

The system projected by Herbert Spencer (born 1820), the major part of which has already appeared, falls into five parts: *First Principles*, 1862, 7th ed., 1889; *Principles of Biology*, 1864-67, 4th ed., 1888; *Principles of Psychology*, 1855, 5th ed., 1890; *Principles of Sociology* (vol. i. 1876, 3d ed., 1885; part iv. *Ceremonial Institutions*, 1879, 3d ed., 1888, part v. *Political Institutions*, 1882, 2d ed., 1885, part vi. *Ecclesiastical Institutions*, 1885, 2d ed., 1886, together constituting vol. ii.); *Principles of Ethics* (part i. *The Data of Ethics*, 1879, 5th ed., 1888; parts ii. and iii. *The Inductions of Ethics* and *The Ethics of Individual Life*, constituting with part i. the first volume, 1892; part iv. *Justice*, 1891). A comprehensive exposition of the system has been given, with the authority of the author, by F.H. Collins in his *Epitome of the Synthetic Philosophy*, 1889.[1] The treatise on *Education*, 1861, 23d ed., 1890, his sociological writings, and his various essays have also contributed essentially to Mr. Spencer's fame, both at home and abroad. The *First Principles* begin with the "Unknowable." Since human opinions, no matter how false they may seem, have sprung from actual experiences, and, when they find wide acceptance and are tenaciously adhered to, must have something in them which appeals to the minds of men, we must assume that every error contains a kernel of truth, however small it be. No one of opposing views is to be accepted as wholly true, and none rejected as entirely false. To discover the incontrovertible fact which lies at their basis, we must reject the various concrete elements in which they disagree, and find for the remainder the abstract expression which holds true throughout its divergent manifestations. No antagonism is older, wider, more profound, and more important than that between religion and science. Here too some most general truth, some ultimate fact must lie at the basis. The ultimate religious ideas are self-contradictory and untenable. No one of the possible hypotheses concerning the nature and origin of things—every religion may be defined as an *a priori* theory of the universe, the accompanying ethical code being a later growth—is logically defensible: whether the world is conceived atheistically as self-existent, or pantheistically as self-created, or theistically (fetichism, polytheism, or monotheism), as created by an external agency, we are everywhere confronted by unthinkable conclusions. The idea of a First Cause or of the absolute (as Mansel, following Hamilton, has proved in his *Limits of Religious Thought*) is full of contradictions. But however widely the creeds diverge, they show entire unanimity, from the grossest superstition up to the most developed theism, in the belief that the existence of the world is a mystery which ever presses for interpretation, though it can never be entirely explained. And in the progress of religion from crude fetichism to the developed theology of our time, the truth, at first but vaguely perceived, that there is an omnipresent Inscrutable which manifests itself in all phenomena, ever comes more clearly into view.

[Footnote 1: Cf. also Fiske's *Outlines of Cosmic Philosophy*, 2 vols., 1874. Numerous critiques and discussions of Spencer's views have been given in various journals and reviews; among more extended works reference may be made to Bowne, *The Philosophy of Herbert Spencer*, 1874; Malcolm Guthrie, *On Mr. Spencer's Formula of Evolution*, 1879, and the same author, *On Mr. Spencer's Unification of Knowledge*, 1882; and T.H. Green, on Spencer and Lewes, *Works*, vol. i.—TR.]

Science meets this ultimate religious truth with the conviction, grasped with increasing clearness as the development proceeds from Protagoras to Kant, that the reality hidden behind all phenomena must always remain unknown, that our knowledge can never be absolute. This principle maybe established inductively from the incomprehensibility of the ultimate scientific ideas, as well as deductively from the nature of intelligence, through an analysis of the product and the process of thought. (1) The ideas space, time, matter, motion, and force, as also the first states of consciousness, and the thinking substance, the ego as the unity of subject and object, all represent realities whose nature and origin are entirely incomprehensible. (2) The subsumption of particular facts under more general facts leads ultimately to a most general, highest fact, which cannot be reduced to a more general one, and hence cannot be explained or comprehended. (3) All thought (as has been shown by Hamilton in his essay "On the Philosophy of the Unconditioned," and by his follower Mansel) is the establishment of relations, every thought involving relation, difference, and (as Spencer adds) likeness. Hence the absolute, the idea of which excludes every relation, is entirely beyond the reach of an intelligence which is concerned with relations alone, and which always consists in discrimination, limitation, and assimilation—it is trebly unthinkable. Therefore: Religion and Science agree in the supreme truth that the human understanding is capable of relative knowledge only or of a knowledge of the relative (Relativity). Nevertheless, according to Spencer, it is too much to conclude with the thinkers just mentioned, that the idea of the absolute is a mere expression for inconceivability, and its existence problematical. The nature of the absolute is unknowable, but not the existence of a basis for the relative and phenomenal. The considerations which speak in favor of the relativity of knowledge and its limitation to phenomena, argue also the existence of a non-relative, whose phenomenon the relative is; the idea of the relative and the phenomenal posits *eo ipso* the existence of the absolute as its correlative, which manifests itself in phenomena. We have at least an indefinite, though not a definite, consciousness of the Unknowable as the Unknown Cause, the Universal Power, and on this is founded our ineradicable belief in objective reality.

All knowledge is limited to the relative, and consists in increasing generalization: the apex of this pyramid is formed by philosophy. Common knowledge is un-unified knowledge; science is partially unified knowledge; philosophy, which combines the highest generalizations of the sciences into a supreme one, is completely unified knowledge. The data of philosophy are—besides an Unknowable Power—the existence of knowable likenesses and differences among its manifestations, and a resulting segregation of the manifestations into those of subject and object. Further, derivative data are space (relations of coexistence), time (relations of irreversible sequence), matter (coexistent positions that offer resistance), motion (which involves space, time, and matter), and force, the ultimate of ultimates, on which all others depend, and from our primordial experiences of which all the other modes of consciousness are derivable. Similarly the ultimate primary truth is the *persistence of force*, from which, besides the indestructibility of matter and the continuity of (actual or potential) motion, still further truths may be deduced: the persistence of relations among forces or the uniformity of law, the transformation and equivalence of (mental and social as well as of physical) forces, the law of the direction of motion (along the line of least resistance, or the line of greatest traction, or their resultant), and the unceasing rhythm of motion. Beyond these analytic truths, however, philosophy demands a law of universal synthesis. This must be the law of *the continuous redistribution of matter and motion*, for each single thing, and the whole universe as well, is involved in a (continuously repeated) double process of *evolution* and *dissolution*, the former consisting in the integration of matter[1] and the dissipation of motion, the latter in the absorption of motion and the disintegration of matter. The law of evolution, in its complete development, then runs: "Evolution is an integration of matter and concomitant dissipation of motion; during which the matter passes from an indefinite, incoherent homogeneity to a definite, coherent heterogeneity; and during which the retained motion undergoes a parallel transformation." This is inductively supported by illustrations from every region of nature and all departments of mental and social life; and, further, shown deducible from the ultimate principle of the persistence of force, through the mediation of several corollaries to it, viz., the instability of the homogeneous under the varied incidence of surrounding forces, the multiplication of effects by action and reaction, and segregation. Finally the principle of equilibration indicates the impassable limit at which evolution passes over into dissolution, until the eternal round is again begun. If it may be said of Hegel himself, that he vainly endeavored to master the concrete fullness of reality with formal concepts, the criticism is applicable to Spencer in still greater measure. The barren schemata of concentration, passage into heterogeneity, adaptation, etc., which are taken from natural science, and which are insufficient even in their own field, prove entirely impotent for the mastery of the complex and peculiar phenomena of spiritual life.

[Footnote 1: Organic growth is the concentration of elements before diffused; cf. the union of nomadic families into settled tribes.]

Armed with these principles, however, Mr. Spencer advances to the discussion of the several divisions of "Special Philosophy." Passing over inorganic nature, he finds his task in the interpretation of the phenomena of life, mind, and society in terms of matter, motion, and force under the general evolution formula. This procedure, however, must not be understood as in any wise materialistic. Such an interpretation would be a misrepresentation, it is urged, for the strict relativity of the standpoint limits all conclusions to phenomena, and permits no inference concerning the nature of the "Unknowable." The *Principles of Biology* take up the phenomena of life. Life is defined as the "continuous adjustment of internal relations to external relations." No attempt is made to explain its origin, yet (in the words of Mr. Sully) it is clear that the lowest forms of life are regarded as continuous in their essential nature with sub-vital processes. The evolution of living organisms, from the lowest to the highest, with the development of all their parts and functions, results from the co-operation of various factors, external and internal, whose action is ultimately reducible to the universal law.

The field of *psychology* is intimately allied with biology, and yet istinguished from it. Mental life is a subdivision of life in general, and may be subsumed under the general definition; but while biological truths concern the connection between internal phenomena, with but tacit or occasional recognition of the environment, psychology has to do neither with the internal connection nor the external connection, but "the connection between these two connections." Psychology in its subjective aspect, again, is a field entirely *sui generis*. The substance of mind, conceived as the underlying substratum of mental states, is unknowable; but the character of those states of which mind, as we know it, is composed, is a legitimate subject of inquiry. If this be carefully investigated, it seems highly probable that the ultimate unit of consciousness is something "of the same order as that which we call a nervous shock." Mind is proximately composed of feelings and the relations between feelings; from these, revived, associated, and integrated, the whole fabric of consciousness is built up. There is, then, no sharp distinction between the several phases of mind. If we trace its development objectively, in terms of the correspondence between inner and outer phenomena, we find a gradual progress from the less to the more complex, from the lower to the higher, without a break. Reflex action, instinct, memory, reason, are simply stages in the process. All is dependent on experience. Even the forms of knowledge, which are *a priori* to the individual, are the product of experience in the race, integrated and transmitted by heredity, and become organic in the nervous structure. In general the correspondence of inner and outer in which mental life consists is mediated by the nervous organism. The structure and functions of this condition consciousness and furnish the basis for the interpretation of mental evolution in terms of "evolution at large, regarded as a process of physical transformation." Nevertheless mental phenomena and bodily phenomena are not identical, consciousness is not motion. They are both phenomenal modes of the unknowable, disparate in themselves, and giving no indication of the ultimate nature of the absolute. Subjective analysis of human consciousness yields further proof of the unity of mental composition. All mental action is ultimately reducible to "the continuous differentiation and integration of states of consciousness." The criterion of truth is the inconceivability of the negation. Tried by this test, as by all others, realism is superior to idealism, though in that "transfigured" form which implies objective existence without implying the possibility of any further knowledge concerning it,—hence in a form entirely congruous with the conclusion reached by many other routes.

Sociology deals with super-organic evolution, which involves the co-ordinated actions of many individuals. To understand the social unit, we must study primitive man, especially the ideas which he forms of himself, of other beings, and of the surrounding world. The conception of a mind or other-self is gradually evolved through observation of natural phenomena which favor the notion of duality, especially the phenomena of sleep, dreams, swoons, and death. Belief in the influence of these doubles of the dead on the fortunes of the living leads to sorcery, prayer, and praise. Ancestor-worship is the ultimate source of all forms of religion; to it can be traced even such aberrant developments as fetichism and idolatry, animal-, plant-, and nature-worship. Thus the primitive man feels himself related not only to his living fellows, but to multitudes of supernatural beings about him. The fear of the living becomes the root of the political, and the fear of the dead the root of the religious, control. A society is an organic entity. Though differing from an individual organism in many ways, it yet resembles it in the permanent relations among its component parts. The Domestic Relations, by which the maintenance of the species is now secured, have come from various earlier and less developed forms; the militant type of society is accompanied by a lower, the industrial type by a higher stage of this development. Ceremonial observance is the most primitive kind of government, and the kind from which the political and religious governments have differentiated. Political organization is necessary in order to co-operation for ends which benefit the society directly, and the individual only indirectly. The ultimate political force is the feeling of the community, including as its largest part ancestral feeling. Many facts combine to obscure this truth, but however much it may be obscured, public feeling remains the primal source of authority. The various forms and instruments of government have grown up through processes in harmony with the general law. The two antithetical types of society are the militant and the industrial—the former implies compulsory co-operation under more or less despotic rule, with governmental assumption of functions belonging to the individual and a minimizing of individual initiative; in the latter, government is reduced to a minimum and best conducted by representative agencies, public organizations are largely replaced by private organizations, the individual is freer and looks less to the state for protection and for aid. The fundamental conditions of the highest social development is the cessation of war. The ideas and sentiments at the basis of Ecclesiastical Institutions have been naturally derived from the ghost-theory already described. The goal of religious development is the final rejection of all anthropomorphic conceptions of the First Cause, until the harmony of religion and science shall be reached in the veneration of the Unknowable. The remaining parts of Mr. Spencer's Sociology will treat of Professional Institutions, Industrial Institutions, Linguistic Progress, Intellectual, Moral, and Aesthetic Progress.

The subject matter of *ethics* is the conduct termed good or bad. Conduct is the adjustment of acts to ends. The evolution of conduct is marked by increasing perfection in the adjustment of acts to the furtherance of individual life, the life of offspring, and social life. The ascription of ethical character to the highly evolved conduct of man in relation to these ends implies the fundamental assumption, that "life is good or bad according as it does, or does not, bring a surplus of agreeable feeling." The ideal of moral science is rational deduction: a rational utilitarianism can be attained only by the recognition of the necessary laws—physical, biological, psychological, and sociological—which condition the results of actions; among these the biological laws have been largely neglected in the past, though they are of the utmost importance as furnishing the link between life and happiness. The "psychological view," again, explains the origin of conscience. In the course of development man comes to recognize the superiority of the higher and more representative feelings as guides to action; this form of self-restraint, however, is characteristic of the non-moral restraints as well, of the political, social, and religious controls. From these the moral control proper has emerged—differing from them in that it refers to intrinsic instead of extrinsic effects—and the element of coerciveness in them, transferred, has generated the feeling of moral compulsion (which, however, "will diminish as fast as moralization increases").

Such a rational ethics, based on the laws which condition welfare rather than on a direct estimation of happiness, and premising the relativity of all pains and pleasures, escapes fundamental objections to the earlier hedonism (*e.g.*, those to the hedonic calculus); and, combining the valuable elements in the divergent ethical theories, yields satisfactory principles for the decision of ethical problems. Egoism takes precedence of altruism; yet it is in turn dependent on this, and the two, on due consideration, are seen to be co-essential. Entirely divorced from the other, neither is legitimate, and a compromise is the only possibility; while in the future advancing evolution will bring the two into complete harmony. The goal of the whole process will be the ideal man in the ideal society, the scientific anticipation of which, absolute ethics, promises guidance for the relative and imperfect ethics of the transition period.

Examination of the actual, not the professed, ideas and sentiments of men reveals wide variation in moral judgments. This is especially true of the "pro-ethical" consciousnesses of external authorities, coercions, and opinions—religious, political, and social—by which the mass of mankind are governed; and is broadly due to variation in social conditions. Where the need of external co-operation predominates the ethics of enmity develops; where internal, peaceful co-operation is the chief social need the ethics of amity results: and the evolution principle enables us to infer that, as among certain small tribes in the past, so in the great cultivated nations of the future, the life of amity will unqualifiedly prevail. The Ethics of Individual Life shows the application of moral judgments to all actions which affect individual welfare. The very fact that some deviations from normal life are now morally disapproved, implies the existence of both egoistic and altruistic sanctions for the moral approval of all acts which conduce to normal living and the disapproval of all minor deviations, though for the most part these have hitherto remained unconsidered. Doubtless, however, moral control must here be somewhat indefinite; and even scientific observation and analysis must leave the production of a perfectly regulated conduct to "the organic adjustment of constitution to [social] conditions."

The Ethics of Social Life includes justice and beneficence. Human justice emerges from sub-human or animal justice, whose law (passing over gratis benefits to offspring) is "that each individual shall receive the benefits and evils of its own nature and its consequent conduct." This is the law of human justice, also, but here it is more limited than before by the non-interference which gregariousness requires, and by the increasing need for the sacrifice of individuals for the good of the species. The egoistic sentiment of justice arises from resistance to interference with free action; the altruistic develops through sympathy under social conditions, these being maintained meanwhile by a "pro-altruistic" sentiment, into which dread of retaliation, of social reprobation, of legal punishment, and of divine vengeance enter as component parts. The idea of justice emerges gradually from the sentiment of justice: it has two elements, one brute or positive, with inequality as its ideal, one human or negative, the ideal of which is equality. In early times the former of these was unduly appreciated, as in later times the latter, the true conception includes both, the idea of equality being applied to the limits and the idea of inequality to the benefits of action. Thus the formula of justice becomes: "Every man is free to do that which he wills, provided he infringes not the equal freedom of any other man "—a law which finds its authority in the facts, that it is an *a priori* dictum of "consciousness after it has been subject to the discipline of prolonged social life," and that it is also deducible from the conditions of the maintenance of life at large and of social life. From this law follow various particular corollaries or rights, all of which coincide with ordinary ethical concepts and have legal enactments corresponding to them. Political rights so-called do not exist; government is simply a system of appliances for the maintenance of private rights. Both the nature of the state and its constitution are variable: the militant type requires centralization and a coercive constitution; the industrial type implies a wider distribution of political power, but requires a representation of interests rather than a representation of individuals. Government develops as a result of war, and its function of protection against internal aggression arises by differentiation from its primary function of external defense. These two, then, constitute the essential duties of the state; when war ceases the first falls away, and its sole function becomes the maintenance of the conditions under which each individual may "gain the fullest life compatible with the fullest life of fellow-citizens." All beyond this, all interference with this life of the individual, whether by way of assistance, restraint, or education, proves in the end both unjust and impolitic. The remaining parts of the *Ethics* will treat of Negative and Positive Beneficence.

If J.S. Mill and Spencer (the latter of whom, moreover, had announced evolution as a world-law before the appearance of Darwin), move in a direction akin to positivism, the same is true, further, of G.H. Lewes (1817-78; *History of Philosophy*, 5th ed., 1880; *Problems of Life and Mind*, 1874 *seq*).

Turning to the discussion of particular disciplines, we may mention as prominent among English logicians,[1] besides Hamilton, Whewell, and Mill, Whately, Mansel, Thomson, De Morgan, Boole (*An Investigation of the Laws of Thought*, 1854); W.S. Jevons (*The Principles of Science*, 2d ed., 1877); Venn (*Symbolic Logic*, 1881; *Empirical Logic*, 1889), Bradley, and Bosanquet. Among more recent investigators in the field of psychology we may name Carpenter, Ferrier, Maudsley, Galton, Ward, and Sully (*The Human Mind*, 1892), and in the field of comparative psychology, Lubbock, Romanes (*Mental Evolution in Animals*, 1883; *Mental Evolution in Man*, 1889), and Morgan (*Animal Life and Intelligence*, 1891). Among ethical writers the following, besides Spencer and Green, hold a foremost place: H. Sidgwick *(The Methods of Ethics*, 4th ed., 1890), Leslie Stephen *(The Science of Ethics*, 1882), and James Martineau *(Types of Ethical Theory*, 3d ed., 1891). The quarterly review *Mind* (vols. i.-xvi. 1876-91, edited by G. Croom Robertson; new series from 1892, edited by G.F. Stout) has since its foundation played an important part in the development of English thought.

[Footnote 1: Cf. Nedich, *Die Lehre von der Quantifikation des Prädikats* in vol. iii. of Wundt's *Philosophische Studien*; L. Liard, *Les Logiciens Anglais Contemporains*, 1878; Al. Riehl in vol. i. of the *Vierteljahrsschrift für wissenschaftliche Philosophie*, 1877 [cf. also appendix A to the English translation of Ueberweg's *Logic*.—TR.].]

German idealism, for which S.T. Coleridge (died 1834) and Thomas Carlyle (died 1881) endeavored to secure an entrance into England, for a long time gained ground there but slowly. Later years, however, have brought increasing interest in German speculation, and much of recent thinking shows the influence of Kantian and Hegelian principles. As pioneer of this movement we may name J.H. Stirling *(The Secret of Hegel*, 1865); and as its most prominent representatives John Caird (*An Introduction to the Philosophy of Religion*, 1880), Edward Caird *(The Critical Philosophy of Immanuel Kant*, 1889; *The Evolution of Religion*, 1893), both in Glasgow, and T.H. Green (1836-82; professor at Oxford; *Prolegomena to Ethics*, 3d ed., 1887; *Works*, edited by Nettleship, 3 vols., 1885-88).[1] In opposition to the hereditary empiricism of English philosophy—which appears in Spencer and Lewes, as it did in Locke, Berkeley, and Hume, though in somewhat altered form—Green maintains that all experience is constituted by intelligible relations. Knowledge, therefore, is possible only for a correlating self-consciousness; while nature, as a system of relations, is likewise dependent on a spiritual principle, of which it is the expression. Thus the central conception of Green's philosophy becomes, "that the universe is a single eternal activity or energy, of which it is the essence to be self-conscious, that is, to be itself and not itself in one" (Nettleship). To this universal consciousness we are related as manifestations or "communications" under the limitations of our physical organization. As such we are free, that is, self-determined, determined by nothing from without. The moral ideal is self-realization or perfection, the progressive reproduction of the divine self-consciousness. This is possible only in terms of a development of persons, for as a self-conscious personality the divine spirit can reproduce itself in persons alone; and, since "social life is to personality what language is to thought," the realization of the moral ideal implies life in common. The nearer determination of the ideal is to be sought in the manifestations of the eternal spirit as they have been given in the moral history of individuals and nations. This shows what has already been implied in the relation of morality to personality and society, that moral good must first of all be a common good, one in which the permanent well-being of self includes the well-being of others also. This is the germ of morality, the development of which yields, first, a gradual extension of the area of common good, and secondly, a fuller and more concrete determination of its content. Further representatives of this movement are W. Wallace, Adamson, Bradley; A. Seth is an ex-member.

[Footnote 1: Cf. on Green the Memoir by Nettleship in vol. iii. of the *Works*.]

The first and greatest of American philosophical thinkers was the Calvinistic theologian Jonathan Edwards (1703-58; treatise on the *Freedom of Will*, 1754; *Works*, 10 vols., edited by Dwight, 1830). Edwards's deterministic doctrine found numerous adherents (among them his son, who bore his father's name, died 1801) as well as strenuous opponents (Tappan, Whedon, Hazard among later names), and essentially contributed to the development of philosophical thought in the United States. For a considerable period this crystallized for the most part around elements derived from British thinkers, especially from Locke and the Scottish School. In 1829 James Marsh called attention to German speculation [1] by his American edition of Coleridge's *Aids to Reflection*, with an important introduction from his own hand. Later W.E. Channing (1780-1842), the head of the Unitarian movement, attracted many young and brilliant minds, the most noted of whom, Ralph Waldo Emerson (1803-82), became a leader among the New England transcendentalists. Metaphysical idealism has, perhaps, met with less resistance in America than in England. Kant and Hegel have been eagerly studied (G.S. Morris, died 1889; C.C. Everett; J. Watson in Canada; Josiah Royce, *The Spirit of Modern Philosophy*, 1892; and others); and *The Journal of Speculative Philosophy*, edited by W.T. Harris, has since 1867 furnished a rallying point for idealistic interests. The influence of Lotze has also been considerable (B.P. Bowne in Boston). Sympathy with German speculation, however, has not destroyed the naturally close connection with the work of writers who use the English tongue. Thus Spencer's writings have had a wide currency, and his system numbers many disciples, though these are less numerous among students of philosophy by profession (John Fiske, *Outlines of Cosmic Philosophy*, 1874).

[Footnote 1: Cf. Porter, *op. cit.*]

In the latest decades the broadening of the national life, the increasing acquaintance with foreign thought, and the rapid development of university work have greatly enlarged and deepened the interest in philosophical pursuits. This is manifested most clearly in the field of psychology, including especially the "new" or "physiological" psychology, and the history of philosophy, though indications of pregnant thought in other departments, as ethics and the philosophy of religion, and even of independent construction, are not wanting. Among psychologists of the day we may mention G.S. Hall, editor of *The American Journal of Psychology* (1887 seq.), G.T. Ladd (*Elements of Physiological Psychology*, 1887), and William James (*Principles of Psychology*, 1890). *The International Journal of Ethics* (Philadelphia, 1890 scq.), edited by S. Burns Weston, is "devoted to the advancement of ethical knowledge and practice"; among the foreign members of its editorial committee are Jodl and Von Gizycki. The weekly journal of popular philosophy, *The Open Court*, published in Chicago, has for its object the reconciliation of religion and science; the quarterly, *The Monist* (1890 seq.), published by the same company under the direction of Paul Carus (*The Soul of Man*, 1891), the establishment of a monistic view of the world. Several journals, among them the *Educational Review* (1891 seq., edited by N.M. Butler), point to a growing interest in pedagogical inquiry. *The American Philosophical Review* (1892 seq., edited by J.G. Schurman, *The Ethical Import of Darwinism*, 1887) is a comprehensive exponent of American philosophic thought.

%4. Sweden, Norway, Denmark, and Holland.%

In *Sweden* an empirical period represented by Leopold (died 1829) and Th. Thorild (died 1808), and based upon Locke and Rousseau, was followed, after the introduction of Kant by D. Boëthius, 1794, by a drift toward idealism. This was represented in an extreme form by B. Höijer (died 1812), a contemporary and admirer of Fichte, who defended the right of philosophical construction, and more moderately by Christofer Jacob Böstrom (1797-1866), the most important systematic thinker of his country. As predecessors of Böstrom we may mention Biberg (died 1827), E.G. Geijer (died 1846), and S. Grubbe (died 1853), like him professors in Upsala, and of his pupils, S. Ribbing, known in Germany by his peculiar conception of the Platonic doctrine of ideas (German translation, 1863-64), the moralist Sahlin (1877), the historian, of Swedish philosophy[1] (1873 seq.) A. Nyblaeus of Lund, and H. Edfeldt of Upsala, the editor of Böstrom's works (1883).

[Footnote 1: Cf. Höffding, *Die Philosophie in Schweden* in the *Philosophische Monatshefte*, vol. xv. 1879, p. 193 seq.]

Böstrom's philosophy is a system of self-activity and personalism which recalls Leibnitz and Krause. The absolute or being is characterized as a concrete, systematically articulated, self-conscious unity, which dwells with its entire content in each of its moments, and whose members both bear the character of the whole and are immanent in one another, standing in relations of organic inter-determination. The antithesis between unity and plurality is only apparent, present only for the divisive view of finite consciousness. God is infinite, fully determinate personality (for determination is not limitation), a system of self-dependent living beings, differing in degree, in which we, as to our true being, are eternally and unchangeably contained. Every being is a definite, eternal, and living thought of God; thinking beings with their states and activities alone exist; all that is real is spiritual, personal. Besides this true, suprasensible world of Ideas, which is elevated above space, time, motion, change, and development, and which has not arisen by creation or a process of production, there exists for man, but only for him—man is formally perfect, it is true, but materially imperfect (since he represents the real from a limited standpoint)—a sensuous world of phenomena as the sphere of his activity. To this he himself belongs, and in it he is spontaneously to develop the suprasensible content which is eternally given him (i.e., his true nature), namely, to raise it from the merely potential condition of obscure presentiment to clear, conscious actuality. Freedom is the power to overcome our imperfection by means of our true nature, to realize our suprasensible capacities, to become for ourselves what we are in ourselves (in God). The ethics of Böstrom is distinguished from the Kantian ethics, to which it is related, chiefly by the fact that it seeks to bring sensibility into a more than merely negative relation to reason. Society is an eternal, and also a personal, Idea in God. The most perfect form of government is constitutional monarchy; the ideal goal of history, the establishment of a system of states embracing all mankind.

J. Borelius of Lund is an Hegelian, but differs from the master in regard to the doctrine of the contradiction. The Hegelian philosophy has adherents in *Norway* also, as G.V. Lyng (died 1884; *System of Fundamental Ideas*), M.J. Monrad (*Tendencies of Modern Thought*, 1874, German translation, 1879), both professors in Christiania, and Monrad's pupil G. Kent (*Hegel's Doctrine of the Nature of Experience*, 1891).

The *Danish* philosophy of the nineteenth century has been described by Höffding in the second volume of the *Archiv für Geschichte der Philosophie*, 1888. He begins with the representatives of the speculative movement: Steffens (see above), Niels Treschow (1751-1833), Hans Christian Oersted (1777-1851; *Spirit in Nature*, German translation, Munich, 1850-51), and Frederik Christian Sibbern (1785-1872). A change was brought about by the philosophers of religion Sören Kierkegaard (1813-55) and Rasmus Nielsen (1809-84; *Philosophy of Religion*, 1869), who opposed speculative idealism with a strict dualism of knowledge and faith, and were in turn opposed by Georg Brandes (born 1842) and Hans Bröchner (1820-75). Among younger investigators the Copenhagen professors, Harald Höffding[1] (born 1843) and Kristian Kroman[2] (born 1846) stand in the first rank.

[Footnote 1: Höffding: *The Foundations of Human Ethics*, 1876, German translation, 1880; *Outlines of Psychology*, 1882, English translation by Lowndes, 1891, from the German translation, 1887; *Ethics*, 1887, German translation by Bendixen, 1888.]

[Footnote 2: Kroman: *Our Knowledge of Nature*, German translation, 1883; *A Brief Logic and Psychology*, German translation by Bendixen, 1890.]

Land (*Mind*, vol. iii. 1878) and G. von Antal (1888) have written on philosophy in *Holland*. Down to the middle of the nineteenth century the field was occupied by an idealism based upon the ancients, in particular upon Plato: Franz Hemsterhuis (1721-90; *Works*, new ed., 1846-50), and the philologists Wyttenbach and Van Heusde. Then Cornelius Wilhelm Opzoomer[3] (1821-92; professor in Utrecht) brought in a new movement. Opzoomer favors empiricism. He starts from Mill and Comte, but goes beyond them in important points, and assigns faith a field of its own beside knowledge. In opposition to apriorism he seeks to show that experience is capable of yielding universal and necessary truths; that space, time, and causality are received along with the content of thought; that mathematics itself is based upon experience; and that the method of natural science, especially deduction, must be applied to the mental sciences. The philosophy of mind considers man as an individual being, in his connection with others, in relation to a higher being, and in his development; accordingly it divides into psychology (which includes logic, aesthetics, and ethology), sociology, the philosophy of religion, and the philosophy of history. Central to Opzoomer's system is his doctrine of the five sources of knowledge: Sensation, the feeling of pleasure and pain, aesthetic, moral, and religious feeling. If we build on the foundation of the first three alone, we end in materialism; if we leave the last unused, we reach positivism; if we make religious feeling the sole judge of truth, mysticism is the outcome. The criteria of science are utility and progress. These are still wanting in the mental sciences, in which the often answered but never decided questions continually recur, because we have neither derived the principles chosen as the basis of the deduction from an exact knowledge of the phenomena nor tested the results by experience. The causes of this defective condition can only be removed by imitating the study of nature: we must learn that no conclusions can be reached except from facts, and that we are to strive after knowledge of phenomena and their laws alone. We have no right to assume an "essence" of things beside and in addition to phenomena, which reveals itself in them or hides behind them. Pupils of Opzoomer are his successor in his Utrecht chair, Van der Wyck, and Pierson. We may also mention J.P.N. Land, who has done good service in editing the works of Spinoza and of Geulincx, and the philosopher of religion Rauwenhoff (1888).

[Footnote 1: Opzoomer: *The Method of Science*, a Handbook of Logic, German translation by Schwindt, 1852; *Religion*, German translation by Mook, 1869.]

On the system of the Hungarian philosopher Cyrill Horváth (died 1884 at Pesth) see the essay by E. Nemes in the *Zeitschrift für Philosophie*, vol. lxxxviii, 1886. Since 1889 a review, *Problems of Philosophy and Psychology*, has appeared at Moscow in Russian, under the direction of Professor N. von Grot.

CHAPTER XVI.

GERMAN PHILOSOPHY SINCE THE DEATH OF HEGEL.

With Hegel the glorious dynasty which, with a strong hand, had guided the fate of German philosophy since the conclusion of the preceding century disappears. From his death (1831) we may date the second period of post-Kantian philosophy,[1] which is markedly and unfavorably distinguished from the first by a decline in the power of speculative creation and by a division of effort. If previous to this the philosophical public, comprising all the cultured, had been eagerly occupied with problems in common, and had followed with unanimous interest the work of those who were laboring at them, during the last fifty years the interest of wider circles in philosophical questions has grown much less active; almost every thinker goes his own way, giving heed only to congenial voices; the inner connection of the schools has been broken down; the touch with thinkers of different views has been lost. The latest decades have been the first to bring a change for the better, in so far as new rallying points of philosophical interest have been created by the neo-Kantian movement, by the systems of Lotze and Von Hartmann, by the impulse toward the philosophy of nature proceeding from Darwinism, by energetic labors in the field of practical philosophy, and by new methods of investigation in psychology.

[Footnote 1: On philosophy since 1831 cf. vol. iii. of J.E. Erdmann's *History*; Ueberweg, *Grundriss*, part iii. §§ 37-49 (English translation, vol. ii. pp. 292-516); Lange, *History of Materialism*; B. Erdmann, *Die Philosophie der Gegenwart* in the *Deutsche Rundschau*, vols. xix., xx., 1879, June and July numbers; (A. Krohn,) *Streifzüge durch die Philosophie der Gegenwart* in the *Zeitschrift für Philosophie und philosophische Kritik*, vols. lxxxvii., lxxxix., 1885-86; (Burt, *History of Modern Philosophy*, 1892), also the third volume of Windelband's *Geschichte der neueren Philosophie*, when it appears.]

%1. From the Division of the Hegelian School to the Materialistic Controversy.%

A decade after the philosophy of Hegel had entered on its supremacy a division in the school was called forth by Strauss's *Life of Jesus*(1835). The differences were brought to light by the discussion of religious problems, in regard to which Hegel had not expressed himself with sufficient distinctness. The relation of knowledge and faith, as he had defined it, admitted of variant interpretations and deductions, and this in favor of Church doctrine as well as in opposition to it. Philosophy has the same content as religion, but in a different form, *i.e.*, not in the form of representation, but in the form of the concept—it transforms dogma into speculative truth. The conservative Hegelians hold fast to the identity of content in the two modes of cognition; the liberals, to the alteration in form, which, they assert, brings an alteration in content with it. According to Hegel the lower stage is "sublated" in the higher, *i.e.*, conserved as well as negated. The orthodox members of the school emphasize the conservation of religious doctrines, their justification from the side of the philosopher; the progressists, their negation, their overcoming by the speculative concept. The general question, whether the ecclesiastical meaning of a dogma is retained or to be abandoned in its transformation into a philosophemc, divides into three special questions, the anthropological, the soteriogical, and the theological. These are: whether on Hegelian principles immortality is to be conceived as a continuance of individual existence on the art of particular spirits, or only as the eternity of the universal reason; whether by the God-man the person of Christ is to be understood, or, on the other hand, the human species, the Idea of Humanity; whether personality belongs to the Godhead before the creation of the world, or whether it first attains to self-consciousness in human spirits, whether Hegel was a theist or a pantheist, whether he teaches the transcendence or the immanence of God. The Old Hegelians defend the orthodox interpretation; the Young Hegelians oppose it. The former, Göschel, Gabler, Hinrichs, Schaller (died 1868; *History of the Philosophy of Nature since Bacon*, 1841 *seq.*), J.E. Erdmann in Halle (1805-92; *Body and Soul*, 1837; *Psychological Letters*, 1851, 6th ed., 1882; *Earnest Sport*, 1871, 4th ed., 1890), form, according to Strauss's parliamentary comparison carried out by Michelet, the "right"; the latter, Strauss, Feuerbach, Bruno Bauer, and A. Ruge, who, with Echtermeyer, edited the *Hallesche*, afterward *Deutsche, Jahrbücher für Wissenschaft und Kunst*, 1838-42, the "left." Between them, and forming the "center," stand Karl Rosenkranz[1] in Königsberg (1805-79), C.L. Michelet in Berlin (p. 16; *Hegel, the Unrefuted World-philosopher*, 1870; *System of Philosophy*, 1876 *seq.*), and the theologians Marheineke (a pupil of Daub at Heidelberg) and W. Vatke (*Philosophy of Religion*, edited by Preiss, 1888). Contrasted with these is the group of semi- or pseudo-Hegelians (p. 596), who declare themselves in accord with the theistic doctrines of the right, but admit that the left represents Hegel's own opinion, or at least the correct deductions from his position.

[Footnote 1: K. Rosenkranz: *Psychology*, 1837, 3d ed., 1863; *Science of the Logical Idea*, 1858; *Studies*, 1839 *seq.*, *New Studies*, 1875 *seq.*; *Aesthetics of the Ugly*, 1853; several works on the history of poetry.]

The following should also be mentioned as Hegelians: the philosopher of history, Von Cieszkowski, the pedagogical writer, Thaulow (at Kiel, died 1883), the philosopher of religion and of law, A. Lasson at Berlin, the aesthetic writers Hotho, Friedrich Theodor Vischer[1] (1807-87), and Max Schasler (*Critical History of Aesthetics*, 1872; *Aesthetics*, 1886), the historians of philosophy, Schwegler (died 1857; *History of Greek Philosophy*, 1859, 4th ed., 1886, edited by Karl Köstlin, whose *Aesthetics* appeared 1869), Eduard Zeller[2] of Berlin (born 1814), and Kuno Fischer (born 1824; 1856-72 professor at Jena, since then at Heidelberg; *Logic and Metaphysics*, 2d ed., 1865). While Weissenborn (died 1874) is influenced by Schleiermacher also, and Zeller and Fischer strive back toward Kant, Johannes Volkelt[3] in Würzburg (born 1848), who started from Hegel and advanced through Schopenhauer and Hartmann, has of late years established an independent noëtical position and has done good service by his energetic opposition to positivism *(Das Denken als Hülfvorstellungs—Thätigkeit und als Aupassungsvorgang* in the *Zeitschrift für Philosophic*, vols. xcvi., xcvii., 1889-90).

[Footnote 1: Vischer: *Aesthetics*, 1846-58; *Critical Excursions*, 1844 *seq.*; several *Hefte* "Altes and Neues". The diary in the second part of the novel *Auch Einer* develops an original pantheistic view of the world.]

[Footnote 2: Zeller: *The Philosophy of the Greeks in its Historical Development*, 5 vols., 3d ed., vol. i. 5th ed. (English translation, 1868 *seq.*); three collections of *Addresses and Essays*, 1865, 1877, 1884.]

[Footnote 3: Volkelt: *The Phantasy in Dreams*, 1875; *Kant's Theory of Knowledge*, 1879; *On the Possibility of Metaphysics*, inaugural address at Basle, 1884; *Experience and Thought, Critical Foundation of the Theory of Knowledge*, 1886; *Lectures Introductory to the Philosophy of the Present Time* (delivered in Frankfort on the Main), 1892.]

The leaders of the Hegelian left require more detailed consideration. In David Friedrich Strauss[1] (1808-74, born and died at Ludwigsburg) the philosophy of religion becomes a historical criticism of the Bible and of dogmatics. The biblical narratives are, in great part, not history (this has been the common error alike of the super-naturalistic and of the rationalistic interpreters), but myths, that is, suprasensible facts presented in the form of history and in symbolic language. It is evident from the contradictions in the narratives and the impossibility of miracles that we are not here concerned with actual events. The myths possess (speculative, absolute) truth, but no (historical) reality. They are unintentional creations of the popular imagination; the spirit of the community speaks in the authors of the Gospels, using the historical factor (the life-history of Jesus) with mythical embellishments as an investiture for a supra-historical, eternal truth (the speculative Idea of incarnation). The God become man, in which the infinite and the finite, the divine nature and the human, are united, is the human race. The Idea of incarnation manifests itself in a multitude of examples which supplement one another, instead of pouring forth its whole fullness in a single one. The (real) Idea of the race is to be substituted for a single individual as the subject of the predicates (resurrection, ascension, etc.) which the Church ascribes to Christ. The Son of God is *Humanity*.

[Footnote 1: Strauss: *The Life of Jesus*, 1835-36, 4th ed., 1840 [English translation by George Eliot, 2d ed., 1893]; the same "for the German People," 1864 [English translation, 1865]; *Christian Dogmatics*, 1840-41; *Voltaire*, 1870; *Collected Writings*, 12 vols., edited by Zeller, 1876-78. On Strauss cf. Zeller, 1874 [English, 1874], and Hausrath, 1876-78.]

In his second principal work Strauss criticises the dogmas of Christianity as sharply as he had criticised the Gospel narrative in the first one. The historical development of these has of itself effected their destruction: the history of dogma is the objective criticism of dogma. Christianity and philosophy, theism and pantheism, dualism and immanence, are irreconcilable opposites. To be able to know we must cease to believe. Dogma is the product of the unphilosophical, uncultured consciousness; belief in revelation, only for those who have not yet risen to reason. In the transformation of religious representations into philosophical Ideas nothing specifically representative is left; the form of representation must be actually overcome. The Christian contraposition of the present world and that which is beyond is explained by the fact that the sensuo-rational spirit of man, so long as it does not philosophically know itself as the unity of the infinite and the finite, but only feels itself as finite, sensuo-empirical consciousness, projects the infinite, which it has in itself, as though this were something foreign, looks on it as something beyond the world. This separation of faith is entirely unphilosophical; it is the mission of the philosopher to reduce all that is beyond the world to the present. Thus for him immortality is not something to come, but the spirit's own power to rise above the finite to the Idea. And like future existence, so the transcendent God also disappears. The absolute is the universal unity of the world, which posits and sublates the individual as its modes. God is the being in all existence, the life in all that lives, the thought in all that think: he does not stand as an individual person beside and above other persons, but is the infinite which personifies itself and attains to consciousness in human spirits, and this from eternity; before there was a humanity of earth there were spirits on other stars, in whom God reflected himself.

Three decades later Strauss again created a sensation by his confession of materialism and atheism, *The Old Faith and the New*, 1872 (since the second edition, "With a Postscript as Preface"),[1] in which he continues the conflict against religious dualism. The question "Are we"—the cultured men of the day—"still Christians?" is answered in the negative. Christianity is a cult of poverty, despising the world, and antagonistic to labor and culture; but we have learned to esteem science and art, riches and acquisition, as the chief levers of culture and of human progress. Christianity dualistically tears apart body and soul, time and eternity, the world and God; we need no Creator, for the life-process has neither beginning nor end. The world is framed for the highest reason, it is true, but it has not been framed by a highest reason. Our highest Idea is the All, which is conformed to law, and instinct with life and reason, and our feeling toward the universe—the consciousness of dependence on its laws—exercises no less of ethical influence, is no less full of reverence, and no less exposed to injury from an irreverent pessimism, than the feeling of the devout of the old type toward their God. Hence the answer to the second question "Have we still a religion?" maybe couched in the affirmative. The new faith does not need a *cultus* and a Church. Since the dry services of the free congregations offer nothing for the fancy and the spirit, the edification of the heart must be accomplished in other ways—by participation in the interests of humanity, in the national life, and, not last, by aesthetic enjoyment. Thus in his last work, which in two appendices reaches a discussion of the great German poets and musicians, the old man returns to a thought to which he had given earlier expression, that the religious *cultus* should be replaced by the *cultus* of genius.

[Footnote 1: English translation by Mathilde Blind, 1873.]

As Strauss went over from Hegelianism to pantheism, so Ludwig Feuerbach[1] (1804-72), a son of the great jurist, Anselm Feuerbach, after he had for a short time moved in the same direction, took the opposite, the individualistic course, only, like Strauss, to end at last in materialism. "My first thought," as he himself describes the course of his development, "was God; my second, reason; my third and last, man." As theology has been overcome by Hegel's philosophy of reason, so this in turn must give place to the philosophy of man. "The new philosophy makes man, including nature as his basis, the highest and sole subject of philosophy, and, consequently, anthropology the universal science." Only that which is immediately self-evident is true and divine. But only that which is sensible is evident (*sonnenklar*); it is only where sensibility begins that all doubt and conflict cease. Sensible beings alone are true, real beings; existence in space and time is alone existence; truth, reality, and sensibility are identical. While the old philosophy took for its starting point the principle, "I am an abstract, a merely thinking being; the body does not belong to my essence," the new philosophy, on the other hand, begins with the principle, "I am a real, a sensible being; the body in its totality is my ego, my essence itself." Feuerbach, however, uses the concept of sensibility in so wide and vague a sense that, supported—or deceived—by the ambiguity of the word sensation, he includes under it even the most elevated and sacred feelings. Even the objects of art are seen, heard, and felt; even the souls of other men are sensed. In the sensations the deepest and highest truths are concealed. Not only the external, but the internal also, not only flesh, but spirit, not only the thing, but the ego, not only the finite, the phenomenal, but also the true divine essence is an object of the senses. Sensation proves the existence of objects outside our head—there is no other proof of being than love, than sensation in general. Everything is perceivable by the senses, if not directly, yet indirectly, if not with the vulgar, untrained senses, yet with the "cultivated senses," if not with the eye of the anatomist or chemist, yet with that of the philosopher. All our ideas spring from the senses, but their production requires communication and converse between man and man. The higher concepts cannot be derived from the individual Ego without a sensuously given Thou; the highest object of sense is man; man does not reach concepts and reason in general by himself, but only as one of two. The nature of man is contained in community alone; only in life with others and for others does he attain his destiny and happiness. The conscience is the ego putting itself in the place of another who has been injured. Man with man, the unity of I and Thou, is God, and God is love.

[Footnote 1: Feuerbach was born at Landshut, studied at Heidelberg and Berlin, habilitated, 1828, at Erlangen, and lived, 1836-60, in the village of Bruckberg, not far from Bayreuth, and from 1860 until his death in Rechenberg, a suburb of Nuremberg. *Collected Works* in 10 vols., 1846-66. The chief works are entitled: *P. Bayle*, 1838, 2d ed., 1844; *Philosophy and Christianity*, 1839; *The Essence of Christianity*, 1841, 4th ed., 1883 [English translation by George Eliot, 1854]; *Principles of the Philosophy of the Future*, 1843; *The Essence of Religion*, 1845; *Theogony*, 1857; *God, Freedom, and Immortality*, 1866. Karl Grün, 1874, C.N. Starcke, 1885, and W. Bolin, 1891, treat of Feuerbach.]

To the philosophy of religion Feuerbach assigns the task of giving a psychological explanation of the genesis of religion, instead of showing reason in religion. In bidding us believe in miracles dogma is a prohibition to think. Hence the philosopher is not to justify it, but to uncover the illusion to which it owes its origin. Speculative theology is an intoxicated philosophy; it is time to become sober, and to recognize that philosophy and religion are diametrically opposed to each other, that they are related to each other as health to disease, as thought to phantasy. Religion arises from the fact that man objectifies his own true essence, and opposes it to himself as a personal being, without coming to a consciousness of this divestment of self, of the identity of the divine and human nature. Hence the Hegelian principles, that the absolute is self-consciousness, that in man God knows himself, must be reversed: self-consciousness is the absolute; in his God man knows himself only. The Godhead is our own universal nature, freed from its individual limitations, intuited and worshiped as another, independent being, distinct from us. God is self objectified, the inner nature of man expressed; man is the beginning, the middle, and the end of religion. All theology is anthropology, for all religion is a self-deification of man. In religion man makes a division in his own nature, posits himself as double, first as limited (as a human individual), then as unlimited, raised to infinity (as God); and this deified self he worships in order to obtain from it the satisfaction of his needs, which the course of the world leaves unmet. Thus religion grows out of egoism: its basis is the difference between our will and our power; its aim, to set us free from the dependence which we feel before nature. (Like culture, religion seeks to make nature an intelligible and compliant being, only that in this it makes use of the supernatural instruments faith, prayer, and magic; it is only gradually that men learn to attack the evils by natural means.) That which man himself is not, but wishes to be, that he represents to himself in his gods as existing; they are the wishes of man's heart transformed into real beings, his longing after happiness satisfied by the fancy. The same holds true of all dogmas: as God is the affirmation of our wishes, so the world beyond is the present embellished and idealized by the fancy. Instead of "God is merciful, is love, is omnipotent, he performs miracles and hears prayers," the statement must be reversed: mercy, love, omnipotence, to perform miracles, and to hear prayers, is divine. In the sacraments of baptism and the Lord's supper Feuerbach sees the truth that water and food are indispensable and divine. As Feuerbach, following out this naturalistic tendency, reached the extreme of materialism, the influence of his philosophy—whose different phases there is no occasion to trace out in detail—had already passed its culmination. From his later writings little more has found its way into public notice than the pun, that man is (*ist*) what he eats (*isst*).

The remaining members of the Hegelian left may be treated more briefly. Bruno Bauer[1] (died in 1882; his principal work is the *Critique of the Synoptics*, in three volumes, 1841-42, which had been preceded, in 1840, by a *Critique of the Evangelical History of John*) at first belonged on the right of the school, but soon went over to the extreme left. He explains the Gospel narratives as creations with a purpose (*Tendenzdichtungen*), as intentional, but not deceitful, inventions, from which, despite their unreality, history may well be learned, inasmuch as they reflect the spirit of the time in which they were constructed. His own publications and those of his brother Edgar are much more radical after the year 1844. In these the brothers advocate the standpoint of "pure or absolute criticism," which extends itself to all things and events for or against which sides are taken from any quarter, and calmly watches how everything destroys itself. As soon as anything is admitted, it is no longer true. Nothing is absolutely valid, all is vain; it is only the criticising, all-destroying ego, free from all ethical ties, that possesses truth.

[Footnote 1: Not to be confused with the head of the Tübingen School, Ferdinand Christian Baur (died 1860).]

One further step was possible beyond Feuerbach and Bruno Bauer, that from the community to the particular, selfish individual, from the criticising, therefore thinking, ego, to the ego of sensuous enjoyment. This step was taken in that curious book *The Individual and his Property*, which Kaspar Schmidt, who died in 1856 at Berlin, published in 1845 (2d ed., 1882), under the pseudonym of Max Stirner. The Individual of whom the title speaks is the egoist. For me nothing is higher than myself; I use men and use up the world for my own pleasure. I seek to be and have all that I can be and have; I have a right to all that is within my power. Morality is a delusion, justice, like all Ideas, a phantom. Those who believe in ideals, and worship such generalities as self-consciousness, man, society, are still deep in the mire of prejudice and superstition, and have banished the old orthodox phantom of the Deity only to replace it by a new one. Nothing whatever is to be respected.

* * * * *

Among the opponents of the Hegelian philosophy the members of the "theistic school," who have above been designated as semi-Hegelians, approximate it most closely. These endeavor, in part retaining the dialectic method, to blend the immanence of the absolute, which philosophy cannot give up and concerning which Hegel had erred only by way of over-emphasis, with the transcendence of God demanded by Christian consciousness, to establish a theism which shall contain pantheism as a moment in itself. God is present in all creatures, yet distinct from them; he is intramundane as well as extramundane; he is self-conscious personality, free creative spirit, is this from all eternity, and does not first become such through the world-development. He does not need the world for his perfection, but out of his goodness creates it. Philosophy must begin with the living Godhead instead of beginning, like Hegel's Logic, with the empty concept of being. For the categories—as Schelling had already objected—express necessary forms or general laws only, to which all reality must conform, but which are never capable of generating reality; the content which appears in them and which obeys them, can only be created by a Deity, and only empirically cognized. This is the standpoint of Christian Hermann Weisse[1] in Leipsic (1801-66), Karl Philipp Fischer[2] in Erlangen (1807-85), Immanuel Hermann Fichte[3] (1797-1879; 1842-65 professor in Tübingen), and the follower of Schleiermacher, Julius Braniss in Breslau (1792-1873). The following hold similar views, influenced, like Weisse and K. Ph. Fischer, by Schelling: Jacob Sengler of Freiburg (1799-1878; *The Idea of God*, 1845 seq.), Leopold Schmid of Giessen (1808-69; cf. p. 516, note), Johannes Huber (died 1879), Moritz Carrière[4] (born 1817), both in Munich, K. Steffensen of Basle (1816-88; *Collected Essays*, 1890), and Karl Heyder in Erlangen (1812-86; *The Doctrine of Ideas*, vol. i. 1874). Chalybaeus at Kiel (died 1862), and Friedrich Harms at Berlin (died 1880; *Metaphysics*, posthumously edited by H. Wiese, 1885), who, like Fortlage and I.H. Fichte, start from the system of the elder Fichte, should also be mentioned as sympathizing with the opinions of those who have been named.

[Footnote 1: Weisse: *System of Aesthetics*, 1830; *The Idea of the Godhead*, 1833; *Philosophical Dogmatics*, 1855. His pupil Rudolf Seydel has published several of his posthumous works; H. Lotze also acknowledges that he owes much to Weisse. Rud. Seydel in Leipsic (born 1835), *Logic*, 1866; *Ethics*, 1874; cf. p. 17.]

[Footnote 2: K. Ph. Fischer: *The Idea of the Godhead*, 1839; *Outlines of the System of Philosophy*, 1848 seq.; *The Untruth of Sensationalism and Materialism*, 1853.]

[Footnote 3: I.H. Fichte: *System of Ethics*, 1850-53, the first volume of which gives a history of moral philosophy since 1750; *Anthropology*, 1856, 3d ed., 1876; *Psychology*, 1864.]

[Footnote 4: Carrière: *Aesthetics*, 1859, 3d ed., 1885; *The Moral Order of the World*, 1877, 2d ed., 1891; *Art in connection with the Development of Culture*, 5 vols., 1863-73.]

The same may be said, further, of Hermann Ulrici[1] of Halle (1806-84), for many years the editor of the *Zeitschrift für Philosophie und philosophische Kritik*, founded in 1837 by the younger Fichte and now edited by the author of this *History*, which, as the organ of the theistic school, opposed, first, the pantheism of the Young Hegelians, and then the revived materialism so loudly proclaimed after the middle of the century. This *Zeitschrift* of Fichte and Ulrici, following the altered circumstances of the time, has experienced a change of aim, so that it now seeks to serve idealistic efforts of every shade; while the *Philosophische Monatshefte* (founded by Bergmann in 1868, edited subsequently by Schaarschmidt, and now) edited by P. Natorp of Marburg, favors neo-Kantianism, and the *Vierteljahrsschrift für wissenschaftliche Philosophie* (begun in 1877, and) edited by R. Avenarius of Zurich, especially cultivates those parts of philosophy which are open to exact treatment.

[Footnote 1: Ulrici: *On Shakespeare's Dramatic Art*, 1839, 3d ed., 1868 [English, 1876]; *Faith and Knowledge*, 1858; *God and Nature*, 1861, 2d ed., 1866; *God and Man*, in two volumes, *Body and Soul*, 1866, 2d ed., 1874, and *Natural Law*, 1872; various treatises on Logic—in which consciousness is based on the distinguishing activity, and the categories conceived as functional modes of this—on Spiritualism, etc.]

The appearance of *materialism* was the consequence of the flagging of the philosophic spirit, on the one hand, and, on the other, of the dissatisfaction of the representatives of natural science with the constructions of the Schelling-Hegelian school. If the German naturalist is especially exposed to the danger of judging all reality from the section of it with which he is familiar, from the world of material substances and mechanical motions, the reason lies in the fact that he does not find it easy, like the Englishman for example, to let the scientific and the philosophico-religious views of the world go on side by side as two entirely heterogeneous modes of looking at things. The metaphysical impulse to generalization and unification spurs him on to break down the boundary between the two spheres, and, since the physical view of things has become part of his flesh and blood, psychical phenomena are for him nothing but brain-vibrations, and the freedom of the will and all religious ideas, nothing but illusions. The materialistic controversy broke out most actively at the convention of naturalists at Göttingen in 1854, when Rudolph Wagner in his address "On the Creation of Man and the Substance of the Soul" declared, in opposition to Karl Vogt, that there is no physiological reason for denying the descent of man from one pair and an immaterial immortal soul. Vogt's answer was entitled "Collier Faith and Science." Among others Schaller (*Body and Soul*, 1855), J.B. Meyer in a treatise with the same title, 1856, and the Jena physicist, Karl Snell,[1] took part in the controversy by way of criticism and mediation. A much finer nature than the famous leaders of materialism—Moleschott (*The Circle of Life*, 1852, in answer to Liebig's *Chemical Letters*), and Louis Büchner, with whose *Force and Matter* (1855, 16th ed., 1888; English translation by Collingwood, 4th ed., 1884) the gymnasiast of to-day still satisfies his freethinking needs—is H. Czolbe (1819-73; *New Exposition of Sensationalism*, 1855; *The Limits and Origin of Human Knowledge*, 1865), who, on ethical grounds, demands the exclusion of everything suprasensible and contentment with the given world of phenomena, but holds that, besides matter and motion, eternal, purposive forms and original sensations in a world-soul are necessary to explain organic and psychical phenomena.

[Footnote 1: Snell (1806-86): *The Materialistic Question*, 1858; *The Creation of Man*, 1863. R. Seydel has edited *Lectures on the Descent of Man*, 1888, from Snell's posthumous writings.]

%2. New Systems: Trendelenburg, Fechner, Lotze, and Hartmann%.

The speculative impulse, especially in the soul of the German people, is ineradicable. It has neither allowed itself to be discouraged by the collapse of the Hegelian edifice, nor to be led astray by the clamor of the apostles of empiricism, nor to be intimidated by the papal proclamation of the infallibility of Thomas Aquinas.[1] Manifold attempts have been made at a new conception of the world, and with varying success. Of the earlier theories[2] only two have been able to gather a circle of adherents—the dualistic theism of Günther (1783-1863), and the organic view of the world of Trendelenburg (1802-72).

[Footnote 2: In 1879 a summons was sent forth from Rome for the revival and dissemination of the Thomistic system as the only true philosophy (cf. R. Eucken, *Die Philosophic des Thomas von Aquino und die Kultur der Neuzeit*, 1886). This movement is supported by the journals, *Jahrbuch für Philosophie und spekulative Theologie*, edited by Professor E. Commer of Münster, 1886 *seq.*, and *Philosophisches Jahrbuch*, edited, at the instance and with the support of the Görres Society, by Professor Const. Gutberlet of Fulda, 1888 *seq.* While the text-books of Hagemann, Stoeckl, Gutberlet, Pesch, Commer, C.M. Schneider, and others also follow Scholastic lines, B. Bolzano (died 1848), M. Deutinger (died 1864) and his pupil Neudecker, Oischinger, Michelis, and W. Rosenkrantz (1821-74; *Science of Knowledge*, 1866-68), who was influenced by Schelling, have taken a freer course.]

[Footnote 2: Trahndorff, gymnasial professor in Berlin (1782-1863), *Aesthetics*, 1827 (cf. E. von Hartmann in the *Philosophische Monatshefte*, vol. xxii. 1886, p. 59 *seq.*, and J. von Billewicz, in the same, vol. xxi. 1885, p. 561 *seq.*); J.F. Reiff in Tübingen: *System of the Determinations of the Will*, 1842; K. Chr. Planck (died 1880): *The Ages of the World*, 1850 *seq.*; *Testament of a German*, edited by Karl Köstlin, 1881; F. Röse (1815-59), *On the Method of the Knowledge of the Absolute*, 1841; *Psychology as Introduction to the Philosophy of Individuality*, 1856. Emanuel Sharer follows Röse. Friedrich Rohmer (died 1856): *Science of God, Science of Man*, in *Friedrich Rohmer's Wissenschaft und Leben*, edited by Bluntschli and Rud. Seele, 6 vols., 1871-92.]

Anton Günther (engaged in authorship from 1827; *Collected Writings*, 1881; *Anti-Savarese*, edited with an appendix by P. Knoodt), who in 1857 was compelled to retract his views, invokes the spirit of Descartes in opposition to the Hegelian pantheism. In agreement with Descartes, Günther starts from self-consciousness (in the ego being and thought are identical), and brings not only the Creator and the created world, but also nature (to which the soul is to be regarded as belonging) and spirit into a relation of exclusive opposition, yet holds that in man nature (body and soul) and spirit are united, and that they interact without prejudice to their qualitative difference. J.H. Pabst (died in 1838 in Vienna), Theodor Weber of Breslau, Knoodt of Bonn (died 1889), V. Knauer of Vienna and others are Güntherians.

Adolf Trendelenburg[1] of Berlin, the acute critic of Hegel and Herbart, in his own thinking goes back to the philosophy of the past, especially to that of Aristotle. Motion and purpose are for him fundamental facts, which are common to both being and thinking, which mediate between the two, and make the agreement of knowledge and reality possible. The ethical is a higher stage of the organic. Space, time, and the categories are forms of thought as well as of being; the logical form must not be separated from the content, nor the concept from intuition. We must not fail to mention that Trendelenburg introduced a peculiar and fruitful method of treating the history of philosophy, viz., the historical investigation of particular concepts, in which Teichmüller of Dorpat (1832-88; *Studies in the History of*

Concepts, 1874; *New Studies in the History of Concepts*, 1876-79; *The Immortality of the Soul*, 2d ed., 1879; *The Nature of Love*, 1880; *Literary Quarrels in the Fourth Century before Christ*, 1881 and 1884), and Eucken of Jena (cf. pp. 17 and 623) have followed his example. Kym in Zurich (born 1822; *Metaphysical Investigations*, 1875; *The Problem of Evil*, 1878) is a pupil of Trendelenburg.

[Footnote 1: Trendelenburg: *Logical Investigations*, 1840, 3d ed., 1870; *Historical Contributions to Philosophy*, 3 vols., 1846, 1855, 1867; *Natural Law on the Basis of Ethics*, 1860, 2d ed., 1868. On Trendelenburg cf. Eucken in the *Philosophische Monatshefte*, 1884.]

Of more recent systematic attempts the following appear worthy of mention: Von Kirchmann (1802-84; from 1868 editor of the *Philosophische Bibliothek*), *The Philosophy of Knowledge*, 1865; *Aesthetics*, 1868; *On the Principles of Realism*, 1875; *Catechism of Philosophy* 2d ed., 1881; E. Dühring (born 1833), *Natural Dialectic*, 1865; *The Value of Life*, 1865, 3d ed, 1881; *Critical History of the Principles of Mechanics*, 1873, 2d ed., 1877; *Course of Philosophy*, 1875 (cf. on Dühring, Helene Druskowitz, 1889); J. Baumann of Göttingen (born 1837), *Philosophy as Orientation concerning the World*, 1872; *Handbook of Ethics*, 1879; *Elements of Philosophy*, 1891; L. Noiré, *The Monistic Idea*, 1875, and many other works; Frohschammer of Munich (born 1821), *The Phantasy as the Fundamental Principle of the World-process*, 1877; *On the Genesis of Humanity, and its Spiritual Development in Religion, Morality and Language*, 1883; *On the Organization and Culture of Human Society*, 1885.

In the first rank of the thinkers who have made their appearance since Hegel and Herbart stand Fechner and Lotze, both masters in the use of exact methods, yet at the same time with their whole souls devoted to the highest questions, and superior to their contemporaries in breadth of view as in the importance and range of their leading ideas—Fechner a dreamer and sober investigator by turns, Lotze with gentle hand reconciling the antitheses in life and science.

Gustav Theodor Fechner[1] (1801-87; professor at Leipsic) opposes the abstract separation of God and the world, which has found a place in natural inquiry and in theology alike, and brings the two into the same relation of correspondence and reciprocal reference as the soul and the body. The spirit gives cohesion to the manifold of material parts, and needs them as a basis and material for its unifying activity. As our ego connects the manifold of our activities and states in the unity of consciousness, so the divine spirit is the supreme unity of consciousness for all being and becoming. In the spirit of God everything is as in ours, only expanded and enhanced. Our sensations and feelings, our thoughts and resolutions are His also, only that He, whose body all nature is, and to whom not only that which takes place in spirits is open, but also that which goes on between them, perceives more, feels deeper, thinks higher, and wills better things than we. According to the analogy of the human organism, both the heavenly bodies and plants are to be conceived as beings endowed with souls, although they lack nerves, a brain, and voluntary motion. How could the earth bring forth living beings, if it were itself dead? Shall not the flower itself rejoice in the color and fragrance which it produces, and with which it refreshes us? Though its psychical life may not exceed that of an infant, its sensations, at all events, since they do not form the basis of a higher activity, are superior in force and richness to those of the animal. Thus the human soul stands intermediate in the scale of psychical life: beneath and about us are the souls of plants and animals, above us the spirits of the earth and stars, which, sharing in and encompassing the deeds and destinies of their inhabitants, are in their turn embraced by the consciousness of the universal spirit. The omnipresence of the divine spirit affords at the same time the means of escaping from the desolate "night view" of modern science, which looks upon the world outside the perceiving individual as dark and silent. No, light and sound are not merely subjective phenomena within us, but extend around us with objective reality—as sensations of the divine spirit, to which everything that vibrates resounds and shines.

[Footnote 1: *Nanna, or on the Psychical Life of Plants*, 1848; *Zend-Avesta, or on the Things of Heaven and the World Beyond*, 1851; *Physical and Philosophical Atomism*, 1855; *The Three Motives and Grounds of Belief*, 1863; *The Day View*, 1879; *Elements of Aesthetics*, 1876; *Elements of Psycho-physics*, 1860; *In the Cause of Psycho-physics*, 1877; *Review of the Chief Points in Psycho-physics*, 1882; *Book of the Life after Death*, 1836, 3d ed., 1887; *On the Highest Good*, 1846; *Four Paradoxes*, 1846; *On the Question of the Soul*, 1861; *Minor Works by Dr. Mises* (Fechner's pseudonym), 1875. On Fechner cf. J. E. Kuntze, Leipsic, 1892.]

The door of the world beyond also opens to the key of analogy. Similar laws unite the here with the hereafter. As intuition prepares the way for memory, and lives on in it, so the life of earth merges in the future life, and continues active in it, elevated to a higher plane. Fechner treats the problem of evil in a way peculiar to himself. We must not consider the fact of evil apart from the effort to remove it. It is the spur to all activity—without evil, no labor and no progress.

Fechner's "psycho-physics," a science which was founded by him in continuation of the investigations of Bernoulli, Euler, and especially of E.H. Weber, wears an entirely different aspect from that of his metaphysics (the "day view," moreover does not claim to be knowledge, but belief—though a belief which is historically, practically, and theoretically well-grounded). This aims to be an exact science of the relations between body and mind, and to reach indirectly what Herbart failed to reach by direct methods, that is, a measurement of psychical magnitudes, using in this attempt the least observable differences in sensations as the unit of measure. Weber's law of the dependence of the intensity of the sensation on the strength of the stimulus—the increase in the intensity of the sensation remains the same when the relative increase of the stimulus (or the relation of the stimuli) remains constant;[1] so that, *e.g.*, in the case of light, an increase from a stimulus of intensity 1 to one of intensity 100, gives just the same increase in the intensity of the sensation as an increase from a stimulus of intensity 2 (or 3) to a stimulus of 200 (or 300)—is much more generally valid than its discoverer supposed; it holds good for all the senses. In the case of the pressure sense of the skin, with an original weight of 15 grams (laid upon the hand when at rest and supported), in order to produce a sensation perceptibly greater we must add not 1 gram, but 5, and with an original weight of 30 grams, not 5, but 10. Equal additions to the weights are not enough to produce a sensation of pressure whose intensity shall render it capable of being distinguished with certainty, but the greater the original weights the larger the increments must be; while the intensities of the sensations form an arithmetical, those of the stimuli form a geometrical, series; the change in sensation is proportional to the relative change of the stimulus. Sensations of tone show the same proportion (3:4) as those of pressure; the sensibility of the muscle sense is finer (when weights are raised the proportion is 15:16), as also that of vision (the relative brightness of two lights whose difference of intensity is just perceptible is 100:101). In addition to the investigations on the threshold of difference there are others on the threshold of stimulation (the point at which a sensation becomes just perceptible), on attention, on methods of measurement, on errors, etc. Moreover, Fechner does not fail to connect his psycho-physics, the presuppositions and results of which have recently been questioned in several quarters,[2] with his metaphysical conclusions. Both are pervaded by the fundamental view that body and spirit belong together (consequently that everything is endowed with a soul, and that nothing is without a material basis), nay, that they are the same essence, only seen from different sides. Body is the (manifold) phenomenon for others, while spirit is the (unitary) self-phenomenon, in which, however, the inner aspect is the truer one. That which appears to us as the external world of matter, is nothing but a universal consciousness which overlaps and influences our individual consciousness. This is Spinozism idealistically interpreted. In aesthetics Fechner shows himself an extreme representative of the principle of association.

[Footnote 1: Fechner teaches: The sensation increases and diminishes in proportion to the logarithm of the stimulus and of the psycho-physical nervous activity, the latter being directly proportional to the external stimulus. Others, on the contrary, find a direct dependence between nervous activity and sensation, and a logarithmic proportion between the external stimulus and the nervous activity.]

[Footnote 2: So by Helmholtz; Hering *(Fechners psychophysisches Gesetz*, 1875); P. Langer *(Grundlagen der Psychophysik*, 1876); G.E. Müller in Göttingen *(Zur Grundlegung der Psychophysik*, 1878); F.A. Müller *(Das Axiom der Psychophysik*, 1882); A. Elsas *(Ueber die Psychophysik*, 1886); O. Liebmann *(Aphorismen zur Psychologie, Zeitschrift für Philosophie*, vol. ci.—Wundt has published a number of papers from his psycho-physical laboratory in his *Philosophische Studien*, 1881 seq. Cf. also Hugo Münsterberg, *Neue Grundlegung der Psychophysik* in *Heft* iii. of his *Beiträge zur experimentellen Psychologie*, 1889 seq). [Further, Delboeuf, in French, and a growing literature in English as A. Seth, *Encyclopedia Britannica*, vol. xxiv. 469-471; Ladd, *Elements of Physiological Psychology*, part ii. chap, v.; James, *Principles of Psychology*, vol. i. p. 533 seq.; and numerous articles as Ward, *Mind*, vol. i.; Jastrow, *American Journal of Psychology*, vols. i. and iii.—TR.]]

The most important of the thinkers mentioned in the title of this section is Rudolph Hermann Lotze (1817-81: born at Bautzen; a student of medicine, and of philosophy under Weisse, in Leipsic; 1844-81 professor in Göttingen; died in Berlin). Like Fechner, gifted rather with a talent for the fine and the suggestive than for the large and the rigorous, with a greater reserve than the former before the mystical and peculiar, as acute, cautious, and thorough as he was full of taste and loftiness of spirit, Lotze has proved that the classic philosophers did not die out with Hegel and Herbart. His *Microcosmus* (3 vols., 1856-64, 4th ed., 1884 seq; English translation by Hamilton and Jones, 3d ed., 1888), which is more than an anthropology, as it is modestly entitled, and *History of Aesthetics in Germany*, 1868, which also gives more than the title betrays, enjoy a deserved popularity. These works were preceded by the *Medical Psychology*, 1852, and a polemic treatise against I.H. Fichte, 1857, as well as by a *Pathology* and a *Physiology*, and followed by the *System of Philosophy*, which remained incomplete (part i. *Logic*, 1874, 2d ed., 1881, English translation edited by Bosanquet, 2d ed., 1888; part ii. *Metaphysics*, 1879, English translation edited by Bosanquet, 2d ed., 1887). Lotze's *Minor Treatises* have been published by Peipers in three volumes (1885-91); and Rehnisch has edited eight sets of dictata from his lectures, 1871-84.[1] Since these "Outlines," all of which we now have in new editions, make a convenient introduction to the Lotzean system, and are, or should be, in the possession of all, a brief survey may here suffice.

[Footnote 1: *Outlines of Psychology, Practical Philosophy, Philosophy of Religion, Philosophy of Nature, Logic and the Encyclopedia of Philosophy, Metaphysics, Aesthetics*, and the *History of Philosophy since Kant*, all of which may be emphatically commended to students, especially the one first mentioned, and, in spite of its subjective position, the last. [English translations of these *Outlines* except the fourth and the last, by Ladd, 1884 seq.] On Lotze cf. the obituaries by J. Baumann (*Philosophische Monatshefte*, vol. xvii.), H. Sommer (*Im Neuen Reich*), A. Krohn (*Zeitschrift für Philosophie*, vol. lxxxi. pp. 56-93), R. Falckenberg (Augsburg *Allgemeine Zeitung*, 1881, No. 233), and Rehnisch (*National Zeitung* and the *Revue Philosophique*, vol. xii.). The last of these was reprinted in the appendix to the *Grundzüge der Aesthetik*, 1884, which contains, further, a chronological table of Lotze's works, essays, and critiques, as well as of his lectures. Hugo Sommer has zealously devoted himself to the popularization of the Lotzean system. Cf., further, Fritz Koegel, *Lotzes Aesthetik*, Göttingen, 1886, and the article by Koppelmann referred to above, p. 330.]

The subject of metaphysics is reality. Things which are, events which happen, relations which exist, representative contents and truths which are valid, are real. Events happening and relations existing presuppose existing things as the subjects in and between which they happen and exist. The being of things is neither their being perceived (for when we say that a thing is we mean that it continues to be, even when we do not perceive it), nor a pure, unrelated position, its position in general, but *to be is to stand in relations*. Further, the *what* or essence of the things which enter into these relations cannot be conceived as passive quality, but only abstractly, as a rule or a law which determines the connection and succession of a series of qualities. The nature of water, for example, is the unintuitable somewhat which contains the ground of the change of ice, first into the liquid condition, and then into steam, when the temperature increases, and conversely, of the possibility of changing steam back into water and ice under opposite conditions. And when we speak of an unchangeable identity of the thing with itself, as a result of which it remains the same essence amid the change of its phenomena, we mean only the consistency with which it keeps within the closed series of forms a_1, a_2, a_3, without ever going over into the series b_1, b_2. The relations, however, in which things stand, cannot pass to and fro between things like threads or little spirits, but are states in things themselves, and the change of the former always implies a change in these inner states. To stand in relations means to *exchange actions*. In order to experience such effects from others and to exercise them upon others, things must neither be wholly incomparable (as red, hard, sweet) and mutually indifferent, nor yet absolutely independent; if the independence of individual beings were complete the process of action would be entirely inconceivable. The difficulty in the concept of causality—how does being a come to produce in itself a different state a because another being b enters into the state [Greek: b]?—is removed only when we look on the things as modes, states, parts of a single comprehensive being, of an infinite, unconditioned substance, in so far as there is then only an action of the absolute on itself. Nevertheless the assumption that, in virtue of the unity and consistency of the absolute or of its impulse to self-preservation, state [Greek: b] in being b follows state [Greek: a] in being a as an accommodation or compensation follows a disturbance, is not a full explanation of the process of action, does not remove the difficulty as to how one state can give rise to another. Metaphysics is, in general, unable to show how reality is made, but only to remove certain contradictions which stand in the way of the conceivability of these notions. The so far empty concept of an absolute looks to the philosophy of religion for its content; the conception of the Godhead as infinite personality (it is a person in a far higher sense than we) is first produced when we add to the ontological postulate of a comprehensive substance the ethical postulate of a supreme good or a universal world-Idea.

By "thing" we understand the permanent unit-subject of changing states. But the fact of consciousness furnishes the only guaranty that the different states a, [Greek: b], y, are in reality states of one being, and not so many different things alternating with one another. Only a conscious being, which itself effects the distinction between itself and the states occurring in it, and in memory and recollection feels and knows itself as their identical subject, is actually a subject which has states. Hence, if things are to be real, we must attribute to them a nature in essence related to that of our soul. Reality is existence for self. All beings are spiritual, and only spiritual beings possess true reality. Thus Lotze combines the monadology of Leibnitz with the pantheism of Spinoza, just as he understands how to reconcile the mechanical view of natural science (which is valid also for the explanation of organic life) with the teleology and the ethical idealism of Fichte. The sole mission of the world of forms is to aid in the realization of the ideal purposes of the absolute, of the world of values.

The ideality of space, which Kant had based on insufficient grounds, is maintained by Lotze also, only that he makes things stand in "intellectual" relations, which the knowing subject translates into spatial language. The same character of subjectivity belongs not only to our sensations, but also to our ideas concerning the connection of things. Representations are results, not copies, of the external stimuli; cognition comes under the general concept of the interaction of real elements, and depends, like every effect, as much upon the nature of the being that experiences the effect as upon the nature of the one which exerts it, or rather, more upon the former than upon the latter. If, nevertheless, it claims objective reality, truth must not be interpreted as the correspondence of thought and its object (the cognitive image can never be like the thing itself), nor the mission of cognition, made to consist in copying a world already finished and closed apart from the realm of spirits, to which mental representation is added as something accessory. Light and sound are not therefore illusions because they are not true copies of the waves of ether and of air from which they spring, but they are the end which nature has sought to attain through these motions, an end, however, which it cannot attain alone, but only by acting upon spiritual subjects; the beauty and splendor of colors and tones are that which of right ought to be in the world; without the new world of representations awakened in spirits by the action of external stimuli, the world would lack its essential culmination. The purpose of things is to be known, experienced, and enjoyed by spirits. The truth of cognition consists in the fact that it opens up the meaning and destination of the world. That which ought to be is the ground of that which is; that which is exists in order to the realization of values in it; the good is the only real. It is true that we are not permitted to penetrate farther than to the general conviction that the Idea of the good is the ground and end of the world; the question, how the world has arisen from this supreme Idea as from the absolute and why just this world with its determinate forms and laws has arisen, is unanswerable. We understand the meaning of the play, but we do not see the machinery by which it is produced at work behind the stage. In ethics Lotze emphasizes with Fechner the inseparability of the good and pleasure: it is impossible to state in what the worth or goodness of a good is to consist, if it be conceived out of all relation to a spirit capable of finding enjoyment in it.

If Lotze's philosophy harmoniously combines Herbartian and Fichteo-Hegelian elements, Eduard von Hartmann (born 1842; until 1864 a soldier, now a man of letters in Berlin) aims at a synthesis of Schopenhauer and Hegel; with the pessimism of the former he unites the evolutionism of the latter, and while the one conceives the nature of the world-ground as irrational will, and the other as the logical Idea, he follows the example of Schelling in his later days by making will and representation equally legitimate attributes of his absolute, the Unconscious. His principal theoretical work, *The Philosophy of the Unconscious*, 1869 (10th ed., 1891; English translation by Coupland, 1884), was followed in 1879 by his chief ethical one, *The Moral Consciousness* (2d ed., 1886, in the *Selected Works*); the two works on the philosophy of religion, *The Religious Consciousness of Humanity in the Stages of its Development*, 1881, and *The Religion of Spirit*, 1882, together form the third chief work (*The Self-Disintegration of Christianity and the Religion of the Future*, 1874, and *The Crisis of Christianity in Modern Theology*, 1880, are to be regarded as forerunners of this); the fourth is the *Aesthetics* (part i. *German Aesthetics since Kant*, 1886; part ii. *Philosophy of the Beautiful*, 1887). The *Collected Studies and Essays*, 1876, were preceded by two treatises on the philosophy of nature, *Truth and Error in Darwinism*, 1875, and *The Unconscious from the Standpoint of Physiology and the Theory of Descent*, published anonymously in 1872, in the latter of which, disguised as a Darwinian, he criticises his own philosophy. Of his more recent publications we may mention the *Philosophical Questions of the Day*, 1885; *Modern Problems*, 1886; and the controversial treatise *Lotzes Philosophy*, 1888.[1]

[Footnote 1: On Hartmann cf. Volkelt in *Nord und Süd*, July, 1881; the same, *Das Unbewusste und der Pessimismus*, 1873; Vaihinger, *Hartmann, Dühring und Lange*, 1876; R. Koeber, *Das philosophische System Ed. v, Hartmann*, 1884; O. Pfleiderer, critique of the *Phänomenologie des sittlichen Bewusstseins (Im neuen Reich)*, 1879; L. von Golther, *Der moderne Pessimismus*, 1878; J. Huber, *Der Pessimismus*, 1876; Weygoldt, *Kritik des philosophischen Pessimismus der neuesten Zeit*, 1875; M. Venetianer, *Der Allgeist*, 1874; A Taubert (Hartmann's first wife), *Der Pessimismus und seine Gegner*, 1873; O. Plümacher, *Der Kampf ums Unbewusste* (with a chronological table of Hartmann literature appended), 1881; the same, *Der Pessimismus in Vergangenheit und Gegenwart*, 1884; Krohn, *Streifzüge* (see above); Seydel (see above). During the year 1882 four publications appeared under the title *Der Pessimismus und die Sittenlehre*, by Bacmeister, Christ, Rehmke, and H. Sommer (2d ed., 1883). [English translation of *Truth and Error in Darwinism* in the *Journal of Speculative Philosophy*, vols. xi.-xiii., and of *The Religion of the Future*, by Dare, 1886; cf. also Sully's *Pessimism*, chap. v.—TR.]]

In polemical relation, on the one hand, to the naïve realism of life, and, on the other, to the subjective idealism of Kant, or rather of the neo-Kantians, the logical conclusion of which would be absolute illusionism, Hartmann founds his "transcendental realism," which mediates between these two points of view (the existence and true nature of the world outside our representations is knowable, if only indirectly; the forms of knowledge, in spite of their subjective origin, have a more than subjective, a transcendental, significance) by pointing out that sense-impressions, which are accompanied by the feeling of compulsion and are different from one another, cannot be explained from the ego, but only by the action of things in themselves external to us, *i.e.*, independent of consciousness, and themselves distinct from one another. The causality of things in themselves is the bridge which enables us to cross the gulf between the immanent world of representations and the transcendent world of being. The causality of things in themselves proves their reality, their difference at different times, their changeability and their temporal character; change, however, demands something permanent, existence, an existing, unchangeable, supra-temporal, and non-spatial substance (whether a special substance for each thing in itself or a common one for all, is left for the present undetermined). My action upon the thing in itself assures me of its causal conditionality or necessity; the various affections of the same sense, that there are many things in themselves; the peculiar form of change shown by some bodies, that these, like my body, are united with a soul. Thus it is evident that, besides the concept of cause, a series of other categories must be applied to the thing in itself, hence applied transcendentally.

The "speculative results" obtained by Hartmann on an "inductive" basis are as follows: The *per se (Ansich)* of the empirical world is the Unconscious. The two attributes of this absolute are the active, groundless, alogical, infinite will, and the passive, finite representation (Idea); the former is the ground of the *that* of the world, the latter the ground of its purposive *what* and *how*. Without the will the representation, which in itself is without energy, could not become real, and without the representation (of an end) the will, which in itself is without reason, could not become a definite willing (relative or immanent dualism of the attributes, a necessary moment in absolute monism). The empirical preponderance of pain over pleasure, which can be shown by calculation,[1] proves that the world is evil, that its non-existence were better than its existence; the purposiveness everywhere perceptible in nature and the progress of history toward a final goal (it is true, a negative one) proves, nevertheless, that it is the best world that was possible (reconciliation of eudemonistic pessimism with evolutionistic optimism). The creation of the world begins when the blind will to live groundlessly and fortuitously passes over from essence to phenomenon, from potency to act, from supra-existence to existence, and, in irrational striving after existence, draws to itself the only content which is capable of realization, the logical Idea. This latter seeks to make good the error committed by the will by bringing consciousness into the field as a combatant against the insatiable, ever yearning, never satisfied will, which one day will force the will back into latency, into the (antemundane) blessed state of not-willing. The goal of the world-development is deliverance from the misery of existence, the peace of non-existence, the return from the will and representation, become spatial and temporal, to the original, harmonious equilibrium of the two functions, which has been disturbed by the origin of the world or to the antemundane identity of the absolute. The task of the logical element is to teach consciousness more and more to penetrate the illusion of the will—in its three stages of childlike (Greek) expectation of happiness to be attained here, youthful (Christian) expectation of happiness to be attained hereafter, and adult expectation of happiness to be attained in the future of the world-development—and, finally, to teach it to know, in senile longing after rest, that only the doing away with this miserable willing, and, consequently, with earthly existence (through the resolve of the majority of mankind) can give the sole attainable blessedness, freedom from pain. The world-process is the incarnation, the suffering, and the redemption of the absolute; the moral task of man is not personal renunciation and cowardly retirement, but to make the purposes of the Unconscious his own, with complete resignation to life and its sufferings to labor energetically in the world-process, and, by the vigorous promotion of consciousness, to hasten the fulfillment of the redemptive purpose; the condition of morality is insight into the fruitlessness of all striving after pleasure and into the essential unity of all individual beings with one another and with the universal spirit, which exists in the individuals, but at the same time subsists above them. "To know one's self as of divine nature, this does away with all divergence between selfwill and universal will, with all estrangement between man and God, with all undivine, that is, merely natural, conduct."

[Footnote 1: Cf. Volkelt, *Ueber die Lust als höchsten Werthmassstab* (in the *Zeitschrift für Philosophie*, vol. lxxxviii.), 1886, and O. Pfleiderer, *Philosophy of Religion*, vol. ii. p. 249 *seq*.]

Religion, which, in common with philosophy, has for its basis the metaphysical need for, or the mystical feeling of, the unity of the human individual and the world-ground, needs transformation, since in its traditional forms it is opposed to modern culture, and the merging of religion (as a need of the heart) in metaphysics is impossible. The religion of the future, for which the way has already been prepared by the speculative Protestantism of the present, is *concrete monism* (the divine unity is transcendent as well as immanent in the plurality of the beings of earth, every moral man a God-man), which includes in itself the abstract monism (pantheism) of the Indian religions and the Judeo-Christian (mono-) theism as subordinate moments. (The original henotheism and its decline into polytheism, demonism, and fetichism was followed by—Egyptian and Persian, as well as Greek, Roman, and German—naturalism, and then by supernaturalism in its monistic and its theistic form. The chief defect of the Christian religion is the transcendental-eudemonistic heteronomy of its ethics.) The *Religion of Spirit* divides into three parts. The psychology of religion considers the religious function in its subjective aspect, faith as a combined act of representation, feeling, and will, in which one of these three elements may predominate—though feeling forms the inmost kernel of the theoretical and practical activities as well—and, as the objective correlate of faith, grace (revealing, redeeming, and sanctifying), which elevates man above peripheral and phenomenal dependence on the world, and frees him from it, through his becoming conscious of his central and metaphysical dependence upon God. The metaphysics of religion (in theological, anthropological, and cosmological sections) proves by induction from the facts of religion the existence, omnipotence, spirituality, omniscience, righteousness, and holiness of the All-one, which coincides with the moral order of the world. Further, it proves the need and the capacity of man for redemption from guilt and evil—here three spheres of the individual will are distinguished, one beneath God, one contrary to God, and one conformable to God, or a natural, an evil, and a moral sphere—and, preserving alike the absoluteness of God and the reality of the world, shows that it is not so much man as God himself, who, as the bearer of all the suffering of the world, is the subject of redemption. The ethics of religion discusses the subjective and objective processes of redemption, namely, repentance and amendment on the part of the individual and the ecclesiastical *cultus* of the future, which is to despise symbols and art.

It is to Hartmann's credit, though the fact has not been sufficiently appreciated by professional thinkers, that in a time averse to speculation he has devoted his energies to the highest problems of metaphysics, and in their elaboration has approached his task with scientific earnestness and a comprehensive and thorough consideration of previous results. Thus the critique of ethical standpoints in the historical part of the *Phenomenology of the Moral Consciousness*, especially, contains much that is worthy of consideration; and his fundamental metaphysical idea, that the absolute is to be conceived as the unity of will and reason, also deserves in general a more lively assent than has been accorded to it, while his rejection of an infinite consciousness has justly met with contradiction. It has been impossible here to go into his discussions in the philosophy of nature—they cannot be described in brief—on matter (atomic forces), on the mechanical and teleological views of life and its development, on instinct, on sexual love, etc., which he very skillfully uses in support of his metaphysical principle.

%3. From the Revival of the Kantian Philosophy to the Present Time.%

%(a) Neo-Kantianism, Positivism, and Kindred Phenomena.%—The Kantian philosophy has created two epochs: one at the time of its appearance, and a second two generations after the death of its author. The new Kantian movement, which is one of the most prominent characteristics of the philosophy of the present time, took its beginning a quarter of a century ago. It is true that even before 1865 individual thinkers like Ernst Reinhold of Jena (died 1855), the admirer of Fries, J.B. Meyer of Bonn, K.A. von Reichlin-Meldegg, and others had sought a point of departure for their views in Kant; that K. Fischer's work on Kant (1860) had given a lively impulse to the renewed study of the critical philosophy; nay, that the cry "Back to Kant" had been expressly raised by Fortlage (as early as 1832 in his treatise *The Gaps in the Hegelian System*), and by Zeller (p. 589). But the movement first became general after F.A. Lange in his *History of Materialism* had energetically advocated the Kantian doctrine according to his special conception of it, after Helmholtz[1] (born 1821) had called attention to the agreement of the results of physiology with those of the Critique of Reason, and at the same time Liebmann's youthful work, *Kant and the Epigones*, in which every chapter ended with the inexorable refrain, "therefore we must go back to Kant," had given the strongest expression to the longing of the time.

[Footnote 1: Helmholtz: *On Human Vision*, 1855; *Physiological Optics*, 1867; *Sensations of Tone*, 1863, 4th ed., 1877 [English translation by Ellis, 2d ed., 1885].]

Otto Liebmann (cf. also the chapter on "The Metamorphoses of the A Priori" in his *Analysis of Reality*) sees the fundamental truth of criticism in the irrefutable proof that, space, time, and the categories are functions of the intellect, and that subject and object are necessary correlates, inseparable factors of the empirical world, and finds Kant's fundamental error, which the Epigones have not corrected, but made still worse, in the non-concept of the thing in itself, which must be expelled from the Kantian philosophy as a remnant of dogmatism, as a drop of alien blood, and as an illegitimate invader which has debased it.

According to Friedrich Albert Lange[1] (1828-75; during the last years of his life professor at Marburg), materialism, which is unfruitful and untenable as a principle, a system, and a view of the world, but useful and indispensable as a method and a maxim of investigation, must be supplemented by formal idealism, which, rejecting all science from mere reason limits knowledge to the sensuous, to that which can be experienced, yet at the same time conceives the formal element in the sense world as the product of the organization of man, and hence makes objects conform to our representations. Above the sensuous world of experience and of mechanical becoming, however, the speculative impulse to construction, rounding off the fragmentary truth of the sciences into a unified picture of the whole truth, rears the ideal world of that which ought to be. Notwithstanding their indefeasible certitude, the Ideas possess no scientific truth, though they have a moral value which makes them more than mere fabrics of the brain: man is framed not merely for the knowledge of truth, but also for the realization of values. But since the significance of the Ideas is only practical, and since determinations of value are not grounds of explanation, science and metaphysics or "concept poetry" (*Begriffsdichtung*) must be kept strictly separate.

[Footnote 1: F.A. Lange: *Logical Studies*, 1877. Cf. M. Heinze in the *Vierteljahrsschrift für wissenschaftliche Philosophic*, 1877, and Vaihinger in the work cited above, p. 610 note.]

Friedrich Paulsen of Berlin (born in 1846; cf. pp. 330, 332, note) sees in the Kantian philosophy the foundation for the philosophy of the future. A profounder Wolff (the self-dominion of the reason), a Prussian Hume (the categories of the understanding are not world-categories; rejection of anthropomorphic metaphysics), and a German Rousseau (the primacy of the will, consideration of the demands of the heart; the good will alone, not deeds nor culture, constitutes the worth of man; freedom, the rights of man) in one person, Kant has withdrawn from scientific discussion the question concerning the dependence of reality on values or the good, which is theoretically insoluble but practically to be answered in the affirmative, and given it over to faith. Kant is in so far a positivist that he limits the mission of knowledge to the reduction of the temporo-spatial relations of phenomena to rules, and declares the teleological power of values to be undemonstrable. But science is able to prove this much, that the belief in a suprasensible world, in the indestructibility of that which alone has worth, and in the freedom of the intelligible character, which the will demands, is not scientifically impossible. Since, according to formal rationalism, the whole order of nature is a creation of the understanding, and hence atomism and mechanism are only forms of representation, valid, no doubt, for our peripheral point of view, but not absolutely valid, since, further, the empirical view of the world apart from the Idea of the divine unity of the world (which, it is true, is incapable of theoretical realization) would lack completion, the immediate conviction of the heart in regard to the power of the good is in no danger of attack from the side of science, although this can do no further service for faith than to remove the obstacles which oppose it. The will, not the intellect, determines the view of the world; but this is only a belief, and in the world of representation, the intelligible world, with which the will brings us into relation, can come before us only in the form of symbols.—While Albrecht Krause (*The Laws of the Human Heart, a Formal Logic of Pure Feeling*, 1876) and A. Classen (*Physiology of the Sense of Sight*, 1877) are strict followers of Kant, J. Volkelt (*Analysis of the Fundamental Principles of Kant's Theory of Knowledge*, 1879) has traced the often deplored inconsistencies and contradictions in Kant down to their roots, and has shown that in Kant's thinking, which has hitherto been conceived as too simple and transparent, but which, in fact, is extremely complicated and struggling in the dark, a number of entirely heterogeneous principles of thought (skeptical, subjectivistic, metaphysico-work, rationalistic, *a priori*, and practical motives) are at which, conflicting with and crippling one another, make the attainment of harmonious results impossible. Benno Erdmann (p. 330) and Hans Vaihinger (pp. 323 note, 331) have given Kant's principal works careful philological interpretation.

Among the various differences of opinion which exist within the neo-Kantian ranks, the most important relates to the question, whether the individual ego or a transcendental consciousness is to be looked upon as the executor of the *a priori* functions. In agreement with Schopenhauer and with Lotze, who makes the subjectivity of space, time, and the pure concepts parallel with that of the sense qualities, Lange teaches that the human individual is so organized that he must apprehend that which is sensuously given under these forms. Others, on the contrary, urge that the individual soul with its organization is itself a phenomenon, and consequently cannot be the bearer of that which precedes phenomena—space, time, and the categories as "conditions" of experience are functions of a pure consciousness to be presupposed. The antithesis of subject and object, the soul and the world, first arises in the sphere of phenomena. The empirical subject, like the world of objects, is itself a product of the *a priori* forms, hence not that which produces them. To the transcendental group belong Hermann Cohen[1] in Marburg, A. Stadler[2], Natorp, Lasswitz (p.17), E. König (p. 17), Koppelmann (p. 330), Staudinger (p. 331). Fritz Schultze of Dresden is also to be counted among the neo-Kantians (*Philosophy of Natural Science*, 1882; *Kant and Darwin*, 1875; *The Fundamental Thoughts of Materialism*, 1881; *The Fundamental Thoughts of Spiritualism*, 1883; *Comparative Psychology*, i. 1, 1892).

[Footnote 1: Cohen: *Kant's Theory of Experience*, 1871, 2d ed., 1886; *Kant's Foundation of Ethics*, 1877; *Kant's Foundation of Aesthetics*, 1889.]

[Footnote 2: Stadler: *Kant's Teleology*, 1874; *The Principles of the Pure Theory of Knowledge in the Kantian Philosophy*, 1876; *Kant's Theory of Matter*, 1883.]

The German positivists[1]:—E. Laas of Strasburg (1837-85), A. Riehl of Freiburg in Baden (born 1844), and R. Avenarius of Zurich (born 1843)—develop their sensationalistic theory of knowledge in critical connection with Kant. Ernst Laas defines positivism (founded by Protagoras, advocated in modern times by Hume and J.S. Mill, and hostile to Platonic idealism) as that philosophy which recognizes no other foundations than positive facts (*i.e.*, perceptions), and requires every opinion to exhibit the experiences on which it rests. Its basis is constituted by three articles of belief: (1) The correlative facts, subject and object, exist and arise only in connection (objects are directly known only as the contents of a consciousness, *cui objecta sunt*, subjects only as centers of relation, as the scene or foundation of a representative content, *cui subjecta sunt*: outside my thoughts body does not exist as body, nor I myself as soul). (2) The variability of the objects of perception. (3) Sensationalism—all specific differences in consciousness must be conceived as differences in degree, all higher mental processes and states, including thought, as the perceptions and experiences, transformed according to law, of beings which feel, have wants, possess memory, and are capable of spontaneous motion. The subject coincides with its feeling of pleasure and pain, from which sensation is distinguished by its objective content. The illusions of metaphysics are scientifically untenable and practically unnecessary. Various yearnings, wants, presentiments, hopes, and fancies, it is true, lead beyond the sphere of that which can be checked by sense and experience, but for none of their positions can any sufficient proof be adduced. As physics has discarded transcendent causes and learned how to get along with immanent causes, so ethics also must endeavor to establish the worth of moral good without excursions into the suprasensible. The ethical obligations arise naturally from human relations, from earthly needs. The third volume of Laas's work differs from the earlier ones by conceding the rank of facts to the principles of logic as well as to perception. Aloys Riehl opposes the theory of knowledge (which starts from the fundamental fact of sensation) as scientific philosophy to metaphysics as unscientific, and banishes the doctrine of the practical ideals from the realm of science into the region of religion and art. Richard Avenarius defends the principle of "pure experience." Sensation, which is all that is left as objectively given after the removal of the subjective additions, constitutes the content, and motion the form of being.

[Footnote 1: Laas: *Idealism and Positivism*, 1879-84. Riehl: *Philosophical Criticism*, 1876-87; Address *On Scientific and Unscientific Philosophy*, 1883. Avenarius (p. 598): *Philosophy as Thought concerning the World according to the Principle of Least Work*, 1876; *Critique of Pure Experience*, vol. i. 1888, vol. ii. 1890; *Man's Concept of the World*, 1891. C. Göring (died 1879; *System of Critical Philosophy*, 1875) may also be placed here.]

With the neo-Kantians and the positivists there is associated, thirdly, a coherent group of noëtical thinkers, who, rejecting extramental elements of every kind, look on all conceivable being as merely a conscious content. This monism of consciousness is advocated by W. Schuppe of Greifswald (born 1836; *Noëtical Logic*, 1878), J. Rehmke, also of Greifswald (*The World as Percept and Concept*, 1880; "The Question of the Soul" in vol. ii. of the *Zeitschrift für Psychologie*, 1891), A. von Leclair (*Contributions to a Monistic Theory of Knowledge*, 1882), and R. von Schubert-Soldern (*Foundations of a Theory of Knowledge*, 1884; *On the Transcendence of Object and Subject*, 1882; *Foundations for an Ethics*, 1887). J. Bergmann[1] in Marburg (born 1840) occupies a kindred position.

[Footnote 1: Bergmann: *Outlines of a Theory of Consciousness*, 1870; *Pure Logic*, 1879; *Being and Knowing*, 1880; *The Fundamental Problems of Logic*, 1882; *On the Right*, 1883; *Lectures on Metaphysics*, 1886; *On the Beautiful*, 1887; *History of Philosophy*, vol. i., *Pre-Kantian Philosophy*, 1892.]

It is the same scientific spirit of the time, which in the fifties led many who were weary of the idealistic speculations over to materialism, that now secures such wide dissemination and so widespread favor for the endeavors of the neo-Kantians and the positivists or neo-Baconians, who desire to see metaphysics stricken from the list of the sciences and replaced by noëtics, and the theory of the world relegated to faith. The philosophy of the present, like the pre-Socratic philosophy and the philosophy of the early modern period, wears the badge of physics. The world is conceived from the standpoint of nature, psychical phenomena are in part neglected, in part see their inconvenient claims reduced to a minimum, while it is but rarely that we find an appreciation of their independence and co-ordinate value, not to speak of their superior position. The power which natural science has gained over philosophy dates essentially from a series of famous discoveries and theories, by which science has opened up entirely new and wide outlooks, and whose title to be considered in the formation of a general view of reality is incontestable. To mention only the most prominent, the following have all posited important and far-reaching problems for philosophy as well as for science: Johannes Müller's (Müller died 1858) theory of the specific energies of the senses, which Helmholtz made use of as an empirical confirmation of the Kantian apriorism; the law of the conservation of energy discovered by Robert Mayer (1842, 1850; Helmholtz, 1847, 1862), and, in particular, the law of the transformation of heat into motion, which invited an examination of all the forces active in the world to test their mutual convertibility; the extension of mechanism to the vital processes, favored even by Lotze; the renewed conflict between atomism and dynamism; further, the Darwinian theory[1] (1859), which makes organic species develop from one another by natural selection in the struggle for existence (through inheritance and adaptation); finally, the meta-geometrical speculations[2] of Gauss (1828), Riemann (*On the Hypotheses which lie at the Basis of Geometry*, 1854, published in 1867), Helmholtz (1868), B. Erdmann (*The Axioms of Geometry*, 1877). G. Cantor, and others, which look on our Euclidean space of three dimensions as a special case of the unintuitable yet thinkable analytic concept of a space of n dimensions. The circumstance that these theories are still largely hypothetical in their own field appears to have stirred up rather than moderated the zeal for carrying them over into other departments and for applying them to the world as a whole. Thus, especially, the Darwinians[3] have undauntedly attempted to utilize the biological hypothesis of the master as a philosophical principle of the world, and to bring the mental sciences under the point of view of the mechanical theory of development, though thus far with more daring and noise than success. The finely conceived ethics of Höffding (p. 585) is an exception to the rule which is the object of this remark.

[Footnote 1: A critical exposition of the modern doctrine of development and of the causes used to explain it is given by Otto Hamann, *Entwickelungslehre und Darwinismus*, Jena, 1892. Cf. also, O. Liebmann, *Analysis der Wirklichkeit*; and Ed. von Hartmann (above, p.

610). [Among the numerous works in English the reader may be referred to the article "Evolution," by Huxley and Sully, *Encyclopedia Britannica*, 9th ed., vol. viii.; Wallace's *Darwinism*, 1889; Romanes, *Darwin and after Darwin*, i. *The Darwinian Theory*, 1892; and Conn's *Evolution of To-day*, 1886.—TR.]]

[Footnote 2: Cf. Liebmann, *Analysis der Wirklichkeit*, 2d ed., pp. 53-59. G. Frege (*Begriffsschrift*, 1879; *The Foundations of Arithmetic*, 1884; *Function and Concept*, 1891; "On Sense and Meaning" in the *Zeitschrift für Philosophie,* vol. c. 1892) has also chosen the region intermediate between mathematics and philosophy for his field of work. We note, further, E.G. Husserl, *Philosophy of Arithmetic*, vol. i., 1891.]

[Footnote 3: Ernst Haeckel of Jena (born 1834; *General Morphology*, 1866; *Natural History of Creation*, 1868 [English, 1875] I *Anthropogeny*, 1874; *Aims and Methods of the Development History of To-day*, 1875; *Popular Lectures*, 1878 seq.—English, 1883), G. Jäger, A. Schleicher *(The Darwinian Theory and the Science of Language*, 1865), Ernst Krause (Carus Sterne, the editor of *Kosmos*) O. Caspari, Carneri (*Morals and Darwinism*, 1871), O. Schmidt, Du Prel, Paul Rée (*The Origin of the Moral Feelings*, 1877; *The Genesis of Conscience*, 1885; *The Illusion of Free Will*, 1885); G.H. Schneider (*The Animal Will*, 1880; *The Human Will*, 1882; *The Good and Ill of the Human Race*, 1883).]

Besides the theory of knowledge, in the elaboration of which the most eminent naturalists[1] participate with acuteness and success, psychology and the practical disciplines also betray the influence of the scientific spirit. While sociology and ethics, following the English model, seek an empirical basis and begin to make philosophical use of statistical results (E.F. Schäffle, *Frame and Life of the Social Body*, new ed., 1885; A. von Oettingen, *Moral Statistic in its Significance for a Social Ethics*, 3d ed., 1882), psychology endeavors to attain exact results in regard to psychical life and its relation to its physical basis—besides Fechner and the Herbartians, W. Wundt and A. Horwicz should be mentioned here. Wundt and, of late, Haeckel go back to the Spinozistic parallelism of material and psychical existence, only that the latter emphasizes merely the inseparability *(Nichtohneeinander)* of the two sides (the cell-body and the cell-soul) with a real difference between them and a metaphysical preponderance of the material side, while the former emphasizes the essential unity of body and soul, and the higher reality of the spiritual side.

[Footnote 1: Helmholtz, Virchow (born 1821), Zöllner (1834-82; *On the Nature of Comets*, 1872), and Du Bois-Reymond (born 1818), who, in his lectures *On the Limits of the Knowledge of Nature*, 1872, and *The Seven World-riddles*, 1880 (both together in 1882, and reprinted in the first series of his *Addresses*, 1886), looks on the origin of life, the purposive order of nature, and thought as problems soluble in the future, but declares, on the other hand, that the nature of matter (atoms) and force *(actio in distant)*, the origin of motion, the genesis of consciousness (of sensation, together with pleasure and pain) from the knowable conditions of psychical life, and the freedom of the will, are absolute limits to our knowledge of nature.]

%(b) Idealistic Reaction against the Scientific Spirit.%—In opposition to the preponderance of natural science and the empirico-skeptical tendency of the philosophy of the day conditioned by it, an idealistic counter-movement is making itself increasingly felt as the years go on. Wilhelm Dilthey[1] abandons metaphysics as a basis, it is true, but (with the assent of Gierke, *Preussische Jahrbücher*, vol. liii. 1884) declares against the transfer of the method of natural science to the mental sciences, which require a special foundation. In spite of his critical rejection of metaphysics, Wilhelm Windelband in Strasburg (born 1848; *Preludes*, 1884) is, like Dilthey, to be counted among the idealists. In opposition to the individualism of the positivists, the folk-psychologists—at their head Steinthal and Lazarus (p. 536); Gustav Glogau[2] in Kiel (born 1844) is an adherent of the same movement—defend the power of the universal over individual spirits. The spirit of the people is not a phrase, an empty name, but a real force, not the sum of the individuals belonging to the people, but an encompassing and controlling power, which brings forth in the whole body processes (*e.g.*, language) which could not occur in individuals as such. It is only as a member of society that anyone becomes truly man; the community is the subject of the higher life of spirit.

[Footnote 1: Dilthey: *Introduction to the Mental Sciences*, part i., 1883; *Poetic Creation* in the Zeller *Aufsätze*, 1887; "Contributions to the Solution of the Question of the Origin of our Belief in the Reality of the External World, and its Validity," *Sitzungsberichte* of the Berlin Academy of Sciences, 1890; "Conception and Analysis of Man in the Fifteenth and Sixteenth Centuries" in the *Archiv für Geschichte der Philosophie*, vols. iv., v., 1891-92.]

[Footnote 2: Glogau: *Sketch of the Fundamental Philosophical Sciences* (part i., *The Form and the Laws of Motion of the Spirit*, 1880; part ii., *The Nature and the Fundamental Forms of Conscious Spirit*, 1888); *Outlines of Psychology*; 1884.]

If folk-psychology, whose title but imperfectly expresses the comprehensive endeavor to construct a psychology of society or of the universal spirit, is, as it were, an empirical confirmation of Hegel's theory of Objective Spirit, Rudolf Eucken[1] (born 1846), pressing on in the Fichtean manner from the secondary facts of consciousness to an original real-life, endeavors to solve the question of a universal becoming, of an all-pervasive force, of a supporting unity ("totality") in the life of spirit (neither in a purely noëtical nor a purely metaphysical, but) in a noölogical way, and demands that the fundamental science or doctrine of principles direct its attention not to cognition by itself, but to the activity of psychical life as a whole.

[Footnote 1: Eucken: *The Unity of Spiritual Life in the Consciousness and Deeds of Humanity*, 1888; *Prolegomena* to this, 1885. A detailed analysis of the latter by Falckenberg is given in the *Zeitschrift für Philosophie*, vol. xc, 1887; cf. above, pp. 17 and 610.]

We have elsewhere discussed the more recent attempts to establish a metaphysic which shall be empirically well grounded and shall cautiously rise from facts.[1] In regard to the possibility of metaphysics three parties are to be distinguished: On the left, the positivists, the neo-Kantians, and the monists of consciousness, who deny it out of hand. On the right, a series of philosophers—e.g., adherents of Hegel, Herbart, and Schopenhauer—who, without making any concessions to the modern theory of knowledge, hold fast to the possibility of a speculative metaphysics of the old type. In the center, a group of thinkers who are willing to renounce neither a solid noëtical foundation nor the attainment of metaphysical conclusions—so Eduard von Hartmann, Wundt,[2] Eucken, Volkelt (pp. 590, 617). Otto Liebmann (born 1840; *On the Analysis of Reality*, 1876, 2d ed., 1880; *Thoughts and Facts*, Heft i. 1882) demands a sharp separation between the certain and the uncertain and an exact estimation of the degree of probability which theories possess; puts the principles of metaphysics under the rubric of logical hypothesis; and, in his *Climax of the Theories*, 1884, calls attention to the fact that experiential science, in addition to axioms necessarily or apodictically certain and empeiremes possessing actual or assertory certainty, needs, further, a number of "interpolation maxims," which form an attribute of our type of intellectual organization *(i.e.*, principles, according to the standard of which we supplement the fragmentary and discrete series of single perceptions and isolated observations by the interpolation of the needed intermediate links, so that they form a connected experience). The most important of these maxims are the principles of real identity, of the continuity of existence, of causality, and of the continuity of becoming. Experience is a gift of the understanding; the premises, as a rule, latent in ordinary consciousness, on whose anticipatory application our experience is based throughout, assert something absolutely incapable of being experienced. If, in order to the production of a "pure experience," we eliminate all subjective additions of the understanding contained in experiential thought (all that cannot be present at the moment or locally at hand, in short, all that cannot be the direct object and content of actual observation), this breaks up into an unordered, unconnected aggregate of discontinuous perceptual fragments; in order that a complete and articulated condition of experience may result, these fragments (the purely factual content of observation, the incoherent matter of perception) must be supplemented and connected by very much that is not observed.

[Footnote 1: R. Falckenberg, *Ueber die gegenwärtige Lage der deutschen Philosophie*, inaugural address at Erlangen, Leipsic, 1890.]

[Footnote 2: Wundt: *Essays*, 1885, including "Philosophy and Science"; *System of Philosophy*, 1889. On the latter cf. Volkelt's paper in the *Philosophische Monatshefte*, vol. xxvii. 1891; and on the *Essays* a notice by the same author in the same review, vol. xxiii. 1887.]

Further, a reaction against crude naturalism is observable in the practical field, though political economists (Roscher) and jurists take a more active part in it than the philosophers. Personally R. von Jhering (1818-92; *Purpose in Law*, 2 vols., 1877-83, 2d ed., 1884-86) stands on idealistic ground, although, rejecting the nativistic and formalistic theory, he is in principle an adherent of "realism," of the principle of interest and social utility (the moral is that Which is permanently useful to society).

Finally, similar motives underlie the growing interest in the history of philosophy. The idealistic impulse seeks the nourishment which the un-metaphysical present denies to it from the great works of the past, and hopes, by keeping alive the classical achievements of previous times, to enhance the consciousness of the urgency and irrepressibleness of the highest questions, and to awaken courage for renewed attempts at their solution. Thus the study of history enters the service of systematic philosophy.

%(c) The Special Philosophical Sciences.%—The more the courage to attack the central problems of philosophy has been paralyzed by the neo-Kantian theory of knowledge and the coming-in of the positivistic spirit, the more lively has been the work of the last decades in the special departments: the transfer of the center of gravity from metaphysics to the particular sciences is the most prominent characteristic of the philosophy of the time. Logic sees century-old convictions shattered and new foundations arising. Psychology has entered into competition with physiology in regard to the discovery of the laws of the psychical functions which depend on bodily processes, while metaphysical questions are forced into the background and there is a growing distrust of the reliability of inner observation. The philosophy of religion is favored with undiminished interest and aesthetics, after long neglect, with a renewal of attention; the philosophy of history is about to reconquer its former rights. There is, moreover, an especially lively interest in ethics; and the investigation of the history of philosophy is more widely extended than ever before. We will close our sketch with a short survey of the particular disciplines.

In the department of *logic* the following should be mentioned as classical achievements: the works of Christoph Sigwart of Tübingen (vol. i. 1873, 2d ed., 1889; vol. ii. 1878), of Lotze (p. 605), and of Wundt (vol. i. *Erkenntnisslehre*, 1880; vol. ii. *Methodenlehre*, 1883). Besides these, Bergmann (p. 620), Schuppe (p. 619), and Benno Erdmann (*Logik*, vol. i. 1892) deserve notice.

In *psychology* the following writers have made themselves prominent: Wilhelm Wundt at Leipsic (born 1832), *Grundzüge der physiologischen Psychologie*, 1874, 3d ed., 1887; A. Horwicz, *Psychologische Analysen auf physiologischer Grundlage*, 1872 *seq*.; Franz Brentano in Vienna (born 1838), *Psychologie vom empirischen Standpunkte*, vol. i. 1874; Carl Stumpf of Munich (born 1848), *Ueber den psychologischen Ursprung der Raumvorstellung*, 1873, *Tonpsychologie*, vol. i. 1883, vol. ii. 1890; Theodor Lipps of Breslau (born 1851), *Grundthatsachen des Seelenlebens*, 1883. The following may be mentioned in the same connection: J.H. Witte, *Das Wesen der Seele*, 1888; H. Münsterberg, *Die Willenshandlung*, 1888, *Beiträge zur experimentellen Psychologie*, 1889 *seq*,; Goswin K. Uphues at Halle, *Wahrnehmung und Empfindung*, 1888, *Ueber die Erinnerung*, 1889; H. Schmidkunz, *Psychologie der Suggestion*, 1892; H. Ebbinghaus, the co-editor of the *Zeitschrift für Psychologie una Physiologie der Sinnesorgane*, 1890 *seq*.; H. Spitta; Max Dessoir, *Der Hautsinn*, in the *Archiv für Anatomie una Physiologie*, 1892. The following works are psychological contributions to the theory of knowledge: E.L. Fischer, *Theorie der Gesichtswahrnehmung*, 1891; Hermann Schwarz, *Das Wahrnehmungsproblem*, 1892. Finally we may add A. Dorner in Königsberg, *Das menschliche Erkennen*, 1887; and E.L. Fischer, *Die Grundfragen der Erkenntnisstheorie*, 1887.

The literature of *moral philosophy* has been substantially enriched by Wundt, *Ethik*, 1886, 2d ed., 1892; and Friedrich Paulsen, *System der Ethik*, 1889, 2d ed., 1891. We may mention, further, Baumann (p. 601); Schuppe, *Grundzüge der Ethik und Rechtsphilosophie*, 1882; Witte, *Freiheit des Willens*, 1882; G. Class in Erlangen, *Ideale und Güter*, 1886; Richard Wallaschek, *Ideen zur praktischen Philosophic*, 1886; F. Tönnies in Kiel, *Gemeinschaft und Gesellschaft*, 1887; A. Döring, *Philosophische Güterlehre*, 1888; Th. Ziegler, *Sittliches Sein und Werden*, 2d ed., 1890; G. Simmel, *Einleitung in die Moralwissenschaft*, vol. i. 1892.

Of the newer works in the field of *aesthetics*, in addition to A. Zeising's *Aesthetische Forschungen*, 1855, C. Hermann's *Aesthetik*, 1875, and Hartmann's *Philosophie des Schönen*, 1887, we may mention the *Einleitung in die Aesthetik* of Karl Groos, 1892, and the following by Lipps: *Der Streit über die Tragödie*, 1890; *Aesthetische Faktoren der Raumanschauung*, 1891; the essay *Psychologie der Komik (Philosophische Monatshefte*, vols. xxiv.-xxv. 1888-89), and *Aesthetische Litteraturberichte*, (in the same review, vol. xxvi. 1890 *seq*.).

Among the writers and works on the *philosophy of history* we may note Conrad Hermann in Leipsic (born 1819), *Philosophie der Geschichte*, 1870; Bernheim, *Geschichtsforschung und Geschichtsphilosophie*, 1880; Karl Fischer, *Ist eine Philosophie der Geschichte wissenschaftlich erforderlich bezw. möglich?* Dillenburg Programme, 1889; Hinneberg, *Die philosophischen Grundlagen der Geschichtswissenschaft* in Sybel's *Historische Zeitschrift*, vol. lxiii. 1889; A. Dippe, *Das Geschichtsstudium mit seinen Zielen und Fragen*, 1891; Georg Simmel, *Die Probleme der Geschichtsphilosophie*, 1892.

In the *philosophy of religion*, which is discussed especially by the theologians, a neo-Kantian and a neo-Hegelian tendency confront each other. The former, dividing in its turn, is represented, on the one hand, by the Ritschlian school—W. Herrmann in Marburg (*Die Metaphysik in der Theologie*, 1876, *Die Religion im Verhältniss zum Welterkennen und zur Sittlichkeit*, 1889), J. Kaftan in Berlin (*Das Wesen der christlichen Religion*, 1881)—and, on the other, by R.A. Lipsius in Jena (born 1830; *Dogmatik*, 1876, 2d ed., 1879; *Philosophie und Religion*, 1885). The latter is represented by A.E. Biedermann of Zurich (1819-85; *Christliche Dogmatik*, 1868; 2d ed., 1884-85), a pupil of W. Vatke, and by Otto Pfleiderer of Berlin (born 1839; *Religionsphilosophie*, 1879; 2d ed., 1883-4). The neo-Kantians base religion exclusively on the practical side of human nature, especially on the moral law, derive it from the contrast between external dependence on nature and the inner freedom or supernatural destination of the spirit, and wish it preserved from all intermixture with metaphysics. According to the neo-Hegelians, on the contrary, the theoretical element in religion is no less essential; and is capable of being purified, of being elevated from the form of representation, which is full of contradictions, into the adequate form of pure thought, capable, therefore, of reconciliation with philosophy. Hugo Delff (*Ueber den Weg zum Wissen und zur Gewissheit zu gelangen*, 1882; *Die Hauptprobleme der Philosophie und Religion*, 1886) follows Jacobi's course.

Among the numerous works on the *history of philosophy*, besides the masterpieces of Zeller, J.E. Erdmann, and Kuno Fischer, the following are especially worthy of attention:

Cl. Bäumker in Breslau, *Das Problem der Materie in der griechischen Philosophie*, 1890; H. Bonitz, *Platonische Studien*, 3d ed., 1886, *Aristotelische Studien*, 1862 seq., *Index Aristotelicus*, 1870, *Kleine Schriften*; P. Deussen (born 1845), *Das System der Vedanta*, 1883, H. Diels in Berlin, *Doxographi Graeci*, 1879; Eucken in Jena (p. 17), *Die Methode der aristotelischen Forschung*, 1872, Address *Ueber den Werth der Geschichte der Philosophie*, 1874; J. Freudenthal in Breslau (born 1839, pp. 63, 118), *Hellenistische Studien, 3 Hefte*, 1879, *Ueber die Theologie des Xenophanes*, 1886; M. Heinze in Leipsic, *Die Lehre vom Logos in der griechischen Philosophie*, 1872; G. Freiherr von Hertling in Munich (born 1843), *Materie und Form und die Definition der Seele bei Aristoteles*, 1871, *Albertus Magnus*, 1880; H. Heussler in Basle (p. 65 note), *Der Rationalismus des XVII. Jahrhunderts in seinen Beziehungen zur Entwickelungslehre*, 1885; Fr. Jodl in Prague (born 1849; pp. 16, 221 note); A. Krohn (1840-89), *Sokrates und Xenophon*, 1874, *Der platonische Staat*, 1876, *Die platonische Frage*, 1878—on Krohn, an obituary by Falckenberg in the *Biographisches Jahrbuch für Alterthumskunde, Jahrg.* 12, 1889; P. Natorp (pp. 88 note, 598), *Forschungen zur Geschichte des Erkenntnissproblems im Alterthum*, 1884; Edmund Pfleiderer in Tübingen (born 1842; p. 113 note[1]), *Empirismus und Skepsis im D. Humes Philosophie*, 1874, *Die Philosophie des Heraklit im Lichte der Mysterienidee*, 1886; K. von Prantl (1820-88), *Geschichte der Logik im Abendlande*, 4 vols., 1855-70; Carl Schaarschmidt (pp. 88 note, 117-118); *Johannes Sarisberiensis*, 1862, *Die Sammlung der platonischen Schriften*, 1866; L. Schmidt in Marburg (born 1824), *Die Ethik der alten Griechen*, 1881; Gustav Schneider, *Die platonische Metaphysik*, 1884; H. Siebeck in Giessen, *Untersuchungen zur Philosophie der Griechen*, 1873, 2d ed., 1888, *Geschichte der Psychologie*, part i. 1880-84; Chr. von Sigwart (born 1830; pp. 17, 118); Heinrich von Stein in Rostock (born 1833), *Sieben Bücher zur Geschichte des Platonismus*, 1862-75; Ludwig Stein in Berne, editor of the *Archiv für Geschichte der Philosophie*, founded in 1877, *Die Psychologie der Stoa*, I. *Metaphysisch-Anthropologischer Theil*, 1886, II. *Erkenntnisstheorie*, 1888, *Leibniz und Spinoza*, 1890; L. Strümpell, *Geschichte der griechischen Philosophie*, 1854, 1861; Susemihl in Greifswald, *Die Politik des Aristoteles*, Greek and German with notes, 1879, further, a series of essays on Plato and Aristotle; Teichmüller (p. 601); Trendelenburg (pp. 600-601), *Aristotelis de Anima*, 2d ed., by Belger. 1887; Th. Waitz, *Aristotelis Organon*, 1844-46; J. Walter in Königsberg, *Die Lehre von der praktischen Vernunft in der griechischen Philosophie*, 1874, *Geschichte der Aesthetik im Alterthum*, 1892; Tob. Wildauer in Innsbruck, *Die Psychologie des Willens bei Sokrates, Platon, und Aristoteles*, 1877, 1879; W. Windelbund in Strasburg (pp. 15-16), *Geschichte der alten Philosophie*, 1888; Theob. Ziegler in Strasburg, *Geschichte der christlichen Ethik*, 1886, 2d ed., with index, 1892; Rob. Zimmermann (pp. 19 note, 331, 536), *Studien und Kritiken*, 1870.

%4. Retrospect.%

In order to avoid the appearance of arbitrary construction we have been sparing with references of a philosophico-historical character. In conclusion, looking back at the period passed over, we may give expression to some convictions concerning the guiding threads in the development of modern philosophy, though these here claim only the rights of subjective opinion.

A mirror of modern culture, and conscious of its sharp antithesis to Scholasticism, modern philosophy in its pre-Kantian period is pre-eminently characterized by naturalism. Nature, as a system of masses moved according to law, forms not only the favorite object of investigation, but also the standard by which psychical reality is judged and explained. The two directions in which this naturalism expresses itself, the mechanical view of the world, which endeavors to understand the universe from the standpoint of nature and all becoming from the standpoint of motion,[1] and the intellectualistic view, which seeks to understand the mind from the standpoint of knowledge, are most intimately connected. Where the general view of the All takes form and color from nature, a content and a mission can come to the mind from no other source than the external world; whether we (empirically) make it take up the material of representation from without or (rationalistically) make it create an ideal reproduction of the content of external reality from within, it is always the function of knowledge, conceived as the reproduction of a completed reality, which, since it brings us into contact with nature, advances into the foreground and determines the nature of psychical activity. As is conceivable, along with dogmatic faith in the power of the reason to possess itself of the reality before it and to reconstrue it in the system of science, and with triumphant references to the mathematical method as a guaranty for the absolute certainty of philosophical knowledge, the noëtical question emerges as to the means by which, and the limits within which, human knowledge is able to do justice to this great problem. Descartes gave out the programme for all these various tendencies—the mechanical explanation of nature, the absolute separation of body and soul (despiritualization of matter), thought the essence of the mind, the demand for certain knowledge, armed against every doubt, and the question as to the origin of ideas. Its execution by his successors shows not only a lateral extension in the most various directions (the dualistic view of the world held by the occasionalists, the monistic or pantheistic view of Spinoza, the pluralistic or individualistic view of Leibnitz; similarly the antithesis between the sensationalism of Locke and Condillac and the rationalism of Spinoza and Leibnitz), but also a progressive deepening of problems, mediated by party strife which puts every energy to the strain. What a tremendous step from the empiricism of Bacon to the skepticism of Hume, from the innate ideas of Descartes to the potential *a priori* of Leibnitz! From the moment when the negative and positive culminations of the pre-Kantian movement in thought—Hume and Leibnitz—came together in one mind, the conditions of the Kantian reform were given, just as the preparation for the Socratic reform had been given in the skepticism of the Sophists and the [Greek: nous] principle of Anaxagoras.

[Footnote 1: Even for Leibnitz the mind is a machine (*automaton spirituale*), and psychical action a movement of ideas.]

Kant, who dominates the second period of modern philosophy down to the present time, is related to his predecessors in a twofold way. In his criticism he completes the noëtical tendency, and at the same time overcomes naturalism, by limiting the mechanical explanation (and with it certain knowledge, it is true) to phenomena and opposing moralism to intellectualism. Nature must be conceived from the standpoint of the spirit (as its product, for all conformity to law takes its origin in the spirit), the spirit from the standpoint of the will. Metaphysics, as the theory of the *a priori* conditions of experience, is raised to the rank of a science, while the suprasensible is removed from the region of proof and refutation and based upon the rock of moral will. In the positive side of the Kantian philosophy—the spirit the law-giver of nature, the will the essence of spirit and the key to true reality—we find its kernel, that in it which is forever valid. The conclusions on the absolute worth of the moral disposition, on the ultimate moral aim of the world, on the intelligible character, and on radical evil, reveal the energy with which Kant took up the mission of furnishing the life-forces opened up by Christianity—which the Middle Ages had hidden rather than conserved under the crust of Aristotelian conceptions entirely alien to them, and the pre-Kantian period of modern times had almost wholly ignored—an entrance into philosophy, and of transforming and enriching the modern view of the world from this standpoint. Kant's position is as opposite and superior to the specifically modern, to the naturalistic temper of the new period, as Plato stands out, a stranger and a prophet of the future, above the level of Greek modes of thought. More fortunate, however, than Plato, he found disciples who followed further in the direction pointed out by that face of the Janus-head of his philosophy which looked toward the future: the ethelism of Fichte and the historicism of Hegel have their roots in Kant's doctrine of the practical reason. These are acquisitions which must never be given up, which must ever be reconquered in face of attack from forces hostile to spirit and to morals. In life, as in science, we must ever anew "win" ethical idealism "in order to possess it." As yet the reconciliation of the historical and the scientific, the Christian and the modern spirit is not effected. For the inbred naturalism of the modern period has not only asserted itself, amalgamated with Kantian elements, in the realistic metaphysics and mechanical psychology of Herbart and in the system of Schopenhauer, as a lateral current by the side of Fichte, Schelling, and Hegel, but, under the influence of the new and powerful development of the natural sciences, has once more confidently risen against the traditions of the idealistic school, although now it is tempered by criticism and concedes to the practical ideals at least a refuge in faith. The conviction that the rule of neo-Kantianism is provisional does not rest merely on the mutability of human affairs. The widespread active study of the philosophy of the great Königsberger gives ground for the hope that also those elements in it from which the systems of the idealists have proceeded as necessary consequences will again find attention and appreciation. The perception of the fact that the naturalistico-mechanical view represents only a part, a subordinate part, of the truth will lead to the further truth, that the lower can only be explained by the higher. We shall also learn more and more to distinguish between the permanent import of the position of fundamental idealism and the particular form which the constructive thinkers have given it; the latter may fall before legitimate assaults, but the former will not be affected by them. *The revival of the Fichteo-Hegelian idealism by means of a method which shall do justice to the demands of the time by a closer adherence to experience, by making general use of both the natural and the mental sciences, and by an exact and cautious mode of argument—this seems to us to be the task of the future.* The most important of the post-Hegelian systems, the system of Lotze, shows that the scientific spirit does not resist reconciliation with idealistic convictions in regard to the highest questions, and the consideration which it on all sides enjoys, that there exists a strong yearning in this direction. But when a deeply founded need of the time becomes active, it also rouses forces which dedicate themselves to its service and which are equal to the work.

THE END.

Printed in Great Britain
by Amazon